T0189566

Communications in Computer and Information Science 1376

More information about this series at http://www.springer.com/series/7899

Satish Kumar Singh · Partha Roy ·
Balasubramanian Raman ·
P. Nagabhushan (Eds.)

Computer Vision and Image Processing

5th International Conference, CVIP 2020
Prayagraj, India, December 4–6, 2020
Revised Selected Papers, Part I

 Springer

Editors
Satish Kumar Singh
Indian Institute of Information
Technology Allahabad
Prayagraj, India

Balasubramanian Raman
Indian Institute of Technology Roorkee
Roorkee, India

Partha Roy
Indian Institute of Technology Roorkee
Roorkee, India

P. Nagabhushan
Indian Institute of Information
Technology Allahabad
Prayagraj, India

ISSN 1865-0929   ISSN 1865-0937   (electronic)
Communications in Computer and Information Science
ISBN 978-981-16-1085-1   ISBN 978-981-16-1086-8   (eBook)
https://doi.org/10.1007/978-981-16-1086-8

This Springer imprint is published by the registered company Springer Nature Singapore Pte Ltd.
The registered company address is: 152 Beach Road, #21-01/04 Gateway East, Singapore 189721, Singapore

Preface

The 5th IAPR International Conference on Computer Vision & Image Processing was focused on image or video processing and computer vision. This year CVIP 2020 was held at the Indian Institute of Information Technology Allahabad, Prayagraj, India. We received submissions on topics such as biometrics, forensics, content protection, image enhancement/super-resolution/restoration, motion and tracking, image or video retrieval, image, image/video processing for autonomous vehicles, video scene understanding, human-computer interaction, document image analysis, face, iris, emotion, sign language and gesture recognition, 3D image/video processing, action and event detection/recognition, medical image and video analysis, vision-based human gait analysis, remote sensing, multispectral/hyperspectral image processing, segmentation and shape representation, image/video security, visual sensor hardware, compressed image/video analytics, document, and synthetic visual processing and Datasets and Evaluation, etc. CVIP is now one of the flagship conferences in the field of Computer Science and Information Technology.

CVIP 2020 received 352 submissions from all over the world from countries including Poland, United Kingdom, United States, Norway, Sweden, Russia, Germany, China, and many others. All submissions were rigorously peer reviewed and 134 papers were finally selected for presentation at CVIP 2020. The Program Committee finally selected all 134 high-quality papers to be included in this volume of Computer Vision and Image Processing (CVIP) proceedings published by Springer Nature.

The conference advisory committee, technical program committee, and faculty members of the Indian Institute of Information Technology Allahabad, Prayagraj, India made a significant effort to guarantee the success of the conference. We would like to thank all members of the program committee and the referees for their commitment to help in the review process and for spreading our call for papers. We would like to thank Ms. Kamya Khatter from Springer Nature for her helpful advice, guidance, and continuous support in publishing the proceedings. Moreover, we would like to thank all the authors for supporting CVIP 2020; without all their high-quality submissions the conference would not have been possible.

December 2020   Satish Kumar Singh

Organization

Patron

Bidyut Baran Chaudhuri   ISI Kolkata, India

General Chair

P. Nagabhushan   IIIT Allahabad, India

General Co-chairs

Balasubramanian Raman   IIT Roorkee, India
Shekhar Verma   IIIT Allahabad, India

Conference Chairs

Partha Pratim Roy   IIT Roorkee, India
Sanjeev Kumar   IIT Roorkee, India
Satish K. Singh   IIIT Allahabad, India
Vrijendra Singh   IIIT Allahabad, India

Local Organizing Committee

Shirshu Varma   IIIT Allahabad, India

Conference Conveners

K. P. Singh   IIIT Allahabad, India
Mohammed Javed   IIIT Allahabad, India
Pritee Khanna   IIITDMJ, India
Shiv Ram Dubey   IIIT Sri City, India

Publicity Chairs

Subrahmanyam Murala   IIT Ropar, India
Shiv Ram Dubey   IIIT Sri City, India
Ashwini K.   GAT Bangalore, India

International Advisory and Programme Committee

Ajita Rattani   Wichita State University, USA
Alireza Alaei   Southern Cross University, Australia

Ankit Chaudhary	The University of Missouri – St. Louis, USA
Ashish Khare	University of Allahabad, India
B. H. Shekhar	Mangalore University, India
Bunil Kumar	Balabantaray NIT Meghalaya, India
Debashis Sen	IIT Kharagpur, India
Emanuela Marasco	George Mason University, USA
Gaurav Gupta	Wenzhou-Kean University, China
Guoqiang Zhong	Ocean University of China, China
J. V. Thomas (Associate Director)	STA ISRO Bangalore, India
Juan Tapia Farias	Universidad de Chile, Chile
Kiran Raja	NTNU, Norway
M. Tanveer	IIT Indore, India
Munesh C. Trivedi	NIT Agartala, India
P. V. Venkitakrishnan (Director CBPO)	ISRO Bangalore, India
Prabhu Natarajan	DigiPen Institute of Technology Singapore, Singapore
Pradeep Kumar	Amphisoft, India
Puneet Gupta	IIT Indore, India
Rajeev Jaiswal	EDPO, ISRO HQ (Bangalore), India
Sahana Gowda	BNMIT, Bengaluru, India
Sebastiano Battiato	Università di Catania, Italy
Sharad Sinha	IIT Goa, India
Somnath Dey	IIT Indore, India
Sule Yildirim Yayilgan	Norwegian University of Science and Technology (NTNU), Norway
Surya Prakash	IIT Indore, India
Thinagaran Perumal	Universiti Putra Malaysia, Malaysia
Watanabe Osamu	Takushoku University, Japan
Mohan S. Kankanhalli	National University of Singapore, Singapore
Ananda Shankar Chowdhury	Jadavpur University, India
Anupam Agrawal	IIIT Allahabad, India
Aparajita Ojha	IIITDM Jabalpur, India
B. M. Mehtre	IDRBT Hyderabad, India
B. N. Chatterji	IIT Kharagpur (Past Affiliation), India
Bir Bhanu	University of California, Riverside, USA
Chirag N. Paunwala	SCET, Surat, India
D. S. Guru	University of Mysore, India
Daniel P. Lopresti	Lehigh University, USA
G. C. Nandi	IIIT Allahabad, India
Gaurav Sharma	University of Rochester, USA
Gian Luca Foresti	University of Udine, Italy
Jharna Majumdar	Nitte Meenakshi Institute of Technology, India
Jonathan Wu	University of Windsor, Canada
Josep Lladós	Universitat Autònoma de Barcelona, Spain

Contents – Part I

Contents – Part II

Contents – Part III

An Approach for Fraction of Vegetation Cover Estimation in Forest Above-Ground Biomass Assessment Using Sentinel-2 Images

Praveen Kumar[1] , Akhouri P. Krishna[1] , Thorkild M. Rasmussen[2] ,
and Mahendra K. Pal[2(✉)]

[1] Department of Remote Sensing, BIT Mesra, Ranchi 835 215, Jharkhand, India
[2] Division of Geosciences and Environmental Engineering, Department of Civil, Environmental
and Natural Resources Engineering, Luleå University of Technology, 971 87 Luleå, Norrbotten
County, Sweden
mahendra.pal@ltu.se

Abstract. Forests are one of the most important components to balance and reg-
ulate the terrestrial ecosystem on the Earth in protecting the environment. Accurate forest above-ground biomass (AGB) assessment is vital for sustainable forest management to recognize climate change and deforestation for mitigation
processes.

In this study, Sentinel 2 remote sensing image has been used to calculate
the fraction of vegetation cover (FVC) in order to accurately estimate the forest
above-ground biomass of Tundi reserved forest in the Dhanbad district located in
the Jharkhand state, India. The FVC is calculated in four steps: first, vegetation
index image generation; second, vegetation index image rescaled between 0 to 1;
third, the ratio of vegetated and non-vegetated areas was calculated with respect
to the total image area, and finally, FVC image is generated.

In this paper, three vegetation indices have been calculated from the Sentinel
2 image, namely: normalized difference vegetation index (NDVI), normalized
difference index 45 (NDI45), and inverted red-edge chlorophyll index (IRECI).
Then, the FVC images were generated from the above vegetation indices individually. The ground FVC values were estimated from 22 different locations from
the study area. Finally, the image based FVC estimates were compared with the
ground estimated FVC. The results show that the IRECI based FVC provided
the best approximation to the ground FVC among the different vegetation indices
tested.

Keywords: Vegetation indices · Fraction of vegetation cover · Forest above
ground biomass · Sentinel 2 images · Optical remote sensing

1 Introduction

Forest are one among the most dominant factors to maintain our terrestrial ecosystem of
the Earth. Especially, climate changes, global warming, clean water, valuable ecosystem

© Springer Nature Singapore Pte Ltd. 2021
S. K. Singh et al. (Eds.): CVIP 2020, CCIS 1376, pp. 1–11, 2021.
https://doi.org/10.1007/978-981-16-1086-8_1

goods and humanity directly depend on forests [1–5]. Forests are also a central factor for the global carbon cycle and atmospheric carbon sinks or sources [6]. Forests are capable of stabilizing atmospheric carbon dioxide concentrations thereby mitigating global warming and climate change [7, 8]. Forest resources have been shrinking faster over the last few decades. As a consequence, the threat to ecosystem as an essential life-support system is also potentially rising. Therefore, it is crucial to study the forest ecosystem to mitigate the above concerns due to the same. The global observation systems and analysis techniques are improving rapidly worldwide to study, monitoring, mapping and understand the forests ecosystem. Remote sensing is one of the fastest and cost-effective geo-spatial monitoring and mapping techniques useful in investigating and observing natural resources. Applications include forest monitoring and recording forest biomass on climate change mitigation and planning for maintaining balance for ecosystem services. The monitoring forests and estimation of forest biomass using satellite data has received increasing attention for many reasons globally. Accurate forest above-ground biomass (AGB) assessment is crucial for sustainable forest management and mitigation processes and to recognize climate change scenario due to deforestation. Biomass assessment via remotely sensed data of a large region is one the cost effective and eco-friendly application of remote sensing technology. Remotely sensed data from the recently launched satellites confer for better ecosystem models and improved land-based inventory systems. The above datasets and improved techniques allow better assessment of forest canopy height, estimation of forest AGB, and carbon stocks [1–5]. At the present time optical remote sensing data are freely available at a global scale. However, the satellite image processing and analysis for quick, accurate and precise forest above ground biomass (AGB) evaluation are still challenging and difficult. Accurate forest aboveground biomass (AGB) assessment is crucial for sustainable forest management to recognize possible climate change and deforestation for mitigation processes.

The Copernicus programme, an Earth observation programme of the European Union aims at achieving a global, continuous, autonomous, high quality, wide range Earth observation capacity [9]. The Copernicus Sentinel missions are collecting a number of data including Sentinel 1 (microwave) and Sentinel 2 (optical) for mapping and monitoring applications [10]. The availability of Sentinel 2 imagery at high spatial resolution (10 m to 60 m) offers a new opportunity to study and assessment for the above-mentioned challenges. Generally, remote sensing techniques do not derive forest biomass directly, but use parameters that are related to forest above ground biomass such as forest height, leaf area index, fraction of vegetation cover (FVC), or net primary production. Because of established relationships with AGB, these parameters or variables are widely incorporated into the mapping of forest AGB. Different methods have been developed to estimate forest biomass with remote sensing and ground data, based on passive and/or active instruments [1–5]. Active sensors, such as light detection and ranging (LiDAR) and synthetic aperture radar (SAR), have the advantage to penetrate the canopy; for this reason, they are considered the most useful tools for providing vertical structure or volumetric forest measures. Passive sensors, such as optical Sentinel 2 provides the vegetation surface cover, spread and chlorophyll contents and FVC in estimation of AGB [11]. Canopy height estimation using multifrequency and multipolarization Radarsat-1 and Sentinel-1 images over hilly forested areas have also been shown to provide significant improvement in AGB evaluation [12]. The top of the canopy digital surface model (TCDSM) also proved to be one of the important parameters. In forest management, carbon storage assessment, and forest stand height measurement.

Tree height is an ecological parameter in its own right and also an important input to the tree growth simulation models [13]. Further, there are several improvements in the data processing and classification techniques have been developed for forest monitoring and mapping using the above datasets (e.g., Sentinel-2) [1–5].

This research aims to apply recently launched optical Sentinel 2 satellite data, collected on December 4, 2019 for estimation of FVC in order to estimate forest above ground biomass. Ground truth data from 22 ground locations with 30 m by 30 m plot size were collected between September 4, 2019 to September 30, 2019 for forest FVC and above ground biomass measurements. In this study, vegetation indices and FVC from Sentinel 2 were calculated and validated with ground truth in order to measure accurately AGB from Tundi reserved forest, Jharkhand, India. The study demonstrated encouraging results in calculated FVC in forest AGB mapping using the freely accessible and high-resolution Sentinel 2 data.

2 Study Area and Datasets

Description of the study area and data details are provided in brief in the following subsection.

2.1 Study Area

In this experiment, Tundi reserved forest in the Dhanbad district of Jharkhand state, India is selected as a study area. There are few isolated hills of varying dimensions scattered in the northern half in this district. The study area covers 144 km^2, and ranges between the latitude 230 52′ 57.37″ N - 230 59′44.62″ N and longitude 860 12′13.49″ E - 860 30′58.28″ E. The type of forest is deciduous and consists of Shorea robusta commonly known locally as "Sal" as the most predominant tree species. Overall forest composition and nature is mixed and the top storey of the forest is with average height around 12 m and maximum height up to 20 m. The test site is dominated by minor hillocks with undulating topography.

The area receives typical monsoon type climate with three marked seasons, the hot, the rainy and winter. Humidity is very high during the rainy season and very low during the hot weather. The hot season extends from February to middle of June. The maximum temperature rises above 45 ^{0}C and hot wind known as "Loo" blows frequently during April to June till onset of monsoon. Thunderstorms usually occur in May, accompanied by a temporary fall in temperature by few degrees. Due to heavy industrialization and mining activities, lot of suspended particles and specks of dusts are found in the atmosphere during this season. The monsoon usually breaks in the middle of June and continues till the end of September. The average rainfall is between 1100 mm to 1200 mm.

2.2 Datasets

The Sentinel 2 multi-spectral image (MSI) Level 1C data collected on December 4, 2019 have been used to assess FVC in this study. The multispectral bands with spatial resolution of 10 m and 20 m were used after resampling to 10 m. The data details are displayed in Table 1. Further, study sites were visited, and ground truth (GT) samples from 22 different locations were collected. The ground measurement for tree heights, and FVC estimate were done.

Table 1. Bands specifications and spectral range of the Sentinel 2 system.

Sub-system	Band number	Wavelength range (μm)	Band central wavelength (μm)	SR(m)
VNIR	1	0.43–0.45	0.443 (Coastal aerosol)	60
	2	0.46–0.52	0.490 (blue)	10
	3	0.54–0.58	0.560 (green)	
	4	0.65–0.68	0.665 (red)	
	5	0.70–0.71	0.705 (Vegetation red edge)	20
	6	0.73–0.75	0.749 (Vegetation red edge)	
	7	0.77–0.79	0.783 (Vegetation red edge)	
	8	0.78–0.90	0.842 (NIR)	10
	8a	0.86–0.88	0.865 (Vegetation red edge)	20
	9	0.93–0.95	0.945 (Water vapor)	60
	10	1.37–1.39	1.375 (SWIR – Cirrus)	
SWIR	11	1.57–1.66	1.610 (SWIR)	20
	12	2.10–2.28	2.190 (SWIR)	

Note: SR = spatial resolution; VNIR = visible/near infrared; SWIR = shortwave infrared

3 Proposed Method

The proposed approach to calculate FVC from sentinel 2 is applied in the following sequential steps.

Step 1. In this step, preprocessing is performed on raw data for radiometric calibration and noise reduction from radiance data. Further, atmospheric correction is performed for eliminating the atmospheric effects and converting radiance data into reflectance data. Furthermore, spatial resampling is performed to bring all the bands of the dataset into similar spatial resolution.

Step 2. In this step, vegetation index (VI) is calculated. In this work three different vegetation indices are calculated to compare the vegetation indices for finding the best among the available indices in FVC calculation. The three different vegetation indices: normalized difference vegetation index (NDVI), normalized difference index 45 (NDVI45), and inverted red-edge chlorophyll index (IRECT) are calculated from Sentinel 2 reflectance data as below.

$$NDVI = \frac{(Band8 - Band4)}{(Band8 + Band4)}. \tag{1}$$

$$NDI45 = \frac{(Band5 - Band4)}{(Band5 + Band4)}. \tag{2}$$

$$IRECI = \frac{(Band7 - Band4)}{(Band5/Band6)}. \tag{3}$$

Suppose the above indices are represented as VI_i, where $i = 1{:}3$, technique for vegetation index calculation. Thus, $VI_1 = NDVI$, $VI_2 = NDI45$, and $VI_3 = IRECI$.

The following process from step 3 to step 5 is applied on each vegetation index individually.

Step 3. In this step, the calculated vegetation indices values are rescaled to 0–1 from each vegetation index individually, as below.

$$VIR = \frac{VI - VI_{min}}{VI_{max} - VI_{min}}, \tag{4}$$

where, VIR is the rescaled vegetation index value, VI is the vegetation index value, VI_{min}, is the minimum vegetation index value and VI_{max} is the maximum vegetation index value.

Further, a threshold vegetation index value (e.g., VIR = 0.5 in this paper) was chosen to distinguish vegetated and non-vegetated pixels in the image.

Step 4. In this step, ratio of vegetated and non-vegetated area with respect to the area of entire study area is calculated. According to the threshold vegetation index chosen in the above step (e.g., 0.5), pixel values more than threshold are counted as vegetated and less than threshold are counted as non-vegetated pixels.

Let us consider total number of pixels in the image is N_{total} and number of vegetated and non-vegetated pixels are $N_{vegetation}$ and $N_{non\text{-}vegetation,}$ respectively. Then ratio of vegetation ($R_{vegetation}$) and non-vegetation ($R_{vegetation}$) areas with respect to entire area are calculated as:

$$R_{vegetation} = \frac{N_{vegetation}}{N_{total}} \text{ and } R_{non-vegetation} = \frac{N_{non-vegetation}}{N_{total}}. \tag{5}$$

Step 5. In this step, the FVC image is generated using the following steps.

The average vegetation index value from vegetated pixels and non-vegetated pixels are calculated as $AVI_{vegetation}$ and $AVI_{nonvegetation}$ respectively. Further, normalized AVI (NAVI) is calculated from the vegetated and non-vegetated pixels as below.

$$NAVI_{vegetation} = R_{vegetation} \times AVI_{vegetation}, \text{ and}$$
$$NAVI_{non-vegetation} = R_{non-vegetation} \times AVI_{non-vegetation}. \tag{6}$$

The FVC is generated as below.

$$F_{vegetationcover} = \frac{VIR - NAVI_{non-vegetation}}{NAVI_{vegetation} - NAVI_{non-vegetation}}. \tag{7}$$

The above model represents the connection of vegetation fraction with VI in the image.

The $NAVI_{vegetation}$ and the $NAVI_{nonvegetation}$ represent the influences of vegetation and non-vegetation in the image pixels.

The above procedure from step 3 to step 5 is repeated individually for each vegetation index generated from the Sentinel 2 image. Suppose vegetation indices images after rescaling are represented as $VIR_i(x,y)$, where $i = 1{:}3$; is the technique for generation of vegetation indices (e.g., $1 = NDVI$, $2 = NDI45$, and $3 = IRECI$ in this paper), and (x,y) is the location of the image pixel, then the general equation for FVC from vegetation indices are represented as below.

$$F_i^{vegetationcover}(x, y) = \frac{VIR_i(x, y) - NAVI_i^{non-vegetation}}{NAVI_i^{vegetation} - NAVI_i^{non-vegetation}}. \tag{8}$$

The effectivity of the above approach was tested on Sentinel 2 image from the study area using three vegetation indices namely NDVI, NDI45 and IRECI.

4 Results and Discussion

The above developed approach was applied on Sentinel-2 as an optical remote sensing image to calculate the FVC in order to calculate forest AGB from Tundi reserved forest, Jharkhand, India. The results are shown in Fig. 1.

Initially, vegetation indices have been calculated to get the information of vegetation amount at each pixel in the image using NDVI (Fig. a (1), NDI45 (Fig. a (2), and IRECI (Fig. a (3) respectively. Subsequently, the developed approach was applied on each vegetation indices to calculate corresponding FVC images (NDVI (Fig. b (1), NDI45 (Fig. b (2), and IRECI (Fig. b (3)).

Additionally, we have collected 22 ground field data with 30 m by 30 m plot size and associated FVC were calculated from the corresponding plots. The sampling sites on the ground were carefully chosen to truly represent the varying conditions of the entire forest diversity of the study area.

To verify the accuracy of FVC results calculated from Sentinel 2, we have rescaled the calculated FVC between 0–1 for both ground truth and the Sentinel 2 data. The results revealed that ground based calculated FVC matched with image FVC with varying degree of accuracy with respect to vegetation indices. The image FVC with respect to ground FVC within one standard deviation are 15, 17, and 20 among 22 points by NDVI, NDI45 and IRECI respectively. The results show that our approach for calculation of FVC from Sentinel 2 produces accuracy of more than 68% for NDVI, 77% for NDI45 and 90% for IRECI based estimations. Thus, the IRECI performs best among the three vegetation indices used in this paper. The results reveal that Sentinel 2 data, combined with the

(a)

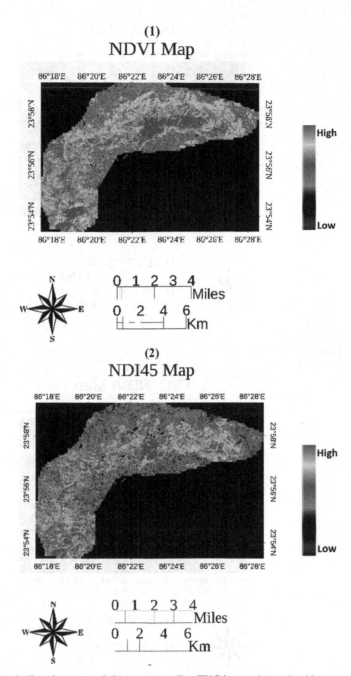

Fig. 1. (a) Vegetation indices image, and (b) corresponding FVC image determined by proposed approach using NDVI (1), NDI45 (2) and IRECI (3) from the study area.

(3)
IRECI Map

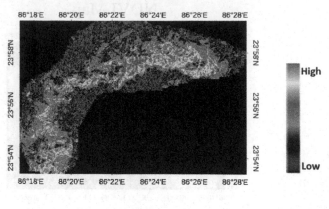

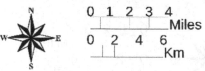

(b)

(1)
FVC_NDVI Map

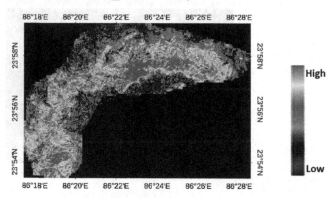

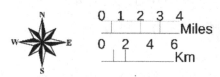

Fig. 1. (*continued*)

(2)
FVC_NDI45 Map

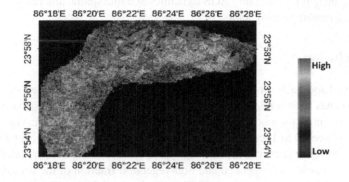

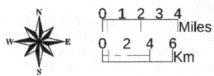

(3)
FVC_IRECI Map

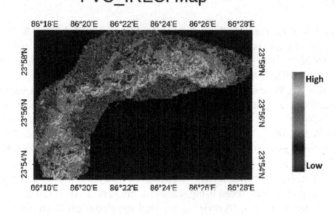

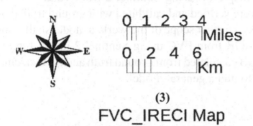

Fig. 1. (*continued*)

developed approach, can be used to monitor forest vegetation expansion and health at high spatio-temporal resolution with improved accuracy.

A linear regression between ground based calculated AGB and FVC will be developed in future work to find a general relationship between FVC and AGB. This work will provide the insight for obtaining AGB dynamics at a fine spatial and temporal resolution with optical remote sensing data.

5 Conclusion

An improved approach for FVC estimation from vegetated terrain has been developed. The method has been implemented mainly in four steps involving vegetation index calculation to quantify the amount of vegetation at each pixel of the image, vegetation index rescaling between 0 to 1, computing the ratio of vegetated and non-vegetated area with respect to the entire survey area, and finally, FVC calculation from rescaled vegetation index and proportion of vegetated and non-vegetated fraction of the image. The developed approach was applied to map FVC using Sentinel 2 from Tundi reserved forest, Jharkhand, India. The results were verified and validated with ground truth demonstrating accuracy of roughly 90%. As a further scope of the work, a model shall be developed for directly calculating forest AGB from FVC using Sentinel 2 in our future research work. Relationship between AGB calculated from ground truth and FVC calculated from Sentinel 2 shall be established to find a general model.

References

1. Agata, H., Aneta, L., Dariusz, Z., Krzysztof, S., Marek, L., Christiane, S., Carsten, P.: Forest aboveground biomass estimation using a combination of sentinel-1 and sentinel-2 data. In: IGARSS 2018–2018 IEEE International Geoscience and Remote Sensing Symposium, pp. 9026–9029. IEEE, July 2018
2. Chen, L., Ren, C., Zhang, B., Wang, Z., Xi, Y.: Estimation of forest above-ground biomass by geographically weighted regression and machine learning with Sentinel imagery. Forests 9(10), 582 (2018)
3. Frampton, W.J., Dash, J., Watmough, G., Milton, E.J.: Evaluating the capabilities of Sentinel-2 for quantitative estimation of biophysical variables in vegetation. ISPRS J. Photogramm. Remote Sens. 82, 83–92 (2013)
4. Nuthammachot, N.A., Phairuang, W., Wicaksono, P., Sayektiningsih, T. Estimating Aboveground biomass on private forest using sentinel-2 imagery. J. Sens. (2018)
5. Zhang, Y., Liang, S., Yang, L.: A review of regional and global gridded forest biomass datasets. Remote Sensing 11(23), 2744 (2019)
6. Timothy, D., Onisimo, M., Cletah, S., Adelabu, S., Tsitsi, B.: Remote sensing of aboveground forest biomass: a review. Tropical Ecol. 57(2), 125–132 (2016)
7. Lu, X.T., Yin, J.X., Jepsen, M.R., Tang, J.W.: Ecosystem carbon storage and partitioning in a tropical seasonal forest in Southwestern China. Ecol. Manage. 260, 1798–1803 (2010)
8. Qureshi, A., Pariva, B.R., Hussain, S.A.: A review of protocols used for assessment of carbon stock in forested landscapes. Environ. Sci. Policy 16, 81–89 (2012)
9. ESA: Copernicus, Overview. ESA. 28 October 2014. Accessed 26 Apr 2016
10. Gomez, M.G.C.: Joint use of Sentinel-1 and Sentinel-2 for land cover classifi-cation: A machine learning approach. Lund University GEM thesis series (2017)
11. Zhang, S., Chen, H., Fu, Y., Niu, H., Yang, Y., Zhang, B.: Fractional vegetation cover estimation of different vegetation types in the Qaidam Basin. Sustainability 11(3), 864 (2019)

12. Kumar, P., Krishna, A.P.: Forest biomass estimation using multi-polarization SAR data coupled with optical data. Curr. Sci. **119**(8), 1316–1321 (2020)
13. Kumar, P., Krishna, A.P.: InSAR based Tree height estimation of hilly forest using multi-temporal Radarsat-1 and Sentinel-1 SAR data. IEEE J. Selected Topics Appl. Earth Observ. Remote Sens. **12**(12), 5147–5152 (2019)

Dynamic Multimodal Biometric System

Prateek Patil[✉] and Suneeta Agarwal

Motilal Nehru National Institute of Technology, Allahabad, India
prateekpatilmnnit@gmail.com

Abstract. A Multimodal Biometric System uses a combination of different biometric modalities for individual's identification/verification, while in the case of unimodal biometric systems, the system uses a single biometric. Unimodal biometric systems have some drawbacks because of intra-class variations, restricted degrees of freedom, possible spoof attacks and non-universality. These drawbacks have been reduced by fusion based multimodal biometric system. Various methods of fusion and data integration strategies have been utilized to combine information in fusion based multimodal systems. By using Biometric modalities dynamically, this paper presents a new approach to further enhance the security by reducing the False Acceptance Rate (FAR) and False Rejection Rate (FRR). Here, a user does not know in which order collected biometrics are being used for testing. The next biometric to be used for testing, totally depends on the result of previously performed test. It will make very difficult for an imposter to fool the system. Three biometrics, Palm print, Knuckle print and Iris are collected in this system. The accuracy of the system is improved to 99.99% with respect to some earlier Models as shown in Table 3.

Keywords: Multimodal biometric system · Unimodal · FAR and FRR

1 Introduction

In today's modern era, Biometrics are more convenient and efficient way in comparison to text based password or tokens for providing better security to the system. A biometric is a physiological or behavioural trait of a person which is unique and can be universally accepted. Some popular biometrics for identification/verification are: face, iris, retina, fingerprints, palm-prints, hand vein and hand geometry. Depending on the security requirement different biometric traits are being used in the systems for identification/verification. A biometric should possess some basic characteristics to be used in a system for identification/verification such as : universality, permanance, uniqueness, measurability and acceptability etc. [1]. Based on the above mentioned characteristics, Palm Print, Knuckle Print and Iris are the biometric traits which have been proved to be better having maximum number of characteristics [1].

In Multimodal biometric system multiple biometric modalities are used together. Multimodal Biometric system reduces the drawbacks of unimodal biometric system. It combines the evidence obtained from different modalities using

© Springer Nature Singapore Pte Ltd. 2021
S. K. Singh et al. (Eds.): CVIP 2020, CCIS 1376, pp. 12–19, 2021.
https://doi.org/10.1007/978-981-16-1086-8_2

an effective fusion scheme. This improves the overall accuracy of the biometric system.

Types of multimodal biometric systems :

1: Using one biometric feature, A multi-sensor system can be developed that obtains data from from various sensors.
2: Multiple algorithms can be implemented for processing a single biometric feature in a system.
3: A system consolidating multiple occurrences of the same body trait.
4: A model which uses multiple templates of the same biometric method obtained with the help of a single sensor.
5: A system which can combine information about the biometric features of the individual to establish his identity.

Following are the steps of any biometric Identification/Verification system:

1: Registration : The biometric information of the user is extracted through a sensor and template is generated after pre-processing and saved in the database.
2: Identification/Verification : Identification (one-to-many matching) involves comparing the captured trait with templates stored in the template database. Verification (one-to-one) involves comparing captured trait corresponding to the template of the claimed identity [2].

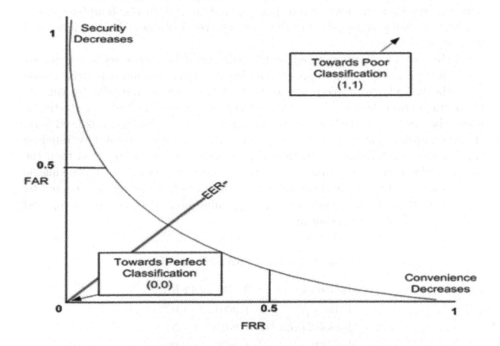

Fig. 1. The curve between FAR and FRR

The Accuracy of the system shows how good the system performs for the desired application. FAR and FRR are the two widely used metrics which are used to determine system's accuracy. FAR is the percentage of imposters who are incorrectly granted access while FRR is the percentage of valid users who are incorrectly denied accessing the system. Applications where high security is must, require a low FAR which has the effect of increasing the FRR. Applications where high security is not a concern, demands low FRR.

The Fig. 1 illustrates that varying the threshold used in the system affects FAR and FRR. Therefore, if the threshold selected is increased to make the access harder, some enrolees may find it more difficult to gain access. Thus, in the case of a biometric verification system, the FRR and the FAR vary in opposite directions. EER is the Equal Error rate, which is the point where FAR = FRR.

2   Proposed Dynamic Multimodal Biometric System

In this system, three biometrics, Palm Print, Knuckle Print and Iris biometrics are chosen to be collected initially. These biometrics are chosen because they satisfy maximum number of basic biometric characteristics as compared to other biometrics [1]. The proposed system uses these biometrics in an order so that the overall FRR and FAR are decreased and the true acceptance rate (TAR) is increased. The relationship between TAR and FRR is TAR = 1 - FRR. The palm print biometric is selected to be used initially and based on the decision here i.e., whether the user's palm print is matching with the template or not (the user is being accepted or rejected respectively) the next biometric is used for further testing.

If the user has been accepted by the palm print biometric section then he/ she is further tested with respect to the iris biometric section otherwise tested with the knuckle print biometric section. If the user is accepted by the iris biometric section then he/she is declared as Genuine user and no more testing is done, else the user is declared as an Imposter. No third biometric is used here. However, after being rejected by the palm print biometric section it is tested by the Knuckle print biometric section. If here also, the user is rejected then the user is declared as an imposter and no third biometric is used. But if the knuckle print is accepted then the third biometric Iris is used. If the use is accepted by iris section then the user is declared as a genuine user, else the user is rejected and the user is declared as an imposter.

Table 1. FAR and FRR of Biometrics

Biometric	FAR	FRR
Palm print [22]	0.00012%	1.02%
Knuckle print [22]	0.001%	1.54%
Iris [23]	0.94%	0.99%

The FAR, FRR and the accuracy of the proposed system have been calculated as follows:

$$FAR = FAR(P) \times FAR(I) + TRR(P) \times FAR(K) \times FAR(I)$$
$$FRR = TAR(P) \times FRR(I) + FRR(P) \times FRR(K) + FRR(P) \times TAR(K) \times FRR(I)4$$

$$Accuracy = 100 - (FAR + FRR)/2[14] \qquad (1)$$

Using the available results of the state of the art work (Table 1) the FAR, FRR and the accuracy of the proposed model are calculated as shown in Table 2.

Table 2. Results for proposed model

Model	FAR	FRR	Accuracy
Proposed dynamic multimodal biometric model	1.05×10^{-7}	9.0×10^{-3}	99.99%

The overall FRR and FAR of the proposed system are 9.0×10^{-3} and 1.05×10^{-7} respectively and the accuracy of the system is 99.99% as shown in Table 2. Table 3 represents the comparison between existing multimodal biometric systems and the Proposed Dynamic Multimodal Biometric System.

In the proposed system, selection of a biometric for testing the user's authenticity is taken dynamically. Here the user does not know with which biometric he/she is being tested next. The biometrics are arranged in this order because the FAR of Palm print is lower in comparison to other two biometrics used in the system and therefore the system does not falsely accept an imposter in the beginning. If the rejection occurs at the beginning, then the knuckle print biometric section is used so that the FRR can be reduced. At the last the iris biometric section is used. The circumvention in the case of iris biometric is lowest, so it will be very difficult for an imposter to fool the system here and thus the security is enhanced because of lack of spoofing. At the initial phase the user's palm print, knuckle print and iris images are collected as input. By using these

Table 3. Comparision table

Multimodal biometric system	Accuracy
Iris and Knuckle print [20]	98.92%
Iris and Palm print [21]	99.20%
Face and Iris [2]	99.43%
Palm print and Knuckle prin [22]	99.92%
Proposed dynamic multimodal biometric system	99.99%

biometrics dynamically, the matching time of the system has been reduced since all the biometrics are not being used for all. This approach is also increasing the security of the system and reducing both the FAR and FRR.

Following are the steps performed by the proposed system :

Figure 2 represents the block model of the proposed Dynamic Multimodal Biometric System.

1: Initially the Inputs for palm print, knuckle print and iris in the form of images are taken by the user.
2: The inputs are processed and are stored as templates in the database.
3: First of all the palm print biometric section is used. Here, the palm print of the user is matched with the stored palm print template.
4: Based on the result of the palm print section the next decision is taken, in the case of acceptance it is tested with the iris biometric section otherwise with the knuckle print biometric section.
5: After being accepted by the palm print biometric section in step 4, the Iris biometric section becomes active and if the user is further accepted by this biometric section, then it is declared as a genuine user else an imposter. No third biometric is used here.
6: On the other hand, if knuckle print section rejects the user then no further testing is performed and the user is treated as an Imposter.
7: But if the user is accepted by knuckle print biometric section then the third biometric, iris, is used for the final decision.
8: If the user has been accepted in step 6, it is then tested by the iris section and if here also it is accepted, then it is declared as a genuine user else rejected considering it as an imposter.

In this model a third biometric, iris is used because the circumvention of iris is very low and the Iris scanner can distinguish dead eyeballs from he living ones, so fooling the system will not be easy. This model can be used for Banking transactions, Hospitals, Military, Online examinations etc. Here, all the three biometrics are not being used all together whereas in the existing fusion based multimodal biometric systems all biometrics are being used together. In fusion based systems, if one biometric trait of a user is poorly forged and the other is very strongly forged, then there are chances that the user may be declared as genuine even if he/she is an imposter. On the other hand, in the proposed Dynamic Multimodal Biometric System, if the system accepts/rejects user's one biometric trait then he/she is being tested with the other selected biometric trait (based on the decision taken by the system). Here, out of 5 cases, all the three biometrics are used in only 2 cases and only two biometrics (palm print and iris/palm print and knuckle print) are used in the remaining 3 cases.

The proposed model can be updated further based on whether the application requires low FRR or low FAR :

• Module 1 : When an application requires low FRR - For this Module Knuckle Print System may be used after being rejected by the Palm Print system. Here, no third biometric is needed to be used. The FRR will go down from

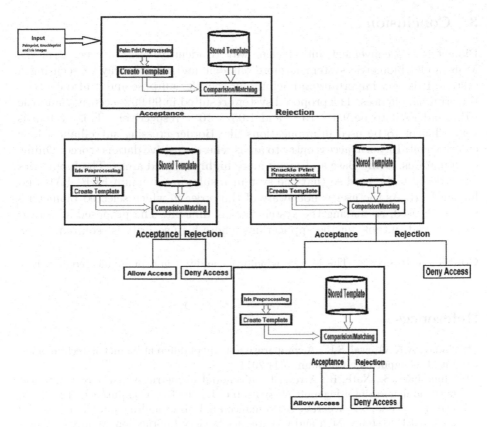

Fig. 2. Proposed dynamic multimodal biometric system

9.0×10^{-3} to 1.5×10^{-4} as shown in Table 4. This module can be used in the applications like Political meetings, Army gathering etc., where presence of all the genuine user is required and for this FRR must be low.

- Module 2 : When an application requires low FAR - For this Module Knuckle Print System may be used after being accepted by the Palm Print system. Here, no third biometric is needed to be used. The FAR will go down from 0.105×10^{-6} to 0.12×10^{-10} as shown in Table 4. This module can be used in the applications like Border crossing, Airport entrance, and highly secured areas where imposter should be rejected and for this FAR must be low.

Table 4. Comparision table

Model	FAR	FRR
Module 1	0.99×10^{-5}	1.5×10^{-4}
Module 2	0.12×10^{-10}	1.5×10^{-2}
Proposed dynamic multimodal biometric model	0.105×10^{-6}	9.0×10^{-3}

3   Conclusion

Biometric is a convenient and efficient way to identify/verify a user. Dynamic Multimodal biometric system is more efficient and reliable way of securing a system. It is very important and helpful for security purpose and it also controls the criminal offences. The proposed system resulted in 99.99% accuracy and the FRR and FAR to be 9.0×10^{-3} and 1.05×10^{-7} respectively. This system is very efficient to be used in applications like Border crossing surveillance, Law enforcement, Physical access entry to areas where sensitive data is stored, Online examinations, Army Base and many more highly secured areas. The biometrics are ordered to be used so that the system results in minimum FRR, FAR and higher TAR. As the user is not aware of the order in which selected biometrics are being used, so making the system fool is difficult. The proposed system is efficient and suitable for the applications where high security is required.

Conflict of Interests. This is my original work and it is not communicated anywhere else.

References

1. Yadav, A.K. Grewal, S.K.: A comparative study of different biometric technologies. Int. J. Comput. Sci. Commun. 5(1) 2014
2. Chaudhary, S., Nath, R.: A robust multimodal biometric system integrating iris, face and fingerprint using multiple svms. Int. J. Adv. Res. Comput. Sci. 7(2) (2016)
3. Dahel, S., Xiao, Q.: Accuracy performance analysis of multimodal biometrics. In: 2003 IEEE Systems, Man and Cybernetics Society Information Assurance Workshop, pp. 170–173. IEEE (2003)
4. Bowyer, K.W., Hollingsworth, K., Flynn, P.J.: Image understanding for iris biometrics: a survey. Comput. Vis. Image Underst. **110**(2), 281–307 (2008)
5. Wildes, R.P.: Iris recognition: an emerging biometric technology. Proc. IEEE **85**(9), 1348–1363 (1997)
6. Boles, W.W., Boashash, B.: A human identification technique using images of the iris and wavelet transform. IEEE Trans. Sign. Proc. **46**(4), 1185–1188 (1998)
7. Parashar, S., Vardhan, A., Patvardhan, C., Kalra, P.K.: Design and implementation of a robust palm biometrics recognition and verification system. In: 2008 Sixth Indian Conference on Computer Vision, Graphics & Image Processing, pp. 543–550. IEEE (2008)
8. Fukumi, M., Akamatsu, N.: A new rule extraction method from neural networks. In: Proceedings of International Joint Conference on Neural Networks IJCNN'99, vol. 6, pp. 4134–4138. IEEE (1999). (Cat. No. 99CH36339)
9. Kumar, B., Thornton, J., Savvides, M., Boddeti, V.N., Smereka, J.M.: Applicationof correlation filters for iris recognition. In: Handbook of Iris Recognition, pp. 337–354. Springer (2013)
10. Sun, Z., Wang, Y., Tan, T., Cui, J.: Improving iris recognition accuracy via cascaded classifiers. IEEE Trans. Syst. Man Cybern. Part C Appl. Rev. **35**(3), 435–441 (2005)
11. Du, Y., Ives, R., Etter, D.M., Welch, T.: Use of one-dimensional iris signatures to rank iris pattern similarities. Opt. Eng. **45**(3), 037201 (2006)

12. Chen, Y., Dass, S.C., Jain, A.K.: Localized Iris image quality using 2-D wavelets. In: Zhang, D., Jain, A.K. (eds.) ICB 2006. LNCS, vol. 3832, pp. 373–381. Springer, Heidelberg (2005). https://doi.org/10.1007/11608288_50
13. Mazur, J.: Fast algorithm for Iris detection. In: Lee, S.-W., Li, S.Z. (eds.) ICB 2007. LNCS, vol. 4642, pp. 858–867. Springer, Heidelberg (2007). https://doi.org/10.1007/978-3-540-74549-5_90
14. Perumal, E. Ramachandran, S.: A multimodal biometric system based on palm print and finger knuckle print recognition methods. Int. Arab J. Inf. Technol. (IAJIT), 12(2) (2015)
15. Laxmi, V., et al.: Palm print matching using LBP. In: 2012 International Conference on Computing Sciences, pp. 110–115. IEEE (2012)
16. Leng, L., Teoh, A.B.J., Li, M., Khan, M.K.: Orientation range for transposition according to the correlation analysis of 2D PalmHash code. In: 2013 International Symposium on Biometrics and Security Technologies, pp. 230–234. IEEE (2013)
17. Razzak, M.I., Yusof, R., Khalid, M.: Multimodal face and finger veins biometric authentication. Sci. Res. Essays 5(17), 2529–2534 (2010)
18. Ruth Karunya, S., Veluchamy, S.: Contactless hand based multimodal biometrics identification system. Res. J. Eng. Sci. 2278, 9472 (2013). ISSN
19. Barde, S., Zadgaonkar, A., Sinha, G.: Multimodal biometrics using face, ear and iris modalities. Int. J. Comput. Appl. 975, 8887 (2014)
20. Singh, S., Kant, C.: FKP and Iris based multimodal biometric system using PCA with NFNN. Available at SSRN 3358136.19 (2019)
21. Gayathri, R., Ramamoorthy, P.: Feature level fusion of palmprint and iris. Int. J. Comput. Sci. Issues (IJCSI), 9(4), 194 (2012)
22. Shanmugalakshmi, R., et al.: Multimodal biometric system for personal identification using palmprint and finger knuckle print fusion techniques (2014)
23. David, Z.: Advanced pattern recognition technologies with applications to biometrics. 1st edition Medical Information Science Reference (2008)

Copy-Move Image Forgery Detection Using Spatio-Structured SIFT Algorithm

Raimoni Hansda, Rajashree Nayak⑩, and Bunil Ku. Balabantaray$^{(\boxtimes)}$⑩

National Institute of Technology Meghalaya, Shillong, India
{rnayak,bunil}@nitm.ac.in

Abstract. Copy-move image forgery detection (CMIFD) via SIFT algorithm is one of the emerging and effective key-point based strategies. This algorithm is robust against large-scale geometric transformations and various attacks during the forgery process. CMIFD via SIFT algorithm accurately localizes the tampered regions rich in structural content at a cost of key-point matching problem and provides inferior detection accuracy with higher rate of false alarm in localizing relatively smoothed and little structured forgery regions. Natural images are highly structured. Pixels in these images preserve sufficient spatial and structural correlation among each other which should be preserved during the feature matching process. However, SIFT algorithm has no provision to preserve structural correlation among key-points. Consequently, detects insufficient number of key-points for images rich in structural content. To alleviate these bottlenecks, we have proposed an efficient CMIFD scheme by (i) integrating spatial and structural information additionally in the SIFT feature descriptor and (ii) utilized an adaptive strategy in selecting optimal number of matched key-points from a pool of candidate key-points. All these modifications enable to minimize the key-point matching problem and localize both structured and smoothed tampered regions accurately. Outperforming behavior of the proposed method is validated via several experimental result analyses.

Keywords: CMIFD · SIFT · Key-points

1 Introduction

In the modern era of digital India, digital images play a vital role in almost all applications whether it is medical imaging, law enforcement, image and computer vision applications, military, forensic applications or various commercial applications. Hence, it becomes indispensable to check the authenticity and originality of the input image before its further use. However, certain user friendly image manipulation tools such as Adobe Illustrator, Adobe Photoshop, PaintShop, ACDSee, Polarr and GIMP enable to modify or tamper the integrity of the original content without providing any mark or clue in the tampered images.

Supported by NIT Meghalaya.

Tampering or image forgery (IF) is performed to hide important information (removing murder weapon from the crime scene) or to mislead the situation (by pasting some fake information in the same scene). By visual perception, one cannot assure the reliability or authenticity of digital images. Hence, detection and localization of forgery region become essential. It becomes more challenging to localize the tampered region in blind image forensics as there is no knowledge about the embedded security marks such as digital watermarks or digital signatures [1]. Among various passive IF techniques, copy-move type image forgery (CMTIF) is one of the commonly encountered manipulating schemes. Figure 1 depicts a typical example of CMTIF. The plain areas from the original image are copied and pasted above the murder weapon in the tampered image to hide the evidence.

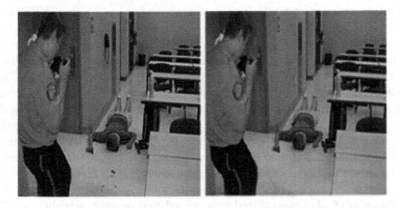

Fig. 1. Typical example of the copy-move image forgery. Left one: Original image; Right one: Tampered/Forged image

CMTIF is generated by copying and pasting some portion of the image content in the same image followed by its post processing [1,2]. Copy-pasting process keeps the intrinsic properties such as color condition, illumination behavior and noise incurred almost intact in both tampered and source images. Post processing operations such as scaling, rotation, shifting and intermediate attacks such as JPEG compression, variation of brightness, color reduction, addition of noise and contrast manipulation provide realistic look to the tampered images [2]. Despite of these challenges, varieties of CMTIF detection methods (CMTIFDMs) have been proposed in literature and are categorized under (i) block-based methods (BBMs) [3–5] (ii) Key-point based methods (KPBMs) [6–12]. Figure 2 depicts the generalized block diagram of either of these CMTIFDMs.

KPBMs solely depend on the selection of interest points or key-points (KPs) of an image. Usually, KPs are extracted along regions rich in entropy contents either by utilizing SIFT [6–11] or SURF [12] algorithms. Each key-point is represented via a feature vector. The detected key-point feature descriptors are matched for localizing the tampered region. In the matching process, presence of

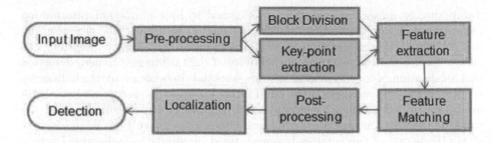

Fig. 2. Generalized steps for the copy-move image forgery detection scheme.

clustered matched areas provides the cue for the tampered region. Matched KPs are found by measuring similarity between these feature vectors. KPBMs provide commendable detection accuracy at a lower computational overload. Unlike BBMs, KPBMs are robust against noise distortions and image compression. Nevertheless, these methods are insensitive to the variations of illumination and geometric transformation [2,11]. However, as compared to SURF, SIFT based methods provide excellent detection accuracy [12] and are invariant to rotation, scaling and variations of illumination. In [6–11] several KPBMs utilizing SIFT feature along with other transforms are provided. In [6], Huang et al. utilized SIFT feature based detection method. Best-Bin-First search method is used in the matching process. Matching threshold value is selected as 0.45 which enabled to obtain lesser number of false positive rate. However, this method suffered from feature-matching problem and also failed to detect small sized forgery region. In [7], Amerini et al. have utilized generalized two nearest neighbours (g2NN) for matching the SIFT descriptor. This method can detect multiple copy-move forgery regions efficiently. In [8], Hashmi et al. applied DWT and SIFT for the detection of forged regions. DWT reduced the computational burden of the feature extraction process by extracting feature vectors only at the LL band of the image whereas, SIFT enables robust detection performance. Hashmi et al. in [9] used SIFT and dyadic wavelet transform (DyWT) for the detection purpose. DyWT is shift-invariant. DyWT with SIFT performed well in presence of different geometric transformations and extracted sufficient number of relevant features for the detection of IF. In [10], Alberry et al. used SIFT for feature extraction and Fuzzy-C-means (FCM) for clustering purposes. FCM enabled to reduce the computational burden of the feature-matching process. In [11], Li et al. proposed an efficient IF detection algorithm by utilizing SIFT algorithm with a lower value of contrast threshold to detect smoothed forged regions. Feature point matching is accomplished by hierarchical-matching scheme which enabled to reduce the computational burden of the matching process. An iterative approach is utilized for the localization of IF. This method efficiently detected small and smooth forgery regions.

Here in this paper, we have suggested a robust key-point based copy-move type forgery detection method by utilizing SIFT feature integrated with spatial and structural information to maintain the spatial homogeneity among key-points. The integrated spatio-structural information enables to detect small as well as smooth copied regions successfully. Besides, key-point matching problem is removed by measuring the similarity among feature vectors using distance function lying in non-euclidean space. Consequently, proposed work provides a faster and efficient IF detection method.

Rest of the paper is organized as follows: Section 2 describes the general steps of SIFT based CMTIFDMs. Section 3 describes the proposed work. Section 4 discusses the performance assessment of our suggested detection method along with some of the existing outperforming CMTIFDMs utilizing SIFT algorithms. Section 5 highlights the outperforming behavior of the proposed work with some future direction.

2   SIFT Based Copy-Move Forgery Detection Methods

This section provides a brief discussion on the generation of robust feature vectors via SIFT algorithm for the detection of copy-move tampered regions. SIFT algorithm is broadly classified into four stages [7]. Stage 1 deals with identification of key-points via the detection of extrema points over different scale spaces. This stage identifies several scale and orientation invariant candidate key-points in the high entropy regions of the image. Stage 2 aims at removing irrelevant and unstable feature points such as low contrast and edge points which are not properly localized. Stage 3 enables to provide rotation invariance by assigning dominant orientation to each of the persisted key-points. Local image gradient direction is utilized to allot one or more orientations to each key-point. Stage 4 ends with the generation of (1×128) dimensional feature vector for each key-point. The generated feature vector is invariant to scale, rotation, location and illumination.

Let the SIFT algorithm is applied to image $I(x, y)$ which generates n number of stable key-points such as $[k_1; k_2; ......; k_n]$ represented by n feature descriptors $[f_1; f_2; ......; f_n]$. Each feature descriptor is described as (1×128) dimensional feature vector. In a nutshell, each key-point k is described as a five dimensional vector and is described in Eq. (1).

$$k = \{x; y; \sigma; \theta; f\} \tag{1}$$

where $(x; y)$ are the coordinates in the image plane, σ, θ are the scale and dominant orientation assigned to the key-point. f is the (1×128) dimensional feature vector. Afterwards, key-points are matched with each other either via Eud based measure [6,9] or by hierarchical point based matching strategy [11].

3   Proposed Method

Primary aim of our proposed work is to integrate spatial and structural information with the robust yet popularly used key-point based feature descriptor SIFT to detect smooth and small sized forgery region. The proposed scheme shows an excellent detection accuracy irrespective of the size (small or regular) and type (structured or smooth) of forgery region at an appreciable computational time. SIFT algorithm effectively detects copy-move forgery regions in presence of various geometric distortions, Gaussian noise or JPEG compressions. However, this algorithm

- provides higher rate of false alarm and inferior detection accuracy in localizing relatively smaller or smooth forged regions due to extraction of insufficient number of key-points.
- fails to extract sufficient distinctive key-points in uniform texture region, in smooth regions and region with little structure. This is because the oriented gradient histogram information in SIFT algorithm does not preserve spatial compatibility around the neighborhood of key-points.
- provides heavy computationally burden during the matching of key-points via Euclidean distance (Eud). Complexity goes on increasing with increase in size of key-points. Moreover, Eud is highly sensitive to noise, outliers and small deformation. Consequently, small change in the input vector results in higher number of false matches in the output.

One probable solution to localize smooth or low contrast copy region is by lowering the contrast threshold as given in method [11]. However, obtaining an optimal strategy to select this value is still an open problem. Moreover, in natural images, neighborhood pixels around the key-point carry strong structural and spatial correlation which cannot be ignored during the similarity measurement of two regions [13]. For this reason, we have exploited structural and spatial information along with the conventional SIFT feature descriptor. The modified feature descriptor is termed as structured spatial histogram (StSH). In stage 4 of SIFT algorithm, along with the generation of (1×128) dimensional feature vector, the spatial mean, covariance and structural information for each bin around the key-point are computed in the neighborhood of (4×4) array of 16 histograms with 8 bins each to generate the feature descriptor StSH. Like oriented histogram, StSH of an image region is insensitive to local affine distortions. StSH not only preserves spatial information of an image region but also retains its structural content efficiently. Global positions of the pixels in image region are effectively captured by StSH. Nevertheless, it is easy to compute and allows easy inclusion in any forgery detection technique. Hence, by incorporating spatial and structural information in the SIFT algorithm, each generic key-point k is represented as eight dimensional vector as given in Eq. (2).

$$k = \{x_p; y_p; \sigma_p; \theta_p; f_p; \mu_p; \Sigma_p; \xi_p\} \quad p = 1, 2, ...8 \tag{2}$$

where, p is the number of bins. $x_p; y_p; \sigma_p; \theta_p; f_p$ are the same at p^{th} bin as described in Eq. (1). Whereas, $\mu_p; \Sigma_p; \xi_p$ denote the mean vector, co-variance vector and structural content vector of the coordinates of pixels x, y in the neighborhood of each key-point contributing to p^{th} bin. These feature vectors are computed as given in Eq. (3).

$$\mu_p = \frac{1}{\sum_{i=1}^{16} \delta_{ip}} \sum_{j=1}^{16} C_j \delta_{jp}$$

$$\Sigma_p = \frac{1}{\sum_{i=1}^{16} \delta_{ip} - 1} \sum_{j=1}^{16} (C_j - \mu_p)(C_j - \mu_p)^T \delta_{jp} \tag{3}$$

$$\xi_p = sqrt\left(\frac{1}{\sum_{i=1}^{16} \delta_{ip} - 1}\right)(C_j - \mu_p)^2 \delta_{jp}$$

where, δ_{jp}: Kronecker delta function.

$$\delta_{jp} = \begin{cases} 1; & if\ j^{th}\ pixel\ lies\ in\ p^{th}\ bin \\ 0; & otherwise \end{cases} \tag{4}$$

C_j denotes the spatial location of pixel j. $C_j = [x; y]^T$. T: Transpose operation. Similarity between key-points k_1 and k_2 are measured as given in Eq. (5).

$$sim(k_1, k_2) = \sum_{p=1}^{8} \rho_1\left(f_p^{(1)}, f_p^{(2)}\right) + \rho_2\left(\mu_p^{(1)}, \mu_p^{(2)}, \Sigma_p^{(1)}, \Sigma_p^{(2)}\right) + \rho_3\left(\xi_p^{(1)}, \xi_p^{(2)}\right)$$

$$\rho_1(\bullet) = \left\| f_p^{(1)} - f_p^{(2)} \right\|_1$$

$$\rho_2(\bullet) = N_1 \exp\left(-\{M^T \Gamma^{-1} M\}^{1/2}\right)$$

$$\rho_3(\bullet) = N_2 \exp\left(-\left\{\frac{\xi_p^{(12)} + c_1}{\xi_p^1 \xi_p^2 + c_1}\right\}\right)$$

$$\tag{5}$$

where, $M = \left(\mu_p^{(1)} - \mu_p^{(2)}\right); \Gamma = \left(\frac{\Sigma_p^{(1)} + \Sigma_p^{(2)}}{2}\right); \Gamma^{-1} > 1$. $\xi_p^{(12)}$ is the mutual structural interrelationship between key-points k_1 and k_2. N_1, N_2 are normalization constants. c_1 is a constant to avoid instability. Superscripts $(1), (2)$ in the parameters correspond to key-point k_1 and k_2 respectively.

3.1 Feature Matching

In the feature matching step, n number of extracted key-points are matched by measuring the Euclidean distances of their corresponding feature descriptors. For k^{th} key-point, let the sim vector contains $(n-1)$ number of sorted similarity distance values as $sim = \{sim_1, sim_2, ... sim_{n-1}\}; sim_1 < sim_2$. Conventionally, based on two nearest neighbors procedure k^{th} key-point is considered to be matched if the condition of distance ratio $sim_i/sim_{i+1} \leq Th$; $i = 1, 2, ...(n-1), Th \in (0, 1)$ holds good. Usually, methods in [9–11] utilized the threshold value Th either 0.6 or 0.8 for the matching of key-points. However, this value may not provide optimal accuracy or may introduce many false matches. To avoid the rate of false matching we have introduced an adaptive strategy to select the value of the distance ratio Th. In our proposed work key-point is considered to be matched if Eq. (6) is satisfied.

$$sim_i\big/sim_{i+1} < \frac{\max{(sim_i)_{i=1}^{n-1}} + \min{(sim_i)_{i=1}^{n-1}}}{2} \quad i = 1, 2, ...(n-1) \qquad (6)$$

where, max(.) and min(.) functions compute the maximum and minimum values of the Euclidean distances (sim) of key-point descriptor with other (n-1) key-point descriptors.

The idea behind this type of strategy is that selecting a fixed Th value of 0.6 or 0.8 may provide appropriate matching for non-smoothed tampered regions but provides inferior detection accuracy with higher rate of false alarm in localizing relatively smoothed and little structured forgery regions. In contrast, the proposed threshold selection strategy is locally adaptive and hence, enables to select optimal number of matched key-points with reduced rate of false matches irrespective of the type of forged region.

After obtaining the matched key-points, the RANSAC algorithm is performed to remove the unwanted outliers followed by the representation of remaining stable feature's matched points in an array $StableMatch$. If $StableMatch \geq 1$ then we will declare the image is forged and co-ordinates of matched points are used to localize the tampered region.

4 Result and Analysis

This section demonstrates the performance analysis of our proposed detection method along with some of the existing methods [9–11] in literature. Both image-level and pixel-level analysis have been performed here. Image-level analysis enables to quantify whether the image under consideration is forged or authentic whereas, pixel-level analysis quantifies the performance accuracy on localizing the forged region. Our proposed work is validated on two benchmark data sets i.e., MICC-F220 [7] and GRIP [14] data sets. MICC-F220 dataset consists of forged images which are of plain copy-move, rotation, scaling or combination of rotation and scaling. GRIP dataset contains smoothed forged regions. The whole simulation is done in Python library OpenCV version 3.4.2 in Anaconda Navigator on Windows 10 (64-bit) operating system, 1.60 GHz processor and 8 GB RAM. Figure 3 shows some of the sample original and forged images from MICC-F220 dataset. The forged/tampered regions are shown in red color rounded shape. Fig. 4 shows the sample forged smooth images from the GRIP dataset. The forgery regions are characterized via masked images. Figure 5 shows the matched feature points of the sample images (as described in Fig. 3) using proposed method along with other compared methods [9–11]. Figure 6 shows localization results of the sample images as described in Fig. 5. From Figs. 5 and 6 it is observed that our proposed work enables to match more number of reliable key-points to achieve an appropriate localization of forged region. Moreover, as compared to other methods, proposed method has almost no false matches to detect the forged region. Fig. 7 shows the forgery detection results for the

Fig. 3. Sample images from MICC-F220 dataset. (a), (c), (e), (g): Original Images. (b), (d), (f), (h): Forged Images

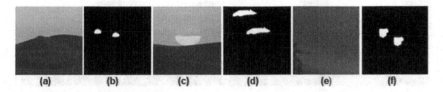

Fig. 4. Sample images from GRIP dataset. (a), (c), (e): Forged Images. (b), (d), (f): Masked Images

smooth images shown in Fig. 4. Methods in [9,10] fail to localize the forgery regions. This is because only SIFT based algorithms can not preserve spatial correlation among key-points. Hence, results for these methods are not shown in Fig. 7. In contrast, our proposed method and method in [11] can localize the smooth forgery regions. Method in [11] utilizes a lower contrast threshold value to keep sufficient amount of key-points in the smooth region. However, this method introduces some false matches (shown in red color arrows) during the matching process. As compared to this method, our proposed method utilizes the notion of structured-spatiogram, hence successfully preserves spatial as well as structural correlation around the neighborhood of stable key-points. Thus, provides superior detection of forgery regions even for smoothed forged region.

Along with localization of forgery regions via key-point matching, different evaluation metrics such as True Positive Rate (TPR), False Positive Rate (FPR), Accuracy, F_1 Score and IoU Score are also computed for analyzing the performance behavior of the compared methods. These evaluation metrics are computed based on Eq. (7). Higher values of TPR, Accuracy, F_1 Score, IoU Score with a lower value of FPR signify better forgery detection performance of the method.

Fig. 5. Matched feature points of some images from MICC-F220 using different Copy-Move detection methods. Column 1: [9], Column 2: [10], Column 3: [11], Column 4: Proposed method.

$$TPR = \frac{TP}{(TP+FN)}; FPR = \frac{FP}{(TN+FP)}$$

$$Accuracy = \frac{(TP+TN)}{(TP+TN+FP+FN)}; F_1\ Score = \frac{2TP}{2TP+FP+FN} \qquad (7)$$

$$IoU\ Score = \frac{TP}{TP+FP+FN}$$

Table 1 records these performance measure values along with processing time (in seconds) for both MICC-F220 and GRIP data sets. From Table 1 it is perceived that in both data sets our proposed method localizes the forgery regions with greater accuracy than other methods. Methods in [11] and our proposed method provide almost similar detection accuracy (99.10% Vs 99.32%) in localizing non-smoothed forged regions in MICC-F200 dataset. However, our proposed method provides better detection accuracy than the method [11] (98.56% Vs 98.12%) in localizing the smoothed forged regions in GRIP dataset.

Besides accuracy, our proposed work provides superior performance in terms of other evaluation metrics. Figure 8 depicts the bar plot of the average values of the quality measures of proposed method along with compared methods for both

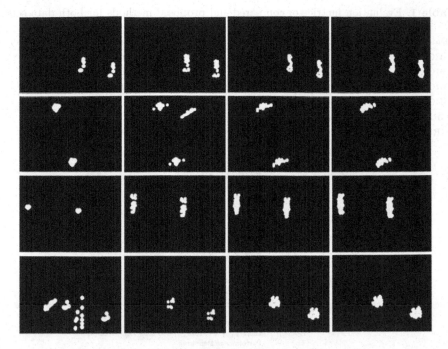

Fig. 6. Localization results of test images in Fig. 5 using different methods. Column 1: [9], Column 2: [10], Column 3: [11], Column 4: Proposed method.

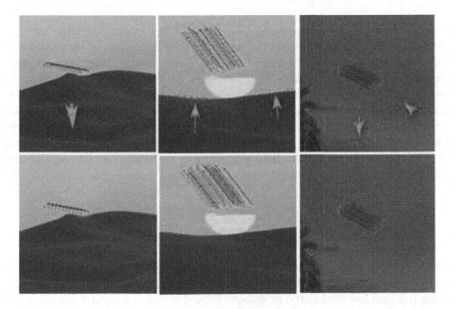

Fig. 7. Copy-move detection results for smoothed regions from GRIP dataset. Row 1: Detection result by using method in [11], Row 2: detection results of Proposed method.

Table 1. Evaluation metrics of compared and proposed methods for both data sets.

Data set	Methods	TPR (%)	FPR (%)	Accuracy (%)	F_1 score	IoU score (%)	Time (sec)
MICC-F220	[9]	92	4	94	93.21	66.67	18
MICC-F220	[10]	99.09	9.09	96	95.12	86.60	16.15
MICC-F220	[11]	100	1.82	99.02	99.10	91.23	3.0
MICC-F220	Proposed	100	1.42	99.27	99.32	93.24	3.86
GRIP	[11]	100	0	98.12	100	89.56	13.9
GRIP	Proposed	100	0	98.56	100	91.16	14.02

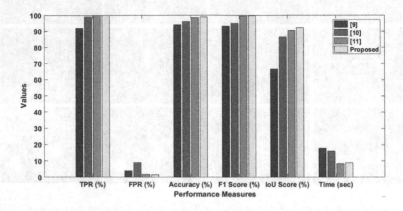

Fig. 8. Average performance measures of different detection methods.

the data set images. In terms of processing time, our method consumes comparatively less processing time than the methods in [9, 10]. Both of these methods utilized computationally expensive L_2 norm based feature matching strategy. In contrast, our method utilizes L_1 norm based feature matching scheme which provides enhanced robust detection results and consumes lesser time than L_2 norm. As compared to the method in [11] our method takes around 0.5 s more time to detect the forged region. Because the method in [11] integrates hierarchical feature point matching scheme. However, as compared to other methods, our proposed method provides excellent performance in localizing either structured or smoothed forgery regions at greater accuracy and manageable computational overload.

5   Conclusion

In this paper, we have suggested an efficient key-point based copy-move forgery detection method which enables to localize not only highly structured tampered regions but also low structured or smooth forged regions at greater accuracy. We have integrated spatial as well as structural content in the SIFT algorithm which facilitates to detect sufficient number of key-points even in smooth tampered regions. Moreover, an adaptive threshold selection strategy has been suggested to minimize the rate of false matches in the matching process. Performance assessment of the proposed work is validated both at image-level and pixel-level and found to be superior than the comparable state-of-the-art methods.

References

1. Farid, H.: A survey of image forgery detection. IEEE Sign. Process. Mag. **2**(26), 16–25 (2009)
2. Christlein, V., Riess, C., Jordan, J., Riess, C., Angelopoulou, E.: An evaluation of popular copy-move forgery detection approaches. IEEE Trans. Inf. Forensics Secur. **7**(6), 1841–1854 (2012)
3. Fridrich, A.J., Soukal, B.D., Lukáš, A.J.: Detection of copy-move forgery in digital images. In: Proceedings of Digital Forensic Research Workshop Citeseer (2003)
4. Muhammad, G., Hussain, M., Bebis, G.: Passive copy move image forgery detection using undecimated dyadic wavelet transform. Digital Invest. **9**(1), 49–57 (2012)
5. Zhao, J., Guo, J.: Passive forensics for copy-move image forgery using a method based on DCT and SVD. Forensic Sci. Int. **233**(1–3), 158–166 (2013)
6. Huang, H., Guo, W., Zhang, Y.: Detection of copy-move forgery in digital images using sift algorithm. In: 2008 IEEE Pacific-Asia Workshop on Computational Intelligence and Industrial Application, vol. 2, pp. 272–276. IEEE (2008)
7. Amerini, I., Ballan, L., Caldelli, R., Del Bimbo, A., Serra, G.: A sift-based forensic method for copy-move attack detection and transformation recovery. IEEE Trans. Inf. Forensics Secur. **6**(3), 1099–1110 (2011)
8. Hashmi, M.F., Hambarde, A.R., Keskar, A.G.: Copy move forgery detection using DWT and SIFT features. In: 2013 13th International Conference on Intelligent Systems Design and Applications, pp. 188–193. IEEE (2013)
9. Hashmi, M.F., Anand, V., Keskar, A.G.: Copy-move image forgery detection using an efficient and robust method combining un-decimated wavelet transform and scale invariant feature transform. Aasri Procedia **9**, 84–91 (2014)
10. Alberry, H.A., Hegazy, A.A., Salama, G.I.: A fast sift based method for copy move forgery detection. Future Comput. Inf. J. **3**(2), 159–165 (2018)
11. Li, Y., Zhou, J.: Fast and effective image copy-move forgery detection via hierarchical feature point matching. IEEE Trans. Inf. Forensics Secur. **14**(5), 1307–1322 (2018)
12. Prasad, S., Ramkumar, B.: Passive copy-move forgery detection using sift, hog and surf features. In: 2016 IEEE International Conference on Recent Trends in Electronics, Information & Communication Technology (RTEICT), pp. 706–710. IEEE (2016)
13. Nayak, R., Patra, D.: New single-image super-resolution reconstruction using MRF model. Neurocomputing **293**, 108–129 (2018)
14. Cozzolino, D., Poggi, G., Verdoliva, L.: Efficient dense-field copy-move forgery detection. IEEE Trans. Inf. Forensics Secur. **10**(11), 2284–2297 (2015)

F-UNet: A Modified U-Net Architecture for Segmentation of Stroke Lesion

Hritam Basak[1]([⊠])(iD) and Ajay Rana[2]

[1] Jadavpur University, Kolkata, India
[2] SRM Institute of Science and Technology, Chennai, India

Abstract. The assessment, prognosis, and treatment of brain stroke are completely dependent on accurate localization and segmentation of stroke lesions. The 2D and 3D convolutional neural networks (CNN) in recent times have been proven to be useful to detect and segment brain stroke lesions very efficiently. However, 2D CNN models cannot detect the three-dimensional spatio-temporal features whereas the 3D CNN models require extremely high computational resources and larger training time due to high memory requirements and hyper-parameter adjustments. To tackle this challenge, in this paper we propose a novel dimension fusion network architecture that can produce similar results as the 3D models, but with very small computational requirements. We also proposed an enhanced loss function for faster convergence than the dice coefficient loss and focal loss functions. Our proposed network was tested on the publicly available ATLAS dataset. The network and the loss function outperformed the existing methods and the state-of-the-art models both in terms of precision (0.6347 ± 0.2876), recall (0.5236 ± 0.2933), DSC (0.5350 ± 0.2763), and faster convergence.

Keywords: Deep learning · Dimension fusion · Brain MRI · Stroke lesion segmentation

1 Introduction

One of the most common cerebrovascular diseases, prevalent among the community between age limits of 40 and 60 is the stroke that contributes to a huge percentage of death worldwide every year [1,2]. Studies show that they can even cause 2 to 5 years of adult disabilities in 37–71% of reported cases globally. Rehabilitation can cause a long-term recovery in an acute condition, though the effectiveness of rehabilitation may also vary based on the neurological developments and damages caused by a stroke in patients. However, there have been significant improvements in recent days in neuro-imaging including brain image analysis and the T1-weighted high-quality MRI images have been instrumental for researchers in the assessment of patients' improvements to treatments or the possibility of gaining back some functionality like a motor speech [4]. In recent days, CNN and DNN models have been significantly useful for segmentation and classification purposes [5–11,35] and provide an end-to-end pipeline for segmentation task which is different from traditional hand-crafted feature extraction

© Springer Nature Singapore Pte Ltd. 2021
S. K. Singh et al. (Eds.): CVIP 2020, CCIS 1376, pp. 32–43, 2021.
https://doi.org/10.1007/978-981-16-1086-8_4

and segmentation in classical image processing problems. The 2-D CNN converts the volumetric data of MRI images into two-dimensional and predicts the result. A loss function is assigned to calculate the loss between predicted results and the actual annotated ground truths and by minimizing these losses, the network improvises its results with increasing iterations. However, some of the spatio-temporal information is lost in this approach and hence recently researchers have shifted towards 3-D CNNs.

To make use of the important circumstantial information of the volumetrical data and to outline and segregate the abnormalities in medical imaging, 3-D CNNs are trained. As it is difficult to meet the computational and memory requirements for 3-D CNNs, they have been avoided mostly, though they might be useful to extract important volumetric information. U-net architectures have also been instrumental in recent days for this purpose [12,13]. To solve the problem of segmentation of stroke-lesion accurately, we proposed a novel dimensionally fused U-net framework (F-UNet) that, despite having a 2-D framework, can also associate with important spatial 3-D information along with the 2-D ones with significantly low resources in terms of memory requirements and dataset.

Secondly, we proposed an enhanced mixing loss function that can significantly improve the convergence of the model. It combines the Focal Loss and Dice Loss functions to enhance the gradient propagation and results in faster convergence than the traditional and widely used Dice loss functions.

2 Related Works

Researchers have been using traditional and handcrafted features for brain MRI segmentation purposes for years and have achieved quite significant results [14]. Kemmling et al. [15] demonstrated a multivariate CTP based segmentation method of MRI images with a probability of infarct voxelwise. Machine learning models such as Random Forest or SVM (Support Vector Machine) were used for this purpose along with the image processing algorithm. For example, a histogram optimization algorithm was used using DWI for ischemic stroke lesion segmentation by Nabizadeh et al. [16]. Mitra et al. [17] suggested a multimodal MRI imaging for the feature extraction and then used the Random Forest method for the lesion segmentation and it reduced the false positive rate significantly. A random-forest-based method was further suggested by Mahmood et al. [18] for acute stroke lesion segmentation which achieved the best result in the ISLES challenge in 2015. Sivakumar et al. [21] proposed an HHET method for internal brain region enhancement followed by an ANFIS classifier for detection and segmentation of stroke lesions from brain MRI. Recently, the emerging deep learning models have shown improvements in segmentation and classification tasks in biomedical applications. Handcrafted features have limitations and depend highly on the skills of feature engineers. Besides, it is difficult to extract features manually from a large dataset. Therefore, Kamnitsas et al. [5] proposed DeepMedic, a 2-D CNN model that achieved a DC score of 0.59 on the ISLES dataset later. Chen et al. [22] achieved a DC score of 0.67 on the test set of the institutional dataset due to a lack of public datasets by using DWI. They implemented a framework that contained features of EDD net and MUSCLE net (Multi-Scale Convolutional Level Net). Cui et al. [23] proposed another 2-D CNN model for the segmentation and classification of carcinoma in nasopharyngeal cases from the MRI dataset. They used cascade architecture for the segmentation of tumors from the MRI images and then classified them into four different regions based on their characteristics.

3   Proposed Methodology

3.1   Feature Extraction Using the Proposed F-UNet

The basic architecture of the network is based on the U-Net backbone with some further modifications. We have developed a symmetric encoder-decoder model that can extract low-level fine surface information along with high-level semantics. The architecture is displayed in Fig. 1. The H, W, and D in Fig. 1(b) are the height, width, and depth of the feature volume whereas C represents the number of channels in the feature map. The recently implemented squeeze and excite block (SE block) has a hyperparameter r, known as a reduction ratio, that can be used to control the computational cost and capacity of the SE block.

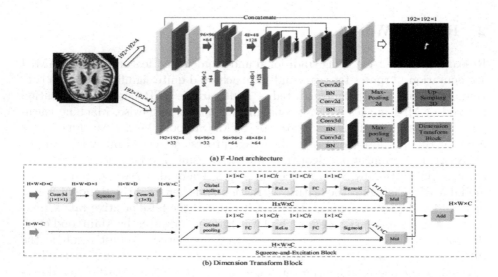

Fig. 1. (a) The F-U-Net architecture where the encoder is slightly modified from the basic 2-D U-Net by adding the 3-D convolutional layer and dimension transfer block. (b) The dimensional transform block where the two different channels indicate the 2-D and 3-D network respectively.

This block opens the connection between different feature channels and can enhance the effect of fusion of 2-D and 3-D features in the dimensional fusion block. In each of these blocks, we add the reduced 3-D branch feature map to the 2-D branch feature map by SE weighted fusion. The block can be considered as a special architectural block, used for the dynamic channel-wise recalibration of the features and thus enabling the network to extract important spatial features. Each channel features are average-pooled to a single value, followed by a dense layer, accompanied by the ReLU activation that adds non-linearity and reduces the channel complexity of output significantly. Finally, followed by another dense layer and sigmoid, each channel receives a smooth gating function and the 'excitation' is the weighting of all feature maps in the side network at a lesser computational cost. Thus, very small stroke regions, having higher importance in biomedical applications, can be detected easily by this approach.

If F_{2d} and F_{3d} represent the feature maps in two and three dimensions respectively, which serves as the input of the dimension transfer block, where C, H, W, D, N represent the number of channels, height, width, depth, and a batch size of the feature map respectively, we first convert F_{3d} having the dimension of N*H*W*D*C to F^*_{3d} of dimension N*H*W*D*1 with the convolution operation using a three dimensional 1*1*1 convolutional block. Next, the dimensionality of F^*_{3d} is squeezed from N*H*W*D*1 to N*H*W*D. To keep the dimension consistent with the 2D feature maps, we then convert the F^*_{3d} with the dimension of N*H*W*D to N*H*W*C by using a 2D 3*3 convolutional block with filter size set to C. If f_d represents the dimensionality reduction operation function, we convert F_{3d} to F'_{3d} by using this function(where F'_{3d} has the dimension of N*H*W*C):

$$F'_{3d} = f_d(F_{3d}) \tag{1}$$

We use the SE block to weight the two different dimensional feature channels and their weighted channel outputs for the sake of better ability of feature expression before fusion. Mathematically,

$$F = f_s(F'_{3d}) + f_s(F_{2d}) \tag{2}$$

(where F has the dimension of N*H*W*C)

F denotes the fused feature map which is obtained as the output of the SE block. The parameters of the complete network and the architecture are further described in Fig. 2. The two different dimensional features are fused in this step where f_s represents the SE block which squeezes and excites as described by [30].

3.2 Loss Function

In medical image analysis, especially in stroke lesion segmentation from brain MRI images, the actual stroke lesion part comprises of a very small region as compared to the entire background and foreground part. Therefore, the

	Feature size	Two-dimensional operation	Feature size	Three-dimensional operation
Input	192×192×4	-	192×192×4×1	-
Convolution block 1	192×192×32	2×(3×3 Conv+ Bn)	192×192×4×3	2×(3×3×3 Conv+ Bn)
Pooling	96×96×32	2×2 max pooling	96×96×2×32	2×2×2 max pooling
Convolution block 2	96×96×64	2×(3×3 Conv+ Bn)	96×96×2×64	2×(3×3×3 Conv+ Bn)
Dimension fusion block 2	96×96×64	-	-	-
Pooling	48×48×64	2×2 max pooling	48×48×1×64	2×2×2 max pooling
Convolution block 3	48×48×128	2×(3×3 Conv+ Bn)	48×48×1×128	2×(3×3×3 Conv+ Bn)
Dimension fusion block 3	48×48×128	-	-	-
Pooling	24×24×128	2×2 max pooling	-	-
Convolution block 4	24×24×256	2×(3×3 Conv+ Bn)	-	-
Dropout	24×24×256	-	-	-
Pooling	12×12×256	2×2 max pooling	-	-
Convolution block 5	12×12×512	2×(3×3 Conv+ Bn)	-	-
Dropout	12×12×512	-	-	-
Up-sampling block 1-4	192×192×32	2×2 Up-sampling[*] 2×(3×3 Conv+ Bn)	-	-
Convolution	192×192×1	1×1 Conv	-	-

Fig. 2. The architecture of the proposed F-U-Net. Up-sampling [*] symbolizes that the particular layer is merged before up-sampling.

traditional loss function may sometimes result in local optima instead of the global one while using them. As a remedy, we proposed a new loss function that addresses the background and foreground voxel imbalance in [31] and it is the combination of two traditional loss functions.

The focal loss is the improved version of widely used binary cross-entropy loss, by adding a regulating factor. It extends the loss range to low loss and reduces the loss of contribution for easier specimens. Mathematically, we define the Focal Loss with the help of binary cross-entropy loss function by the following equation:

$$L_F(x, GT) = \begin{cases} -log(x) \sum_{j=1}^{n_0} a(1-x)^b, \text{ when GT}=1 \\ -log(1-x) \sum_{j=1}^{n} (1-a)x^b, \text{ otherwise} \end{cases} \quad (3)$$

where GT $\in \{0, 1\}$ represents the pixel-level ground truth, x represents the probability value of model prediction and can have value in the range [0, 1], n0 and n1 represent the pixel count in class 0 and class 1 respectively, a and b are the modulating variables and can have values in the range (0, 1] and [0, 5] respectively, and can be set according to the requirements. The dice loss alleviates the problem of foreground and background pixel imbalance by modifying the Dice Similarity Coefficient score between the annotated GT and the predicted sample results, hence performs better in the segmentation tasks.

$$L_D(x, GT) = 1 - \frac{2 \sum\limits_{j=1}^{n} x_j GT_j + c}{\sum\limits_{j=1}^{n} x_j^2 + \sum\limits_{j=1}^{n} GT_j^2 + c} \tag{4}$$

where, c is a modulating variable that can have values in the range [0, 1] and prevents the problem of zero in the denominator. Thus, it allows gradient propagation of the negative samples too.

We proposed a mixture of these two losses and named it as Improved Mixing Loss for faster convergence. To keep the positive gradient in each iteration, we inverted the value of L_D and took a logarithm of it. Next, we added the focal loss to it to explore whether these two losses have reinforcement characteristics or not. But, as the focal loss is defined as the summation of all the voxel probabilities, we used a $1/n$ factor to the focal loss to make it an average of the voxel probabilities and to keep it in a comparable range to the dice loss which plays a significant role in the gradient propagation. Mathematically, our proposed loss function is:

$$L(x, GT) = \frac{1}{n} L_F(x, GT) - log[L_D(x, GT)] \tag{5}$$

3.3 Implementation

We have selected the transverse section images in the preprocessing step and region of interest having diagonal coordinates of (15, 20) and (185, 225) have been cropped from the corresponding images that eliminate the unnecessary details from the image and enlarges the actual lesion part. Next, we resized the cropped portion of the image to the specified dimension of 192*192 to feed in the network. This step was performed with the help of the bilinear interpolation method. Next, we integrated all the processed images with spatial arrangements of two upper slices and one lower size that formed a matrix having a dimension of 192*192*4. In the down-sampling phase of the U-Net, the initial number of filet has been set to 32 to both the 2D and 3D channels of the network. The numbers of convolution filters are doubled after every single pooling layer and finally, the number of filters is set to 512 for the 2D channel and batch normalization was done after every convolution operation for the stability of the training process. The hyperparameter r of the dimension transfer block is set to 16 and the values of modulating variables a, b in the Focal loss function are set to 1.1 and 0.48 whereas c in the Dice loss function is set to have value 1. SGD optimizer with a learning rate of 1e-6 was used and all the additional parameters were set similar to the one mentioned by Kingma et al. [32].

4   Results and Discussions

In this section, we compared our result with the existing state of the art results from 2D and 3D U-Nets and also compare the superiority of our proposed loss function with the existing ones. We used the publicly available ATLAS dataset for the training and validation of our method. The dataset contains 229 instances of 233*197*189 MRI T1 sequence scans and delineates the various stages of stroke lesions. We have used 80% of the dataset (183 slices) from the entire dataset distribution for the training set and the remaining 20% for validating the results. The cause for this split-approach is to reduce the biasing that might be caused by selecting 80% from a single patient data volume as all the slides might not contain the lesions. The quantitative measurement indices are represented by the following equations:

If True Positive (TP) means that a positive voxel is correctly predicted as positive; False Positive (FP) means that a negative voxel is mistakenly classified as positive; False Negative means that a positive voxel is incorrectly classified as negative, then:

$$Precision = \frac{TP}{TP + FP} \qquad (6)$$

$$Recall = \frac{TP}{FN + TP} \qquad (7)$$

$$DSC = \frac{2TP}{2TP + FN + FP} \qquad (8)$$

4.1 Comparison with State-of-the-Art Results

We experimented with both the original U-Net architecture, where the parameter settings are similar to the one described in [33], and the transformed one where batch normalization was added after every convolution layer for the stability purpose, and the number of convolution layers was also reduced. Furthermore, we also compared our result with the 3D U-Net model result and was based on the precision, recall, and DSC scores, and the batch size was set to 32 for all the cases, except the 3D U-Net, where the batch size was set to 4 due to a large number of memory requirements. Table 1 shows how better our model is as compared to different U-Net architectures.

We compared the result of the F-U-Net with the existing state-of-the-art methods (SegNet, DeepLab v3, and PSP network) to prove the superiority of the performance of our proposed method. Google DeepLab series has the latest member named DeepLab v3 which has the feature of encoder-decoder structure accompanied by Atrous Spatial Pyramid Pooling. SegNet also performs

Table 1. Comparison of results with existing U-Net models (the results are presented in the form of mean − standard deviation)

Method	No. of Parameter	Precision	Recall	DSC	Global DSC
3D U-Net (transformed)	22997826	0.5528 ± 3239	0.4740 ± 0.3102	0.4720 ± 0.2752	0.7088
2D U-Net (transformed)	7771297	0.5509 ± 0.3303	0.5041 ± 0.3037	0.4957 ± 0.2899	0.7137
2D U-Net (original)	31090593	0.5624 ± 0.2149	0.4840 ± 0.3004	0.4869 ± 0.2837	0.7120
Proposed method	8640163	0.6347 ± 0.2876	0.5236 ± 0.2933	0.5350 ± 0.2763	0.7229

Table 2. Comparison of results with existing state-of-the-art models (the results are presented in the form of mean − standard deviation)

Method	Precision	Recall	DSC	Global DSC
LINDA	0.44 ± 0.30	0.51 ± 0.36	0.44 ± 0.34	-
ALI	0.30 ± 0.24	0.56 ± 0.32	0.35 ± 0.25	-
Lesion GNB	0.29 ± 0.19	0.70 ± 0.31	0.38 ± 0.30	-
Clusterize	0.15 ± 0.16	0.80 ± 0.22	0.24 ± 0.20	-
PSP	0.5001 ± 0.2920	0.4711 ± 0.2870	0.4458 ± 0.2589	0.6730
SegNet	0.3850 ± 0.2851	0.3322 ± 0.3113	0.3191 ± 0.2426	0.6001
U-Net	0.5520 ± 0.3301	0.5041 ± 0.3011	0.5011 ± 2799	0.7149
DeepLab v3	0.5630 ± 0.3273	0.4465 ± 0.2756	0.4530 ± 0.3049	0.7105
Ours	0.6347 ± 0.2876	0.5236 ± 0.2933	0.5350 ± 0.2763	0.7229

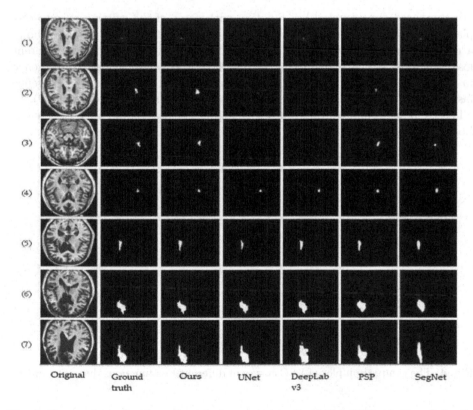

Fig. 3. Comparison of our result with the ground truth, U-Net, PSP net, DeepLab v3, and SegNet for different test cases. The seven cases are arranged with the increasing size of the stroke lesion area.

well in the segmentation task where non –linear up-sampling and unpooling in the downsampling are two important features. Pyramid pooling and Atrous convolution are the two important features used in the Pyramid Scene Parsing network for retrieval of important context information. The first five results of the Table 2 represents the results obtained from [34] on the same dataset and were not performed in our experiments, whereas the second half of the results are the recently developed deep learning-based approach that was explained beforehand. It is observed from Fig. 3 that most of the models find it quite difficult to identify and segment the lesion when the foreground is very small compared to the background, whereas our model performs quite well in these cases (row 1–3). In the last two rows, it is observed that the lesion boundary is fuzzy, still, our network performs significantly well as it can extract 3D spatio-temporal features from the images.

4.2 Loss Validation

We compared our proposed loss function with some of the existing ones to display the superiority in performance in the segmentation task. Figure 4 shows a comparison plot of rising DSC scores with increasing iterations in different loss functions. We have found that dice coefficient loss has the least convergence in the early stages of training, however, it overtakes the focal loss convergence faster in the later stages of training (i.e. after iteration number close to 40). In all cases, our method converges faster than the Focal Loss and Dice Coefficient Loss.

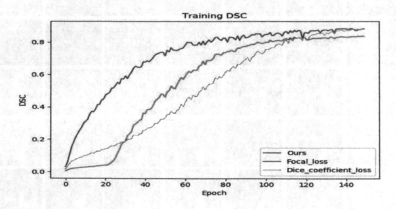

Fig. 4. The comparison plot of DSC curves in different loss functions during training.

5   Conclusion and Future Work

The importance of stroke lesion detection and segmentation has a huge impact on the clinical prognosis. This helps physicians to quickly assess the condition of the patient as well as the necessity and planning of surgery can also be planned. In this paper, we proposed a novel architecture for 3D context features extraction and segmentation of brain lesions from MRI images with very low computational resources. Furthermore, we also proposed a new loss function and compared our result with the existing state-of-the-art results. Our network performed comparatively between segmentation as well as localization of stroke lesion. Our proposed loss function also converges faster than the two popular loss functions, Focal Loss and Dice Coefficient Loss, most commonly used in segmentation task. Further, we can improve the performance by experiments on dimension fusion blocks and incorporating more 3D information. The proposed method can also be evaluated on a larger dataset for further assessment of the effectiveness of the approach.

References

1. Redon, J., et al.: Stroke mortality and trends from 1990 to 2006 in 39 countries from Europe and Central Asia: implications for control of high blood pressure. Eur. Heart J. **32**(11), 1424–1431 (2011)
2. Donkor, E.: Stroke in the 21st century: a snapshot of the burden, epidemiology, and quality of life. Stroke Res. Treat. **2018**, 1–10 (2018)
3. Mayo Clinic. 2020. Stroke - Symptoms And Causes. https://www.mayoclinic.org/diseases-conditions/stroke/symptoms-causes/syc20350113. Accessed 12 June 2020
4. Neumann, A., et al.: Interrater agreement for final infarct MRI lesion delineation. Stroke **40**(12), 3768–3771 (2009)
5. Kamnitsas, K., et al.: Efficient multi-scale 3D CNN with fully connected CRF for accurate brain lesion segmentation. Med. Image Anal. **36**, 61–78 (2017)
6. Guerrero, R., et al.: White matter hyperintensity and stroke lesion segmentation and differentiation using convolutional neural networks. NeuroImage: Clin. **17**, 918–934 (2018)
7. Atlason, H., Love, A., Sigurdsson, S., Gudnason, V., Ellingsen, L.: SegAE: unsupervised white matter lesion segmentation from brain MRIs using a CNN autoencoder. NeuroImage Clin. **24**, 102085 (2019)
8. Joshi, S.: Ischemic stroke lesion segmentation by analyzing MRI images using deep convolutional neural networks. HELIX **8**(5), 3721–3725 (2018)
9. Praveen, G., Agrawal, A., Sundaram, P., Sardesai, S.: Ischemic strokelesion segmentation using stacked sparse autoencoder. Comput. Biol. Med. **99**, 38–52 (2018)
10. Liu, L., Chen, S., Zhang, F., Wu, F.-X., Pan, Y., Wang, J.: Deep convolutional neural network for automatically segmenting acute ischemic stroke lesion in multi-modality MRI. Neural Comput. Appl. **32**(11), 6545–6558 (2019). https://doi.org/10.1007/s00521-019-04096-x
11. Nazari-Farsani, S., Nyman, M., Karjalainen, T., Bucci, M., Isojärvi, J., Nummenmaa, L.: Automated segmentation of acute stroke lesions using a datadriven anomaly detection on diffusion weighted MRI. J. Neurosci. Methods **333**, 108575 (2020)
12. Weng, Y., Zhou, T., Li, Y., Qiu, X.: NAS-Unet: neural architecture search for medical image segmentation. IEEE Access **7**, 44247–44257 (2019). https://doi.org/10.1109/ACCESS.2019.2908991

13. Zhang, J., Lv, X., Sun, Q., Zhang, Q., Wei, X., Liu, B.: SDResU-Net: separable and dilated residual U-net for MRI brain tumor segmentation. Curr. Med. Imaging Former. Curr. Med. Imaging Rev. **15** (2019)

14. Shao, W., Huang, S., Liu, M., Zhang, D.: Querying representative and informative super-pixels for filament segmentation in bioimages. IEEE/ACM Trans. Comput. Biol. Bioinform. **17**(4), 1394–1405 (2019)

15. Kemmling, A., et al.: Multivariate dynamic prediction of ischemic infarction and tissue salvage as a function of time and degree of recanalization. J. Cereb. Blood Flow Metab. **35**(9), 1397–1405 (2015)

16. Nabizadeh, N., Kubat, M., John, N., Wright, C.: Automatic ischemic stroke lesion segmentation using single MR modality and gravitational histogram optimization based brain segmentation. In: Proceedings of the International Conference on Image Processing, Computer Vision, and Pattern Recognition (IPCV), p. 1 (2014)

17. Mitra, J., et al.: Lesion segmentation from multimodal MRI using random forest following ischemic stroke. NeuroImage **98**, 324–335 (2014)

18. Mahmood, Q., Basit, A.: Automatic ischemic stroke lesion segmentation in multispectral MRI images using random forests classifier. In: Crimi, A., Menze, B., Maier, O., Reyes, M., Handels, H. (eds.) BrainLes 2015. LNCS, vol. 9556, pp. 266–274. Springer, Cham (2016). https://doi.org/10.1007/978-3-319-30858-6_23

19. Maier, O., et al.: ISLES 2015 - a public evaluation benchmark for ischemic stroke lesion segmentation from multispectral MRI. Med. Image Anal. **35**, 250–269 (2017)

20. Chyzhyk, D., Dacosta-Aguayo, R., Mataró, M., Graña, M.: An active learning approach for stroke lesion segmentation on multimodal MRI data. Neurocomputing **150**, 26–36 (2015)

21. Sivakumar, P., Ganeshkumar, P.: An efficient automated methodology for detecting and segmenting the ischemic stroke in brain MRI images. Int. J. Imaging Syst. Technol. **27**(3), 265–272 (2017)

22. Chen, L., Bentley, P., Rueckert, D.: Fully automatic acute ischemic lesion segmentation in DWI using convolutional neural networks. NeuroImage: Clin. **15**, 633–643 (2017)

23. Cui, S., Mao, L., Jiang, J., Liu, C., Xiong, S.: Automatic semantic segmentation of brain gliomas from MRI images using a deep cascaded neural network. J. Healthc. Eng. **2018**, 1–14 (2018)

24. Chen, Y., Zhu, Y., Jiang, J., Guan, W.: Comparison of contrast-enhanced ultrasound targeted biopsy versus standard systematic biopsy for prostate cancer detection. Ultrasound Med. Biol. **45**, S125 (2019)

25. Shin, H., et al.: Deep convolutional neural networks for computer-aided detection: CNN architectures, dataset characteristics and transfer learning. IEEE Trans. Med. Imaging **35**(5), 1285–1298 (2016)

26. Ji, S., Xu, W., Yang, M., Yu, K.: 3D convolutional neural networks for human action recognition. IEEE Trans. Pattern Anal. Mach. Intell. **35**(1), 221–231 (2013)

27. Li, X., Chen, H., Qi, X., Dou, Q., Fu, C., Heng, P.: H-Dense UNet: hybrid densely connected UNet for liver and tumor segmentation from CT volumes. IEEE Trans. Med. Imaging **37**(12), 2663–2674 (2018)

28. Sudre, C.H., Li, W., Vercauteren, T., Ourselin, S., Jorge Cardoso, M.: Generalised Dice Overlap as a Deep Learning Loss Function for Highly Unbalanced Segmentations. In: Cardoso, M.J., et al. (eds.) DLMIA/ML-CDS -2017. LNCS, vol. 10553, pp. 240–248. Springer, Cham (2017). https://doi.org/10.1007/978-3-319-67558-9_28

29. Ghiasi-Shirazi, K.: Competitive cross-entropy loss: a study on training single-layer neural networks for solving nonlinearly separable classification problems. Neural Process. Lett. **50**(2), 1115–1122 (2018). https://doi.org/10.1007/s11063-018-9906-5

30. Hu, J., Shen, L., Sun, G.: Squeeze-and-excitation networks. In: Proceedings of the IEEE Conference on Computer Vision and Pattern Recognition, pp. 71327141 (2018)

31. Lin, T.Y., Goyal, P., Girshick, R., He, K., Dollár, P.: Focal loss for dense object detection. In: Proceedings of the IEEE International Conference on Computer Vision, pp. 2980–2988 (2017)

32. Kingma, D.P., Ba, J.: Adam: A method for stochastic optimization. arXivpreprint arXiv:1412.6980 (2014)

33. Ronneberger, O.: Invited talk: U-net convolutional networks for biomedical image segmentation. Bildverarbeitung für die Medizin 2017. I, pp. 3–3. Springer, Heidelberg (2017). https://doi.org/10.1007/978-3-662-54345-0_3

34. Ito, K.L., Kim, H., Liew, S.L.: A comparison of automated lesion segmentation approaches for chronic stroke T1-weighted MRI data. Hum. Brain Mapp. **40**(16), 4669–4685 (2019)

35. Chattopadhyay, S., Basak, H.: Multi-scale Attention U-Net (MsAUNet): A Modified U-Net Architecture for Scene Segmentation. arXiv preprint arXiv:2009.06911 (2020)

Radial Cumulative Frequency Distribution: A New Imaging Signature to Detect Chromosomal Arms 1p/19q Co-deletion Status in Glioma

Debanjali Bhattacharya[1], Neelam Sinha[1(✉)], and Jitender Saini[2]

[1] International Institute of Information Technology, Bangalore, India
neelam.sinha@iiitb.ac.in
[2] National Institute of Mental Health and Neuroscience, Bangalore, India

Abstract. Gliomas are the most common primary brain tumor and are associated with high mortality. Gene mutations are one of the hallmarks of glioma formation, determining its aggressiveness as well as patients's response towards treatment. The paper presents a novel approach to detect chromosomal arms 1p/19q co-deletion status non-invasively in low-graded glioma based on its textural characteristics in frequency domain. For this, we derived *Radial Cumulative Frequency Distribution (RCFD)* function from Fourier power spectrum of consecutive glioma slices. Multi-parametric MRIs of 159 grade-2 and grade-3 glioma patients, having biopsy proven 1p/19q mutational status (non-deletion: $n = 57$ and co-deletion: $n = 102$) was used in this study. Different RCFD textural features were extracted to quantify MRI image signature pattern of mutant and wildtype glioma. Owing to skewed dataset we have performed RUSBoost classification; yielding average accuracy of 73.5% for grade-2 and 83% for grade-3 glioma subjects. The efficacy of the proposed technique is discussed further in comparison with state-of-art methods.

Keywords: Glioma · Polar FFT · Radial cumulative frequency distribution · RUSBoost classifier

1 Introduction

Glioma is caused by abnormal and uncontrollable growth of glial cells of brain. The onset and progression of glioma followed by patient's response and overall survival rate is greatly influenced by different characteristics of glioma. In this regard the genetic alteration is one biggest risk factor that cannot be ignored as a cause of glioma. It is seen that only 5%–10% of all glioma are hereditary. For most of the cases it is not inherited at birth but it builds up over time as a result of mutation in DNA sequence of gene. Deeper genetic analyses of larger numbers of glioma samples reforms the old WHO classification of CNS tumor in the year 2016 by introducing molecular characteristics in addition to histology, leading to progress in glioma diagnosis and treatment planning [1]. It is evident that glioma with mutations are clinically and genetically very distinct from tumors

S. K. Singh et al. (Eds.): CVIP 2020, CCIS 1376, pp. 44–55, 2021.
https://doi.org/10.1007/978-981-16-1086-8_5

with wildtype genes and have better prognosis in estimating positive response to radiotherapy [3]. Hence, it is essential to determine 1p/19q co-deletion status in patients suffering from glioma in order to establish effective treatment strategies. Currently the popular approaches for determining mutation are DNA sequencing, immune-histochemical staining and FISH test [4]. But all of these techniques are invasive in nature, as the analysis require *ex-vivo* postoperative or biopsy tissues. Moreover these methods are limited in assessing the glioma's heterogeneity. Hence the objective of our study is to propose a new approach that could able to predict mutational status in glioma in a non-invasive manner. There are few imaging studies reported in literature that predict the presence of gene mutation in glioma non-invasively using multi-modal medical images [3,5–9,12–14]. However some of these studies failed to show promising results in determining the mutational status in individual patients [5–7,9].

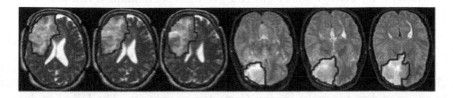

Fig. 1. T2-W MRI of 3 consecutive glioma slices of one subject with 1p/19q co-deletion *(column1 to column3)* and 1p/19q non-deletion *(column4 to column6)*. The glioma portion is highlighted in yellow color (Color figure online)

While exploring the MR images of glioma in individual patient visually, it was observed that the inter-slice texture pattern in majority of gliomas occurred due to mutation are homogeneous in nature; while the inter-slice MRI texture pattern is random and heterogeneous in cases of wildtype gliomas. It was also observed that, this heterogeneity increases with increase in glioma grades for both mutant and wildtype cases. In order to establish the validity of this visual observation, our study aims to differentiate mutant and wildtype gliomas after modeling textural properties of tissue by its spatial frequency content. To achieve this, we have come up with a new function, called *"Radial Cumulative Frequency Distribution (RCFD)"* that could quantify the changes in dominant orientation of tissue alignment across consecutive glioma slices. We hypothesize that changes in dominant tissue orientation is insignificant in glioma occurred due to mutation. This in-turn could reflect the presence of texture homogeneity in mutant gliomas.

The present research contributory work is different from previously reported work [3,5–9,12–14] in that, *it utilizes frequency space texture measures and its pattern analysis to detect molecular marker of glioma in a non-invasive way by multi-parametric structural MRI*. There is recent study that have showed the potential of frequency spectrum analysis in measuring tissue alignment in standard MRI for patients having Multiple Sclerosis [16]. Thus for advancing the treatment and diagnosis of glioma patients, spatial frequency-space analysis to characterize glioma texture could open a new direction in predicting mutational status non-invasively by conventional MRI.

2   Proposed Methodology

2.1   Radial Cumulative Frequency Distribution (RCFD)

In order to examine the nature of tissue anisotropy across glioma slices, we derived radial cumulative frequency distribution (RCFD). RCFD describes the how cumulative frequency of the power spectrum varies radially (with radius 'r') as a function of angle θ. Thus in the context of MR image analysis, the function RCFD can estimate the dominant direction of tissue alignment in a specific slice. For a given tumor image which is a function $f = [x, y]$, where $x, y \in R^2$, the two dimensional (2D) Fourier transform (FT) in discrete domain is defined as

$$F[u, v] = \sum_{x=0}^{M-1} \sum_{y=0}^{N-1} f[x, y] e^{[-j2\pi(\frac{xu}{N} + \frac{yv}{N})]} \tag{1}$$

In Eq. 1, $F[u, v]$ is the Fourier spectrum of $f[x, y]$ where, u, v are the spatial frequencies and x, y are the spatial Cartesian coordinate. The FT of an image normally has lots of low frequencies that are generally located at the center part in Fourier space and contains more image information than its high frequency components that spreads away from the center. Since FT is commonly defined on Cartesian grids, so in order to capture the frequency distribution profile along a specific direction, we expressed FT in Eq. 1 in terms of its polar coordinates. Hence polar FT (PFT) can be formed by transforming spatial and frequency coordinates from Cartesian to Polar using the following Eqs. 2

$$\begin{aligned} x &= r \cos \theta; y = r \sin \theta \\ u &= \rho \cos \psi; v = \rho \sin \psi \end{aligned} \tag{2}$$

Substituting Eqs. 2 in Eqs. 1 we can define the Polar FT as below

$$F[\rho, \psi] = \sum_{\theta=0}^{2\pi} \sum_{r=0}^{R} f[r, \theta] e^{[-j2\pi\rho r \cos(\theta - \psi)]} \tag{3}$$

Equation 3 represents the expression of PFT that converts the spatial position radius and angle (r, θ) into the frequency radius and angle (ρ, ψ). However unlike the rectangular grid system where the grid points are evenly spaced throughout, in case of polar grid, the edge points of polar grid are fairly sparser. Sparsity reduces gradually as we move towards center, resulting denser grid points at the center of polar grid. Therefore to achieve similar densities as observed at the polar grid center, the Cartesian grid is required to be oversampled. In this study PFT is computed by interpolating rectangular 2D Fourier magnitudes into the corresponding polar grids. The FT and the corresponding PFT of three consequtive glioma slices is shown in Fig. 2.

Fig. 2. Power spectrum using FFT *(top row)* and PFT *(bottom row).* The first row shows the FFT and PFT spectrum of one subject with G3 1p/19q co-deleted glioma. The last row shows the same for one subject with G3 1p/19q non-deleted glioma.

The conversion of traditional FFT to PFT helps to derive two functions: (1) The size of dominant texture which is the distribution of frequencies across all angles and can be formulated as

$$D(r) = \sum_{\theta=0}^{2\pi} F(\rho, \psi) \qquad (4)$$

(2) The direction of dominant texture which is the distribution of all frequencies in a specific direction and can be formulated as

$$O(\theta) = \sum_{r=0}^{R} F(\rho, \psi) \qquad (5)$$

Equation 4 and Eq. 5 represent the average spectrum in one-dimension. In context of MRI analysis these two functions represent the texture of tumor tissues. In the proposed study the analysis is based on the second function (Eq. 5) since the size of dominant texture (Eq. 4) hardly ever changes because the predominance of in-general low frequency pattern of MRI. Hence we define RCFD as *the cumulative distribution of all frequencies in a specific direction.* Finally, RCFD of tumor volume is obtained by taking the mean RCFD (MRCFD) of successive tumor slices. Thus the three-dimensional RCFD is derived as

$$MRCFD = \frac{1}{n} \sum_{n=1}^{3} O_n(\theta) \qquad (6)$$

Here, 'n' represents the number of tumor slices. The value of n is 3 as we have consider three consecutive MR slices as described in Sect. 3.1.

2.2   Feature Extraction

Glioma classification based on 1p/19q mutational status was performed by extracting the following features from RCFD function:

(i) Change in dominant direction of tissue alignment:
In Fourier space, pixels have tendency to group along the direction of tissue alignment. Hence to calculate the dominant direction of tissue alignment, covariance
matrix was computed from glioma RCFD. Let, X_i and X_j denote the RCFD of
two successive tumor images as computed using Eq. 5, then covariance between
X_i and X_j is calculated as

$$Cov_{i,j} = \sigma(X_i, X_j) = E[(X_i - E(X_i)(X_i - E[X_i)]] \tag{7}$$

where $Cov_{i,j} \in R^{d x d}$ and 'd' describes the dimensions of random variable. Thus
for the 2D data, covariance matrix would be reduced to

$$Cov_{1,2} = \begin{bmatrix} \sigma_{11} & \sigma_{12} \\ \sigma_{21} & \sigma_{22} \end{bmatrix} \tag{8}$$

Clearly the diagonal (variance) and off-diagonal (covariance) elements in
Eq. 8 captures the amount of spread and orientation respectively. Therefore
in order to assess the nature of tissue alignment in consecutive glioma slices,
the covariance matrix would measure how much the two $MRCFD$ varies with
respect to each other. This further leads to measure the dominant direction
of tissue alignment. This is calculated from largest Eigen vector of covariance
matrix. The change in dominant tissue alignment in successive slices of mutant
and wildtype tumor is used as feature for classification.
(ii) Energy of $MRCFD$: It describes the radial frequency variation of images.
(iii) Peaks energy: The energy of dominant peaks obtained from $MRCFD$. The
dominant peaks were identified as those, where the peaks had a magnitude of
≥ 0.7. Thus the threshold value was set to 0.7 to extract the dominant peaks.
So, more the number of dominant peaks, more will be the energy and vice versa.
(iv) Difference in successive peak height: The mean difference in successive peak
height measures the type of texture. If the difference is more it indicates rapid
drop of $MRCFD$ function which in-turn capture the fine texture of tumor tissue. Likewise smaller difference indicates course texture when the function drops
slowly due to its oscillatory nature.
(v) Euclidean distance: Mean Euclidean distance between two successive
$MRCFD$ was calculated to measure the closeness between two distributions.

2.3   RUSBoost Classification

In given dataset, the mutated glioma class includes 64.15% of data and the
wildtype glioma class includes 35.85% of data which clearly indicates the problem of class imbalance. This problem was addressed by RUSBoost classification.
The main advantage of RUSBoost classifier over traditional machine learning
classifiers lies in its efficacy of handling class imbalance problem. In RUSboost
classifier random-under-samoling (RUS) and the standard boosting procedure
Adaboost are used in combination for better modelling of minority class with
simultaneous elimination of majority class [15].

Let, in dataset 'V', 'n' examples are represented by tuple (x_k, y_k) where x_k is a point in feature space 'X', and y_k be the class label in a set of class label 'Y'. The RUSBoost algorithm begins with initializing the weight of each example to $1/n$. If the total number of iterations are denoted by 'P', then P weak hypothesis H_t are iteratively trained ($t = 1$ to P) using some classification algorithm '$WeakLearn$' as follows: First, the majority class examples are removed using RUS until the majority and minority class examples are equal (1:1). This will result a new training dataset V_t' having a new weight distribution W_t'. In the next step, V_t' and W_t' are passed to '$WeakLearn$' (base learner) in order to create the weak hypothesis H_t. Based on actual training dataset 'V' and weight distribution 'W_t', the pseudo-loss δ_t is calculated. After this, the weight distribution for the next iteration W_{t+1} is updated using weight update parameter a_t followed by normalization. Finally, after 'P' iterations the final hypothesis $\Theta(x)$ is returned as a weighted vote of the each weak hypothesis.

3   Results

3.1   Dataset

The study utilizes TCIA public access database [2] for collecting MRI images of 1p/19q co-deleted and 1p/19q non-deleted glioma. Study subjects include 1mm thick sliced T1 post contrast (T1C-W) and 3mm thick sliced T2-W preoperative MR scans of 159 patients (non-deleted: $n = 57$ and co-deleted: $n = 102$) having grade-2 (G2) and grade-3 (G3) glioma. Total 477 MR slices (for each LGG subject 3 slices were used which incorporate the one with the largest tumor diameter, one below it and one above it) were used in this study. The histopathological sub-types of LGG include astrocytomas, oligoastrocytoma and oligodendroglioma. All subjects had biopsy proven 1p/19q co-deletion or non-deletion status. Figure 1 shows 3 consecutive T2-W MR slices of one subject with and without 1p/19 co-deletion. Glioma portion was extracted from selected MR slices using the ground truth of segmented glioma provided by TCIA which was used as a mask for segmentation purpose. This segmented glioma was thereafter used for the entire analysis.

MATLAB R2018a software was used to write the code and followed by running it on a machine with Intel(R) Core(TM) i3 4005U CPU 1.70GHz processor with 4.00 GB RAM. The Fourier spectrum of successive glioma tissues for one 1p/19q co-deleted and 1p/19q non-deleted glioma sample in Cartesian and polar coordinates are shown in Fig. 2. Figure 3 shows the three RCFDs for three consecutive glioma slices as well as the direction of largest Eigen vector of the covariance of two consecutive RCFDs. From Fig. 3, it is clear that similar pattern in RCFDs of two consecutive glioma yields similar dominant orientations which was computed from Eigen vector of covariance matrix. Hence the dominant direction of tissue alignment of glioma volume will not differ much in case of similar pattern of RCFD. Conversely dominant orientation of tissue alignment would be highly distinct, if RCFD pattern of consecutive glioma slices differs.

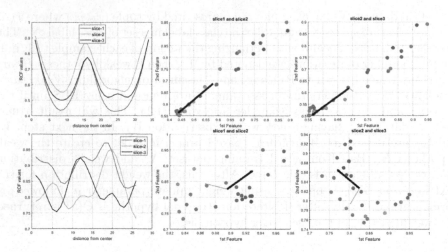

Fig. 3. RCFD profile of PFT *top row* of one G3 glioma with 1p/19q co-deletion *first column* and 1p/19 non-deletion *second column*. The direction of largest Eigen vector is plotted in second row (for slice-1 and slice-2) and third row (for slice-2 and slice-3) that illustrates negligible change in dominant orientation of tissue alignment for 1p/19q co-deleted glioma slices; whereas this change is highly significant in case of 1p/19q non-deleted glioma

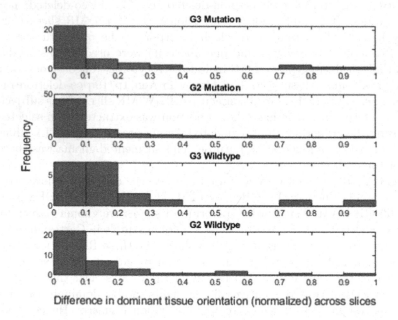

Fig. 4. Histogram plot of change in dominant orientation across glioma slices of all G3 subjects in a specific class. The 4 different histograms are shown for 4 different classes: G3-Mutation, G3-wildtype, G2-Mutation and G2-Wildtype.

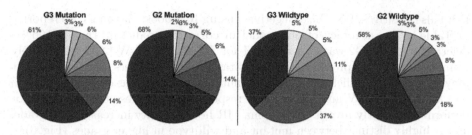

Fig. 5. Illustration of consistency using Histogram Pie chart. The largest area in the pie chart is shown in dark blue color. The value in this area shows the percentage of subjects that yields minimum change (ranges 0 to 0.1 of histogram plot in Fig. 4) in tissue orientation across glioma slices. The pie chart clearly depicts the percentage of subjects having negligible change in tissue orientation is more in mutant cases compare to wildtype.

3.2 More Consistency in Dominant Orientation of Tissue Alignment Across Slices of Mutant Class Compared to Wildtype

In order to study the consistency in dominant direction of tumor tissues across slices, the histogram of the difference in dominant tissue orientation across slices is plotted for all subjects in a specific class and shown in Fig. 4. The illustration of histogram is shown in Fig. 5 with the help of respective pie chart which captures the proportion of subject in histogram. In T2-W MR data, about 86% of G3 mutant and 90% of G2 1p/19q co-deleted subjects showed similar RCFD across glioma slices where the difference in dominant orientation varies from 0° to 21° (0 to 0.2 in histogram). For 1p/19q non-deleted cases the same was observed only in 58% for G3 and 65% for G2 glioma subjects. In other words we can say that the dominant direction of tissue alignment is more consistent across 1p/19q co-deleted glioma slices compared to glioma that occurred due to 1p/19 non-deletion. Using T1-W images this consistency occurs in 61% of G3 mutant and 37% of G3 wildtype subjects. In case of G2 the same was observed in 68% of mutant and 58% of wildtype subjects.

Using RUSBoost, over 99% training accuracy was obtained as compared to other standard classifiers like Naive Bayes, SVM and logistic regression that yield training accuracy in the range of only 60% to 65%. It was quite expected as the traditional classifies tend to classify almost all positive examples (minority) as negative (majority) class in case of data imbalance. All extracted features as discussed in Sect. 2.2 are fed to RUSBoost classifier. The test data label was predicted by 10-fold cross validation. The performance measures like sensitivity (the ratio of correct positive predictions to the total positives examples and measured as: TP/TP+FN), specificity (the ratio of the number of correct negative predictions to the total number of negatives and measured as: TN/TN+FP), F-score (It is the harmonic mean of precision and recall and measured as: 2TP/2TP+FP+FN) and accuracy (the ratio of the total number of correct predictions to the total number of subjects in a dataset and measured as: TP+TN/TP+FP+TN+FN; where TP: True Positives, TN: True Negetives,

FP: False Positives, FN: False Negetives) using RUSboost classifiers are reported in Table 1. The accuracy of our model in correctly predicting the 1p/19q co-deletion status in G2 was 74% and 73% for T1-W and T2-W LGG respectively. Compared to G2, improved result was obtained with G3 cases. For G3 the accuracy in correctly predicting the 1p/19q mutational status was obtained as 82.6% and 82.3% for T1-W and T2-W LGG respectively. The result of classification performance clearly reveals that glioma MR heterogeneity increases with grades and is highly distinct between mutant and wildtype in higher grades (Fig. 6).

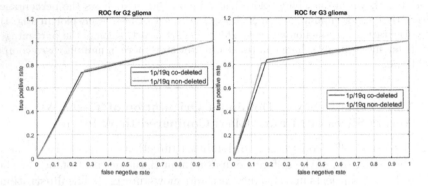

Fig. 6. Illustration of result with ROC curves

4   Discussion

The study proposed a novel approach using RCFD function to assess the variability in frequency texture for prediction of 1p/19q co-deletion using multi-contrast MRI sequences. Cytogenetics with special emphasis on techniques like FISH test has been the gold standard to predict such chromosomal anomalies [4]. However the high cost, influence of cellular phenomenon and hybridization artifact can make the interpretation and performance of FISH test challenging [10,12]. Besides, the information regarding tumor properties which in turn affect the optimal therapy is difficult to obtain from such analyses [10]. Alternatively, there exist a few research works that reported 1p/19q mutational status might be detected with help of multi-modal medical image analyses [3,5–7,9–14]. However few of these studies failed to show promising results in determining the mutational status in individual patients [5–8] in spite of using advance imaging modalities like PWI, DWI, MR spectroscopy [7] and FET-PER images [9]. Iwadate et al.[11] used clinical radiology features to detect 1p/19q co-deletion from 11C–methionine PET images and found that the technique to be helpful to distinguish tumors caused due to 1p/19q co-deletion and 1p/19q non-deletion. Alongside there are studies reported in literature that have shown some promise in detecting 1p/19q status non-invasively using MR images [3,10,13,14]. Tamim

Niazi [3] and Yuqi Han et al. [13] used Radiomics to determine 1p/19q co-deletion in patients. Although radiomics is an emerging techniques in the field of clinical research the present feature extraction methodologies are inconvenient and consume time; thereby increasing the complexity in many medical applications especially if it involves clinical big data. Moreover inappropriate feature selection method in radiomics can be adverse over the performance of radiomics as there is no established method to select the most relevant features.

Table 1. Performance measures of RUSBoost classifier along with obtained accuracy of other classifiers like SVM, Naive Bayes (NB), Logistic Regression (LR) and Logit Boost (LB).

Glioma/contrast	Mutation status	RUSBoost				SVM	NB	LR	LB
		Sensitivity	Specificity	F-Score	Accuracy				
G2/T1	Mutated	0.73	0.75	0.77	74%	54.5%	56%	63%	64.5%
	Wildtype	0.75	0.73	0.69					
G2/T2	Mutated	0.72	0.74	0.75	73%	54.4%	56.2%	60.2%	62%
	Wildtype	0.74	0.72	0.67					
G3/T1	Mutated	0.85	0.8	0.85	82.6%	58%	60%	62%	64%
	Wildtype	0.8	0.85	0.77					
G3/T2	Mutated	0.83	0.81	0.84	82.3%	63%	64.1%	66.2%	67.1%
	Wildtype	0.81	0.83	0.77					

Comparing with the state-of-the-art techniques, in the current study we have proposed a different methodology that utilized frequency-texture characteristics of glioma in order to predict 1p/19q co-deletion status. In this regard RCFD was proposed to quantify the signature pattern that could help in detecting 1p/19q co-deletion status. We hypothesised that changes in dominant orientation of tissue alignment (computed from RCFD) is insignificant in glioma occurred due to 1p/19q co-deletion. This was established by statistical visualizations; here, by histogram and pie chart. All extracted features were integrated and fed into RUSBoost classifier to predict 1p/19q co-deletion status. While analysing the performance with other classifiers like SVM, naive Bayes, logistic regression and Logit-boost, RUSBoost classifier was found to be best in classifying the glioma sub-types based on its mutational status with mean accuracy of 73.5% for G2 and 82.5% for G3 glioma (mean accuracy obtained with (i) SVM = 59.5%; (ii) naive Bayes (NB) = 58.2%; (iii) logistic regression (LR) = 61%; and (iv) Logit Boost (LB) = 65.13%). We have also compared the efficacy of the proposed technique with the state-of-art methods that studied the similar problem and utilized the same TCIA dataset. It is to be noted that without any kind of data augmentation our study outperforms the result reported in literature [10] that yield accuracy of 63.3% and 75.6% using T1W and T2W MRI respectively. The result of our study outperforms another state-of-the-art study reported by Fellah S. [7] where 1p/19q co-deletion status was determined with more than 40% misclassification rates using multimodal MRI. The result of our study is comparable with the result reported by Tamim Niazi et al. [3], where 82.43% classification accuracy was obtained, when their model was applied on unseen set.

To the best of our knowledge there is no previous work done reported in literature that examined frequency-texture characteristics to detect MRI image signature pattern of 1p/19q co-deleted glioma. The most important clinical implications of our study is that it could eventually help to assess the tumor heterogeneity in glioma sub-types; further allowing non-invasive assessment of mutational status during the entire course of treatment. Thus in clinical practice the proposed technique can be potentially used as a confirmatory test of glioma mutation without need of surgical biopsies. Future studies should include additional texture features in order to improve diagnostic accuracy.

5 Conclusion

The study proposed a novel MRI image signature to detect 1p/19q co-deletion status in LGG. The proposed RCFD function classified glioma with and without mutation satisfactorily from preoperative MRI. Thus it could be used as a predictive MRI bio-marker in non-invasive genetic analysis of glioma.

Acknowledgment. The authors of this paper would like to thank Visvesvaraya PhD scheme for Electronics and IT (MEITY), Govt. of India, for its fellowship towards research in IIIT, Bangalore.

References

1. Louis, D.N., et al.: The 2016 world health organization classification of tumors of the central nervous system: a summary. Acta Neuropathologica **131**(6), 803–820 (2016). https://doi.org/10.1007/s00401-016-1545-1
2. Erickson, B., Akkus, Z., et al.: Data from LGG-1p19qDeletion. Cancer Imaging Arch. (2017). https://doi.org/10.7937/K9/TCIA.2017.dwehtz9v
3. Rathore, S., Chaddad, A., Bukhari, N.H., Niazi, T.: Imaging signature of 1p/19q co-deletion status derived via machine learning in lower grade glioma. In: Mohy-ud-Din, H., Rathore, S. (eds.) RNO-AI 2019. LNCS, vol. 11991, pp. 61–69. Springer, Cham (2020). https://doi.org/10.1007/978-3-030-40124-5_7
4. Scheie, D., Andresen, P.A., et al.: Fluorescence in situ hybridization (FISH) on touch preparations: a reliable method for detecting loss of heterozygosity at 1p and 19q in oligodendroglial tumors. Am. J. Surg. Pathol. **30**(7), 828–37 (2006)
5. Latysheva, A., et al.: Dynamic susceptibility contrast and diffusion MR imaging identify oligodendroglioma as defined by the 2016 WHO classification for brain tumors: histogram analysis approach. Neuroradiology **61**(5), 545–555 (2019). https://doi.org/10.1007/s00234-019-02173-5
6. Kebir, S., Weber, M., et al.: Hybrid 11C-MET PET/MRI Combined with "machine learning" in glioma diagnosis according to the revised glioma WHO classification 2016. Clinical Nuclear Medicine **44**(3), 214–220 (2019)
7. Fellah, S.D., Caudal, A.M., et al.: Multimodal MR imaging (diffusion, perfusion, and spectroscopy): is it possible to distinguish oligodendroglial tumor grade and 1p/19q codeletion in the pretherapeutic diagnosis? AJNR Am. J. Neuroradiol. **34**(7), 1326–1333 (2013)

8. Brown, R., Zlatescu, M., et al.: The use of magnetic resonance imaging to noninvasively detect genetic signatures in oligodendroglioma. Clin. Cancer Res. **14**(8), 2357–2362 (2008)
9. Jansen, N.L., Schwartz, C., et al.: Prediction of oligodendroglial histology and LOH 1p/19q using dynamic FET-PET imaging in intracranial WHO grade II and III gliomas. Neuro Oncol. **14**(12), 1473–80 (2012)
10. Akkus, Z., Ali, I., et al.: Predicting deletion of chromosomal arms 1p/19q in low-grade gliomas from MR images using machine intelligence. J. Digit. Imaging **30**(4), 469–476 (2017)
11. Iwadate, Y., Shinozaki, N., et al.: Molecular imaging of 1p/19q deletion in oligodendroglial tumours with 11C-methionine positron emission tomography. J. Neurol. Neurosurg. Psychiatry **87**(9), 1016–21 (2016)
12. Bhattacharya, D., Sinha, N., Saini, J.: Detection of chromosomal arms 1p/19q codeletion in low graded glioma using probability distribution of MRI volume heterogeneity. In: Proceedings of IEEE Region 10 Conference- TENCON-2019, pp: 2695–2699 (2019)
13. Han, Y., et al.: Non-invasive genotype prediction of chromosome 1p/19q co-deletion by development and validation of an MRI-based radiomics signature in lower-grade gliomas. J. Neuro-Oncol. **140**(2), 297–306 (2018). https://doi.org/10.1007/s11060-018-2953-y
14. Zhou, H., Vallieres, M., et al.: MRI features predict survival and molecular markers in diffuse lower-grade gliomas. Neuro Oncol. **19**(6), 862–870 (2017)
15. Seiffert, C., Khoshgoftaar, T.M.: RUSBoost: a hybrid approach to alleviating class imbalance. IEEE Trans. Syst. Man Cybern. - Part A: Syst. Hum. **40** (2010)
16. Sharma, S., Zhang, Y.: Fourier transform power spectrum is a potential measure of tissue alignment in standard MRI: a multiple sclerosis study. PLOS One **12**, e0175979 (2017)

CT Scan Transformation from a Sharp to a Soft Reconstruction Kernel Using Filtering Techniques

Julia Lasek[1,2] and Adam Piórkowski[1,2(✉)]

[1] Medical Simulation Technologies Sp. z oo,
Miechowska 5b m 4, 30–055 Cracow, Poland
[2] Department of Biocybernetics and Biomedical Engineering,
AGH University of Science and Technology,
A. Mickiewicza 30 Av., 30–059 Cracow, Poland
pioro@agh.edu.pl

Abstract. Computed tomography images can be reconstructed using different kernels, depending on the purpose of the examination. Sharp kernels allow the edges of objects such as bones or calcifications to be more precisely defined than is possible with soft kernels; however, they also produce more noise, which makes soft tissue segmentation much more difficult, e.g. in case of a heart modeling.

In this paper, image denoising results are demonstrated for images reconstructed with different kernels. The CT scans of the same patient were reconstructed with 8 kernels: B26f, B30f, B31f, B35f, B36f, B41f, B46f and B50f. All the images were filtered using denoising filters: Anisotropic Diffusion, Gaussian Smoothing, Non-Local Means, and Sigma Filter. The similarity of the images to reference images (B26f) was calculated using SSIM. The results show that filtering can substantially increase the similarity between images reconstructed with a hard or soft kernel.

Keywords: Cardiac CT segmentation · CCTA · Reconstruction kernel · Denoising · SSIM

1 Introduction

Computed tomography (CT) is a widely used method of medical imaging. CT scans are based on X-ray projections, and various algorithms are used to create cross-sectional images of the body. The reconstruction filters depend on the type of tomography and the diagnostic purpose; they may be referred to as algorithm, convolution filter or kernel. The choice of filter parameters has a fundamental impact on spatial resolution and image noise. Therefore, filter selection depends on what tissues are needed for imaging. For soft tissues like the brain or mediastinum, a softer kernel that decreases noise is preferred. When there is a need

© Springer Nature Singapore Pte Ltd. 2021
S. K. Singh et al. (Eds.): CVIP 2020, CCIS 1376, pp. 56–65, 2021.
https://doi.org/10.1007/978-981-16-1086-8_6

for imaging of the lung or bony structures, a sharp kernel that generates images with higher noise, but better spatial resolution is more suitable [15].

A problem occurs when a different kernel should be used than was originally assumed. Changing the algorithm changes how the raw data are processed, so it is necessary to have raw data if a different reconstruction filter needs to be applied. Due to the space limitations of PACS (Picture Archiving and Communication System), raw projections are usually not stored during standard clinical routines because they require much more computer storage than processed images [10]. Therefore, there is usually no easy way to further change an image's reconstruction kernel. The standard protocols used for CCTA (Coronary Computed Tomography Angiography) are for assessing the condition of the coronary vessels. Siemens scanners often use two dedicated kernels: B26f (cardiac, soft, for tissue) and B46f (cardiac, medium-sharp, designed specifically for accurate assessment of coronary calcifications and stents with 3D edge-preserving noise-reduction techniques) [5, 11–13].

The B26f kernel gives a smooth definition of tissues and has less noise, but it blurs the edges of objects with higher density, therefore the B46 kernel is used to visualize them [1, 8, 18]. Unfortunately, the noise in images reconstructed with sharper kernels makes segmentation difficult. An example of an aortic contour with the use of Active Contour algorithm is shown (Fig. 1). The ABsnake (ImageJ) implementation was performed here with the default parameters. For the initial selection (Fig. 1(a)), the algorithm determined different contours for the same CT scan using different kernels. In the case of a soft kernel (B26f), the selection was correct (Fig. 1(b)), but for kernels that generate a noisier image the selection was definitely incorrect (Fig. 1(c), 1(d)). Therefore, in some cases there is a need to transform an image that was reconstructed with a hard kernel to one that is reconstructed with a soft kernel.

1.1 Related Works

There are many post-processing noise-reduction approaches that do not rely on raw data; they can partially solve the discussed problem and can be directly applied to a reconstructed image. Examples include the linear smoothing filter, Anisotropic Diffusion, the Bilateral filter or the Non-Local Means filter. The choice of filter is based on the fact that classic CT images are corrupted with additive Gaussian noise after reconstruction [9]. The objective of this research was to check whether using denoising filters instead of reconstructing new images from raw data makes it possible to reconstruct an image with a hard kernel so that it looks like it has been reconstructed with a soft kernel. This method can be used as segmentation pre-processing or when there is a need for visual comparison of CT volume render, e.g. using 3D Slicer [4, 6]. Several pieces of research that raise this subject have already been presented [21].

Using a convolutional neural network (CNN), Lee et al. [10] showed the possibility of converting a reconstructed image to one that is reconstructed with a different kernel, but without the use of raw data. By measuring the point spread function (PSF), Ohkubo et al. [14] demonstrated a method of image

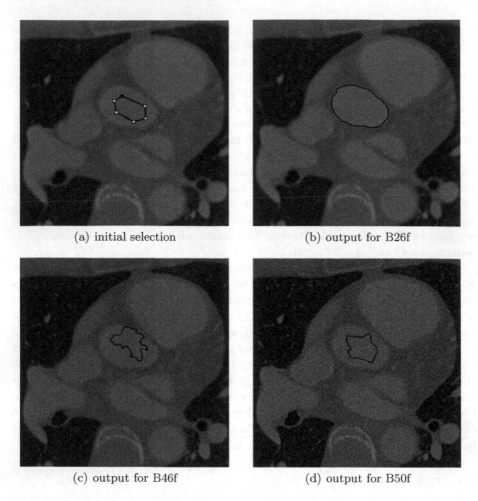

(a) initial selection

(b) output for B26f

(c) output for B46f

(d) output for B50f

Fig. 1. How the choice of reconstruction kernel affects aorta segmentation using Active Contour. Initial selection (a), output for scans reconstructed with the B26f (b), B46f (c) and B50f (d) kernels.

filtering that can be used to obtain similar quality images to those reconstructed with different kernels.

2 Materials and Methods

2.1 The Dataset

The collected CCTA images were acquired from a Siemens SOMATOM Definition Flash scanner. The dataset includes CT scans (611 slices) reconstructed with the analytical reconstruction method using 8 kernels: smooth (B26f); medium smooth (B30f, B31f, B35f, B36f); medium (B41f, B46f); and medium sharp

(B50f); 'B' means standard kernel for the body [19]. Cross-sections present various mediastinum tissues (Fig. 2). The pixel spacing value for all images was 0.4 × 0.4 mm; slice thickness was 0.6 mm, and the resolution was 512 × 512 pixels. The images reconstructed with B26f kernels were the softest. As showed in [1,19], B26f kernel (non-iterative) gives the highest Contrast-to-Noise Ratio (CNR), so these images were used as reference images in our research. The data were processed in the Digital Imaging and Communications in Medicine (DICOM) format, depth of 12 bit.

2.2 Denoising Filters

Many different filtration methods are available [3,7,17]. In this work, the authors limited themselves to the most promising ones, which were selected after preliminary analysis. Image processing was executed using an ImageJ (version 1.52p; National Institutes of Health, Bethesda, MD, USA) environment [16]. The filters used in this research are available as ImageJ plugins: Anisotropic Diffusion, Gaussian Smoothing, Non-Local Means, and Sigma Filter. All filters except Gaussian smoothing were edge-preserving filters that smooth noise and retain sharp edges without affecting image details. The variables in the two-dimensional parameter space were checked with Anisotropic Diffusion and the Sigma Filter.

2.3 Evaluation

After image processing, each image was compared to the reference image (reconstructed with B26f kernel). The Structural Similarity Index SSIM [20] is a method of image comparison commonly used in this type of research [2]. SSIM was calculated (Formula 1) for each filtered image with a wide parameter space of the chosen filters. The best filter parameters were determined experimentally for each filter and kernel type (Fig. 3). Subsequently, the average value was taken for particular parameters for each tested projection of dataset.

$$SSIM(x,y) = \frac{(2\mu_x\mu_y + C_1) + (2\sigma_{xy} + C_2)}{(\mu_x^2 + \mu_y^2 + C_1)(\sigma_x^2 + \sigma_y^2 + C_2)} \tag{1}$$

where: μ_x, μ_y are mean values of compared signals, σ_x, σ_y, σ_x^2, σ_y^2 and σ_{xy} are standard deviations, variances and covariance of respective signals, C_1, C_2 are small constant values to avoid division by zero problem.

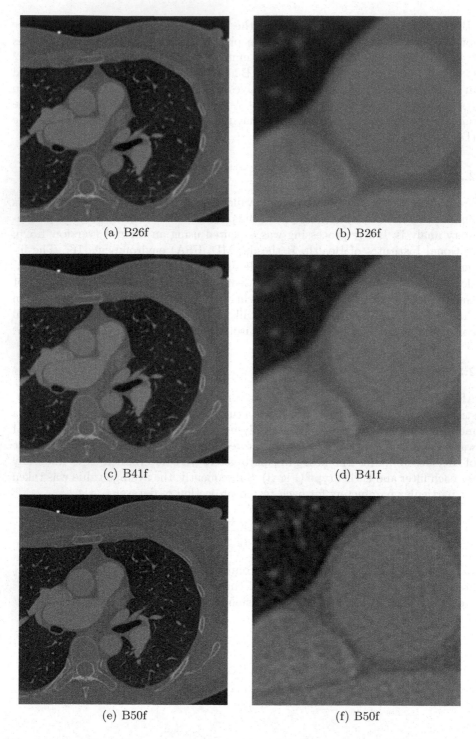

(a) B26f   (b) B26f

(c) B41f   (d) B41f

(e) B50f   (f) B50f

Fig. 2. Examples of projections reconstructed with different kernels: B26f (a, b), B41f (c, d) and B50f (e, f).

3   Results

The results of comparing the SSIM of images reconstructed with different kernels after filtering are shown in Table 1 and Fig. 4. The presented values are averages for all cross-sections. The sigma filter gave the best similarity between the filtered image and the image reconstructed with the soft kernel. The SSIM between images reconstructed with the B50f kernel and those reconstructed with the B26f kernel is 0.9985046. The SSIM between images reconstructed with the B50f kernel after filtering with the sigma filter and those reconstructed with the B26f kernel is 0.9997693. Anisotropic Diffusion gave higher image similarity for filter parameters selected for a single cross-section, but after averaging for all slices and kernels this value is slightly lower than for the sigma filter. This is caused by the edge threshold height parameter, which has different maximum SSIM values for each slice. The Gaussian filter produced a small improvement in similarity because the edges of tissues were not preserved. The highest SSIM values for soft and medium kernels (from B30f to B41f) were achieved using the Non-Local Means filter, but it gave the lowest similarity for images filtered with B46f and B50f.

The sharpest B50f kernel produced the largest differences before and after filtering. The B36f kernel produced images whose similarity to the reference image was not significantly increased using any filtering method.

Table 1. SSIM values for different kernels and filters.

	Original images	Anisotropic diffusion	Gaussian	Non-local means	Sigma
B30f	0.9999468	**0.9999675**	0.9999534	0.9999670	0.9999565
B31f	0.9997377	0.9997747	0.9997417	**0.9997955**	0.9997673
B35f	0.9997655	0.9997606	0.9997655	**0.9997881**	0.9997863
B36f	0.9998382	0.9998319	0.9998382	**0.9998412**	0.9998368
B41f	0.9997371	**0.9997766**	0.9997430	0.9997966	0.9997692
B46f	0.9996439	0.9998178	0.9998137	0.9997879	**0.9998232**
B50f	0.9985046	**0.9997718**	0.9997564	0.9992609	0.9997693
Mean	0.9995962	0.9998144	0.9998017	0.9997482	**0.9998155**
StDev	0.0004906	0.0000724	0.0000763	0.0002243	**0.0000681**

The visual filtering results are shown in Fig. 5. As can be observed, the noise is reduced and the edges near tissues are well preserved.

4   Summary

This study describes the filtering of CT images reconstructed with different kernels. The results show that this is an effective method of increasing the similarity between images reconstructed with a hard or soft kernel. Images after filtering are visually of better quality, which could increase the diagnostic value of these

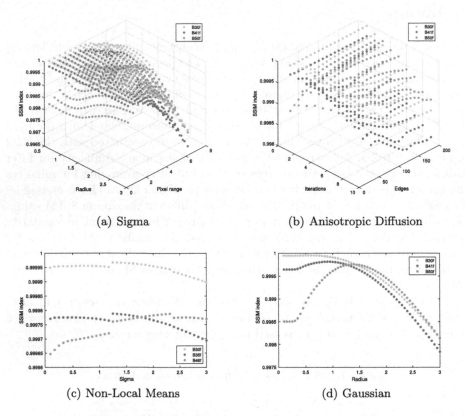

(a) Sigma   (b) Anisotropic Diffusion

(c) Non-Local Means   (d) Gaussian

Fig. 3. SSIM values for space parameters after Sigma (a), Anisotropic diffusion (b), Non-local means (c) and Gaussian (d) filtering.

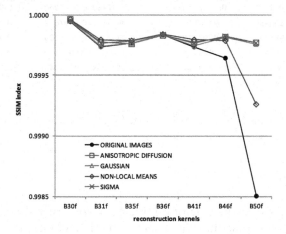

Fig. 4. Graphs of maximum SSIM index values for different filters.

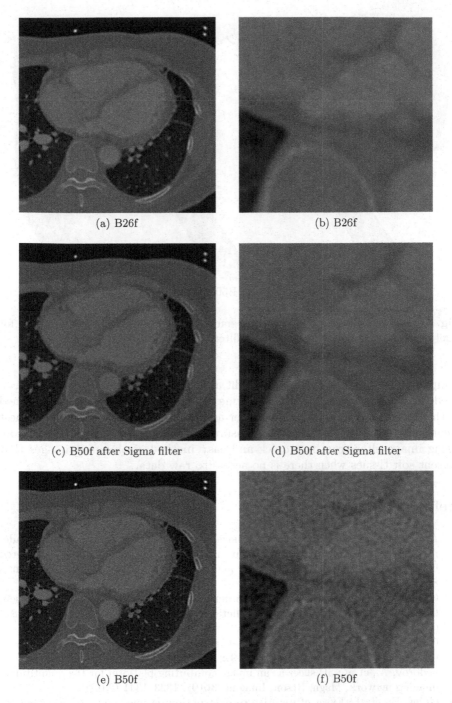

Fig. 5. One of the cross-sections reconstructed with the B26f kernel (a, b), reconstructed with the B50f kernel and filtered with Sigma filter (c, d), reconstructed with the B50f kernel (e, f).

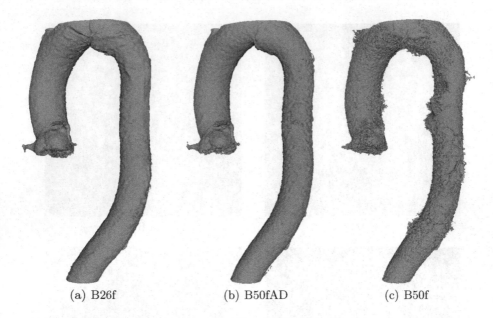

(a) B26f   (b) B50fAD   (c) B50f

Fig. 6. An example of descending aorta segmentation in 3D Slicer (region growing) for B26f (a), B50f after anisotropic diffusion filtering (b), and B50f (c) kernels.

computer tomography images and might allow them to be used when there is a need for visual comparison of CT volume render (Fig. 6). The results obtained in the experiment indicated Sigma filter as the method which gives the highest mean value of the SSIM similarity measure and its smallest standard deviation. Using image filters can be a quick and easy method of obtaining images that present soft tissues when there is no access to raw data.

References

1. Arcadi, T., Maffei, E., Mantini, C., Guaricci, A., La Grutta, L., Martini, C., Cademartiri, F.: Coronary CT angiography using iterative reconstruction vs. filtered back projection: evaluation of image quality. Acta Bio Medica Atenei Parmensis **86**(1), 77–85 (2015)
2. Chen, W., et al.: Low-dose CT image denoising model based on sparse representation by stationarily classified sub-dictionaries. IEEE Access **7**, 116859–116874 (2019)
3. Czerwinski, D.: Digital smoothing filter implementation in cloud computing environment. Przeglad Elektrotechniczny **92**(3), 61–64 (2016)
4. Fedorov, A., et al.: 3D slicer as an image computing platform for the quantitative imaging network. Magn. Reson. Imaging **30**(9), 1323–1341 (2012)
5. Güler, E., et al.: Effect of iterative reconstruction on image quality in evaluating patients with coronary calcifications or stents during coronary computed tomography angiography: a pilot study. Anatol. J. Cardiol. **16**(2), 119 (2016)

6. Kikinis, R., Pieper, S.D., Vosburgh, K.G.: 3D slicer: a platform for subject-specific image analysis, visualization, and clinical support. In: Jolesz, F.A. (ed.) Intraoperative Imaging Image-Guided Therapy, pp. 277–289. Springer, New York (2014). https://doi.org/10.1007/978-1-4614-7657-3_19

7. Knas, M., Cierniak, R.: Computed tomography images denoising with Markov random field model parametrized by Prewitt mask. In: Choraś, R.S. (ed.) Image Processing & Communications Challenges 6. AISC, vol. 313, pp. 53–58. Springer, Cham (2015). https://doi.org/10.1007/978-3-319-10662-5_7

8. Kociołek, M., Strzelecki, M., Obuchowicz, R.: Does image normalization and intensity resolution impact texture classification? Comput. Med. Imaging Graph. **81**, 101716 (2020)

9. Kumar, M., Diwakar, M.: A new exponentially directional weighted function based CT image denoising using total variation. J. King Saud Univ.-Comput. Inf. Sci. **31**(1), 113–124 (2019)

10. Lee, S.M., et al.: CT image conversion among different reconstruction kernels without a sinogram by using a convolutional neural network. Korean J. Radiol. **20**(2), 295–303 (2019)

11. Lim, T.H.: Practical Textbook of Cardiac CT and MRI. Springer, Heidelberg (2015). https://doi.org/10.1007/978-3-642-36397-9

12. McCollough, C.H.: Translating protocols between scanner manufacturer and model (2010). Technology Assessment Initiative: Summit on CT Dose

13. Mileto, A., Guimaraes, L.S., McCollough, C.H., Fletcher, J.G., Yu, L.: State of the art in abdominal CT: the limits of iterative reconstruction algorithms. Radiology **293**(3), 491–503 (2019)

14. Ohkubo, M., Wada, S., Kayugawa, A., Matsumoto, T., Murao, K.: Image filtering as an alternative to the application of a different reconstruction kernel in CT imaging: feasibility study in lung cancer screening. Med. Phys. **38**(7), 3915–3923 (2011)

15. Romans, L.: Computed Tomography for Technologists: A Comprehensive Text. Lippincott Williams & Wilkins, Philadelphia (2018)

16. Schneider, C.A., Rasband, W.S., Eliceiri, K.W.: NIH image to imagej: 25 years of image analysis. Nat. Methods **9**(7), 671–675 (2012)

17. Stanke, L., et al.: Towards to optimal wavelet denoising schemea novel spatial and volumetric mapping of wavelet-based biomedical data smoothing. Sensors **20**(18), 5301 (2020)

18. Szostek, K., Piórkowski, A., Kempny, A., Banyś, R., Gackowski, A.: Using computed tomography images for a heart modeling. J. Med. Inf. Technol. **19**, 75–84 (2012)

19. Völgyes, D., Pedersen, M., Stray-Pedersen, A., Waaler, D., Martinsen, A.C.T.: How different iterative and filtered back projection kernels affect computed tomography numbers and low contrast detectability. J. Comput. Assist. Tomogr. **41**(1), 75–81 (2017)

20. Wang, Z., Bovik, A.C., Sheikh, H.R., Simoncelli, E.P.: Image quality assessment: from error visibility to structural similarity. IEEE Trans. Image Process. **13**(4), 600–612 (2004)

21. Węgliński, T., Fabijańska, A.: Poprawa jakości obrazów tomograficznych o niskiej dawce promieniowania. Informatyka, Automatyka, Pomiary w Gospodarce i Ochronie Środowiska (4), 7–9 (2013)

Development of an Automated Monitoring and Warning System for Landslide Prone Sites

Ankita Saldhi[1]([✉]) [iD] and Subrat Kar[1,2] [iD]

[1] Department of Electrical Engineering, IIT Delhi, New Delhi, India
`subrat@ee.iitd.ac.in`
[2] Bharti School of Telecom Technology and Management, IIT Delhi, New Delhi, India

Abstract. The objective is to detect landslide and report it as soon as it is detected so that appropriate measures can be taken in time in order to reduce the loss of life and infrastructure and to issue advisories to the public. A camera surveillance system with an image processing algorithm for 24/7 monitoring of flow is proposed to detect landslides. The warning system (up to the issuance of a Common Alerting Protocol alert) is also developed. We develop an algorithm that processes the camera feed and accounts for the factors like frames per second (FPS), structural similarity, resolution of the camera and optical flow in order to detect the occurrence of a landslide. Using a network of such cameras and communicating over the network results in a distributed intelligent system. We also estimate the deterioration caused by the disaster from the output image to estimate the extent of the damage incurred.

Keywords: Landslide · Structural similarity · Deterioration · Optical flow · Frame

1 Introduction

1.1 Traditional Techniques for Detection of Landslides

A landslide is a sudden down-slope movement of a mass of mud, debris, rock or soil under the force of gravity. This is essentially due to a decrease in the shear strength of the slope material, due to an increase in the shear stress borne by the material or due to a combination of the two. A change in the stability of a slope can be caused by a number of factors, acting together or alone. This slope movement can also happen under-water.

The technologies which can be used to detect landslides can be broadly classified as those which (a) predict landslide, (b) detect landslide just when it has occurred and those for (c) post landslide analysis. Our main objective is to detect landslide as soon as it has occurred so that a warning alert can be issued. There are various techniques available that detect the landslide [3]. Some of these are discussed below:

© Springer Nature Singapore Pte Ltd. 2021
S. K. Singh et al. (Eds.): CVIP 2020, CCIS 1376, pp. 66–77, 2021.
https://doi.org/10.1007/978-981-16-1086-8_7

(i) Photogrammetric methods of landslide monitoring: This technique is primarily applied in mining areas for monitoring ground movements. The image representing an overall view of the area is formed by installing special three-dimensional cameras at height and photographs are taken via a set of such cameras. The quality of the images depends on the resolution of the camera used. Although the quality of images obtained using this technique is quite good, the complete system and setup turn out to be very costly.

(ii) Ground based geodetic techniques: Vertical and horizontal networks of sensors are deployed in the area under observation and control equipment in the area prone to deformation. The movement of the nodes in the horizontal and vertical directions is used to determine the movement. Though accurate and reliable, this technique is costly to implement.

(iii) Fibre-optic sensing system for detecting landslides and monitoring debris flow: Generally landslides, avalanches and other similar activities like debris flow, rock falls, etc. produce prominent ground vibrations. These hazards are usually detected by measuring these ground vibrations. Although the magnitude of ground vibrations produced by landslides is much less than that produced by earthquakes, the vibrations produced by the former have a high frequency. As a result, these vibrations can be measured/detected within a short distance. Fiber optic sensors are used for the detection of various physical signals. With proper distribution, design and deployment of these sensors, a network can be formed which can detect landslides and other similar activities in the region covered by it. As the optical fiber is very costly, these sensors involve huge monetary investment.

(iv) Terrestrial Laser Scanning (TLS): Terrestrial laser scanning uses light detection and ranging technique (LiDAR). LiDAR produces three-dimensional images of the area under observation. The range of the sensors using LiDAR is approximately 100–300. The longest range can be around 2 km. The images produced are good quality colored 3D images. For the purpose of making an observation, the LiDAR is mounted on a stand that provides a good vertical and horizontal view. The TLS technique has a disadvantage – although the vertical resolution of the results is good, the horizontal resolution is poor. For the 3D representation of the images, snapshots are taken from different angles and the final image is then reconstructed from these multiple 2D images. This increases the complexity of the overall system.

1.2 Drawbacks of Traditional Techniques for Landslide Detection and Advantages of the Proposed Approach

In some of the traditional techniques for detecting landslides, various sensors are used to detect the landslide but most of them get destroyed or just flow away with the landslide. So another such disastrous happening cannot be reported using these sensors. This is not the case in the proposed approach as it uses a camera feed which does not need to be installed in the disaster-prone area. Some other traditional techniques mentioned above are useful in post disaster scenarios but don't provide an instantaneous trigger to commence the restorative action. The proposed methodology stands out because of its response time of landslide detection and cost-effectiveness without compromising performance. We have chosen to use image processing as a technique of choice due to its simplicity, ease of implementation and potential for deployment in a networked camera feed system [10,12,15]. Depending on the structure and relative position of various objects in the video feed [6], information about their relative positions and movement relative to each other can be extracted using image processing [2]. Typically, we use image segmentation, object tracking and, finally, object recognition to achieve this [1]. There are various metrics available to compare two images which depend upon pixel values such as mean square error (MSE), peak signal to noise ratio (PSNR), structural similarity index (SSIM) and histogram based methods [11]. The metrics like mean square error and peak signal to noise ratio are used to detect the difference between consecutive frames of a video but mean square error detects only perceived errors whereas peak signal to noise ratio is slightly biased towards over smoothed results as it is a least squares result. Structural similarity index is more useful if the perceived difference in the structure of the image is to be detected. So SSIM turns out to be more promising.

The approach used is to use a network of cameras and process their video feed to determine if a landslide has occurred by implementing image processing methodologies like structural similarity index and optical flow [9]. This methodology was tested on several videos of landslides. A formula for output deterioration was also devised which considered factors like frames per second (FPS), structural similarity, distance of camera and resolution of camera. By using networked cameras in the landslide prone area, a distributed intelligent system can be obtained and it can be a much efficient way to reduce the time elapsed between the occurrence of disaster and raising an alarm. The system detects landslide and this information is processed appropriately to initiate disaster mitigation instantaneously.

2   The Proposed Methodology and Results

2.1   The Proposed Approach and Its Implementation

The approach makes use of a camera, processes the video feed and uses a measure called structural similarity index (SSIM) as well as optical flow and hence determines if a landslide has occurred. A graded approach was followed to get the final system. First a single camera was used. The SSIM and optical flow [9] were able to detect landslide in some of the cases but failed in some others. So a network of cameras was used to get the view of the area from more than one angle and the resultant system was able to successfully detect the landslides. A diagram of our proposed method can be given as in Fig. 1.

A landslide prone area can be kept under surveillance of a network of cameras each having the logic developed. Most of the processing can be done at the edge devices and the final result is derived from the individual result of the feed

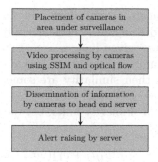

Fig. 1. A block schematic depicting the steps taken in the proposed approach

processing at each individual camera node by the head server. The transmission of images in network cameras is digital and uses security and transmission features of the TCP/IP protocol and hence, faster. Taking this into account, a distributed intelligent system can be obtained.

The methodology makes use of optical flow estimation using the Lucas-Kanade method [8] and a metric called structural similarity index which is a parameter to compare two images. Optical flow describes the motion of image objects within consecutive frames. The motion can be caused by the movements of objects within the frame or by the movement of the camera. Here, the camera is kept at rest so the only resultant motion is due to objects in the frame. Optical flow describes a 2D vector field where each vector is a displacement vector showing the movement of points from first frame to second. There are various methods for estimation of optical flow. We have used Lucas Kanade method based on differentials. The Lucas Kanade method assumes that the flow is essentially constant in a local neighbourhood of the pixel under consideration and the pixel intensities of an object do not change between consecutive frames. The brightness constancy equation can be given as in Eq. 1.

$$I(x, y, t) = I(x + u, y + v, t + 1) \tag{1}$$

where I = intensity of a pixel at (x,y) position at time t, x = x-coordinate of pixel, y = y-coordinate of pixel, u = change in x-coordinate of pixel in next frame, v = change in y-coordinate of pixel in next frame

The Lucas Kanade method uses least squares method to solve the basic optical flow constraint for all the pixels in the neighbourhood. Optical flow has many common use cases and some of them are video compression, segmentation, structure from motion and video stabilization.

Structural similarity index is a measure that differentiates two images on the basis of structural similarities and dissim- ilarities. This metric is essentially a full reference metric that requires two images and quantifies the similarity. Structural similarity takes into account that strong inter-dependencies of pixels are caused when the pixels are spatially close. Some areas where this metric is commonly used include image/video quality assessment i.e. comparing the quality of an image/video against a standard one, image similarity comparison i.e. comparing two images for the mathematical establishment of a number that signifies how much similar two given images are, etc. The latter one is the most prevalent use case of this similarity measure. Image classification, training and classifying images based on their similarity are some other fields of application of SSIM.

The formula for structural similarity index between two images i and j of the same size is given as follows:

$$S(i,j) = \frac{(2\mu_i\mu_j + c_1)(2\sigma_{ij} + c_2)}{(\mu_i^2 + \mu_j^2 + c_1)(\sigma_i^2 + \sigma_j^2 + c_2)} \qquad (2)$$

where S(i,j) = structural similarity between i and j, μ_i = average of i, μ_j = average of j, σ_i^2 = variance of i, σ_j^2 = variance of j, σ_{ij} = covariance of i and j, $c_1 = (k_1 L)^2$, $c_2 = (k_2 L)^2$, $k_1 = 0.1$, $k_2 = 0.1$, L = dynamic range of the pixel-values

The structural similarity index is a decimal value ranging from -1 to 1. It is based on three comparison measures defined between the two windows i and j of same size. These are structure (ST), contrast (C) and luminescence (L) which are given as follows:

$$ST(i,j) = \frac{(\sigma_{ij} + c_3)}{(\sigma_i\sigma_j + c_3)} \qquad (3)$$

$$C(i,j) = \frac{(2\sigma_i\sigma_j + c_2)}{(\sigma_i^2 + \sigma_j^2 + c_2)} \qquad (4)$$

$$L(i,j) = \frac{(2\mu_i\mu_j + c_1)}{(\mu_i^2 + \mu_j^2 + c_1)} \qquad (5)$$

where c1 and c2 are same as given in Eq. 1 and c3=c2/2

SSIM can then be written as a weighted combination of these comparative measures as given in Eq. 6.

$$S(i,j) = [ST(i,j)^x . C(i,j)^y . L(i,j)^z] \qquad (6)$$

When x = y = z = 1, Eq. 6 is reduced to Eq. 2.

Structural similarity and estimation of optical flow were used to compare various frames and an alert was raised when a landslide was detected. The threshold used for SSIM was determined initially at the time of system setup by calibrating the system against camera properties i.e. resolution of the camera, its location, frames per second and processing power of the platform being used. This threshold is set before the installation of the complete system by supervising the images produced by the camera and determining the change in pixels caused by movement constrained by the camera parameters as described before. This approach along with the motion vectors (which provide information regarding magnitude and direction of motion) produced by optical flow estimation are used to determine landslide. One important feature the whole setup had to handle

(a) Frame 0   (b) Frame 372

(c) Frame 0 - Bottom   (d) Frame 372 - Bot-
Right Quadrant   tom Right Quadrant

Fig. 2. Different frames of video feed processing of landslide (a) Frame 0 (b) Frame 372 (c) Frame 0 - Bottom Right Quadrant (d) Frame 372 - Bottom Right Quadrant

was to differentiate the movement of vehicles and similar movements from landslides. In the case of these usual movements, the motion is gradual and changes smoothly with time whereas in the case of a landslide there is an abrupt change in motion vectors occurring at a greater magnitude within a shorter period of time which can be determined using motion vectors of optical flow estimation obtained using the network of cameras. There also exists a possibility that in the absence of sufficient points of interest in the frame the optical flow estimation using Lucas-Kanade method may not perform as expected but since there is a network of cameras present, the complete network together is able to impart the required information successfully. The corners are usually the points of interest since if it is any other part, it becomes difficult to determine whether an object is moving or not if the motion is lateral. The points of interest in our case are detected using Shi-Tomasi algorithm [14]. As the information available at a camera is processed by that node itself and then only it is sent to the server, most of the computation is handled by the nodes themselves hence contributing to better performance of the overall system. The network must operate in star topology where all information is provided to the head end server for its processing. Only the compressed result is passed on to the head server by individual camera nodes to get the final result when a landslide has occurred and to raise an alarm if required. However, the performance under rainfall and dark night scenarios falls under the future scope of study.

The approach was tested on landslide videos and was found to detect landslide successfully. Figure 2(a) is the initial frame of one such feed. This is a frame before the occurrence of a landslide. Using structural similarity index and optical flow estimation using Lucas-Kanade method, detection of landslide was tried upon. Figure 2(b) is the frame in which the methodology thus implemented indicates the occurrence of landslide. Depending upon the threshold used and location of camera it can be inferred if there is sufficient change in the image and if it is of interest. Then the logic was implemented to find the quadrant in which maximum change was observed. As detected by the code, maximum change was observed in the bottom right quadrant. Figure 2(c) is the quadrant from the initial frame. Figure 2(d) is the quadrant from the frame in which the maximum effect of the landslide can be observed.

Figure 3(a) shows the landslide detection using optical flow estimation. The points of interest as detected by the algorithm in an initial frame can be clearly spotted in this figure. Figure 3(b) depicts the points of interest as well as the motion vectors captured during the landslide. Figure 3(c) depicts the optical flow motion vectors and the points of interest detected at the end of the landslide. These motion vectors played a critical role in providing the information when a landslide occurred. To get the motion vectors, the present frame and present points of interest are passed to the next frame which in turn detects the occurrence of these points in the next frame. A status is returned by it confirming the position of points in the next fame. This operation is continued in a loop to run over the video feed of the camera.

The logic and algorithm used for the system can be best described as follows:

- Calibrate the system to find the threshold value before installation against camera parameters like resolution of the camera, its location, frames per second and processing power of the platform being used
- determine the structural similarity index between frames of video feed using Eq. 2
  - given two windows i and j of common size N × N, determine the average of i, average of j
  - determine variance of i, variance of j, co-variance of i and j
  - incorporate the constants as described in Eq. 2
  - substitute the values in Eq. 2
- determine points of interest (corner points in this case) in the current frame
- pass these points and the current frame as input to the next frame
- use the status obtained in the previous step and the points of interest in the next frame to determine motion vectors
- loop over these steps to process the video feed of cameras
- make each camera send the result to the head end server
- head end server processes results from all the camera feeds to come to a final conclusion whether a landslide has occurred or not and raises the alarm accordingly

Next, this had to be related with time to measure deterioration caused by the disaster. Factors that needed to be taken into account include SSIM value and fps of the camera. Assuming camera of the same resolution, it was deduced that output deterioration (D) can be found using the relationship depicted in Eq. 7.

$$D = k \cdot \int \frac{1}{fps \cdot SSIM(n)} \tag{7}$$

(a) Optical flow estimation: motion vectors in the initial frame

(b) Optical flow estimation: motion vectors in the frame captured during landslide

(c) Optical flow estimation: motion vectors in the frame captured after landslide

Fig. 3. (a) Optical flow estimation: initial frame (b) Optical flow estimation: frame during a landslide (c) Optical flow estimation: frame captured after landslide

Table 1. Platform and language experimented with on that platform

Platform used	Language Python	Language C/C++	Language OpenCL
Laptop	2.6 min	17 s	—
Raspberry Pi	24.2 min	2.1 min	—
FPGA	—	—	3.6 s

where $1/fps$ = time between two consecutive frames, SSIM(n) = SSIM between nth and $(n - 1)$th frame since deterioration started, k = constant

The integration is over the time period of deterioration. As the practical measurement of time is discrete and fps is constant, Eq. 8 is obtained.

$$D = k \cdot \sum \frac{1}{fps \cdot SSIM(n)} = k \cdot \frac{1}{fps} \cdot \sum \frac{1}{SSIM(n)} \tag{8}$$

where the summation is over time period of deterioration

Depending on the resolution of the camera, the relative distance between cameras and fps we can set the threshold for SSIM and output deterioration. Using the above methodology, for the case of said video, the output deterioration obtained was 29.1091. The greater the value of D the greater is deterioration. So a formula for output deterioration was devised which considered factors like fps, SSIM, relative distance of the cameras and resolution of the camera. The approach also made use of optical flow to get the surveillance information of the area and determine and raise an alarm when the landslide occurred.

2.2 Comparison of Performance on Three Different Hardware Platforms

In order to improve the processing speed, the next step was to implement the proposed approach on (i) a general-purpose commonly available computing platform (e.g. PC/laptop) (ii) a cost-effective UNIX based simple computing unit (e.g. Raspberry Pi, BeagleBone, etc.) (iii) a dedicated hardware (e.g. Application Specific Integrated Circuit (ASIC), Field Programmable Gate Arrays (FPGA), etc.) [4,7,13]. This was tested using platforms like PC/laptop, Raspberry Pi, FPGA using languages like Python, C and OpenCL. A table summarizing the platform and the language used on it is represented using Table 1.

A reference video was tested on various platforms using various programming languages. The video which took 24.2 min on Raspberry Pi using Python consumed 2.1 min using C language on the same platform. This reference video took 2.6 min on core i3 system with 4 GB RAM (laptop) using Python and 17 s using C. As expected, the best performance was observed with FPGA using C and OpenCL which completed processing the video using the proposed methodology in 3.6 s. This made use of writing the host code in C/C++ which contained the logic for providing input data and getting output data and writing the kernels in OpenCL which were used for mapping the main logic onto the FPGA for better performance. Some experimental results of time taken to process a reference video as per given algorithm considering other parameters is shown in Table 2. The results clearly indicate the effect of change in various parameters on deterioration and time taken to process the given feed.

Table 2. Experimental result of time taken to process as per given algorithm considering other parameters

Sampling factor	Frame rate (FPS)	Image pixels	Time taken
1	30	1080 × 1920	54.444 s
1	30	720 × 1280	19.3405 s
1	30	480 × 720	6.11413 s
1	60	1080 × 1920	98.2286 s
1	60	720 × 1280	47.2185 s
1	60	480 × 720	47.2185 s
1/2	30	1080 × 1920	25.9159 s
1/2	30	720 × 1280	9.98076 s
1/2	30	480 × 720	2.98166 s
1/2	60	1080 × 1920	47.2682 s
1/2	60	720 × 1280	23.4947 s
1/2	60	480 × 720	6.32783 s
1/3	30	1080 × 1920	17.4076 s
1/3	30	720 × 1280	6.97176 s
1/3	30	480 × 720	2.19271 s
1/3	60	1080 × 1920	35.5181 s
1/3	60	720 × 1280	15.0471 s
1/3	60	480 × 720	5.17862 s
1/6	30	1080 × 1920	9.89446 s
1/6	30	720 × 1280	3.48532 s
1/6	30	480 × 720	1.28597 s
1/6	60	1080 × 1920	19.127 s
1/6	60	720 × 1280	8.8422 s
1/6	60	480 × 720	2.85575 s
1/10	30	1080 × 1920	6.0444 s
1/10	30	720 × 1280	2.043 s
1/10	30	480 × 720	0.724244 s
1/10	60	1080 × 1920	11.083 s
1/10	60	720 × 1280	5.03317 s
1/10	60	480 × 720	1.50941 s

3   Conclusion and Future Scope of Study

Metric of structural similarity index and optical flow estimation were used as key image processing techniques to detect the landslide. A formula for output deterioration was devised which considered factors like FPS, structural similarity, location of the camera and resolution of the camera. A distributed intelligent system was proposed as the methodology holds a provision of using network cameras and works much faster where each camera processes its information. Next step was to improve the processing speed and implement this on various platforms. This was tested using platforms like PC/laptop, Raspberry Pi and FPGA using languages like Python, C and OpenCL. The best performance was observed with FPGA using C and OpenCL.

The performance of the proposed approach under dark night scenarios and rainfall conditions is under testing and constitutes the future scope of study.

References

1. Ning, J., Zhang, L., Zhang, D., Wu, C.: Robust object tracking using joint color-texture histogram. Int. J. Pattern Recognit. Artif. Int. **23**(7), 1245–1263 (2009)
2. Mohan, A., Poobal, S.: Crack detection using image processing: a critical review and analysis. Alexandria Eng. J. **57**(2), 787–798 (2018)
3. Hare, Y., Vatti, R.A., Dande, R., Vinchurkar, P.: Landslide detection techniques: a survey. Int. J. Electr. Electron. Comput. Sci. Eng. 1(1) (2014). ISSN: 2348 2273
4. Marwa, C., Bahri, H., Sayadi, F., Atri, M.: Image processing application on graphics processors. Int. J. Image Process. **8**(3), 66 (2014)
5. Uhlemann, S., Wilkinson, P.B., Chambers, J.E., Maurer, H., et al.: Interpolation of landslide movements to improve the accuracy of 4D geoelectrical monitoring. J. Appl. Geophys. **12**, 93–105 (2015)
6. Chen, R., Tong, Y., Yang, J., Wu, M.: Video foreground detection algorithm based on fast principal component pursuit and motion saliency. Comput. Intell. Neurosci. **2019**, 11 (2019). AID 4769185
7. Kalaiselvi, T., Sriramakrishnan, P., Somasundaram, K.: Performance of medical image processing algorithms implemented in CUDA running on GPU based machine. Int. J. Intell. Syst. Appl. **10**, 58–68 (2018)
8. Baker, S., Matthews, I.: Lucas-Kanade 20 years on: a unifying framework. Int. J. Comput. Vis. **56**, 221–255 (2004)
9. Patel, D.M., Upadhyay, S.: Optical flow measurement using Lucas Kanade method. Int. J. Comput. Appl. **6**, 6–10 (2013)
10. Su, Y., Zhao, Q., Zhao, L., Gu, D.: Abrupt motion tracking using a visual saliency embedded particle filter. Pattern Recogn. **47**, 1826–1834 (2014)
11. Tan, H., Yu, P., Li, X., Yang, Y.: Digital image similarity metrics and their performances. In: 2011 2nd International Conference on Artificial Intelligence, Management Science and Electronic Commerce (AIMSEC), Dengleng, vol. 2011, pp. 3922–3925 (2011)
12. Ramesh, O., Gupta, P.V.K.M.: A real time hardware and software co-simulation of edge detection for image processing system. Int. J. Eng. Res. Trends (IJERT) **2**(8), 1695–1701 (2013)

13. Georgis, G., Lentaris, G., Reisis, D.: Acceleration techniques and evaluation on multi-core CPU, GPU and FPGA for image processing and super-resolution. J. Real-Time Image Process. **16**, 1207–1234 (2019)
14. Shi, J., Tomasi, C.: Good features to track. In: 9th IEEE Conference on Computer Vision and Pattern Recognition, pp. 593–600. Springer (1994)
15. Bouwmans, T., Zahzah, E.H.: Robust PCA via principal component pursuit: a review for a comparative evaluation in video surveillance. Comput. Vis. Image Underst. **122**, 22–34 (2014)

Deep Neural Network for Pneumonia Detection Using Chest X-Rays

Himadri Mukherjee[1(✉)], Bubai Das[1], Sahana Das[1], Ankita Dhar[1],
Sk Md Obaidullah[2], K. C. Santosh[3], Santanu Phadikar[4], and Kaushik Roy[1]

[1] Department of Computer Science, West Bengal State University, Kolkata, India
[2] Department of Computer Science and Engineering, Aliah University, Kolkata, India
[3] Department of Computer Science, The University of South Dakota,
Vermillion, SD, USA
santosh.kc@ieee.org
[4] Department of Computer Science and Engineering, Maulana Abul Kalam
Azad University of Technology, Kolkata, India

Abstract. In resource-constrained regions, pneumonia detection is a major challenge which otherwise often proves to be fatal. Since several decades (WHO reports), as chest X-rays provide us visual difference (changes in texture, for example) between normal and abnormal regions, radiologists use them to detect Pneumonia in addition to other sources of data. In this paper, we propose deep neural network that is designed to extract differences in textures from abnormal regions (related to pneumonia). In our experiments, we achieve the highest accuracy of 99.13% using publicly available data: "Chest X-ray Images (Pneumonia)" [13]. The results outperformed handcrafted feature-based tools and other state-of-the-art works.

Keywords: Pneumonia identification · Deep learning · Chest X-ray

1 Introduction

Pneumonia is an infection of the chest that affects both lungs. It is caused by bacteria, virus or fungus and mostly occurs in places with excessive air pollution. Though people of any age can become affected, the old and the very young are more prone to the infection. Air sacs of the lungs become inflamed and filled with pus causing cough with phlegm. The methods of diagnosis include blood tests, pulse oximetry, sputum test and most importantly chest X-ray. The more severe instances are investigated by pleural fluid culture and CT Scan [1,2].

Due to pollution and poverty the risk of pneumonia is high in the third-world countries than in the developed countries. In the US, there are nearly 1 million cases of pneumonia each year and approximately 50,000 deaths [3,4]. According to an estimate given by the WHO, more than four million people world-wide die due to pneumonia and other diseases caused by air-pollution. More than 150 million people, mostly children below the age of five become infected with

S. K. Singh et al. (Eds.): CVIP 2020, CCIS 1376, pp. 78–87, 2021.
https://doi.org/10.1007/978-981-16-1086-8_8

pneumonia each year [5]. Problems are usually aggravated because the disease is not diagnosed on time. Accurate and timely diagnosis might make a difference between life and death. Though it is a common disease, accurate diagnosis of pneumonia is difficult. It requires thorough analysis of chest images by expert clinicians. In Africa alone there is a deficit of 2.3 million clinical staff including doctors [6].

It is very important to detect pneumonia at an early stage for proper treatment. Negligence or misinterpretation of clinical reports in this stage can prove to be fatal. There are many places in the World with little medical support where death due to delayed detection of pneumonia is common. The field of artificial intelligence has developed significantly in the last decade and has influenced healthcare in numerous ways. Researchers have posed interest in development of autonomous systems to aid in healthcare (if not treatment, at least detection). Pneumonia can be detected from chest X-ray images which is itself a challenging job and demands experienced radiologists [7]. Automating such a task is even harder.

Rajpurkar et al. [7] developed a system to detect pneumonia from chest X-ray images. They designed a 121 layer convolutional neural network which was trained on the ChestX-ray14 dataset. They compared their system's performance with that of radiologists and obtained better F1 score for all the 14 diseases embodied in the dataset. Mubarok et al. [8] experimented with the performance of residual network and mask regional CNN for detecting pneumonia. They performed tests on the Kaggle RSNA pneumonia detection challenge dataset consisting of 26.684 instances. They obtained a better accuracy of 85.60% with residual network as compared to mask-RCNN which produced an accuracy of 78.06%. However, the specificity for the former was higher (94.83%) as compared to the later (85.54%).

Ayan and Unver [4] employed deep learning for the purpose of detecting pneumonia form chest X-ray images. They experimented on a dataset consisting of 5856 instances out of which 1583 were normal samples. Two CNN architectures namely Xception and Vgg16 were applied independently along with transfer learning. A higher accuracy of 87% was reported for VGG16 as compared to Xception (82%). They also reported the fact that Xception produced better result for detecting pneumonia instances while Vgg16 was more successful for detecting normal cases.

Chapman et al. [9] studied the performance of expert-crafted rules, Bayesian networks and decision trees for detecting pneumonia from chest X-ray images. The experiments were performed on a dataset of 292 out of which 75 were cases of pneumonia. The expert rule-based system produced a highest sensitivity of 0.92 and the decision tree-based approach produced the lowest (0.857). However, decision tree produced better precision and specificity values as compared to the other two techniques. Contreras-Ojeda et al. [10] attempted to detect pneumonia using texture-based analysis of ultrasound images. Their dataset consisted of 29 images out of which 14 had pneumonia. They extracted several textural metrics like mean, variance, median, kurtosis, standard deviation and skewness and concluded that such features have the capability to detect pneumonia from ultrasound images. Correa et al. [11] used patters of distribution of brightness of ultrasound lungs images for detecting pneumonia. They experimented with 60 images obtained from 21 children aged below 5. Out of them, 15 had pneumonia. The dataset yielded a total of 1450 and 1605 positive and negative feature vectors respectively. This was followed by the application of neural network-based classification which produced a sensitivity value of 90.9% and a specificity of 100%.

Islam et al. [3] used compressed sensing and deep learning for detection of pneumonia. They experimented on a dataset from Kaggle consisting of 5863 images and reported an accuracy of 97.34%. Jakhar and Hooda [12] presented a deep learning-based framework with CNN for automatic identification of pneumonia. They experimented with the Chest X-ray Images (pneumonia) dataset having a total of 5863 samples. They compared the performance of several other machine learning techniques and reported an accuracy of 84% with the CNN-based technique.

Researchers have proposed disparate approaches for detection of pneumonia from images. There are some works which were done on the present dataset as well. Here, a deep neural network-based approach is presented for detection of pneumonia from chest X-rays. The main objective of this work is to reduce the misclassification rate as far as possible. This is very critical in the domain of healthcare. In the rest of the paper, the dataset is discussed in Sect. 2 followed by the deep neural network-based framework in Sect. 3. The handcrafted feature-based approach is discussed in Sect. 3 followed by the analysis of results in Sect. 5. Finally the conclusion is presented in Sect. 6.

2   Dataset

Data is an extremely important aspect for any experiment. The dataset used for developing models should portray different real world characteristics for the development of robust systems. The experiments were performed on the publicly available Chest X-ray Images (pneumonia) dataset in Kaggle [13]. It consists of 5863 X-ray images out of which 4273 images are pneumonia affected and the rest are normal. The images portray real world conditions. In some of the X-rays, the patient had leaned to a side and hence skewed X-ray was obtained. Some of the images had foreign objects. In several X-rays there was presence of noise and texts. It was also noted that the X-ray images were of disparate sizes. The distance of the patient from the acquisition module also varied for different images. Moreover, the captured X-ray frames for disparate patients were also different at times. Handling such characteristics is very challenging for any autonomous system. Some instances from the dataset is presented in Fig. 1.

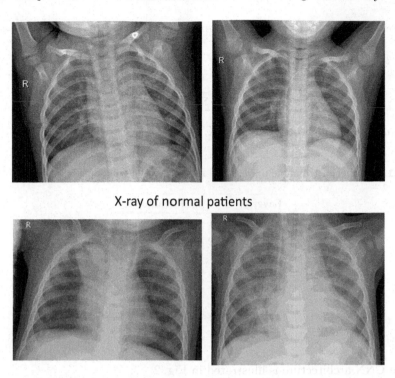

X-ray of normal patients

X-ray of pneumonia patients

Fig. 1. X-rays of normal and pneumonia patients.

3   Deep Neural Network: Custom CNN

Deep learning [14]-based approaches have recently received attention from researchers across the globe. Such techniques have produced very good results and at several instances have superseded standard handcrafted feature-based systems. Convolutional Neural Networks [15] are one such deep learning-based systems. It consists of 3 major components namely convolution, pooling and dense layer. Convolution layer consists of filters which are responsible for extracting important information. The pooling layer is responsible for reducing the dimension of data. The dense layer is a fully connected layer which is responsible for classification.

In the present experiment, a custom CNN was designed for identification of pneumonia from the Chest X-rays. The images were fed to the 1st convolution layer having 32, 5*5 filters whose outputs were passed to the 2nd, 3*3 convolution layer with 16 filters after pooling. This output was again pooled and passed through 2 dense layers of 256 and 50 dimensions with ReLU activation (Equation (1)). The final layer was a 2 dimensional dense layer with softmax activation (Eq. (2)). The number of trainable parameters in the different convolution and dense layers are tabulated in Table 1.

$$f(y) = max(0, y), \tag{1}$$

where, y is the input to a neuron.

$$\sigma(a)_j = \frac{e^{a_j}}{\sum_{k=1}^{K} e^{a_k}}, \tag{2}$$

where, a is an input vector of length K.

Table 1. Number of trainable parameters in each of the convolution and dense layers.

Layer	# Parameters
Convolution 1	2432
Convolution 2	4624
Dense 1	409856
Dense 2	12850
Dense 3	102
Total	429864

The CNN architecture is illustrated in Fig. 2.

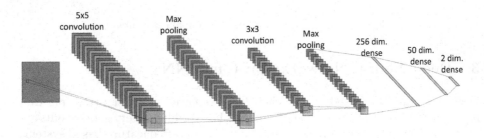

Fig. 2. The used CNN architecture.

4   Handcrafted Features

The performance of handcrafted feature-based approach was also tested in this study. Local Binary Pattern (LBP) were extracted from each of the images. It is a simple but robust texture operation. It works by taking the threshold of the neighbours of a pixel and outputs a binary number. Different applications prefer this method because it is computationally simple and has discriminative power. LBP brings together different conventional statistical and structural models of texture analysis. Most important feature of LBP is its ability to handle monotonic gray-scale images, e.g. it is capable of highlighting variations. Since this method is computationally simple LBP can be easily used to analyze images in any demanding real-world situation. The extracted features were fed to different popular classifiers like SVM, Decision table, J48, Simple logistic, Multilayer perceptron and Random forest. The handcrafted feature-based framework is illustrated in Fig. 3.

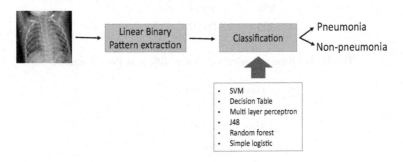

Fig. 3. Handcrafted feature-based framework.

5   Results and Analysis

The images were fed to the CNN with a cross validation evaluation technique. The training iterations and the batch size was initially set to 100. The number of folds of evaluation were varied from 5 to 10 and the best result was obtained for 8 folds as demonstrated in Table 2.

Table 2. Obtained accuracies for different folds of cross validation.

Folds	Accuracy (%)
5	98.45
6	98.65
7	98.89
8	**99.13**
9	99.08
10	99.09

Next, the training were varied for 8 fold cross validation. Experiments were done with lower as well as higher values with respect to 100 iterations but no improvement in result was obtained. The results for different training iterations is presented in Table 3. Finally, the batch size was also varied on either side of 100 instances (initial setup) and accuracy dropped on increasing as well as decreasing the batch size. The different results on varying the batch size is presented in Table 4.

Table 3. Obtained accuracies for different training iterations.

Iterations	Accuracy (%)
50	98.99
100	**99.13**
200	99.11
300	99.11
400	98.92

Table 4. Obtained accuracies for different batch sizes.

Batch	Accuracy (%)
50	98.65
100	**99.13**
150	99.09
200	98.96

The confusion matrix for the best result is presented in Table 5. It is seen that percentage of misclassification for non-pneumonia cases was a bit higher as compared to the pneumonia cases (1.58% and 0.61% respectively). One probable reason for this is perhaps the skew in some of the images. Moreover, there were many cases which had noises in the form of white lines in the sides which also perhaps led to the confusion. In the case of pneumonia images, presence of different foreign objects was observed in the X-ray images which hampered the model. In the case of both the classes, an impression of the heart in the X-rays was observed which further added to the confusion. The ROC curve for this result (best accuracy = 99.13%) along with the AUC value is presented in Fig. 4.

Table 5. Inter-class confusions for the best result using 8 fold cross validation, 100 epochs and 100 instance batch size.

	Non pneumonia	Pneumonia
Non-pneumonia	1558	25
Pneumonia	26	4247

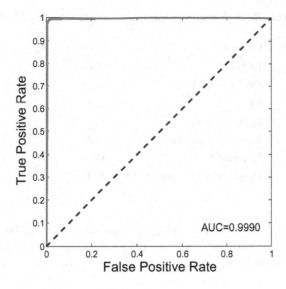

Fig. 4. ROC and AUC for the best result (Accuracy=99.13%).

Different performance metrics in the thick of precision, sensitivity, specificity, false discovery rate and F1-score was also computed for both the classes based on the best result which are presented in Table 6.

Table 6. Values of different performance metrics for the best result.

Metrics	Values
Sensitivity	0.9842
Specificity	0.9939
Precision	0.9836
Negative predictive value	0.9941
False positive rate	0.0061
False negative rate	0.0158
F1 score	0.9839

5.1 Comparative Study

Handcrafted Features: The obtained results for the different classifiers (as discussed in Sect. 3) using LBP features is presented in Table 7. It is noted that the best performance was obtained with CNN-based approach.

Table 7. Performance of different classifiers using LBP.

Classifier	Accuracy (%)
LibSVM	89.65
Decision table	91.70
J48	92.88
Simple logistic	93.61
Multilayer perceptron	94.59
Random forest	95.18
Proposed technique (CNN)	99.13

Comparison with Existing Works: The performance of the proposed approach was compared with established works in literature which is summarized in Table 8. The methodologies are discussed in Sect. 1.

Table 8. Comparison with established works in literature.

Work	Accuracy (%)
Islam et al. [3]	97.34
Jakhar and Hooda [12]	84
Proposed technique (CNN)	99.13

6   Conclusion

In this paper, a system is presented for pneumonia detection from Chest X-rays using deep neural networks. Experiments were performed on over 5K images and an average precision of 0.9836 was obtained. There was presence of noise and foreign objects in some of the images. Some of the images had a skew and texts. In future, pre processing will be performed to remove such aspects to obtain better recognition. The system will also be tuned and optimized to work in mobile platform for easier accessibility. We will experiment with a larger and more robust dataset in future and also test the performance of other handcrafted features. We also plan to experiment with the network architecture for improving the system's performance. Finally, we will equip the system to categorize the degree of infection from the X-rays for making the results more informative.

References

1. https://www.medicalnewstoday.com/articles/151632.php#treatment visited on 7.5.2020
2. https://www.mayoclinic.org/diseases-conditions/pneumonia/diagnosis-treatment/drc-20354210 visited on 7.5.2020
3. Islam, S.R., Maity, S.P., Ray, A.K., Mandal, M.: Automatic detection of pneumonia on compressed sensing images using deep learning. In: 2019 IEEE Canadian Conference of Electrical and Computer Engineering (CCECE), pp. 1–4. IEEE (2019)
4. Ayan, E., Unver, H.M.: Diagnosis of pneumonia from chest X-ray images using deep learning. In: 2019 Scientific Meeting on Electrical-Electronics & Biomedical Engineering and Computer Science (EBBT), pp. 1–5. IEEE (2019)
5. World Health Organization, Household Air Pollution and Health [Fact Sheet], WHO, Geneva, Switzerland (2018). http://www.who.int/newa-room/fact-sheets/detail/household-air-pollution-and-health
6. Naicker, S., Plange-Rhule, J., Tutt, R.C., Eastwood, J.B.: Shortage of healthcare workers in developing countries-Africa. Ethn. Dis. **19**(1), 60 (2009)
7. Rajpurkar, P., et al.: Chexnet: Radiologist-level pneumonia detection on chest x-rays with deep learning (2017). arXiv preprint arXiv:1711.05225
8. Al Mubarok, A.F., Dominique, J.A., Thias, A.H. : Pneumonia detection with deep convolutional architecture. In: 2019 International Conference of Artificial Intelligence and Information Technology (ICAIIT), pp. 486–489. IEEE (2019)
9. Chapman, W.W., Fizman, M., Chapman, B.E., Haug, P.J.: A comparison of classification algorithms to automatically identify chest X-ray reports that support pneumonia. J. Biomed. Inform. **34**(1), 4–14 (2001)
10. Contreras-Ojeda, S.L., Sierra-Pardo, C., Dominguez-Jimenez, J.A., Lopez-Bueno, J., Contreras-Ortiz, S.H.: Texture analysis of ultrasound images for pneumonia detection in pediatric patients. In: 2019 XXII Symposium on Image, Signal Processing and Artificial Vision (STSIVA), pp. 1–4. IEEE (2019)
11. Correa, M., et al.: Automatic classification of pediatric pneumonia based on lung ultrasound pattern recognition. PLoS ONE **13**(12), e0206410 (2018)
12. Jakhar, K., Hooda, N.: Big data deep learning framework using keras: a case study of pneumonia prediction. In: 2018 4th International Conference on Computing Communication and Automation (ICCCA), pp. 1–5. IEEE (2018)
13. https://www.kaggle.com/paultimothymooney/chest-xray-pneumonia visited on 7.5.2020
14. LeCun, Y., Bengio, Y., Hinton, G.: Deep learning. Nature **521**(7553), 436–444 (2015)
15. Olivas-Padilla, B.E., Chacon-Murguia, M.I.: Classification of multiple motor imagery using deep convolutional neural networks and spatial filters. Appl. Soft. Comput. **75**, 461–472 (2019)
16. Ahonen, T., Hadid, A., Pietikainen, M.: Face description with local binary patterns: application to face recognition. IEEE Trans. Pattern Anal. Mach. Intell. **28**(12), 2037–2041 (2006)

Handwriting Recognition on Filled-in Forms Using CNN

Akshada Shinde[1], Adwait Bhave[2(✉)], and Y. V. Haribhakta[3]

[1] Department of Computer Engineering, College of Engineering, Pune, India
shindeaa18.comp@coep.ac.in
[2] Technical Head, Algoanalytics Pvt Ltd., Pune, India
abhave@algoanalytics.com
[3] Faculty of Computer Engineering, College of Engneering, Pune, India
ybl.comp@coep.ac.in

Abstract. Handwriting recognition is the most complex research area in computer vision. Automation of Form documents such as bank cheques, bank account opening forms, Patient admission forms, driving license forms, etc. is the necessity of most industries and government sectors. There has been a lot of work going on in the Optical character recognition (OCR) techniques for English text but it's not giving promising results for recognition of ambiguous characters. We propose a recognition model, built on a nested convolutional neural network which improves the accuracy for ambiguous characters such as 2 and z, 5 and S, etc. Depending on the results of the experiments using the EMNIST dataset for training, validation, and testing, the new approach that uses CNN as a feature extractor and end classifier achieved a better recognition rate than previous models. The system integrates preprocessing, word extraction, classification whether it is printed or handwritten, segmentation, and character recognition together. The system's output is an editable key-value paired text.

Keywords: Form documents · Handwriting recognition · CNN · OCR

1 Introduction

Handwriting Recognition is a critical issue in the area of pattern recognition and computer vision. Extensive research into this area has brought substantial progress from classical methods, right up to human competitiveness. Filling out forms is one of the oldest and widely used methods for gathering information in various fields from the applicants. Automation of the scanning process of Form documents such as bank cheques, bank account opening forms, Patient admission forms, driving license forms, etc. can lead to office productivity and reduce time consumption. With the recent advancement in technologies, it is possible to make the availability of offline collected information online for faster access in the near future. To get more accurate recognized results, the extraction

© Springer Nature Singapore Pte Ltd. 2021
S. K. Singh et al. (Eds.): CVIP 2020, CCIS 1376, pp. 88–98, 2021.
https://doi.org/10.1007/978-981-16-1086-8_9

of the text plays an important role. Extracting data from handwritten document form may have several problems. Moreover, it has been observed that in offices the forms that are being distributed are static, which means the fields do not change rapidly over time. So, it is a good idea to go first for a handwritten data extraction system that is form specific.

Before success in deep learning, there are classical techniques carried heavy limitations in two key areas: 1) Character extraction Individual characters are recognized by ease with OCR. In Cursive handwriting, characters are connected which poses more issues with segmentation. It is hard to explicate handwriting with no clear separation between characters. 2) Feature extraction includes properties like number of strokes, pixel distribution, aspect ratio, distance from the image center, and reflection.

Nowadays recent success in deep learning, CNN is a state of the art of handwriting recognition which achieves excellent results in digit recognition. But when it comes to alphabets, it is not giving promising results due to ambiguity in characters (such as 5 and S; 2 and Z).

Inspired by the advancement in Convolutional Neural Networks, we propose a system that tries to minimize the problem of ambiguous character recognition. The system is limited to English text only. The preprocessing, word extraction, segmentation and recognition are integrated into one system.

2   Related Work

Some work has been carried out to establish different methods and algorithms capable of recognizing handwriting character.

A.G. Hochuli [3] proposed a segmentation free method that uses CNN classifiers one for string length classification and another for classification of digits. The digit classification comprises three classifiers responsible for the classification of isolated digits, 2-digit, and 3-digit strings. Those classifiers are used based on the outputs of the length classifier. The experiments were conducted on NIST SD19, where the strings only contain numeric data.

D. Nasien, H. Haron and S. Yuhani [2] presented a handwriting recognition model for English character identification which uses the Freeman Chain Code as a representation technique of image. An FCC method that uses 8-neighbourhood and Randomized algorithms are used to generate the FCC. FCC is generated from the characters that are used as the features for classification. SVM is used for classification. The problem in this proposed model is the length of FCC depends on the starting points chosen for the generation of FCC.

Darmatasia [1], proposed the deep learning model i.e. CNN for identifying handwritten characters on the form document. The preprocessing, character segmentation and recognition are integrated into one system. Segmentation is done by CCL method. He used a convolutional neural network for feature extraction. Then characters are classified using linear SVM with L2 regularization and L1 loss function. The system fails to extract the Region of Interest(ROI) which contains the connected character.

Hallale et al. [5] proposed a directional method for feature extractions on English handwritten characters. He developed a feature extraction technique with the conventional input pixel technique by using directional pattern matching. The data classified depending on the similarity between the vector features of training data and the vector features of testing data.

Mor et al. [7] proposed a CNN model with two convolutional layers and a fully connected layer for the classification of EMNIST characters. He developed an Android app for handwriting character recognition, obtaining 87.1% accuracy over EMNIST alphanumeric data.

3 Data and Methodology

3.1 Dataset

EMNIST dataset [8] basically the Extended MNIST created from NIST SD 19 [6] dataset. There are five different splits provided in this dataset.

- By Class: 62 unbalanced classes (uppercase alphabets + lowercase alphabets + digits)
- By Merge: 47 unbalanced classes (uppercase alphabets + lowercase alphabets + digits)
- Balanced: 47 balanced classes (uppercase alphabets + lowercase alphabets + digits)
- Letters: 26 balanced classes (uppercase alphabets)
- Digits: 10 balanced classes (digits)

We have used College concession forms for our work, the sample form image shown in Fig. 1. Also We have used EMNIST Balanced 47 classes in this work, to avoid classification errors resulting from misclassification between upper and lower case letters.

3.2 Proposed Method

In proposed approach, CNN is used as feature extractor to extract the input character features. Lecun and Bengio introduced CNN in 1995 in the paper [4]. It achieves best performance for local spacial correlation on image.

CNN is a subset of deep learning models which allows us to extract higher representations of an image. CNN takes the input image as raw data, trains the model, and then extracts the features for better classification. In general, CNN contains three layers: convolution, pooling, and last one fully-connected.

In a convolution operation, the kernel window slides through input images then calculates dot product of its input and filters pixel values. This makes it possible to emphasize the relevant features at convolution. With this computation, you detect a specific feature from the image input and generate convolved features that highlight the important features. These transformed features will often adjust to reduce the loss of prediction, depending on the kernel values affected by

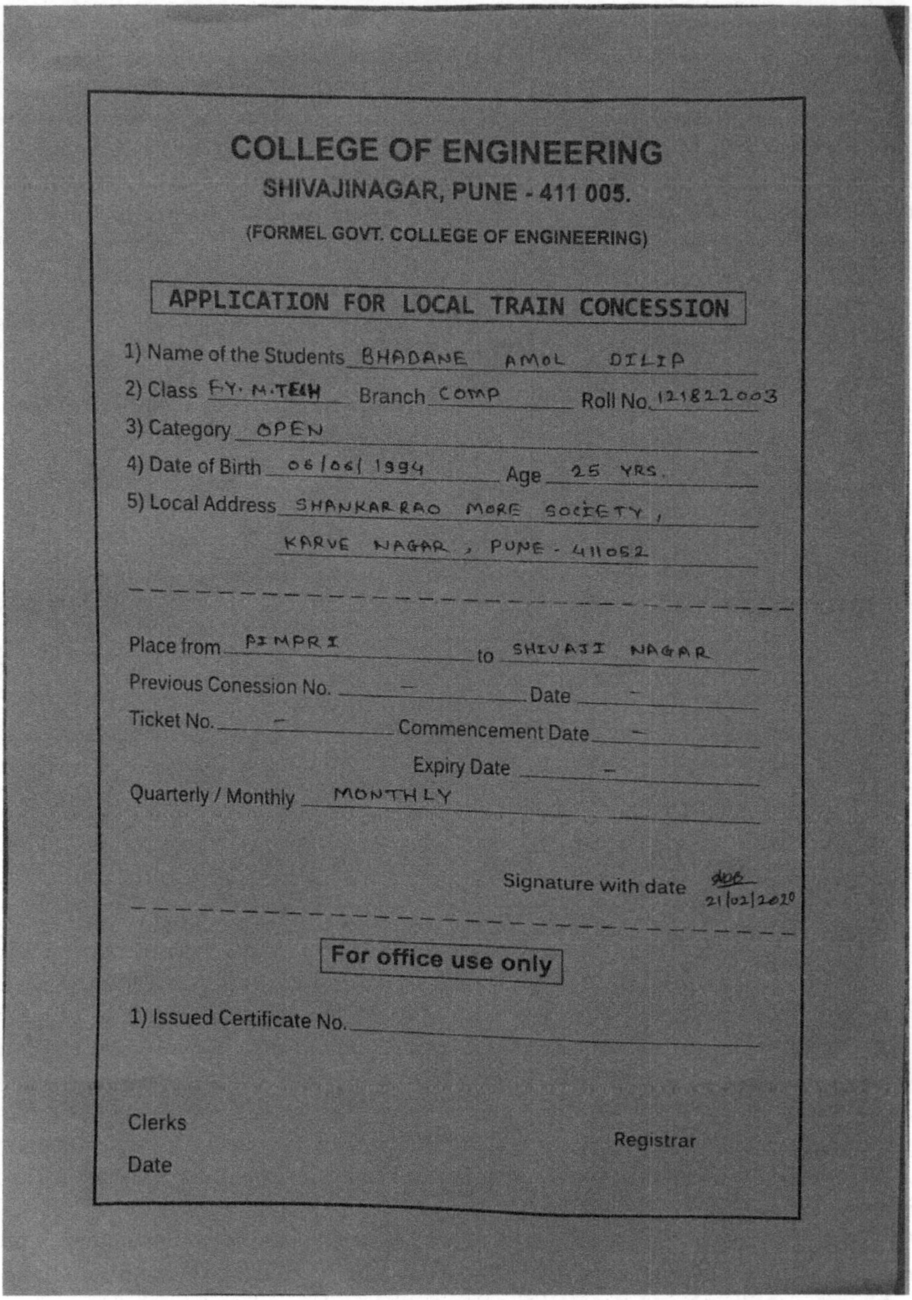

COLLEGE OF ENGINEERING
SHIVAJINAGAR, PUNE - 411 005.
(FORMEL GOVT. COLLEGE OF ENGINEERING)

APPLICATION FOR LOCAL TRAIN CONCESSION

1) Name of the Students BHADANE AMOL DILIP
2) Class F.Y. M.TECH Branch COMP Roll No. 121822003
3) Category OPEN
4) Date of Birth 06/06/1994 Age 25 YRS.
5) Local Address SHANKARRAO MORE SOCIETY, KARVE NAGAR, PUNE - 411052

Place from PIMPRI to SHIVAJI NAGAR
Previous Conession No. - Date -
Ticket No. - Commencement Date -
Expiry Date -
Quarterly / Monthly MONTHLY

Signature with date 21/02/2020

For office use only

1) Issued Certificate No.

Clerks
Date
Registrar

Fig. 1. Sample form image

the gradient descent. CNN uses max pooling to simplify convolutional output information with a max summary to minimize data size and processing time. This permits you to determine the features that produce the highest impact and reduces the risk of overfitting. We flatten the feature outputs to column vectors and feed-forward it to a Fully connected layer (FCL). The FCL involves neurons, weights, and biases. It links neurons in one layer to neurons in the next layer. It is a decision layer which is used for the classification of images in different categories by training a machine.

The last layer of CNN is Softmax or Logistic layer. It remains at the end of a FC-layer. Logistic is used for binary classification whereas softmax is for multi-label classification.

The proposed architecture of nested CNN is as shown in Fig. 1. The main network in which CNN used for feature extraction and classification. It consists of two sets of convolutional layers followed by a subsampling layer.

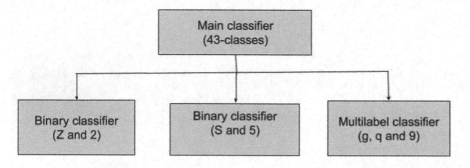

Fig. 2. Block diagram of Nested classification

The output of the first two convolutional layers have 32 feature maps with 28×28 pixels. The filter size that is used for convolution, is 5×5 for the first layer, 3×3 for the second one. The first Max Pooling layer's output is 14×14 with 32 feature maps. The third and fourth convolutional layers have similar parameters used in the first two except the feature map, 64. The output second Max pooling layer is 7×7 with 64 feature maps. The second Max Pooling layer's output is transposed into a vector feature followed by two dense layers. Softmax function used for activation to classify character image. The main network architecture is shown in Fig. 3.

The same architecture with different sets of layers used for binary classifiers. Instead of softmax function sigmoid function is used to classify the characters. In binary classification, binary cross entropy is used as a loss function.

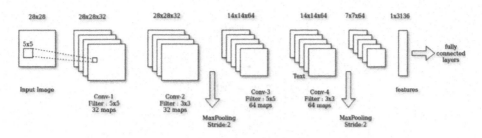

Fig. 3. Architecture of Convolutional neural network

3.3 Handwriting Recognition System

we build a handwriting recognition system to identify the handwriting characters on filled-in form document and convert it into an editable key-value pair text. The flow of the system shown in Fig. 3.

The system consists of five stages: preprocessing, word extraction, classification of words whether it is printed or handwritten, segmentation of handwriting text and classification of handwriting characters. Preprocessing step involves gray conversion, binarization, noise removal using gaussian filter, horizontal and vertical lines removal using morphology of image processing like erode, dilation etc. For word extraction, simple technique is adopted to detect the contour of the words in the text line. The output of word extraction step is used to check whether the given cropped word is printed or handwritten, binary classifier used for the seperation.

We build a handwriting recognition system to identify the handwriting characters on filled-in form document and convert it into an editable key-value pair text. The flow of the system shown in Fig. 3.

The system consists of five stages: preprocessing, word extraction, classification of words whether it is printed or handwritten, segmentation of handwriting text and classification of handwriting characters. Preprocessing step involves gray conversion, binarization, noise removal using gaussian filter, horizontal and vertical lines removal using morphology of image processing like erode, dilation etc. For word extraction, simple technique is adopted to detect the contour of the words in the text line. The output of word extraction step is used to check whether the given cropped word is printed or handwritten, binary classifier used for the seperation.

Handwritten words are segmented using column sum method where foreground pixels are summed after inversion of image and then with specific threshold value, characters are segmented. While printed words are recognize using google's tesseract model. The handwriting characters then given to our proposed system to recognize characters.

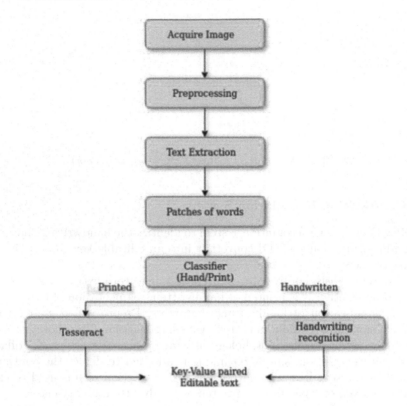

Fig. 4. Flow of handwriting character recognition on form document

3.4 Performance Evaluation

In this research, nested CNN architecture used to recognize ambiguous characters such as 2 and Z, 5 and S etc. The proposed method is evaluated by using accuracy, precision, recall and f1-score.

4   Results and Discussion

In this research, we evaluate the proposed method using EMNIST dataset for training, validation and testing. We approximately selected 1,03,271 sample images for training, 17199 sample images for validation and 17200 sample images for testing. Data divided in the proportion of 80% for training, 10% for validation and 10% for testing purposes. We also evaluate precision, recall and f1-score.

We implement the proposed method using processor Intel(R) Core TM i5-8250 CPU @ 1.6 GHz × 8 (4 physical core with each core having 2 hyper threads), Memory 16.00 GB RAM, Hard disk 1 TB, Linux operating system.

As seen the results from Table 1, the proposed method gives the best accuracy, precision, and recall except for the characters 9, q and g. As there are variety of writing these characters. On merger of uppercase, lowercase and numerical characters, it is hard to recognize characters like O and 0, 1 and l. It is because there is no difference in writing those characters.

Table 1. Accuracy of handwriting recognition

Method	Dataset	No of classes	Accuracy (%)	Precision	Recall	F1-score
CNN (4 classifiers) One main multi- classifiers + 2 binary classifiers + 3-class classifier	EMNIST (upper + lower + num)	43	89.97	90.00	90.00	90.00
	2 and Z	2	88.50	89.00	89.00	89.00
	5 and S	2	88.73	90.00	89.00	89.00
	9, q and g	3	86.66	87.00	87.00	87.00

Based on the results in Table 2, the proposed method achieves the best accuracy using EMNIST dataset both for training and testing. Darmatasia [1] proposed a method which gives accuracy better than our proposed method but he has tested for digits + uppercase letters while in our research we evaluated our model for uppercase, lowercase and numeric characters. The proposed system gives 91.13% accuracy on 5 different test form documents. The plot of training and validation accuracy is shown in Fig. 5. From the Fig. 6, we can say that Adam optimizer doesn't fluctuate more as the number of epochs increases. Also, it is faster than other algorithm

Table 2. Comparison of proposed model's accuracy with the relevant study

Author	Method	Dataset	No of classes	Accuracy (%)
Nasien et al. 2010 [2]	Freeman Chain Code +SVM	NIST (upper)	26	88.46
		NIST (lower)	26	86.00
Hallale & Salunke 2013 [5]	12 directional Feature + similarity	NIST (num + upper)	36	88.26
Darmatasia, 2016 [1]	CNN+SVM L1 Loss Function(dual) and L2 regularization	NIST(upper)	26	93.06
		NIST (lower)	26	86.21
		NIST (num + upper)	36	91.37
Mor et al. 2019 [7]	CNN (2 conv + 1 dense)	EMNIST (Num +upper +lower)	62	87.10
Proposed method	**CNN 1 main multi-classifiers + 2 binary classifiers + 3 class classifier**	**EMNIST (uppercase + lowercase + num)**	**43**	**89.97**
		(2 and Z binary classifier)	**2**	**88.50**
		(5 and S binary classifier)	**2**	**88.71**
		(9, g and q multi-label classifier)	**3**	**86.66**

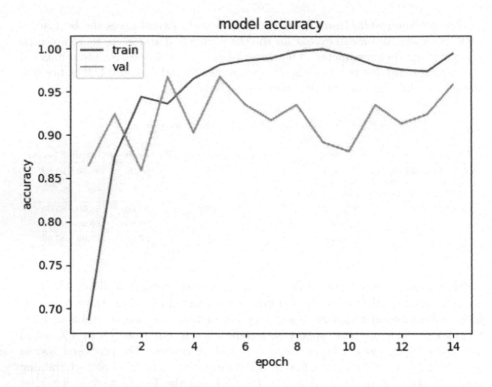

Fig. 5. The Accuracy plot of training and validation samples

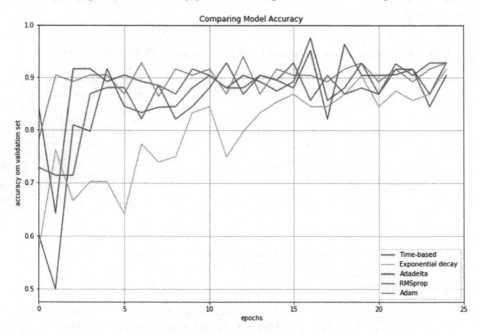

Fig. 6. Comparison of different optimizers on EMNIST data

5   Conclusion and Future Work

In this work, we used CNN as a powerful feature extractor and end classifier. The objective of recognizing handwritten text from a filled form has been met successfully. The proposed system is able to recognize ambiguous characters to some extent. The proposed method has been used to build an automatic handwriting recognition system on form documents. We have successfully integrated the text extraction and recognition system. Also, we tested our model for college concession sample forms to convert it in editable text and produce the outputs in key-valued pairs.

In the future, the proposed system may include many new methodologies to handle cases that presently are difficult to handle. This will include a method to handle the ambiguity between characters like 0 and O, 1 and lowercase l, as it is very hard to separate by classification method. By looking into the surrounding characters of those characters, it can be possible to detect it purely.

References

1. Fanany, M.I.: Handwriting recognition on form document using convolutional neural network and support vector machines (CNN-SVM). In: 2017 5th International Conference on Information and Communication Technology (ICoIC7), pp. 1–6. IEEE, May 2017
2. Nasien, D., Haron, H., Yuhaniz, S.S.: Support vector machine (SVM) for English handwritten character recognition. In: 2010 Second International Conference on Computer Engineering and Applications, vol. 1, pp. 249–252. IEEE, March 2010
3. Hochuli, A.G., Oliveira, L.S., Britto Jr., A.S., Sabourin, R.: Handwritten digit segmentation: is it still necessary? Pattern Recogn. **78**, 1–11 (2018)
4. LeCun, Y., Bengio, Y.: Convolutional networks for images, speech, and time series. In: The Handbook of Brain Theory and Neural Networks, vol. 3361, no. 10 (1995)
5. Hallale, S.B., Salunke, G.D.: Twelve directional feature extraction for handwritten English character recognition. Int. J. Recent Technol. Eng. **2**(2), 39–42 (2013)
6. Grother, P.J.: NIST special database 19 handprinted forms and characters database. National Institute of Standards and Technology (1995)
7. Sengar, A.M.N., Professor, S.A.: handwritten text recognition using tensorflow. Int. J. Eng. Adv.Technol (2019)
8. Cohen, G., Afshar, S., Tapson, J., Van Schaik, A.: EMNIST: extending MNIST to handwritten letters. In: 2017 International Joint Conference on Neural Networks (IJCNN), pp. 2921–2926. IEEE, May 2017
9. Sharma, N., Patnaik, T., Kumar, B.: Recognition for handwritten English letters: A. Int. J. Eng. Innov. Technol. (IJEIT) **2**(7), 318–321 (2013)
10. Shruthi, A.: Offline Handwritten Word Recognition using Multiple Features with SVM Classifier for, pp. 5989–5995 (2015)
11. Jindal, A., Amir, M.: Automatic classification of handwritten and printed text in ICR boxes. In: Souvenir 2014 IEEE International Advance Computing Conference IACC 2014, pp. 1028–1032 (2014)
12. Song, S., Zhan, Z., Long, Z., Zhang, J., Yao, L.: Comparative study of SVM methods combined with voxel selection for object category classification on fMRI data. PLoS ONE **6**(2), e17191 (2011)

13. Andrew, N.G.: Neural network and Deep learning, offered by Stanford University@deeplearning.ai
14. Andrew, N.G.: Convolutional neural network, offered by Stanford University @deeplearning.ai
15. Gonzalez, R.C.: Digital Image Processing, 3rd edn. Pearson Education India (2016)

A Two Side Histogram Shifting Based Reversible Data Hiding Technique in Encrypted Images

Ruchi Agarwal[✉] and Manoj Kumar

Babasaheb Bhimrao Ambedkar University, Lucknow, India

Abstract. Reversible data hiding means lossless recovery of hidden data as well as the original cover, but it lacks the security, to get over this problem, reversible data hiding in encrypted covers came into existence. Many reversible data hiding algorithms have been introduced by researchers but most of them have some flaws such as lack of complete reversibility, low embedding capacity, less security and others. This paper, introduces a simple iterative method which combines encryption and embedding schemes to increase the embedding capacity and security with the use of two side histogram shifting with reference to the peak point. The proposed work is divided into two methods: one uses side information while other does not. Results obtained after comparison of proposed work and existing works, proves the efficiency of scheme.

Keywords: Encryption · Embedding capacity · Histogram shifting · Random permutation · Reversible data hiding

1 Introduction

In this growing era of multimedia and advance information technology, data security is one of the biggest issues among researchers. One of the solutions to this issue is data hiding which is performed in different forms (steganography, digital watermarking etc.). Data hiding refers to the act of embedding sensitive/secret data into the cover medium secretly. Data hiding is applicable in various fields where covert communication is enforced such as information communication, medical imaging, military imaging, law enforcement, forensics, legal matters and many more. Techniques based on data hiding mostly results in distortion of cover image which is not acceptable when the data transferred is quite sensitive. In sensitive fields, even a single bit of information is important, hence reversible data hiding (RDH) schemes are required. To resolve the distortion effect, RDH has been introduced for exact recovery of both the original image content and embedded message losslesly. The main motive of RDH techniques is to embed secret data into the original image and after successful extraction of secret data, the original image is also to be perfectly recovered with zero percentage of bit error rate. In 1997, Barton [1] introduced the first RDH scheme. After that, many RDH schemes [2–8,12] were proposed by researchers which can be broadly

© Springer Nature Singapore Pte Ltd. 2021
S. K. Singh et al. (Eds.): CVIP 2020, CCIS 1376, pp. 99–112, 2021.
https://doi.org/10.1007/978-981-16-1086-8_10

classified into two categories: Difference Expansion (DE) based techniques and Histogram Shifting (HS) techniques. Under these categories, many algorithms were proposed with an aim to upraise the payload capacity as well as visual quality. A DE based algorithm was first introduced in the classical work of Tian [4]. In Tian's method the secret data is embedded by expanding the differences of neighbouring pixel pairs but faces overflow/underflow problem after embedding, which was overcome by the side information also called as location map. Further, many improvements [5–7] were proposed with high embedding capacity and low distortion. In [8], Ni et al. proposed histogram shifting algorithm which does not need any side information to retrieve the embedded information and cover image. In this method, firstly a pixel pair (most occurring pixel and least occurring pixel) is obtained with the help of image histogram and then shifting is performed to make the space for data embedding. Later on, this method was further studied and based on this, schemes [9,10] were proposed. In [10], block-based HS is proposed in which the same method as described in [8] is applied in all the blocks of image that enhances the embedding capacity and reduces the distortion in the marked images. Lee et al. [11] put forward a new technique with the help of difference image histogram instead of original image histogram. All these traditional RDH methods were applied over plaintext images. Since images are the major source for data hiding, so during their transmission over public network they may suffer against many attacks. Thus, for secure image transmission, confidentiality of transmitted data is utmost needed. Thus, the protection of digital media transmitted over public networks against tampering, copying, illegal accessing etc. is still required. Encryption is one of the simplest and secure way by which owner can hide the original data by encrypting it and send to the authorised user where the user can retrieve original data by decrypting the received data.

Reversible data hiding when imposed on encrypted domain becomes more challenging as encrypted images loses the correlation among pixels that had to be used to embed data in the plaintext domain. However, to achieve the security of cover image and secret data many reversible techniques were proposed which combine data hiding and encryption schemes. With the aim to fulfil this requirement, Zhang et al. [13] in 2011 introduced a first reversible data hiding in encrypted domain (RDH-ED). In [13], the basic idea was to flip the LSBs of original data to embed secret data, however, the scheme could not be proven so fruitful on theoretical basis for the extraction of hidden data and hence the original cover image. Improved versions of Zhang's scheme were proposed in [14,15], which were also not fully reversible. In [16], a new scheme which utilizes histogram modification was proposed by Qian et al. to embed the secret data. LSB compression of encrypted images in a RDH scheme was used by Zhang [18]. The main feature of this work was separability, i.e. image recovery and data extraction were independent to each other. Zhang and Qian [19] increases the efficiency of [18] by making use of low-density parity-check (LDPC) code for compression of LSBs to create space for data embedding. In addition to these, other algorithms [17,20–27] were also proposed by authors by combining encryption and embedding algorithms for data hiding in encrypted images. The main drawback of all these algorithms is the compulsion of using the side information (location map), it is note worthy that location map is itself a type of data hiding which leads to recursion and hence results in low embedding capacity and high time complexity. In this paper, we propose a new RDH-ED scheme which combines encryption and histogram shifting to embed two binary watermarks, (a string of 1's and 0's) on both side of the peak point (the count of most occurring pixel in an image) with and without use of any additional side information. The embedding capacity is almost two times the value of peak point which is further increased by implementing the proposed scheme first on whole image and then on all the non-overlapping blocks of image to enhance the embedding capacity upto two bits per pixel.

Contribution of the proposed method can be summarized as- The proposed scheme is secure as it utilizes pseudo random number generator (PRNG) scheme for encryption which is secure against any polynomial adversary. The iterative property of scheme enhances the embedding capacity at each level of iteration. At the first level of iteration the embedding capacity reaches upto 2 bpp which is notably good. The algorithm is iterative and easy to implement having less computational complexity. The proposed scheme is applicable in many sensitive fields such as medical imaging, military, law enforcement, legal matters etc. where every bit of information is important and apart from that the scheme may be utilized where high embedding capacity along with the security is required.

The rest of the paper is organized as follows: In Sect. 2 related work is discussed, Sect. 3 describes the proposed scheme, Sect. 4 discuss about the experimental results of the proposed work followed by comparison of proposed work with existing scheme in Sect. 5 and Sect. 6 concludes the proposed work.

2   Related Work

In the past few years, many techniques based on histogram shifting for reversible data hiding were proposed. The basic idea behind these schemes is to embed the secret data into the peak point of original cover histogram. In [8], Ni et al. first introduced the histogram shifting method using peak point and a zero point. Firstly, the histogram is shifted by making use of zero and peak point so that space can be created along the side of peak point and secondly, data is inserted into the created spaces. The process can be summarized as:

Let, I be the image whose histogram H is generated. Peak point and zero point are denoted by p and z respectively. Afterwards, pixels shifting is done on the basis of following conditions: If $p > z$, left shifting of the histogram is done, otherwise, right shifting of the histogram is done.

1. For embedding process, scan the image for value p, once the value p is obtained, check the value of the secret bit if it is '1' and $p < z$, then the pixel value is incremented by 1; if the value of secret bit is '0', the pixel value p remains the same. For $p > z$ case, check the value of secret bit if it is '1', decrement the pixel value p by 1; if secret bit founds to be '0', the pixel value p remains the same.

2. For extraction process, the watermarked image for $p < z$ is scanned again, secret bit '1' is extracted if $p + 1$ is encountered and if p is encountered '0' is extracted. For $p > z$: secret bit '1' is extracted if $p - 1$ is encountered and if p is encountered '0' is extracted.

With almost similar ideas, other techniques [29–31] were also proposed in plaintext and encrypted domain. Agrawal et al. [28] proposed an algorithm in which instead of zero point, second peak was used point with the motive to reduce distortion. Li et al. [29] explored the shifting of histogram in encrypted images with the help of asymmetric encryption by expanding and shifting the histogram of images with an aim to embed the secret data into the cover images. RDH-ED algorithm discussed in [30], uses two watermarks for embedding in the encrypted medical image. The first watermark is embedded in the encrypted medical image by using bit replacement method and the second watermark is embedded by utilizing the concept of the histogram modification in the marked encrypted image. With the generalisation of this idea, we introduced a new iterative histogram shifting method, for encrypted covers. The proposed scheme instead of shifting histogram on either side of peak point, shifts the histogram on both the sides of peak point of encrypted image and after shifting, the embedding of watermark is done. The watermark could be single string of 1's and 0's, for reflecting two spaces next to peak point, we embed two different watermarks W_1 and W_2. The proposed scheme utilizes two concepts: first, which does not require any location map or side information for watermark extraction but only the key information is needed for decryption and second, which requires side information and the decryption key.

3   Proposed Scheme

The schematic diagram of the proposed work is depicted in Fig. 1. In this paper, a new reversible data hiding scheme using iterative histogram shifting in encrypted domain is introduced. The proposed scheme consists of five subtasks: encryption, embedding, double layer encryption, extraction and recovery of original image.

3.1   Encryption

Interchanging the pixel position values or scrambling the pixels position to create scrambled image is performed using the permutation method [33]. We used random permutation for image encryption using a seed value which controls the random number generation using pseudo random number generator. A random permutation is a method to permute a fixed number of elements from a given set of elements. Random permutation is being used for encryption to take the advantage of the facts that no polynomial adversary can decrypt the permutation based encryption and frequency of pixels occurring in original and encrypted image remains the same. Encryption procedure is same for both the methods of embedding i.e. m1 (without side information) and m2 (with side information). Encryption scheme is performed as follows:

1. Generate a seed value using random number generator.
2. Permute the pixel positions of $I_{i,j}$ using the seed value to obtain the encrypted image $E_{i,j}$ (where (i,j) are the pixel positions).

3.2 Data Embedding Procedure

For data embedding, the histogram of encrypted image E is obtained and the peak point of image is found in the generated histogram. Afterwards, the space on both sides of image is created and embedding of watermark bits is performed as described below. For both the methods, the shifting of histogram towards left, right and resultant histogram (which shows shifting on both the sides together) are shown in Fig. 2.

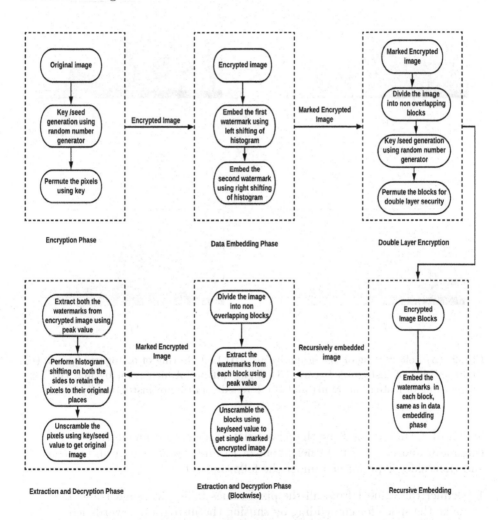

Fig. 1. Sketch of proposed work.

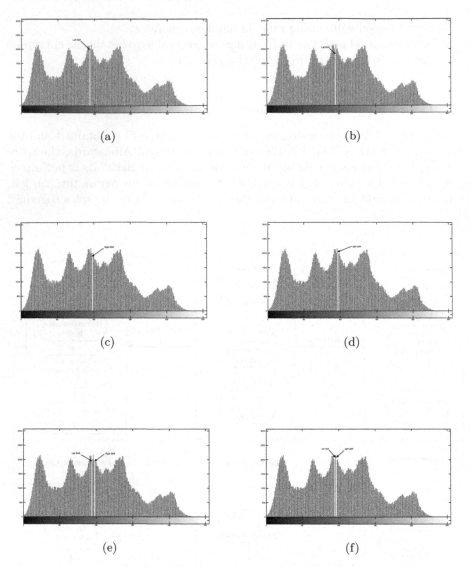

Fig. 2. **(a)** Left shifting of histogram by m1, **(b)** Left shifting of histogram by m2, **(c)** Right shifting of histogram by m1, **(d)** Right shifting of histogram by m2, **(e)** Two side shifting of histogram by m1 and **(f)** Two side shifting of histogram by m2.

Method 1 (m1). Let P be the peak point of encrypted image E, $P-1$ is left neighbour and $P+1$ is right neighbour of P. Shifting of histogram towards left and right sides is performed under the following rules:

1. Deduct the value 1 from all the pixel values falling in range 1 and $P-2$ to make the space for embedding by shifting the histogram towards left.

2. Add 1 to all the pixel values in range $P+2$ and 254 to make the space for embedding by shifting the histogram towards right.

3. After shifting, the vacant space is created for data embedding and both the watermarks W_1 and W_2 are embedded into the left and right vacant spaces by the following rules:

   (a) For W_1 : Scan the image $E_{i,j}$ for value $P-1$ in the histogram, check the watermark value to be inserted if it is '1' subtract 1 from the corresponding pixel value in the image E and thus its histogram value $P-1$ changed to $P-2$; if the watermark value to be embedded is '0', $P-1$ remains same.

   (b) For W_2 : Scan the image $E_{i,j}$ for value $P+1$ in the histogram, check the watermark value to be inserted if it is '1' add 1 in the corresponding pixel value in the image E and thus its histogram value $P+1$ changed to $P+2$; if the watermark value to be embedded is '0', $P+1$ remains same.

Method 2 (m2)

1. Subtract 1 from all the pixel values in range 1 and $P-1$ to make the space for embedding by left shifting the histogram.

2. Increment all the pixel values by 1 in range $P+1$ and 254 to make the space for embedding by right shifting the histogram.

3. Once the space is created for data embedding, watermark bits are embedded into the left and right space by the following rules:

   (a) For first watermark: Scan the image $E_{i,j}$ for value P in the histogram, check the watermark value to be embedded if it is '1' subtract 1 from the corresponding pixel value in the image E and thus its histogram value P changed to $P-1$; if the watermark value to be embedded is '0', P remains same.

   (b) For second watermark: Again scan the image $E_{i,j}$ for value P, check the watermark value to be embedded if it is '1' add 1 in the corresponding pixel value in the image E and thus its histogram value P changed to $P+1$; if the watermark value to be embedded is '0', P remains same.

   In this method, second watermark will be dependent on first, therefore the second watermark will be extracted before the first watermark.

Fig. 3(a) and 3(b) shows the watermarked encrypted histograms for methods m1 and m2 respectively.

The embedding capacity upto this point is limited to the value of peak point, hence to enhance embedding capacity, we divide the encrypted watermarked image into non intersecting blocks and perform the same procedure on each and every block, a type of iterative function is performed to meet desirable embedding capacity. Also, iterative embedding strengthens our algorithm due to occurrence of more distortion in encrypted images.

3.3   Extraction and Recovery of Original Image

In this segment, the secret bits (watermarks W_1 and W_2) are elicited and then original image is losslessly retrieved. Extraction is the just reverse process of embedding procedure. The receiver without any need of side information and only with the help of peak point information first extracts the second water-

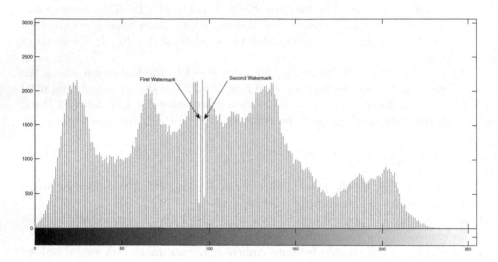

(a) Histogram of embedded image using m1

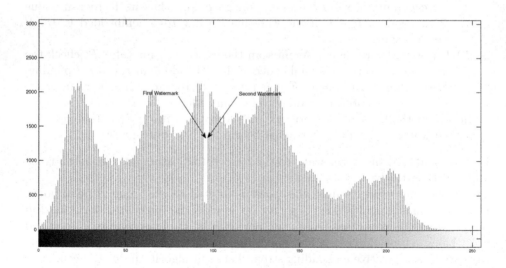

(b) Histogram of embedded image using m2

Fig. 3. Histograms of images when both the watermarks are embedded.

mark and then the first watermark or vice versa for method m1. Let E' be the watermarked encrypted image and $E'_{i,j}$ be the pixel value at i,j^{th} position. Extraction procedures for the methods m1 and m2 follow the following steps:

Method 1 (m1)

1. Scan the encrypted watermarked image E' for $P+2$ and $P+1$ values, if $P+1$ is encountered, '0' is extracted otherwise if encountered value is $P+2$, extract bit '1' and subtract one from all the pixel values ranging in $P+2$ and 254. This leads to extraction of second watermark W_2.
2. Again, scan E' for $P-2$ and $P-1$ values, if the value encountered is $P-2$, extract '1' as watermark bit otherwise if encountered value is $P-1$, extract bit '0', add one to all the pixel values ranging in 0 and $P-2$. This leads to extraction of first watermark W_1.

The above mentioned steps are independent to each other i.e., the order of execution does not matter and hence step 1 and step 2 can be executed in any order.

Method 2 (m2) . In this method, the receiver with the help of side information i.e. peak point value information performs the following steps for extraction of both the watermarks (W_1 and W_2):

1. Scan the encrypted watermarked image E' for P and $P+1$ values, if the result encountered is $P+1$, bit '1' is extracted otherwise if encountered value is P, extract bit '0' and subtract one from all the pixel values ranging in $P+1$ and 254. This leads to extraction of second watermark W_2.
2. Again, scan E' for P and $P-1$ values, if the value encountered is $P-1$, extract '1' otherwise if encountered value is P, extract bit '0', add one to all the pixel values ranging in 0 and $P-1$. This leads to extraction of first watermark W_1.

In the above mentioned steps, the order of execution matters, therefore extraction of second watermark will be performed before first.

A similar extraction procedure will be followed for the extraction of watermarks, when image is divided into non intersecting blocks. In that case, first, the extraction is performed followed by shifting of histograms for all the blocks and afterwards, the watermark bits from whole image are extracted.

After the extraction process, recovery of image is performed using decryption key. The receiver with the help of seed value generates the same sequence of pixel positions and then reverse random permutation is processed on the encrypted image (watermarks removed). The resultant image is identical to original image bit by bit, which shows lossless recovery.

4 Discussion and Experimental Results

The proposed methodology has been imposed on various test images, in Fig. 4, we are showing the result of proposed work only for one image. First of all, an original image is encrypted and then two watermarks are embedded on both sides of the peak point of histogram. Figure 4 clearly states that the histogram of original image and encrypted image are same, as the encryption procedure used in the proposed scheme is based on random permutation which just scrambles the pixel positions and does not change the pixel values. The embedding capacity is relatively low, therefore to enhance the payload, the block wise iterative embedding is used. The same method discussed above is applied on each and every block and before this the blocks are scrambled too. For security purpose, double layer encryption is applied i.e. pixel and block permutation both are used so that attacker cannot get any information about original pixel positions. The last image shown in Fig. 4 is the difference between original and recovered image which shows full black image (all pixels are zero) that is, both the original and recovered images are identical. Thus, the results obtained after experimental study show the lossless recovery of both watermarks and the original image.

We have performed the proposed work in MATLAB on more than 12 standard test images [34] of size 512×512 but due to space limitation results for only seven images are shown in the paper. All the pixel values are integers ranging between $[0-255]$. The payload capacity is shown in Table 1 and Table 2 for different block sizes for methods m1 and m2 respectively. The embedding capacity for Peppers image raise up to 2 bpp when block size is 2×2 as clearly shown in Table 2 for m2 which is notably good.

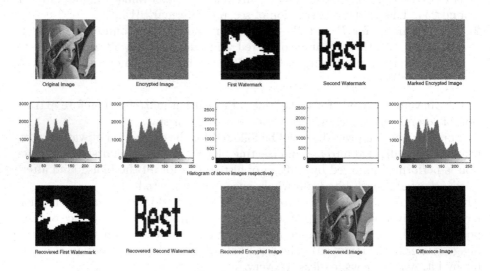

Fig. 4. Results of proposed work.

5 Comparison

Comparison of the proposed scheme is done with recent work by Ge et al. [32]. The results of comparison are shown in Table 3. Obtained results show the effectiveness of proposed work. In [32], two different rules (r1) and (r2) are proposed with different block sizes which are having direct impact on embedding capacity, we compared their rules r1 and r2 with the proposed methods m1 and m2 and found that for the given block sizes m1 and m2 both achieve better results than r1 and r2 in terms of payload capacity. For an instance, the embedding capacity of Lena image with block size 2 of [32] for rule r1 and r2 are 0.0850 and 0.0821 respectively. Whereas for the same image and dimensions, the embedding capacity of proposed approach for methods m1 and m2 are 0.1018 and 0.3768 which is not only slightly better but have an immense rise of about 20% and 359% when compared with [32], this proves the potency of the proposed scheme.

Table 1. Embedding capacity in bits for different block sizes by method 1 (m1)

Test images	Embedding capacity (bits)							
	2×2	4×4	8×8	16×16	32×32	64×64	128×128	256×256
Peppers	108360	127578	116259	96753	76830	56559	37749	24840
Airplane	3 4343	46283	47546	44143	38937	32807	27149	22754
Lena	26687	33477	3 2583	27812	22241	16531	11409	7670
Baboon	6767	9827	10647	10068	9428	7845	6450	3980
Boat	25568	37956	40372	38330	33512	26833	18822	12862
Barbara	17904	24589	24824	21781	17489	12671	8322	5797
Zelda	24053	32359	29297	23387	17662	12738	8828	5978

Table 2. Embedding capacity in bits for different block sizes by method 2 (m2)

Test images	Embedding capacity (bits)							
	2×2	4×4	8×8	16×16	32×32	64×64	128×128	256×256
Peppers	499798	336297	209166	137248	92738	61310	38568	23832
Airplane	111947	100461	80885	61702	48039	36610	27702	22422
Lena	98798	71012	55904	37355	26015	17695	11420	7266
Baboon	76331	37489	27513	19705	13654	9859	7238	5313
Boat	97144	77922	65204	50394	39022	29506	20395	13244
Barbara	88213	57448	44732	30498	20841	13868	8580	5942
Zelda	95501	66670	52197	32223	20681	13515	8797	5661

Table 3. Comparison of Embedding capacity(bpp) with block size 2 and 4 between proposed work and [32]

Test images	2×2				4×4			
	r1	r2	m1	m2	r1	r2	m1	m2
Boat	0.0728	0.0707	0.1975	0.3705	0.1209	0.1213	0.1447	0.2972
Barbara	0.0466	0.0458	0.0683	0.3365	0.0735	0.0733	0.0937	0.2191
Baboon	0.0166	0.0170	0.0258	0.2911	0.0323	0.0324	0.0374	0.1430
Airplane (F16)	0.1108	0.1086	0.1310	0.4270	0.1690	0.1695	0.1765	0.3832
Lena	0.0850	0.0821	0.1018	0.3768	0.1289	0.1285	0.1297	0.2709
Peppers	0.0516	0.0518	0.4133	1.9067	0.0884	0.0883	0.4866	1.2828

6   Conclusion

This paper proposed a new scheme for reversible data hiding based on two side shifting of histogram in encrypted domain. Double layer encryption is used for the security of original image. Also, iterative embedding is proposed i.e. first the scheme is applied on single image and then block wise implementation is performed. In this paper, two methods for data embedding are proposed with and without side information. Both of the methods produce notably good results on the basis of embedding capacity when compared with recently published work. In future, multiple layer approach can be implemented using this scheme to further enhance the embedding capacity. Although the scheme has some limitations also such as there is the noise impact on the method due to the fragile nature of reversible data hiding schemes and hence the proposed scheme is not robust against geometrical attacks like zooming, cropping, rotation etc. Also, on increasing level of iteration the computational complexity of the scheme may increase.

References

1. Barton, J.M.: Method and apparatus for embedding authentication information within digital data, U.S. Patent 5,646,997, 8 July 1997
2. Shi, Y.Q., Ni, Z., Zou, D., Liang, C., Xuan, G.: Lossless data hiding: fundamentals, algorithms and applications. In: Proceedings IEEE International Symposium on Circuits and System, vol. 2, pp. 33–36 (2004)
3. Shi, Y.Q.: Reversible data hiding. In: Proceedings International Workshop Digital Watermarking, pp. 1–12 (2004)
4. Tian, J.: Reversible data embedding using a difference expansion. IEEE Trans. Circuits Syst. Video Technol. **13**(8), 890–896 (2003)
5. Thodi, D.M., Rodriguez, J.J.: Expansion embedding techniques for reversible watermarking. IEEE Trans. Image Process. **16**(3), 721–730 (2007)
6. Fallahpour, M.: Reversible image data hiding based on gradient adjusted prediction. IEICE Electron. Exp. **5**(20), 870–876 (2008)

7. Hu, Y., Lee, H.K., Li, J.: DE-based reversible data hiding with improved overflow location map. IEEE Trans. Circuits Syst. Video Technol. **19**(2), 250–260 (2009)

8. Ni, Z., Shi, Y.Q., Ansari, N., Su, W.: Reversible data hiding. IEEE Trans. Circuits Syst. Video Technol. **16**(3), 354–362 (2006)

9. Van Leest, A., van der Veen, M., Bruekers, F.: Reversible image watermarking. In: Proceedings IEEE International Conference on Information Processing, vol. 2, pp. II-731-II-734, September 2003

10. Fallahpour, M., Sedaaghi, M.H.: High capacity lossless data hiding based on histogram modification. IEICE Electron. Exp. **4**(7), 205–210 (2007)

11. Lee, S.-K., Suh, Y.-H., Ho, Y.-S.: Reversiblee image authentication based on watermarking. In Proceedings IEEE International Conference on Multimedia and Expo, pp. 1321–1324, July 2006

12. Ma, K., Zhang, W., Zhao, X., Yu, N., Li, F.: Reversible data hiding in encrypted images by reserving room before encryption. IEEE Trans. Inf. Forensics Security. **8**(3), 553–562 (2013)

13. Zhang, X.: Reversible data hiding in encrypted image. IEEE Signal Process. Lett. **18**(4), 255–258 (2011)

14. Zhang, W., Ma, K., Yu, N.: Reversibility improved data hiding in encrypted images. Signal Process. **94**(1), 118–127 (2014)

15. Hong, W., Chen, T.-S., Wu, H.-Y.: An improved reversible data hiding in encrypted images using side match. IEEE Signal Process. Lett. **19**(4), 199–202 (2012)

16. Qian, Z., Zhang, X., Wang, S.: Reversible data hiding in encrypted JPEG bitstream. IEEE Trans. Multimedia **16**(5), 1486–1491 (2014)

17. Yu, J., Zhu, G., Li, X., Yang, J.: An improved algorithm for reversible data hiding in encrypted image. In: Shi, Y.Q., Kim, H.-J., Pérez-González, F. (eds.) IWDW 2012. LNCS, vol. 7809, pp. 384–394. Springer, Heidelberg (2013). https://doi.org/10.1007/978-3-642-40099-5_32

18. Zhang, X.: Separable reversible data hiding in encrypted image. IEEE Trans. Inf. Forensics Security **7**(2), 826–832 (2012)

19. Zhang, X., Qian, Z., Feng, G., Ren, Y.: Efficient reversible data hiding in encrypted images. J. Vis. Commun. Image Represent. **25**(2), 322–328 (2014)

20. Liao, X., Shu, C.: Reversible data hiding in encrypted images based on absolute mean difference of multiple neighboring pixels. J. Vis. Commun. Image Represent. **28**, 21–27 (2015)

21. Huang, F., Huang, J., Shi, Y.Q.: New framework for reversible data hiding in encrypted domain. IEEE Trans. Inf. Forensics Security **11**(12), 2777–2789 (2016)

22. Cao, H., Gao, T., You, Z., Cheng, R.: High capacity reversible data hiding in encrypted image based on image encoding and POB. J. Franklin Inst. **357**(13), 9107–9126 (2020)

23. Gao, X., Pan, Z., Gao, E., Fan, G.: Reversible data hiding for high dynamic range images using two-dimensional prediction-error histogram of the second time prediction. Signal Process. **173**, 107579 (2020)

24. Long, M., Zhao, Y., Zhang, X., Peng, F.: A separable reversible data hiding scheme for encrypted images based on Tromino scrambling and adaptive pixel value ordering. Signal Process. **176** 107703 (2020)

25. Qian, Z., Zhang, X.: Reversible data hiding in encrypted images with distributed source encoding. IEEE Trans. Circuits Syst. Video Technol. **26**(4), 636–646 (2016)

26. Shi, Y.Q., Li, X., Zhang, X., Wu, H.T., Ma, B.: Reversible data hiding: advances in the past two decades. IEEE Access **4**, 3210–3237 (2016)

27. Li, X., Zhang, W., Gui, X., Yang, B.: Efficient reversible data hiding based on multiple histograms modification. IEEE Trans. Inf. Forensics Security **10**(9), 2016–2027 (2015)
28. Agrawal, S., Kumar, M.: An improved reversible data hiding technique based on histogram bin shifting. In: Nagar, A., Mohapatra, D.P., Chaki, N. (eds.) Proceedings of 3rd International Conference on Advanced Computing, Networking and Informatics. SIST, vol. 43, pp. 239–248. Springer, New Delhi (2016). https://doi.org/10.1007/978-81-322-2538-6_25
29. Li, M., Li, Y.: Histogram shifting in encrypted images with public key cryptosystem for reversible data hiding. Signal Process. **130**, 190–196 (2017)
30. Kittawi, N., Al-Haj, A.: Reversible data hiding in encrypted images. In: 2017 8th International Conference on Information Technology (ICIT), Amman, pp. 808–813 (2017)
31. Jia, Y., Yin, Z., Zhang, X., Luo, Y.: Reversible data hiding based on reducing invalid shifting of pixels in histogram shifting. Signal Process. **163**, 238–246 (2019)
32. Ge, H., Chen, Y., Qian, Z., Wang, J.: A high capacity multi-level approach for reversible data hiding in encrypted images. IEEE Trans. Circuits Syst. Video Technol. **29**(8), 2285–2295 (2019)
33. Zhou, J., Liu, X., Au, O.C., Tang, Y.Y.: Designing an efficient image encryption-then-compression system via prediction error clustering and random permutation. IEEE Trans. Inf. Forensics Secur. **9**(1), 39–50 (2014)
34. Miscelaneous gray level images. http://decsai.ugr.es/cvg/dbimagenes/g512.php

Security of Digital Images Based on Stream Cipher and MDS Matrix

Abdul Gaffar$^{(\boxtimes)}$, Anand B. Joshi , and Dhanesh Kumar

Department of Mathematics and Astronomy, University of Lucknow,
Lucknow 226007, UP, India

Abstract. Stream ciphers are extensively used over a wide range of applications including security of digital data. In this paper, a method for securing different types of images (binary, gray scale, true color and index) based on stream cipher (RC4A) and MDS (Maximum Distance Separable) matrix is proposed. The proposed scheme is based on the cryptographic Permutation-Substitution Network (PSN) and hence achieves Shannon's confusion-diffusion characteristics required for a robust encryption algorithm. The scheme encrypts a digital image into a random-like image from human visual as well as statistical point of view. Several encryption evaluation metrics are applied on test images to empirically assess the performance and efficiency of the proposed method. The consequences of these statistical and security tests support the concreteness of the proposed approach.

Keywords: Stream cipher · RC4 · RC4A cipher · MDS matrix · PSN

1 Introduction

Symmetric key ciphers are the ciphers in which same key is used for encryption and decryption and these are broadly categorized in two parts: stream ciphers and block ciphers. Stream ciphers are extremely fast and simple in design as compared to block ciphers. The stream ciphers have been implemented in a large number of applications. A5/1 [1] (stream cipher) is used to secure over-the-air communication in the global service for mobile network. E0 [2], the stream cipher is used to secure the signals in bluetooth. In reference to the data security, encryption is the best choice wherein intelligible data (plain data) is encrypted to an unintelligible data (cipher data) by a suitable encryption algorithm. This paper proposes security of digital image data by using RC4A [3] (a variant of RC4 [4]) stream cipher and MDS matrix [5].

Supported by the UGC (University Grants Commission), India under grant number [415024].

RC4 is a stream cipher based software which is used extensively over a wide range of applications due to its amazing speed and simplicity. It became part of popular protocols and standards such as WEP (Wired Equivalent Privacy) in 1997, WPA (Wireless Protected Access) in 2003. It was implemented in SSL (Secure Sockets Layer) in 1995 and TLS (Transport Layer Security) connections in 1999. An MDS matrix [5] is a maximum distance separable matrix and is utilized for resisting differential attack. Moreover, as the key expansion algorithm is one the important factor of any secure encryption algorithm, so the proposed method utilizes the key expansion algorithm of AES cipher [5] for 10 rounds.

The remaining matter of the paper has been put in the following order: Sect. 2 gives a bird view of the related works, Sect. 3 introduces preliminaries which includes stream cipher and RC4 cipher. Section 4 describes RC4A stream cipher. Section 5 depicts the flowchart of the proposed encryption and decryption methods while Sect. 6 discusses simulation results and security assessment. Finally, Sect. 7 concludes the paper followed by the references.

2   Related Works

Mondal et al. [7] in 2015 proposed a technique for image encryption which is based on LFSR (Linear Feedback Shift Register) and RC4 keystream generator. The scheme works on PSN. Here, LFSR is used for pixel shuffling while RC4 is used for substituting pixel intensities of the intermediate encrypted image with the keystreams generated using RC4 cipher via XOR operation. The statistical outcomes vindicate the performance of the scheme. Alani and Iesawi [9] in 2018 proposed an algorithm for gray image encryption using Hénon map and RC4. Encryption evaluation metrics vindicate that the algorithm is proficient for real-time encryption and transmission of gray images. Susanto et al. [10] in 2020 proposed a novel technique for gray image security using Arnold chaotic map, bit-shift and stream encryption. The proposed method is assessed using different statistical and visual tests including differential analysis and these tests support the efficiency of the proposed method. Besides these, RC4 stream cipher has also been used in [6,8].

It is noticeable that all the papers mentioned above are for either gray scale or RGB (true color) image encryption only. None of the paper considers binary or index images. As far as we are aware of the encryption algorithms/methods, this the first method that encrypts binary, gray scale, true color as well as index images.

3   Preliminaries

3.1   Stream Cipher

It is a symmetric key cipher wherein plain-text (input) digits are enciphered bit-by-bit via XOR-ing the input bits with the bits of the pseudo-random bit generator (keystream). As XOR (exclusive-or) is a symmetric operation so, the decryption takes place in the same way as the encryption.

3.2 RC4 Stream Cipher

RC4 was structured in 1987 by Ronald Linn Rivest for RSA (Rivest, Shamir, and Adleman) data security. It is a stream cipher used extensively over a wide range of applications. It has been integrated into popular protocols, namely BitTorrent, WPA, WEP and TLS, SSL connections. Being miraculous for its performance and simpleness, multiple weakness [11] have been discovered. It is biased specifically when the first few bytes are not discarded or random keys are not used. For RC4 algorithm refer to Fig. 1, wherein S denotes an array of length Q (= 256), T denotes the temporary vector while K and l indicate the secret key and length of key (K) respectively.

KSA	PRGA
for $u = 0$ to $Q^* - 1$	$u = 0$
$S[u] = u$	$v = 0$
$T[u] = K[u \bmod l]$	Output Generation Loop
end for	$u = (u + 1) \bmod Q$
	$v = (v + S[u]) \bmod Q$
$v = 0$	swap $(S[u], S[v])$
for $u = 0$ to $Q - 1$	$t = (S[u] + S[v]) \bmod Q$
$v = (v + S[u] + T[u]) \bmod Q$	Output $= S[t]$ (keystream)
swap $(S[u], S[v])$	
end for	
* $Q = 256$	

Fig. 1. KSA (Key Scheduling Algorithm) and PRGA (Pseudo-Random Generation Algorithm) of RC4 stream cipher

4 RC4A Stream Cipher

RC4A cipher is an effort to improve the security as well as speed of the RC4 cipher and was proposed by S. Paul and B. Preneel in 2004. The main weakness in the RC4 cipher is that few initial output bytes generated by PRGA are strongly correlated thereby leaking information about the secret key. So, RC4 cipher was improved keeping in mind this weakness, by using more number of variables thereby reducing the correlation between the initial output bytes of the generated keystream.

4.1 RC4A Algorithm

It is built on the exchange shuffle norm of RC4 cipher in order to achieve a random distribution of a deck of cards. The algorithm runs in two phases. The

Fig. 2. KSA and PRGA of $RC4A$ stream cipher

first one is the key scheduling algorithm and the another one is the pseudo-random generation algorithm. As compared to RC4, it is more secure since there are nearly 2^{3392} secret internal states whereas for RC4, the internal states are only 2^{1700}.

Key Scheduling Algorithm (KSA). The KSA is used to turn an identity permutation of arrays or boxes S_1 and S_2 into a pseudo-random permutation of elements $\{0, 1,..., 255\}$. The pseudo-code is given in Fig. 2 (left side).

Pseudo-Random Generation Algorithm (PRGA). It is used to produce keystreams K_1 and K_2 via the updated states S_1 and S_2 obtained from the KSA. The pseudo-code is given in Fig. 2 (right side). Keystream K_1 is generated in the same fashion as in RC4 but here it is evaluated on state S_2 instead on S_1. Keystream K_2 is generated using the state array S_2 and index v_2 keeping index u fixed. The output ($S_2[u] + S_2[v_2]$) is evaluated on S_1 instead of S_2.

5   Flowchart of the Proposed Method

The pictorial representation of the proposed encryption and decryption methods is depicted in Fig. 3. It is noticeable that for encryption case (left to right in Fig. 3), the internal loop consists of permutation, diffusion and substitution stages, where each stage itself is an encryption stage and these stages together form a PSN [12]. The whole process iterates for r rounds. The stages are discussed in Subsects. 5.3, 5.4 and 5.5 respectively. Note that, decryption takes place in the opposite order of the encryption process, i.e., substitution, diffusion and then permutation (see Fig. 3 from right to left).

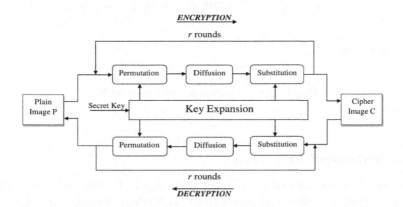

Fig. 3. Flowchart of the proposed method

5.1   Key Expansion

To improve the diffusion and confusion properties [12] of the proposed encryption method, we utilize key expansion algorithm of AES [5] for 128-bit secret key. Arrange the 16-byte secret key, k_1 = {00, 0f, 06, 01, 05, 0a, 02, d1, a8, 39, 0b, e8, c1, 87, 11, 8d} (in hexadecimal) into four words as $z[0]$ = {00, 0f, 06, 01}, $z[1]$ = {05, 0a, 02, d1}, $z[2]$ = {a8, 39, 0b, e8} and $z[3]$ = {c1, 87, 11, 8d}, where each word is of four bytes. Now, apply the key expansion algorithm given in Fig. 4 to generate additional forty words ($z[4], z[5], ..., z[43]$) required for ten rounds encryption and decryption processes. The round constant $Rcon_u$ for u^{th} round is a four byte word and is given as, $Rcon_u$ = {$R_c[u]$, 00, 00, 00}, where the values of $R_c[u]$ to be used in key expansion algorithm (see step (*) of Fig. 4) are given in Table 1. Now, we briefly explain the underlined operation 'TEMP(y)', used in step (*) of Fig. 4, where TEMP = SubWord(RotWord). This operation takes place whenever u is a multiple of four and is evaluated in two steps.

1. Circular left shift of y (= $z[u-1]$) by 1-byte.
   For instance, if y = $[x_0, x_1, x_2, x_3]$, then RotWord($[x_0, x_1, x_2, x_3]$) = $[x_1, x_2, x_3, x_0]$.

2. Replace each byte of $[x_1, x_2, x_3, x_0]$ using AES S-box (see Subsect. 5.2)
   i.e., SubWord($[x_1, x_2, x_3, x_0]$) = $[S(x_1), S(x_2), S(x_3), S(x_0)]$.
   So, TEMP(y) = $[S(x_1), S(x_2), S(x_3), S(x_0)]$.

$$
\begin{aligned}
&\text{Input} = \{z[0], z[1], z[2], z[3]\} \\[6pt]
&\text{for } u = 4 \text{ to } 43 \\
&\quad y = z[u-1] \\
&\quad\quad \text{if } u \ (\text{mod } 4) = 0 \\
&\quad\quad\quad y = z[u-4] \oplus \text{TEMP}(y) \oplus \text{R}_c[u/4] \quad\text{--- (*)} \\
&\quad\quad \text{else } y = z[u-4] \oplus y \\
&\text{end for}
\end{aligned}
$$

Fig. 4. Key expansion algorithm of AES

5.2   Generation of AES S-box

AES S-box [5] is a matrix of 16×16 elements in which rows and columns have values in the range of $00 - 0f$ (hexadecimal). The substitution-box maps a 1-byte input 'a' to a 1 byte output, '$t = S(a)$'. The input (a) and the output (t) are taken as polynomials over Galois Field of two elements, $GF(2)$. The process for computing any element in S-box is given as follows:

1. Map the input to its inverse (multiplicative) in $GF(2^8) = GF(2)/f(x)$, $f(x) = (x^8 + x^4 + x^3 + x + 1)$. Note that '0' (the identity) is self-mapped.
2. Transform the inverse via (1)

$$
t = h \oplus (h <<< 1) \oplus (h << 2) \oplus (h <<< 3) \oplus (h <<< 4) \oplus 63_{16} \qquad (1)
$$

where h represents the multiplicative inverse of input a, $\oplus$ is XOR operator, $<<<$ is the left bit-wise circular shift operator and constant 63_{16} ($= 01100011)_2$ is given in hexadecimal. For instance, if we have to look S-box output corresponding to input say, $3d$ (in hexadecimal). Then using step 1, we find its multiplicative inverse as bb and via step 2, we get $(27)_{16}$ as output. The set of ten round keys obtained by implementing the key expansion algorithm (Fig. 4) for 128-bit secret key are given in Table 2.

Table 1. Values of $R_c[u]$ in hexadecimal

u	1	2	3	4	5	6	7	8	9	10
$R_c[u]$	1	2	4	8	10	20	40	80	1b	36

Table 2. Different round keys (in hexadecimal) to be used for encryption and decryption processes

Secret key	00	0f	06	01	05	0a	02	d1	a8	39	0b	e8	c1	87	11	8d
Round 1	16	8d	5b	79	13	87	59	a8	bb	be	52	40	7a	39	43	cd
Round 2	06	97	e6	a3	15	10	bf	0b	ae	ae	ed	4b	d4	97	ae	89
Round 3	8a	73	a2	eb	9f	63	1d	e0	31	cd	f0	ab	e5	5a	5e	2d
Round 4	3c	2b	7a	32	a3	48	67	d2	92	85	97	79	77	df	c9	54
Round 5	b2	f6	5a	c7	11	be	3d	15	83	3b	aa	6c	f4	e4	63	38
Round 6	fb	0d	5d	78	ea	b3	60	6d	69	88	ca	01	9d	6c	a9	39
Round 7	eb	de	4f	26	01	6d	2f	4b	68	e5	e5	4a	f5	89	4c	73
Round 8	cc	f7	c0	c0	cd	9a	ef	8b	a5	7f	0a	c1	50	f6	46	b2
Round 9	95	ad	f7	93	58	37	18	18	fd	48	12	d9	ad	be	54	6b
Round 10	0d	8d	88	06	55	ba	90	1e	a8	f2	82	c7	05	4c	d6	ac

5.3   Permutation Stage

Let the size of plain image I be $U \times V$. Since we know that the KSA of RC4 (see Fig. 1) produces an array S which is a random permutation of $\{0, 1, 2,..., Q-1\}$ elements, $Q = 256$. Therefore, this array S can be used as a bijective map [12]. For this, we replace Q by U (rows of I) in KSA of RC4 and generate an array $S(= \phi)$ of U elements and this ϕ is used for shuffling rows of the plain image matrix I. Similarly, we again replace Q by V (columns of I) in KSA of RC4 and generate an array $S(= \varphi)$ of V elements and this φ is used for shuffling columns of the image matrix I. The permutation algorithm is given as follows:

Permutation Algorithm

Input: Plain image matrix I, arrays ϕ and φ for permuting rows and columns
of I respectively

Output: Cipher image matrix E

    for $r = 1$ to U

        $J_r \leftarrow I_{\phi[r]+1}$ (Row permutation)

    end for

    for $c = 1$ to V

        $C_c \leftarrow J_{\varphi[c]+1}$ (Column permutation)

    end for

In the permutation algorithm, $I_{\phi[r]+1}$ denotes $(\phi[r] + 1)^{th}$ row of I and it is mapped to r^{th} row of image matrix J. Similarly, $J_{\varphi[c]+1}$ denotes $(\varphi[c] + 1)^{th}$ column of J and it is mapped to c^{th} column of image matrix C. Note that, for decryption case the permutation algorithm works in reverse order, i.e., first columns of cipher image are shuffled using column permutation array φ and then rows are shuffled using row permutation array ϕ.

5.4 Diffusion Stage

To attain the required diffusion property [12], this process is applied to every $B \times B$ sized block I_b in the plain image I over the Galois Field $GF(2^8)$ and is given in (2), where B represents the variable sized block and is calculated by the format of the plain image and M_d denotes the MDS matrix [5] obtained from 4×4 random permutation matrices and is given in (4).

$$E_b = (M_d \cdot I_b \cdot M_d)_{2^8} \tag{2}$$

$$I_b = (M_d^{-1} \cdot E_b \cdot M_d^{-1})_{2^8} \tag{3}$$

$$M_d = \begin{bmatrix} 4 & 2 & 1 & 3 \\ 1 & 3 & 4 & 2 \\ 2 & 4 & 3 & 1 \\ 3 & 1 & 2 & 4 \end{bmatrix} \text{ and } (M_d^{-1})_{2^8} = \begin{bmatrix} 71 & 216 & 173 & 117 \\ 173 & 117 & 71 & 216 \\ 216 & 71 & 117 & 173 \\ 117 & 173 & 216 & 71 \end{bmatrix} \tag{4}$$

It is noticeable that when the plain image I is a gray scale or a true color image, then the size of block matrix I_b is 4×4 (bytes) and the size of I_b is 32×32 bits ($= 4 \times 4$ bytes) in case of binary format image. It is important to note that if $U \times V$ (size of plain image I) is indivisible by $B \times B$, then the diffusion process is applied to the region $B \lfloor U/B \rfloor \times B \lfloor V/B \rfloor$ only, where $\lfloor . \rfloor$ is the *floor* function. Since we apply the diffusion process for each encryption round, so the change in any one pixel of the original image results in the modification of $B \times B$ pixels in each cipher round. So, the minimum number of rounds/iterations required to modify $U \times V$ pixels is given by (5).

$$\#round_{min} = \lceil log_{B \times B}(U \times V) \rceil = \lceil log_2(UV)/2log_2(B) \rceil \tag{5}$$

where $\lceil . \rceil$ denotes the *ceiling* function. Also, note that decryption of this cipher stage is processed by using (3), where M_d^{-1} is the inverse of matrix M_d over $GF(2^8)$ and is given in (4).

5.5 Substitution Stage

In this cipher stage, pixels of the original image are substituted using the keystreams K_1 and K_2 generated by PRGA of RC4A cipher (see Fig. 2) via a secret key k_1 (128-bit). Plain image pixels are first bitwise XOR-ed with the keystream K_1 and then with the keystream K_2. Equation (6) shows the substitution process for encryption case while for decryption case it is shown by (7).

$$E_1 = I \oplus K_1$$
$$E_2 = E_1 \oplus K_2 \tag{6}$$

$$E_1 = E_2 \oplus K_2$$
$$I = E_1 \oplus K_1 \tag{7}$$

where $\oplus$ is XOR operation, K_1 and K_2 are keystreams and I denotes the plaintext. It is noticeable that all the encryption stages mentioned, that is, permutation, diffusion and substitution constitutes a 'cipher round'. Moreover, the secret key (k_1) which is of 128-bit (16 bytes), is only used for key expansion and not for any cipher round. The proposed method makes use of ten rounds for encryption and decryption. The enciphering (or deciphering) keys for each round are listed in Table 2.

6   Simulation Results and Security Assessment

The proposed method is simulated in *MATLAB R2015a*, under the Windows 10 environment with *Core i5* (7th *Gen*) CPU and $8GB$ memory. To empirically estimate the efficiency of the proposed scheme, different types of images such as binary, gray scale, true color and index images are considered.

6.1   Key Space Analysis

The space of all possible permutations of a key constitutes a key space of the crypto algorithm. In order to resist brute-force attack, chosen-cipher-text attack, known-plain-text attack, etc., key space should be very large. As in our proposed scheme, the key is of size 128-bit, producing a key space of 2^{128} which is very large.

6.2   Key Sensitivity Analysis

It is one of the essential criterion for the encryption algorithm to be robust. Moreover, high sensitivity is desired to secure the cryptographic algorithm from attackers. The sensitivity test is analyzed in two facets:

1. Encryption: how dissimilar are two encrypted images E_1 and E_2 with reference to the same plain image I using the cipher keys c_1 and c_2 which differ from each other only by 1 bit.
2. Decryption: how dissimilar are two deciphered images P_1 and P_2 with reference to the same encrypted image E_1 using the two decryption keys λ_1 and λ_2, both of which differ from the encryption key c_1 only by 1 bit.

The consequences of the key sensitivity analysis with respect to encryption and decryption are shown in Fig. 5, whence we infer that the encryption algorithm based on RC4A stream cipher is very sensitive and thus ensures the property of confusion [12].

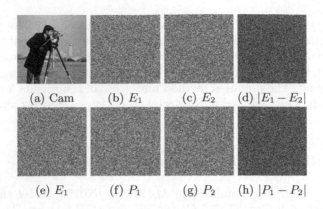

Fig. 5. Key sensitivity consequences: (a) plain image (Cameraman), (b) encrypted image $E_1 = Enc(I, c_1)$, (c) $E_2 = Enc(I, c_2)$, (d) difference between E_1 and E_2, (e) encrypted image E_1, (f) decrypted image $P_1 = Dec(E_1, \lambda_1)$, (g) $P_2 = Dec(E_1, \lambda_2)$ and (h) difference between P_1 and P_2

6.3   Histogram Analysis

Histogram is a demonstration of pixel distributions of an image. As secure crypto algorithm turns an original image into a random-like image, so the histogram of the enciphered image should be distributed uniformly. Figure 6 shows histogram of several original and encrypted images. One can observe from Fig. 6 that the histogram of encrypted images is approximately uniform endorsing that the encrypted images are random-like.

6.4   Entropy Analysis

This analysis is commonly utilized to measure the randomness of an image, say E and it can be calculated using (8).

$$H(E) = -\sum_{i=1}^{2^N} Pr(e_i) \log_2(Pr(e_i)) \tag{8}$$

where e_i represents the ith value in E, $Pr(e_i)$ is the probability of e_i and N denotes number of bits used to represent a pixel and for a gray scale image $N = 8$. The entropy values of the cipher images (Figs. 6L–6n) are 7.9974, 7.9973, and 7.9990 respectively which are very closed to ideal value 8 and are better than the entropy values reported in [6–10,15,16] .

6.5   NPCR and UACI Tests

Number of Pixel Change Rate (NPCR) [13] and the Unified Averaged Changed Intensity (UACI) are commonly used tests for estimating the resistance of differential attack [14]. The values of these tests between crypto (or cipher) images E_1 and E_2 can be calculated using (9) and (10) respectively.

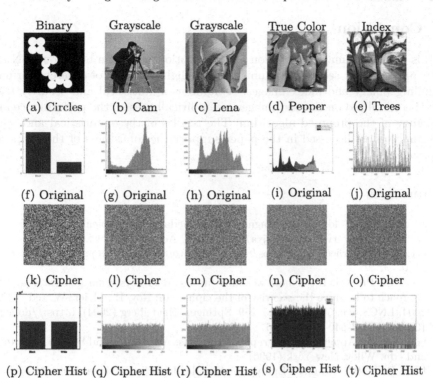

(a) Circles   (b) Cam   (c) Lena   (d) Pepper   (e) Trees

(f) Original   (g) Original   (h) Original   (i) Original   (j) Original

(k) Cipher   (l) Cipher   (m) Cipher   (n) Cipher   (o) Cipher

(p) Cipher Hist (q) Cipher Hist (r) Cipher Hist (s) Cipher Hist (t) Cipher Hist

Fig. 6. Histogram analysis on original and encrypted images

$$NPCR = \sum_{r=1}^{U}\sum_{s=1}^{V} \frac{\beta(r,s)}{UV} \times 100\% \tag{9}$$

$$UACI = \sum_{r=1}^{U}\sum_{s=1}^{V} \frac{|E_1(r,s) - E_2(r,s)|}{255 \cdot (UV)} \times 100\% \tag{10}$$

where $\beta(r,s) = 0$ if $E_1(r,s) = E_2(r,s)$ else $\beta(r,s) = 1$ and U, V denote the rows, columns of the image respectively. $E_1(r,s)$ and $E_2(r,s)$ are the pixels of the crypto images prior to and after alteration of one-pixel of the plain image. NPCR score calculated for different images (Figs. 6b–6d) is 90.6094% while UACI score lies in the range 33.3728–33.4638%. Note that, if the reported NPCR score is greater than the theoretical NPCR value (99.5693%) then the NPCR test is passed. Also, if the UACI score lies in the open interval (33.2225, 33.7016)% then the UACI test is passed. The proposed method passes both the tests and outperforms the methods [6–10, 16] that fail to resist differential attack.

7   Conclusion

In this paper, an image encryption and decryption algorithm based on PSN has been proposed for secure communication of digital images of different formats including binary and index images. A number of statistical and security tests have been utilized on the test images to empirically assess the performance and efficiency of the proposed algorithm. The results of these statistical and security analyses as discussed in the paper support the robustness of the proposed approach.

References

1. Briceno, M., Goldberg, I., Wagner, D.: A pedagogical implementation of A5/1 (1999). https://cryptome.org/jya/a51-pi.htm. Accessed 9 Oct 2020
2. https://grouper.ieee.org/groups/802/15/Bluetooth/core_10_b.pdf. Accessed 9 Oct 2020
3. Paul, S., Preneel, B.: A new weakness in the RC4 keystream generator and an approach to improve the security of the cipher. In: Roy, B., Meier, W. (eds.) FSE 2004. LNCS, vol. 3017, pp. 245–259. Springer, Heidelberg (2004). https://doi.org/10.1007/978-3-540-25937-4_16
4. Schneier, B.: Applied Cryptography: Protocols, Algorithms and Source Code in C, 2nd edn. Wiley, New York (1996)
5. FIPS PUB 197: Advanced Encryption Standard (AES), National Institute of Standards and Technology (2001). http://csrc.nist.gov/publications/fips/fips197/fips-197.pdf. Accessed 9 Oct 2020
6. Ismael, R.S., Youail, R.S., Wahhab, S.: Image encryption by using RC4 algorithm. Eur. Acad. Res. **2**, 5833–5839 (2014)
7. Mondal, B., Sinha, N., Mandal, T.: A secure image encryption algorithm using LFSR and RC4 key stream generator. In: Nagar, A., Mohapatra, D.P., Chaki, N. (eds.) Proceedings of 3rd International Conference on Advanced Computing, Networking and Informatics. SIST, vol. 43, pp. 227–237. Springer, New Delhi (2016). https://doi.org/10.1007/978-81-322-2538-6_24
8. Bhowmick, A., Sinha, N., Arjunan, R.V., Kishore, B.: Permutation-Substitution architecture based image encryption algorithm using middle square and RC4 PRNG. In: Proceedings of International Conference on Inventive Systems and Control (ICISC), Coimbatore, pp. 1–6 (2017). https://doi.org/10.1109/ICISC.2017.8068729
9. Dena, A., Salah, I.: Image encryption algorithm based on RC4 and Henon map. J. Theoret. Appl. Inf. Technol. **96**, 7065–7076 (2018)
10. Susanto, A., Setiadi, D.R.I., Sari, C.A., Sarker, M.K.: Triple layer image security using bit-shift, chaos and stream encryption. Bull. Electr. Eng. Inf. **9**, 980–987 (2020). https://doi.org/10.11591/eei.v9i3.2001
11. Fluhrer, S., Mantin, I., Shamir, A.: Weaknesses in the key scheduling algorithm of RC4. In: Vaudenay, S., Youssef, A.M. (eds.) SAC 2001. LNCS, vol. 2259, pp. 1–24. Springer, Heidelberg (2001). https://doi.org/10.1007/3-540-45537-X_1
12. Shannon, C.E.: Communication theory of secrecy systems. Bell Syst. Tech. J. **28**, 656–715 (1949)
13. Wu, Y., Noonan, J.P., Agaian, S.: NPCR and UACI randomness tests for image encryption. J. Selected Areas Telecommun. (JSAT) **1**, 31–38 (2011)

14. Biham, E., Shamir, A.: Differential cryptanalysis of the Data Encryption Standard, Springer, Heidelberg (1993). https://doi.org/10.1007/978-1-4613-9314-6
15. Fawaz, Z., Noura, H., Mostefaoui, A.: An efficient and secure cipher scheme for images confidentiality preservation. Signal Process. Image Commun. **42**, 90–108 (2016). https://doi.org/10.1016/j.image.2016.01.009
16. Deb, S., Biswas, B., Bhuyan, B.: Advanced image encryption scheme using snow stream cipher. In: Hitendra Sarma, T., Sankar, V., Shaik, R.A. (eds.) Emerging Trends in Electrical, Communications, and Information Technologies. LNEE, vol. 569, pp. 785–794. Springer, Singapore (2020). https://doi.org/10.1007/978-981-13-8942-9_67

Retinal Vessel Segmentation Using Joint Relative Entropy Thresholding on Bowler Hat Transform

Md. Iman Junaid$^{(\boxtimes)}$, U. R. Jena, and Pranaba K. Mishro

Veer Surendra Sai University of Technology, Burla 768018, Odisha, India

Abstract. Retinal vessel segmentation is a method of analyzing the tree like vessel structure in a fundus image. This is to support the diagnosis of different ophthalmology diseases, such as: arteriosclerosis, retinal occlusions and diabetic retinopathy. In this work, we suggest an automated retinal vessel segmentation scheme which involves three steps. First, the retinal image enhancement using Bowler Hat Transform (BHT) for improving the appearance of the image and for converting it to a form better suited for further analysis. Second, the use of matched filter for detection of retinal vessels from the enhanced image using a Gaussian shaped function. Third, the use of joint relative entropy (JRE) for obtaining an optimal threshold value for thresholding. A set of standard fundus images (from DRIVE dataset) are used for testing the efficiency of the suggested scheme. Experimental outcomes show the superiority of the proposed method in terms of the average accuracy, specificity and sensitivity. The efficiency of the suggested scheme is evaluated in comparison with the existing methods. It is to be noted that the suggested scheme is found to be substantially better.

Keywords: BHT enhancement · Matched filter · JRE thresholding

1 Introduction

Retinal image analysis plays a crucial role in retinal pathology for an ophthalmologist for detection and diagnosis. This provides a high rate of information for diagnosing glaucoma, diabetic retinopathy or macular degeneration [1]. These are related with abnormality variation in retinal vessel structure [2]. Therefore, the variations in the anatomy of articular and vascular structures have a principal diagnostic significance. Retinal vessel segmentation consists of wide-range schemes used to implement, automate, identify, localize and extract the retinal vessel structures.

In the literature, the retinal segmentation techniques are broadly classified into two groups. These are rule based and machine learning based techniques. Rule based techniques generally deals with specific rules regarding the framework of algorithm, such as: kernel based, vessel tracking, adaptive local thresholding, etc. Machine Learning method uses a manually segmented image (ground truth)

S. K. Singh et al. (Eds.): CVIP 2020, CCIS 1376, pp. 126–136, 2021.
https://doi.org/10.1007/978-981-16-1086-8_12

to form a labelled dataset which is further used as training dataset. Villalobos-Castaldi et al. [3] suggested an approach using second local entropy for retinal vessel segmentation. A thresholding value is used from the static features of the Gray level co-occurance matrix (GLCM). Marin et al. [4] suggested a scheme supervised method using 7D vector formed from gray scale and moment invariant features. The method used neural network for classifying the vessels in a retinal image. In [5,6], the authors suggested neural network based scheme using the features from GLCM. They used gamma correction and geometric transformations simultaneously with the classifier. Further, Jiang et al. [7] suggested deep convolutional neural network in place of the conventional neural network with similar features for training data set. Yan et al. [8] proposed a method based on the pixel wise loss in the thickness of vessels in training. The method adopts the segmentation levels based on the thickness of the vessels.

Ali et al. [9] suggested a K-means clustering based unsupervised scheme for binarizing gray scales. Shah et al. [10] proposed an unsupervised scheme using Gabor filter and multi-scale line detector. In [9,10], the fundus image is enhanced in Gabor wavelet followed by a median filtering for eliminating false positive points. Maheshwari et al. [11] used local binary pattern for extracting statistical feature from the fundus image. The method used support vector machine for classification. Sundaram et al. [12] suggested the hybridization of multi-scale line detector with bottom hat transform for enhancing the retinal vessels. They also used morphological operations for eliminating the discontinuities. However, noise occurs in the process of exaggeration in the fundus images. This is due to the difference in the lower intensity between the background and the vessel surface. Further, it is challenging to preserve the minute vessels, while segmenting. Since the presently used algorithms have the capability in detection of relatively low vessel pixels classification in a correct manner, they are not likely used for implementing it into an automate system. Eventhough the accuracy for these approaches is sensible, delineating the minute vessels and the non vessel region is taken into account.

To address these problem, we propose here a bowler-hat transform based enhancement technique with joint relative entropy (JRE) thresholding. The proposed method is an unsupervised approach for enhancing the contrast of retinal vessels in comparison to its background. In this paper, the Bowler-hat transform (BHT) is implemented for contrast enhancement in the process of retinal vessel enhancement. This makes the junction points brighter. As a result, the vascular network remains connected at the junctions when segmentation techniques are applied on it. Further, it helps in discriminating between thin and thick vessels. In the next stage, an optimized matched filter is used on the enhanced images for delineating the retinal vessels from the background. The optimized matched filter uses a two dimensional Gaussian shaped kernel for improvising the segmentation performance in the retinal images. The matched filter kernel is designed with three input points. The feasibility of the points is dependent on the orientation, thickness of vessel structures and the pixel intensity profile. Finally, JRE based thresholding is implemented on the resulting response of the matched filter for identifying retinal vessels.

The suggested technique is experimented with multiple retinal images obtained from the DRIVE dataset [13]. The database provides testing images along with the reference images for the evaluation purpose. The performance of the suggested technique evaluated in comparison with the recent methods in terms of the quantitative evaluation parameters (accuracy, specificity and sensitivity). The rest of the paper is arranged as: in Sect. 2, the suggested technique is expressed in details, the result analysis is described in Sect. 3. The performance of the proposed method is concluded in Sect. 4.

2 Suggested Technique

At first, the green channel of the input image is taken and then it is enhanced using Bowler-Hat transform [14]. The enhanced image is applied to the matched filter. The next step is to obtain a matched filter (MF) responded image by use of particular values for σ (intensity profile), L_s (distance of the neighboring pixels), and θ (angular position) on the input image. Once we get the response image, it is then multiplied with a mask in elemental-wise manner, and then it is normalized in the range of 0 and 1. The third step is to get the gray level co-occurance matrix (GLCM) [15] which requires the gray level counts from the previous retinal image extract. Further, the resulting image is reformed to be represented in spatial domain by multiplying the normalized image with highest possible intensity value. This gives a distinctive gray level count. Before producing the JRE threshold value which is applied over the MF responded image to get final vessel extraction [3], the calculation of GLCM in the last stage, is normalized. This is delivered to a functional method. This is to include total number of intensity level for existing in the MF responded image. For calculation of thresholding value, a function is defined which gets iteration on the intensity-levels being passed as an argument. To calculate the probability associated with two quadrants: X and Z. From the above operation, the threshold value of the responded image is included to give us the retinal image with distinct vessels. The resulting images are validated using different evaluation indices for realizing the algorithm's efficiency. The algorithm for the proposed work is explained as shown in Fig. 1.

2.1 Image Enhancement Using Bowler-Hat Transform

The method is a combination of morphological operations on an image obtained from two different structural element banks as described by Sazak et al. [14]. The structural banks are dependent on the varying radii for disk elements. A series of morphological operations are performed on a given image (I) using a disk-shaped the structural elements to form the stack of images as:

$$\{I_{disk}\} = \{I \circ b_d : \forall d \in [1, d_{max}]\} \tag{1}$$

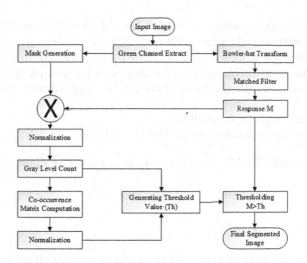

Fig. 1. Schematic diagram of the suggested joint relative entropy thresholding on Bowler Hat Transform.

From this, the I_{disk} images with vessel segments broader than the d are preserved, while other are eliminated. Similarly, stack of images with line shaped structural elements are expressed as:

$$\{I_{line}\} = \{max_\theta(\{I \; o \; b_d : \forall \theta\}) : \forall d \in [1, d_{max}]\} \tag{2}$$

where, the orientation of $\theta \in [0, 180]$. The resulting length of vessel segments with lengthier than d along the orientation of θ will retain, others get eliminated. The enhanced image is formed by combining the resulting stacks in (1) and (2), as the maximum deviations of the stack differences. This is expressed as:

$$I_{enh} = max_d(|I_{line} - I_{disk}|) \tag{3}$$

2.2 Vessel Extraction Based on Matched Filter

Matched Filter is an essential tool for detection of vascular structures from the enhanced fundus image. In general, a Gaussian representation is used for the cross-sectional strength profiling in the retinal vessels. Hence, it is efficient in detecting the piece wise linearly segmented vessels in the retinal image. Therefore, a 2D based MF is designed as follows:

$$K(x, y) = -e^{\frac{-x^2}{2\sigma^2}} \; \forall |y| \le \frac{L_s}{2} \tag{4}$$

where σ is the profiling strength, L_s is the vessel length assuming fixed directions. For this detection, the Gaussian kernel is revolved around 0 to 180° at an angle of 15°. The rotational matrix $R(i)$ is given as:

$$R(i) = \begin{bmatrix} cos\theta \, (i) & -sin\theta \, (i) \\ sin\theta \, (i) & cos\theta \, (i) \end{bmatrix} \tag{5}$$

An array of 12 kernels is convoluted with enhanced image (element-wise multiplication fashion) and only the pixel with maximum response is considered for further analysis. Once the matched filter response (M) is obtained, the mask is used in labeling the belongingness of a pixel in the Region of Interest (ROI) and removing those pixels that lie outside the ROI. There are two ways of generating the mask:

- Thresholding the green channel extract.
- Disc type erosion operation on the threshold image.

Let M_s be the mask, the MF response (M) is obtained as shown below.

$$M = conv(I_{enh}, K) * M_s \qquad (6)$$

2.3   Generation of GLCM

This is generally used for texture, feature analysis and obtaining spatial dependency of gray levels in an image [15]. The values under the study of GLCM generally consists the P_{ij} which indicates the relative frequencies between two neighboring pixels i and j separated by a distance d.

Let us consider an image of size $M \times N$ having L intensity levels $G = \{0, 1, 2, ..., L - 1\}$. The image I is expressed as $I = \{f(x, y)\}_{M \times N}$ where $f(x, y)$ is an intensity value. Therefore, a GLCM of an image I with gray level L can written as $[T_{ij}]_{L \times L}$; where T_{ij} represents total number of pixel transitioning from gray level i to gray level j. To describe it in a simple manner we could say that each element in the matrix indicates the number of times intensity value i is following j. The MF response is analyzed for the values of retinal vessels. To calculate the value of T_{ij} angle between two pixels is considered to be $0°$.

$$T_{ij} = \sum_{m=1}^{M} \sum_{n=1}^{N} \begin{cases} 1, & if \ f(m,n) = i \ and \ f(m, n+1) = j \\ 0, & otherwise \end{cases} \qquad (7)$$

The transition probability P_{ij} can be obtained by the following equation

$$P_{ij} = \frac{T_{ij}}{\sum\limits_{k}^{L-1} \sum\limits_{l}^{L-1} T_{kl}} \qquad (8)$$

Using the threshold value (Th), GLCM of the image is divided into four quadrants (W, X, Y and Z)as in Fig. 2. In accordance to [16], the intensity values of pixels beyond the thresholding is marked as fore ground and the rest is marked as background. Quadrants W and Y gives the information about the pixel transitioning within the backgrounds (BB) and foregrounds (FF) respectively. Correspondingly, the quadrants X and Z relates to the transitioning between foreground and background, noted by FB and BF. These quadrants are categorized into 2 groups. They are local quadrants (W and Y) and joint quadrants (X and Z). Here, we consider the joint quadrants only. Therefore, the probabilities of these quadrants can be expressed as in the following equations.

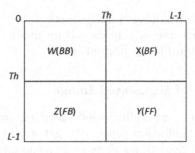

Fig. 2. Quadrants in a co-occurrence matrix.

$$\left[\begin{array}{cc} P_W^{Th} = \sum_{i=0}^{Th} \sum_{j=0}^{Th} P_{ij} & P_X^{Th} = \sum_{i=0}^{Th} \sum_{j=Th+1}^{L} P_{ij} \\ P_Y^{Th} = \sum_{i=Th+1}^{L-1} \sum_{j=Th+1}^{L-1} P_{ij} & P_Z^{Th} = \sum_{i=Th+1}^{L-1} \sum_{j=0}^{Th} P_{ij} \end{array} \right] \tag{9}$$

2.4 Segmentation Using JRE Thresholding

Entropy is a parameter that indicates the measurement of uncertainty of the source image. Relative entropy is defining the relative probability of textural information among them [16]. A smaller value of this parameter is noted when they have closer probability distributions and vice-versa. Using two different probability distributions original (p) and processed (h) image, the parameter is expressed as:

$$J(p; h) = \sum_{j=0}^{L-1} p_j log \frac{p_j}{h_j} \tag{10}$$

$$\left[\begin{array}{cc} h_{ij|W}{}^{Th} = q_W{}^{Th} = \frac{P_W^{Th}}{(Th+1)(Th+1)} & h_{ij|X}{}^{Th} = q_X{}^{Th} = \frac{P_X^{Th}}{(Th+1)(L-Th-1)} \\ h_{ij|Y}{}^{Th} = q_Y{}^{Th} = \frac{P_Y^{Th}}{(L-Th-1)(L-Th-1)} & h_{ij|Z}{}^{Th} = q_Z{}^{Th} = \frac{P_Z^{Th}}{(L-Th-1)(Th+1)} \end{array} \right] \tag{11}$$

The GLCM can be used in the expansion of the 1st ordered relative entropy into 2nd ordered joint relative entropy (11). Here, h_{ij}^{Th} be the transitioning probability using the thresholding value Th. Therefore, the probability of the threshold images is shown in (11). Using (9) and (11) in (10) can be rewritten as:

$$J(\{p_{ij}\}; \{h_{ij}^{Th}\}) = -H(\{p_{ij}\}) - (P_W{}^{Th} log(q_W{}^{Th}) + P_X{}^{Th} log(q_X{}^{Th})$$
$$+ P_Y{}^{Th} log(q_Y{}^{Th}) + P_Z{}^{Th} log(q_Z{}^{Th})) \tag{12}$$

With the use of the computed thresholding value, the retinal vessels are isolated from its back ground. This is achieved by considering the quadrants X and Z. Therefore, $P_X^{Th} log(q_X^{Th}) + P_Z^{Th} log(q_Z^{Th})$ from (12), gives more accurate edge detection. Hence, JRE threshold can be expressed as:

$$Th_{JRE} = arg[min_{Th \in G}\ H_{JRE}(Th)] \tag{13}$$

where, $H_{JRE}(Th) = -(P_X^{Th}log(q_X^{Th}) + P_Z^{Th}log(q_Z^{Th}))$. The Entropy $H_{JRE}(Th)$ is computed for the each intensity levels within quadrants X and Z, and the optimal thresholding value Th_{JRE} from (13).

2.5   Post-processing of Segmented Image

Post-processing techniques generally include filtering and change detection. It is another step in the application process to get a better and accurate result of the segmented image. Sometimes there exist some misclassified pixels which remain isolated therefore affecting the results. The vessels might contain gaps which can be mistakenly identified as non-vessels. To remove it we apply length filtering using 8-connected neighborhood pixel labeling propagation. Similarly, there may be some falsely identified vessel pixels in the ROI. To remove them firstly we have estimated the total pixels. Further, the classification of connecting pixels is carried out by assigning non-vessel pixels in the connecting regions. The accuracy of segmentation is optimized by changing the pixel count limit.

3   Result Analysis

This section gives the segmentation results obtained using the suggested technique in comparison to the existing methods. Qualitative and quantitative analysis is presented for validation. In qualitative analysis, the image quality is observed while in quantitative analysis, performance evaluating parameters are used with respect to the reference images.

3.1   Qualitative Analysis

Here, twenty fundus images from the DRIVE database is taken for the evaluation. Figure below is an example of the results using the suggested technique.

The proposed method is simulated using MATLAB software with a work bench setup of i5 processor. The computation time taken to process one image is approximately 2.8 s. The Fig. 3 is an example of one image from the set of images in which (a) column shows the green channel images of DRIVE database, (b) column contains the original reference images and (c) column contains segmented results from the suggested technique. This analysis generally helps us in identifying how close our proposed method is with respect to ground truth image. This is evaluated in terms of performance evaluation parameters. From Fig. 3, it is clear that some vessels have become distinct after applying BHT enhancement technique which helps to distinguish between smaller and larger vessels. Further, it is taken under account in the quantitative analysis.

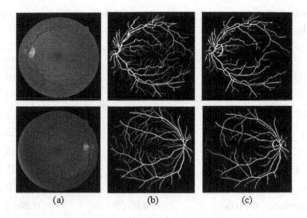

Fig. 3. Segmentation results from fundus image dataset (a) green channel extract images (b) reference images (c) segmented results.

3.2 Quantitative Analysis

The performance of the suggested scheme is evaluated using $Sensitivity = TP/(TP+FN)$, $Specificity = TN/(TN+FP)$ and $Accuracy = (TP+TN)/(TP+TN+FN+FP)$. Here, sensitivity demonstrates the capability of the proposed method to detect pixels belonging to vessel areas. Specificity indicates the potential of non-vessel pixels to be observed. Accuracy gives the vessel and non-vessel pixels correctly identified to the number of pixels in the image.

Table 1. Quantitative analysis of state-of-the-art models in comparison to the proposed model.

Images	Sensitivity	Specificity	Accuracy	Images	Sensitivity	Specificity	Accuracy
I1	0.7545	0.9624	0.9512	I2	0.7648	0.9638	0.9429
I3	0.6938	0.9712	0.9466	I4	0.7001	0.9696	0.9535
I5	0.6911	0.9768	0.9518	I6	0.6823	0.9785	0.9590
I7	0.7222	0.9655	0.9381	I8	0.6735	0.9811	0.9526
I9	0.6542	0.9872	0.9642	I10	0.7438	0.9428	0.9447
I11	0.7176	0.9592	0.9511	I12	0.6854	0.9772	0.9563
I13	0.6592	0.9882	0.9620	I14	0.7415	0.9612	0.9412
I15	0.7938	0.9622	0.9407	I16	0.6867	0.9771	0.9584
I17	0.6689	0.9854	0.9620	I18	0.7161	0.9632	0.9521
I19	0.8098	0.9617	0.9507	I20	0.7709	0.9712	0.9498
-	-	-	-	Average	0.7165	0.9702	0.9514

Table 2. Quantitative assessment of the suggested technique in comparison to the existing methods.

Method	Average sensitivity	Average specificity	Average accuracy
Odstrcilik [17]	0.7060	0.9693	0.9340
Frangi [18]	0.6565	0.9505	0.9270
Jiang-Mojon [19]	0.6363	0.9662	0.9212
Singh [20]	0.6735	0.9721	0.9459
Ali [9]	0.6906	0.9657	0.9425
Sundaram [10]	0.6900	0.9401	0.9301
Saha [12]	0.6821	0.9673	0.9470
Proposed approach	0.7165	0.9702	0.9514

Table 1 gives the average values of the evaluation indices for those images. The obtained values are 0.9514, 0.9702 and 0.7165 for accuracy, specificity and sensitivity respectively. The calculation of these parameters is mainly based on the comparison of pixels between ground truth images and proposed segmented images. Misclassification of pixels will critically affect the results. Table 2 gives a comparative analysis of different approaches using the average values of the same evaluation indices.

The suggested technique is examined using multiple methods as in Table 2. They all use the same dataset for validating the purpose. The classical matched filter used to threshold the filter response. In [9,12], the authors worked on unsupervised machine learning approaches for classifying the vessel regions. Sundaram et al. [10] used bottom hat transform for enhancing vessels in the fundus image. Odstrcilik et al. [17] applied the Kittler minimum error thresholding method. In [20], the authors utilized the local entropy thresholding. Frangi et al. [18] methods were obtained by filtering. Jiang-Mojon [19] proposed multithreshold probing. Table 2 shows the superior performance of the suggested technique over the existing methods. This shows the detection capability of the suggested work is higher than the existing approaches.

4   Conclusion

The suggested technique presents a new direction towards the segmentation of vessels in a fundus images. The described methodology proposes a segmentation method using JRE thresholding method with the MF on a BHT enhanced retinal image. The BHT applied here enhances the green channel extracted image. The MF response is obtained of the enhanced image for vessel detection. The JRE thresholding is providing a suitable thresholding value for the extraction of retinal vessels in comparison to the other MF. The suggested technique is experimented on multiple set of fundus images from DRIVE dataset for computing different evaluation indices. Furthermore, the efficacy of the suggested technique is found to be effective and robust in comparison to the other models.

References

1. Fathi, A., Naghsh-Nilchi, A.R.: Automatic wavelet-based retinal blood vessels segmentation and vessel diameter estimation. Biomed. Signal Process. Control **8**(1), 71–80 (2012)
2. Chakraborti, T., Jha, D.K., Chowdhury, A.S., Jiang, X.: A self-adaptive matched filter for retinal blood vessel detection. Mach. Vis. Appl. **26**(1), 55–68 (2014). https://doi.org/10.1007/s00138-014-0636-z
3. Villalobos-Castaldi, F.M., Edgardo, M., Felipe-Riverón, E.M., Sánchez-Fernández, L.P.: A fast, efficient and automated method to extract vessels from fundus images. J. Vis. **13**, 263–270 (2010)
4. Marin, D., Arturo, A., Manuel, E., Jose, M.: A new supervised method for blood vessel segmentation in retinal images by using gray-level and moment invariant based features. IEEE Trans. Med. Imaging **30**(1), 146–158 (2011)
5. Rahebi, J., Hardalaç, F.: Retinal blood vessel segmentation with neural network by using gray-level co-occurrence matrix-based features. J. Med. Syst. **38**, 85 (2014)
6. Liskowski, P., Krawiec, K.: Segmenting retinal blood vessels with deep neural networks. IEEE Trans. Med. Imaging **35**, 2369–2380 (2016)
7. Jiang, Y., Zhang, H., Tan, N., Chen, L.: Automatic retinal blood vessel segmentation based on fully convolutional neural networks. Symmetry **11**(9), 1112 (2019)
8. Yan, Z., Yang, X., Cheng, K.T.: Joint segment-level and pixel-wise losses for deep learning based retinal vessel segmentation. IEEE Trans. Biomed. Eng. **65**(9), 1912–1923 (2018)
9. Ali, A., Wan Zaki, W.M.D., Hussain, A.: Blood vessel segmentation from color retinal images using K-means clustering and 2D Gabor wavelet. In: Ntalianis, K., Croitoru, A. (eds.) APSAC 2017. LNEE, vol. 428, pp. 221–227. Springer, Cham (2018). https://doi.org/10.1007/978-3-319-53934-8_27
10. Shah, S.A., Shahzad, A., Khan, M.A., Lu, C.K., Tang, T.B.: Unsupervised method for retinal vessel segmentation based on Gabor wavelet and multiscale line detector. IEEE Access **7**, 167221–167228 (2019)
11. Maheshwari, S., Kanhangad, V., Pachori, R.B., Bhandary, S.V., Acharya, U.R.: Automated glaucoma diagnosis using bit-plane slicing and local binary pattern techniques. Comput. Biol. Med. **105**, 72–80 (2019)
12. Sundaram, R., Ravichandran, K.S., Jayaraman, P., Venkatraman, B.: Extraction of blood vessels in fundus images of retina through hybrid segmentation approach. Mathematics **2**(2), 169 (2019)
13. Digital Image for Vessel Extraction (DRIVE) Database. http://www.isi.uu.nl/Research/Databases/DRIVE/. Accessed May 2016
14. Çigdem, S., Carl, J.N., Boguslaw, O.: The multiscale bowler hat transform for blood vessel enhancement in retinal images. Pattern Recognit. **88**, 739–750 (2019). https://doi.org/10.1016/j.patcog.2018.10.011
15. Haralick, R.M., Shanmuga, K., Dinstein, I.: Textural features for image classification. IEEE Trans. Syst. Man Cybern. **3**(6), 610–621 (1973)
16. Yang, C.W., Ma, D.J., Wang, C.M., Wen, C.H., Le, C.S., Chang, C.: Computer-aided diagnostic detection system of venous beading in retinal images. Opt. Eng. **39**(5), 1293–1303 (2000)
17. Odstrcilik, J., et al.: Retinal vessel segmentation by improved matched filtering: evaluation on a new high-resolution fundus image database. IET Image Process. **7**, 373–383 (2013). https://doi.org/10.1049/iet-ipr.2012.0455

18. Frangi, A.F., et al.: Mulitscale vessel enhancement filtering. Med. Image Comput. Comput.-Assist. Interv. **1497**, 130–137 (1998)
19. Jiang, X., Mojon, D.: Adaptive local thresholding by verification based multithreshold probing with application to vessel detection in retinal images. IEEE Trans. Pattern Recogn. Anal. Mach. Intell. **25**, 131–137 (2003)
20. Singh, N.P., Kumar, R., Srivastava, R.: Local entropy thresholding based fast retinal vessels segmentation by modifying matched filter. In: International Conference on Computing, Communication & Automation, pp. 1166–1170. IEEE (2015)

Semantic Segmentation of Nuclei from Breast Histopathological Images by Incorporating Attention in U-Net

R. Rashmi[1], Keerthana Prasad[1(✉)], and Chethana Babu K. Udupa[2]

[1] Manipal School of Information Sciences, Manipal Academy of Higher Education, Manipal, India
keerthana.prasad@manipal.edu
[2] Kasturba Medical College, Manipal Academy of Higher Education, Manipal, India
chethana.babu@manipal.edu

Abstract. Breast cancer is a major disease in the world and is detected by histopathological image analysis. The structure and characteristics of nuclei contributes largely in the decision of malignancy of a tumor. There exists several medical image processing techniques based on traditional and CNN methods to segment nuclei from breast histopathological images. However, these algorithms use hand crafted features and depend on availability of large annotated dataset. Moreover, heterogeneous structure and characteristic of nuclei makes it non trivial task. In this context, this paper presents an encoder decoder based CNN architecture to semantically segment nuclei from breast histopathological images. A new attention mechanism is used to extract feature from the nuclei regions at multiple scales. The proposed architecture is evaluated on breast histopathological images and achieved an mIoU of 0.77.

Keywords: Semantic segmentation · U-Net · Histopathology · CNN

1 Introduction

Breast cancer is one of the highest death causing disease in women. Detecting cancer in an early stage helps in reducing the risk to human life. The tumours in the breast are initially identified by utilizing mammogram. The classification of these tumours as malignant and benign is based on histopathological image analysis since it captures microscopic structure of the tumour. However, manual analysis of histopathological images is tedious, requires domain expertise and are prone to human errors. Hence, an automated decision support system for breast histopathological image analysis is need of the hour.

The analysis of breast histopathological image is largely dependent on the structural characteristics and spatial distribution of nucleus which determines the malignancy of the tumour. For example, hyperchromatism, mitotic cell division, prominent nucleoli etc. are characteristics of malignant nuclei in a

© Springer Nature Singapore Pte Ltd. 2021
S. K. Singh et al. (Eds.): CVIP 2020, CCIS 1376, pp. 137–148, 2021.
https://doi.org/10.1007/978-981-16-1086-8_13

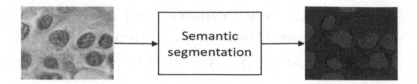

Fig. 1. An illustration of nuclei semantic segmentation.

histopathological image. Hence, the development of automated Computer Aided Diagnostic (CAD) system to analyze breast histopathological images is dependent on accurate detection and segmentation of nuclei. Figure 1 illustrates the process of semantic segmentation of nuclei from breast histopathological images. However, nuclei segmentation in breast histopathological images using medical image processing is challenging due to heterogeneous structure of cells, variations in illumination, poor staining process etc.

In general, traditional image processing methods which include preprocessing, segmentation, feature extraction and classification are used to segment nuclei. Several methods such as image thresholding [11], active contours [4], clustering [3], watershed [19] etc. are extensively used to segment nuclei. But, these traditional approaches depends on hand crafted features which may fail to capture all the variations in the data. Recent developments in deep learning led Convolutional Neural Network (CNN) to be a popular choice for segmentation of nuclei since it can be trained in an end-to-end fashion and also capture the correlation between pixels (spatial information). Several algorithms such as U-Net [18], FCN [13], DeeplabV3+ [1] are widely used to perform semantic segmentation which is a process of labelling every pixel in a given image. One of the major drawbacks of CNN is its dependence on large annotated dataset. The lack of standard dataset with annotations for semantic segmentation of histopathological images limits the development of CNN based algorithms for nuclei segmentation.

This paper presents a new CNN architecture based on U-Net [18] to semantically segment nuclei from breast histopathological images. The proposed architecture uses an attention mechanism to extract features from nuclei regions at multiple scales. In general, the spatial information captured by the CNN is dependent on the size of the filter. In this context, the present study investigates the impact of spatial information on semantic segmentation of nuclei. Moreover, this paper analyses the dependence of the proposed algorithm on size of the training data. The contributions of the paper can be summarized as follows,

- A modified U-Net architecture is proposed which provides attention to nuclei at multiple scales. This ensures the segmentation of smaller and lightly stained nuclei from breast histopathological images.
- An analysis on the effect of filter size on semantic segmentation of nuclei is presented.

- This paper investigates the dependence of the proposed architecture on the size of the dataset for semantic segmentation of nuclei.

The present paper is divided into five sections. The Sect. 2, describes the recent developments in nuclei segmentation from breast histopathological images. The Sect. 3, describes the adopted methodology of the study. A discussion on the obtained results is presented in Sect. 4 and conclusion is presented in Sect. 5.

2 Related Works

There is a considerable amount of literature on nuclei segmentation in breast histopathological images using medical image processing techniques [2,14,16, 20,22]. However, there are still several challenges in nuclei segmentation from breast histopathological images such as heterogeneous structure of nuclei, poor staining process, lack of annotations etc. In general, there are two approaches for segmenting nuclei: traditional image processing techniques and CNN based methods. This section summarizes the recent developments in nuclei segmentation from breast histopathological images using traditional and CNN based approaches.

2.1 Traditional Methods

The traditional approach for nuclei segmentation uses pipe lined process which depends on the knowledge about the histopathological images [19,23]. Moreover, these methods utilize hand crafted features tailored for a specific dataset. In [11], authors utilized image thresholding to segment nuclei. However, these methods fail when the intensity and texture within the nuclei changes. Also, the accuracy of segmentation depends on the selection of threshold value which is challenging. Watershed based segmentation is a popular choice for segmenting nuclei [19,23]. Authors of [19], presented a marker-controlled watershed-based technique to segment the cancerous nuclei at different scales and used different markers in Hematoxylin & Eosin (H&E) stained whole digital slide images of the breast. In an another study [3], a method to classify Usual Ductal Hyperplasia (UDH), Atypical Ductal Hyperplasia (ADH), and Ductal Carcinoma In Situ (DCIS) from the breast tissues was developed. Initially, the input image is converted to LAB colour space and the segmentation was performed by using clustering and watershed-based segmentation algorithm. In [10], the authors proposed a method for automatic nuclei detection using probability map and watershed-based segmentation algorithms. In few literatures, region growing algorithms are used to segment nuclei [21]. However, these algorithms are dependent on hand crafted features. Also, these methods are tailored for a specific dataset.

2.2 CNN Based Methods

In the recent years CNN has become a popular choice for semantic segmentation. Several authors have explored encoder decoder based architectures to perform

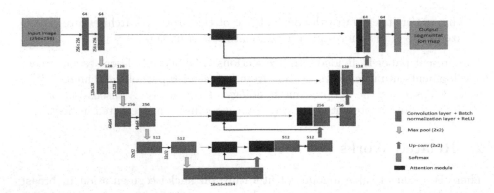

Fig. 2. Modified U-Net architecture with attention module.

semantic segmentation [1,13,18]. However, these algorithms may fail to segment fine and small scale objects. Hence, several studies were focused on incorporating attention mechanism to CNN [5–7,9,12,15,24,25]. These attention mechanisms are generally used to focus on the object of interest by utilizing a attention coefficients. However, identifying these attention coefficients in a learnable way is challenging [12]. Moreover these CNN based approaches are dependent on dataset which limits their applicability.

3   Methodology

The adopted methodology for nuclei semantic segmentation from breast histopathological images includes a pre-processing step known as colour normalization. Subsequently, a CNN model (modified U-Net) is utilized to segment the nuclei. The details of the adopted methodology is presented in this section.

3.1   Pre-processing: Colour Normalization

In general, histopathological images undergoes variations in colour during the process of image acquisition. These variations result in a wrong analysis of images and may alter the end result. Hence, a pre-processing step known as colour normalization is adopted to handle these variations. Colour normalization is a process of transferring the colour distribution of the template image to the target image. In the present study, Reinhard method [17] is utilized to transfer the colour distribution of the template image to the target image. The details of this method can be found in [17].

3.2   Semantic Segmentation: Modified U-Net

This paper uses a modified version of U-Net model developed by Olaf Ronneberger et al. [18] to semantically segment nuclei. This architecture uses encoders to extract features and decoders to localize the class labels. Also skip connections are employed from encoders to decoders to ensure accurate segmentation. In the present study, the U-Net architecture is modified to provide attention to nuclei and the details are given below. The architecture of the modified U-Net is shown in Fig. 2.

Encoder: The encoding path of the proposed architecture is similar to the U-Net architecture. It consists of four blocks where each block consists of two sets of convolution layer, batch normalization layer and Rectified Linear Unit (ReLU). At the end of every block, maxpooling layer is applied to reduce the dimension of the feature maps and transfer most prominent features to the deeper layers. The convolutional layer convolves learnable filters with an input image to detect patterns. Convolution layers are followed by batch normalization layer which prevent over fitting and introduces regularizing effect. At the bottle neck a convolutional layer with 1024 filters is applied followed by batch normalization layer and ReLU activation function. The output of this is passed to the decoder to infer the class labels for every pixel.

Decoder: The decoder groups similar pixels together and produces the segmentation map. The decoder of the proposed model consists of four blocks similar to encoder. Each block of decoder initially applies upconv operation and applies two sets of convolution layer, batch normalization layer and ReLU activation function. The upconv operation is used to increase the dimension of the feature maps by 2. The upconv operation consists of upsampling operation followed by convolution layer (2×2). The encoder uses maxpool operation which results in loss of spatial resolution. In the traditional U-Net architecture, skip connections are employed from corresponding encoding layer to decoding layer to compensate for the loss of spatial information due to usage of maxpool layer. In the skip connection, the corresponding feature maps from encoding layer is concatenated with the feature maps of decoding layer. But this provides an approximate representation of the feature maps and fails to capture finer boundaries of nuclei and lightly stained nuclei. Hence, in the present study, a new attention module is introduced in the skip connection to capture features from nuclei regions at multiple scales. The details of the attention module is presented in Sect. 3.2. The output of this attention module is concatenated with the upsampled feature maps of the corresponding layer in the decoder. These concatenated feature maps are then passed through convolution layers. Lastly, Softmax layer is used which produces the class probability distribution for each pixel and is given as follows,

$$\Phi(c_i, x, \theta) = \frac{e^{c_i}}{\sum_l^C e^{C_l}} \tag{1}$$

The kernel weights are initially assigned by using the approach of [8]. The dropout layers are used to prevent the model from over fitting. The model is trained by using Adam optimizer with learning rate set to 0.0001.

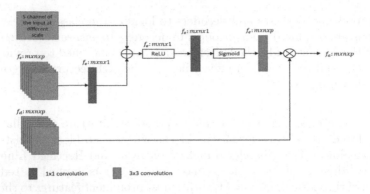

Fig. 3. Description of the attention module.

Attention Module: In general there exist additive and multiplicative attention modules. In the present study, multiplicative attention module is utilized since it is more efficient. To semantically segment nuclei, it is beneficial to enable the model to focus more on nuclei regions than background regions. This helps in detecting smaller and lighter nuclei thereby increasing the accuracy of the semantic segmentation. In this context, an attention module is developed to mask the features of pixels belonging to background regions. This enables the model to give more attention to nuclei regions which aids in effective segmentation nuclei pixels. This attention module is introduced in the skip connection and the details are presented below.

In the present study, S channel from HSV colour space is used to mask the features of background pixel in the skip connections. In the S channel the nuclei pixels are distinct from the background pixels which aids in easier masking of background pixels. The input image is converted to HSV colour space and resized to several scales such as 256×256, 128×128, 64×64 and 32×32. Let this be represented as $S = \{s_1, s_2, s_3, s_4\}$. These different scales are used in different levels of skip connections. That is, s_1 is used in the attention module of first skip connection where the feature dimension is 256×256, s_2 is used in the attention module of second level skip connection where the feature dimension is 128×128 and so on. Let the feature maps from the encoder be represented as f_e and upsampled feature maps from the decoder be represented as f_d. Let the dimension of the f_e and f_d be $m \times n \times p$. The features maps from the encoders (f_e) are initially passed through a 1×1 convolution operation which reduces the dimension of f_e to $m \times n \times 1$. This feature map is subsequently added with the corresponding scale of the S ($m \times n \times 1$). In the present study, S channel is selected since it discriminates nuclei more efficiently from the back ground tissues. This addition of f_e with S channel aids in compensating for the loss of information which occurs during the maxpool operation and also allows the model to focus on nuclei regions. This is passed through a ReLU activation function followed by 1×1 convolution operation, batch normalization layer and sigmoid activation function. These feature maps are passed through a convolution layer with p filters to obtain the attention coefficients f_a. Finally, an element wise multiplication operation is utilized to multiply feature maps f_a and f_d. These features are subsequently concatenated with the upsampled features of the decoding layers. Figure 3 describes the attention module of the proposed system.

4   Results and Discussion

In the present study, The proposed model is utilized to semantically segment breast histopathological images. The performance of the model is evaluated by using various metrics such as precision, recall, F1-score, accuracy and mean Intersection over Union (mIoU). The various results obtained are presented in this section.

4.1   Dataset

In the present study, breast histopathological images are collected from Kasturbha Medical College, Manipal, India. The dataset consists of breast histopathological images taken at 400x magnification. The images were captured at 1600 × 1200 resolution. Manual annotations for nuclei are created for 360 image samples. Sample images are shown in Fig. 4 along with annotations. In the present study, the dataset is divided into train and test split consisting of 318 and 42 images respectively.

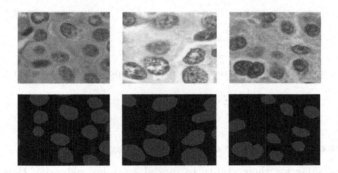

Fig. 4. Sample breast histopathological images and its corresponding annotations.

4.2   Selection of Filter Size for the Proposed Model

In general, convolutional layer uses filters to extract features. These filters represent various patterns which are learnt by the model during back propagation. Filters can be of varying size such as 3 × 3, 5 × 5, 7 × 7 etc., which defines the receptive field of the model. The spatial information captured by the model is dependent on the size of the filters. However, larger filters result in increased parameters of the model making it difficult to train the model. Hence the filter size is considered as one of the hyper-parameter which needs to be tuned. Moreover, the selection of filter size depends on the object of interest and the image size. In this context, an experiment is carried out where the performance of the proposed architecture with varying filter size is compared.

In this study, the proposed architecture is modified to have different filter size. Two additional models were developed with filter size 5×5 and 7×7. The performance of these three models were compared and the metrics are shown in Table 2. From the metrics it is observed that the proposed architecture with (5×5) and (3×3) filters size perform competitively with an mIoU of 0.76 and 0.77 respectively. However, when the filter size is increased to 7×7, the proposed architecture produces low mIoU (in the order of 0.68). This result is acceptable since the input image size to the model is 256×256. This analysis did not show an improvement in the mIoU as the filter size increases. Hence, at 400x magnification, it is observed that 3×3 filters are more suitable as compared to 7×7 and 5×5.

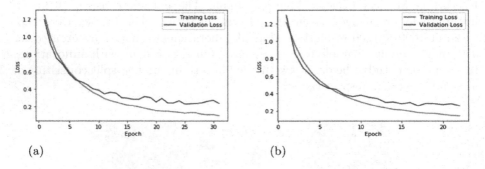

(a)   (b)

Fig. 5. Training and validation loss curves of the proposed (a) and U-Net (b) architecture.

4.3   Effect of Dataset Size on Semantic Segmentation

CNNs are popular for their ability to model complex patterns. However, their dependency on large annotated dataset limits their applicability in the medical image processing. Hence in this study, an analysis is carried out to evaluate the performance of the proposed CNN architecture based on the training dataset size. In the present study, different training split with varying training set size such as 100, 200 and 318 are considered. The proposed model is trained on these training splits and the performance metrics of these models are presented in Table 3. It is observed that the accuracy of the model increases with the increase in the training data. With 100 training samples the proposed model has poor mIoU of 0.71 and the mIoU of the model increases up to 0.77 with 318 training samples.

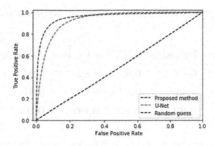

Fig. 6. ROC curve comparison of U-Net and the proposed method.

4.4 Comparison with U-Net

In the present study the proposed architecture is compared with U-Net [18] since the proposed architecture is based on U-Net. The training and validation loss curve of the proposed architecture and the U-Net [18] is shown in Fig. 5 (a) and 5 (b) respectively. Table 1 shows the performance metrics of U-Net and the proposed architecture. It is observed that the U-Net has lower recall and precision values as compared to the proposed architecture. This indicates that U-Net has produced higher false positives and false negatives. Figure 7 shows the nuclei segmentation results of U-Net and the proposed architecture. It is seen that the proposed architecture is able to detect lightly stained and small nuclei since it captures features at multiple scales. Also, the mIoU of the proposed architecture (0.77) is significantly greater than the U-Net (0.66). The false negatives produced by U-Net are highlighted in yellow circles. Figure 6, shows the Receiver Operating Characteristic (ROC) curve of U-Net and the proposed method for nuclei semantic segmentation of breast histopathological images. The area under the curve (Fig. 6) for the proposed method is greater than the U-Net. This demonstrates that the proposed architecture has higher accuracy than U-Net.

Table 1. Performance metrics of U-Net and the proposed architecture.

Methods	Precision	Recall	F1-score	Accuracy	mIoU
U-Net [18]	0.75	0.82	0.77	0.89	0.66
The proposed architecture	**0.89**	**0.85**	**0.86**	**0.93**	**0.77**

Table 2. Performance comparison of the proposed architecture with varying filter size.

Filter size	Precision	Recall	F1-score	Accuracy	mIoU	Parameters
(3 × 3)	**0.89**	**0.85**	**0.86**	0.93	**0.77**	21,623,590
(5 × 5)	**0.89**	0.84	**0.86**	**0.94**	0.76	55,050,022
(7 × 7)	0.80	0.78	0.79	0.90	0.68	105,189,670

Table 3. Performance comparison of the proposed architecture with varying dataset size.

Dataset size	Precision	Recall	F1-score	Accuracy	mIoU
100	0.85	0.80	0.82	0.91	0.71
200	0.86	0.82	0.83	0.91	0.72
318	**0.89**	**0.85**	**0.86**	**0.93**	**0.77**

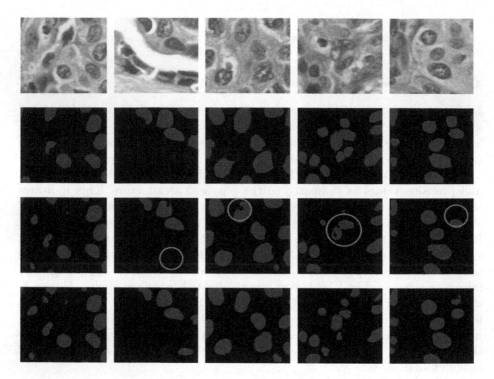

Fig. 7. This figure shows the results of nuclei segmentation by the proposed algorithm (fourth row) and the U-Net (third row). The false negatives of U-Net algorithm is highlighted in yellow circles. (Color figure online)

5   Conclusion

This paper has presented a modified U-Net architecture to semantically segment nuclei from breast histopathological images. A new attention mechanism is proposed to extract features from nuclei regions at multiple scales. The proposed architecture achieved an mIoU of 0.77 which is significantly greater than the U-Net (0.66) thereby validating the efficiency of the proposed attention module. This paper has experimentally demonstrated the dependence of the proposed architecture on size of the dataset. It is identified that the proposed CNN model benefits from larger training data and an improvement in mIoU of 0.06 was observed. Moreover, the evidence from this study suggests that at 400x magnification, 3×3 size filters are more suitable for nuclei semantic segmentation. In future, this work can be extended to segment nuclei from 100x magnification.

References

1. Chen, L.C., Papandreou, G., Kokkinos, I., Murphy, K., Yuille, A.L.: Deeplab: semantic image segmentation with deep convolutional nets, atrous convolution, and fully connected CRF. IEEE Trans. Pattern Anal. Mach. Intell. **40**(4), 834–848 (2017)
2. Cui, Y., Zhang, G., Liu, Z., Xiong, Z., Hu, J.: A deep learning algorithm for one-step contour aware nuclei segmentation of histopathology images. Med. Biol. Eng. Comput. **57**(9), 2027–2043 (2019). https://doi.org/10.1007/s11517-019-02008-8
3. Dundar, M.M., et al.: Computerized classification of intraductal breast lesions using histopathological images. IEEE Trans. Biomed. Eng. **58**(7), 1977–1984 (2011)
4. Fatakdawala, H., et al.: Expectation-maximization-driven geodesic active contour with overlap resolution (emagacor): application to lymphocyte segmentation on breast cancer histopathology. IEEE Trans. Biomed. Eng. **57**(7), 1676–1689 (2010)
5. Fu, J., et al.: Dual attention network for scene segmentation. In: Proceedings of the IEEE Conference on Computer Vision and Pattern Recognition, pp. 3146–3154 (2019)
6. Han, S., et al.: Optimizing filter size in convolutional neural networks for facial action unit recognition. In: Proceedings of the IEEE Conference on Computer Vision and Pattern Recognition, pp. 5070–5078 (2018)
7. Harley, A.W., Derpanis, K.G., Kokkinos, I.: Segmentation-aware convolutional networks using local attention masks. In: Proceedings of the IEEE International Conference on Computer Vision, pp. 5038–5047 (2017)
8. He, K., Zhang, X., Ren, S., Sun, J.: Delving deep into rectifiers: surpassing human-level performance on ImageNet classification. In: Proceedings of the IEEE International Conference on Computer Vision, pp. 1026–1034 (2015)
9. Huang, Z., Wang, X., Huang, L., Huang, C., Wei, Y., Liu, W.: CCNet: criss-cross attention for semantic segmentation. In: Proceedings of the IEEE International Conference on Computer Vision, pp. 603–612 (2019)
10. Kost, H., Homeyer, A., Bult, P., Balkenhol, M.C., van der Laak, J.A., Hahn, H.K.: A generic nuclei detection method for histopathological breast images. In: Medical Imaging 2016: Digital Pathology, vol. 9791, p. 97911E. International Society for Optics and Photonics (2016)
11. Kowal, M., Filipczuk, P., Obuchowicz, A., Korbicz, J., Monczak, R.: Computer-aided diagnosis of breast cancer based on fine needle biopsy microscopic images. Computers Biol. Med. **43**(10), 1563–1572 (2013)
12. Li, K., Wu, Z., Peng, K.C., Ernst, J., Fu, Y.: Tell me where to look: guided attention inference network. In: Proceedings of the IEEE Conference on Computer Vision and Pattern Recognition, pp. 9215–9223 (2018)
13. Long, J., Shelhamer, E., Darrell, T.: Fully convolutional networks for semantic segmentation. In: Proceedings of the IEEE Conference on Computer Vision and Pattern Recognition, pp. 3431–3440 (2015)
14. Mittal, H., Saraswat, M.: An automatic nuclei segmentation method using intelligent gravitational search algorithm based superpixel clustering. Swarm Evol. Comput. **45**, 15–32 (2019)

15. Oktay, O., et al.: Attention U-Net: learning where to look for the pancreas. arXiv preprint arXiv:1804.03999 (2018)
16. Paramanandam, M., et al.: Automated segmentation of nuclei in breast cancer histopathology images. PloS One **11**(9), e0162053 (2016)
17. Reinhard, E., Adhikhmin, M., Gooch, B., Shirley, P.: Color transfer between images. IEEE Comput. Graph. Appl. **21**(5), 34–41 (2001)
18. Ronneberger, O., Fischer, P., Brox, T.: U-Net: convolutional networks for biomedical image segmentation. In: Navab, N., Hornegger, J., Wells, W.M., Frangi, A.F. (eds.) MICCAI 2015. LNCS, vol. 9351, pp. 234–241. Springer, Cham (2015). https://doi.org/10.1007/978-3-319-24574-4_28
19. Veta, M., Van Diest, P.J., Kornegoor, R., Huisman, A., Viergever, M.A., Pluim, J.P.: Automatic nuclei segmentation in H&E stained breast cancer histopathology images. PloS One **8**(7), e70221 (2013)
20. Wan, T., Zhao, L., Feng, H., Li, D., Tong, C., Qin, Z.: Robust nuclei segmentation in histopathology using ASPPU-Net and boundary refinement. Neurocomputing **408**, 144–156 (2020)
21. Wang, P., Hu, X., Li, Y., Liu, Q., Zhu, X.: Automatic cell nuclei segmentation and classification of breast cancer histopathology images. Signal Process. **122**, 1–13 (2016)
22. Xie, L., Qi, J., Pan, L., Wali, S.: Integrating deep convolutional neural networks with marker-controlled watershed for overlapping nuclei segmentation in histopathology images. Neurocomputing **376**, 166–179 (2020)
23. Yi, F., Huang, J., Yang, L., Xie, Y., Xiao, G.: Automatic extraction of cell nuclei from H&E-stained histopathological images. J. Med. Imaging **4**(2), 027502 (2017)
24. Zhao, H., et al.: PSANet: point-wise spatial attention network for scene parsing. In: Ferrari, V., Hebert, M., Sminchisescu, C., Weiss, Y. (eds.) ECCV 2018. LNCS, vol. 11213, pp. 270–286. Springer, Cham (2018). https://doi.org/10.1007/978-3-030-01240-3_17
25. Zhao, T., Wu, X.: Pyramid feature attention network for saliency detection. In: Proceedings of the IEEE Conference on Computer Vision and Pattern Recognition, pp. 3085–3094 (2019)

Automated Diagnosis of COVID-19 from CT Scans Based on Concatenation of Mobilenetv2 and ResNet50 Features

Taranjit Kaur$^{(\boxtimes)}$ and Tapan Kumar Gandhi

Department of Electrical Engineering, Indian Institute of Technology, Delhi, Hauz Khas,
New-Delhi 110016, India
{Taranjit.Kaur,tgandhi}@ee.iitd.ac.in

Abstract. Timely and precise identification of COVID19 is an arduous task due
to the shortage and the inefficiency of the medical test kits. As a result of which
medical professionals have turned their attention towards radiological images like
Computed Tomography (CT) scans. There have been continued attempts on creating deep learning models to detect COVID-19 using CT scans. This has certainly
reduced the manual intervention in disease detection but the reported detection
accuracy is limited. Motivated by this, in the present work, an automatic system
for COVID-19 diagnosis is proposed using a concatenation of the Mobilenetv2
and ResNet50 features. Typically, the features from the last convolution layer of
the transfer learned Mobilenetv2, and the last average pooling layer of the learned
ResNet50 are fused to improve the classification accuracy. The fused feature vector along with the corresponding labels is used to train an SVM classifier to give
the output. The proposed technique is validated on the benchmark COVID CT
dataset comprising of a total of 2482 images with 1252 positive and 1230 negative
cases. The experimental results reveal that the proposed feature fusion strategy
achieves a validation accuracy of 98.35%, F1-score of 98.39%, the precision of
99.19%, and a recall of 97.60% for detecting COVID-19 cases with 80% training
and 20% validation scheme. The obtained results are better than the comparison
models and the existing state of artworks reported in the literature.

Keywords: Diagnosis · COVID-19 · Feature fusion

1 Introduction

Last year in December, an outbreak of coronavirus infection (SARS-CoV-2) started
in Wuhan, China [1–3]. By January 2020 end, the World Health Organization (WHO)
proclaimed it to be a global pandemic [3]. Health officials and researches are working
together to understand the COVID-19 pathogenesis. They are trying hard to develop
strategies that can control its spread. One main obstacle in combating the pandemic
spread is the inefficiency and scarcity of tests. The contemporary pathogenic testing forms its basis on reverse transcription-polymerase chain reaction (RT-PCR) and
sequencing of nucleic acid from the virus. The efficacy of nucleic acid testing is reliant

© Springer Nature Singapore Pte Ltd. 2021
S. K. Singh et al. (Eds.): CVIP 2020, CCIS 1376, pp. 149–160, 2021.
https://doi.org/10.1007/978-981-16-1086-8_14

on factors like the accessibility and number of test kits in the area affected. However, the reproducibility and perfection of the testing kits are also a major concern as the nucleic acid tests have to be reiterated numerous times before it is finally confirmed. Pathogenic lab testing although it is the gold standard it is time-taking with substantial false-negative outcomes. In such a scenario, clinicians have turned their attention towards radiological images that have proven to be an important diagnostic tool for COVID-19 detection. Radiographical alterations in Computer Tomography (CT) scans of COVID-19 cases show ground-glass opacities in the initial phase and pulmonary consolidation in the advanced phase [4]. Distinctive CT scans may aid the prompt screening of suspicious cases [5]. As a result, based on the graphical features existing in CT images, a clinical diagnosis can be provided before the pathogenic test, thus saving crucial time for pandemic control. In addition to that, the wide availability of the CT scanners makes this task faster. Further, to ease the burden of the radiologists and the medical professionals deep learning techniques like Convolutional Neural Networks (CNN) have evolved that can provide an automatic interpretation of whether the scan is COVID positive or not [6–8]. Chen et al. [9] developed a UNet++ model to excerpt features from the CT scans to classify them as COVID positive or COVID negative. The authors used 40 thousand CT scans from 106 patients for model training. The model did well both on per-patient and per-image basis reaching a sensitivity value of 100% and 94.34%. The model was comparable to the diagnosis of an expert radiologist for 27 prospective patients. The designed model reduced the radiologist reading time by nearly 65%. Wang et al. [10] proposed an inception transfer learning model for COVID-19 diagnosis. The model was tested on 325 COVID and 740 pneumonia affected images. The authors achieved a validation accuracy of nearly 80%. Zhao et al. [11] designed a transfer learned DenseNet model for the categorization of CT scans into COVID and Non-COVID classes. The authors obtained an F1 score of 85.3% and an accuracy value of 84.7% on a dataset comprising of 275 COVID and 195 Non-COVID scans. Loey et al. [12] compared five deep transfer learned (DTL) model for COVID-19 detection using the dataset prepared by [11]. The authors combined theses DTL models with classical augmentation and Conditional Generative Adversarial Networks (CGAN). GoogleNet, AlexNet, VGGNet16, VGGNet19, and ResNet50 were used for investigation. The authors concluded that ResNet 50 is the finest in rendering a test accuracy of 82.91%. Soares et al. [13] provided a larger dataset of 1252 positive CT Scans and 1230 as non-infected. The authors used the eXplainable Deep Learning approach (xDNN) to recognize if the subject is affected by SAR-Cov-2 or not. They attained an accuracy of 97.38% with an F score of 97.31%. The systematic analysis of the literature reveals that COVID-19 detection using CT scans of the chest is drawing the researcher's attention due to the limited availability of detection kits. Also, timely and accurate identification of COVID-19 from CT images is tedious and challenging for the radiologists. As the number of cases is surging up day by day, the automatic COVID-19 diagnosis mechanism is the necessity of the hour that will help in speedy detection of the virus at different stages and release the pressure of manually annotating the slices over the health care professionals. This will also increase opportunities for faster patient recovery. Motivated by this, there has been increasing efforts on the development of deep learning models for COVID-19 diagnosis as these approaches do not require handcrafted features or sophisticated feature selection and classification methods. However, the reported works are difficult to reproduce as CT scan data used in their work is not publically available. To counteract this, Soares et al. [13] provided a benchmark dataset with 2482 CT scans. Although the effort is appreciable, deep learning models usually require huge labeled training datasets to render good accuracy. If the training data set is smaller, CNN leads to overfitting. To mitigate this, transfer learned Deep CNN (DCNN) model, i.e., explainable DNN has been explored in [13] but the detection accuracy is less. Inspired by the advantage of the transfer learning in working on a small pathological dataset and with the aim to improvise the detection accuracy over existing works, the present paper proposes an algorithm based on the concatenation of features from the ResNet 50 and mobinenetv2 architectures for the automated detection of COVID-19 from CT images.

2 Database and Performance Evaluation Measures

2.1 COVID Dataset Description

For the analysis of the proposed feature concatenation based approach, the COVID19-CT dataset collected by Soares et al. [13] has been used. It comprises of CT scans of 60 subjects affected by SARS-COV-2 and images from another 60 subjects not infected by SARS-COV-2. So, the database has a total of 2482 images with 1252 positive and 1230 negative [13]. The train and test split statistics for this dataset is given in Table 1. Sample COVID and non- COVID scans are presented in Fig. 1. Also, in the present work, performance metrics like Recall, Precision, Accuracy, F-score, and Area under the Curve (AUC) are chosen to validate the performance of the proposed approach.

Table 1. Data split statistics

Data set	COVID	Non-COVID	Total
Train	1003	983	1986
Validation	250	246	496

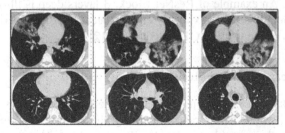

Fig. 1. Sample COVID (upper row) and non-COVID (lower-row) images available in the dataset

3 Proposed Methodology

3.1 Mobilenetv2

The architecture of Mobilenetv2 is inspired by the Mobilenetv1 [14]. It employs depth-wise separable convolutions as the basic constructing blocks. In contrast to the V1 structure, it adds two new features: a) Linear bottleneck in between the layers, and b) Shortcut connections in between bottlenecks [14]. The basic structure is shown below as Fig. 2. Mobilenetv2 is chosen in the present work because of its memory-efficient nature. It is faster than other models for the same value of classification accuracy [15]. In contrast to Mobilenetv1, it uses two times fewer operations, and 30% fewer parameters [14, 15]. It is specifically tailored for mobile and resource-constrained environments. This makes its implementation and storage easy on a simple computing platform which makes it advantageous for real-time scenarios [15].

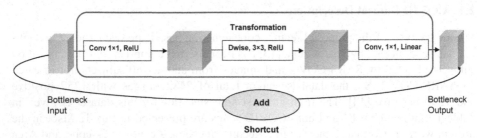

Fig. 2. Building blocks of Mobilenetv2

3.2 ResNet50

ResNet50 is a pretrained network that is 50 layers deep [16]. It has 48 convolutional layers, one max-pooling, and one average pooling layer. In its architecture, shortcut connections have been introduced that skip three layers with non-linearities (ReLU) along with 1×1 convolution layers. This helps in mitigating the gradient vanishing problem in deep networks. An example of ResNet Block, 3 layers deep is illustrated in Fig. 3 below [16]. ResNet50 has been explicitly chosen because of its superior performance than other models on the COVID CT scan dataset [12].

3.3 Proposed Feature Fusion Mechanism

The proposed feature concatenation scheme is divided into four phases. First is the data preparation phase, second is the transfer learning phase, third is the feature extraction and feature fusion phase, and last is the classification phase. The ensuing sub-sections briefly describe all the four phases.

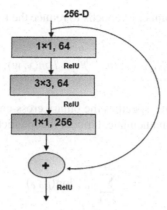

Fig. 3. ResNet 3-layer block example

Data Preparation Phase

The dataset is divided in the proportion 8:2, i.e., 80% of the total images in the dataset is used for training and 20% is used for validation as per the works by [13]. For better generalization and to prevent overfitting data augmentation is used for training data.

Transfer Learning Phase

Transfer learning is the most effective utilization of the power of the deep models for the smaller dataset as getting millions of annotated images for Deep CNN training is expensive and challenging. In transfer learning, attributes of the established pre-trained models like Mobilenetv2 [14, 15] and ResNet-50 [16] trained on huge labeled image dataset is used for cross-domain image classification tasks. It is seen that the initial layers of these pre-trained models contain only edge and color-related information. More specific attributes are contained in later layers. As a result of which parameters of the early layers require no or very less fine-tuning [17]. Motivated by this, in the present work we have fine-tuned only the last three layers of the chosen pre-trained models. The approach for fine-tuning works by extracting all the layers of the network except the last three. Then the layers are shifted to the new classification task by substituting the last three layers with a fully connected ('fc') layer, a softmax layer, and a classification output layer. The size of the 'fc' layer is set to the size equal to the number of classes in the new classification problem [18, 19]. For the present work, the value is taken as two, equal to the number of classes, i.e., COVID and Non-COVID. Summarizing the same mathematically: Let $Model = \{Mobilenetv2, ResNet50\}$ be the set of the chosen pre-trained architectures. Let (X_{input}, Y_{output}) be the current CT scan image dataset; having 'N' images with the set of labels as $Y_{output} = \{y|y \in \{Non\text{-}COVID; COVID\}\}$. The training and validation sets are represented as (X_{train}, Y_{train}) and (X_{val}, Y_{val}). The training data is further divided into mini-batches (n), such that $(X_i, Y_i) \in (X_{train}, Y_{train})$; $i = 1, 2, ..., N/n$. Iterative optimization of the pre-trained model, $m \in Model$ is carried out using 'n' for a specific number of epochs to reduce the loss, L as given in Eq. (1) by weight updation.

$$L(w, X_i) = 1/n \sum_{x \in X_i, y \in Y_i} l(m(x, w), y) \tag{1}$$

In the above expression, $l(.)$ specifies the binary cross-entropy loss function defined in Eq. (2) and $m(x, w)$ is the mathematical model that predicts a category 'y' for feature input 'x' and weight 'w'.

$$l = - \sum_{c=1}^{M} y_{o,c} \log(p_{o,c}) \tag{2}$$

In Eq. (2), M is the number of classes, 'y' indicates whether label 'c' is the right categorization for observation 'o', and 'p' is the probability that observation 'o' belongs to label class 'c'. Solving, the above equations will result in a transfer learned model.

It is significant to mention that the models are fine-tuned separately on the CT scan dataset and thereafter used in the next phase.

Feature Extraction and Fusion Phase

After training the models on the newer CT image dataset separately via the transfer learning concept, features are extracted from both the learned models. For Mobilenetv2, features are deduced from the last convolutional layer ('Conv_1'), and for ResNet50 features are extracted by performing activations onto the last average pooling layer ('avg_pool') of the model. Thereafter the features are concatenated together to form a feature vector of dimension 1×63232.

Classification Phase

In this phase, the feature vector formulated by concatenating along with the corresponding labels is used to train an SVM classifier. SVM is a supervised learning method and works by creating an optimal hyperplane [20]. Considering a group of N training examples (x_i, y_i), x_i represents a pattern in feature space (d-dimensional) and $y_i \in \{-1,1\}$ be the class output label. Let $K(x_i, x_j)$, be the kernel value matrix and α_i be the Lagrange coefficients to be computed through optimization. The SVM output is obtained by the maximizing the quadratic optimization function given below as

$$\max \ W(\alpha) = -\frac{1}{2} \sum_{i}^{N} \sum_{j}^{N} \alpha_i \alpha_j y_i y_j K(x_i; \ x_j) + \sum_{i}^{N} \alpha_i \tag{3}$$

The above equation is subject to condition $0 \le \alpha_i \le C, \forall i$ and $\sum_{i}^{N} \alpha_i y_i = 0$.

Thereafter the trained SVM is utilized to provide predictions for the validation dataset. The complete procedure is summarized as Fig. 4.

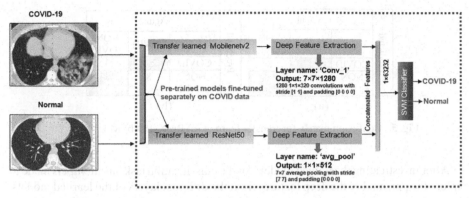

Fig. 4. Proposed concatenated network

4 Results

4.1 Experimental Settings

Table 1 summarizes the COVID images used in each set. i.e., training, and validation. Images are resized to fit the dimensions of the Input layer of the comparison transfer learned models, i.e., an image input is changed to a size equal to $224 \times 224 \times 3$. These learned models are fitted for 20 epochs with a mini-batch size of 180 with early stopping criteria. Further, the weight parameters are trained via 'Adam' with the initial learning rate as 0.0006. Also, binary cross-entropy is employed as a loss function. The learned models are implemented in MATLAB 19a and executed on a system with Intel Core i7-4500U CPU, 8 GB RAM, and 1.8 GHz processor.

4.2 Results

This section provides the results of using the proposed feature fusion-based technique for the binary classification of CT images as COVID and Non-COVID. Table 2 gives the results for transfer learned ResNet50 and Mobilenetv2 models. The tabular entries indicate that the learned Mobilenetv2 model achieves validation accuracy of 97.74%, precision of 98.78%, F1 score of 97.78%, and AUC of 99.88%. The outcomes are better than the learned ResNet50 model that attained the value of 97.12%, 96.83%, 97.21%, and 99.73% for different performance measures. Figure 5 illustrates the confusion matrix for the transfer learned models. The number of FN+FP is less in the learned Mobilenetv2, i.e., 11 than in ResNet 50 resulting in small misclassification error.

Table 2. Performance metrics for the transfer learned models on the validation data set

Model	Precision	Recall	Accuracy	F1-score	AUC
ResNet50	96.83%	97.60%	97.12%	97.21%	99.73%
Mobilenetv2	98.78%	96.80%	97.74%	97.78%	99.80%

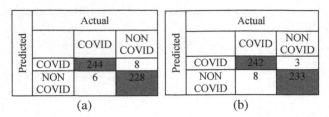

Fig. 5. Confusion matrix for transfer learned (a) ResNet50(b) Mobilenetv2

After investigating the trained models for the classification task, an attempt is made to explore the potential of the deep features from the different layers of the learned models. Moreover, experimentations are also done on fusing the activations from different layers. Experimentation reveals that best results are attained when the activations from 'Conv_1' (Mobilenetv2) and 'avg_pool' (ResNet 50) are combined. The detection results are given in Table 3. Interestingly, as given in Table 3, the proposed feature fusion-based approach performs the finest by achieving a validation accuracy of 98.35%, precision of 99.19%, F1-score of 98.39%, recall of 97.60%, and AUC of 99.88%. The results are better than solely using the activations from the 'avg_pool; and 'Conv_1' layer that reached a validation accuracy of 96.71% and 97.94% respectively. The fusion results are in consensus with the fact that the deeper layers of the model like 'Conv_1' excerpt the image texture and shape-related information which is decisive for classification. Also, the dominant features like positional invariant and rotational ones are obtained from the activations of the pooling layer. Combining, these features has resulted in improved performance. Furthermore, the investigation also reveals that a larger feature vector (62720) from a 'Conv_1' has better performance in contrast to a smaller feature vector (512) from 'avg_pool' which justifies its contribution. Figure 6 illustrates the confusion matrix using features from 'avg_pool', 'Conv_1', and from both layers. The number of FN + FP is least in the proposed feature fusion-based approach, i.e., 8 in contrast to 16 and 10 resulting from deep features of the learned models.

Table 3. Performance metrics using deep features from transfer learned model

Model	Precision	Recall	Accuracy	F1-score	AUC
ResNet50-'avg_pool' features	96.43%	97.20%	96.71%	96.81%	99.44%
Mobilenetv2-'Conv_1' features	97.24%	98.80%	97.94%	98.02%	99.77%
Proposed (same partition as [13])	99.19%	97.60%	98.35%	98.39%	99.88%
Proposed (5-fold cross validation)	98.88%	98.88%	98.87%	98.88%	98.87%

(a)

Predicted	Actual	
	COVID	NON COVID
COVID	243	9
NON COVID	7	227

(b)

Predicted	Actual	
	COVID	NON COVID
COVID	247	7
NON COVID	3	229

(c)

Predicted	Actual	
	COVID	NON COVID
COVID	247	5
NON COVID	3	231

Fig. 6. Confusion matrix using features from (a) 'avg_pool' (b) 'Conv_1' (c) both 'avg_pool' & 'Conv_1'

5 Discussion

Apart from exploring the efficacy of the ResNet50 and Mobilenetv2 model for COVID detection and proposing a feature fusion strategy, a comparative analysis with the recent works is also carried out. The analysis has been restricted to the works reported on the same dataset [13]. Table 4 presents the performance comparison of the proposed methodology for COVID-19 detection with the reported techniques as available in the literature. The authors in [13] have proposed x-DNN for COVID detection using features from the VGG-16 fully connected layer. They also experimented with other models like GoogleNet, VGG16, Alexnet, Decision Trees, and AdaBoost classifiers. The proposed feature fusion-based algorithm, as investigated in the present work is superior to x-DNN as it resulted in an accuracy value of 98.35% and F-score 98.39% better than x-DNN for which accuracy and F1-score were 97.38% and 97.31% respectively. Also, the results using the proposed feature fusion strategy are superior to deep bidirectional long short-term memory network with mixture density network (DBM) network proposed in the works by [21]. The results are comparable to those attained via the DBM+Memetic Adaptive Differential Evolution (MADE) algorithm for which the validation accuracy was marginally better, i.e., 98.37%. The proposed feature fusion strategy is advantageous in the context that it does not need any optimization algorithm for tuning the hyper-parameters of the network unlike the works by Pathak et al. [21] that have utilized MADE for tuning the hype-parameters of the DBM model.

Solely to contrast the performance of the proposed algorithm on multiple datasets, the COVID19-CT dataset collected by He et al. [11, 23] has also been used in the present work. It comprises of 397 non-COVID scans and 349 positive COVID scans. The images are of varying sizes. Moreover, the training, validation, and the test sets are created by partitioning the data the ratio 0.6, 0.15, and 0.25 [11, 23] resulting in 191, 234; 60,58; & 98, 105 COVID and non-COVID images in the training, validation, and the test pools. The experimental results on this dataset are summarized in Table 5. Clearly, the proposed algorithm reaches to ceiling level of classification performance by attaining a test accuracy of 84.24% and an F1-score of 83.16%. Also, the proposed feature fusion strategy when validated under a five-fold data partitioning scheme results in an accuracy of 88.21% and 87.06%. The results are better than the comparison counterparts e.g. CRNet [23], CVR-Net [24], MNasNet1.0 [25], and Light CNN [26] that reached to an accuracy value of 73%, 78%, 81.77%, and 83% respectively.

Table 4. Comparative analysis of the proposed feature fusion strategy with the existing works using the same database as [13]

Technique	Accuracy	Precision	Recall	F1 score	AUC
xDNN [13]	97.38%	99.16%	95.53%	97.31%	97.36%
GoogleNet [13]	91.73%	90.20%	93.50%	91.82%	91.79%
VGG16 [13]	94.96%	94.02%	95.43%	94.97%	94.96%
Alexnet [13]	93.75%	94.98%	92.28%	93.61%	93.68%
Decision Tree [13]	79.44%	76.81%	83.13%	79.84%	79.51%
AdaBoost [13]	95.16%	93.63%	96.71%	95.14%	95.19%
DBM [21]	97.23%	98.14%	97.68%	97.89%	97.71%
DBM+MADE [21]	98.37%	98.74%	98.87%	98.14%	98.32%
EfficientNet [22]	98.99%	99.20%	98.80%	-	-
Proposed (fixed partition)	**98.35%**	**99.19%**	**97.60%**	**98.39%**	**99.88%**
Proposed (5-fold CV)	**98.87%**	**98.88%**	**98.88%**	**98.88%**	**98.87%**

Table 5. Comparative analysis of the proposed strategy with the existing works [23]

Method	Accuracy	F1 score
VGG-16 [23]	76.00%	76.00%
ResNet-18 [23]	74.00%	73.00%
ResNet-50 [23]	80.00%	81.00%
DenseNet-121 [23]	79.00%	79.00%
DenseNet-169 [23]	83.00%	81.00%
EfficientNet-b0 [23]	77.00%	78.00%
EfficientNet-b1 [23]	79.00%	79.00%
CRNet [23]	73.00%	76.00%
CVR-Net [24]	78.00%	78.00%
MNasNet1.0 [25]	81.77%	83.56%
ShuffleNet-v2-x1.0 [25]	74.38%	75.70%
Light CNN [26]	83.00%	83.33%
Proposed algorithm (using same partition as [23])	**84.24%**	**83.16%**
Proposed algorithm (5-fold cross validation)	**88.21%**	**87.06%**

6   Conclusion

In the present work, an effective algorithm based upon the concatenation of Mobilenetv2 and ResNet50 features is proposed for classifying the chest CT scans as COVID or normal. To analyze the texture content present in the CT scans, higher-level features are extracted from the deeper layer 'Conv_1' and 'avg_pool' of the transfer learned Mobilenetv2 and ResNet50 model and thereafter fused. The fused feature vector is then utilized for SVM classifier training. The predictions on the validation data reveal that with feature fusion a ceiling level of the classification accuracy is achieved. It achieved a validation accuracy of 98.35% better than the comparison models and the existing state of artworks on the same dataset. The outcomes presented in the paper will aid in speedy detection of this virus at the different phases whether initial or severe. Such a detection system will also increase the opportunities for fast recovery of patients worldwide thereby releasing the pressure off the medical professionals and the healthcare system around the world. Forthcoming works will be dedicated to implementing the model on a real-time basis to assists medical professionals in providing a timely and accurate diagnosis.

References

1. Huang, C., et al.: Clinical features of patients infected with 2019 novel coronavirus in Wuhan, China. Lancet **395**, 497–506 (2020)
2. Zhu, N., et al.: A novel coronavirus from patients with pneumonia in China, 2019. N. Engl. J. Med. **382**, 727–733 (2020)
3. Zhou, F., et al.: Clinical course and risk factors for mortality of adult inpatients with COVID-19 in Wuhan, China: a retrospective cohort study. Lancet **395**, 1054–1062 (2020)
4. Bernheim, A., et al.: Chest CT findings in coronavirus disease-19 (COVID-19): relationship to duration of infection. Radiology **295**, 200463 (2020)
5. Koo, H.J., Lim, S., Choe, J., Choi, S.-H., Sung, H., Do, K.-H.: Radiographic and CT features of viral pneumonia. Radiographics **38**, 719–739 (2018)
6. Gozes, O., et al.: Rapid ai development cycle for the coronavirus (covid-19) pandemic: initial results for automated detection & patient monitoring using deep learning ct image analysis. arXiv Prepr. arXiv2003.05037 (2020)
7. Choe, J., et al.: Deep learning–based image conversion of CT reconstruction kernels improves radiomics reproducibility for pulmonary nodules or masses. Radiology **292**, 365–373 (2019)
8. Kermany, D.S., et al.: Identifying medical diagnoses and treatable diseases by image-based deep learning. Cell **172**, 1122–1131 (2018)
9. Chen, J., et al.: Deep learning-based model for detecting 2019 novel coronavirus pneumonia on high-resolution computed tomography: a prospective study. medRxiv (2020)
10. Wang, S., et al.: A deep learning algorithm using CT images to screen for Corona Virus Disease (COVID-19). medRxiv (2020)
11. Zhao, J., Zhang, Y., He, X., Xie, P.: COVID-CT-dataset: a CT scan dataset about COVID-19. arXiv Prepr. arXiv2003.13865 (2020)
12. Loey, M., Smarandache, F., Khalifa, N.E.M.: A deep transfer learning model with classical data augmentation and CGAN to detect COVID-19 from chest CT radiography digital images (2020)
13. Soares, E., Angelov, P., Biaso, S., Froes, M.H., Abe, D.K.: SARS-CoV-2 CT-scan dataset: a large dataset of real patients CT scans for SARS-CoV-2 identification. medRxiv (2020)
14. Howard, A.G., et al.: Efficient convolutional neural networks for mobile vision applications. arXiv Prepr. arXiv1704.04861 (2017)
15. Sandler, M., Howard, A., Zhu, M., Zhmoginov, A., Chen, L.-C.: Mobilenetv2: inverted residuals and linear bottlenecks. In: Proceedings of the IEEE Conference on Computer Vision and Pattern Recognition, pp. 4510–4520 (2018)

16. He, K., Zhang, X., Ren, S., Sun, J.: Deep residual learning for image recognition. In: Proceedings of the IEEE Conference on Computer Vision and Pattern Recognition, pp. 770–778 (2016)
17. Yosinski, J., Clune, J., Bengio, Y., Lipson, H.: How transferable are features in deep neural networks? In: Advances in Neural Information Processing Systems, pp. 3320–3328 (2014)
18. Sonawane, P.K., Shelke, S.: Handwritten devanagari character classification using deep learning. In: 2018 International Conference on Information, Communication, Engineering and Technology (ICICET), pp. 1–4 (2018)
19. Lu, S., Lu, Z., Zhang, Y.-D.: Pathological brain detection based on AlexNet and transfer learning. J. Comput. Sci. **30**, 41–47 (2019)
20. Graf, H.P., Cosatto, E., Bottou, L., Dourdanovic, I., Vapnik, V.: Parallel support vector machines: the cascade SVM. In: Advances in Neural Information Processing Systems, pp. 521–528 (2005)
21. Pathak, Y., Shukla, P.K., Arya, K.V.: Deep bidirectional classification model for COVID-19 disease infected patients. IEEE/ACM Trans. Comput. Biol. Bioinform. (2020)
22. Silva, P., et al.: COVID-19 detection in CT images with deep learning: a voting-based scheme and cross-datasets analysis. Inform. Med. Unlocked **20**, 100427 (2020)
23. He, X., et al.: Sample-efficient deep learning for COVID-19 diagnosis based on CT scans. medRxiv (2020)
24. Hasan, M., Alam, M., Elahi, M., Toufick, E., Roy, S., Wahid, S.R., et al.: CVR-Net: a deep convolutional neural network for coronavirus recognition from chest radiography images. arXiv Prepr. arXiv2007.11993 (2020)
25. Saqib, M., Anwar, S., Anwar, A., Blumenstein, M., et al.: COVID19 detection from radiographs: is deep learning able to handle the crisis? (2020)
26. Polsinelli, M., Cinque, L., Placidi, G.: A light CNN for detecting COVID-19 from CT scans of the chest. arXiv Prepr. arXiv2004.12837 (2020)

An Ensemble Method for Efficient Classification of Skin Lesion from Dermoscopy Image

B. H. Shekar⑩ and Habtu Hailu⁽✉⁾

Mangalore University, Mangalagangothri, Karnataka, India

Abstract. Nowadays, skin cancer is growing-up due to exposure to Ultraviolet (UV) radiation emanating from the sun light. Among several categories of skin lesion, melanoma is the most deadly cancerous kind. Diagnosing skin lesion in its early stage have a great chance to cure the disease. Researchers have proposed several computer-aided diagnosis techniques to detect skin lesions. In this work, we present an ensemble model to classify skin lesion using a pre-trained DenseNet and InceptionV3 algorithms. The fully layered fine-tuned technique is applied to both the algorithms which are previously explored for ImageNet dataset. The fine-tuned algorithms are utilized to train on the HAM10000 dataset. The classification results obtained due to the pre-trained models are concatenated in the average ensemble method. The experimentation on the standard datasets confirm the classification accuracy of 91% and indicates that the proposed approach is a promising as compared to the previously developed approaches.

Keywords: Deep learning · DenseNet · InceptionV3 · Ensemble learning · Skin lesion classification

1 Introduction

Globally in each year, 132,000 new melanoma and 2 to 3 million non-melanoma skin cancer patients appear which shows that the rate of skin cancer incidence is drastically growing-up [1,2]. The major cause for this is due to ultraviolet (UV) radiation which is the most significant spectrum of sunlight that can destroy the DNA under the skin cell that leads to excess development of skin cells resulting in skin cancer. The main cause of UV to reach our surroundings is the evacuation of the level of the ozone layer [3,4]. The most usual categories of skin lesions are squamous cell carcinoma, melanoma, basal cell carcinoma, Benign, Actinic keratosis, Melanocytic nevi, Vascular lesions, and Dermatofibroma [5–7]. Melanoma is the most serious cancerous kind of skin lesion, which is the cause for 9000 mortality in 2017 in United States [8] only. If melanoma is diagnosed in its early stage, nearly 95% of the cases have a possibility to cure, especially basal cell and squamous cell carcinomas are highly curable cases [9].

© Springer Nature Singapore Pte Ltd. 2021
S. K. Singh et al. (Eds.): CVIP 2020, CCIS 1376, pp. 161–178, 2021.
https://doi.org/10.1007/978-981-16-1086-8_15

Skin lesion is primarily detected manually by using human naked eyes, which require a magnifying and illuminated skin images. Among several procedural techniques, the most common methods (ABCD) rule, Menzies 7-point checklist and 3-point checklist are used to detect the melanoma in the early stages [10,11]. Reports on the performance of clinical dermatologists on diagnostic accuracy have claimed 80% for a dermatologist who have ten years and more experience, whereas dermatologist who have 3 to 5 years experience were able to reach only 62% [12]. This shows that for detecting skin lesion with a better accuracy, years of experience over difficult situations plays a great role. Applying machine learning techniques on dermoscopic image to classify malignant and benign lesion becomes popular task because of the ability to detect patterns in digital images. Deep learning methods exhibit better performance in detection and classification of various diseases by means of medical image examination [5,13].

Several studies have been prompted to classify skin lesion from dermascopic images. Barata et al. [14] uses a global and local features for the detection of melanoma in dermoscopy images. They have compared the effect of color and texture features for lesion classification and concluded that a combination of features leads to better performance. In the work of Codella et al. [15] a combination of support vector machine (SVM), sparse coding techniques and deep learning are applied on International Skin Imaging Collaboration (ISIC) dataset to recognize/classify dermoscopy images. A convolutional network with transfer learning is developed by Cıcero et al. [16] on a custom dataset of skin image to get better performance in the skin lesion classification task.

In the recent days, we have been witnessing the application of deep learning for many of the medical image analysis problems. Among these, Esteva et al. [17] applied a pretrained CNN technique, GoogleNet and Inception v3 for image classification. In order to tackle the difficulties of classifying skin lesion, Lopez et al. [18] presented a pretrained VGGNet algorithm with the transfer learning method. The ISIC dataset is used for testing the proposed method. In 2017, Krizhevsky et al. [19] applied a deep CNN on a large dataset of ImageNet LSVRC-2010. The number of different classes after classification is 1000. Codella et al. [20] proposed an ensemble of deep residual network and fully CNN in combination with SVM, hand-coded feature extractor and sparse coding method to segment and detect melanoma cases on a dataset of International Symposium on Biomedical Imaging (ISBI). To classify the dermoscopy image dataset of ISBI 2017 into three different classes, Harangi et al. [21] employ an ensemble technique that fuses the classification output of four different deep neural network algorithms. Tan et al. [22] used a feature optimization technique considering Particle Swarm Optimization (PSO) for the purpose of classification of skin lesion into benign and malignant. Dermofit Image Library, PH2, and Dermnet are the datasets used for evaluation.

In addition to these works, most recently Hekler et al. [23] implements a deep learning network for skin lesion classification into malignant melanoma and benign nevus that could help human for the histopathologic melanoma diagnosis. To enhance the performance of skin lesion classification, a dilated convolution of deep learning technique is applied on four pretrained algorithms (VGG16, VGG19, MobileNet and InceptionV3) by [5]. They have used transfer learning for the extraction of features from the images. Chaturvedi et al. [4] proposed a transfer learning on pretrained MobileNet algorithm and evaluated on HAM10000 dataset to classify into seven different classes. In Pratiwi et al. [13], CNN model is proposed for the detection of skin cancer from HAM10000 dermoscopy image. In the work of Khan et al. [24], an ensemble of pretrained ResNet-50 and ResNet-101 through transfer learning based feature extraction is employed for skin lesion classification. The features extracted are fed to SVM for classification. Even though, several attempts are done for classification of skin lesions, still there is lack of generality in their capability of classification and have not achieved better accuracy because of the complexities in the image itself [4].

In this study, we proposed an ensemble method that fuses the two most common pretrained deep convolutional neural networks, namely DenseNet and InceptionV3, which are pretrained on approximately 1.28 million images. In most of the cases these two algorithms outperform in the HAM10000 dataset [25] as we explore from the previous works. We use a fine tuning technique for the feature extraction (discussed in the methodology in detail). The proposed model is trained and tested on HAM10000 dataset [25] that consists of 10015 dermoscopy images. The rest of the paper is outlined as follows. Section 2 introduces the proposed method which details about dataset description, data pre-processing techniques, data augmentation and the proposed architecture. Section 3 present experimental findings. Finally, Discussion and Conclusions are given in Sect. 4.

2   Proposed Methodology

In this section, we present the details of the proposed methodology which include the dataset used for training and evaluation, data pre-processing and augmentation techniques, and the architecture of the proposed method.

2.1   Dataset

To train, validate and test the proposed model, we have used a collection of dermatoscopic images namely Human Against Machine with 10000 training images (HAM10000) dataset which is available publicly on International Skin Imaging Collaboration (ISIC). The dataset accommodates 10015 dermatoscopic images gathered from different populations by using a variety of modalities. The dataset is not equally distributed for each type of lesions, 6705 Melanocytic nevi (nv) images, 1113 Melanoma (mel) images, 1099 Benign keratosis (bkl) images, 514

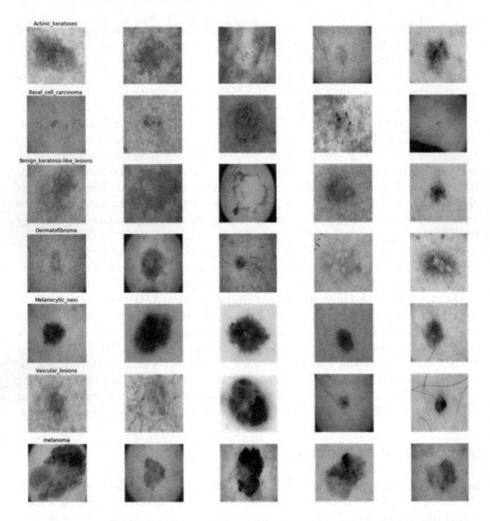

Fig. 1. Randomly selected sample images for each cancer type from the HAM10000 dataset.

Basal cell carcinoma (bcc) images, 327 Actinic keratosis (Akiec) images, 142 Vascular (vasc) images and 115 Dermatofibroma (df) images. All images are stored with 600 × 450 pixels resolution. This indicates that, more than 50% of the dataset is imbalanced to only one type of lesion namely Melanocytic nevi. Figure 1 shows five sample images from each lesion types.

2.2 Data Pre-processing

The pixel resolutions of all the images used in this study are 600 × 450. To make the size of these images compatible with our models (DenseNet and InceptionV3), we downscale the pixel resolution to 256 × 192 by using Keras Image-DataGenerator. Then normalization of the dataset is performed by dividing the pixel values of the images by 255.0. Finally, we divide the dataset for the training (8111 images), validation (902 images) and testing (1002 images) sets.

2.3 Data Augmentation

For deep learning algorithms, to get a better performance, a large amount of data is required. But still, acquiring an adequate amount of data is the main challenge in the area. One best solution to increase the dataset size is the data augmentation technique as it raises the dataset size without eliminating the structure of the data. In our study, the first data augmentation techniques used is a rotation operation with a range randomly between 0 and 60°. The other concern in image data preparation is, objects of interest in the image may be off-centred by several means. To handle this problem, we apply width shifting and height shifting with a range of 0.2. At last, shear and random zooming operations are applied with a range of 0.2.

2.4 Proposed Architecture

Recently, for image classification, CNN become the state-of-the-art method because it achieved excellent performance on a well-known datasets such as MINIST [26] and ImageNet [27]. There are several varieties of CNN algorithms for image classification task, such as AlexNet [19], GoogLeNet [28], ResNet [29], DenseNet [30], VGGNet [31], InceptionV3 [32] and others. In our work, we perform the classification of skin lesion by using an ensemble method which encompasses well-established deep learning architectures that have shown better accuracy in the previous works, namely DenseNet and InceptionV3. These architectures are available as a pretrained model that were initially trained with ImageNet dataset that contains around 1.28 million natural images with 1000 classes. We use the weights and biases from the pretrained model to initialize learning on our dataset, and then a fine-tuning technique is applied on all the layers in the selected architectures. The details are presented in the following subsections.

The DenseNet Architecture: The DenseNet architecture proposed by Huang et al. [30] contains all the layers which are directly connected to each other to optimize the flow of information between the layers. That means, each layer in the network receive information from all the antecedent layers and feeds its output to all the consequent layers. A concatenation operation is performed in every layer to merge the inputs from the previous layers. Equation 1 presents the input feature map fetched to the ith layer from all the preceding layers [33]. The connectivity pattern in each layer of a single dense block is illustrated in Fig. 2. DenseNet is one of the best performer method on ImageNet dataset where it performs 0.773 on top-1 and 0.936 on top-5 retrievals.

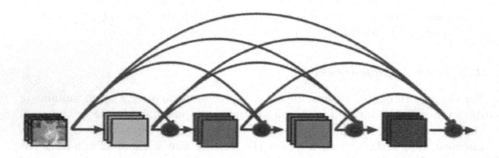

Fig. 2. A layout of single dense block which has 5 layers.

$$x_i = H_i(x_0, x_1, ..., x_{i-1}) \tag{1}$$

Here, x_i is the output of the ith layer and H_i is the composite function that represent the operations such as rectified linear units (ReLU), Batch Normalization (BN), and Convolution (Conv).

In our work, we have used the variant of DenseNet that is named as DenseNet-201, which has 4 dense blocks and 201 layers. Figure 3 shows a DenseNet architecture with three dense blocks. In each dense block, there is a composition layer which performs sequentially BN and ReLU and then a 3 × 3 convolution operations. The convolution operation is used to provide the concatenated output feature map, say for example, to transform the input feature maps x_0, x_1, x_2 to output feature map x_3 by using Eq. 1. The Batch Normalization operation is used to normalize the input of each layer [34] in order to decrease the absolute difference between data and make the relative difference higher.

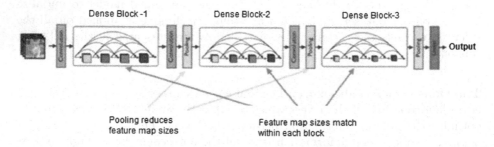

Fig. 3. A deep DenseNet with 3 dense block.

The other operation which is part of composition layer is the ReLU, which is applied in DenseNet architecture. Equation 2 describes how the ReLU operation works.

$$ReLu(x) = \begin{cases} x, & \text{if } x > 0. \\ 0, & \text{otherwise.} \end{cases} \tag{2}$$

The changing of feature map size due to the down-sampling layers in convolutional networks makes difficult to perform the concatenation operation. To facilitate down-sampling, the Densenet architecture separates the whole network into various dense blocks that are connected densely. As shown in Fig. 3, there are transition layers between these densely connected dense blocks used to perform convolution and pooling operation. In this work, these transition layers include three different operations namely batch normalization, 1×1 convolution and a 2×2 average pooling operation [30]. Beside, a bottleneck layer is incorporated within the dense blocks before a 3×3 convolution layer. It consists of BN, ReLU and a 1×1 convolution layer. The 1×1 convolution operation in this layer makes the network computationally efficient by reducing the number of input feature maps to the 3×3 convolution operation in the dense block. This layer make DenseNet method effective by reducing the complexity and size of the model. The main benefits of DenseNet, when compared to other methods, are presented below.

- *Only a few parameters:* Since the feature maps from the preceding layers acts like an input for the current layer, many feature maps can be reused to learn by some convolution kernels.
- *Capability to reduce over fitting:* The dense connection in the DenseNet network built short paths from the beginning to the end layers. Due to this, the loss function provides additional guidance for each layer. Consequently, the dense connection protects the over-fitting problem in a better way, particularly it is a good choice for learning from the small size of data.
- *Layers are deeper:* Because all layers are linked directly to each other, the network has highly deep architecture.

The InceptionV3 Architecture: By enhancing the GoogleNet [28] network, Szegedy et al. [32] proposed an algorithm called InceptionV3. The major enhancement is reducing the size of the parameters by concatenating the convolutional filters which have different sizes into a new filter. Consequently the computational complexity of the model is decreased. Figure 4 illustrates the architecture of InceptionV3. This model scores an error rate of 3.5% on top-5 and 17.3% on top-1 of ImageNet dataset.

In this network, the number of parameters is reduced by replacing the convolution filters of size greater than 3×3 (e.g. 5×5 or 7×7) by a sequence of 3×3 convolution layers. The computational cost of a large spatial filter convolution is expensive [32]. In addition to this, spatial factorization into asymmetric convolutions is applied. This means, replacing an $n \times n$ filters by two layer asymmetric filters of $n \times 1$ followed by $1 \times n$. The InceptionV3 network has 42 layers and the detail of the network that is shown in Fig. 4 is presented in Table 1.

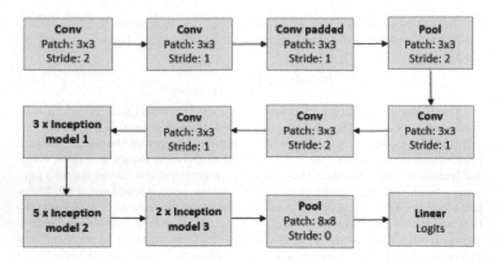

Fig. 4. The architecture of InceptionV3.

Table 1. The detailed outline of InceptionV3 architecture. The input size column also represents the output size of the previous layer.

Type of layer	Patch size/stride	Input size
Conv	$3 \times 3/2$	$299 \times 299 \times 3$
Conv	$3 \times 3/1$	$149 \times 149 \times 32$
conv padded	$3 \times 3/1$	$147 \times 147 \times 32$
Pool	$3 \times 3/2$	$147 \times 147 \times 64$
Conv	$3 \times 3/1$	$73 \times 73 \times 64$
Conv	$3 \times 3/2$	$71 \times 71 \times 80$
Conv	$3 \times 3/1$	$35 \times 35 \times 192$
Pool	8×8	$8 \times 8 \times 2048$
Linear	Logits	$1 \times 1 \times 2048$
Softmax	Classifier	$1 \times 1 \times 1000$

Fine Tuned Ensemble: To increase the image classification accuracy on a dataset which do not have sufficient amount of annotated images, an ensemble of DNN is a powerful technique, which makes a decision by combining the prediction results from multiple models [21]. In our work, we have explored an ensemble of two well-known pretrained CNN algorithms, DenseNet and InceptionV3. Firstly, the two methods (DenseNet and IncptuionV3) are fine-tuned and trained on our dataset individually, and then the best performed model is saved. The fine tuning technique is applied by freezing all the layers of the networks prior to the final fully connected layer. A fully connected layer of the pretrained networks is removed and replaced by a new fully connected layer that have seven neurons which is equivalent to the number of classes in the prediction task. Finally, classification is performed by fusing saved models by averaging technique. An averaging of a models' prediction is an ensemble learning technique that predicts based on the predictions obtained by each model. It considers each model equally for average calculation and used to bring down the variance in the final neural network model [21]. Figure 5 presents the model architecture of the current work.

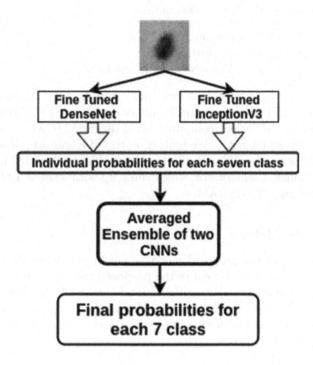

Fig. 5. The proposed ensemble architecture.

3   Experimental Details

In this section, we present the details of the experimental setup, the evaluation metrics and results with a detailed discussion on the experimentation.

3.1   Experimental Setup

In the current study, we perform a classification task using two fine-tuned DNN methods and then we have employed an ensemble technique. The proposed models are trained for 40 epochs with a batch size of 32 on our dataset. The evaluation of the model is done using 902 sample images from the validation set and 1002 sample images from the test set. We have considered Adam optimizer to optimize learning with a learning rate of 0.0001, the minimum learning rate is set to 0.1×106. We have used the Top 1 accuracy, which is the standard performance measure in CNN studies [19]. Firstly, we have compared the classification accuracy obtained on the HAM10000 dataset considering

- Fine-tuned denseNet algorithm
- Fine-tuned InceptionV3 algorithm and
- An ensemble method of DenseNet and InceptionV3.

In addition, the best accuracy result from our evaluation is compared with other previous studies which have better performance and done on HAM10000 dataset. To program the model for our computer aided diagnosis (CAD) system, we use python programming language. We built it on top of Keras deep learning framework for neural networks [35] with the tensorflow [36] back-end. The training is performed on Google Collaborator, which come up with a single 12 GB NVIDIA Tesla K80 GPU and 12 GB RAM.

3.2   Evaluation Metrics

The overall testing of the proposed model is performed using 1002 unseen test dataset. To assess the achievement of the proposed model, we use several evaluation metrics, namely precision, recall, accuracy, and F1-Score. For each of the 7 groups' precision, Recall, and F1-score are determined. Also, the weighted average which is a good measure for unbalanced dataset is also calculated for recall, precision and f1-score.

3.3   Experimental Results

This part narrate the assessment outcomes of the proposed method empirically and graphically on the HAM10000 dataset. As shown in Tables 2, 3 and 4, the experimental result for DenseNet, InceptionV3, and the Ensemble of the two models respectively is presented with precision, recall, and f1score on the HAM10000 dataset for seven classes. Accordingly, for individual models, namely DenseNet and InceptionV3, the Melanocytic nevi class which has the maximum number of the test sample (678 out of 1002) scores the highest precision, recall, and f1-score. For Melanocytic nevi class, DenseNet scores 95%, 96% and 95%

Table 2. Precision, recall, and F1-score for each class due to DenseNet model.

Class name	Precision	Recall	F1-score
akiec	0.94	0.57	0.71
bcc	0.92	0.79	0.85
bkl	0.73	0.83	0.78
df	0.92	0.73	0.81
nv	0.95	0.96	0.95
mel	0.93	0.93	0.93
vasc	0.71	0.71	0.71

Table 3. Precision, recall, and F1-score for each class due to Inceptionv3 model.

Class name	Precision	Recall	F1-score
akiec	0.70	0.57	0.63
bcc	0.93	0.74	0.82
bkl	0.66	0.78	0.71
df	0.83	0.67	0.74
nv	0.84	0.95	0.95
mel	0.81	0.93	0.87
vasc	0.74	0.69	0.71

and InceptionV3 scores 94%, 95% and 95% precision, recall, and f1-score respectively. The ensemble method scores the highest precision of 100% for Melanoma and Dermatofibroma, the highest recall of 96% for Melanocytic nevi, and 96% f1-score for melanoma classes. Quantitatively, Table 5 demonstrates the accuracy, weighted precision, weighted recall and weighted f1-score of our ensemble network and the two fine-tuned network for test dataset. A weighted average of precision, recall, and f1-score for DenseNet 90%, 89% and 89%; for InceptionV3 88%, 88% and 88%; and for Ensemble model 91%, 91% and 91% in the given order is recorded. We have also computed the training-validation accuracy curves for the proposed method. The training-validation accuracy curve for DenseNet and InceptionV3 models are demonstrated in Fig. 6 and Fig. 7 respectively. The graphs exhibit that there is a high increasing rate of accuracy until 25th epoch and there-after 25th epoch, the graph becomes converge in both models. Another evaluation metric that is applied in this study is to visualize the classification performance using confusion matrix which is described in terms of correctly classified and wrongly classified test samples. The proposed method performance is presented in Figs. 8, 9 and 10 for DenseNet, InceptionV3, and Ensemble models respectively on HAM10000 dataset that contain seven classes. The diagonals of a confusion matrix from top-left to bottom-right are correctly classified samples, and all other cells out of this diagonal represent wrongly classified samples.

Table 4. Precision, recall, and F1-score for each class due to Ensemble approach.

Class name	Precision	Recall	F1-score
akiec	0.87	0.71	0.78
bcc	0.98	0.86	0.92
bkl	0.74	0.86	0.80
df	1.00	0.73	0.85
nv	0.95	0.96	0.95
mel	1.00	0.93	0.96
vasc	0.77	0.75	0.76

Table 5. The evaluation metrics(%) of the proposed methods.

ModelName	WeightedPrecision	WeightedRecall	WeightedF1Score	Accuracy	Loss
DenseNet	90	89	89	89.42	53.36
InceptionV3	88	88	88	87.82	55.55
Ensemble	91	91	91	90.91	38.33

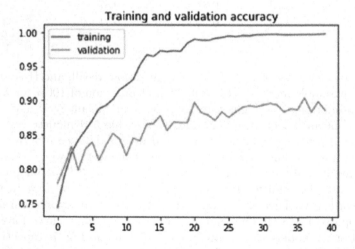

Fig. 6. The classification accuracy curve due to DenseNet model.

Finally, we have made a comparative study with the existing state-of-the-art methods that are validated on the HAM10000 dataset as shown in Table 6. The highest outcome of proposed architecture is indicated by making bold. The comparison in the table indicates that the proposed method achieves better when compared to existing algorithms.

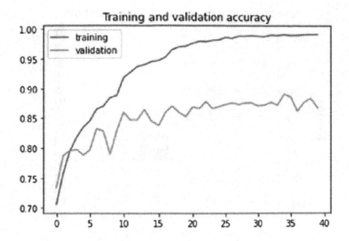

Fig. 7. The classification accuracy curve due to Inceptionv3 model.

Table 6. The Comparative analysis of the proposed method with the existing methods.

Method	Model used	Precision	Recall	F1 score	Accuracy
Khan et al. [24]	Resnet-50 and Resnet-101	90.14	89.71	-	89.9
SS Chaturvedi et al. [4]	MobileNet	89	83	83	83.15
Shahin et al. [37]	Ensemble (ResNet and InceptionV3)	86.2	79.6	-	89.9
MAR Ratul et al. [5]	InceptionV3	89	89	89	89.81
RA Pratiwi et al. [13]	VGG19	78.21	96.40	86.36	87.64
Our method (ensemble)	DenseNet and InceptionV3	91	91	91	90.91

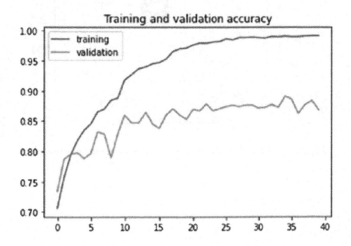

Fig. 8. The confusion matrix due to DenseNet model.

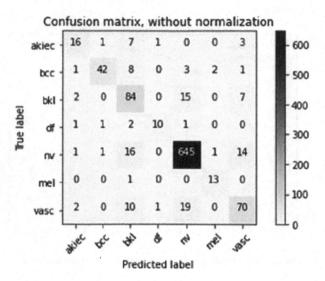

Fig. 9. The confusion matrix due to Inceptionv3 model.

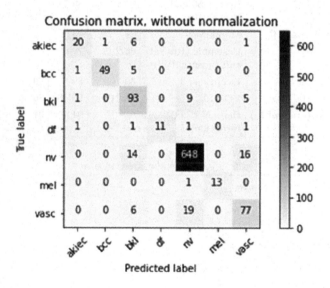

Fig. 10. The confusion matrix due to Ensemble model.

4   Discussion and Conclusions

The diagnosis and detection of skin cancer is the complex task due imbalanced number of training samples. In the previous section, we have presented the experimental results with well-known metrics numerically and graphically. It is evident from the experimental results (see Tables 2 and 3) that the DenseNet and InceptionV3 scores the highest precision, recall and f1-score with respect to Melanocytic nevi class which has large number of samples. This class has 678 samples out of which 67% is considered for the test dataset. In the Ensemble model, there is no single class that possess a good score than the other classes with respect to all the evaluation metrics as indicated in the Table 4. But, almost in all evaluation metrics for all individual classes, the ensemble model achieves a better performance than DenseNet and InceptionV3 models. By observing the classification rate of every individual class obtained from the experimental analysis, it is clear that almost all classes that have large categories have better classification rates whereas those images from small classes are highly misclassified.

In addition, as the multi-class classification report shows in Table 5, the ensemble model records a better classification accuracy when compared with the individual models in terms of accuracy, loss, and weighted average of precision, recall, and f1-score. It achieves an accuracy of 91%, loss of 38.33% and an equal score for weighted precision, recall, and f1-score of 91% for the unseen test datasets. We have observed that concatenating two or more models together by using various ensembling techniques can improve the prediction capability and generalization ability of a classification model.

The confusion matrix also gives a clear illustration by comparing the True label and Predicted label for each sample in the test set. Even if most of the images are classified correctly, due to the presence of high similarity in the inter-class and the variability due to intra-class between images in some classes in the training data makes it impossible to reach high classification capability for each class. The comparative process indicates that the proposed method achieves better performance in terms of precision, f1-score, and accuracy. In terms of recall, our model is in the second rank next to Pratiwi et al. '[13]'. But our model is much better than this model in view of precision and hence better f1-score is registered by the proposed study.

In summary, in the current work, we have employed a new ensemble method for skin lesion classification by using deep learning. In our proposed method, the fine-tuned technique is applied on DenseNet and InceptioV3 networks. These algorithms were pretrained on ImageNet dataset which is a large image dataset with 1000 different classes. For our task, we remove the last fully-connected layer of the algorithms and replace it with a new fully-connected layer that is appropriate for our classification task on the HAM10000 dataset which has 7 classes. After we train the algorithms on our dataset separately, we concatenate the results by the average ensemble technique. Experimentation is performed on the test dataset and achieved an accuracy of 89.42%, 87.82% and 91% for DenseNet, InceptionV3 and ensemble models respectively. From the experimental result, we observe that through the fusion of two methods, the model scores better performance than individual architectures. Moreover, the comparative study shows that the result of the proposed method achieves better performance in most of the parameters, when compared to the existing state-of-the-art methods. Although the proposed method has improved accuracy, it still needs improvement to tackle the overfitting problem and to increase the accuracy by using different regularization techniques.

References

1. WHO: Skin cancers WHO (2017)
2. Narayanan, D.L., Saladi, R.N., Fox, J.L.: Ultraviolet radiation and skin cancer. Int. J. Dermatol. **49**(9), 978–986 (2010)
3. Parkin, D., Mesher, D., Sasieni, P.: 13 cancers attributable to solar (ultraviolet) radiation exposure in the UK in 2010. Br. J. Cancer **105**(2), S66–S69 (2011)
4. Chaturvedi, S.S., Gupta, K., Prasad, P., et al.: Skin lesion analyser: an efficient seven-way multi-class skin cancer classification using MobileNet. arXiv preprint arXiv:190703220 (2019)
5. Ratul, A.R., Mozaffari, M.H., Lee, W.S., Parimbelli, E.: Skin lesions classification using deep learning based on dilated convolution, bioRxiv, p. 860700 (2019)
6. Gandhi, S.A., Kampp, J.: Skin cancer epidemiology, detection, and management, medical. Clinics **99**(6), 1323–1335 (2015)
7. Damsky, W., Bosenberg, M.: Melanocytic nevi and melanoma: unraveling a complex relationship. Oncogene **36**(42), 5771–5792 (2017)
8. Rogers, H.W., Weinstock, M.A., Feldman, S.R., Coldiron, B.M.: Incidence estimate of nonmelanoma skin cancer (keratinocyte carcinomas) in the US population, 2012. JAMA Dermatol. **151**(10), 1081–1086 (2015)
9. Thörn, M., Ponté, F., Bergström, R., Sparén, P., Adami, H.O.: Clinical and histopathologic predictors of survival in patients with malignant melanoma: a population-based study in Sweden. JNCI: J. Natl. Cancer Inst. **86**(10), 761–769 (1994)
10. Binder, M., Schwarz, M., Winkler, A., Steiner, A., Kaider, A., Wolff, K., et al.: Epi-luminescence microscopy: a useful tool for the diagnosis of pigmented skin lesions for formally trained dermatologists. Arch. Dermatol. **131**(3), 286–291 (1995)
11. Gachon, J., Beaulieu, P., Sei, J.F., Gouvernet, J., Claudel, J.P., Lemaitre, M., et al.: First prospective study of the recognition process of melanoma in dermatological practice. Arch. Dermatol. **141**(4), 434–438 (2005)
12. Morton, C., Mackie, R.: Clinical accuracy of the diagnosis of cutaneous malignant melanoma. Br. J. Dermatol. **138**(2), 283–287 (1998)
13. Pratiwi, R.A., Nurmaini, S., Rini, D.P.: Skin lesion classification based on convolutional neural networks. Comput. Eng. Appl. J. **8**(3), 203–216 (2019)
14. Barata, C., Ruela, M., Francisco, M., Mendonça, T., Marques, J.S.: Two systems for the detection of melanomas in dermoscopy images using texture and color features. IEEE Syst. J. **8**(3), 965–979 (2013)
15. Codella, N., Cai, J., Abedini, M., Garnavi, R., Halpern, A., Smith, J.R.: Deep learning, sparse coding, and SVM for melanoma recognition in dermoscopy images. In: Zhou, L., Wang, L., Wang, Q., Shi, Y. (eds.) MLMI 2015. LNCS, vol. 9352, pp. 118–126. Springer, Cham (2015). https://doi.org/10.1007/978-3-319-24888-2_15

16. Cicero, F.M., Oliveira, A.H.M., Botelho, G.M., da Computaçao, C.D.C.: Deep learning and convolutional neural networks in the aid of the classification of melanoma. In: Conference on Graphics, Patterns and Images, SIBGRAPI (2016)
17. Esteva, A., Kuprel, B., Novoa, R.A., Ko, J., Swetter, S.M., Blau, H.M., et al.: Dermatologist-level classification of skin cancer with deep neural networks. Nature **542**(7639), 115–118 (2017)
18. Lopez, A.R., Giro-i Nieto, X., Burdick, J., Marques, O.: Skin lesion classification from dermoscopic images using deep learning techniques. In: 2017 13th IASTED International Conference on Biomedical Engineering (BioMed), pp. 49–54. IEEE (2017)
19. Krizhevsky, A., Sutskever, I., Hinton, G.E.: ImageNet classification with deep convolutional neural networks. Adv. Neural Inf. Process. Syst. **25**, 1097–1105 (2012)
20. Codella, N.C., Nguyen, Q.B., Pankanti, S., Gutman, D.A., Helba, B., Halpern, A.C., et al.: Deep learning ensembles for melanoma recognition in dermoscopy images. IBM J. Res. Dev. **61**(4/5), 1–5 (2017)
21. Harangi, B.: Skin lesion classification with ensembles of deep convolutional neural networks. J. Biomed. Inform. **86**, 25–32 (2018)
22. Tan, T.Y., Zhang, L., Neoh, S.C., Lim, C.P.: Intelligent skin cancer detection using enhanced particle swarm optimization. Knowl.-Based Syst. **158**, 118–135 (2018)
23. Hekler, A., Utikal, J.S., Enk, A.H., Berking, C., Klode, J., Schadendorf, D., et al.: Pathologist level classification of histopathological melanoma images with deep neural networks. Eur. J. Cancer **115**, 79–83 (2019)
24. Khan, M.A., Javed, M.Y., Sharif, M., Saba, T., Rehman, A.: Multi-model deep neural network based features extraction and optimal selection approach for skin lesion classification. In: 2019 International Conference on Computer and Information Sciences (ICCIS), pp. 1–7. IEEE (2019)
25. Tschandl, P., Rosendahl, C., Kittler, H.: The HAM10000 dataset, a large collection of multisource dermatoscopic images of common pigmented skin lesions. Sci. Data **5**, 161–180 (2018)
26. LeCun, Y.: The MNIST database of handwritten digits (1998). http://yann.lecun.com/exdb/mnist/
27. Russakovsky, O., Deng, J., Su, H., Krause, J., Satheesh, S., Ma, S., et al.: ImageNet large scale visual recognition challenge. Int. J. Comput. Vis. **115**(3), 211–252 (2015)
28. Szegedy, C., Liu, W., Jia, Y., Sermanet, P., Reed, S., Anguelov, D., et al.: Going deeper with convolutions. In: Proceedings of the IEEE Conference on Computer Vision and Pattern Recognition, pp. 1–9 (2015)
29. He, K., Zhang, X., Ren, S., Sun, J.: Deep residual learning for image recognition. In: Proceedings of the IEEE Conference on Computer Vision and Pattern Recognition, pp. 770–778 (2016)
30. Huang, G., Liu, Z., Van Der Maaten, L., Weinberger, K.Q.: Densely connected convolutional networks. In: Proceedings of the IEEE Conference on Computer Vision and Pattern Recognition, pp. 4700–4708 (2017)
31. Simonyan, K., Zisserman, A.: Very deep convolutional networks for large-scale image recognition. arXiv preprint arXiv:14091556 (2014)
32. Szegedy, C., Vanhoucke, V., Ioffe, S., Shlens, J., Wojna, Z.: Rethinking the inception architecture for computer vision. In: Proceedings of the IEEE Conference on Computer Vision and Pattern Recognition, pp. 2818–2826 (2016)
33. Zhang, J., Lu, C., Li, X., Kim, H.J., Wang, J.: A full convolutional network based on DenseNet for remote sensing scene classification. Math. Biosci. Eng. **16**(5), 3345–3367 (2019)

34. Ioffe, S., Szegedy, C.: Batch normalization: accelerating deep network training by reducing internal covariate shift. arXiv preprint arXiv:150203167 (2015)
35. Chollet, F., et al.: Keras (2015)
36. Abadi, M., Agarwal, A., Barham, P., Brevdo, E., Chen, Z., Citro, C., et al.: Tensorflow: large scale machine learning on heterogeneous distributed systems. arXiv preprint arXiv:160304467 (2016)
37. Shahin, A.H., Kamal, A., Elattar, M.A.: Deep ensemble learning for skin lesion classification from dermoscopic images. In: 2018 9th Cairo International Biomedical Engineering Conference (CIBEC), pp. 150–153. IEEE (2018)

A Two-Phase Splitting Approach for the Removal of Gaussian-Impulse Noise from Hyperspectral Images

Hazique Aetesam[1]($^\boxtimes$), Suman Kumar Maji[1], and Jérôme Boulanger[2]

[1] Department of Computer Science and Engineering, Indian Institute of Technology Patna, Patna 801103, Bihar, India
{hazique.pcs16,smaji}@iitp.ac.in
[2] MRC Laboratory of Molecular Biology, Cambridge Biomedical Campus, Francis Crick Avenue, Cambridge, UK
jeromeb@mrc-lmb.cam.ac.uk

Abstract. In this paper, we design a framework for denoising hyperspectral images (HSI) using Maximum a posteriori (MAP) criterion with emphasis on Gaussian-impulse noise which is the characteristic of HSI data. We derive fidelity terms with respect to Gaussian-Laplacian distribution to collectively remove mixed Gaussian noise and sparse high intensity impulse noise. We split the degradation model into two parts to facilitate removal of residual noise encountered, while separately handling the two noise cases. Behaviour of this residual noise, often rendered as artefacts in the final results, is handled by proper tuning of hyperparameters in our objective function. Experimental results on synthetic data are conducted in the noise range of 20 dB to 5 dB for Gaussian noise and 0.5% to 20% for impulse noise. Quantitative and qualitative denoising results on synthetic and real HSI data illustrate the effectiveness of our method against the state-of-the-art techniques.

Keywords: Hyperspectral image · Image denoising · Gaussian-impulse noise · Laplacian distribution

1 Introduction

Hyperspectral Imaging (HSI) is the application of remote sensing for capturing image data beyond the visible parts of electromagnetic spectrum in order to observe reflectance from real scenes, spanning across a wide wavelength range from 400 nm to 2500 nm [17]. It facilitates visualization of areas which are not visible through conventional cameras. Its application areas range from agriculture [1], object detection, mineral exploration to military surveillance [28], pharmaceuticals [9], medicine [15], etc.; to name a few.

Noise, however, introduced during the image acquisition process deteriorates the visual quality of the acquired images and is characterized by grainy texture, horizontal and vertical stripes in the images. Noise affects the subsequent

© Springer Nature Singapore Pte Ltd. 2021
S. K. Singh et al. (Eds.): CVIP 2020, CCIS 1376, pp. 179–190, 2021.
https://doi.org/10.1007/978-981-16-1086-8_16

applications of object tracking, spectral unmixing and classification tasks from the HSI data. In HSI, noise is characterised by Gaussian noise as well as sparse noise [5]. Image denoising is a class of algorithms that are used to mitigate the effect of noise from acquired images.

One of the earliest references of HSI denoising can be seen in the work of [16] where signal dependent nature of noise in spectral domain is handled by exploiting the dissimilarity of signal along spatial and spectral dimension and working in the derivative domain using wavelet shrinkage operator. A filtering-based approach called Color Spectrum filtering is utilized based on the assumption that under a normal scenario, the spectrum is smooth [19]. Here, noisy channel is detected based on de-correlation with neighbouring channels. Also, assumption of Gaussian noise as the only source of noise [14] can have limiting performance on such methods. A Bayesian framework is adopted in [8] by modelling noise as non-identical and independently distributed Mixture of Gaussian (MoG) using Low Rank Matrix Factorization (LRMF) strategy to imitate the complex nature of HSI noise.

Total Variation (TV) based methods can be seen in many works. An optimization framework is designed using Split-Bregman as the optimization technique using 2D Total Variation (TV) along spatial dimension and 1D TV in the spectral dimension [3]. Similar work can be found in [2]. Using lexicographical ordering of data to exploit low rank behavior of clean data, Augmented Lagrange Multiplier (ALM) is used in [29] to recover clean HSI data from its noisy observation. A combination of nuclear norm, ℓ_1-norm regularization and TV regularization is adopted in a unified framework in [11]. Nuclear norm is used to exploit spectral low rank property while TV regularization is used as prior to preserve piece-wise smooth regions of the image. Similar approach is applied using spatio-spectral TV augmented with group low rank property in [13]. Using ALM as the optimization strategy in a variational framework is exploited by combinations of TV regularization, ℓ_1-norm regularization and frebonius norm.

Sparse dictionary of spectral signature in HSI data is used as prior for restoration of coloured (RGB) hyperspectral data [4]. Sparse dictionary learning is explored by establishing redundancy and correlation (RAC) along spatial dimension by global RAC and along spectral dimension by local RAC to remove noise from spatio-spectral dimensions [30]. An iterative non-local strategy is delivered in [22] using decomposition of 3rd order tensor to 4th order tensors to obtain non-local similarity along spatial direction and global similarity along spectral direction. Similarly, non-local self similarity along with low-rank approximation is focused in the works of Chang et al. [7]. In a method proposed in [23], utilizing the low-rank property of clean HSI data, noisy image is reconstructed using robust principal component analysis (RPCA). Authors in [25] effectively denoised HSI data using non-local spatial similarity and low rank constraint along spectral dimension. Similar techniques using non-local similarity and low-rank behaviour along spatial-spectral dimension is explored in works of [24]. A novel approach is devised in [10] using hypothesis testing based on Kullback-Leibler Divergence (KLD) for approximating Poisson distributed HSI data by

Gaussian distribution and vice-versa. The proposed method is tested with applications to Compact Reconnaissance Imaging Spectrometer for Mars (CRISM).

In this paper, we intend to design a MAP based variational framework for the removal of mixed Gaussian and random-valued impulse noise from HSI data. As we will discuss in the proposed section, we split the image degradation model for HSI into two parts and fit a Maximum a posteriori (MAP) estimator to the resultant model. The ensuing variational model helps in better recovery of noisy data and artefacts, as has been shown in the experimental section.

Rest of the paper is organised as follows. We discuss image degradation model faced in HSI data in Sect. 2 and set a background for our proposed technique to be discussed in Sect. 3. We have conducted extensive experiments on synthetically corrupted (Subsect. 4.1) and real HSI data (Subsect. 4.2) in Sect. 4. Finally, paper is concluded in Sect. 5.

2   HSI Degradation Model and Objective

Image formation of HSI data is generally modelled as [5]:

$$f = u + g + s \tag{1}$$

where $u \in R^{wh \times c}$ is the clean data corrupted by additive Gaussian noise g with mean 0 and variance σ_n^2 (approximated by normal distribution $g \sim \mathcal{N}(0, \sigma_n^2)$) and additive impulse/sparse noise approximated by Laplacian distribution with given location (0) and scale parameter (σ_s); denoted by $s \sim \mathcal{L}(0, \sigma_n)$. w, h and c are the width, height and number of spectral bands in the image respectively. To exploit spatio-spectral correlation among different bands of HSI data, Casorati matrix representation is employed [29] (by vectorisation of all HSI bands to obtain a 2D matrix). As a result, each band is reshaped into a vector of size $wh \times 1$ to produce a resultant 2D matrix of size $wh \times c$ obtained by concatenation of all the bands together. This helps in proper utilisation of similarity among neighbouring pixels in surrounding layers. A combination of Gaussian-impulse corrupted data is represented by observation f. Impulse noise affects limited number of pixels but affects them heavily and there is no easy way to recover impulse corrupted noisy pixels. Impulse noise can be fixed valued impulse noise (FVIN) or random-valued impulse noise (RVIN) [12]. Salt-and-pepper noise is a FVIN where pixels are randomly replaced by two extreme values $[u_{\min}, u_{\max}]$. RVIN, on the other hand, replaces pixels with any random value in the range $[u_{\min}, u_{\max}]$ and hence, is a more practical assumption [5,11,12,29] in HSI data. We have therefore made the same noise assumption for modelling our degradation scenario.

Our objective is to recover an image $\hat{u}$, from the observed noisy data f, which will be visually as close as possible to u. Following Bayesian formulation we have:

$$\hat{u} = \arg\max_u p(u|f) = \arg\max_u p(f|u) \cdot p(u) \tag{2}$$

Maximizing Eq. (2) is same as minimizing the negative log-likelihood of the function (due to monotonically increasing property of log function):

$$\hat{u} = \arg\min_u - \log p(u|f) = \arg\min_u - \log(p(f|u) + p(u)) \tag{3}$$

We derive our variational formulation by modelling the likelihood term $p(f|u)$ in accordance with the appropriate noise model and the prior term $p(u)$ with respect to the property we intend to achieve in our denoised image.

3   Proposed Denoising Framework

We propose to re-write Eq. (1) i.e., the image formation model by splitting it into two parts with the help of a new variable v such that:

$$\begin{cases} v = u + g \\ f = v + s \end{cases} \tag{4}$$

The variable v now accounts only for the Gaussian noise degradation of u and then by adding impulse noise s to Gaussian corrupted v leads us to the final composite noisy image f.

Since v is a Gaussian corrupted observation, its MAP estimator can be written as:

$$\hat{u} = \arg\min_{u} - \log\left(\frac{1}{\sqrt{2\pi\sigma_g^2}}\exp\left(-\frac{(v-u)^2}{2\sigma_g^2}\right)\right) - \log p(u) \tag{5}$$

The prior term can be modelled as Gibbs prior:

$$p(u) = e^{-\alpha R(u)}, \ \alpha > 0 \tag{6}$$

We choose the Total Variation (TV) prior because of its high quality denoising ability while preserving the high frequency details of the image [18]. We therefore choose $R(u) = |\nabla u|$, where ∇ is the gradient operator. Substituting in Eq. (5), we obtain:

$$\hat{u} = \arg\min_{u}\left(\frac{(v-u)^2}{2\sigma_g^2} + \alpha|\nabla u|\right) \tag{7}$$

which can be equivalently written as:

$$\hat{u} = \arg\min_{u} \frac{1}{2}\|v - u\|_2^2 + \|\nabla u\|_1 \tag{8}$$

Similarly f is corrupted by additive impulse noise s on v, which is already a Gaussian corrupted image. Its MAP estimator is therefore given by fitting the likelihood term with laplacian distribution [12] and is given by (using the same expression for $p(v) = |\nabla v|$):

$$\hat{v} = \arg\min_{v} - \log\left(\frac{1}{2\sigma_s}\exp\left(-\frac{|f-v|}{\sigma_s}\right)\right) - \log p(v) \tag{9a}$$

$$\hat{v} = \arg\min_{v}\left(\frac{|f-v|}{\sigma_s} + |\nabla v|\right) \tag{9b}$$

This is equivalent to minimizing the following energy functional:

$$\hat{v} = \arg \min_{v} \|f - v\|_1 + \|\nabla v\|_1 \tag{10}$$

We propose to club Eq. (8) and Eq. (10) in a successive manner, such that:

$$\begin{cases} \hat{v} = \arg \min_{v} \ \|f - v\|_1 + \lambda_1 \|\nabla v\|_1 \\ \hat{u} = \arg \min_{u} \ \frac{1}{2}\|\hat{v} - u\|_2^2 + \lambda_2 \|\nabla u\|_1 \end{cases} \tag{11}$$

It is important to mention here that ℓ_2 data fidelity term $\| \cdot \|_2^2$ penalises loss considering Gaussian distribution of noise with TV as the regularization term ($\|\nabla u\|_1$) utilizing prior information from clean data. Similarly, ℓ_1 data fidelity term $\| \cdot \|_1$ penalises loss considering laplacian distribution (impulse) of noise with TV regularization on ($\|\nabla v\|_1$). Also, from a different point of view, ℓ_1-norm fidelity term is characterized by the contrast invariant property and lack of continuous dependence on data [6]. As a result of separate TV regularization terms, we are able to remove residual Gaussian and impulse noise from our restored data while successively handling the effects of both noise sources. Minimizing Eq. (11) with respect to v and u gives us the following:

$$v_{k+1} = v_k - \alpha \left[\left(\frac{(f - v_k)}{\sqrt{(f - v_k)^2 + \delta}} \right) + \lambda_1 \ \mathrm{div} \left(\frac{\nabla v_k}{|\nabla v_k|_\gamma} \right) \right] \tag{12a}$$

$$u_{k+1} = u_k - \alpha \left[(\hat{v} - u_k) + \lambda_2 \ \mathrm{div} \left(\frac{\nabla u_k}{|\nabla u_k|_\beta} \right) \right] \tag{12b}$$

Eq. (12a) and Eq. (12b) are the solutions obtained using first order optimization technique like gradient descent to obtain the solutions for true image $\hat{u} \sim u$. u_k and v_k are the corresponding solutions obtained at iteration k. In Eq. (12a), initial data v_0 is set with noisy observation f. Optimal value of v obtained at $\hat{v}$ is free from impulse noise but it still contains residual Gaussian noise. To remove this residual noise, $\hat{v}$ is used as initial value of u to obtain optimized value of u at $\hat{u}$. δ, β and γ are very small positive constant terms introduced in order to avoid division by zero and α is the step size. λ_1 and λ_2 are the regularization hyperparameters. As discussed in the experimental section, values of hyperparameters are obtained after optimising them for the best metric result.

4   Experiments and Discussion

In this section, we conduct experiments on synthetic and real HSI datasets to test the potential applicability of our technique over state-of-the-art methods available in the literature for denoising HSI data. For quantitative evaluation, we have used the Peak Signal to Noise ratio (PSNR) and Structural Similarity (SSIM) [20] metrics. SSIM is a reliable metric used to compare the

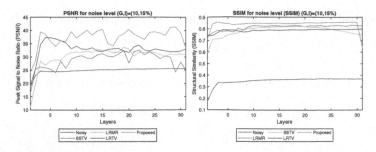

Fig. 1. Quantitative results for *Beers* dataset synthetically corrupted by Gaussian-impulse noise at level $(G, I) = (10 \text{ dB}, 15\%)$.

restoration results perceived by Human Visual System. For comparison, we use three techniques; namely: Hyperspectral Image Restoration Using Low-Rank Matrix Recovery (LRMR) [29], Reducing Mixed Noise from Hyperspectral Images- Spatio-Spectral Total Variation (SSTV) [3] and Total-Variation Regularized Low-Rank Matrix Factorization for Hyperspectral Image Restoration (LRTV) [11].

Table 1. (Mean) Peak Signal to Noise Ratio ((M)PSNR)

Images	Noise levels	Noisy	LRMR [29]	SSTV [3]	LRTV [11]	Proposed
Boat	(20, 0.5)	37.93483	45.80103	45.19565	52.44666	53.93978
	(18, 1)	37.0977	41.12151	40.97859	49.6807	50.18706
	(15, 5)	33.72437	39.51454	38.99611	42.12812	43.52601
	(12, 10)	30.57734	36.46679	34.49019	38.95098	39.05433
	(10, 15)	27.66936	31.93391	29.60225	34.39635	35.32598
	(5, 20)	20.76654	27.80054	25.07054	28.00373	30.59371
Bridge	(20, 0.5)	40.38278	46.3108	42.53173	48.3635	49.37724
	(18, 1)	38.07408	42.29087	40.27125	44.33467	45.20096
	(15, 5)	35.19445	39.92664	37.74431	41.51511	42.90052
	(12, 10)	31.57236	35.8077	33.49365	37.88711	38.60369
	(10, 15)	29.24674	33.00381	31.81953	34.54515	35.73806
	(5, 20)	22.70886	26.58061	24.63656	28.25876	29.50857
Beers	(20, 0.5)	36.76521	38.04239	41.37883	47.8976	49.47953
	(18, 1)	35.87462	37.98006	40.97298	43.7326	47.20774
	(15, 5)	33.71041	35.27898	36.18821	39.73153	42.00363
	(12, 10)	28.08486	32.33426	33.90704	35.24768	39.0979
	(10, 15)	24.86433	30.55156	31.80095	32.10115	37.30939
	(5, 20)	19.65303	25.92655	28.67122	33.89089	34.67122

4.1 Results on Synthetic Data

In this section, we replicate the real degradation scenario in HSI data. As discussed in the introduction and proposed method section, images are synthetically corrupted with Gaussian noise of specific signal to noise ratio (SNR) in dB followed by random-valued impulse noise specified in terms of percentage. These synthetic noise cases are input to our benchmark techniques as well as our proposed method.

We have obtained our images from two different sources: University of South Carolina-Signal and Image Processing Institute (USC-SIPI)[1] [21] consisting of volumes segregated according to the nature of images: textures, aerials, miscellaneous and sequences. All images are available in coloured and grayscale formats with 8 bits/pixel in three different sizes: 256 × 256, 512 × 512 and 1024 × 1024. To avoid the computational burden encountered especially in comparing techniques in terms of their execution time, we have considered images of size 256 × 256 in grayscale format. We have normalized all images in the range [0...1] to prevent bias caused when obtaining metric results.

Table 2. (Mean) Structural Similarity ((M)SSIM)

Images	Noise levels	Noisy	LRMR [29]	SSTV [3]	LRTV [11]	Proposed
Boat	(20, 0.5)	0.891291	0.988813	0.983416	0.998113	0.999761
	(18, 1)	0.7878	0.979479	0.967263	0.987904	0.994547
	(15, 5)	0.717871	0.867266	0.826562	0.88981	0.897009
	(12, 10)	0.627649	0.822675	0.803021	0.844951	0.854914
	(10, 15)	0.543288	0.753964	0.732339	0.778921	0.781214
	(5, 20)	0.295264	0.640181	0.620974	0.660521	0.675606
Bridge	(20, 0.5)	0.917747	0.96997	0.95184	0.989784	0.997745
	(18, 1)	0.834082	0.981924	0.980616	0.983476	0.984256
	(15, 5)	0.752072	0.909482	0.889814	0.926699	0.946144
	(12, 10)	0.709628	0.857968	0.842594	0.878801	0.899524
	(10, 15)	0.659368	0.795371	0.801447	0.806718	0.823504
	(5, 20)	0.556002	0.694112	0.684578	0.717476	0.732012
Beers	(20, 0.5)	0.966358	0.985767	0.978484	0.990221	0.993756
	(18, 1)	0.93884	0.955679	0.937405	0.96555	0.988339
	(15, 5)	0.787316	0.908123	0.890531	0.92555	0.943737
	(12, 10)	0.522937	0.862337	0.858968	0.880237	0.909475
	(10, 15)	0.350952	0.812621	0.806346	0.831097	0.858242
	(5, 20)	0.136451	0.652621	0.628371	0.714205	0.73973

---

[1] http://sipi.usc.edu/database/database.php.

To further study the effect of denoising along spectral dimension by different methods including ours, we have used clean multi-spectral datasets obtained over wavelength range 400 nm to 700 nm with 31 spectral bands from CAVE database[2] [27]. Images are obtained using multi-spectral CCD camera with spatial resolution of 512 × 512 pixels along spatial directions separated by wavelength of 10 nm along spectral domain in 16 bit PNG format. The entire database contains 32 images organised into 5 scene types: stuffs, skin and hair, paints, food and drinks and real and fake.

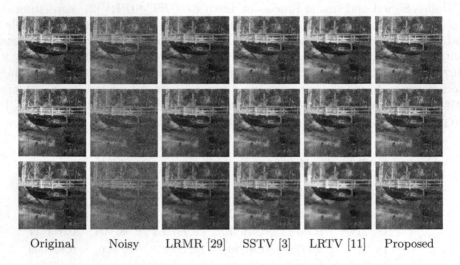

Original   Noisy   LRMR [29]   SSTV [3]   LRTV [11]   Proposed

Fig. 2. Visual results of synthetically corrupted bridge image at varying levels of Gaussian-impulse noise. **Row 1:** $(G, I) = (12\text{ dB}, 10\%)$; $(\lambda_1, \lambda_2) = (1e - 3, 1e - 4)$, **Row 2:** $(G, I) = (10\text{ dB}, 15\%)$; $(\lambda_1, \lambda_2) = (0.5e - 3, 0.5e - 3)$ and **Row 3:** $(G, I) = (5\text{ dB}, 20\%)$; $(\lambda_1, \lambda_2) = (1e - 2, 1e - 3)$

All the images used as synthetic data are corrupted by a combination of Gaussian-Impulse noise of varying levels. SNR is used to specify Gaussian noise levels of particular variance. Higher the SNR, lesser is the noise (lesser is the variance) and vice-versa. SNR is specified in decibel (dB). Impulse noise is specified in terms of percentage (%). More is the percentage of impulse noise, more is the intensity of noise. We have conducted our experiments by corrupting all data with six different levels of Gaussian-impulse noise: $(G, I) = (20\text{ dB}, 0.5\%), (18\text{ dB}, 1\%), (15\text{ dB}, 5\%), (12\text{ dB}, 10\%), (10\text{ dB}, 15\%)$ and $(5\text{ dB}, 20\%)$. Figure 1 shows the layer-wise PSNR and SSIM comparison for one noise level: $(10\text{ dB}, 15\%)$ for beers dataset (from CAVE database) for layers 1 to 31. We can clearly see that the proposed technique outperforms the competing algorithms. In Table 1 and Table 2 respectively, we provide PSNR and

---

[2] https://www.cs.columbia.edu/CAVE/databases/multispectral/.

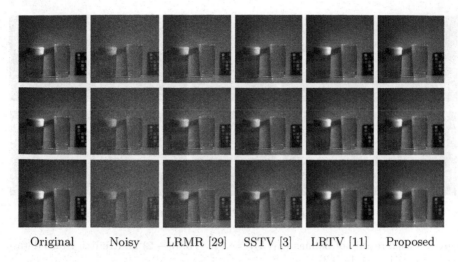

Original   Noisy   LRMR [29]   SSTV [3]   LRTV [11]   Proposed

Fig. 3. Visual results of synthetically corrupted beers [26] image at varying levels of Gaussian-impulse noise. **Row 1:** $(G, I) = (12$ dB, $10\%)$; $(\lambda_1, \lambda_2) = (0.8e - 4, 1e - 5)$, **Row 2:** $(G, I) = (10$ dB, $15\%)$; $(\lambda_1, \lambda_2) = (1.5e - 3, 1e - 3)$ and **Row 3:** $(G, I) = (5$ dB, $20\%)$; $(\lambda_1, \lambda_2) = (1e - 2, 1e - 1)$

SSIM for SIPI datasets and mean PSNR and mean SSIM for CAVE dataset multichannel *beers* image. In terms of quantitative evaluation, the proposed method gives the best metric values signifying better denoising over the others.

We present visual results for three different noise cases $((12$ dB, $10\%)$, $(10$ dB, $15\%)$ and $(5$ dB, $20\%))$ in Fig. 2 and Fig. 3 for bridge and beers datasets respectively. For *beers* dataset, we have shown results of layer 24. We can clearly observe that our proposed technique is able to remove noise of all levels from both datasets without introducing unnecessary artefacts and without loss of detailed structures in images. Although LRTV shows closer PSNR and SSIM values (over the other methods) against our proposed technique, details in bridge images are almost lost in LRTV. In addition to that, we can observe ringing artefacts for noise level $(10$ dB, $15\%)$ for *beers* dataset in LRTV.

4.2 Results on Real Data

To check the performance of the proposed technique on a practical HSI scenario, we have conducted experiments on two real HSI datasets. Both the images are obtained from Airborne Visible/Infrared Imaging Spectrometer (AVIRIS) sensor. Test site for *Indian Pines*[3] is present in north-west Indiana obtained over spatial resolution of 145 × 145 pixels with reflectance bands over range 0.4 to 2.5 μm with 200 bands. The area covered by the image is two-third agricultural

---

[3] http://lesun.weebly.com/hyperspectral-data-set.html.

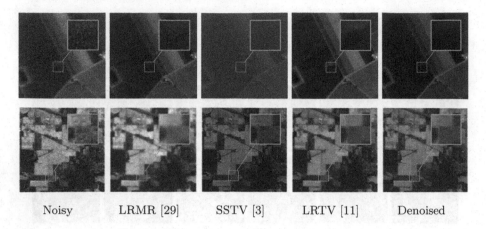

Noisy   LRMR [29]   SSTV [3]   LRTV [11]   Denoised

Fig. 4. Visual results of Salinas $(\lambda_1, \lambda_2) = (2e-3, 1e-2)$ and Indian Pines dataset $(\lambda_1, \lambda_2) = (1e-4, 1e-3)$.

and one-third forest. Our second dataset is a 224 channels image from *Salinas Valley*[4], California covering an area with 512×217 pixels in spatial dimension.

In Fig. 4, we have shown results for *Salinas* and *Indian pines* dataset for layer 3 and 111 respectively. We have chosen these layers in real data with a view of high grainy texture rendered by high levels of noise. With fairly smooth regions in *Salinas* dataset, we can see that our technique performs best among all competing methods. This becomes more evident in magnified sections of images where LRMR performs worst and SSTV develops a white cover upon restoration. On the other hand, large sections of residual artefacts can be seen in left side region of LRTV results. As far as *Indian pines* dataset is concerned, the proposed technique preserves the details while significantly removing the granular effects of noise. Details are particularly smoothed out in LRMR while noise is not properly removed in SSTV. LRTV still provides a better compromise between these two extremes.

5   Conclusion

In this paper, we have proposed a novel image denoising technique for HSI data corrupted by a mixture of Gaussian-impulse noise. We have designed our variational framework by modelling image degradation using a combination of Gaussian-Laplacian distribution. Splitting the degradation model into two parts and developing step-wise denoising framework provides necessary denoising gains with special consideration for the removal of residual artefacts. Experimental results on synthetically corrupted data and real HSI data suggest utility of our technique in real scenario. As a future work, we intend to work on learning based techniques to utilize the result of learning-based denoiser as prior into the

---

[4] http://www.ehu.eus/ccwintco/index.php/.

MAP based iterative optimization techniques. Further, exploring the low-rank behaviour of HSI data can help mitigate computational complexity incurred and lessen burden of large size in HSI data.

References

1. Adão, T., et al.: Hyperspectral imaging: a review on UAV-based sensors, data processing and applications for agriculture and forestry. Remote Sens. **9**(11), 1110 (2017)
2. Aggarwal, H.K., Majumdar, A.: Generalized synthesis and analysis prior algorithms with application to impulse denoising. In: Proceedings of the 2014 Indian Conference on Computer Vision Graphics and Image Processing, pp. 1–7 (2014)
3. Aggarwal, H.K., Majumdar, A.: Hyperspectral image denoising using spatio-spectral total variation. IEEE Geosci. Remote Sens. Lett. **13**(3), 442–446 (2016)
4. Arad, B., Ben-Shahar, O.: Sparse recovery of hyperspectral signal from natural RGB images. In: Leibe, B., Matas, J., Sebe, N., Welling, M. (eds.) ECCV 2016. LNCS, vol. 9911, pp. 19–34. Springer, Cham (2016). https://doi.org/10.1007/978-3-319-46478-7_2
5. Calatroni, L., De Los Reyes, J.C., Schonlieb, C.B.: Infimal convolution of data discrepancies for mixed noise removal. SIAM J. Imaging Sci. **10**(3), 1196–1233 (2017)
6. Chan, T.F., Esedoglu, S.: Aspects of total variation regularized l1 function approximation. SIAM J. Appl. Math. **65**(5), 1817–1837 (2005)
7. Chang, Y., Yan, L., Zhong, S.: Hyperspectral image denoising via spectral and spatial low-rank approximation. In: 2017 IEEE International Geoscience and Remote Sensing Symposium (IGARSS), pp. 4193–4196. IEEE (2017)
8. Chen, Y., Cao, X., Zhao, Q., Meng, D., Xu, Z.: Denoising hyperspectral image with non-iid noise structure. IEEE Trans. Cybern. **48**(3), 1054–1066 (2017)
9. Hamilton, S.J., Lodder, R.A.: Hyperspectral imaging technology for pharmaceutical analysis. In: Biomedical Nanotechnology Architectures and Applications, vol. 4626, pp. 136–147. International Society for Optics and Photonics (2002)
10. He, L., O'Sullivan, J.A., Politte, D.V., Powell, K.E., Arvidson, R.E.: Quantitative reconstruction and denoising method hyber for hyperspectral image data and its application to crism. IEEE J. Sel. Top. Appl. Earth Obs. Remote Sens. **12**(4), 1219–1230 (2019)
11. He, W., Zhang, H., Zhang, L., Shen, H.: Total-variation-regularized low-rank matrix factorization for hyperspectral image restoration. IEEE Trans. Geosci. Remote Sens. **54**(1), 178–188 (2015)
12. Huang, T., Dong, W., Xie, X., Shi, G., Bai, X.: Mixed noise removal via Laplacian scale mixture modeling and nonlocal low-rank approximation. IEEE Trans. Image Process. **26**(7), 3171–3186 (2017)
13. Ince, T.: Hyperspectral image denoising using group low-rank and spatial-spectral total variation. IEEE Access **7**, 52095–52109 (2019)
14. Li, A., Chen, D., Lin, K., Sun, G.: Hyperspectral image denoising with composite regularization models. J. Sens. **2016**, 1–9 (2016)
15. Lu, G., Fei, B.: Medical hyperspectral imaging: a review. J. Biomed. Opt. **19**(1), 010901 (2014)
16. Othman, H., Qian, S.E.: Noise reduction of hyperspectral imagery using hybrid spatial-spectral derivative-domain wavelet shrinkage. IEEE Trans. Geosci. Remote Sens. **44**(2), 397–408 (2006)

17. Rasti, B., Scheunders, P., Ghamisi, P., Licciardi, G., Chanussot, J.: Noise reduction in hyperspectral imagery: overview and application. Remote Sens. **10**(3), 482 (2018)
18. Rudin, L.I., Osher, S., Fatemi, E.: Nonlinear total variation based noise removal algorithms. Phys. D: Nonlinear Phenom. **60**(1–4), 259–268 (1992)
19. Toivanen, P.J., Kaarna, A., Mielikainen, J.S., Laukkanen, M.: Noise reduction methods for hyperspectral images. In: Image and Signal Processing for Remote Sensing Viii, vol. 4885, pp. 307–313. International Society for Optics and Photonics (2003)
20. Wang, Z., Bovik, A.C., Sheikh, H.R., Simoncelli, E.P.: Image quality assessment: from error visibility to structural similarity. IEEE Trans. Image Process. **13**(4), 600–612 (2004)
21. Weber, A.G.: The USC-SIPI image database version 5. USC-SIPI Rep. **315**(1) (1997)
22. Xu, F., Bai, X., Zhou, J.: Non-local similarity based tensor decomposition for hyperspectral image denoising. In: 2017 IEEE International Conference on Image Processing (ICIP), pp. 1890–1894. IEEE (2017)
23. Xu, F., Chen, Y., Peng, C., Wang, Y., Liu, X., He, G.: Denoising of hyperspectral image using low-rank matrix factorization. IEEE Geosci. Remote Sens. Lett. **14**(7), 1141–1145 (2017)
24. Xue, J., Zhao, Y., Liao, W., Chan, J.C.W.: Nonlocal low-rank regularized tensor decomposition for hyperspectral image denoising. IEEE Trans. Geosci. Remote Sens. **57**(7), 5174–5189 (2019)
25. Xue, J., Zhao, Y., Liao, W., Kong, S.G.: Joint spatial and spectral low-rank regularization for hyperspectral image denoising. IEEE Trans. Geosci. Remote Sens. **56**(4), 1940–1958 (2017)
26. Yasuma, F., Mitsunaga, T., Iso, D., Nayar, S.: Generalized assorted pixel camera: post-capture control of resolution, dynamic range and spectrum. Tech. rep. (November 2008)
27. Yasuma, F., Mitsunaga, T., Iso, D., Nayar, S.K.: Generalized assorted pixel camera: post-capture control of (2008)
28. Yuen, P.W., Richardson, M.: An introduction to hyperspectral imaging and its application for security, surveillance and target acquisition. Imaging Sci. J. **58**(5), 241–253 (2010)
29. Zhang, H., He, W., Zhang, L., Shen, H., Yuan, Q.: Hyperspectral image restoration using low-rank matrix recovery. IEEE Trans. Geosci. Remote Sens. **52**(8), 4729–4743 (2013)
30. Zhao, Y.Q., Yang, J.: Hyperspectral image denoising via sparse representation and low-rank constraint. IEEE Trans. Geosci. Remote Sens. **53**(1), 296–308 (2014)

Enhancement of Deep Learning in Image Classification Performance Using VGG16 with Swish Activation Function for Breast Cancer Detection

Debendra Muduli$^{(\boxtimes)}$, Ratnakar Dash, and Banshidhar Majhi

National Institute of Technology Rourkela, Odisha, India

Abstract. Breast cancer is one of the main reasons for death among women throughout the whole world. The mortality rate of breast cancer is controlled by early detection and diagnosis. In this paper, we proposed a CAD model based on a deep convolutional neural network that helps the radiographer with medical imaging analysis. We have applied a novel modification to the VGG16 model with a Swish activation function for mammogram classification. Firstly, we have cropped and normalized the ROI images from two publicly available mammogram databases called MIAS and DDSM. Secondly, we applied the augmentation method for avoiding the over-fitting problem. After augmentation, the resultant images are combined and train with the proposed CAD model. We have considered the five-fold cross-validation method and the best fine-tuning strategy to represent transfer learning's importance during the training. Our proposed model experimented with a publicly available dataset called DDSM and achieves better accuracy of 97.15% compared to other existing methods.

Keywords: Convolution neural network · VGG · Deep learning · Transfer learning · Computer-aided diagnosis

1 Introduction

Breast cancer is the leading cause of death among women all over the world. According to the report published by the American Cancer Society, the death rate of women is 41,760, and men are 500. In India, breast cancer is also a primary disease among women, and the mortality rate is 87,090 per year. So early detection and diagnosis is the only way to prevent breast cancer death rate. The non-invasive technique called mammogram is a famous screening test for breast cancer with different advantages like a non-radioactive and proper resolution. The mammography is useful for detecting micro classification, representing the early sign of cancer [1,2].

Until now, most of the CAD models based on different machine learning techniques provide accurate results in various real-time applications without any involvement of human [3,4]. There are numerous issues like high computational cost, data loss during transmission, better bandwidth frequency required

© Springer Nature Singapore Pte Ltd. 2021
S. K. Singh et al. (Eds.): CVIP 2020, CCIS 1376, pp. 191–199, 2021.
https://doi.org/10.1007/978-981-16-1086-8_17

for medical video transmission, robust model, and accurate detection of cancer. By solving all these issues, various methods have proposed in different applications like deep learning for brain tumor classification [5], edge-based cloud for pathological detection, and classification [6], hand-written word recognition [7]. From several CNN based experiments, we have inspired to design a deep learning-based CAD model for breast cancer classification. But deep CNN models require large datasets for training. In the case of a medical domain like breast cancer, a large dataset is not available. Experimentally, to train a CNN model, we require an ample memory space and more computational time. The CNN model suffering over-fitting problem with small amount of dataset. Various proposed CNN models [8] based on a small amount of dataset. With overcome all these above problems, the main contributions of the paper are listed below:-

a. Provide a novel modification of the VGG16 model with a Swish activation function.
b. Investigating the importance of the transfer learning technique with the best fine-tuning process.
c. Aim of the work is to provide the best fine-tuning method for the CNN model, which helps the researchers to design the CNN based classifier model.

The remainder of the paper is arranged as follows: related works described in Sect. 2, proposed methodology in Sect. 3, experimental result and discussion in Sect. 4 and conclusion with future work in Sect. 5.

2   Related Works

The deep learning-based convolutional network plays a significant role in the field of medical image processing. A deep feature based CNN model proposed by [9], where the intensity and deep features are extracted automatically and used for tumor classification. Here GLCM features are used to train the model. Touahri et al. [10] have proposed a CNN model based on LBP(local binary pattern) textural features. Rahman et al. [8] have developed a modified version of the state of deep CNN models called InceptionV3 and ResNet50. Here they have added two fully connected layers and changed the output layer. During the experiment, they have frozen the first seven layers of the InceptionV3 model and add two fully connected layer with replacing the last layer to Softmax layer for binary classification. Similarly, they have applied the same process two other CNN model called ResNet50 except for frozen first six layers. Chougrad et al. [11] have explored the importance of transfer learning and experimented with the different deep CNN models with the best fine-tuning strategy.

From the literature review, we observed that transfer learning plays a significant role in various deep learning approaches. This technique is beneficial in the medical domain, with a small amount of datasets [12]. Till now, different existing models based on a small dataset with the CNN model, and the transfer learning method not fully explored. Thus, there is a scope for further improvement in deep learning techniques by utilizing a modified state of art CNN architecture.

3   Proposed Methodology

The CNN models provide a high success rate in various medical image applications like tumor segmentation, classification, and diagnosis. These present works inspired us to build a CNN based CAD model for breast cancer classification. The proposed CAD model consists of three key stages: preprocessing of the dataset, novel modification of VGG16 with Swish activation function, fine-tuned the proposed CAD model. The proposed CNN based CAD model shown in Fig. 1. In the proposed CAD model, firstly, the ROI of each image is extracted and normalized by the global contrast normalization (GCN) technique. Secondly, different image processing methods augment the normalized image. Thirdly, the augmented images trained with the fine-tuned CAD model with the Swish activation function. Fourthly, we have tested the model with test images. Finally, the experimented result is compared with some existing works.

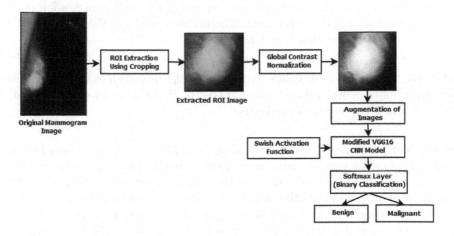

Fig. 1. Overview of proposed CNN based CAD model

3.1   Preprocessing and Augmentation of Dataset

To enhance the performance of the modified CNN model, the preprocessing of the dataset is must require. The mammogram images contain unnecessary artifact information, which provides a low-quality image. For better classification results, we need only the cancerous region except for the whole image. We have used a manual cropping process to extract the region of interest (ROI) from each image based on the information like coordinate and radius value provided by radiographer [3,4]. Here we used 479 and 502 images from two class benign and malignant in the case of DDSM [13] and 66 and 52 from MIAS [14]. To maintain common input space, we have employed a pixel normalization technique called global contrast normalization (GCN). This technique calculates each image pixel's mean value and subtracts the mean value from each pixel of an image. To aim of reducing the over-fitting of the proposed CNN model, we have augmented the small dataset, MIAS [14] and DDSM [13] with different image processing techniques like (a) rotated with angles varies from -50^0 to 50^0 with variation five steps, (b) each image flipping vertically and horizontally (c) each image gamma-corrected with ranging from 0.6 to 1.3. Here, we used five-fold cross-validation methods, each fold; the total augmented training images 21,180 to train the proposed CAD model.

3.2   Modified VGG16 Model with Swish Activation Function

The CNN model provides good image classification results with the help of activation function [12,15]. In our proposed work, we have replaced the Relu activation function with Swish [15]. We have added drop out and L2 regularization methods for avoiding the over-fitting problem. We have fine-tuned the weights of the network by frozen some layer and resuming the back-propagation on the unfrozen layer during the experiment. The architectural specification of VGG16 model and Swish activation is as follows:

VGG16. For a large scale image recognition task, Simonyan et al. [16] proposed a convolutional neural network called VGG16. It contains 13 convolutional, 5 pooling, and 3 number of dense layers.

Swish Activation. The Swish activation function [15] is a non-linear function that maintains the value of the neurons within a particular range and is fed to the next layer for further computation. It has a non-monotonicity property, which will distinguish itself from other activation functions with better performance. It has several advantages over Relu like; it generates a small negative output value for respective small negative input values due to non-monotonicity. It improves the flow of gradient. The smoothness is another property which plays an important aspect during generalization and optimization operation. This activation function optimized the model's means, convergence towards the minimum cost. Here, we have considered the learnable parameter α is 1.0. It is defined in Eq. 1.

$$Swish(x) = x \times Sigmoid(x \times \alpha) \tag{1}$$

Here, a Sigmoid function is defined by Eq. 2.

$$Sigmoid(x) = \frac{1}{1 + e^{-\alpha x}} \tag{2}$$

The function Relu is defined in Eq. 3.

$$Relu(x) = max(0, x) \tag{3}$$

Each layer of the modified VGG16 model shown in Fig.2. To train a CNN model, we required a large amount of dataset. In, medical domain large amount of dataset is not available. To overcome this problem, a machine learning technique introduced called transfer learning. In this method, the CNN model learns the background knowledge during a problem solving and reuse it for another problem-solving process. In the proposed CAD model, we have considered a state-of-art convolutional model called VGG-16, which based on transfer learning and fine-tuning.

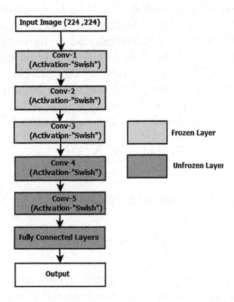

Fig. 2. Overview of proposed CNN based CAD model with Frozen and Unfrozen Layers.

4 Experimental Results and Discussion

The experiment of the proposed model conducted on a personal computer with a 2.80 GHz Xeon processor and 64 GB of RAM. The GPU card supported for this experiment is Nvidia GeForce GTX1080 Ti, which has 3584 CUDA cores. The proposed modified model simulated in python language with Keras API based on Tensor-flow backend with the Windows-10 operating system.

The original VGG16 [16] model trained with images of ImageNet with fixed size 224 × 224. To maintain the structure, we have resized our normalized augmented images to 224× 224 with Chanel 3. The rest of the layers are the same as the original VGG16 model, with little changes in the fully connected layer. We have considered 1024, 1024, and 2 neurons for three dense layers. We have applied the dropout and L2 regularization method for avoiding the over-fitting problem. In the last fully connected layer, a soft-max function is used to decide the final class label.

We have investigated different possible combinations of optimal layers for fine-tuning during the training of the proposed CAD model with the transfer learning technique. The best fine-tuning combination of the proposed CAD model by freezing the layers from Conv-1 to Conv-3 and unfrozen layers Conv-4, Conv-5 with fully connected layers, are fine-tuned weights by resuming back-propagation with a small learning rate 0.0001. During the experiment, we have recognized the number of unfrozen convolution layers exceed Conv-4, the overall accuracy of the proposed model decreased. The best optimal fine-tuning combination of layers shown in Fig. 2. During the training, deep neural network parameters are varying with their magnitude. So we have used ADAM [17] optimization technique to train them. It finds the individual learning rate for each parameter. We have set the learning rate of the ADAM optimizer is 0.0001. For minimizing over-fitting, we employed one of the regularization types called L2 regularization and dropout. The L2 regularization penalizes large weight and prefers smaller ones, and the penalty of the weight matrix W_i is defined in Eq. 4.

$$Reg(\hat{w}) = \sum_j \sum_k \hat{w}_{j,k}^2 \tag{4}$$

Then the loss function $\hat{l}$ is computed as in Eq. 5

$$\hat{l} = \frac{1}{M} \sum_{j=1}^{M} \hat{l}_j + \Theta \times Reg(\hat{w}) \tag{5}$$

Here, M is the number of samples, and θ is the hyper-parameter, which controls the regularization strength. Here we have considered $\theta = 1$ for the best result. Accordingly, we have added a drop out layer with a probability of 0.5. The proposed modified model trained with Relu and Swish activation function.

In the VGG16, at first, the recent success of Swish activation motivates us to replace the Relu activation with Swish activation. After the replacement, we trained the model with a merged dataset to learn the feature representation for the mammogram classification task. The trained model weights are saved and used to further train the model with the best fine-tuning combinations, where the frozen layers are freeze to extract the features from mammogram images. We have applied a Five-fold cross-validation method to validate the performance of our proposed model. In every fold, the DDSM [13] dataset has divided into train, validation, and test random split with ratio 60:20:20. Then the train set combined with MIAS [14] dataset to creates a merged dataset with a size 706 number of images. The same process was repeated five times. The final performance of the model is decided by averaging the values obtained from each fold. The modified VGG16 model trained with 500 epochs with batch size 128 images. The training and validation performance of the modified VGG16 model with the Swish activation function on the merged dataset is shown in Fig. 3 and 4.

During testing, we observed that the proposed model with the Swish activation function provides 97.15% accuracy as compare to Relu. The five-fold average result is shown in Table 1. The experimented result is compared with different existing works shown in Table 2. From Table 2, it is proved that our proposed model yields superior classification accuracy as compared to other existing methods.

Table 1. The five-fold average accuracy obtained when fine-tuning the modified VGG16 model with the DDSM dataset in (%).

Model name	Accuracy	Recall	Specificity	F1 Score
Modified VGG16 +Relu	96.95	97.07	96.83	96.86%
Modified VGG16 +Swish	**97.15**	**97.08**	**97.22**	**97.07%**

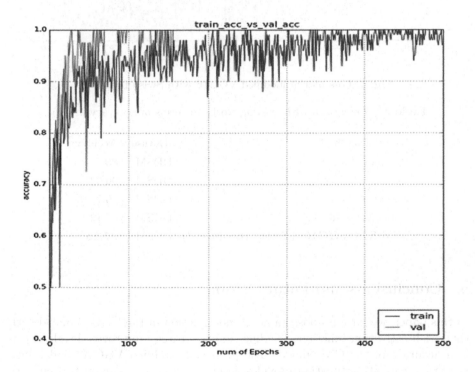

Fig. 3. Accuracy plot of modified VGG16 with Swish function

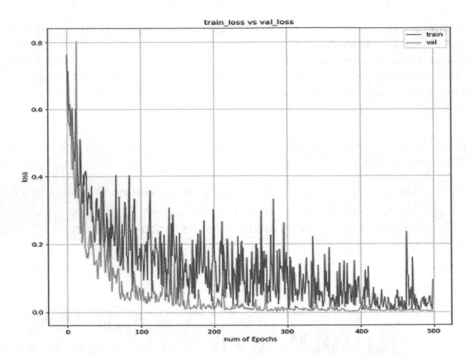

Fig. 4. Loss plot of modified VGG16 with Swish function

Table 2. Comparison with existing works in terms of accuracy in (%).

Existing methods	Dataset	Accuracy
Rahman et al. [8]	DDSM	85.7
Touahri et al. [10]	DDSM	96.32
Jiao et al. [9]	DDSM	96.7
Chougrad et al. [11]	DDSM	97.12
Modified VGG16 +Swish (proposed)	DDSM	**97.15**

5   Conclusions and Future Scope

In this paper, we have proposed a novel modification of the VGG16 model with
the Swish activation function. The fine-tuning strategy improves the classification accuracy of the CNN model. The proposed modified VGG16 model with
the Swish activation function provides good accuracy as compare to Relu. We
can experiment with the proposed method with other deep learning models and
different mammogram datasets in the future. Our proposed model is based on
binary classification; We can test the model for multi-class. Other imaging techniques can use the learning process to improve the classification accuracy of the
proposed model.

References

1. Bray, J., Ferlay, I., Soerjomataram, R.L., Siegel, L.A., Torre, A.: Jemal, Global cancer statistics 2018: globocan estimates of incidence and mortality worldwide for 36 cancers in 185 countries. CA A Cancer J. Clin. **68**(6), 394–424 (2018)
2. Society, A.C.: Breast cancer facts & figure **2017–2018** (2017)
3. Muduli, D., Dash, R., Majhi, B.: Automated breast cancer detection in digital mam- mograms: a moth flame optimization based elm approach. Biomed. Signal Process. Control **59**, 101912 (2020)
4. Beura, S., Majhi, B., Dash, R.: Mammogram classification using two dimensional discrete wavelet transform and gray-level co-occurrence matrix for detection of breast cancer. Neurocomputing **154**, 1–14 (2015)
5. Nayak, D.R., Dash, R., Majhi, B.: Automated diagnosis of multi-class brain abnor- malities using MRI images: a deep convolutional neural network based method. Pattern Recognition Letters (2020)
6. Hossain, M.S., Muhammad, G.: Emotion recognition using secure edge and cloud computing. Inf. Sci. **504**, 589–601 (2019)
7. Das, D.: H-wordnet: a holistic convolutional neural network approach for hand- written word recognition, IET Image Processing **14**(11), 1794–1805 (2020)
8. Rahman, A.S.A., Belhaouari, S.B., Bouzerdoum, A., Baali, H., Alam, T., Eldaraa, A.M.: Breast mass tumor classification using deep learning. In: 2020 IEEE Interna- tional Conference on Informatics, IoT, and Enabling Technologies (ICIoT), IEEE, 2020, pp. 271–276 (2020)
9. Jiao, Z., Gao, X., Wang, Y., Li, J.: A deep feature based framework for breast masses classification. Neurocomputing **197**, 221–231 (2016)
10. Touahri, R., AzizI, N., Hammami, N.E., Aldwairi, M., Benaida, F.: Automated breast tumor diagnosis using local binary patterns (LBP) based on deep learn- ing classification. In: 2019 International Conference on Computer and Information Sciences (ICCIS), IEEE, 2019, pp. 1–5 (2019)
11. Chougrad, H., Zouaki, H., Alheyane, O.: Deep convolutional neural networks for breast cancer screening. Comput. Methods Programs Biomed. **157**, 19–30 (2018)
12. Pan, S.J., Yang, Q.: A survey on transfer learning. IEEE Trans. Knowl. Data Eng. **22**(10), 1345–1359 (2010)
13. Heath, M., Bowyer, K., Kopans, D., Moore, R., Kegelmeyer, W.P.: The digital database for screening mammography. In: Proceedings of the 5th International Workshop on Digital Mammography, Medical Physics Publishing, 2000, pp. 212–218 (2020)
14. Suckling, P.: The mammographic image analysis society digital mammogram database, Digital Mammo, pp. 375–386 (1994)
15. Ramachandran, P., Zoph, B., Le, Q.V.: Searching for activation functions (2017). arXiv:1710.05941
16. Simonyan, K., Zisserman, A.: Very deep convolutional networks for large-scale image recognition, arXiv preprint arXiv:1409.1556 (2014)
17. Bengio, Y.: Practical recommendations for gradient-based training of deep archi- tectures. In: Montavon, G., Orr, G.B., Müller, K.-R. (eds.) Neural Networks: Tricks of the Trade. LNCS, vol. 7700, pp. 437–478. Springer, Heidelberg (2012). https://doi.org/10.1007/978-3-642-35289-8_26

Multi-stream CNN for Face Anti-spoofing Using Color Space Analysis

Purva Mhasakar[✉], Srimanta Mandal, and Suman K. Mitra

Dhirubhai Ambani Institute of Information and Communication Technology,
Gandhinagar, Gujarat, India
{201601082,srimanta_mandal,suman_mitra}@daiict.ac.in

Abstract. Face recognition systems are one of the fastest, accurate and most accessible biometric modalities. These systems are widely used in a variety of applications such as ID verification in phones, surveillance, border control and security checks in payment methods. However, these face recognition systems are prone to major security threats due to different types of spoof attacks (presentation attacks). To address this issue, we propose a multi-stream CNN based architecture for analyzing different color spaces of face images. Different color spaces help us to discriminate between real and spoof images. In order to consider local information, we consider analyzing patches instead of the entire image. We evaluate our architecture on different benchmark databases such as CASIA-FASD, MSU-USSA, and REPLAY-ATTACK to see its efficiency as compared to other approaches.

Keywords: Face anti-spoofing · Biometric authentication · Presentation attacks · Multi-stream CNN · Deep learning

1 Introduction

Biometric authentication is the most secure and convenient way for access control in a security process. These authentication systems verify the captured biometric data with the stored data. The forms of data can be fingerprints, face, iris, voice, and other physiological characteristics. Among these modalities, face plays a significant role. Especially in different security applications such as surveillance [20,29], border control [21,23], online commerce [9,15], and so on. The popularity of face biometrics has increased due to the advent of new and efficient image processing and pattern recognition techniques.

Due to its wide usage and easily accessible nature, face biometric systems possess serious threats. Spoof attacks, also known as presentation attacks are the source of major security threats faced by these face recognition systems. A spoof attack is said to occur when a person tries to impersonate some other individual, in order to gain access into the system. We discuss this in detail, with the help of Fig. 1, where we show an example of image of a real person and spoof attacks taken from the CASIA-FASD [32] dataset. In Fig. 1, image (a) represents a real person

© Springer Nature Singapore Pte Ltd. 2021
S. K. Singh et al. (Eds.): CVIP 2020, CCIS 1376, pp. 200–211, 2021.
https://doi.org/10.1007/978-981-16-1086-8_18

while the other three represent spoof attacks. Image (b) exhibits a printed photograph attack, in which the attacker is trying to impersonate some other person by holding his photograph in front of the security camera. In image (c) attacker holds a printed photograph in which the eyes region has been cut out from the photograph. Hence, the attacker uses the photograph as a mask. Image (d) exhibits a video attack in which we observe that the attacker is attempting to trick the security camera by placing a video of some other person in front of the camera.

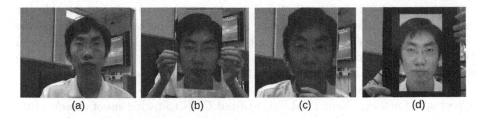

Fig. 1. Figure shows (a) real face (b) spoof attack by using printed photograph (c) spoof attack by using printed photograph with cut eyes (d) spoof attack using video from CASIA-FASD database.

In order to prevent spoof attacks, we need to build robust security system. In this paper, we propose a multi-stream CNN based approach to analyze different color spaces, and integrate complementary information to discriminate between real and spoof face images. Since different color spaces contain various aspects of color and intensity information, the combination is able to bring the differences between real and spoof images. Hence, the combined deep feature is robust to different kind of spoofing. Moreover, patch-level CNN is considered to take advantage of discriminative information that are present in local level instead of the entire image. The main contributions of this paper are:

1. We analyze different color spaces to bring out the right combination of color spaces that helps in classifying real and spoof images.
2. To focus on local discriminating information, patch level CNN are employed.

2   Related Work

With the increase in the use of face biometric systems, building a robust system is necessary. Therefore many researchers have been working on eliminating all the threats, by identifying various spoof attacks.

In the early years researchers were utilizing eye blinking and head motion to detect spoof attacks. Tan et al. [27] in their research utilised the difference between motion deformation patterns present in real 3D faces and the 2D face photos used in creating spoof attack. They used the lambertian reflectance model along with the Difference of Gaussian (DoG) to highlight these differences in the movements. Similarly, Pan et al. [18] took advantage of the fact that humans tend to blink eyes once in every 2–4 s. They used the information provided by this motion to detect face spoof attacks. Bao et al. [2] proposed an approach to detect the motion of face using an optical-flow system to detect spoof attacks (presentation attacks) caused by using prints and planar screens. But these methods were not able to work against attacks such as video replay attacks and photographs with eyes portion cut out.

Määtt et al. [17] and Chingovska et al. [5] used local binary patterns (LBP) for understanding the structure of micro-textures present in the face. Kose and Dugelay [12] suggested to utilise the differences between reflective characteristics of live faces and masks in order to identify spoof attacks. Raghavendra et al. [22] advocate the use of bands belonging to multiple spectrum to tackle the issue of print attacks. To build a face anti-spoofing method, they leverage the complementary details present in various bands. Dhamecha et al. [8] explored the domain of thermal imaging to determine spoof attacks. They also created a database consisting of thermal images for spoof attacks as well as real faces.

In the recent years, researchers have been using deep learning methods to detect spoof attacks. Yang et al. [31] utilized CNN to tackle spoof attacks. Preprocessing step involved extraction of face and its landmarks. This information was passed to the CNN for training. Further, the features obtained from the classifier were passed to an SVM classifier. Shao et al. [25] proposed to create a face anti-spoofing method to prevent 3D masks attacks by utilising the feature of facial dynamics. They train a deep convolutional network for capturing this information. Moreover in [30], Xu et al. use the information from multiple frames of a video and pass it to the LSTM-CNN architecture. Lucena et al. [16] also used deep learning based approach. They used transfer learning by adding more layers to the pre-trained VGG16 [26] architecture.

3   Proposed Approach

In this section, we discuss about the preprocessing steps and their significance followed by generation of patches and its advantages. Further we discuss about the architecture of our proposed multi-stream CNN model. With the help of Fig. 2, we illustrate a flowchart of our proposed approach. It describes various steps of our proposed approach, such as extracting useful information from the input image, performing color space analysis, patch generation and providing patches as input to CNN streams in multi-stream CNN. Each of these steps are elaborated in the following subsections.

3.1   Preprocessing

Preprocessing techniques have a crucial role in enhancing the performance of CNN based approaches. These techniques help us enhance the input features and eliminate the unwanted background features. For performing the task of face anti-spoofing, the datasets consist of videos for every subject. The videos comprise of several types of spoof attacks like print, replay and video attacks. As the first preprocessing step, we randomly extract frames from every input video. In order to remove the unnecessary background information, we perform face detection followed by cropping. For face detection we use the Haar-Cascade

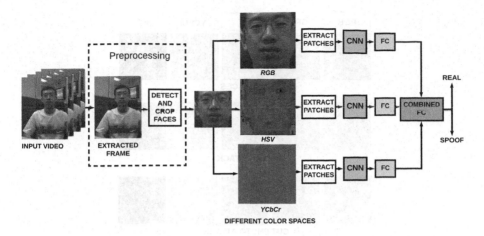

Fig. 2. Figure illustrates various steps in our proposed approach

[7] algorithm which uses a cascade of classifiers to detect the face region. After detection, face is cropped from the frame. The outputs obtained are of different sizes. The proposed multi-stream CNN network requires the input to be of fixed size, but reshaping the images to a constant size would lead to loss of information. In the subsequent subsections, we discuss how we tackle this issue with the help of patch generation.

3.2   Color Space Analysis

After preprocessing, we obtain face images from the input videos. In the next step, we highlight the differences between fake and spoof faces using color space analysis. We consider HSV, YCbCr, RGB and GRAY color spaces. We also consider High Frequency Component of images for the analysis. RGB uses the red, green and blue components to form the image. In YCbCr space, Y is the intensity component, and the Cb, Cr are the blue and red color components with respect to green. In HSV, H depicts the purity of a color, whereas S denotes the degree to which a color is diluted by white light, and V represents the intensity values. Gray scaling of images, represents the images in shades of gray depending upon the brightness levels of RGB components. The high frequency component of images (High frequency Images) are obtained by subtracting the low pass filtered gray-scale image from the original gray-scale image.   Different color spaces and the high frequency components of the real and spoof face images are shown in Fig. 3. One can observe that the gray scale face images and extracting its high frequency components does not help us to discriminate between real and spoof images. However, the color spaces like HSV and YCbCr contain more discriminative information. RGB carries correlated color information, YCbCr contains uncorrelated color and intensity information, but the representation is not practical for human interpretation. However, HSV color space is more meaningful for the same purpose. Thus, all these color spaces complement each

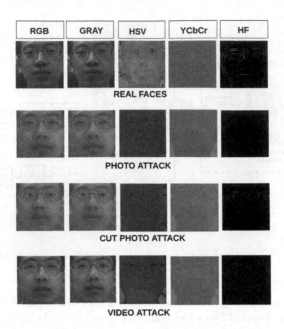

Fig. 3. Figure shows face images in different color spaces and their high frequency components.

other in different aspects. This implies that analyzing these color spaces and integrating their information will be beneficial to distinguish between real and spoof face images.

3.3　Patch Generation

After converting the input images to various color maps, our next step is to pass these images to our network. However, our model requires all the input images to be of a fixed size, but the cropped faces from the preprocessing step provides face images with different dimension. Resizing the color maps to a fixed dimension, would lead to loss of local information. Hence we extract overlapping patches of fixed size from the images. The main objective of extracting patches, and use them for input instead of images is to utilize the local information. Moreover, patch generation would help in increasing the number of samples for training.

3.4　Feature Extraction and Classification

As discussed in the above subsections, we advocate the use color space analysis to highlight the differences between real and spoof images. We observe that different color spaces contain sufficient information to discriminate between real and spoof images. Hence, a combination of these color spaces can be utilized to make our model more robust to different kind of attacks. This shall make our network architecture more efficient.

Hence, we propose to use multi-stream CNN network, which is formed by concatenation of the fully connected layers of two or more CNN network streams. The patches belonging to different color spaces (RGB, HSV, YCbCr) can be simultaneously passed to independent CNN streams in the multi-stream CNN network. Hence, for a given input image our network will learn features extracted from different color spaces and fuse this information. We make our model efficient and robust by providing it with these rich features.

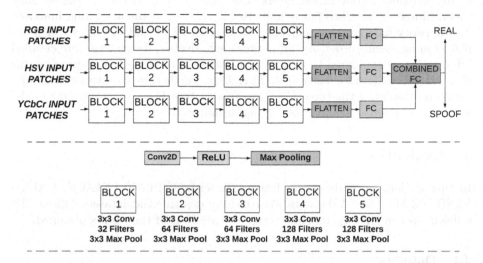

Fig. 4. Figure shows the architecture diagram of multi-stream CNN consisting of three CNN network streams

We perform various experiments to determine which combination of color spaces would give better performance when passed to the multi-stream CNN network. Since grayscale and high frequency components of face images did not provide good results, we do not consider it. For the experiments, we consider patches created from RGB, HSV and YCbCr component of images. We use the accuracy metrics to determine the suitable combination. Accuracy is the fraction of predictions our model got right. The Table 1 consists of various combinations along with their results. After these experiments we conclude that three-stream CNN with RGB, HSV and YCbCr color spaces obtains the highest accuracy.

Table 1. Analysis of Combinations of Color Spaces

Color space	Type of Multi-stream CNN	Accuracy obtained
RGB, HSV	Two-stream CNN	97.62%
HSV, YCbCr	Two-stream CNN	91.03%
RGB, YCbCr	Two-stream CNN	98.14%
RGB, HSV, YCbCr	**Three-stream CNN**	**99.86%**

The combination of images by RGB, HSV and YCbCr color spaces gives better performance. This is because these color spaces are quite effective in skin color detection, as reported by Shaik et al. [24], and the color of facial images play an important role in detecting spoofs. Therefore, we use a multi-stream CNN consisting of three CNN network streams.

As shown in Fig. 4 each CNN network stream takes in RGB, HSV and YCbCr patches respectively. With the help of Fig. 4 we explain that every block in the figure consists of convolution layers. The max pooling layers are placed after them. Moreover, rectified linear unit (ReLU) is used as the activation function. The network has convolutional filter maps with 32,64 and 128 sizes which are placed in increasing order. As our network gets deeper, it extracts more detailed information as compared to its previous layers. In order to keep capturing this detailed information we increase the filter sizes. Further, we concatenate the fully connected layers of the three CNN streams to fuse them together. Our model learns rich features and gives better performance.

4   Evaluation

In this section, we evaluate our framework with REPLAY-ATTACK, CAISA-FASD and MSU-USSA datasets. We concisely describe the datasets, followed by a discussion on the experimental setup and analysis of the results obtained.

4.1   Datasets

REPLAY-ATTACK [6]: This dataset is made of recordings of 50 subjects, who present print and video attacks. These attacks have been captured using both, hand-based devices and fixed-support devices. Additionally, the attacks have been recorded in two illumination conditions : adverse and controlled. We divide this dataset into training and testing parts.

CASIA-FASD [32]: This dataset consists of replay, print and cut-print attacks which have been captured for 50 subjects. Each subject's video is recorded in different illumination conditions as well as different resolutions. This dataset has assigned 20 subjects for training and 30 for testing.

MSU-USSA [19]: This dataset comprises of recordings captured from different mediums such as camera of tablets, mobile phones and computers. It consists of 1000 subject recordings, which are shot in different light conditions. Additionally, the dataset also consists of subject diversity.

4.2   Results and Discussion

For every database, we create a training set for the multi-stream CNN models. The training set consists of videos. From each video we extract random frames. After extraction of frames, we detect the faces using Haar Cascade algorithm and crop that region. Further, we apply color spaces on these face images followed by extraction of random patches. We performed experiments to determine optimal number of frames to be extracted from input video, the number of random patches to be extracted from a given frame and optimal patch size. We took input videos from the REPLAY-ATTACK database to perform these experiments. Table 2 summaries our experiment. From the Table 2 we observe that 20 random patches of 96 × 96 size extracted from 25 frames gives us optimal results. After

Table 2. Determining optimal parameters

No. of frames	No. of patches extracted every frame	Size of each patch	Accuracy obtained
10	20	64 × 64	97.36%
10	20	96 × 96	98.00%
10	20	150 × 150	97.50%
10	40	64 × 64	98.17%
10	40	96 × 96	99.10%
10	40	150 × 150	97.29%
25	20	64 × 64	99.24%
25	20	96 × 96	**99.86%**
25	20	150 × 150	99.20%
25	40	64 × 64	98.26%
25	40	96 × 96	98.60%
25	40	150 × 150	96.12%

extraction of patches, we pass them as input to the CNN. The patches belonging to a live face are assigned label 1, while the patches extracted from spoof attack images have label 0.

We have proposed the use of multi-stream CNN consisting of three CNN network streams. In Fig. 4 we can view the details of each layer for the three stream CNN. In every CNN stream we have used five convolutional layers. We use 32, 64, 64, 128 and 128 as the progressive sizes of every layers. Max pooling and Relu layers are inserted after each convolutional layer. We have used sigmoid as the activation function and Adam is used as the optimizer.

For measuring the performance in the field of biometrics, EER (Equal Error Rate) and HTER (Half Total Error Rate) are widely used. We have used these metrics to evaluate the results and provide comparison with other methods. EER and HTER are defined using the FAR (False Acceptance Rate) and FRR (False Rejection Rate). FAR is the rate at which the testing model, matches the biometric sample of an imposter to an actual user. While, FRR is the rate at which, biometric sample of a user is rejected, despite belonging to an actual user. The unique point, where FAR and FRR are both equal is termed as EER.

Table 3. EER (%) and HTER (%) on REPLAY-ATTACK and CASIA-FASD

Datasets:	REPLAY-ATTACK		CASIA-FASD	
Methods	EER	HTER	EER	HTER
L. Li et al. [14] (VGG)	8.40%	4.30%	5.20%	–
L. Li et al. [14] (DPCNN)	2.90%	6.10%	4.50%	–
Z. Boulkenafet et.al [4]	0.10%	2.20%	**2.10%**	–
J. Yang et al. [31]	2.14%	–	4.92%	–
Yousef Atoum et al. [1]	0.79%	**0.72%**	2.67%	**2.27%**
Z. Xu et al. [30]	0.40%	2.90%	6.20%	7.34%
Proposed	**0.07%**	2.08%	3.12%	4.12%

Table 4. EER (%) and HTER (%) on MSU-USSA

Reference	EER	HTER
de Freitas Pereira et.al. [10]	14.20%	–
Yousef Atoum et al. [1]	0.35%	0.21%
Boulkenafet et.al. [3]	3.50%	–
Gan et.al. [11]	4.8%	–
Wen et.al. [28]	5.80%	–
Haoliang Li et al. [13]	**0.0%**	7.0%
Proposed	1.12%	**0.10%**

Furthermore, the average of FAR values and FRR values is termed as HTER. The results obtained are reported in Tables 3 and 4. By analyzing them, we conclude that our proposed approaches give promising results and can help mitigate threats from face anti-spoof attacks. Additionally, we perform a cross-database experiment to measure the capability of generalization. We used CAISA-FASD and REPLAY-ATTACK to perform this cross dataset test on the testing sets. Hence, model trained on one dataset was used to perform testing for another dataset. We reported HTER values of 34% on the CASIA-FASD and 38.72% on the REPLAY-ATTACK. These values are found comparable to the other state-of-the-art methods.

5   Conclusion

Face anti-spoofing is gaining immense attention from researchers and organisations working in the domain of face based biometric systems. In this paper, we have used different color spaces to differentiate between real and spoof. The method has been developed based on multi-stream CNN architecture that helps us to build a robust and efficient model by combining features from different color spaces. In order to focus on local information, patches have been considered instead of the entire image. The proposed approach is validated with a few benchmark datasets. The results obtained are very encouraging and significantly better than many existing methods.

References

1. Atoum, Y., Liu, Y., Jourabloo, A., Liu, X.: Face anti-spoofing using patch and depth-based cnns. In: 2017 IEEE International Joint Conference on Biometrics (IJCB), pp. 319–328. IEEE (2017)
2. Bao, W., Li, H., Li, N., Jiang, W.: A liveness detection method for face recognition based on optical flow field. In: 2009 International Conference on Image Analysis and Signal Processing, pp. 233–236. IEEE (2009)
3. Boulkenafet, Z., Komulainen, J., Hadid, A.: Face antispoofing using speeded-up robust features and fisher vector encoding. IEEE Signal Process. Lett. **24**(2), 141–145 (2016)
4. Boulkenafet, Z., Komulainen, J., Li, L., Feng, X., Hadid, A.: OULU-NPU: a mobile face presentation attack database with real-world variations. In: 2017 12th IEEE International Conference on Automatic Face & Gesture Recognition (FG 2017), pp. 612–618. IEEE (2017)
5. Chingovska, I., Anjos, A., Marcel, S.: On the effectiveness of local binary patterns in face anti-spoofing. In: 2012 BIOSIG-Proceedings of the International Conference of Biometrics Special Interest Group (BIOSIG), pp. 1–7. IEEE (2012)
6. Chingovska, I., Anjos, A., Marcel, S.: On the effectiveness of local binary patterns in face anti-spoofing (2012)
7. Cuimei, L., Zhiliang, Q., Nan, J., Jianhua, W.: Human face detection algorithm via haar cascade classifier combined with three additional classifiers. In: 2017 13th IEEE International Conference on Electronic Measurement & Instruments (ICEMI), pp. 483–487. IEEE (2017)
8. Dhamecha, T.I., Nigam, A., Singh, R., Vatsa, M.: Disguise detection and face recognition in visible and thermal spectrums. In: 2013 International Conference on Biometrics (ICB), pp. 1–8. IEEE (2013)
9. Feng, W., Zhou, J., Dan, C., Peiyan, Z., Li, Z.: Research on mobile commerce payment management based on the face biometric authentication. Int. J. Mob. Commun. **15**(3), 278–305 (2017)
10. de Freitas Pereira, T., Anjos, A., De Martino, J.M., Marcel, S.: LBP - TOP based countermeasure against face spoofing attacks. In: Park, J.-I., Kim, J. (eds.) ACCV 2012. LNCS, vol. 7728, pp. 121–132. Springer, Heidelberg (2013). https://doi.org/10.1007/978-3-642-37410-4_11
11. Gan, J., Li, S., Zhai, Y., Liu, C.: 3d convolutional neural network based on face anti-spoofing. In: 2017 2nd International Conference on Multimedia and Image Processing (ICMIP), pp. 1–5. IEEE (2017)
12. Kose, N., Dugelay, J.L.: Reflectance analysis based countermeasure technique to detect face mask attacks. In: 2013 18th International Conference on Digital Signal Processing (DSP), pp. 1–6. IEEE (2013)
13. Li, H., He, P., Wang, S., Rocha, A., Jiang, X., Kot, A.C.: Learning generalized deep feature representation for face anti-spoofing. IEEE Trans. Inf. Foren. Security **13**(10), 2639–2652 (2018)

14. Li, L., Feng, X., Boulkenafet, Z., Xia, Z., Li, M., Hadid, A.: An original face anti-spoofing approach using partial convolutional neural network. In: 2016 Sixth International Conference on Image Processing Theory, Tools and Applications (IPTA), pp. 1–6. IEEE (2016)
15. Lin, W.H., Wang, P., Tsai, C.F.: Face recognition using support vector model classifier for user authentication. Electronic Commerce Res. Appl. **18**, 71–82 (2016)
16. Lucena, O., Junior, A., Moia, V., Souza, R., Valle, E., Lotufo, R.: Transfer learning using convolutional neural networks for face anti-spoofing. In: Karray, F., Campilho, A., Cheriet, F. (eds.) ICIAR 2017. LNCS, vol. 10317, pp. 27–34. Springer, Cham (2017). https://doi.org/10.1007/978-3-319-59876-5_4
17. Määttä, J., Hadid, A., Pietikäinen, M.: Face spoofing detection from single images using texture and local shape analysis. IET Biometrics **1**(1), 3–10 (2012)
18. Pan, G., Sun, L., Wu, Z., Lao, S.: Eyeblink-based anti-spoofing in face recognition from a generic webcamera. In: 2007 IEEE 11th International Conference on Computer Vision, pp. 1–8. IEEE (2007)
19. Patel, K., Han, H., Jain, A.: Secure Face Unlock: Spoof Detection on Smartphones. IEEE Trans. Inf. Forensic and Security **20**(20), 30 (2016)
20. Pham, V.H., Tran, D.P., Hoang, V.D.: Personal identification based on deep learning technique using facial images for intelligent surveillance systems. Int. J. Mach. Learn. Comput. **9**(4), 465–470 (2019)
21. Raghavendra, R., Busch, C.: Improved face recognition by combining information from multiple cameras in automatic border control system. In: 2015 12th IEEE International Conference on Advanced Video and Signal Based Surveillance (AVSS), pp. 1–6. IEEE (2015)
22. Raghavendra, R., Raja, K.B., Venkatesh, S., Busch, C.: Extended multispectral face presentation attack detection: an approach based on fusing information from individual spectral bands. In: 2017 20th International Conference on Information Fusion (Fusion), pp. 1–6. IEEE (2017)
23. del Rio, J.S., Moctezuma, D., Conde, C., de Diego, I.M., Cabello, E.: Automated border control e-gates and facial recognition systems. Computers & Security **62**, 49–72 (2016)
24. Shaik, K.B., Ganesan, P., Kalist, V., Sathish, B., Jenitha, J.M.M.: Comparative study of skin color detection and segmentation in HSV and YCBCR color space. Procedia Comput. Sci. **57**(12), 41–48 (2015)
25. Shao, R., Lan, X., Yuen, P.C.: Deep convolutional dynamic texture learning with adaptive channel-discriminability for 3d mask face anti-spoofing. In: 2017 IEEE International Joint Conference on Biometrics (IJCB), pp. 748–755. IEEE (2017)
26. Simonyan, K., Zisserman, A.: Very deep convolutional networks for large-scale image recognition. arXiv preprint arXiv:1409.1556 (2014)
27. Tan, X., Li, Y., Liu, J., Jiang, L.: Face liveness detection from a single image with sparse low rank bilinear discriminative model. In: Daniilidis, K., Maragos, P., Paragios, N. (eds.) ECCV 2010. LNCS, vol. 6316, pp. 504–517. Springer, Heidelberg (2010). https://doi.org/10.1007/978-3-642-15567-3_37
28. Wen, D., Han, H., Jain, A.K.: Face spoof detection with image distortion analysis. IEEE Trans. Inf. Forensics and Security **10**(4), 746–761 (2015)
29. Wheeler, F.W., Weiss, R.L., Tu, P.H.: Face recognition at a distance system for surveillance applications. In: 2010 Fourth IEEE International Conference on Biometrics: Theory, Applications and Systems (BTAS), pp. 1–8. IEEE (2010)
30. Xu, Z., Li, S., Deng, W.: Learning temporal features using LSTM-CNN architecture for face anti-spoofing. In: 2015 3rd IAPR Asian Conference on Pattern Recognition (ACPR), pp. 141–145. IEEE (2015)

31. Yang, J., Lei, Z., Li, S.Z.: Learn convolutional neural network for face anti-spoofing. arXiv preprint arXiv:1408.5601 (2014)

32. Zhang, Z., Yan, J., Liu, S., Lei, Z., Yi, D., Li, S.Z.: A face antispoofing database with diverse attacks. In: 2012 5th IAPR International Conference on Biometrics (ICB), pp. 26–31. IEEE (2012)

Multi-focus Fusion Using Image Matting and Geometric Mean of DCT-Variance

Manali Roy$^{(\boxtimes)}$ and Susanta Mukhopadhyay

Indian Institute of Technology (ISM), Dhanbad, India

Abstract. Optical lenses installed in most imaging devices suffer from the limited depth of field due to which objects get imaged with varying sharpness and details, thereby losing essential information. To cope with the problem, an effective multi-focus fusion technique is proposed in this paper based on a focus measure obtained from the statistical properties of an image and its DCT-bandpass filtered versions. The focus information obtained is eventually converted into a decision trimap using fundamental image processing operations. This trimap largely discriminates between the focussed and defocussed pixels and expedites the fusion process by acting as an input to a robust image matting framework to obtain a final decision map. Experimental results illustrate the superiority of the proposed approach over other competing multi-focus methods in terms of visual quality and fusion metrics.

Keywords: Multifocus fusion · DCT · Geometric mean · Focus measure · Robust image matting

1 Introduction

Multi focus image fusion happens to be a widely accepted solution to solve the defocus problem for digital images where objects at different focal depths appear to be out-of-focus. It aims to integrate several partially focused images of a similar scene captured under different focal settings to produce an all-in-focus image [5]. The homogeneously focussed fused image contains more information compared to the source images. Fusion approaches are mainly performed in these domains, i.e., a) Spatial, b) Transform, and c) Hybrid. Unlike the transform domain (which tends to introduce brightness or contrast distortion in the result), the spatial domain (pixel-based and region-based) methods exploit the spatial consistency between the pixel values for better focus analysis. The performance of conventional window-based spatial methods depends on a fixed block size, which often generates blocking artifacts on object boundaries due to block-based computation of focus measure. Moreover, the fixed block size may not produce equally good results for all the source images. Region-based methods are introduced to solve the above problem, which splits/segments the image into focussed and defocused regions. However, the accuracy of the segmentation greatly influences the final result. To achieve a perfect segmentation, optimization approaches are adopted to generate several image matting algorithms [14].

© Springer Nature Singapore Pte Ltd. 2021
S. K. Singh et al. (Eds.): CVIP 2020, CCIS 1376, pp. 212–223, 2021.
https://doi.org/10.1007/978-981-16-1086-8_19

Multi-focus fusion algorithms are being developed, employing image matting techniques to refine the focussed region maps [2,4]. In this paper, a multi-focus fusion algorithm is proposed where a matting algorithm based on color sampling is used to segment the background from the foreground. The focussed and defocussed regions are roughly obtained by using a focus measure derived from statistical properties lying within the bandpass filtered versions of an image. The primary highlights of the paper are:

- The focus measure is derived using geometric mean from bandpass filtered versions of the source image.
- The focus information is incorporated into an image matting model to obtain accurate weight decision maps.
- The algorithm performs equally well for both registered, unregistered and artificial multi-focus image pairs.

The course of the paper is organized as follows: Sect. 2.1 briefly introduces the preliminary concepts used in the proposed work. Section 3 outlines the proposed algorithm in detail. Experimental results and discussions are presented in Sect. 4. Lastly, the paper is concluded in Sect. 5.

2   Preliminaries

2.1   Image Matting in Multi-focus Fusion

For natural images, the majority of the pixels either belong to the definite foreground or definite background. However, pixels lying on the junction separating the foreground and background cannot be assigned completely to either of them. The image matting technique is used for accurate separation of the foreground from the background using the foreground opacity as a parameter. In this framework, an image $I(x,y)$ can be viewed as a linear combination of foreground $I_f(x,y)$ and background $I_b(x,y)$ as presented in Eq. 1.

$$I(x,y) = \alpha(x,y)I_f(x,y) + (1-\alpha)(x,y)I_b(x,y) \tag{1}$$

where $\alpha(x,y)$ is the foreground opacity or alpha matte and lies between [0,1]. Constraining $\alpha = 0$ or 1 reduces the matting problem into a classic problem of binary segmentation. Matting method deals with appropriate estimation of alpha values (α) for indefinite or mixed pixels (lying at the intersection). Equation 1 is clearly an under-constrained problem as it contains three unknown variables i.e., α, I_f and I_b to be determined from single input image, I. So, a user needs to provide a 3-pixel image known as 'trimap', which clearly divides the input image into three regions: definite foreground, definite background, and unknown regions. This trimap fastens the process of solving the unknown variables to obtain the alpha matte. The alpha matte obtained in Fig. 1(c) uses the trimap in Fig. 1(b) to separate the foreground from the background.

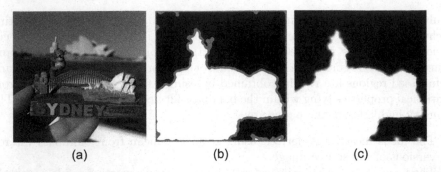

Fig. 1. (a) Source image (Focus on Foreground); (b) Trimap of (a); (c) Alpha Matte;

2.2 Variance as Focus Measure

Operators based on grayscale pixel intensity statistics such as variance, standard deviation, and other variants are widely used in extracting focus information from images [7]. Statistics based operators take advantage of meaningful patterns existing within the images. A well-focused image is expected to have high variance due to a wide-spread edge or non-edge like responses, whereas for blurry images, the value of variance is lower. Theoretically, variance effectively gives us an idea about the spread of pixel intensity values about the mean value and mathematically defined as,

$$\sigma^2 = \frac{\sum(x_i - \bar{x})^2}{n - 1} \qquad (2)$$

3 Proposed Algorithm

This section contains detailed description of the proposed scheme divided into three subsections, a) focus map generation, b) trimap formation and c) fusion based on image matting. The process flowchart is pictorially given in Fig. 3.

3.1 Generation of Focus Maps

The focus information from the source images is extracted using an efficient in-focus measure, which exploits the consistent statistical properties exhibited by the source image along with its bandpass filtered versions. It is to be noted that instead of using a single bandpass filter, a bank of filters is applied to retain the whole of data in a different format without loss of any information. To obtain the bank of filters, block-based (8 × 8) DCT is chosen due to a) excellent energy compaction properties, b) reduced computation cost, and c) good estimator of image sharpness. The 2-D block based DCT transform of an $N \times N$ block of an image, $I(x,y)$ is given by,

$$F(u,v) = \frac{2}{N}C(u)C(v)\sum_{x=0}^{N-1}\sum_{y=0}^{N-1}\cos\frac{(2x+1)u\pi}{2N}\cos\frac{(2y+1)v\pi}{2N}I(x,y) \qquad (3)$$

where $u, v = 0, 1, 2, \ldots N - 1$.

$$C(u) = \begin{cases} \frac{1}{\sqrt{2}}, & u = 0 \\ 1, & otherwise \end{cases}, \quad C(v) = \begin{cases} \frac{1}{\sqrt{2}}, & v = 0 \\ 1, & otherwise \end{cases}$$

Eq. 3 gives N^2 (i.e., 64) number of basis images (Fig. 2b). Excluding the top-left basis image (i.e., F(0,0) representing mean intensity, marked by the red cross), the rest of the $N^2 - 1$ basis images constitute the bank of bandpass filters (bf_m where $m = 1 \ldots N^2 - 1$, marked by green square) which retains frequencies lying within the desired range. A set of bandpass filtered images, I_m where $m = 1 \ldots N^2 - 1$ is obtained after filtering the source image with each of the filters, thereby producing 63 feature images in total (Fig. 2c,d,e). As stated earlier, defocus regions have smaller values of variance (σ^2), but for a blurry patch with a complex pattern, a large value of variance causes it to be falsely marked as focussed. To avoid such outliers, variance calculated using Eq. 3 for all the feature images are combined using geometric mean. Theoretically, the geometric mean is not affected by data fluctuations, gives more weight to smaller values, and is easy to compute. Mathematically, the geometric mean of variances is defined as follows,

$$g(x) = \sqrt[n]{\prod_{n=1}^{N^2-1} \sigma_n^2(x)} \tag{4}$$

Now, for a pair of source images (say I_i and I_j), the corresponding focus maps (fm_i and fm_j) are obtained by carrying out simple difference operation between their geometric variance maps as given below,

$$fm_i = g_i(x) - g_j(x), \quad fm_j = g_j(x) - g_i(x) \tag{5}$$

where $g_i(x)$ and $g_j(x)$ are the variance maps obtained from Eq. 4 for i^{th} and j^{th} source image respectively.

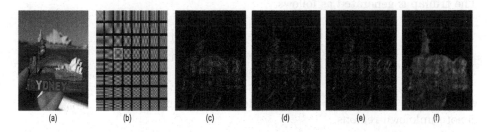

(a)   (b)   (c)   (d)   (e)   (f)

Fig. 2. (a) Source image (Focus on Foreground); (b) DCT basis functions; (c),(d),(e) Filtered versions of (a) using (b) (Contrast-corrected for better visualization in the manuscript); (f) Focus Map (f_i)

3.2   Trimap Generation

After obtaining the focus information using Eq. 5, this section outlines the steps involved in trimap generation. The individual focus maps are binarized in two stages, a) the first stage of binarization involves comparing each pixel value with the global maximum intensity value using Eq. 6 and b) the second stage of binarization is performed using a threshold parameter T to obtain the definite focussed pixels as expressed in Eq. 7.

$$f_b^1 = \begin{cases} 1, & fm > \max\{fm\} \\ 0, & otherwise \end{cases} \quad (6) \qquad f_b^2 = \begin{cases} 1, & fm - \max\{fm\} > T \\ 0, & otherwise \end{cases} \quad (7)$$

Equation 6 gives a coarse yet believable focussed binary region which requires further iterations of processing to remove isolated pixels, small holes generated within the focussed region and fragments of regions caused due to image noise. Therefore, further processing of the binary map obtained at Eq. 6 is carried out by a hole filling operation which fills up existing holes within the definite region followed by application of window based median filter to remove isolated pixels and fragmented regions. The next stage of processing involves iterative skeletonization followed by a final median filtering to effectively remove the scattered pieces. So, mathematically the entire processing equation can be presented as,

$$(f_b^1)' = Med[Skel\{Med(f_b^1, w), i\}] \tag{8}$$

where w and i refers to the sliding window used for median filter and iterations of skeletonization respectively. From Eq. 7 and Eq. 8, the definite focussed region of a source image can be defined as,

$$f_d(x, y) = \begin{cases} 1, & (f_b^1)' = 1 \text{ or } f_b^2 = 1 \\ 0, & otherwise \end{cases} \tag{9}$$

The trimap is generated as follows,

$$t_{map} = \begin{cases} 1, & \text{if } f_d = 1 \text{ and } max\{f_d\} = 0 \\ 0, & \text{if } f_d = 0 \text{ and } max\{f_d\} = 1 \\ 0.5 & otherwise \end{cases} \tag{10}$$

where $t_{map} = 0$ or $t_{map} = 1$ signifies definite focus or defocus and $t_{map} = 0.5$ denote unknown regions.

3.3   Fusion Using Matting

The final step of the proposed work is to generate the alpha matte(α) for the source images using the trimap generated in the previous section. To obtain appropriate alpha values for indefinite pixels, a matting based approach based on color sampling is adopted [13]. The matting algorithm estimates the initial value of alpha for unknown pixels using 'good' sample pairs of foreground and background pixels from the neighborhood. The good samples can express the color of the unknown pixel as a convex combination of themselves. To select the 'best' sample pair from the probable candidates, a 'distance ratio' is defined, which associates each pair with a confidence value. The initial matte is further refined by minimizing the following energy function by solving a graph labeling problem as a random walk.

$$E = \sum_{z \in I} [\hat{f}_z(\alpha_z - \hat{\alpha_z})^2 + (1 - \hat{f}_z)(\alpha_z - \delta(\hat{\alpha_z} > 0.5))^2] + \lambda \cdot J(\alpha, a, b) \qquad (11)$$

Here $\hat{\alpha_z}$ and $\hat{f}_z$ are the initial alpha and confidence value estimated at the sampling step respectively, δ stands for boolean function and $J(\alpha, a, b)$ denotes the additional neighbourhood energy term around 3×3 pixels for further improvement. Minimizing the energy term, $J(\alpha, a, b)$ means finding suitable values for constants α, a and b for which the energy term is optimized.

Now, let α_f be the final alpha matte obtained after solving Eq. 11, the fused image can be represented as linear combination of the source images with respect to the alpha matte (α_f).

$$I_f = \alpha_f I_i(x, y) + (1 - \alpha_f) I_j(x, y) \qquad (12)$$

4   Experimental Results and Discussion

This section discusses and compares the experimental performance of the proposed approach in terms of objective and subjective evaluation with other fusion approaches.

4.1   Experimental Setup

Table 1. Experimental Parameters

Name	Value
Median filter (Window size, w)	8×8
Skeletonization (Iterations, i)	5
Binarization (Threshold, T)	128

The experimental setup adopted for testing the proposed approach includes datasets, execution environment, fusion metrics and methods for visual comparison. The algorithm is tested using two multi-focus datasets, a) Lytro Dataset

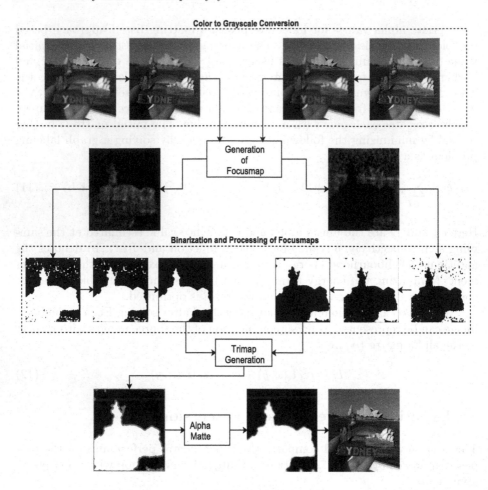

Fig. 3. Process flowchart for the proposed approach

[8] consisting of registered multifocus pairs and b) Pxleyes Dataset [1] containing unregistered multi-focus image pairs submitted as a part of photography contest. The experiments are performed over MATLAB R2015a, installed over 64-bit windows platform having Intel 2.30 GHz Core i5 CPU and 4GB RAM. The algorithm has been quantitatively compared with four equivalent fusion methods, GD [9], DWT-AB [6], MWGF [17] and GCF [12] using the following fusion metrics, mutual information (MI_{AB}^{F}) [11], Piella's metric (Q_o) [10], feature mutual information (FMI) [3], Xydeas's metric (Q_{AB}^{F}) [15] and Zhao's metric (P'_{blind}) [16]. The parameters used for the experiment and average value for individual metrics for both the datasets are presented in Table 1 and Table 2 respectively.

4.2 Subjective Evaluation

A good fusion algorithm should not introduce or enhance extra features, artifacts, or inconsistencies in the fused result. In this section, the visual quality of the results from the proposed method is compared with other standard fusion algorithms to study their relative performances. Figure 4 and Fig. 5 presents the results for registered source pairs from the Lytro dataset, whereas Fig. 6 and Fig. 7 portrays the same using unregistered source pairs from the Pxleyes dataset. For both the datasets, GD based method produces fusion results with increased contrast and brightness (as marked by red boxes in Fig. 4c and Fig. 5c). Besides, it also blurs out the foreground (Fig. 6c) and creates visible shadows around light (dark) color objects against a darker (lighter) background. This distortion can be attributed to the poor wavelet-based reconstruction of fused coefficients in the gradient domain. Similarly, results from the DWT-AB method suffer from color distortion, as evident from random color spots scattered over the fused result (green-blue spots in Fig. 6d-red box and Fig. 7d-black box). GCF method extracts the salient regions using a gaussian curvature filter followed by a focus criterion that combines spatial frequency and local variance. The performance of the method is illustrated in Fig. 4e, 5e (red box) where the fused result has picked up pixels from the source image with defocussed foreground. For unregistered source pair (Fig. 6e-red box and Fig. 7e-black box), staircase/block effect can be observed along the boundary of the objects. For MWGF based method, the fusion performance for registered source pair is visually appealing without visible distortions (Fig. 4f, 5f, 7f), yet for some unregistered pair, it creates a blurred effect along the border (Fig. 6). Results from the proposed method (Fig. 4h, 5h, 6h, 5h) are best in terms of visual quality with no pixel/color distortion, maximum preservation of source image information. The superiority of the approach is further validated by the highest value of fusion metric obtained for individual datasets, as listed in Table 2.

Table 2. Average objective evaluation on multifocus image sets

Images	Metrics	GD [9]	DWT-AB [6]	MWGF [17]	GCF [12]	Proposed
				Methods		
Lytro (512 × 512)	MI_{AB}^F	0.5322	1.0773	1.1872	1.1115	**1.2118**
	Q_o	0.8981	0.9401	0.9305	0.9399	**0.9435**
	FMI	0.8938	0.9050	0.9059	**0.9062**	0.9061
	Q_{AB}^F	0.7079	0.7230	0.7245	0.7309	**0.7340**
	P_{blind}'	0.7640	0.8290	0.7749	0.8441	**0.8513**
Pxyeles	MI_{AB}^F	0.3747	0.6325	0.8303	0.8929	**0.9579**
	Q_o	0.7910	0.8643	0.8586	0.8701	**0.8839**
	FMI	0.8812	0.8927	0.8897	0.9026	**0.9028**
	Q_{AB}^F	0.5911	0.6128	0.6808	0.7024	**0.7027**
	P_{blind}'	0.5191	0.5731	0.5629	0.7222	**0.7281**

Fig. 4. Registered source image and fusion results: (a) Focus on the foreground; (b) Focus on background; (c) GD based result; (d) DWT-AB result; (e) GCF based result; (f) MWGF based result; (g) Generated Alpha Matte; (h) Result using proposed method

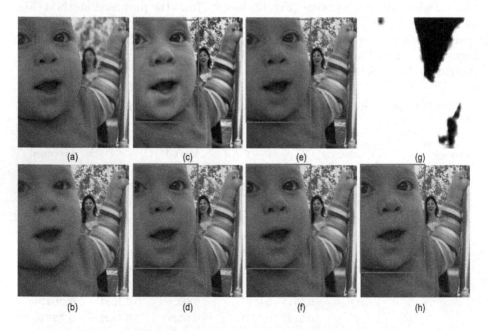

Fig. 5. Registered source image and fusion results: Same order as in Fig. 4

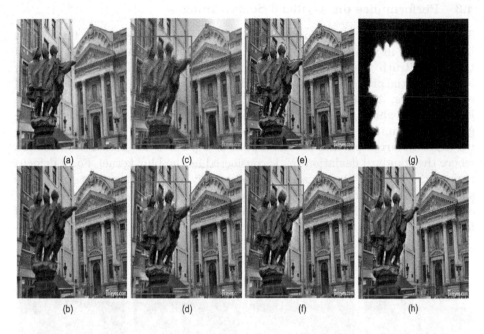

Fig. 6. Unregistered source image and fusion results: Same order as in Fig. 4

Fig. 7. Unregistered source image and fusion results: Same order as in Fig 4

4.3   Performance on Artificial Source Images

The performance of the algorithm for artificial multi-focus source images has been studied in this section. In case of artificial source images, availability of the groundtruth all-in-focus image helps us to compare the quality of fusion achieved by the proposed algorithm. Figure 8 presents the results for two artificial source images. Additionally, a reference based image quality metric, i.e., SSIM is calculated which gives us a reasonably higher accuracy with repsect to the ground truth image. Irrespective of the source images being real or artifical, the defocussed blurred patches around a pixel is expressed as gaussian convolution where the standard deviation (σ) is considered as the blur kernel. For a defocus region, the value of the square of standard deviation, i.e., variance will have smaller values in comparison to a focussed region. It uses statistical averaging on the variances of DCT filtered bandpass responses to measure the degree of focus.

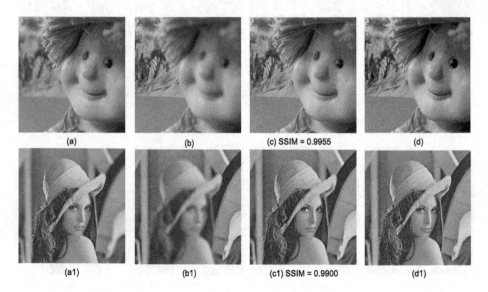

Fig. 8. Performance on artificial images: (a),(a1) Focus on Foreground; (b),(b1) Focus on Background; (c),(c1) Fused by the proposed algorithm; (d),(d1) Groundtruth image

5   Conclusion

This paper proposes a multi-focus fusion algorithm that exploits first-order statistics to extract the salient regions from a partially focused image. The source images are subjected to a bank of bandpass filters to obtain multiple filtered versions, which is statistically combined using the geometric mean of variance. The focus map is gradually converted into a 3-pixel trimap, which acts as an input to an image matting model to achieve perfect fusion results. The qualitative and quantitative efficacy of the proposed method is confirmed by performing experiments using suitable multi-focus datasets and fusion metrics.

References

1. www.pxleyes.com
2. Chen, Y., Guan, J., Cham, W.K.: Robust multi-focus image fusion using edge model and multi-matting. IEEE Trans. Image Process. **27**(3), 1526–1541 (2017)
3. Haghighat, M.B.A., Aghagolzadeh, A., Seyedarabi, H.: A non-reference image fusion metric based on mutual information of image features. Comput. Electric. Eng. **37**(5), 744–756 (2011)
4. Li, S., Kang, X., Hu, J., Yang, B.: Image matting for fusion of multi-focus images in dynamic scenes. Inf. Fusion **14**(2), 147–162 (2013)
5. Liu, Y., Wang, L., Cheng, J., Li, C., Chen, X.: Multi-focus image fusion: a survey of the state of the art. Information Fusion (2020)
6. Liu, Y., Wang, Z.: Multi-focus image fusion based on wavelet transform and adaptive block. J. Image Graph. **18**(11), 1435–1444 (2013)
7. Maruthi, R., Sankarasubramanian, K.: Multi focus image fusion technique in spatial domain using an image variance as a focus measure. i-Manager's J. Fut. Eng. Technol. **5**(3), 24 (2010)
8. Nejati, M., Samavi, S., Shirani, S.: Multi-focus image fusion using dictionary-based sparse representation. Inf. Fus. **25**, 72–84 (2015)
9. Paul, S., Sevcenco, I.S., Agathoklis, P.: Multi-exposure and multi-focus image fusion in gradient domain. J. Circ. Syst. Comput. **25**(10), 1650123 (2016)
10. Piella, G., Heijmans, H.: A new quality metric for image fusion. In: Proceedings 2003 International Conference on Image Processing (Cat. No. 03CH37429). vol. 3, pp. III-173. IEEE (2003)
11. Qu, G., Zhang, D., Yan, P.: Information measure for performance of image fusion. Electronics lett. **38**(7), 313–315 (2002)
12. Tan, W., Zhou, H., Rong, S., Qian, K., Yu, Y.: Fusion of multi-focus images via a gaussian curvature filter and synthetic focusing degree criterion. Appl. Optics **57**(35), 10092–10101 (2018)
13. Wang, J., Cohen, M.F.: Optimized color sampling for robust matting. In: 2007 IEEE Conference on Computer Vision and Pattern Recognition, pp. 1–8. IEEE (2007)
14. Wang, J., Cohen, M.F.: Image and video matting: a survey. Now Publishers Inc. (2008)
15. Xydeas, C., Petrovic, V.: Objective image fusion performance measure. Electronics Lett. **36**(4), 308–309 (2000)
16. Zhao, J., Laganiere, R., Liu, Z.: Performance assessment of combinative pixel-level image fusion based on an absolute feature measurement. Int. J. Innov. Comput. Inf. Control **3**(6), 1433–1447 (2007)
17. Zhou, Z., Li, S., Wang, B.: Multi-scale weighted gradient-based fusion for multi-focus images. Inf. Fusion **20**, 60–72 (2014)

Deep Learning Based Lens for Mitigating Hospital Acquired Infections

Pratibha Gawali[1], Ritika Latke[2], Prashant Bartakke[1], and Anant Shinde[3(✉)]

[1] Department of Electronics and Telecommunication Engineering,
College of Engineering, 411005 Pune, India
ppb.extc@coep.ac.in
[2] Baystate Wing Hospital, Palmer 01069, MA, USA
[3] Department of Biomedical Engineering, University of Massachusetts,
Amherst 01003, MA, USA
Anantshinde@umass.edu

Abstract. The WHO has recommended 'frequent hand washing' as means to curtail the spread of 'Public Health Emergencies of International Concern.' Improvement in the seven step hand wash compliance rate has been shown to reduce the spread of hospital acquired infections. Most of the hand hygiene compliance identification systems developed over the years have restricted their focus on tracking the movement of healthcare workers to and from the hand wash station. However, these systems have failed to detect if the seven step hand wash were performed or not. We proposed and implemented a computer vision and artificial intelligence based system to detect seven steps of the hand wash process. We used the Visual Geometry Group-16 (VGG-16) network combined with the Long Short Term Memory (LSTM) module as a classification system. We developed the hand wash database of 3000 videos to train and optimize the parameters of the VGG16-LSTM model. The optimized model detects different steps of handwash with high accuracy and near real time detection ability. This system will prove to be useful for improving hand wash compliance rate and to curb the spread of infectious diseases.

Keywords: Hand wash process · Computer vision · Hand hygiene compliance · VGG16 · LSTM

1 Introduction

In the last 12 years, WHO has declared 'Public Health Emergencies of International Concern (PHEIC)' on five occasions. Four out of these five diseases including 'COVID-19 pandemic' were infectious disease spreading with human to human contact. WHO has reported that 'hand hygiene is the most effective way to prevent the spread of COVID-19.' Absence, inadequate, and/or insufficient access to the clean water, the crunch of time for the health care staff, and lack of awareness of the importance pertaining to the hand wash practices have

S. K. Singh et al. (Eds.): CVIP 2020, CCIS 1376, pp. 224–235, 2021.
https://doi.org/10.1007/978-981-16-1086-8_20

caused some significant concerns in maintaining the appropriate hand-hygiene. Consequently, deficiency of hand-hygiene has aided the spread of various infectious diseases. We may observe poor hand sanitization practices in various settings across the globe. Hospital-Acquired Infections (HAIs) is one example of such settings where inappropriate hand-hygiene practice in the hospital environment may lead to severe infections from patients to the health care staff or vice-versa. Therefore, learning an appropriate hand-wash method and being compliant to hand-hygiene standards are two crucial steps to prevent the spread of the pathogens which lead to HAIs. Low hand-hygiene compliance is directly correlated to higher HAIs and may cause increased HAIs related casualties. In the USA many health-related systems record a low hand hygiene compliance rate which causes higher HAIs [5]. The prevalence rate of infection acquired in Intensive Care Units (ICUs) vary from 9.1% to 50% in the USA [2,10,16]. The World Health Organization (WHO) and the Centers for Disease Control and Prevention (CDC) have recommended all the health care workers (HCWs) to take enough time to engage in the Hand Wash Process (HWP) [6]. Despite these recommendations, healthcare workers' hand wash compliance rates are low reflecting in HAIs numbers.

These high HAIs numbers suggest the need for preventive measures such as monitoring HWP. There are two ways of monitoring HWP; one way is the direct observation process and the second way is the indirect observation process. The direct observation process consists of visual observation and the indirect observation includes observation using electronic devices. In the direct observation method, individuals who record the data may have raters' bias which can lead to incorrect data collection [7]. This shows the need to use the indirect observation method which is free from subjective data errors. The indirect observation method avoids rater bias and innate human errors, therefore making it a more objective data collection method to measure the hand wash compliance.

There are many Indirect Observation Methods that have been implemented using different technologies such as Electronic monitoring system [5,8,18], Radio Frequency Identification (RFID) System [3,4], Sensors [17], Bluetooth Based [11], Zigbee Based, and Ultrasonic Systems [14]. Above mentioned electronic monitoring techniques merely provide feedback alerting HCWs if they miss performing necessary hand wash. The RFID and other tracking based systems are helpful in identifying locations of HCWs and their visits to hand wash stations [11,15]. None of these methods check if the hand wash is completed by following all seven steps recommended by WHO guidelines [12]. A system should be implemented to check if all the suggested steps of the hand wash process are followed.

Lacey and colleagues have developed a camera and processor based system to check the HWP [13]. In this system, the camera is used for capturing and processor is used for data transfer as well as detection. Their system detects hand motion and classifies motion patterns using the Support Vector Machine algorithm. Although this is the only reported testing system to identify steps of hand wash they failed to report important performance parameters such as training and testing accuracies.

In this article, we proposed and developed a hand wash detection system using deep learning architecture. In this system, a mobile camera system is used to supervise the movement of the HWP and deep learning architecture is used to classify seven steps of HWP. We developed a database of 3000 videos where each video represents one of the seven steps. Training, validation, and testing accuracies for proposed deep learning architecture are reported.

2   Methodology

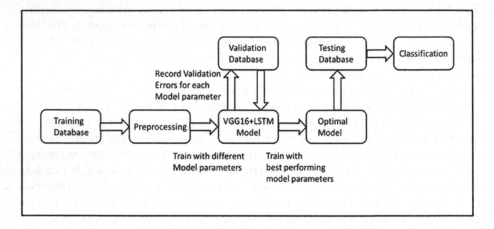

Fig. 1. A flowchart for the proposed hand wash detection system.

A methodology for the proposed hand wash detection system is described in four sections namely database creation, preprocessing of data, train deep learning architecture using database videos, and classification and identification of hand wash steps (see Fig. 1).

2.1   Database Creation

Since there is no standard image or video HWP database available we created a video database at the Centre of Excellence in Signal and Image Processing, College of engineering, Pune. We used a tripod- camera setup with a white background. We used a camera (Micromax Selfie E460 smartphone, Micromax Smartphone manufacturer, Gurugram, Haryana, India) with 16MP resolution and a framerate of 30 frames per second. The camera was placed at a height of 50 cm from the plane white surface. We recorded HWP performed by 130(80 male, 50 female) volunteers using alcohol-based hand rub (Dettol hand sanitizer,

Reckitt Benckiser pty Ltd., Elandsfontein 1406, South Africa). Volunteers performed the WHO recommended seven step HWP at 20 cm distance from the camera device (see Fig. 2). Each video represents a single data point in the database. All volunteers gave verbal consent to participate in the research.

We partitioned the database into three parts- training, validation, and testing. Videos recorded from different groups of volunteers were used for three parts of the database. Each video is a 20 s duration and has recorded one of the seven steps of HWP. We extracted frames from each video at 30 frames per second which are fed as input to deep learning model.

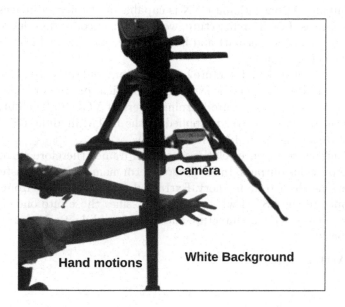

Fig. 2. Database creation laboratory setup.

2.2 Pre-processing Dataset

We applied image processing techniques on input data such as resizing frames, normalization, and segmentation. Random rotation and horizontal flips of images were performed which adds variation to the database. An increase in database variation helped the extraction of more features improving the robustness of the training algorithm in the process. Following preprocessing, steps were performed to prepare images for VGG16-LSTM architecture.

1. Convert the given image into an array format.
2. Input images captured by the camera vary in size, therefore before it is applied to the convolutional neural network (CNN) it needs to be resized to 224 × 224 × 3. (requirement of VGG16)

3. Segmentation is used to separate HWP from the background.
4. Images are rotated in a plane at random degrees of rotation between 0 to 180°.

Once the preprocessing of the database is completed it is ready to be fed into the VGG16- LSTM architecture.

2.3   Training of Dataset Using VGG16 - LSTM Architecture

Sequence of frames or video classification is not possible by the image classification technique. A conventional CNN is capable of classifying images but does not classify videos. In our architecture, we used the encoder-decoder model with VGG16 network as encoder part and LSTM as decoder part which is more suitable for video classification.

The VGG16 network architecture has three types of layers: first is input data, second is feature learning and the last one is classification. In our experiment, we used only input data and feature learning layers of VGG16. The output of the VGG16's feature learning layer is applied to the LSTM module. LSTM module is a type of Recurrent Neural Network (RNN).

RNN contains recurrence relations between frames therefore current output depends on previous outputs. In RNN short term memory is used instead of that LSTM uses long short term memory. Extracted feature sequence from VGG16 is given as input to the LSTM which further classifies those into one of the seven HWP steps. The VGG16 architecture and LSTM module used in our system are described below.

VGG16 Architecture

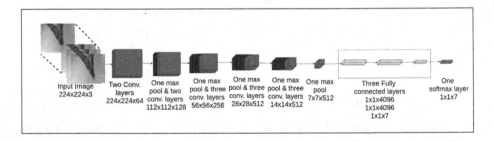

Fig. 3. VGG16 network architecture.

VGG16 network architecture consists of a convolution layer followed by the pooling layer at every stage with 16 layers in total (see Fig. 3). A convolutional layer has filters of size 3×3 and stride of 1×1 while filters of size 2×2 and stride of 2×2 are used for the pooling layer. Input images applied to the network are of fixed size $224 \times 224 \times 3$. Different layers of VGG16 network are described below.

1. Convolutional Layer - The first two layers (CONV64 × 2) have a number of filters so that at the end, the volume becomes 224 × 224 × 64 also known as feature maps. The convolution layer is used for extracting features from the input images. Every convolution layer is followed by a nonlinear function namely ReLU improving discrimination power of the network. These layers extract low level features namely edges, texture at the early stages while high level features namely parts, shapes towards later stages. These high level features might be effective for Hand wash steps detection.

2. Max Pooling Layer/Average pooling Layer - This layer is used for reducing the size of feature maps. This layer obviously has no parameters and is responsible for reducing the height and width by half thus resulting in a volume of 112 × 112 × 64. Max/Average from the 2 × 2 grid is found and passed on to the next layer. Max/Average pooling layer retains variability of output generated at the layer.

3. Dropout Layer - This layer ensures avoiding overfitting of the model during the training period. The dropout probability has been set in the range of 0.3 to 0.5.

4. Fully Connected Layer - This layer follows a bunch of the convolutional and pooling layers as shown in Fig. 3. In this layer, all the neurons are connected to each other. Here we flatten the output of the final pooling layer to form a feature vector and apply it to three fully connected layers with 4096 nodes.

5. Softmax layer - The final layer of the VGG16 network architecture is a softmax layer with seven output nodes. This layer assigns a probability value to the feature vector output of the fully connected layer which is interpreted as belonging to a certain class. Thus, the classification could be done on the basis of these probabilities. As mentioned earlier, the proposed system uses the LSTM module for classification hence we do not use the softmax layer of VGG16 network.

Recurrent Neural Network - Long Short Term Memory (RNN-LSTM)
RNN is a feedforward network with memory components. RNN applies the same function to every element in the input data sequence. Its output depends on current and previous elements of the sequence. The output is fed back to the network resulting in recurrence. RNN's memory stores cell states which proves to be helpful in the processing of input data sequences. In RNN, backpropagation through time of the long sequence of features may encounter the problem of gradient vanishing or explosion. In chain rule, multiplication of small gradients for N network layers results in exponential decrease also known as gradient vanishing. In contrast, multiplication of large gradient values for network layers results in exponential increase also known as gradient explosion [1]. These problems directly affect the model training and weight matrix updation. Long short term memory (LSTM) structure avoids the gradient vanishing and explosion problems since it has long term dependence and nonlinear modeling nature enabling handling of long sequences of data [1].

LSTM utilises a cell state Ct-1 for storing the long term states and transfer of information to these cell states are controlled with three gates namely input, output, and forget gate. Current input Xt and previous output ht-1 are fed to all gates. These inputs are multiplied with gate specific weight matrix W(gate) followed by addition of bias b(gate). These gates are constructed using sigmoid function as a smooth curve is in the range of 0 to 1 and differentiable as well. Pointwise multiplications are carried out to generate Ct and ht shown in Fig. 4.

Main feature of the LSTM gates is selection of input data, output data, and forget irrelevant data. Previous cell state Ct-1 when entered into the module it discards feature vectors which are irrelevant for the further process of training using forget gate(Ft). Using input gate (It) new cell state C't is added into the module. C't and relevant data from previous cell state Ct-1 (after discarding parts using the forget gate) are combined to generate Ct [9]. Hyperbolic tangent activation function is used to distribute the gradients which allow Ct cell states information flow without vanishing or exploding problems. Structure of LSTM module and its gate functions are shown in Fig. 4.

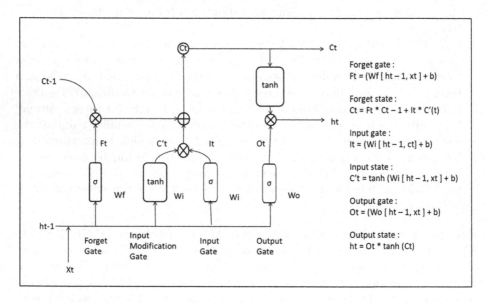

Fig. 4. LSTM module with all gates equations.

VGG16-LSTM Architecture

VGG16 architecture accepts input from HWP video database. Frames are extracted from the stepwise videos and features of steps are generated. Features extracted from the VGG16 are applied to the LSTM module as input and it predicts respective steps of HWP (see Fig. 5).

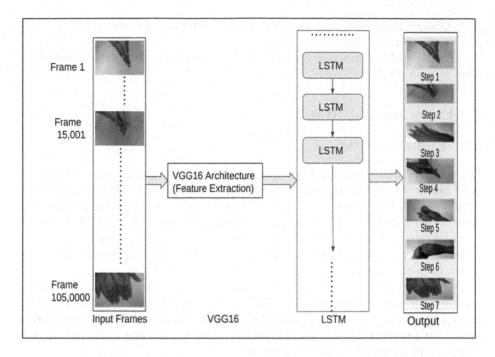

Fig. 5. VGG16-LSTM architecture for hand wash classification.

2.4   Classification of HWP Steps

Softmax layer of LSTM network with 7 neurons is used to classify features extracted from VGG16 network. The training is carried out using mini-batch gradient descent optimiser. This optimiser takes fewer epochs for acceptable training and validation accuracy. Testing accuracy is computed by predicting classes of steps in test videos and ground truth.

2.5   Performance Evaluation Parameter

Accuracy of the model is estimated from classification results categorised into true positives (TP), true negatives (TN), false positives (FP) and false negatives (FN).

$$Accuracy = TP + TN/(TP + TN + FP + FN) \tag{1}$$

Range of accuracy is 0 to 1, 1 being highest. Loss - Natural choice of loss function happens to be cross entropy as this work is targeted as multiclass classification. Cross entropy loss is defined as follows.

$$L_{cross-entropy} = (-1/N) \sum_{1}^{N} p_i log(\hat{p}_i) \tag{2}$$

p_i = Ground truth probability distribution, usually one hot vector.
$\hat{p}_i$ = Predicted probability distribution

The value of loss function increases if the model classification results deviate from ground truth.

3   Experimental Results

3.1   Evaluation of Model

Experiments were performed using a HWP database generated by following WHO recommended seven step HWP. We have created our database in a video format; a 20 s long video of each HWP step was recorded using a Micromax camera. A total number of videos in the database is 3000, which are further categorised into training, validation, and testing. Data augmentation is applied to increase an artificial variation in the training database which further improves accuracy of the model.

Weights and biases of VGG16 layers were set in the beginning using He initialization technique. A dropout value of 0.5 was used for both VGG16 and LSTM. In LSTM hidden layers, ReLU activation function was used. Hyper-parameters for training proposed VGG16 LSTM architecture are as follows. Table 1 gives a summary of all hyper parameter settings.

Table 1. Hyper-parameters for training.

Hyper-parameter	Values
Optimiser	Stochastic Gradient Descent
Learning rate	0.00005
Epochs	150
Mini-batch size	64
Early stopping patience parameter	10

Training, validation loss and accuracy are plotted against epochs as shown in Fig. 6. Classification accuracies (Training, Validation, and Testing) for HWP using the VGG16- LSTM model are listed in Table 2. We recorded the final training loss of 0.123 and validation loss of 0.1950 for our model.

In Table 2, training, validation and testing accuracy of VGG16 - LSTM model are listed for each step of HWP. It is observed that validation accuracies of step2 and step6 are lower than others. Testing accuracies of steps 2, 3, 5, and 6 are lower compared to the rest of the steps. Prediction time for classification of 20 sec videos into seven steps is around 40 s.

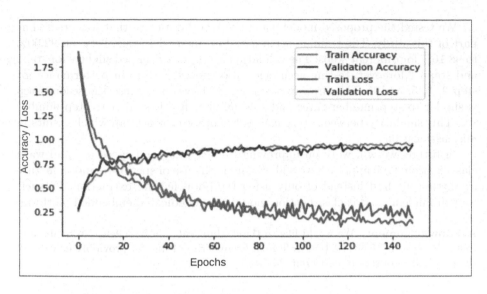

Fig. 6. Accuracy/Loss Vs Epochs for VGG16 LSTM architecture.

Table 2. Training, Validation and Testing Accuracy (%) of each step.

Model steps	Training accuracy	Validation accuracy	Testing accuracy
Step1	98.00	96.00	94.00
Step2	92.00	86.48	71.23
Step3	97.00	93.52	80.01
Step4	96.50	96.50	86.52
Step5	97.00	93.00	79.39
Step6	95.02	89.00	73.03
Step7	98.10	97.12	96.00

We have implemented the proposed model on HP Z230 workstation with Intel Xeon processor E3-1200 v3, four cores, and 32 GB RAM. The model was designed with Python programming language in the Anaconda environment using OpenCV, Scikit-learn, Tensor Flow, and Keras libraries.

4   Discussion and Conclusion

We proposed a computer vision based classification system for identifying steps of WHO recommended hand wash process. The proposed model uses VGG16 and LSTM as encoder and decoder respectively. There was no standard HWP image or video database available. We created a HWP database of 3000 videos recording seven steps of hand wash recommended by WHO.

We tested the proposed model using the HWP database that was created as part of this study. The training accuracies for our model range between 92.00% to 98.10% for different steps. The validation accuracies dropped slightly for step2 and step6. Moreover, testing accuracies also showed a drop in performance for step 2, 3, 5, and 6. This drop in accuracy is observed because the second step is similar to step number three and step number five is similar to step number six. This similarity between steps causes feature vector overlap which results in misclassification.

In future, we will work on improving the accuracy and speed of hand wash classification. One approach we will explore is the use of spatial-temporal feature extraction method instead of only using temporal feature extraction. Further, we will implement this classification module on a dedicated embedded platform.

Acknowledgement. We would like to thank the Center of Excellence in Signal and Image Processing (COE-S&IP), College of Engineering, Pune for providing us with all the required resources to carry out this work.

References

1. Al-Abri, S., Lin, T.X., Tao, M., Zhang, F.: A derivative-free optimization method with application to functions with exploding and vanishing gradients. IEEE Control Syst. Lett. **56**(3), 1247–1293 (2020)
2. Armellino, D., Hussain, E., Schilling, M.E., Senicola, W., Eichorn, A., Dlugacz, Y., Farber, B.F.: Using high-technology to enforce low-technology safety measures: the use of third-party remote video auditing and real-time feedback in healthcare. Clinical Infectious Diseases **54**(1), 1–7 (2012)
3. Baslyman, M., Rezaee, R., Amyot, D., Mouttham, A., Chreyh, R., Geiger, G., Stewart, A., Sader, S.: Real-time and location-based hand hygiene monitoring and notification: proof-of-concept system and experimentation. Personal and Ubiquitous Comput. **19**(3–4), 667–688 (2015)
4. Boudjema, S., Dufour, J., Aladro, A., Desquerres, I., Brouqui, P.: Medihandtrace®: a tool for measuring and understanding hand hygiene adherence. Clinical Microbiol. Infection **20**(1), 22–28 (2014)
5. Boyce, J.M., Cooper, T., Dolan, M.J.: Evaluation of an electronic device for real-time measurement of alcohol-based hand rub use. Infection Control Hospital Epidemiol. **30**(11), 1090–1095 (2009)
6. Camins, B.C., Fraser, V.J.: Reducing the risk of health care-associated infections by complying with CDC hand hygiene guidelines. Joint Commission J. Qual. Patient Saf. **31**(3), 173–179 (2005)
7. Challenge, F.G.P.S.: Who guidelines on hand hygiene in health care: a summary. Geneva: World Health Organization **119**(14), 1977–2016 (2009)
8. Cheng, V.C., Tai, J.W., Ho, S.K., Chan, J.F., Hung, K.N., Ho, P.L., Yuen, K.Y.: Introduction of an electronic monitoring system for monitoring compliance with moments 1 and 4 of the who" my 5 moments for hand hygiene" methodology. BMC Infectious Diseases **11**(1), 151–153 (2011)
9. Greff, K., Srivastava, R.K., Koutník, J., Steunebrink, B.R., Schmidhuber, J.: LSTM: a search space odyssey. IEEE Trans. Neural Networks Learn. Syst. **28**(10), 2222–2232 (2016)

10. Homa, K., Kirkland, K.B.: Determining next steps in a hand hygiene improvement initiative by examining variation in hand hygiene compliance rates. Quality Manage. Healthcare **20**(2), 116–121 (2011)
11. Jain, S., et al.: A low-cost custom HF RFID system for hand washing compliance monitoring. In: IEEE 8th International Conference on ASIC, pp. 975–978 (2009)
12. Kilpatrick, C., Pittet, D.: Who save lives: clean your hands global annual campaign. a call for action (2011)
13. Lacey, G., Llorca, D.F.: Hand washing monitoring system, US Patent 8,090,155 (2012)
14. Levchenko, A., Boscart, V., Ibbett, J., Fernie, G.: Distributed IR based technology to monitor hand hygiene of healthcare staff. In: 2009 IEEE Toronto International Conference Science and Technology for Humanity (TIC-STH), pp. 252–255 (2009)
15. Levchenko, A.I., Boscart, V.M., Fernie, G.R.: Hand hygiene monitoring and real-time prompting system. IEEE Int. Syst. Conf. SysCon **2012**, 1–5 (2012)
16. di Martino, P., Ban, K.M., Bartoloni, A., Fowler, K.E., Saint, S., Mannelli, F.: Assessing the sustainability of hand hygiene adherence prior to patient contact in the emergency department: a 1-year postintervention evaluation. Am. J. Infection Control **39**(1), 14–18 (2011)
17. Polgreen, P.M., Hlady, C.S., Severson, M.A., Segre, A.M., Herman, T.: Method for automated monitoring of hand hygiene adherence without radio-frequency identification. Infection Control Hospital Epidemiol. **31**(12), 1294–1297 (2010)
18. Swoboda, S.M., Earsing, K., Strauss, K., Lane, S., Lipsett, P.A.: Electronic monitoring and voice prompts improve hand hygiene and decrease nosocomial infections in an intermediate care unit. Critical care med. **32**(2), 358–363 (2004)

Edge Detection on Medical Images Using Intuitionistic Fuzzy Logic

Nidhi Tripathi$^{(\boxtimes)}$, Deepak Kumrawat, Venkata Keerthi Gottimukkala,
S. Jeevaraj, and W. Wilfred Godfrey

ABV-IIITM, Gwalior, India
{jeevaraj,godfrey}@iiitm.ac.in

Abstract. The edges make the image analysis easy by discarding unwanted data and preserving only essential information about the image boundary. In order to improve edge detection accuracy on medical images, this paper presents a novel edge detection algorithm based on Attanassov's Intuitionistic fuzzy set theory. The proposed intuitionistic divergence measure is applied to medical images, and edge detection was performed. The edge detection results are measured by MSE and PSNR parameters. According to the measurement parameters, the results were analyzed and found to be more accurate and more noise-robust than the methods based on fuzzy and other intuitionistic fuzzy set theory and traditional edge detection methods.

Keywords: Edge detection · Intuitionistic fuzzy set · Fuzzy set · Divergence measure · Medical images

1 Introduction

Edge detection is an essential aspect in the field of digital image processing. It is a crucial step for producing an efficient medical image as it identifies abnormal growths automatically. It is a fundamental tool in feature detection and feature extraction.

Edge detection becomes a complicated task and consumes more time when an image is corrupted by noise. Edges can be found in many directions, so a set of templates that represent different directions of edges (edge profiles) are used to find all the edges present in the image.

Generally, image edges are vague, so direct edge detection will detect broken and discontinued edges. Therefore, prior processing is the first step to any edge detection method to detect clear and accurate edges. The edge detection process steps are filtering, enhancement, detection, and localization [15]. Filtering is used to diminish the noise in an image without vanishing the right edges. Enhancement is used so that the quality of edges becomes more accurate than earlier. Detection is used to determine which edge pixels are supposed to be dismissed as noise and which edge pixels are to be preserved. Localization is used for the detection of the accurate location of an edge in an image.

© Springer Nature Singapore Pte Ltd. 2021
S. K. Singh et al. (Eds.): CVIP 2020, CCIS 1376, pp. 236–246, 2021.
https://doi.org/10.1007/978-981-16-1086-8_21

In literature, one of the first method for edge detection was proposed by Sobel, but the Sobel edge detector couldn't detect all true edges properly, i.e., the edges were discontinued and broken. Besides, Prewitt proposed another similar edge detection method, but this edge detector was also sensitive to noise. Later on, Robert came up with another method, but it gives minor details only. Afterward, Canny also came up with another method for edge detection, which was much more complicated and time-consuming and showed some false edges due to noise. In all the classical edge detection methods, the edges are discontinuous and broken [12].

The conventional methods could not handle the noise present in the image. So, a fuzzy-based approach for edge detection was used as it can represent inexact and imprecise information. Later, the intuitionistic fuzzy-based approach has been developed to model more uncertainties than fuzzy, present in real-life situations to get much more accurate results.

Fuzzy logic is an extension of crisp logic, which can model vague information [9]. Unlike a crisp set, which has only two possibilities: either an element belongs or does not belong to a set, a fuzzy set defines an element's degree of belongingness in a set. This degree of belongingness, called membership degree, lies in [0, 1]. In the fuzzy set, a non-membership degree is taken as one minus membership degree. This is not always the case due to a lack of knowledge, as the membership function cannot always be precisely defined. So, Intuitionistic fuzzy set [10] has been proposed as an extension to fuzzy set that includes membership and non-membership degree.

$$A = [x, \mu_A(x), \nu_A(x)] \tag{1}$$

where x is the pixel value, $\mu_A(x)$ is the membership degree of x and $\nu_A(x)$ is the non-membership degree of x in intuitionistic fuzzy set A [5,6].

It measures a lack of knowledge in the form of a hesitation degree.

$$\pi_A(x) = 1 - \mu_A(x) - \nu_A(x) \tag{2}$$

where $\pi_A(x)$ is the hesitation degree of x, $\mu_A(x)$ is the membership degree of x and $\nu_A(x)$ is the non-membership degree of x in intuitionistic fuzzy set A.

Uncertainty plays a crucial role in decision making, so there arises a need to consider as many uncertainties as possible to get better results. It considers more uncertainty than fuzzy logic, so it is expected to give better results in vague scenarios [8].

Edge detection filters [1] unwanted data and preserves necessary information. So, it is necessary to select a robust edge detector [4] to get the best outcomes in all the conditions. In this work, an attempt has been made to develop a novel edge detection technique using intuitionistic fuzzy logic [7] which gives comparatively better results than the currently existing techniques. It helps save countless lives every day and improves the quality of life of patients across the world. It is well known that medical images are not uniformly illuminated, so the image boundaries are not clearly visible. So, there are many more uncertainties than other images, and as intuitionistic fuzzy considers more uncertainties than fuzzy, it is of great use.

2 Related Work

In the literature, there exist many methods for edge detection. Majority of the edge detection algorithms normally convolute filter operators and take the input image and then the overlapping map of the input image part to output signals. In this process, edges can be lost due to the noise.

2.1 Literature Review of Divergence Measure

It is vital to define dissimilarity/divergence between intuitionistic fuzzy sets (IFSs) since it has applications in various fields, including image segmentation and decision-making.

An IF-divergence(Intuitionistic fuzzy- divergence) can be defined as a measure of difference that should satisfy the following rational properties [14]:

- It is a symmetrical and non-negative measure of the two IF-sets.
- The IF-divergence of an IF-set is zero by itself.
- The further equivalent the two IF-sets are, the smaller the IF-divergence between them is.
- In fuzzy sets, the IF-divergence for fuzzy sets becomes a divergence.

Some of the existing divergence measures are the following:

1. **Rajeev et al.'s [13] Divergence Measure**

   Rajeev et al. [13] have defined an intuitionistic fuzzy divergence measure based on the fuzzy entropy measure of intuitionistic fuzzy sets.

   The fuzzy entropy measure of an intuitionistic fuzzy set can be defined as:

$$E_\beta(B) = \frac{1}{n} \sum_{i=1}^{n} \left[1 - (\mu(b_i) + \nu(b_i))^\beta \cdot e^{1-(\mu(b_i)+\nu(b_i))^\beta} \right], \text{where } \beta \in [0,1]$$

   Intuitionistic fuzzy divergence measure can be defined between P and Q as:

$$IFD(P,Q) = \left(\frac{E_\beta(P) + E_\beta(Q)}{2} \right) - E_\beta \left(\frac{P+Q}{2} \right)$$

2. **Hassan M. et al.'s [2] Divergence Measure**

   Intuitionistic fuzzy divergence measure can be defined between P and Q as :

$$IFD(P,Q) = \sum_i \sum_j 4 - (1 - \mu_P(x_{ij}) + \mu_Q(y_{ij})) \cdot e^{\mu_P(x_{ij})-\mu_Q(y_{ij})} - (1 + $$
$$\mu_P(x_{ij}) - \mu_Q(y_{ij})) \cdot e^{\mu_Q(y_{ij})-\mu_P(x_{ij})} - (1 + \pi_P(x_{ij}) - \pi_Q(y_{ij})) \cdot e^{\pi_Q(y_{ij})-\pi_P(x_{ij})}$$
$$- (1 - \pi_P(x_{ij}) + \pi_Q(y_{ij})) \cdot e^{\pi_P(x_{ij})-\pi_Q(y_{ij})}$$

3. **Vlachos et al.'s [3] Divergence Measure**

Intuitionistic fuzzy divergence measure can be defined between P and Q as:

$$IFD_{VS}(P,Q) = \sum_{i=1}^{n} [\mu_P(x_i) \ln \left(\frac{\mu_P(x_i)}{(1/2) \cdot (\mu_P(x_i) + \mu_Q(x_i))} \right)$$

$$+ \nu_P(x_i) \ln \left(\frac{\mu_P(x_i)}{(1/2) \cdot (\nu_P(x_i) + \nu_Q(x_i))} \right)]$$

4. **Zhang & Jiang's [3] Divergence Measure**

Intuitionistic fuzzy divergence measure between P and Q can be defined as:

$$IFD_{ZJ}(P,Q) = \sum_{i=1}^{n} [\left(\frac{\mu_P(x_i) - \nu_P(x_i) + 1}{2} \right)$$

$$\cdot \ln \left(\frac{\mu_P(x_i) - \nu_P(x_i) + 1}{(1/2) \cdot (2 + (\mu_P(x_i) - \nu_P(x_i)) + (\mu_Q(x_i) - \nu_Q(x_i)))} \right)$$

$$+ \left(\frac{\nu_P(x_i) - \mu_P(x_i) + 1}{2} \right) \cdot \ln \left(\frac{\nu_P(x_i) - \mu_P(x_i) + 1}{(1/2) \cdot (2 + (\nu_P(x_i) - \mu_P(x_i)) + (\nu_Q(x_i) - \mu_Q(x_i)))} \right)]$$

5. **Wei and Ye's [3] Divergence Measure**

Intuitionistic fuzzy divergence measure between P and Q:

$$IFD_{WY}(P,Q) = \sum_{i=1}^{n} [\mu_P(x_i) \ln \left(\frac{\mu_P(x_i)}{(1/2) \cdot (\mu_P(x_i) + \mu_Q(x_i))} \right)$$

$$+ \nu_P(x_i) \ln \left(\frac{\nu_P(x_i)}{(1/2) \cdot (\nu_P(x_i) + \nu_Q(x_i))} \right)$$

$$+ \pi_P(x_i) \ln \left(\frac{\pi_P(x_i)}{(1/2) \cdot (\pi_P(x_i) + \pi_Q(x_i))} \right)]$$

6. **Mao et al.'s [3] Divergence Measure**

Intuitionistic fuzzy divergence measure between P and Q:

$$IFD_M(P,Q) = \sum_{i=1}^{n} [\pi_P(x_i) \ln \left(\frac{\pi_P(x_i)}{(1/2) \cdot (\pi_P(x_i) + \pi_Q(x_i))} \right)$$

$$+ \Delta_P(x_i) \ln \left(\frac{\Delta_P(x_i)}{(1/2) \cdot (\Delta_P(x_i) + \Delta_Q(x_i))} \right)]$$

The most critical drawback of above existing edge detection techniques based on intuitionistic fuzzy sets [11] is that: Although many researchers have defined various divergence measures on the class of intuitionistic fuzzy sets and tried to use it for edge detection, these approaches have given good results for only specific images, i.e., the same algorithm or technique cannot apply to all images.

In the proposed method, we have introduced a generalizing parameter alpha, which helps in giving good results for all images.

3   Proposed Divergence Measure

This section includes the newly proposed divergence measure, the axioms of divergence measure, and edge detection steps.

3.1   Chaira Method and Its Drawbacks

The intuitionistic fuzzy divergence measure between the images P and Q proposed by Chaira method is:

$$IFD(P,Q) = \sum_i \sum_j (2 - (1 - \mu_P(x_{ij}) + \mu_Q(y_{ij})) \cdot e^{\mu_P(x_{ij}) - \mu_Q(y_{ij})} -$$

$$(1 + \mu_P(x_{ij}) - \mu_Q(y_{ij})) \cdot e^{\mu_Q(y_{ij}) - \mu_P(x_{ij})}) + (2 - (1 - \mu_P(x_{ij}) + \mu_Q(y_{ij}) + \pi_Q(y_{ij})$$

$$- \pi_P(x_{ij})) \cdot e^{\mu_P(x_{ij}) - \mu_Q(y_{ij}) - (\pi_Q(y_{ij}) - \pi_P(x_{ij}))} - (1 + \pi_P(x_{ij}) - \pi_Q(y_{ij}) + \mu_P(x_{ij})$$

$$- \mu_Q(y_{ij})) \cdot e^{\pi_Q(y_{ij}) - \pi_P(x_{ij}) - (\mu_P(x_{ij}) - \mu_Q(y_{ij}))})$$

In the Chaira method, a combination of a, b, and other parameters are to be chosen by hit and trial method for each image separately, which is a complicated task.

We have introduced a new parameter called alpha α, which is first varied by hit and trial method to see where it is generalizing the divergence measure to get better results. Then that value of alpha is kept fixed for generalizing the divergence measure. It is the parameter that generalizes the divergence measure proposed by Chaira. It is different from the Chaira method's parameters as it is a parameter for generalizing the divergence measure rather than getting a better result for specific images.

3.2   The Newly Proposed Distance Measure

The extent of information between the membership degrees of pixels (x_{ij}) & (y_{ij}) of images P and Q respectively, is given as:

1. due to $\mu_P(x_{ij})$ and $\mu_Q(y_{ij})$:

$$e^{\mu_P(x_{ij})} / e^{\mu_Q(y_{ij})}$$

2. due to $\mu_P(x_{ij}) + \Pi_P(x_{ij})$ and $\mu_Q(y_{ij}) + \Pi_Q(y_{ij})$:

$$e^{\mu_P(x_{ij}) + \Pi_P(x_{ij})} / e^{\mu_Q(y_{ij}) + \Pi_Q(y_{ij})}$$

due to $\mu_P(x_{ij})$ and $\mu_Q(y_{ij})$ the divergence between images P and Q may be stated as:

$$D_1(P,Q) = \sum_{i=1}^n \sum_{j=1}^n \frac{\alpha}{1+\alpha} \cdot [1 - (1 - \mu_P(x_{ij})) \cdot e^{\mu_P(x_{ij}) - \mu_Q(y_{ij})}$$

$$- \mu_Q(x_{ij}) \cdot e^{\mu_Q(y_{ij}) - \mu_Q(x_{ij})}]$$

Similarly, the divergence of image Q against image P can be written as:

$$D_1(Q, P) = \sum_{i=1}^{n} \sum_{j=1}^{n} \frac{\alpha}{1+\alpha} \cdot [1 - (1 - \mu_Q(y_{ij})) \cdot e^{\mu_Q(y_{ij}) - \mu_P(x_{ij})}$$
$$- \mu_Q(y_{ij}) \cdot e^{\mu_P(x_{ij}) - \mu_Q(y_{ij})}]$$

So, the total divergence between the pixels (x_{ij}) and (y_{ij}) of the images P and Q due to $\mu_P(x_{ij})$ and $\mu_Q(y_{ij})$ is:

$$D(P, Q) = D_1(P, Q) + D_1(Q, P) = \sum_{i=1}^{n} \sum_{j=1}^{n} \frac{\alpha}{1+\alpha} \cdot [2 - (1 - \mu_P(x_{ij})$$
$$+ \mu_Q(y_{ij})) \cdot e^{\mu_P(x_{ij}) - \mu_Q(y_{ij})} - (1 - \mu_Q(y_{ij}) + \mu_P(x_{ij})) \cdot e^{\mu_Q(y_{ij}) - \mu_P(x_{ij})}].$$

Similarly, the total divergence between the pixels (x_{ij}) and (y_{ij}) of images P and Q due to $\mu_P(x_{ij}) + \pi_P(x_{ij})$ and $\mu_Q(y_{ij}) + \pi_Q(y_{ij})$ is:

$$D(P, Q) = \sum_{i=1}^{n} \sum_{j=1}^{n} \frac{\alpha}{1+\alpha} \cdot (2 - [1 - (\mu_P(x_{ij}) - \mu_Q(y_{ij})) + (\pi_Q(y_{ij}) - \pi_P(x_{ij}))]$$
$$\cdot e^{\mu_P(x_{ij}) - \mu_Q(y_{ij}) - (\pi_Q(y_{ij}) - \pi_P(x_{ij}))} - [1 - (\pi_Q(y_{ij}) - \pi_P(x_{ij})) + (\mu_P(x_{ij}) - \mu_Q(y_{ij}))]$$
$$\cdot e^{\pi_Q(y_{ij}) - \pi_P(x_{ij}) - (\mu_P(x_{ij}) - \mu_Q(y_{ij}))}).$$

The intuitionistic fuzzy divergence measure between the images P and Q, IFD, is obtained by adding above two Equations and which can be written as:

$$IFD(P, Q) = \sum_i \sum_j \frac{\alpha}{1+\alpha} \cdot [(2 - (1 - \mu_P(x_{ij}) + \mu_Q(y_{ij})) \cdot e^{\mu_P(x_{ij}) - \mu_Q(y_{ij})}$$
$$- (1 + \mu_P(x_{ij}) - \mu_Q(y_{ij})) \cdot e^{\mu_Q(y_{ij}) - \mu_P(x_{ij})}) + (2 - (1 - \mu_P(x_{ij}) + \mu_Q(y_{ij}) + \pi_Q(y_{ij})$$
$$- \pi_P(x_{ij})) \cdot e^{\mu_P(x_{ij}) - \mu_Q(y_{ij}) - (\pi_Q(y_{ij}) - \pi_P(x_{ij}))} - (1 + \pi_P(x_{ij}) - \pi_Q(y_{ij}) + \mu_P(x_{ij})$$
$$- \mu_Q(y_{ij})) \cdot e^{\pi_Q(y_{ij}) - \pi_P(x_{ij}) - (\mu_P(x_{ij}) - \mu_Q(y_{ij}))})].$$

3.3   Axioms

Divergence measure is a function which holds the following axioms:
Axiom 1: $IFD(A, B) \geq 0$;
Axiom 2: $IFD(A, B) = 0$; if and only if $A = B$.
where A and B are two intuitionistic fuzzy sets.
Our proposed divergence measure has satisfied both axioms which can be proved easily. Hence the proof is omitted.

3.4   Steps for Edge Detection

Edges can be present in many different directions, so a set of 16 templates are used to reflect all possible orientations of the edges to detect them. Now they are placed over the image, and to find the edges of the image; the similarity is computed. The choice of templates is crucial as it reflects the type and direction of edges. As all existing edge detectors have some or the other drawbacks, there is a need to design a new edge detection model. Here, a novel divergence measure is designed using intuitionistic fuzzy logic. In general, a divergence measure helps in finding similarities between pixels. The proposed divergence measure is a generalization over the Chaira method, where we try to obtain good results by varying only α and keeping other parameters a and b constant.

Now, this proposed divergence measure will be used in generating edge detected image following the below steps:T-

1. An image is taken as input and converted into a gray scale image.
2. The image is normalized and these normalized values of pixels are taken as corresponding membership degree.
3. A set of 16 templates are taken which represent different edge profiles.
4. The divergence measure between each pixel of the 3×3 window and 3×3 template is calculated by placing the centre of template at each pixel position of normalized image. The following divergence measure is used:

$$
IFD(P,Q) = \sum_i \sum_j \frac{\alpha}{1+\alpha} \cdot [(2 - (1 - \mu_P(x_{ij}) + \mu_Q(y_{ij})) \cdot e^{\mu_P(x_{ij}) - \mu_Q(y_{ij})} - (1 + \mu_P(x_{ij})
$$

$$
- \mu_Q(y_{ij})) \cdot e^{\mu_Q(y_{ij}) - \mu_P(x_{ij})}) + (2 - (1 - \mu_P(x_{ij}) + \mu_Q(y_{ij}) + \pi_Q(y_{ij}) - \pi_P(x_{ij}))
$$

$$
\cdot e^{\mu_P(x_{ij}) - \mu_Q(y_{ij}) - (\pi_Q(y_{ij}) - \pi_P(x_{ij}))} - (1 + \pi_P(x_{ij}) - \pi_Q(y_{ij}) + \mu_P(x_{ij}) - \mu_Q(y_{ij}))
$$

$$
\cdot e^{\pi_Q(y_{ij}) - \pi_P(x_{ij}) - (\mu_P(x_{ij}) - \mu_Q(y_{ij}))})].
$$

Here, x_{ij}, y_{ij} represents pixel values of image window and template respectively, where each pixel value is defined as an intuitionistic fuzzy set. α is a parameter. $\mu_X(x_{ij})$ and $\mu_Y(y_{ij})$ represents membership values of x_{ij}, y_{ij} in X and Y respectively. $\pi_X(x_{ij})$ and $\pi_Y(y_{ij})$ represents hesitation degree of x_{ij}, y_{ij} in X and Y respectively.

5. The minimum of the nine divergence values is computed in step 4.
6. Step 4 is repeated for all the 16 templates.
7. The maximum of the 16 values is obtained after applying all the 16 templates.
8. Assign the maximum value at that pixel position where the template's center was placed over the image.
9. Repeat step 4 to step 8 for all pixel positions.
10. The above steps result in a new intuitionistic divergence matrix.
11. The intuitionistic fuzzy divergence matrix is thresholded, and the thin morphological operator is also applied.
12. An edge detected image is obtained as a result.

4   Results and Discussion

This section has compared the proposed method with an Interval type-2 fuzzy systems (IT2FSs) based edge detection method, type-1 fuzzy systems (T1FSs) edge detection method, and the chaira edge detection method. Later the resulting images are also shown.

4.1   Comparison Between Proposed Method and Other Methods

This section compares the results based on the two parameters discussed previously: MSE and PSNR are shown.

On the application of the proposed divergence measure and other methods to images, it is found that the mean squared error, which uses the proposed divergence measure, is lesser as compared to that of other methods. On applying the proposed divergence measure, for combinations of a and b used, it was found that the results are best when alpha = 0.6. When the value of alpha is taken less than 0.3, the edges were found to be missing. Furthermore, when the alpha value is taken greater than 0.6, thick edges were obtained, thereby increasing the MSE. So, it was found that for a specific combination of a and b, the range of alpha should be between 0.3 and 0.6.

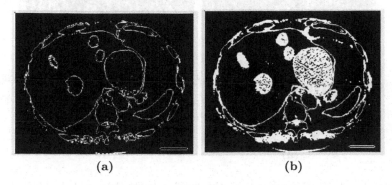

(a)   (b)

Fig. 1. (a) $a = 1$, $b = 0.7$, alp = 0.57, threshold = 0.098 (b) $a = 1$, $b = 0.7$, threshold = 0.098

MSE and PSNR are inversely proportional to each other. So, when the value of MSE is less, PSNR will be more. So, the greater is the value of PSNR better are the results (Table 1 and 2).

Table 1. MSE table

Images	Proposed method	Chaira method	T1FSs method	IT2FSs method
Cameraman	0.1137	0.1691	0.1452	0.1181
Moon	0.0769	0.1036	0.0984	0.0787
CTscan 1	0.1242	0.2284	0.1837	0.1469
CTscan 2	0.0919	0.3190	0.1539	0.1231
CTscan 3	0.1102	0.3613	0.2035	0.1424

Table 2. PSNR table

Images	Proposed method	Chaira method	T1FSs method	IT2FSs method
Cameraman	57.57	55.84	56.54	57.44
Moon	59.27	57.97	58.23	59.20
CTscan 1	57.18	54.54	55.52	56.49
CTscan 2	58.49	53.09	56.29	57.26
CTscan 3	57.70	52.55	55.07	56.62

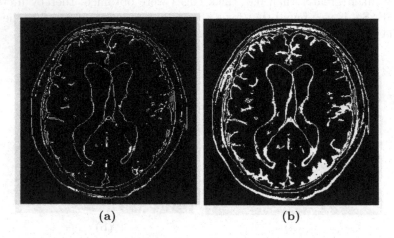

(a)   (b)

Fig. 2. (a) $a = 1$, $b = 0.7$, alp $= 0.57$, threshold $= 0.098$ (b) $a = 1$, $b = 0.7$, threshold $= 0.098$

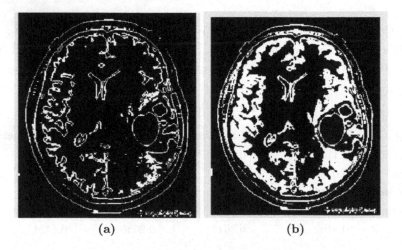

(a)   (b)

Fig. 3. (a) $a = 1$, $b = 0.7$, alp $= 0.6$, threshold $= 0.098$ (b) $a = 1$, $b = 0.7$, threshold $= 0.098$

The values of a and b were determined by hit and trial method and are kept fixed for all sets of images. Results with $a = 1.0$ and $b = 0.7$ are shown for each image. The value of α is kept near 0.6, to get better results for all images. Taking images given by Canny as the ground truth, the proposed method's results were found to be better than the other methods.

5   Conclusion

In this paper, a novel method is presented using intuitionistic fuzzy set theory for image edge detection. The proposed intuitionistic fuzzy divergence measure has been implemented for edge detection on several images. The results have been compared with the results given by the method proposed by Chaira, and Interval type-2 fuzzy systems(IT2FSs) based edge detection method, type-1 fuzzy systems(T1FSs) based edge detection method. The outcomes acquired were noted to be better than other methods. These results demonstrate the efficacy of the method proposed. This work can be further extended in the future by taking into consideration the uncertainty to achieve much better outcomes.

References

1. Abdallah, A., Ayman, A.: Edge detection in digital images using fuzzy logic technique. World Acad. Sci. Eng. Technol. **51**, 178–186 (2009)
2. Alsufyani, A., El-Owny, H.B.M.: Exponential intuitionistic fuzzy entropy measure based image edge detection. Int. J. Appl. Eng. Res. **13**(10), 8518–8524 (2018)
3. Ansari, M.D., Mishra, A.R., Ansari, F.T.: New divergence and entropy measures for intuitionistic fuzzy sets on edge detection. Int. J. Fuzzy Syst. **20**(2), 474–487 (2018)
4. Ansari, M.D., Singh, G., Singh, A., Kumar, A.: An efficient salt and pepper noise removal and edge preserving scheme for image restoration. Int. J. Comput. Technol. Appl. **3**(5), 1848–1854 (2012)
5. Atanassov, K.T.: Intuitionistic fuzzy sets. In: Intuitionistic fuzzy sets, pp. 1–137. Springer (1999)
6. Atanassov, K.: Intuitionistic fuzzy sets, theory, and applications. Fuzziness and Soft Computing (1999)
7. Becerikli, Y., Karan, T.M.: A new fuzzy approach for edge detection. In: Cabestany, J., Prieto, A., Sandoval, F. (eds.) IWANN 2005. LNCS, vol. 3512, pp. 943–951. Springer, Heidelberg (2005). https://doi.org/10.1007/11494669_116
8. Bustince, H., Burillo, P.: Vague sets are intuitionistic fuzzy sets. Fuzzy Sets Syst. **79**(3), 403–405 (1996)
9. Chaira, T.: Fuzzy Set and its Extension. Wiley, Hoboken (2019)
10. Chaira, T., Ray, A.K.: A new measure using intuitionistic fuzzy set theory and its application to edge detection. Appl. Soft Comput. **8**(2), 919–927 (2008)
11. Grzegorzewski, P.: Distances between intuitionistic fuzzy sets and/or interval-valued fuzzy sets based on the Hausdorff metric. Fuzzy Sets Syst. **148**(2), 319–328 (2004)
12. Jain, R., Kasturi, R., Schunck, B.G.: Machine Vision, vol. 5. McGraw-Hill, New York (1995)

13. Kaushik, R., Bajaj, R.K., Kumar, T.: On intuitionistic fuzzy divergence measure with application to edge detection. Procedia Comput. Sci. **70**, 2–8 (2015)
14. Montes, I., Pal, N.R., Janiš, V., Montes, S.: Divergence measures for intuitionistic fuzzy sets. IEEE Trans. Fuzzy Syst. **23**(2), 444–456 (2015). https://doi.org/10.1109/TFUZZ.2014.2315654
15. Trucco, E., Verri, A.: Introductory Techniques for 3-D Computer Vision, vol. 201. Prentice Hall, Englewood Cliffs (1998)

Border to Border Distance Based Method for Detecting Juxta-Pleural Nodules

R. Jenkin Suji$^{(\boxtimes)}$ (iD), W. Wilfred Godfrey(iD), and Joydip Dhar(iD)

Atal Bihari Vajpayee Indian Institute of Information Technology and Management,
Gwalior, Madhya Pradesh, India
{suji,godfrey,jdhar}@iiitm.ac.in

Abstract. Accurate detection and segmentation of lung structures play a vital role in computer based lung cancer detection and diagnosis. Lung segmentation is challenging when the nodules are attached to the pleural walls of the lung boundary. This paper presents a novel methodology on detecting the lung structures to include the juxta-pleural nodules by calculating the shortest distance between two borders of the two consecutive slices. The proposed methodology is tested with some sample CT slices on Lung Image Database Consortium and Image Database Resource Initiative dataset. This work validates and demonstrates that the sequence based image processing is useful for detecting the nodules attached to the lung boundaries, juxta-pleural nodules.

Keywords: Juxta-pleural lung nodule · Sequence based · Lung parenchyma segmentation

1 Introduction

Pulmonary nodules are one of the major symptoms of the lung cancer detection and diagnosis [4]. Pulmonary nodules are defined as round or oval in appearance and the size of the nodule is not more than 30 mm in diameter. Computer tomography (CT) images are the most sensitive and cheapest methods for detecting the pulmonary nodules at early stages of lung cancer. Computer based methods use CT images for detecting the pulmonary nodules at the early stages in order to reduce mortality rate and increase the survival rate.

Pulmonary nodules are classified in to juxta-pleural nodules, juxta-vascular nodules and isolated nodules. Juxta-pleural nodules are those nodules attached to the lung boundary or pleural wall of the lung. Juxta-vascular nodules are those nodules attached to the blood vessels of the lung. Isolated nodules are those nodules which are not attached to the neighbouring structures of the lung such as blood vessels, pleural wall etc.

This work was carried out at ABV- IIITM Gwalior, India with funding from DST, Govt. of India.

S. K. Singh et al. (Eds.): CVIP 2020, CCIS 1376, pp. 247–259, 2021.
https://doi.org/10.1007/978-981-16-1086-8_22

Computer based methods for lung cancer detection and diagnosis consists of the following stages –Lung segmentation, Candidate lung nodule detection, Feature extraction and Lung nodule classification.

Accurate segmentation of the lung structures are very essential for accurately detecting the candidate nodules. Segmentation of the lung structures are very challenging due to inhomogeneity of the lung. This inhomogeneity is compounded by the challenge that the nodules have more or less similar voxel intensities as the body region and the tissue region surrounding the lung [2,11]. Due to this, in the presence of juxta-pleural lung nodules, segmentation of the lung is challenging and conventional algorithms fail to include the nodules attached to the neighboring structures of the lung within the lung contour.

The proposed method is a image sequence based method for lung segmentation. Typical methods for lung segmentation are intensity based, template based, model based, deep learning based etc. This paper presents a border to border method for detecting the juxta-pleural nodules attached to the pleural wall of the lung. Section 2 describes the literature survey on various methods for detecting the juxta-pleural nodules, Sect. 3 explains the methodology on detecting the juxta-pleural nodules using border to border distance method. Section 4 analyses the proposed method on various lung CT images of LIDC-IDRI dataset and Sect. 5 concludes with conclusion and future direction.

2   Literature Survey

Lung Segmentation approaches can be broadly classified as slice based and scan based methods. Scan based methods process the entire volume in a single go to obtain the lung contour, for instance application of a global threshold on a scan volume etc. Scan based approaches process the thoracic volume one by one. Now, the scan based methods may be either processed independently or in sequence. Traditional lung segmentation methods are categorised into thresholding based, region based, model based and machine learning based methods [6]. Traditional methods are very good in segmenting the nodules when the nodules are not attached to the neighbouring structures of the lung. But they fail to include the nodules when the nodules are attached to the neighbouring structures of the lung. Below, a literature survey on various methods for detecting the juxta-pleural nodules are given.

Saraswathi and Sheela [7] proposed a method for detecting the shape and size based juxta-pleural nodules located on the lung boundary using optimal critical point selection algorithm. Initially suspected nodule region is obtained using bidirectional chain code and optimal critical point selection algorithm. Then the shape and size features are extracted and the nodules are classified using support vector machines and random forest classifiers. They used CT images from LIDC dataset and their method is able to detect the nodules in a short time duration.

Jinke Wang and Haoyan Guo [12] proposed an automatic method for segmenting the lung parenchyma images including juxta pleural nodules using contour tracing and correction methods. They extracted the chest skin boundary using image aligning, morphological operation and connected region analysis and the lung contour of the right and left lungs are segmented using diagonal based border tracing with maximum cost path algorithm. Then the lung parenchyma is refined using arc-based border smoothing and concave based border correction. They evaluated their method on 45 chest CT lung volumes with volume difference of 11.15 ± 69.63 cm^3, volume overlap error of $3.5057 \pm 1.3719\%$, average surface distance of 0.7917 ± 0.2741 mm, root mean square distance of $.6957 \pm 0.6568$ mm, maximum symmetric absolute surface distance of 21.3430 ± 8.1743 mm, and average time-cost required is 2 s per image.

Sariya and Ravishankar [8] proposed a method for classifying the juxta-pleural nodules using ray casting algorithm and neural networks. Zhang Yang et al. [13] proposed a method for segmenting the pulmonary nodules on CT images especially for juxta-pleural and juxta-vascular nodules. They extracted the lung parenchyma using region growing, morphological operations, edge detection, curvature calculation and inflection points extraction from CT images. Later the nodules are segmented using graph-cut, ray casting and geodesic methods. They tested their method on 258 nodules and they proved better results while comparing with the other traditional approaches.

Ganesh Singadkar et al. [9] proposed an automatic method for segmenting the lung parenchyma including the juxta-vascular and juxta-pleural nodules using curvature based border correction. They identified the dominant points of the concave and convex region of the lung boundary and those dominant points are connected through dominant point marching algorithm. They tested 36 CT lung volumes from LIDC dataset and achieved a 96.97% average volumetric overlap fraction, 2.324% average under segmentation rate and 0.79% average over segmentation rate. Their method took on an average of 182.448 sec for processing each CT volume and 0.953 sec for processing each slice which is comparatively performed faster than the manual segmentation performed by the radiologists.

Heewon Chung et al. [3] implemented an automatic method using active contour model and Bayesian method for segmenting the lung structures with juxta-pleural nodules. They used Chan-Vese model for extracting active lung contours and Bayesian approach for predicting the lung images from the previous frame of the segmented lung contour. They used concave points detection and Hough transform for eliminating the false positives. They tested their method with 16873 images and 314 images having juxta pleural nodules and achieved dice similarity coefficient of 0.9809, modified hausdorff distance of 0.4806, sensitivity of 0.9785, specificity of 0.9981, accuracy of 0.9964 and juxta-pleural nodule detection rate of 96%.

Huidrom et al. [5] proposed a lung segmentation method for segmenting the lung structures in order to include the juxta-pleural nodules. Initially they used thresholding methods for segmenting the lung structures and later they used boundary analysis methods to include the juxta-pleural nodules. They analysed 10 CT images from LIDC dataset and 10 images from Regional Institute of Medical Sciences (RIMS) dataset. They achieved 99% accuracy, 99% sensitivity, 99%

specificity, 99% dice similarity coefficient, 99% overlap measure, 99% positive predictive value in both the datasets.

Among the above methods Ganesh Singadkar [9] and Heewon Chung [3] used sequence of images for detecting juxta-pleural nodules. While the above papers show promising results, there is scope for further refinements of the methodologies and their works required to be validated by large and inclusive datasets.

The basis for this work is as follows: Given a sequence of frames consisting of a motion scheme, the frame sequence evolves smoothly with an associated degree of similarity or coherence between two successive frames. By analyzing this sequence of frames, if the degree of influence of the stochastic process on the scene evolution can be estimated, an event can be identified and other operations including interpretation and prediction can be carried out depending on the application. Thus, in order to observe and interpret to infer a dynamic system state/frame transition, a model describing the normal evolution of the states/frames is required. This is considered as the reference model. To detect the dynamic system state inconsistencies, the dynamic system state/frame is compared with the reference model state/frame and the inconsistencies are measured and quantified. After quantification of the inconsistencies, the reference model may be once more used to update the inconsistencies.

The major contributions of this paper are

1. A Border to Border distance based juxta-pleural nodule detection method to identify the juxta-pleural nodules.
2. Validation of the proposed approach using LIDC-IDRI dataset.

3   Proposed Methodology

The method proposed in this work processes the slices in sequence to identify juxta-pleural nodule.

3.1   Border to Border Distance Based Juxta-Pleural Nodule Detection Method to Identify the Juxta-Pleural Nodules

Given the N successive chest CT image slices from a single scan volume, the lung region in a single slice is identified as left lobe and right lobe. Identification and separation of left and right lobe is carried out using centroid information. The rest of the processing is performed over either lobes separately in an identified fashion as described herein. We denote the lung contour state vector of the ith frame by C_i, which denotes the contour of either lobe. The sequence of frames may be C_1, C_2, ... C_N. The sequence of the frames denote the spatial location of the scan, top to bottom along the axial axis. It is also assumed that this sequence evolves according to the following system model:

$$C_i = f(C_{i-1}, w_i) \tag{1}$$

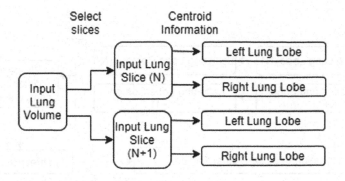

Fig. 1. First steps in processing of Lung CT slices

where f is a system transition function specific to this frame sequence and this determines the change in the size of lung contour for a pair of frames in the sequence. This change in size can be positive or negative and specifically, this depends on the lung phase, discussed later and physical dimensions of the organ etc. and w denotes the sudden inconsitency/error that may be introduced along the lung contour due to presence of juxta-pleural nodule.

Here, the Euclidean distance is used to compute the shortest distance between two arbitrary points from the two consecutive slices.

On a lung CT scan without juxta-pleural nodules, there are no sudden inconsistencies in the successive lung contours and hence the $w_i = 0$ for such scans. A positive value of w_i denotes a large variation in the successive lung contour in comparision with the previous lung contour. Estimating this w_i, by comparing the successive lung contours gives sufficient information on the presence or absence of a juxta-pleural nodule in the successive frames. On successive scans which comprise of juxta-pleural nodules, the w_i remains zero for all frames (denoting natural evolution)in the sequence except those frame sequences or pairs which comprise of a frame denoting a non-noduled slice and a noduled slice in either order.

Hence, the problem of identifying juxta-pleural nodules from lung contour is reduced to identifying non-zero w_i. The problem of redrawing the lung contour is reduced to finding the natural evolution of the lung contour from the previous frame.

Assuming that C_{n-1} is a normal lung contour from $(n-1)^{th}$ frame without juxta-pleural nodule and C_n is the lung contour from successive and adjacent n^{th} frame whose contour has been affected due to the existence of a juxta-pleural nodule. One way of finding out non-zero w_n is to find the difference and check if the difference is above a threshold.

$$\text{Difference} = C_{n-1} - f(C_{n-1}, w_n) = C_{n-1} - C_n \qquad (2)$$

If the difference is significant, then this may denote the presence of a juxta-pleural nodule.

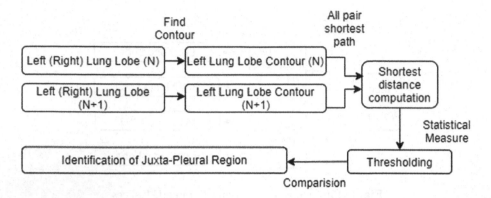

Fig. 2. Later steps in processing of Lung CT slices

3.2   Computation of Difference

Let C_{n-1}^k denote the contour coordinates from the lung contour of $(n-1)^{th}$ frame and C_n^k denote the contour coordinates from the lung contour of nth frame, k denotes that the variable refers to contour coordinates. Each of these contours comprise of $|C_{n-1}^k|$ coordinates and $|C_n^k|$ coordinates respectively. The shortest distance is computed from the nth frame lung contour coordinates, C_n^k to $(n-1)^{th}$ frame contour coordinates, C_{n-1}^k. This resulting distance is a vector of length $|C_n^k|$, called D_{n-1}^n. Let thresh be the threshold obtained by some of the statistical measures on the distribution of the distance vector. This can be mean, median, standard deviation, variance or even may be obtained by applying Otsu thresholding. If m denotes the mean of this distance vector and s denote the standard deviation of this distance vector. The decision on if this threshold is to be used for finding the nodule is as follows:

if $thresh \leq (m+s)$ **then**
    do not apply thresholding
else
    apply thresholding
end if

Non-application of thresholding indirectly implies that there are no juxta-pleural nodules in the nth frame lung contour. On the other hand the application of thresholding denotes the possibility of the presence of juxta-pleural nodule.

Another way of applying thresholding to locate the juxta-pleural nodules is to obtain constant values for threshold and compare the same with the statistical measures. For instance, a nodule is present

if $statistical parameter \leq constant$ **then**
    nodule not present
else
    nodule is present
end if

The set of contour co-ordinates from C_n^k whose D_{n-1}^n values in the distance vector are greater than the threshold are selected and marked on a two dimensional frame to obtain the juxta-pleural nodule contour.

4 Results and Discussion

4.1 Datasets Used

The proposed work can be tested with Lung Image Database Consortium and Image Database Resource Initiative public dataset [1]. This dataset has 1018 CT scans of 1012 patients. Each CT scan has multiple 2D CT slices and a corresponding XML file that records the result of two phase annotation process performed by four radiologists in a blinded and unblinded manner.

4.2 Step by Step Results on Processing of 2D Image Slices

Figures 3, 4, 5, 6, 7 8 show the step by step results obtained on processing two consecutive image slices. Figures 3(a) & (b) refer to LIDC-IDRI - 0022, slices 99 and 100. As per the radiologists annotation, the nodule is set to begin from slice 100 onwards.

The two 2-D image slices are input to thresholding and morphology based lung segmentation pipeline [10]. The output obtained are the left and right lobes as shown in Fig. 3(c) & (d). The contours of these lung region is obtained as shown in Fig. 4(a) & (b) and they are overlaid on top of each other as shown in 5. The red contour shows the contour of the lung region as in Fig. 4(a) and blue contour shows the contour of the lung region as in Fig. 4(b).

From these overlapping contours, the coordinates of the contour are obtained and shortest distant points from one contour to the other contour is obtained and the distance of such points are also tabulated. That is, assuming the contour corresponding to 99th slice as first contour and the contour corresponding to 100th slice as second contour, the points along the second contour from all points of the first contour are obtained as well as the points along the first contour from all points of the second contour are obtained and their corresponding distances stored.

Figure 6(a) shows the lines drawn between all points of first contour to shortest point coordinates of second contour. Similarly, Fig. 6(b) shows the line drawn between all points of second contour to shortest point coordinates of first contour.

Now a threshold constant of 2.0 is used and the standard deviation of all the stored distances is computed. If the standard deviation is beyond 2, this means that there is a significant change in the lung contour which may possibly have been due to a lung nodule along the lung contour.

The juxta-pleural nodule region is then found out by listing all those shortest points from one contour to another which contribute to a significant change in

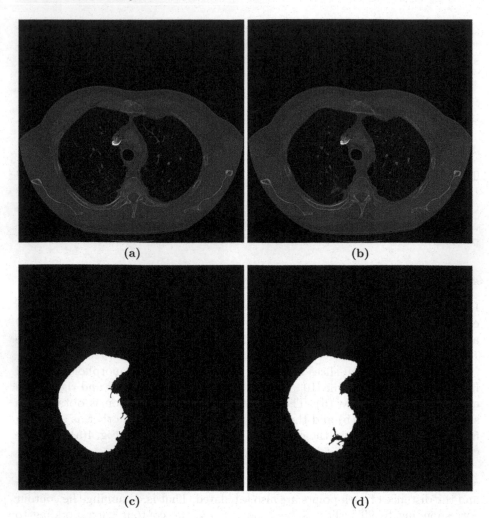

Fig. 3. (a) original image - slice number 99 of LIDC-IDRI-0022 volume (b) original image - slice number 100 of LIDC-IDRI-0022 volume (c) Segmented Left lobe of slice number 99 of LIDC-IDRI-0022 volume (d) Segmented Left lobe of slice number 100 of LIDC-IDRI-0022 volume

lung contour. The distance is significant when the distance of the points is greater than the Otsu threshold of the distance vector. Figure 7 shows the distribution of the distances through a histogram and the red line is the Otsu threshold.

As shown in Fig. 8 the points which contribute to the significant variation in the distances are marked as lung nodule and are highlighted by the square.

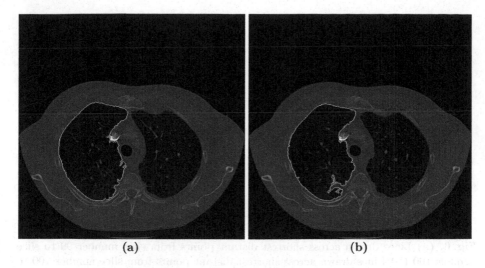

Fig. 4. (a) Left lobe contour of slice number 99 of LIDC-IDRI-0022 volume (b) Left lobe contour of slice number 100 of LIDC-IDRI-0022 volume

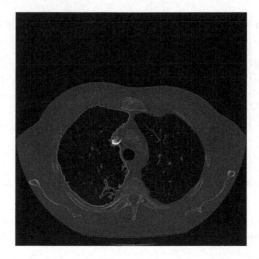

Fig. 5. Left lobe contours of slice number 99 & 100 of LIDC-IDRI-0022 volume overlaid

Table 1 shows the previous slice number and the current slice number. For a specific previous slice number and current slice number, each row presents the average shortest distance between the all coordinate points in lung contour from the previous slice to the current slice and current slice to the previous slice with respect to the left lobe and the right lobe. The bold values clearly show that there exist a nodule in the left lobe between the 99th slice to 110th slice.

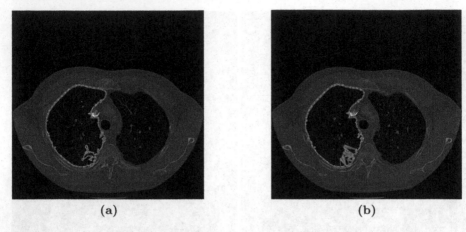

(a)   (b)

Fig. 6. (a) Lines drawn across shortest distant points from slice number 99 to slice number 100 **(b)** Lines drawn across shortest distant points from slice number 100 to slice number 99

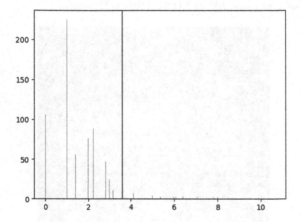

Fig. 7. Distribution of lengths of Lines drawn across shortest distant points from slice number 99 to slice number 100 with the Otsu threshold distance in red

Table 2 shows the results obtained on slices of a single image volume with various values of the standard deviation. It can be observed that the standard deviation of constant 3 is optimal than other values.

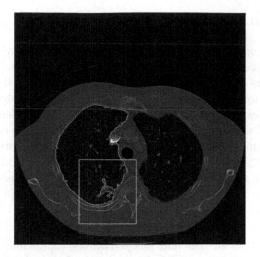

Fig. 8. The region of interest shown by square around Juxta-pleural nodule region

Table 1. Distance measures of LIDC-IDRI-0022 volume

S.No	Previous Slice No	Current Slice No	Distance Length (in mm)			
			Left Lobe		Right Lobe	
			Pre to Cur	Cur to Pre	Pre to Cur	Cur to Pre
1	99	100	**8.4540**	0.9501	0.9957	0.9837
2	100	101	**8.1590**	1.6692	1.0828	1.084
3	101	102	**9.2790**	2.7870	1.5444	1.3409
4	102	103	**8.6793**	3.7123	1.7730	1.8248
5	103	104	**10.400**	4.2058	0.9485	0.9635
6	104	105	**9.2633**	4.5890	1.0814	1.0316
7	105	106	**8.1943**	6.0045	1.5030	1.3946
8	106	107	**8.4527**	7.5222	1.4755	1.6339
9	107	108	**7.1294**	7.9784	1.5353	1.4998
10	108	109	**6.0944**	7.5761	1.4346	1.4906
11	109	110	**3.8293**	3.1888	1.3375	1.3154

Table 2. Sensitivity analysis of varying standard deviation

Measures	Standard deviation			
	2	3	4	5
Sensitivity	90.65	88.13	64.71	47.71
Specificity	82.01	86.38	89.98	91.75
Accuracy	82.79	86.58	87.92	88.14

5   Conclusion

This paper has proposed as well as demonstrated a simple while novel method for detection of juxta-pleural lung nodules from radiological images obtained from patients. The novelty of the proposed system is that the images are not processed in isolation but they are processed in sequence to calculate the shortest distance between two slices helps in segmentation of juxta-pleural lung nodules. The demonstrated work applied the border to border shortest distance algorithm for the nodule segmentation task. Further, this work successfully validates and demonstrates that sequence based information useful for nodule segmentation and can be used in random with other medical image processing applications.

References

1. Armato III, S.G., et al.: The lung image database consortium (LIDC) and image database resource initiative (IDRI): a completed reference database of lung nodules on CT scans. Med. Phys. **38**(2), 915–931 (2011)
2. Cavalcanti, P.G., et al.: Lung nodule segmentation in chest computed tomography using a novel background estimation method. Quantit. Imaging Med. Surg. **6**(1), 16 (2016)
3. Chung, H., Ko, H., Jeon, S.J., Yoon, K.H., Lee, J.: Automatic lung segmentation with juxta-pleural nodule identification using active contour model and Bayesian approach. IEEE J. Trans. Eng. Health Med. **6**, 1–13 (2018)
4. Dhara, A.K., Mukhopadhyay, S., Khandelwal, N.: Computer-aided detection and analysis of pulmonary nodule from CT images: a survey. IETE Tech. Rev. **29**(4), 265–275 (2012)
5. Huidrom, R., Chanu, Y.J., Singh, K.M.: Automated lung segmentation on computed tomography image for the diagnosis of lung cancer. Computación y Sistemas **22**(3), 907–915 (2018)
6. Mansoor, A., et al.: Segmentation and image analysis of abnormal lungs at CT: current approaches, challenges, and future trends. Radiographics **35**(4), 1056–1076 (2015)
7. Saraswathi, S., Sheela, L.M.I.: Detection of juxtapleural nodules in lung cancer cases using an optimal critical point selection algorithm. Asian Pacific J. Cancer Prevent. APJCP **18**(11), 3143 (2017)
8. Sariya, K., Ravishankar, M.: Classifying juxta-pleural pulmonary nodules. In: Satapathy, S.C., Biswal, B.N., Udgata, S.K., Mandal, J.K. (eds.) Proceedings of the 3rd International Conference on Frontiers of Intelligent Computing: Theory and Applications (FICTA) 2014. AISC, vol. 328, pp. 597–603. Springer, Cham (2015). https://doi.org/10.1007/978-3-319-12012-6_66
9. Singadkar, G., Mahajan, A., Thakur, M., Talbar, S.: Automatic lung segmentation for the inclusion of juxtapleural nodules and pulmonary vessels using curvature based border correction. J. King Saud Univ. Comput. Inf. Sci. (2018)
10. Suji, R.J., Bhadouria, S.S., Dhar, J., Godfrey, W.W.: Optical flow methods for lung nodule segmentation on LIDC-IDRI images. J. Digit. Imaging **33**(5), 1306–1324 (2020). https://doi.org/10.1007/s10278-020-00346-w
11. Tan, Y., Schwartz, L.H., Zhao, B.: Segmentation of lung lesions on CT scans using watershed, active contours, and Markov random field. Med. Phys. **40**(4), 043502 (2013)

12. Wang, J., Guo, H.: Automatic approach for lung segmentation with juxta-pleural nodules from thoracic CT based on contour tracing and correction. Comput. Math. Methods Med. **2016** (2016)
13. Yang, Z., et al.: Robust pulmonary nodule segmentation in CT image for juxta-pleural and juxta-vascular case. Curr. Bioinform. **14**(2), 139–147 (2019)

Appearance-Invariant Entry-Exit Matching Using Visual Soft Biometric Traits

V. Vinay Kumar[1(✉)] (iD) and P. Nagabhushan[2]

[1] Department of Studies in Computer Science, University of Mysore, Mysuru, India
[2] Indian Institute of Information Technology Allahabad, Prayagraj, India

Abstract. The problem of appearance invariant subject re-identification for Entry-Exit surveillance applications is addressed. A novel Semantic Entry-Exit matching model that makes use of ancillary information about subjects such as height, build, complexion, and clothing color to endorse exit of every subject who had entered private area is proposed in this paper. The proposed method is robust to variations in appearances such as clothing, carrying, and head masking. Each describing attribute is given equal weight while computing the matching score, and hence the proposed model achieves high rank-k accuracy on benchmark datasets. The soft biometric traits used as a combination though, cannot achieve high rank-1 accuracy, it helps to narrow down the search to match using reliable biometric traits such as gait and face whose learning and matching time is costlier when compared to the soft biometrics.

Keywords: Entry-exit surveillance · Appearance-invariant person re-identification · Camera forbidden zones

1 Introduction

Intelligent video surveillance systems overcame the limitations in the human ability to diligently watch and monitor multiple live video surveillance footages [1]. The intelligent video surveillance domain witnessed extensive research in the past two decades, thus extending its applications to intruder detection and validation, crime prevention, elderly people, and children monitoring. Today, public places such as shopping malls, airports, buses, and rail stations are completely under surveillance ambit except in few areas such as toilets and changing rooms, which are referred to as *private areas* where installing surveillance cameras is considered a breach of privacy. This is often seen as a hindrance to security systems in crime prevention and public safety. As a solution, the notion of Entry-Exit surveillance (EES) [2] deals with the monitoring of subjects entering and exiting private areas. The key objective is to assure that the subjects who had entered private areas exit in time without much variations in their appearances that may lead to suspicion. Every subject who enters the private area is labeled and saved in the gallery, and every subject who exits the private area is considered as a probe and has to be matched with subjects available in the gallery.

© Springer Nature Singapore Pte Ltd. 2021
S. K. Singh et al. (Eds.): CVIP 2020, CCIS 1376, pp. 260–269, 2021.
https://doi.org/10.1007/978-981-16-1086-8_23

1.1 Relevance of the Problem

The problem of entry-exit matching can be related to a person re-identification problem where the aim is to match subjects moving between surveillance ambits of non-overlapping cameras. For every probe subject, the matching subject in the gallery set should have a high matching rank when compared with other subjects. A detailed survey on person re-identification can be found in [3,4]. In conventional person re-identification systems, it is assumed that the subject is to be matched across camera views on the same day, and hence the issue of variation in the appearance of subjects due to change in clothing is under-addressed. However, in entry-exit surveillance, the temporal gap between entry and exit where the subjects move out of surveillance ambit envisage the possibility of change in the appearance of subjects with respect to clothing, carrying, and head masking. Traces of appearance invariant subject re-identification solutions available in the literature include analysis of gait and motion patterns in [5]. However, state of the art gait recognition algorithms suffers due to variations in the walking directions. Face biometric trait is another promising attribute for subject re-identification that can be robust to changes in clothing and carrying conditions. However, capturing of face attributes is limited to very few frames due to the distance of subjects from the camera. Adding to it, the possibility of face occlusions due to subjects overlapping as well as religious and cultural practices in unconstrained environments limits the extraction of face attributes from surveillance videos.

On the other hand, visual soft biometric attributes such as clothing color, height, body-build, accessories possessed by the subjects can be extracted from low-resolution video frames. Most of the current state of the art person re-identification methods mainly focus on clothing attributes for matching. However, in entry-exit surveillance, due to the possibility of variations in the clothing of subjects, relatively less importance must be attributed to clothing color but cannot be completely dropped as it has a high discriminating ability in the majority of the cases. The probability of change in clothing in places such as toilets and baby feeding rooms is relatively lower when compared to that of dress changing rooms in clothing outlets. Hence, it is necessary to analyze the reliability of clothing color in different scenarios. The height of the subjects is most view-invariant as reported in [6] and capturing of the attribute during subjects' appearance in a predefined region of interest in the camera view scene (entrances of private the areas in Entry-Exit surveillance scenario), makes it reliable. Similarly, build of the subjects can be captured by computing the height to width ratio provided the video footages are captured from a still camera with no variations in the view angle. Unlike the height attribute, build attribute is pose-variant. However, computing the vertical projections of the silhouettes of the segmented subjects' bounding boxes makes it discriminative. Lastly, skin complexion can be another promising attribute if illumination variations in the multiple camera views are handled.

The above discussed soft biometrics are unique in nature and are to be given equal weight for their discriminative ability under different scenarios. Also, as one soft biometric attribute cannot single-handedly identify subjects due to intra-class variations and inter-class similarities, combinations of these attributes, to an extent, can predict the subjects by matching them with the gallery samples.

1.2 Motivations and Contributions

With the above discussion, it can be inferred that though soft biometrics are not entirely reliable to recognize subjects, they provide prominent clues and help in narrowing down the search. Also, learning of soft biometrics is computationally faster as compared to the classical visual biometrics such as face and gait. This motivates us to explore the efficiency of soft biometrics in Entry-Exit matching.

The innovations accomplished in this paper can be summarized as follows:

- First, a set of hybrid features representation that is robust to possible appear-ance variations is introduced.
- An ensemble-based approach for handling heterogeneous matching results from individual soft biometrics.
- Matching analysis based on single-camera as well as two-camera based Entry-Exit surveillance model.

The proposed method is evaluated using the EnEx dataset [2] that comprises of Entry-Exit surveillance data using Single-camera and EnExX dataset [13] that also comprises of Entry-Exit surveillance data but using two field-of-view-overlapping cameras.

2   Statement of the Problem

Given the input images of subjects that are segmented from the surveillance video frames, the aim is to represent each subject with a set of highly discrim-inative soft biometric features such as clothing color, height, body-build, and complexion. Features from the subjects that are classified to have entered pri-vate areas are extracted and are saved in the gallery with labels. For every sub-ject who exits from a private area, features are extracted and are matched with samples in the gallery, and the matching score is computed with each labeled subject. Certainly, 100% classification accuracy cannot be expected from rank-1 but from rank-k predictions, and the goal is to find the value of k with which the search can be narrowed down from n to k where k<<n.

3   Proposed Model

The proposed subject recognition model is outlined in two modules, as described below.

- Feature Representation: A novel feature representation that comprises a set of features that include clothing color as well as subjects height, body-build, and complexion is introduced, thus making the model robust to clothing changes. Detailed discussion on each individual feature types can be found in the next subsection.

– Learning and Recognition: Each feature type is analyzed for its discriminative and correlating abilities on inter-class and intra-class samples, respectively, and the transformation function that maximizes the inter-class separability and intra-class associativity is computed. Subject recognition is performed based on the collective confidence of the visual soft biometrics ensembles.

3.1 Feature Representation

A set of heterogeneous features represents the individual subject, as discussed below.

Clothing Color. The given input image of the subject is decomposed into the head, torso, and leg regions based on [7]. Torso and leg regions are individually analyzed. Low-level features such as color and texture used in conventional person re-identification methods exhibit high discriminative ability on different camera views. The computational complexity of color features is faster as compared to texture features [8], and hence the proposed model is confined to color features.

RGB color space is robust to variations in translation, rotation, and scaling factors but suffers from temporal light changes outdoor throughout the day as well as illumination variations due to different camera views. HSV color space is interpreted as color space commonly perceived by humans and is considered efficient enough for color-based analysis, the RGB to HSV color transformation is time-consuming and slows down learning. On the other hand, the YCbCr color space clearly differentiates the luminance and color components. The Y component corresponds to luminance, and Cb and Cr components correspond to chrominance where Cb is blue-difference chrominance, and Cr is red-difference chrominance, and the computational complexity of RGB to YCbCr transformation is of the order $h \, X \, w$ where h and w are height and width of the input subject image. Histograms of Cb and Cr components of the torso and leg regions are computed for each subject and are concatenated to a single feature vector.

Height. Height is one of the prominent features that helps in narrowing down the search by clustering subjects of similar heights. The height of the subject is captured with reference to the entrance of private areas. As the features of the subjects who enter private areas are saved in the gallery only on confirmation of his/her entry, learning is done in time. Also, during exit, the subjects have to cross the entrance first, and hence, height is captured with other sets of features. As the height feature captured is the relative height and not the actual height, it is normalized to the values between 0 and 1.

Body-Build. Extracting height features near to the entrances of private areas also provide scope for extracting build of the subject by computing the maximum height to width ratio of the bounding boxes of the subjects when they cross the entrance. Variations in the pose of the subject are the major challenge to be addressed. Vertical projection profile is computed for the bounding boxes, and threshold t is determined with experiments to eliminate hand and leg swings, thus segmenting the subject image based on torso distribution.

Skin Complexion. Skin complexion is another essential visual attribute that helps in grouping subjects with the same complexion. The segmented head region is analyzed for skin components using the YCbCr color model with the threshold for skin detection, as reported in [9]. The skin region is segmented from the front, lateral and oblique views except for the back view.

3.2   Matching

For each feature type, Linear Discriminant Analysis (LDA) is applied for data disassociation, by projecting the feature matrix onto a subspace that maximizes the ratio of inter-class to intra-class distribution, using the Fisher's criterion.

For every class C_i (individual), the separability d_i between samples $s \in C_i$ is computed using

$$d_i = \sum (s - \bar{s}_i)(s - \bar{s}_i)' \tag{1}$$

where $\bar{s}_i$ is the mean of the class C_i

The intra-class separability matrix d for n classes is given by

$$d = \sum_{i=1}^{n} d_i \tag{2}$$

and the intra-class compactness is given by

$$Q = 1/d \tag{3}$$

The disassociativity matrix D between classes is computed using

$$D = \sum_{i=1}^{n} m_i(\bar{s}_i - \bar{s})(\bar{s}_i - \bar{s})' \tag{4}$$

where m_i is the number of training samples in class C_i and $\bar{s}$ is the overall mean.

The transition matrix T that maximizes the spread between the classes and compactness within the classes is given by

$$T = |D||Q| \tag{5}$$

So, given a probe subject p, the features are extracted and every soft biometric is operated with transition function in Eq. 5 and the classification is performed for every soft biometric by computing the euclidean distance of the probe with every gallery sample and thus all the gallery classes are ranked for every soft biometric. Subject recognition is done based on the collective voting decision among the different soft biometrics ensemble thus giving equal prominence for each soft biometric. Confidence Cf is computed for every gallery class C_i for each soft biometric f using

$$Cf(C_i, f) = \frac{n - rank(C_i, f) + 1}{n} \tag{6}$$

Hence, the Collective confidence CF of the model for each gallery class C_i is

$$CF(C_i) = \sum_{j=1}^{f} \frac{Cf(C_i, j)}{f} \tag{7}$$

Rank for every gallery class is assigned based on the collective confidence calculated using Eq. 7.

4 Experiments and Discussions

The proposed method is tested using the EnEx dataset as well as EnExX dataset. EnEx dataset provides EES data using a single camera, and EnExX dataset provides EES data using two cameras. However, EnExX dataset can be used for single camera-based analysis as well. Firstly, with a single camera view where the camera is placed so as to view the entrance of private areas without intruding the privacy of the public. Here, the camera captures flipped views of subjects during entry and exit where generally back view of the subject is visible during entry and front view during exit, or if the camera is placed so as to have a lateral view of the subject, then entry-exit shall have left-right flipped view variations. Next, with two view-overlapping cameras so as to have 360° view of the subject where one camera compliment the other by having a flipped view of the subject simultaneously.

4.1 Experimental Setup

The input to the system is the images of the subjects extracted from video frames of the datasets using [10] deeply learned people detection method. The frames are background subtracted before applying the people detectors. Two sets of images - gallery and probes. Gallery set contains images captured while subjects entered, whereas probe set contained images captured while subjects exited. Figure 1 shows sample images of subjects in the gallery and probe using a single camera, and Fig. 2 shows sample images of subjects in the gallery and probe using two cameras. The image pair in the first row shows the entry of the subject captured in two different cameras and the second row shows subject exiting the private area

The height and body-build attributes are captured when the subject crossed the entrances of private areas, and other attributes such as clothing color and skin complexion were extracted after normalizing the input images to the standard size of 128×64. Then the input images are decomposed into the head, torso, and leg regions, and these are converted to the YCbCr color model, and histograms

Fig. 1. Sample Entry-Exit image pair with variation in appearance from EnExX dataset [13] using Single Camera

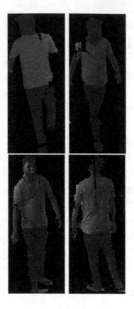

Fig. 2. Sample Entry-Exit image pair with variation in appearance from EnExX dataset captured using two cameras

of Cb and Cr components are extracted with 24 bins per channel for each region of a subject. Skin regions are extracted from each input image, and the mean of Cb and Cr components are computed.

Initially, simulations were carried out on the EnEx dataset, here the size of the private area, which is the gallery, was assumed to be 10, 25, and 50, respectively. The gallery contained 30 training images for each subject, among which five images provided height and body-build metrics. Hence, the height and body-build attributes are trained separately. For every probe subject, a single image that contained all the attributes was selected to match with all the samples in the gallery. Later, the simulations were extended to EnExX dataset, where pair of images for clothing and skin complexion attributes are provided for training and testing, and the features are concatenated to a single vector for representation.

The notion of Entry-Exit surveillance is novel and the proposed model is first of its kind that solved Entry-Exit matching which involved appearance invariant person re identification. However, comparative analysis is provided with [11] and [12] methods that includes soft biometrics by evaluating them on the EnEx and EnExX dataset. Tables 1, 2, 3 and 4 provide matching scores of the proposed method in comparison with [11] and [12].

Table 1. Matching rates on EnEx dataset, gallery size = 25

Gallery size = 25			
Rank	1	5	10
RS-KISS	0.079	0.316	0.486
Ensemble Learning	0.094	0.367	0.491
Proposed model	0.231	0.489	0.867

Table 2. Matching rates on EnEx dataset, gallery size = 50

Gallery size = 50			
Rank	1	5	10
RS-KISS	0.071	0.283	0.423
Ensemble Learning	0.082	0.326	0.463
Proposed model	0.217	0.466	0.812

4.2 Discussion

With the results, it is evident that the state of the art person re-identification systems suffers due to variations in the clothing of the subjects and hence the demand for active research in appearance-invariant person re-identification. Variations in the appearances account for clothing, height due to change in foot wears and complexion due to applying cosmetics. Hence, collective confidence of the attributes are considered than weighted averaging. The proposed model, though, is robust to clothing variations, it suffers due to uniformity in height, build and complexion of subjects of the same race. Also, the extraction of skin attributes from subjects who cover the entire body with religious attires is challenging. The height attribute though, looks promising, it suffers due to variations in head accessories of the subjects. Overall, the evaluation results of the proposed model on the EES specific datasets can be used as a benchmark by the research community to compare their works on the EES matching problem using visual soft biometrics.

Table 3. Matching rates on EnExX dataset, gallery size = 25

Gallery size = 25			
Rank	1	5	10
RS-KISS	0.091	0.352	0.533
Ensemble Learning	0.162	0.431	0.616
Proposed model	0.366	0.581	0.891

Table 4. Matching rates on EnExX dataset, gallery size = 50

Gallery size = 50			
Rank	1	5	10
RS-KISS	0.088	0.263	0.411
Ensemble Learning	0.113	0.412	0.493
Proposed model	0.342	0.563	0.838

5   Conclusion

With this paper, it can be inferred that in real-time tracking, it is important
to narrow down the search based on predictions using visual attributes whose
learning and recognition are faster than the reliable attributes such as gait whose
learning and recognition rates are higher and faster with the narrow galleries.
Collective confidence based matching provides equal weightage to all the soft
biometrics considered. The proposed novel Entry-Exit subject matching method
shows good rank-10 accuracy on the standard datasets and thus enkindle competitive research in the Entry-Exit surveillance domain.

Acknowledgements. This work has been supported by The University Grants Commission, India.

References

1. Sulman, N., Sanocki, T., Goldgof, D., Kasturi, R.: How effective is human video
   surveillance performance? In: 19th International Conference on Pattern Recognition, ICPR 2008, pp. 1–3, 8–11 December 2008
2. Vinay Kumar, V., Nagabhushan, P., Roopa, S.N.: Entry–exit video surveillance: a
   benchmark dataset. In: Chaudhuri, B.B., Nakagawa, M., Khanna, P., Kumar, S.
   (eds.) Proceedings of 3rd International Conference on Computer Vision and Image
   Processing. AISC, vol. 1022, pp. 353–364. Springer, Singapore (2020). https://doi.
   org/10.1007/978-981-32-9088-4_30
3. Yu, H.X., Zheng, W.S., Wu, A., Guo, X., Gong, S., Lai, J.H.: Cross-view asymmetric metric learning for unsupervised person re-identification. In: Proceedings of
   the IEEE International Conference on Computer Vision and Pattern Recognition
   (2019)

4. Karanam, S., Wu, Z., Rates-Borras, A., Camps, O. and Radke, R.J.: A systematic evaluation and benchmark for person re-identification: features, metrics, and datasets. In: IEEE Transactions on Pattern Analysis and Machine Intelligence, vol. 41, no. 3, pp. 523–536, 1 March 2019. https://doi.org/10.1109/TPAMI.2018.2807450

5. Chin-Poo, L., Chiat, W., Alan, T., Kian, L.: Review on vision-based gait recognition: representations, classification schemes, and datasets. Am. J. Appl. Sci. **14**, 252–266 (2017). https://doi.org/10.3844/ajassp.2017.252.266

6. Moctezuma, D., Conde, C., De Diego, I.M., et al.: J. Image Video Proc. **2015**, 28 (2015). https://doi.org/10.1186/s13640-015-0078-1

7. Iat-Fai, L., Jing-Jing, F., Ming, T.: Automatic body feature extraction from a marker-less scanned human body. Comput. Aided Des. **39**, 568–582 (2007). https://doi.org/10.1016/j.cad.2007.03.003

8. Shahbahrami, A., Borodin, D., Juurlink, B.: Comparison between color and texture features for image retrieval (2008)

9. Kolkur, S., Kalbande, D., Shimpi, P., Bapat, C., Jatakia, J.: Human skin detection using RGB. HSV, and YCbCr color models (2017). https://doi.org/10.2991/iccasp-16.2017.51

10. Kokul, T., Ramanan, A., Pinidiyaarachchi, U.A.J.: Online multi-person tracking-by-detection method using ACF and particle filter. In: 2015 IEEE Seventh International Conference on Intelligent Computing and Information Systems (ICICIS), Cairo, pp. 529–536 (2015)

11. Yang, Y., Liu, X., Ye, Q., Tao, D.: Ensemble learning-based person re-identification with multiple feature representations. Complexity **2018**, 12 (2018). Article ID 5940181. https://doi.org/10.1155/2018/5940181

12. Tao, D., Jin, L., Wang, Y., Yuan, Y., Li, X.: Person re-identification by regularized smoothing KISS metric learning. IEEE Trans. Circuits Syst. Video Technol. **23**(10), 1675–1685 (2013)

13. Vinay Kumar, V., Nagabhushan, P.: Monitoring of people entering and exiting private areas using computer vision. Int. J. Comput. Appl. **177**(15), 1–5 (2019)

A Nonlocal Spatial Coherent Fuzzy C-Means Clustering for Bias Field Correction in Brain MR Images

Pranaba K. Mishro$^{(\boxtimes)}$, Sanjay Agrawal, and Rutuparna Panda

VSS University of Technology, Burla 768018, India

Abstract. Bias field in magnetic resonance (MR) images is caused due to the varying gradient driven eddy current in the MR image scanner. This results in intensity inhomogeneity (IIH) in the MR image. Therefore, bias field correction is a fundamental requisite in the tissue investigation procedure. The existing solutions used fuzzy c-means (FCM) algorithm with non-local spatial information. However, the use of only local spatial information may lead to poor segmentation of tissue regions. In this paper, we suggest a nonlocal spatial coherent FCM clustering scheme for bias field correction. A similarity measure is computed using a Gaussian kernel for local spatial information. A nonlocal coherence factor is incorporated into the objective function and membership matrix for separating the non-discriminable tissue regions in the brain MR images. The suggested scheme is analyzed in comparison with different existing methods. It is experimented with different modalities of synthetic and clinical brain MR images. The method is validated using standard cluster validation and quality evaluation indices. The results indicate the superiority of the proposed methodology compared with state-of-the-art approaches.

Keywords: Bias field correction · MR image analysis · FCM clustering

1 Introduction

Magnetic resonance (MR) imaging is an important clinical image analyzing tool for the diagnostic laparotomies. In brain images, it plays a vital role in analyzing the tissue structure and diagnosing brain diseases. However, noise and bias field or intensity inhomogeneity (IIH) affects the quality of the image in practice. Further, the complex tissue boundaries are inherent challenges with brain MR image analysis. Therefore, it is essential to eliminate such artifacts for achieving better segmentation accuracy. In the literature, filtering, surface fitting, segmentation and histogram based approaches are found to address the problem. Among these approaches, fuzzy C-means (FCM) clustering based segmentation is a fundamental technique used for bias field correction (BFC) and delineating the tissue regions [1–3]. In recent years, many modifications on the conventional FCM technique are reported [4–14].

In [4], the authors suggested a modified FCM (MFCM) technique. The objective function of the method is formulated by using local spatial information. It biases the

© Springer Nature Singapore Pte Ltd. 2021
S. K. Singh et al. (Eds.): CVIP 2020, CCIS 1376, pp. 270–281, 2021.
https://doi.org/10.1007/978-981-16-1086-8_24

intensity values towards piecewise homogeneous labels. This approach helps in correcting the bias field in brain tissue regions. However, the method is tested with single feature data only. Szilagyi et al. [5] suggested a multi stage hybrid FCM for varying IIH in the tissue regions of brain MR images. Despotovic et al. [6] presented a spatial FCM (SFCM) algorithm for BFC in brain MR images. The method compensates the bias field by including neighboring information while computing the membership values. However, these methods eliminate bias filed at the cost of increased computational complexity. Ji et al. [7] proposed a possibilistic FCM algorithm for estimating IIH within the tissue regions. The method used the local contextual information in computing the objective function. Further, the authors used the prior and posterior probabilities for computing the spatial information. It is integrated with orthogonal polynomials for computing the bias field in the brain MR images [8]. However, the estimation of spatial information is limited to its local neighboring pixels. This may result in assigning data points of same tissue region to different clusters.

Tu et al. [9] suggested the coherent local intensity clustering (CLIC) approach for estimating the IIH in the brain MR images. The method included a total variation factor as a local coherent intensity criterion for optimal solution. However, the method is less effective in complex inhomogeneous environment. Cong et al. [10] suggested a bias field estimation approach using its local and global information (BFELGI). A Gaussian kernel map is used for incorporating the local spatial information, whereas global information is included as a regularization factor. The method is found to be effective in reducing small level of BFC in brain MR images. However, the presence of noise in MR image may result in inaccurate tissue regions. Shan et al. [11] suggested a contour based region fitting scheme for BFC in brain MR images. The spatial information is computed from the probabilities of intensity levels in its neighborhood. Borys et al. [12] suggested N3 correction on the k-harmonic means for estimating the bias field. However, the performance of the method is limited with the complex structure brain MR images. Mahata et al. [13] incorporated local contextual information and Gaussian fuzzy clusters (LCIGFC) in formulating the cost function and membership matrix of the FCM algorithm. A slowly varying Gaussian space is implemented iteratively for modeling the bias field. Song and Zhang [14] incorporated a nonlocal coherence factor in the FCM clustering scheme for BFC in brain MR images. The objective function is formulated using a Gaussian kernel based local spatial information and a global mean factor. In these techniques, the BFC and segmentation of the tissue regions are carried out simultaneously.

From the above discussions, it is observed that the FCM based schemes used local and nonlocal spatial information for BFC and segmentation of tissue regions in brain MR images. However, the coherence between the local and nonlocal spatial information in correcting the bias field is missing in state-of-the-art methods. This has motivated us to suggest a nonlocal spatial coherent FCM (NSCFCM) clustering approach for BFC and tissue region segmentation in brain MR images. The method includes local spatial information and nonlocal regularization factor in the objective function and the membership matrix for BFC and tissue region segmentation. The suggested scheme is tested with various forms of synthetic and real brain MR images and validated using standard evaluation indices. The method is formulated by using the statistical and FCM based methods in our published articles [15, 16]. The performance of the proposed scheme is compared with recently published articles. The remained paper is arranged as: Sect. 2 explains briefly the related methods. The proposed methodology is discussed in Sect. 3. The outcomes and their analysis is presented in Sect. 4. The proposed methodology is concluded in Sect. 5.

2 Related Methods

This section briefly elaborates the recent methods suggested in solving the problem on hand. The discussed methods are used for comparison also. Let $A = \{a_1, ..., a_M\}$ is a brain MR image with M number of pixels. The image is affected by bias field, resulting in intensity inhomogeneity within the tissue regions. FCM algorithm is employed to partition the image M into v number of clusters by minimizing the objective function.

$$J_{FCM} = \sum_{i=1}^{v} \sum_{j=1}^{M} u_{ij}^m \|a_j - c_i\|^2, \tag{1}$$

where, u_{ij} is a membership value of a pixel a_j in i^{th} cluster. $\|.\|$ is an Euclidian norm, $m(>1)$ is the fuzzifier, defining the degree of fuzziness in the partition. Here, the membership matrix satisfies the condition $u_{ij} \in [0\,1] | \sum_{i=1}^{v} u_{ij} = 1$ and $0 < \sum_{j=1}^{M} u_{ij} < M$.

The SFCM Method

The method is formulated by introducing a weight factor in the objective function of the FCM algorithm. Here, the weight factor in combination with the existing distance measure in the membership matrix is used for BFC in brain MR images. The modified objective function is expressed as [6]:

$$J_{SFCM} = \sum_{i=1}^{v} \sum_{j=1}^{M} u_{ij}^m (1 - S_{ij}) \|a_j - c_i\|^2, \tag{2}$$

where S_{ij} is the weight factor used in formulating the new distance measure as $(1 - S_{ij})\|a - c_i\|^2$. This introduce the neighboring information in combination with the gray scale differences. The method is useful in preserving the structural details as well as the edge information, while performing BFC in the tissue regions. However, the effect of nonlocal spatial information from the similar structures are not considered in this approach.

The CLIC Method

The method formulates a convergence mechanism for BFC in brain MR images by introducing the spatially coherent local intensities. The spatial coherent information is computed from the similarity of each pixel in its neighborhood. The similarity measure is formulated using a Gaussian kernel weight parameter. The objective function of the technique is expressed as [9]:

$$J_{CLIC} = \sum_{i=1}^{v} \sum_{j=1}^{M} u_{ij}^m \sum_{r \in \Omega_j} D\|a_j - b_j c_i\|^2, \tag{3}$$

where, b_jc_i is the cluster prototype. $D = M(r-j)$ is the Gaussian kernel weight parameter. The method is found to be effective with smoothly varying intensity values in a local region (Ω_j) of an image. However, only the local neighboring information is considered for computing the similarity measure. This gives poor performance with the bias field affected brain MR images with noise.

The BFELGI Method

The method is formulated using the local and global spatial information for BFC in brain MR images. The local neighboring information is incorporated by using a Gaussian kernel mapping space, whereas nonlocal spatial information is included as a global regulating parameter. The weight among the local and global spatial information helps in estimating the bias field information. An improved objective function is formulated using the weight among the local and global information for estimating the bias field information. This is written as [10]:

$$J_{BFELGI} = \sum_{i=1}^{v}\sum_{j=1}^{M} u_{ij}^m \sum_{r\in\Omega_j} D\|a_j - b_jc_i\|^2 + \sum_{i=1}^{v}\sum_{j=1}^{M} \left(a_j u_{ij}^m (1 - u_{ij}^{m-1}) + \beta_j u_{ij}^m \sum_{r\in\Omega_j} D\|\bar{a}_j - b_jc_i\|^2 \right)$$

(4)

where, β_j is the balancing weight in between the local and nonlocal neighboring information. Rest of the parameter are same as in (3). The computation of global information reduces the complexity in parameter setting, while correcting the bias field.

The LCIGFC Method

The method used local contextual information for obtaining the belongingness of a particular tissue type into a region. Further, a Gaussian function is used to compute the bias field caused due to IIH in the tissue regions of the brain MR image. The method used local and nonlocal membership values for generating the cluster centers. The objective function is denoted as [13]:

$$J_{LCIGFC} = \sum_{i=1}^{v}\sum_{j=1}^{M} u_{ij}^m \left\| \frac{a_j}{b_j} - c_i \right\|^2 + \beta \sum_{i=1}^{v}\sum_{j=1}^{M} f_{ij} \tau_{ij}^m \left\| \frac{\bar{a}_j}{b_j} - c_i \right\|^2,$$

(5)

where, u_{ij} and τ_{ij} are the global and local membership values, f_{ij} is the probability of belongingness of the pixel a_j into the ith cluster and b_j is the estimated bias field. β is the parameter controlling the effect of spatial information. However, the execution time is high due to the iterative computation of the pixel labels.

3 Proposed Methodology

The proposed method is formulated by incorporating the local and nonlocal spatial information in computing the objective function and the membership matrix of the standard FCM algorithm. The local spatial information is included as a similarity measure. This is obtained by using a Gaussian kernel space for discriminating the MR data in its neighborhood. Further, a nonlocal spatial regularization factor is incorporated for compensating

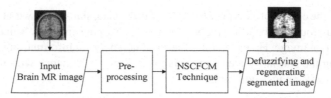

Fig. 1. Representation block diagram of the suggested technique.

the non-discriminable tissue regions. A representation block diagram of the suggested technique is given in Fig. 1.

Here, $A = \{a_1, \cdots, a_M\}$ is the biased MR image with M number of data points, where $a_j = x_j b_j$ is the jth biased data of the actual data x_j with a bias field data b_j. The nonlocal weighted mean value (y_j) of the image is expressed as:

$$y_j = \sum_{l \in \omega_j^r} \omega_{jl} a_l, \qquad (6)$$

where, ω_j^r is the region of interest with radius r around a_l, ω_{jl} is the nonlocal regularization factor of an image. This value is computed from the similarity measure of a data point in its neighborhood with the constraint conditions $0 \leq \omega_{jl} \leq 1$ and $\sum_l \omega_{jl} = 1$.

Mathematically, this value is computed as:

$$\omega_{jl} = e\left(-\|Na_j - Na_l\|_{2\sigma}^2 / h\right), \qquad (7)$$

where, σ is the standard deviation, Na_j and Na_l are the neighboring grayscale vectors of the data point at j^{th} pixel. h is a control factor for adjusting the deviation of the similarity measure. The objective function of the proposed methodology is formulated by introducing the local neighborhood information and nonlocal weighted mean value, as:

$$J_{NSCFCM} = \sum_{i=1}^{v} \sum_{j=1}^{M} u_{ij}^m \sum_{r \in \Omega_j} D\left[\beta_j(1 - S_{ij})\|a_j - b_j c_i\|^2 + (1 - \beta_j)\|y_j - b_j c_i\|^2\right], \qquad (8)$$

where, the pixel data (a_j) belongs to the ith cluster with membership value (u_{ij}). The scalar exponent (m) defines the degree of fuzziness, Ω_j is the selective region of data point (a_j) with radius r, $b_j c_i$ is the ith cluster prototype, S_{ij} is the weighted term of Gaussian kernel assigned for the pixel value a_j, $b_j c_i$ is the cluster prototype with bias field, β_j is a balancing factor among local spatial information and nonlocal weighted mean value. This can be calculated as:

$$\beta_j = \frac{1}{1 + \sigma_a/\bar{a}^2}, \qquad (9)$$

where, $\bar{a}$ is the mean intensity value and σ_a is the standard deviation of a pixel data in the same window. The inclusion of a data point in a specific cluster (tissue region) is determined in terms of its membership matrix. The membership value and the cluster centers are computed using the following expressions:

$$
u_{ij} = \frac{\sum\limits_{r \in \Omega_j} M \left[\beta_j (1 - S_{ij}) \| a_j - b_j c_i \|^2 + (1 - \beta_j) \| y_j - b_j c_i \|^2 \right]^{-1/(m+1)}}{\sum\limits_{l=1}^{v} \left(\sum\limits_{r \in \Omega_j} M \left[\beta_j (1 - S_{ij}) \| a_j - b_j c_i \|^2 + (1 - \beta_j) \| y_j - b_j c_i \|^2 \right]^{-1/(m+1)} \right)},
$$

(10)

$$
c_i = \frac{\sum\limits_{j=1}^{M} \sum\limits_{r \in \Omega_j} M b_j \left[\beta_j (1 - S_{ij}) a_j - (1 - \beta_j) y_j \right] u_{ij}^m}{\sum\limits_{j=1}^{M} \sum\limits_{r \in \Omega_j} M b_j^2 (1 - \beta_j S_{ij}) u_{ij}^m}
$$

(11)

Further, the bias field data is estimated as:

$$
b_j = \frac{\sum\limits_{i=1}^{v} \sum\limits_{r \in \Omega_j} M c_i \left[\beta_j (1 - S_{ij}) a_j + (1 - \beta_j) y_j \right] u_{ij}^m}{\sum\limits_{i=1}^{v} \sum\limits_{r \in \Omega_j} M c_i^2 (1 - \beta_j S_{ij}) u_{ij}^m}.
$$

(12)

Membership values (10) and cluster center (11) are computed and updated iteratively for their optimal values. The bias field data is estimated using (12). The proposed scheme converges to the actual values using iterative conditional mode. Finally, all tissue regions are extracted and combined to form the bias field corrected brain MR image having distinctive tissue areas.

4 Results and Discussion

This section presents the outcomes of the proposed methodology in comparison to the recently published works. The suggested technique is simulated with $i5$ processor using MATLAB. A set of T1, T2, PD and clinical brain MR images are used for the performance comparison. Various volumes of synthetic brain MR images are abstracted from the BrainWeb dataset [17] and clinical data are taken from IBSR database [18]. The percentage of noise shows the variation of the gray scale intensities with the influence of noise. For example, 7% noise indicates the variation of actual intensity value by $\pm 7\%$. Similarly, IIH percentage shows the degradation of intensities in presence of IIH. For each synthetic brain MR images, a selected volume of 51 slices are chosen depending on the presence of all tissue regions. A selected volume of 21 slices of t1-w real MR images are also experimented. The suggested scheme is compared with the recently published SFCM [6], CLIC [9], BFELGI [10], LCIGFC [13] methods.

276   P. K. Mishro et al.

Qualitative Evaluation

This analysis provides a visual appreciation for the resulting segmented brain MR images with BFC. Figures (2, 3 and 4) presents the outcomes of the suggested method in comparison to existing models. The analysis is presented with multiple volumes of brain MR images with different IIH and noise levels. The non-intersecting bias field corrected tissue region is supported using the histogram analysis, as in Fig. 5.

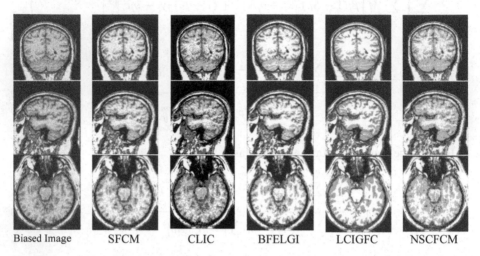

Biased Image   SFCM   CLIC   BFELGI   LCIGFC   NSCFCM

Fig. 2. Input T1-w brain MR images (20% IIH) and segmented results with different methods.

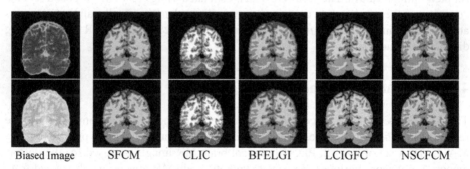

Biased Image   SFCM   CLIC   BFELGI   LCIGFC   NSCFCM

Fig. 3. Input T2 and PD-w brain MR images (20% IIH) and segmented results with different methods.

The segmented outcomes of different techniques using an input volume (20%IIH) of brain MR image are presented in Fig. 2. Row wise, the input and segmented images are presented for the coronal, sagittal and transversal views of T1-w brain MR images. From the visual observations, the clarity and discrimination of the tissue regions are better in comparison to the other methods. The outcomes from the suggested method gives distinguishable tissue matters without noise. This may be due to the use of coherence

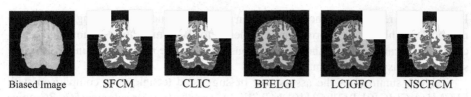

| Biased Image | SFCM | CLIC | BFELGI | LCIGFC | NSCFCM |

Fig. 4. Input T1-w real brain MR images with IIH and segmented results with different methods.

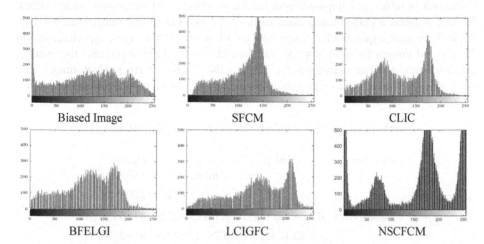

Fig. 5. Histogram of the outcomes with different methods.

factor between the local and nonlocal spatial information in computing the objective function and the membership matrix.

A similar trend is perceived with T2 and PD-w MR images. The outcomes are presented in Fig. 3. In this figure, only the tissue portion is presented on stripping the skull using a morphological operation. In Fig. 4, the visual assessment of the suggested technique using the clinical image is presented in comparison to the other methods. It is to be noted that the selected images are clinically normal. Further, they contain significant tissue regions. The bias field correction performance is further supported by relative histogram analysis. The histogram of an image with bias field shows a flat area in the inter tissue region. This makes the tissue regions inseparable. The suggested technique creates a valley in between the tissue area, indicating the removal of bias field. Figure 5 shows the histograms of different approaches (SFCM [6], CLIC [9], BFELGI [10], LCIGFC [13]) in comparison to the suggested technique.

Quantitative Evaluation
The qualitative analysis is carried out with a set of standard fuzzy partition evaluation index: classification entropy (V_{CE}) and partition coefficient (V_{PC}) [19], and quality evaluation index: mean square error (MSE) and peak signal to noise ratio (PSNR) [20]. Tables 1, 2 and 3 presents the numerical assessment of the proposed scheme in comparison to the SFCM [6], CLIC [9], BFELGI [10], LCIGFC [13] methods. The superiority of the suggested technique is observed for all modalities of brain MR image at different

IIH level. The reason being the incorporation of the coherence term relating the local and nonlocal neighborhood information. This leads to the computation of nonintersecting clusters, indicating BFC in the tissue regions. Further, the method is found to be more suitable in noisy environment.

Table 1 summarizes the assessment of suggested technique in comparison with SFCM [6], CLIC [9], BFELGI [10], LCIGFC [13] methods. Four volumes (5%–7% noise and 20%–40% IIH) of MR images are experimented on all the compared approaches. Each data in table are computed from the mean value of 51 successive image slices. Table 2 presents a performance assessment of T2 and PD-w MR images at 20% IIH. Table 3 presents a quantitative assessment of T1-w real MR images, experimented on 21 selected images from '20Normal_T1' dataset. Lastly, Table 4 presents the average execution time of different methods for resulting the bias field corrected MR images. The comparison is carried out using for the outcomes as presented in Fig. 2. Same simulation

Table 1. Assessment of different methods using T1-w MR images.

Image volume	Methods	Cluster validation		Quality validation	
		V_{PC}	V_{CE}	MSE	PSNR
5% noise + 20% IIH	SFCM [6]	0.7812	0.1724	48.25	32.59
	CLIC [9]	0.7831	0.1448	41.62	32.87
	BFELGI [10]	0.7856	0.1427	37.32	33.49
	LCIGFC [13]	0.8234	0.1213	35.57	35.62
	NSCFCM	**0.8603**	**0.0812**	**31.25**	**37.55**
7% noise + 20% IIH	SFCM	0.7814	0.1774	52.57	30.12
	CLIC	0.7824	0.1542	48.63	32.28
	BFELGI	0.7865	0.1323	45.26	31.79
	LCIGFC	0.8163	0.1120	42.37	34.01
	NSCFCM	**0.8546**	**0.0889**	**39.56**	**34.30**
5% noise + 40% IIH	SFCM	0.7981	0.1954	49.61	28.78
	CLIC	0.8047	0.1769	46.83	30.57
	BFELGI	0.8034	0.1432	45.45	31.28
	LCIGFC	0.8144	0.1212	40.38	34.36
	NSCFCM	**0.8437**	**0.0958**	**35.42**	**36.83**
7% noise + 40% IIH	SFCM	0.7123	0.1856	55.74	28.34
	CLIC	0.7416	0.1765	50.32	31.05
	BFELGI	0.7762	0.1512	48.26	32.86
	LCIGFC	0.7635	0.1208	42.53	33.94
	NSCFCM	**0.8157**	**0.1043**	**40.70**	**34.25**

setup is used for presenting a fair comparison. Bold fonts are used in tables to mark the best values.

Table 2. Assessment of different methods using T2 and PD-w MR images.

Image volume	Methods	Cluster validation		Quality validation	
		V_{PC}	V_{CE}	MSE	PSNR
5% noise + 20% IIH	SFCM	0.7653	0.1986	52.78	30.09
	CLIC	0.7675	0.1765	49.53	31.84
	BFELGI	0.7785	0.1587	44.38	34.11
	LCIGFC	0.7982	0.1342	40.75	34.21
	NSCFCM	**0.8417**	**0.1015**	**35.76**	**38.73**
5% noise + 20% IIH	SFCM	0.7786	0.2079	55.87	27.67
	CLIC	0.7765	0.1892	52.48	31.87
	BFELGI	0.7889	0.1765	46.47	32.58
	LCIGFC	0.8097	0.1532	42.56	33.89
	NSCFCM	**0.8345**	**0.1252**	**38.26**	**37.16**

Table 3. Assessment of different methods using clinical MR images.

Image volume	Methods	Cluster validation		Quality validation	
		V_{PC}	V_{CE}	MSE	PSNR
T1-w	SFCM	0.7512	0.2125	68.37	22.95
	CLIC	0.7535	0.1984	62.54	25.87
	BFELGI	0.7745	0.1762	54.87	28.43
	LCIGFC	0.7983	0.1519	48.62	32.08
	NSCFCM	**0.8380**	**0.1210**	**41.25**	**34.33**

Table 4. Comparison of average execution time.

Methods	SFCM	CLIC	BFELGI	LCIGFC	NSCFCM
Average execution time (Sec)	**59.86**	65.73	95.68	112.28	70.25

From this table, it is noted that the suggested technique takes more execution time in comparison to SFCM and CLIC. This may be due to the use of the coherence term relating the local and nonlocal spatial information. Nevertheless, the outcomes are better than the other methods.

5   Conclusion

In this paper, the suggested NSCFCM technique is experimented for eliminating the bias field in the brain MR images. The method delineates the biased tissue regions in presence of abnormalities in the tissue boundaries. This may be due to inclusion of nonlocal regularization factor in combination with the local spatial information in computing the objective function and the membership matrix. The use of nonlocal regularization factor aids in including more accurate data points into a cluster, whereas the local spatial information helps in discriminating the non-homogeneous data points. This also eliminates spurious blobs significantly and resolves the problem of noise incurred in the image. The suggested scheme is investigated on various volumes of MR images with different levels of IIH. A standard set of evaluation indices are used for validation. The results show the proficiency and robustness of the suggested technique towards BFC in MR images. However, the running time is little higher than the SFCM and CLIC, but lower than the other compared techniques.

Acknowledgement. This work is supported by PhD scholarship grant under TEQIP-III, VSS University of Technology, Burla.

References

1. Vovk, U., Pernus, F., Likar, B.: A review of methods for correction of intensity inhomogeneity in MRI. IEEE Trans. Med. Imaging **26**(3), 405–421 (2007)
2. Dora, L., Agrawal, S., Panda, R., Abraham, A.: State-of-the-art methods for brain tissue segmentation: a review. IEEE Rev. Biomed. Eng. **10**, 235–249 (2017)
3. Mishro, P.K., Agrawal, S., Panda, R., Abraham A.: A novel type-2 fuzzy C-means clustering for brain MR image segmentation. IEEE Trans. Cybern. (2020)
4. Ahmed, M.N., Yamany, S.M., Mohamed, N., Farag, A.A., Moriarty, T.: A modified fuzzy c-means algorithm for bias field estimation and segmentation of MRI data. IEEE Trans. Med. Imaging **21**(3), 193–199 (2002)
5. Szilágyi, L., Szilágyi, S.M., Benyó, B., Benyó, Z.: Intensity inhomogeneity compensation and segmentation of MR brain images using hybrid c-means clustering models. Biomed. Signal Process. Control **6**(1), 3–12 (2011)
6. Despotovic, I., Vansteenkiste, E., Philips, W.: Spatially coherent fuzzy clustering for accurate and noise-robust image segmentation. IEEE Signal Process. Lett. **20**(4), 295–298 (2013)
7. Ji, Z.X., Sun, Q.S., Xia, D.S.: A modified possibilistic fuzzy c-means clustering algorithm for bias field estimation and segmentation of brain MR image. Comput. Med. Imaging Graph. **35**(5), 383–397 (2011)
8. Ji, Z., Liu, J., Cao, G., Sun, Q., Chen, Q.: Robust spatially constrained fuzzy c-means algorithm for brain MR image segmentation. Pattern Recogn. **47**(7), 2454–2466 (2014)
9. Tu, X., Gao, J., Zhu, C., Cheng, J.Z., Ma, Z., Dai, X., Xie, M.: MR image segmentation and bias field estimation based on coherent local intensity clustering with total variation regularization. Med. Biol. Eng. Comput. **54**(12), 1807–1818 (2016)
10. Cong, W., et al.: A modified brain MR image segmentation and bias field estimation model based on local and global information. Comput. Math. Methods Med. **2016**, 1–12 (2016)
11. Shan, X., Gong, X., Nandi, A.K.: Active contour model based on local intensity fitting energy for image segmentation and bias estimation. IEEE Access. **6**, 49817–49827 (2018)

12. Borys, D., Serafin, W., Frackiewicz, M., Psiuk-Maksymowicz, K., Palus, H.: A phantom study of new bias field correction method combining N3 and KHM for MRI imaging. In: International Conference on SITIBS, pp. 314–319. IEEE (2018)
13. Mahata, N., Kahali, S., Adhikari, S.K., Sing, J.K.: Local contextual information and Gaussian function induced fuzzy clustering algorithm for brain MR image segmentation and intensity inhomogeneity estimation. Appl. Soft Comput. **68**, 586–596 (2018)
14. Song, J., Zhang, Z.: Brain tissue segmentation and Bias field correction of MR image based on spatially coherent FCM with nonlocal constraints. Comput. Math. Methods Med. **201**, 1–13 (2019)
15. Mishro, P.K., Agrawal, S., Panda, R., Abraham, A.: Novel fuzzy clustering based bias field correction technique for brain magnetic resonance images. IET Image Proc. **14**(9), 1929–1936 (2020)
16. Mishro, P.K., Agrawal, S., Panda, R.: A fuzzy C-means clustering approach to HMRF-EM model for MRI brain tissue segmentation. In: International Conference on CERA, pp. 371–376. IEEE (2017)
17. BrainWeb: Simulated Brain Database. http://bic.mni.mcgill.ca/brainweb/. Accessed: Mar-Apr, 2020
18. IBSR. http://www.cma.mgh.harvard.edu/ibsr/. Accessed: Mar-Apr, 2020
19. Wu, K., Yang, M.S.: A cluster validity index for fuzzy clustering. Pattern Recogn. Lett. **26**(9), 1275–1291 (2005)
20. Ndajah, P., Kikuchi, H., Yukawa, M., Watanabe, H., Muramatsu, S.: An investigation on the quality of denoised images. Int. J. Circuit Syst. Signal Process. **5**(4), 423–434 (2011)

Securing Biometric Data over Cloud via Shamir's Secret Sharing

Nishant Raj and Debanjan Sadhya[✉]

ABV-Indian Institute of Information Technology and Management Gwalior,
Gwalior, India
debanjan@iiitm.ac.in

Abstract. In this modern age, most enterprises use a biometric-based model for automated identity authentication. Biometric data are sometimes stored over the cloud for better accessibility and scalability. However, cloud storage poses many threats in terms of data privacy and security since it is relatively easy for intruders to access this information. To address this issue, we propose a framework based on Shamir's Secret Sharing (SSS). In this model, the biometric data is divided into different shares and distributed over various cloud data centers such that no single share reveals complete information about the data. Instead, a subset of the shares is required to reconstruct the original biometric features. We have tested this approach for fingerprint images on the benchmark FVC2002-DB1 database. Our empirical results reveal that the information leaked by the shares about the corresponding base images is approximately 33%. The performance of such models also significantly reduces in comparison to the baseline models. Hence our work provides a holistic framework for securely storing biometric data over the cloud.

Keywords: Biometrics security · Shamir's secret sharing · Cloud storage

1 Introduction

Fast development in the cloud computing facility benefits the users in terms of transmission, storage, and data processing. These properties also facilitate biometric-based authentication to grow both in terms of storage and information sharing among different organizations. However, the privacy of the data is a major concern while storing biometric information over a single cloud server. Importantly, biometric features are permanent and cannot get replaced once stolen. A wide variety of adversarial attack models exist which aim to compromise the stored information. Specific instances of these attacks include hillclimbing and privacy invasion [5]. In the worst case, the stored templates of the biometric traits could be utilized for gaining access to other applications in which the genuine users had previously enrolled.

Biometric template protection (BTP) schemes are designed to provide robust security guarantees against various biometric threat models. The ISO/IEC Standard 24745 on Biometric Information Protection defines two major components

S. K. Singh et al. (Eds.): CVIP 2020, CCIS 1376, pp. 282–292, 2021.
https://doi.org/10.1007/978-981-16-1086-8_25

for any BTP scheme: pseudonymous identifier and auxiliary data [13]. Based upon the generation technique of these two pieces of information, BTP schemes are broadly categorized as either cancelable biometrics or biometric cryptosystems [11]. Both of these design principles employ a transformation function to convert the biometric features from their base domain to a transformed domain. However, these schemes are not directly applicable in a cloud-based environment due to their relatively slow computational speed. Furthermore, the performance of the resulting model considerably degrades due to the incurred loss of information in the transformation process (especially for cancelable biometric techniques) [12].

1.1 Contributions

In this paper, we develop a framework based on Shamir's Secret Sharing (SSS) for securely storing biometric data over the cloud. SSS is a well-established technique for sharing data in a distributed environment. In our work, we divide a biometric image into multiple shares and distribute them over physically separated cloud data centers (CDC) during the enrolment phase. Since SSS is a threshold based technique, an adversary would require to concurrently access a minimum number of CDCs for recovering the original biometric image. Based on the fact that CDCs are kept physically separated over a wide geographic location, the chances of the adversary in reconstructing the original biometric image becomes significantly low. We also empirically investigate the amount of feature-based information that each share leaks about the original image. Finally, we analyze the effects of directly using the shares during authentication on the system performance.

2 Related Work

The foundation of the SSS scheme was developed by Shamir [15] long back in 1979. In this work, the author used a threshold-based approach to divide the images into n different shares so that at least k shares are required to regenerate the original image. An extension of this idea was made by Sreekumar et al. [17] in which they introduced a Permutation Ordered Binary (POB) Number System. In this scheme, a secret was divided into different shares based on their POB value. The original secret was then recovered by converting the POB values of shares into their corresponding decimal forms. A combination of Shamir's Secret Sharing and POB Secret Sharing schemes has also been presented [16]. However, a significant disadvantage of such techniques is that the shares reveal partial information about the base image. This limitation was later addressed by Sadhya et al. [14], wherein the notion of *perfect secrecy* was utilized.

Some techniques have been used to ensure the privacy and security of data over the cloud. Kumar et al. [7] used Elliptic curve cryptography (ECC) to ensure the secure storage of data. The authors proposed to divide the data into two different parts as public and private sections. This division was based on the access of the data to a particular set of users. Since the data gets stored over the cloud in a plain-text format, it is vulnerable to different kinds of attacks. In order to address this problem, both the public and private sections were encrypted using ECC. However, this encryption-based approach is also vulnerable to several performance and accuracy issues [18]. Alsolami et al. [3] proposed *cloud-id-screen* for secure storage and authentication of biometric fingerprint data over the cloud. In this approach, the feature was first extracted from the biometric image and a pair-table was built based on the distance between the minutiae points. This table was divided into different subsets, which were then distributed over different CDCs.

The security and privacy issues of cloud based remote biometric authentication was recently addressed by Kaur and Khanna [6]. In their work, the authors proposed a random-distance based cancelable biometric scheme for securing applications hosted over different servers. The developed scheme was characterized by desirable properties such as non-invertibility and revocability due to the underlying cancelable transformation functions. A comprehensive study on security and privacy issues of cloud and their mitigation through facial recognition was performed by Kumar et al. [8]. In their proposed approach, the authors encrypted facial features for ensuring the security of the biometrics data.

3   Shamir's Secret Sharing

In the standard SSS scheme, a data D is divided into n different parts so that any combination of k parts will reconstruct the original data. However, even the complete information of $k-1$ parts will not reveal any information about the data. This threshold-based scheme is functionally based on the notion of polynomial interpolation. If k distinct points are given in a 2-dimensional plane, then there will be a unique polynomial of degree $k-1$ that can be formed from those points. Without loss of generality, let us choose a numerical data D representing pixel values in an image. To divide the image into parts (D_i) having a threshold of k, we pick a random polynomial of degree $k-1$ having constant term equal to the value of the data (acting as the secret). A generalized polynomial can be represented as:

$$q(x) = c_0 + c_1 x + c_2 x^2 + \cdots + c_{k-1} x^{k-1} \tag{1}$$

In Eq. (1), the constant term of the polynomial is set as $c_0 = D$. To divide the data into n shares, we vary the value of x in the polynomial. The secret can be recovered by using Lagrange interpolation over the combination of any k out of n shares. In this numerical method, a unique polynomial of degree $n-1$ can be generated which passes through n distinct points $\{(x_1, y_1), (x_2, y_2), \ldots (x_n, y_n)\}$. The equation of the polynomial is:

$$p(x) = \sum_{j=1}^{n} p_j(x) \tag{2}$$

where

$$p_j(x) = y_j \prod_{k=1 k \neq j}^{n} \frac{x - x_k}{x_j - x_k} \tag{3}$$

The constant terms from the polynomials are finally extracted for forming the reconstructed image.

4 Methodology

In our proposed approach, we split a fingerprint image into multiple shares and distribute them in separate CDCs. This technique enhances the security of storing biometric information over a cloud-based platform. The architecture of the framework is shown in Fig. 1. The following sub-sections describe the steps followed in our proposed approach.

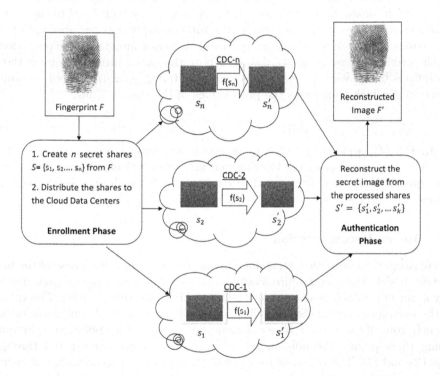

Fig. 1. The proposed framework for storing biometric data over CDCs.

4.1 Share Generation

Let us denote the extracted fingerprint image during the enrolment phase by F. We also fix two model parameters during this initial stage. We represent the total number of shares in which we would divide the biometric fingerprint image by n. Also, let k denote the minimum number of shares required to reconstruct the original biometric image. Both of these model parameters characterize the (n, k) SSS scheme. Next, we construct a polynomial of degree $k - 1$ corresponding to each pixel of the biometric image following Eq. (1). Specifically speaking, the constant term of the polynomial (viz. c_0) is equated to the pixel value, and the rest of the coefficients are generated randomly. Finally, n points are generated from each polynomial by varying the value of x. Each of these points will contribute as a corresponding pixel in the n different shares. Let us denote the individual shares by s_i, where $i = \{1, 2, \ldots, n\}$.

4.2 Image Filtering

One important property of the SSS scheme is that it follows additive and multiplicative homomorphism. This implies that any addition or multiplication operations (with constants) performed over the shares can be translated to the reconstructed image as well [4]. These properties further imply that performing certain operations over Shamir's shares is equivalent to performing the same operations on the original biometric image. Let us denote the shares after performing these operations by s_i'. We can represent a generic filtering operation as an encoding function $\mathcal{F}$ which transforms the pixel values of the shares. Thus,

$$\mathcal{F} : s_i(x, y) \rightarrow s_i'(x, y) \, , \, i = \{1, 2, \ldots n\} \tag{4}$$

In Eq. (4), $s_i(x, y)$ and $s_i'(x, y)$ represent the pixel intensity values of the ith share before and after the filtering operation respectively. Although we have not employed any such filters on the biometric shares, such an avenue might be explored in later studies.

4.3 Image Reconstruction

We perform the image reconstruction during the authentication phase of the biometric model. Since we require least k shares to regenerate the original image, any k out of available n shares are randomly chosen for this purpose. The values of the corresponding pixels from all the k shares are extracted, which are subsequently considered as the k base points in the Lagrange interpolation technique. Using these points, the polynomials of degree $k - 1$ are constructed through Eqs. (2) and (3). The constant terms of the constructed polynomials will correspond to the pixel values of the original image. The final reconstructed fingerprint image is denoted by F'.

4.4 Similarity Score

We have used the minutiae-based matching scheme of [2] for calculating the similarity score between any two fingerprint images. The feature extraction process itself is adopted from the work of Abraham [1]. We have specifically used this method for estimating the amount of information revealed by each share about the corresponding fingerprint image. For an efficient matching process, we have built a database that contains the minutiae points of the original finger-print image and the corresponding shares in the form of a matrix. During the matching process, each share's minutiae points are compared with the minutiae points of their corresponding fingerprint sample. The final similarity scores s lies between $s \in [0,1]$ with zero representing no matching minutiae and unity indicating complete matching minutiae sets.

5 Experimental Results and Analysis

We have divided our empirical simulations into two sections. In the first section, we inspect the similarity between a fingerprint image and its corresponding shares. Subsequently, we exclusively focus on the performance aspects of the SSS based model in the second part. In all of our experiments, we have used the FVC2002-DB1 benchmark dataset [10]. This dataset contains eight finger-print samples from 100 subjects, thereby totaling to 800 images. All the samples of dimension 388×374 were captured by the TouchView II optical sensor. Throughout the entire simulation process, we have varied the values of (n, k) for the following three settings: (3,2), (5,3), and (7,5). It should be noted that these specific values have been commonly used in other related works.

5.1 Share Analysis

A common limitation of the SSS scheme is that the shares reveal some sensitive information (viz. parameter values) due to the presence of correlated information among the image pixels [9]. In this section, we analyze this property for biometric fingerprint images via both qualitative and quantitative approaches. It can be distinctly observed in Fig. 2 that the shares do indeed reveal some structural information of the ridges in the fingerprint images. This pattern is noted for all the three scenarios involving the values of n and k. As already stated, the revelation of partial pixel information is a significant limitation of the SSS scheme. However, it is also essential that we perform a quantitative analysis of this similarity since fingerprint matching is performed on the basis of the extracted feature points. To achieve this objective, we estimate the similarity scores of the base fingerprint images with the correspondingly generated shares (viz. genuine matching). Noticeably, we have opted for feature-based matching (as against pixel-based matching) since features form the core of any biometric model. Figure 3 presents the box-plots of the similarity scores for all three sce-narios. The statistical metrics of these scores are also presented in Table 1. As observable, all the three cases resulted in almost identical scores with an average of ≈ 0.33. Hence, we can empirically state that neither the number of shares nor the threshold affects the similarity score. However, a larger value of k directly increases the security of the scheme since the adversary has to simultaneously acquire at least k distinct shares from physically separated CDCs.

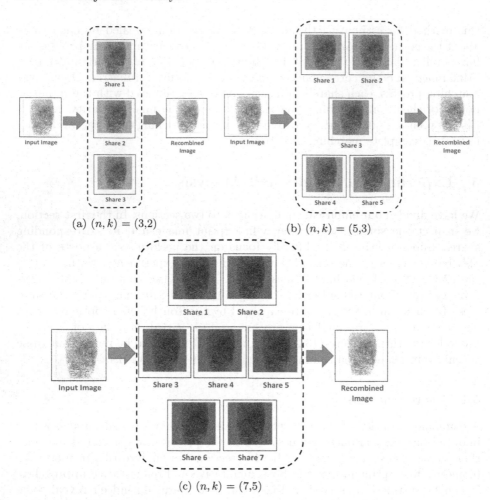

(a) $(n, k) = (3, 2)$

(b) $(n, k) = (5, 3)$

(c) $(n, k) = (7, 5)$

Fig. 2. Qualitative analysis of the similarity between the base fingerprint image and the corresponding shares.

The value of s also implies the amount of matching information present between the shares and the corresponding original fingerprint image. The contents of Table 1 hence indicate that approximately 33% of minutiae information is retained in the generated shares on average. As demonstrated in the later simulations, an adversary does not gain any significant advantage through directly using these shares during authentication. It should be noted that the similarity score between an original image and its reconstructed version is always one.

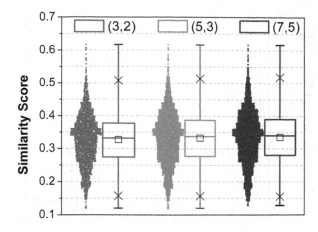

Fig. 3. Box-plots of the similarity scores for various system settings.

Table 1. Statistical analysis of the similarity scores. max(s) is the maximum of s, min(s) is the minimum of s, $\mu(s)$ is the average of s, $\sigma(s)$ is the standard deviation of s, and $\tilde{s}$ is the median of s.

Setting	max(s)	min(s)	$\mu(s)$	$\sigma(s)$	$\tilde{s}$
(3,2)	0.6166	0.1205	0.3271	0.0774	0.3315
(5,3)	0.6166	0.1205	0.3331	0.0797	0.3378
(7,5)	0.6166	0.1286	0.3354	0.0804	0.3405

5.2   Performance Analysis

Now we analyze the performance of the biometric model solely based on the shares. We evaluate the Equal Error Rate (EER) of the model when an adversary attempts to present a compromised share instead of the original fingerprint during authentication. The scores presented in the previous section represent the genuine matching cases in which every fingerprint is matched with its corresponding shares. For estimating the impostor scores, we have checked the similarity between the fingerprints of two different persons. Specifically speaking, we have compared the fingerprint image of the ith person with the shares of the $(i+1)^{th}$ person. Using this protocol creates an equal number of cases for both genuine and impostor matches. The resulting ROC and DET curves are depicted in Fig. 4. Noticeably, this scenario results in the EERs of 13.15%, 14.86% and 12.46% corresponding to (3,2), (5,3) and (7,5) respectively. However, these values directly correspond to the minutiae-based feature extractor which we have used in our simulations. Hence for an unbiased comparison, we have also evaluated the baseline results for the FVC-2002-DB1 database. It is observed that the EER decreases to 5.75% when we base our comparisons directly on the fingerprint images and not the shares. Hence this result reiterates the loss of information incurred in the generated shares. The security of the model is also vindicated due to the non-suitability of utilizing the compromised shares during authentication.

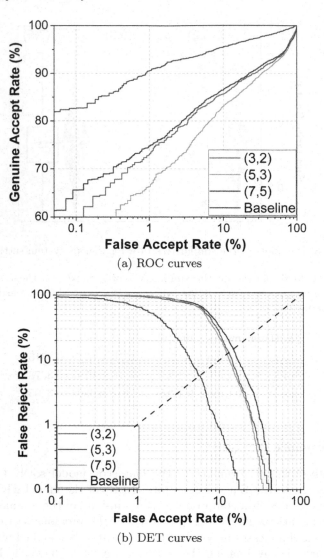

(a) ROC curves

(b) DET curves

Fig. 4. Comparative analysis based on the performance curves. In Fig. 4b, The points where the black dashed diagonal line intersect with the curves represent the corresponding EERs.

6   Conclusion

Storing biometric information over a cloud-based platform is a beneficial prospect. However, such a model provides a single point of adversarial attack in compromising the stored biometric features. In this work, we have proposed a threshold-based approach for securely storing biometric data over physically separated cloud data centers. Our framework is structurally based on the notion of Shamir's secret sharing wherein a secret (fingerprint image in our case) is divided into multiple shares. We have used the minutiae-based similarity score to check the percentage information revealed by each share, which we empirically estimated to be 33% for the FVC-2002-DB1 database. Furthermore, the recognition accuracy of the model substantially decreased if we performed the matching based on the shares. Our present work could be further extended by exploiting the homomorphic property of the SSS scheme. Since this technique follows additive and multiplicative homomorphism, we can implement several image enhancement filters on the stored shares. Investigating the effects of these filters on the model performance can be an extension of our work.

References

1. Abraham, J., Kwan, P., Gao, J.: Fingerprint matching using a hybrid shape and orientation descriptor. In: Yang, J., Nanni, L. (eds.) State of the Art in Biometrics. IntechOpen, Rijeka (2011). https://doi.org/10.5772/19105. (Chapter 2)
2. Alilou, V.K.: Fingerprint matching: a simple approach (2020). https://www.mathworks.com/matlabcentral/fileexchange/44369-fingerprint-matching-a-simple-approach
3. Alsolami, F., Alzahrani, B., Boult, T.: Cloud-id-screen: secure fingerprint data in the cloud. In: 2018 IEEE 4th International Conference on Identity, Security, and Behavior Analysis (ISBA), pp. 1–8. IEEE (2018)
4. Benaloh, J.C.: Secret sharing homomorphisms: keeping shares of a secret secret (extended abstract). In: Odlyzko, A.M. (ed.) CRYPTO 1986. LNCS, vol. 263, pp. 251–260. Springer, Heidelberg (1987). https://doi.org/10.1007/3-540-47721-7_19
5. Jain, A.K., Nandakumar, K., Nagar, A.: Biometric template security. EURASIP J. Adv. Signal Process **2008** (2008). https://doi.org/10.1155/2008/579416
6. Kaur, H., Khanna, P.: Privacy preserving remote multi-server biometric authentication using cancelable biometrics and secret sharing. Future Gener. Comput. Syst. **102**, 30–41 (2020). https://doi.org/10.1016/j.future.2019.07.023. http://www.sciencedirect.com/science/article/pii/S0167739X18330553
7. Kumar, A., Lee, B.G., Lee, H., Kumari, A.: Secure storage and access of data in cloud computing. In: 2012 International Conference on ICT Convergence (ICTC), pp. 336–339. IEEE (2012)
8. Kumar, S., Singh, S.K., Singh, A.K., Tiwari, S., Singh, R.S.: Privacy preserving security using biometrics in cloud computing. Multimed. Tools Appl. **77**(9), 11017–11039 (2018). https://doi.org/10.1007/s11042-017-4966-5
9. Lathey, A., Atrey, P.K.: Image enhancement in encrypted domain over cloud. ACM Trans. Multimed. Comput. Commun. Appl. (TOMM) **11**(3), 1–24 (2015). https://doi.org/10.1007/s11042-017-4966-5
10. Maltoni, D., Maio, D., Jain, A.K., Prabhakar, S.: Handbook of Fingerprint Recognition. Springer Science & Business Media, London (2009). https://doi.org/10.1007/978-1-84882-254-2
11. Manisha, Kumar N: Cancelable biometrics a comprehensive survey. Artif. Intell. Rev. **53**, 3403–3446 (2020). https://doi.org/10.1007/s10462-019-09767-8
12. Nandakumar, K., Jain, A.K.: Biometric template protection: bridging the performance gap between theory and practice. IEEE Signal Process. Mag. **32**(5), 88–100 (2015)

13. Rathgeb, C., Uhl, A.: A survey on biometric cryptosystems and cancelable biometrics. EURASIP J. Inform. Secur. **2011**(1), 3 (2011). https://doi.org/10.1186/1687-417X-2011-3

14. Sadhya, D., Agarwal, A., Raman, B.: Perfectly secure Shamir's secret sharing scheme for privacy preserving image processing over cloud. In: Proceedings of the 11th Indian Conference on Computer Vision, Graphics and Image Processing. ICVGIP 2018, Association for Computing Machinery, New York, NY, USA (2018)

15. Shamir, A.: How to share a secret. Commun. ACM **22**(11), 612–613 (1979). https://doi.org/10.1145/359168.359176

16. Singh, P., Agarwal, N., Raman, B.: Don't see me, just filter me: towards secure cloud based filtering using Shamir's secret sharing and POB number system. In: Proceedings of the Tenth Indian Conference on Computer Vision, Graphics and Image Processing, p. 12. ACM (2016)

17. Sreekumar, A., Sundar, S.B.: An efficient secret sharing scheme for n out of n scheme using POB-number system. Hack **2009**, 33 (2009)

18. Wu, Z., Tian, L., Li, P., Wu, T., Jiang, M., Wu, C.: Generating stable biometric keys for flexible cloud computing authentication using finger vein. Inform. Sci. **433**, 431–447 (2018)

DarkGAN: Night Image Enhancement Using Generative Adversarial Networks

Prasen Alaspure$^{(\boxtimes)}$, Praful Hambarde , Akshay Dudhane,
and Subrahmanyam Murala

Computer Vision and Pattern Recognition Lab, IIT Ropar, Rupnagar, India
{2018eem1017,2018eez0001,2017eez0001,subbumurala}@iitrpr.ac.in

Abstract. Low light image enhancement is one of the challenging tasks in computer vision, and it becomes more difficult when images are very dark. Recently, most of low light image enhancement work is done either on synthetic data or on the images which are considerably visible. In this paper, we propose a method to enhance real-world night time images, which are dark and noisy. The proposed DarkGAN consists of two pairs of Generator - Discriminator. Moreover, the proposed network enhances dark shades and removes noise up to a much extent, with natural-looking colors in the output image. Experimental results evaluation of the proposed method on the "See In the Dark" dataset demonstrates the effectiveness of the proposed model compared with other state-of-the-art methods. The proposed method yields comparable better results on qualitative and quantitative assessments when compared with the existing methods.

Keywords: Low-light image enhancement · Generative Adversarial Networks

1 Introduction

The images captured in the day time look pretty, good and more colorful, but at night it isn't so. Images taken at night are generally very dark, highly suffered from noise and blurred. Due to a lack of visibility and low contrast, the images taken at night convey very little information. Nowadays, major work in the field of object detection [23], depth estimation [13–15] human action recognition [3], and image de-hazing [7–9] is done by considering day time vision only as working in night vision for given tasks is very challenging. These tasks become more difficult when images are incredibly dark.

Object detection, tracking, extraction and classification are the most important tasks to automate any robotic operation. To perform all these operations smoothly even in the dark, objects should be clearly visible without which the whole operation can be misguided. Hence first, we need to enhance dark shades

Electronic supplementary material The online version of this chapter (https:// doi.org/10.1007/978-981-16-1086-8_26) contains supplementary material, which is available to authorized users.

so that objects can be seen even in a very dark environment. We also need to remove noise, blur effect and then proceed with further operations.

In computer vision, most of low light image enhancement work is done either on synthetic data or the images which considerably visible. In traditional methods of image enhancement, Histogram Equalization [28] is used to improve contrast by stretching pixel intensities but it often produces unrealistic effects in images, another method of Log transformation makes darker pixels brighter but this could lead to loss of information.

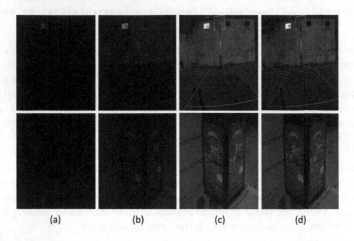

Fig. 1. Sony's short exposure image reconstructed as JPG using (a) Sony Imaging Edge application, (b) Rawpy library, (c) Proposed Method's output on (b), and (d) Ground truth image.

Dong *et al.* [6] take the inverse of dark channel prior [16] treat it as a hazy image then de-haze it and again inverted back which helps in removing dark shades. However, this method lacks the necessary physical model to support the imaging process of low-light images. The Retinex theory proposed by Land *et al.* [24] is based on the color image can be decomposed into two factors such as reflectance and illumination assumption. Single-scale Retinex (SSR) [22] and multiscale Retinex (MSR) [21] treats the reflectance as the final enhanced result which often looks unnatural and frequently appears to be over enhanced.

The recent development in the field of deep learning attracts many researchers to work on low light image enhancement. Multi-layer perceptrons [2], deep autoencoders [26], convolutional networks [19,34], stacked sparse denoising autoencoders (SSDA) [1,33] and trainable non-linear reaction diffusion (TNRD) [5] but unfortunately most of the methods are trained on synthetic data such as adding Gaussian or salt & pepper noise. In EnlightenGAN [20] researchers consider considerably visible images but the proposed method is focused on very dark images in which very little information is visible.

Some state-of-the-art methods Dong *et al.* [6], SRIE [10], NPEA [29], LIME [12], RRM [25] and ALSM [30] we have compared in this paper. It is observed

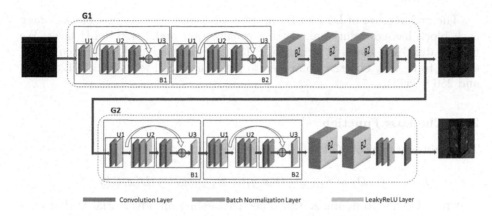

Fig. 2. The proposed DarkGAN (Generator 1 and Generator 2) architecture.

that these methods work well when low light images have very low or negligible noise, which is not a real-world scenario. On the other hand, when images are very dark and noisy, these methods failed to produce real colors in the output images. Figure 1 demonstrates the overall view of this research paper.

2   Proposed Method

In Generative adversarial networks (GANs) [11], Generator G tries to learn to map from the random noise vector z to output image y. Generator G always produces 'fake' images and Discriminator D tries to discriminate between 'real' and 'fake' images. This is unsupervised learning in which both Generator G and Discriminator D are trained together in an adversarial manner until Generator G fools the Discriminator D. This concept further extended from unsupervised to supervised by conditional GANs [27] in which Generator G tries to learn to map from observed image x and random noise vector z to y. After the success of Image-to-Image Translation with conditional adversarial networks [18], we are further extending this concept. We have proposed cGAN based Dark Night Image Enhancement using Generative Adversarial Networks (DarkGAN) for night time image enhancement.

2.1   The Network Architecture

The proposed DarkGAN architecture consists of two pairs of Generator *i.e.* (G1 and G2) and Discriminator *i.e.* (D1 and D2) models. In which the first pair is for coarse-level enhancement and the second pair for fine-level enhancement. The architecture of G1 and G2 are consists of residual blocks [17] as shown in Fig. 2. Each residual block [17] consists of 3 units as shown in Fig. 2 and each unit has convolutional, batch normalization and the LeakyReLU layer. The features of the first unit are added to third unit pixel-wise except for the last block in each Generator.

The architecture of D1 and D2 are the same and consists of 4 blocks where each block has convolutional, batch normalization and LeakyReLU layer. We used 'PatchGAN' based Discriminator [18] in which we found that patch size of 64×64 to be very effective compared to patch sizes of 1×1, 32×32, 128×128 and 256×256.

2.2   The Loss Function

The main objective of cGAN [11] is given by

$$\mathcal{L}_{cGAN}(G, D) = \mathbb{E}_{x,y}[\log D(x, y)] + \mathbb{E}_{x,z}[\log(1 - D(x, G(x, z)))] \tag{1}$$

where G tries to minimize this objective against an adversarial D that tries to maximize it, i.e.

$$G^* = \arg \min_G \max_D \mathcal{L}_{cGAN}(G, D) \tag{2}$$

The L1 loss function combined with GAN loss defined as.

$$G^* = \arg \min_G \max_D \mathcal{L}_{cGAN}(G, D) + \lambda \mathcal{L}_{L1}(G) \tag{3}$$

where L1 loss is

$$\mathcal{L}_{L1}(G) = \mathbb{E}_{x,y,z}[||y - G(x, z)||_1] \tag{4}$$

We have tried replacing L1 with L2 but it did not work well, output images were showing unwanted sharpening which was making images look unrealistic. We also found that the combined loss of cGAN and L1 was creating much blurry output images. To overcome this problem, we have decided to go with a combination of cGAN, L1 and SSIM loss for G1 and combination of cGAN, L1 and multiscale SSIM loss for G2. The main objective for the proposed DarkGAN is defined as given below:

$$G_1^* = \arg \min_G \max_D \mathcal{L}_{cGAN}(G, D) + \lambda \mathcal{L}_{L1}(G) + SSIM \tag{5}$$

$$G_2^* = \arg \min_G \max_D \mathcal{L}_{cGAN}(G, D) + \lambda \mathcal{L}_{L1}(G) + MS\_SSIM \tag{6}$$

where, SSIM et al. [31] is structural similarity index and MS SSIM et al. [32] is multi scale structural similarity index.

2.3   Training

We train the networks from scratch using the combined loss of cGAN + λ*(L1) + SSIM as G1 loss function and the combined loss of cGAN + λ*L1 + MS SSIM as G2 loss function. While training, input to the network is a short exposure image from "See In the Dark (SID) Dataset" [4].

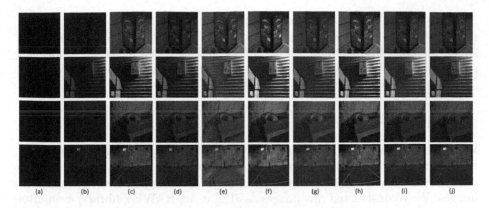

Fig. 3. Comparison of results over different state-of-the-art methods (a) raw image constructed as JPG, (b) input image, (c) Dong [6], (d) SRIE [10], (e) NPEA [29], (f) LIME [12], (g) RRM [25], (h) ALSM [30], (i) Proposed Method and (j) Ground truth

We train the G1-D1 pair for 40 epochs with a learning rate of 0.0002 and while G1-D1 training, the G2-D2 pair is kept in an ideal state. After 40 epochs, training of G1-D1 pair stopped and G2-D2 pair training starts with using G1 in a testing mode such that, the first input image is given to G1 and then applied to G2. Here we assume that G1 is trained at its best and further enhancement is provided by G2. G2-D2 pair is trained for 60 epochs with learning rate of 0.0001. We used Adam optimizer and λ is fixed at 100 in both the pairs during training.

3   Experiments and Results

3.1   The Dataset

In this paper, we use "See In the Dark" (SID) dataset [4] for both training and testing purposes. The dataset contains short exposure and long exposure raw images from Sony and Fuji cameras where all images in the dataset are real-world night time images. Short exposure images are input images and long exposure images are their corresponding ground truth images. Short exposure images (input images) are so dark such that when they are constructed as JPG, we saw almost nothing. So, to use them for training and testing purposes, we first reconstructed them using the Rawpy library. We used images from both Sony and Fuji cameras for training and testing but we keep training and testing images separately. The target of the proposed method is night time dark image enhancement and we did not consider any day time images here.

3.2   Experimental Set-up

Since the prime focus of the proposed method is to enhance real-world dark images of the night time, we prefer to use the SID dataset [4] as it contains real-world very dark images of the night time. The dataset has very fewer images, we choose 200 images for training and 20 images for testing from both sony and fuji camera. We avoid common images from both of these while training. At a later stage, we found that training images are not sufficient and hence we go for data augmentation. We increase the dataset by rotating, flipping and transposing images which finally turn out to be a set of 1400 images.

3.3   Qualitative Analysis

We have compared the results of the proposed method with several state-of-the-art methods as shown in Fig. 3. As we can see in Fig. 3(a) images are so dark such that we saw absolutely nothing when raw images constructed as JPG images. We reconstructed raw images as JPG using RAWPY library, even after this reconstruction very little information is visible as shown in Fig. 3(b) and these images are used as the input images in this proposed method for training and testing.

When tested on these input images as shown in Fig. 3(b), all methods are enhancing dark shades but they failed to produce natural colors as input images are very noisy. NPEA [29] introduces many artifacts in the output images, outputs of SRIE [10] are bit dark and slightly blurred, RRM [25] is producing more blurred output images, when viewed in zoom mode artifacts can be easily observed in Dong [6], LIME [12] and ALSM [30].

The proposed DarkGAN method when applied to input image it is enhancing dark shades with preserving the natural color, removing most of the noise, reducing blurred effect and removing most of the artefacts.

We have used official codes released by the respective authors to implement existing methods.

3.4   Quantitative Analysis

We have evaluated the results of the proposed and existing methods using PSNR, MSE and multi-scale SSIM evaluation. Here, Fig. 4 shows a comparative analysis of the different state-of-the-art methods including the proposed method over standard evaluation parameters. The proposed method outperforms than others on each parameter. From the qualitative and quantitative analysis, it is clear that the proposed DarkGAN gives outstanding results over state-of-the-art methods. This evaluation is done on 20 testing images, we show only a few images here and others are enclosed in the supplementary material.

3.5   Ablation Study

Analysis Using Different Loss Functions. We have tested different loss functions to achieve better results. We begin with cGAN + L1 loss in G1 and cGAN + L2 loss in G2 but it is observed that L2 loss is producing unwanted sharpening of images that do not look realistic. The combination of cGAN + L1 + SSIM loss always performs better with lambda multiplies with L1 loss when

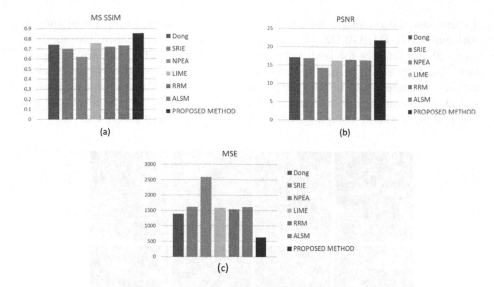

Fig. 4. Comparison of different state-of-the-art methods with proposed method on quantitative parameters (a) Multi Scale SSIM, (b) PSNR and (c) MSE tested on 20 images.

used as loss functions for both G1 and G2. But, it is observed that we got a slightly better improvement when SSIM is replaced by MS SSIM as loss for G2. The comparison using several quantitative parameters such as multi-scale SSIM, PSNR and MSE of various loss functions used for G1 and G2 is shown in Table 1. A total of 20 testing images are used for these evaluations.

Table 1. Quantitative analysis of different loss functions for G1 and G2

Loss fo G1	Loss for G2	MS SSIM	PSNR	MSE
L1	L2	0.8185	21.58	694.6
L2	L1	0.8437	20.64	719.79
L1 + SSIM	L2 + SSIM	0.8466	21.42	659.17
L1 + SSIM	L1 + SSIM	0.8495	21.77	**620.58**
L1 + SSIM	L1 + MS SSIM	**0.8537**	**21.87**	630.68
L1 + SSIM	L2 + MS SSIM	0.8422	21.79	647.38
L1 + MS SSIM	L1 + MS SSIM	0.8258	21.75	724.94

Analysis Using Different Generator Architectures. We perform an ablation analysis using different Generator architectures to evaluate the performance of the second pair (G2-D2) in the proposed network. We consider two networks, the first one with a single pair (G1-D1) and another network with combined of both pairs (G1-D1, G2-D2). We perform qualitative and quantitative analysis using 20 test images for both network output results. The comparative qualitative analysis is shown in Fig. 5. The quantitative analysis over standard evaluation parameters like PSNR, MSE and multi-scale SSIM is shown in Table 2. In Fig. 5 we can clearly see that output of G1 is a bit darker, noisy and less information is visible compared with the combined output of G1-G2.

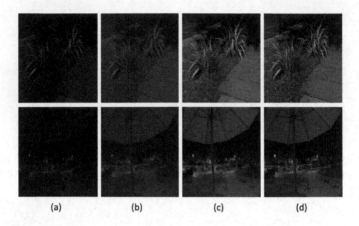

Fig. 5. (a) Input image, (b) Output of G1, (c) Output of combined G1-G2 and (d) Ground truth

Table 2. Ablation analysis

	MS-SSIM	PSNR	MSE
G1	0.6911	18.05	1385.81
G1-G2	**0.8537**	**21.87**	**630.68**

4 Conclusion

In this paper, we have proposed a novel deep network DarkGAN for very dark and noisy image enhancement. The proposed DarkGAN consists of the duel Generator-Discriminator networks. Among which the first Generator-Discriminator pair designed for the major visibility improvement while the second pair aimed at precise fine enhancement. The performance of the proposed DarkGAN has been compared both qualitatively and quantitatively with the existing state-of-the-art methods for low-light image enhancement. We are also looking forward to working on high-resolution images as the proposed network does not yields much better results on high-resolution images.

References

1. Agostinelli, F., Anderson, M.R., Lee, H.: Adaptive multi-column deep neural networks with application to robust image denoising. In: Advances in Neural Information Processing Systems, pp. 1493–1501 (2013)
2. Burger, H.C., Schuler, C.J., Harmeling, S.: Image denoising: can plain neural networks compete with BM3D? In: 2012 IEEE Conference on Computer Vision and Pattern Recognition, pp. 2392–2399. IEEE (2012)
3. Chaudhary, S., Murala, S.: Deep network for human action recognition using weber motion. Neurocomputing **367**, 207–216 (2019)
4. Chen, C., Chen, Q., Xu, J., Koltun, V.: Learning to see in the dark. In: Proceedings of the IEEE Conference on Computer Vision and Pattern Recognition, pp. 3291–3300 (2018)
5. Chen, Y., Pock, T.: Trainable nonlinear reaction diffusion: a flexible framework for fast and effective image restoration. IEEE Trans. Pattern Anal. Mach. Intell. **39**(6), 1256–1272 (2016)
6. Dong, X., et al.: Fast efficient algorithm for enhancement of low lighting video. In: 2011 IEEE International Conference on Multimedia and Expo, pp. 1–6. IEEE (2011)
7. Dudhane, A., Biradar, K.M., Patil, P.W., Hambarde, P., Murala, S.: Varicolored image de-hazing. In: Proceedings of the IEEE/CVF Conference on Computer Vision and Pattern Recognition, pp. 4564–4573 (2020)
8. Dudhane, A., Hambarde, P., Patil, P., Murala, S.: Deep underwater image restoration and beyond. IEEE Signal Process. Lett. **27**, 675–679 (2020)
9. Dudhane, A., Murala, S.: RYF-Net: deep fusion network for single image haze removal. IEEE Trans. Image Process. **29**, 628–640 (2019)
10. Fu, X., Zeng, D., Huang, Y., Zhang, X.P., Ding, X.: A weighted variational model for simultaneous reflectance and illumination estimation. In: Proceedings of the IEEE Conference on Computer Vision and Pattern Recognition, pp. 2782–2790 (2016)
11. Goodfellow, I., et al.: Generative adversarial nets. In: Advances in Neural Information Processing Systems, pp. 2672–2680 (2014)
12. Guo, X., Li, Y., Ling, H.: Lime: low-light image enhancement via illumination map estimation. IEEE Trans. Image Process. **26**(2), 982–993 (2016)
13. Hambarde, P., Dudhane, A., Murala, S.: Single image depth estimation using deep adversarial training. In: 2019 IEEE International Conference on Image Processing (ICIP), pp. 989–993. IEEE (2019)
14. Hambarde, P., Dudhane, A., Patil, P.W., Murala, S., Dhall, A.: Depth estimation from single image and semantic prior. In: 2020 IEEE International Conference on Image Processing (ICIP), pp. 1441–1445. IEEE (2020)
15. Hambarde, P., Murala, S.: S2DNet: depth estimation from single image and sparse samples. IEEE Trans. Comput. Imaging **6**, 806–817 (2020)
16. He, K., Sun, J., Tang, X.: Single image haze removal using dark channel prior. IEEE Trans. Pattern Anal. Mach. Intell. **33**(12), 2341–2353 (2010)
17. He, K., Zhang, X., Ren, S., Sun, J.: Deep residual learning for image recognition. In: Proceedings of the IEEE Conference on Computer Vision and Pattern Recognition, pp. 770–778 (2016)
18. Isola, P., Zhu, J.Y., Zhou, T., Efros, A.A.: Image-to-image translation with conditional adversarial networks. In: Proceedings of the IEEE Conference on Computer Vision and Pattern Recognition, pp. 1125–1134 (2017)

19. Jain, V., Seung, S.: Natural image denoising with convolutional networks. In: Advances in Neural Information Processing Systems, pp. 769–776 (2009)
20. Jiang, Y., et al.: Enlightengan: deep light enhancement without paired supervision. arXiv preprint arXiv:1906.06972 (2019)
21. Jobson, D.J., Rahman, Z.u., Woodell, G.A.: A multiscale retinex for bridging the gap between color images and the human observation of scenes. IEEE Trans. Image Process. 6(7), 965–976 (1997)
22. Jobson, D.J., Rahman, Z., Woodell, G.A.: Properties and performance of a center/surround retinex. IEEE Trans. Image Process. 6(3), 451–462 (1997)
23. Kuang, H., Chen, L., Chan, L.L.H., Cheung, R.C., Yan, H.: Feature selection based on tensor decomposition and object proposal for night-time multiclass vehicle detection. IEEE Trans. Syst. Man Cybern. Syst. 49(1), 71–80 (2018)
24. Land, E.H.: The retinex theory of color vision. Sci. Am. 237(6), 108–129 (1977)
25. Li, M., Liu, J., Yang, W., Sun, X., Guo, Z.: Structure-revealing low-light image enhancement via robust retinex model. IEEE Trans. Image Process. 27(6), 2828–2841 (2018)
26. Lore, K.G., Akintayo, A., Sarkar, S.: LLNet: a deep autoencoder approach to natural low-light image enhancement. Pattern Recogn. 61, 650–662 (2017)
27. Mirza, M., Osindero, S.: Conditional generative adversarial nets. arXiv preprint arXiv:1411.1784 (2014)
28. Pizer, S.M.: Contrast-limited adaptive histogram equalization: speed and effectiveness stephen m. pizer, r. eugene johnston, james p. ericksen, bonnie c. yankaskas, keith e. muller medical image display research group. In: Proceedings of the First Conference on Visualization in Biomedical Computing, Atlanta, Georgia, 22–25 May 1990. p. 337. IEEE Computer Society Press (1990)
29. Wang, S., Zheng, J., Hu, H.M., Li, B.: Naturalness preserved enhancement algorithm for non-uniform illumination images. IEEE Trans. Image Process. 22(9), 3538–3548 (2013)
30. Wang, Y.F., Liu, H.M., Fu, Z.W.: Low-light image enhancement via the absorption light scattering model. IEEE Trans. Image Process. 28(11), 5679–5690 (2019)
31. Wang, Z., Bovik, A.C., Sheikh, H.R., Simoncelli, E.P.: Image quality assessment: from error visibility to structural similarity. IEEE Trans. Image Process. 13(4), 600–612 (2004)
32. Wang, Z., Simoncelli, E.P., Bovik, A.C.: Multiscale structural similarity for image quality assessment. In: The Thrity-Seventh Asilomar Conference on Signals, Systems & Computers, vol. 2, pp. 1398–1402. IEEE (2003)
33. Xie, J., Xu, L., Chen, E.: Image denoising and inpainting with deep neural networks. In: Advances in Neural Information Processing Systems, pp. 341–349 (2012)
34. Zhang, K., Zuo, W., Chen, Y., Meng, D., Zhang, L.: Beyond a Gaussian denoiser: Residual learning of deep CNN for image denoising. IEEE Trans. Image Process. 26(7), 3142–3155 (2017)

Cancelable Biometric Template Generation Using Convolutional Autoencoder

Gourav Siddhad$^{(\boxtimes)}$ ⓘ, Pritee Khanna ⓘ, and Aparajita Ojha

PDPM Indian Institute of Information Technology, Design and Manufacturing,
Jabalpur, Jabalpur, India
{gourav.siddhad,pkhanna,aojha}@iiitdmj.ac.in

Abstract. Convolutional autoencoders are a great tool for extracting features from images and compressing them to a lower dimension called latent space. A latent space vector is generated from the input images by extracting the relevant and the most useful features required for approximating the images. In the proposed work, a convolutional autoencoder is used for feature extraction, random noise and random convolution are used for generating cancelable template from these features. This architecture has been trained for palm vein, wrist vein, and palm print images combined from different datasets namely, CASIA, CIEPUT, and PolyU. The proposed method has been experimented and evaluated for various modalities such as palm print, palm vein, and wrist vein. The evaluation of these methods has been done in three different scenarios for addressing different uses and attacks possible.

Keywords: Autoencoder · Cancelable biometric · Non-invertible transforms · Random convolution · Random noise

1 Introduction

Biometric identities are unique to an individual and therefore are more reliable than token or knowledge-based identifiers. In a biometric recognition system, these identifiers are stored in the database directly. If stolen by an attacker, then these identifiers can be used for illegitimate access to a system [5,24]. This puts the system at risk and once lost, a biometric can not be recovered [10,11].

To secure a biometric identity, it is distorted in a non-invertible way by using a user-specific token to create a pseudo-identity (cancelable template). The pseudo-identities generated for a user with different tokens are also distinct [10,23]. During enrolment, pseudo-identity is stored in the database which is used while authentication for similarity matching. During an attack, if a pseudo-identity is compromised, then a new pseudo-identity can be generated without compromising the original biometric [19]. Similarly, for a user, many pseudo-identities can be generated and stored across various biometric systems. The process is supposed to fulfil the properties like *non-invertibility, cancelability, revocability,* and *diversity* [10,11,23].

© Springer Nature Singapore Pte Ltd. 2021
S. K. Singh et al. (Eds.): CVIP 2020, CCIS 1376, pp. 303–314, 2021.
https://doi.org/10.1007/978-981-16-1086-8_27

Real-time applications of biometric systems such as forensics require not only accurate but fast systems. Hand-held devices like smartphones and tablets which use biometrics for the privacy of data and the system also require a quick and accurate response. Therefore, biometric recognition methods required for such applications should be storage and computationally efficient. This work proposes an autoencoder based biometric template protection method, which generates templates of low dimension and supports faster storage and retrieval of templates. Size of the transformed template reduces to 25% of the original biometric image with the proposed method and yet ensuring the performance. The method has promising results, especially on the lower end devices.

Rest of the work is discussed as follows. Section 2 describes the related works in cancelable biometrics domain. Section 3 explains the feature extraction process and the proposed methodology. Results are described and compared with other methods in Section 4, along with performance and cancelability analysis. Finally, the work is concluded in Section 5.

2   Related Work

Non-invertible transforms and biometric salting are two ways to generate cancelable templates [10]. Non-invertible transforms use one-way functions to prevent invertibility of templates. Biometric salting distorts templates using random data followed by one or more operations to make them non-invertible. *random projection* [22], *random noise* [16] and *random convolution* [17] based transforms are used for biometric salting.

Non-invertible transforms modify biometric data by mapping it to a new random sub-space using a non-invertible mapping function. Ratha et al. [23] proposed cartesian, polar, and surface folding transforms to map minutiae features into random space. Hashing based transformations make use of hash functions to transform the feature vector into non-invertible space. Index of first order (IFO) proposed by Kim and Teoh [13] is based on index-of-max (IoM) hashing which is a variation of locality sensitive hashing (LSH). IFO maps real-valued fingerprint features to max ranked discrete index hashed codes. Gomez et al. [7] used bloom filters (referred as BF here) to generate cancelable templates. Bloom filters are computed after performing a structure preserving feature rearrangement on extracted feature blocks to generate cancelable templates. Ali and Tahir [4] proposed a non-invertible transform-based integration of encrypted and decrypted features for iris images. The cancelable template is generated by encrypting the features of the iris image extracted using 2D gabor filter and stored in the database. The templates are decrypted only during template matching.

In random projection, biometric data is salted by projecting it on random sub-space such that the pairwise distances between points are preserved. Balwant and Deshmukh [6] proposed a cancelable biometric method using local binary patterns (LBP) and random projection (referred as LBP-RP here). An LBP features histogram is generated and random projection is performed using an orthonormal key. The template is generated by performing pairwise quantization. The performance of this method was increased by using local ternary patterns (LTP) instead of LBP. Kumar and Rawat [15] suggested random permutation locality preserving projection (RP-LPP) which generates a low dimensional representation of the biometric image using LPP. A user-specific random permutation matrix is used to provide cancelability to templates.

A random noise based method proposed by Kaur and Khanna [11] (referred as XOR here) extracted log-gabor features which are XORed with gaussian random noise followed by median filtering to get non-invertible templates. Later, they proposed a random distance method (RDM) based cancelable scheme, where median filtering is performed on euclidean distances between random noise and log-gabor features and stored as features [12]. Another method by Lee et al. [16] generates cancelable templates using multiple images of a user during training to generate a set of codes, hadamard product is performed for non-invertibility and noise is embedded after finding coherent regions.

Random convolution based transformations make use of random kernels to convolve the biometric image or features to generate cancelable templates. One such method by Maiorana et al. [17] can be applied to any biometric whose template can be represented as a set of sequences. The original sequence is decomposed into non-overlapping parts using a key (random number). Linear convolution is performed on these parts to obtain the transformed sequence. Wang and Hu [25] proposed the use of curtailed circular convolution. From minutiae points, a pair-minutiae vector is obtained through pairwise minutiae matching, which is quantized to generate a binary vector. A random binary vector is used to perform circular convolution with the feature vector to generate cancelable fingerprint templates.

Recently, Nguyen et al. [18] proposed a novel hybrid method to achieve cancelability by using two random keys. The first key is used to generate random orthonormal matrix for the projection of the extracted biometric features. The second key is used for fuzzy commitment method to generate the helper data. For authentication purpose, the second key is stored as a hash in the database alongside helper data.

Some recent works utilized deep neural networks for either feature extraction or cancelability of biometric images. Jang and Cho [8] proposed a deep table-based hashing (DTH) framework that extracts features from the convolutional neural network (CNN). Binary code is generated from these features using the index of hash table. Noise embedding and intra-normalization are used to distort biometric data. Phillips et al. [21] enhanced BioCapsule by using deep learning techniques for pre-processing and feature extraction. Also, they extended BioCapsule's domain from iris to face recognition. Multi-task (cascaded) convolutional neural network (MTCNN) method (a combination of three CNNs) was used for alignment, segmentation and facial landmark detection. After detection and segmentation, FaceNet is used to extract facial features and classification is done using support vector machine (SVM).

Generally, the template size in cancelable biometric methods is too high to efficiently handle the storage and computation requirements in low-end devices.

To address this issue, an autoencoder based cancelable biometric method is proposed to generate low-dimensional templates with the following highlights:

1. Convolutional Autoencoder is developed to fit in this particular scenario of template generation instead of using a pre-trained model.
2. Template size is reduced to 25% of the original biometric image.
3. Only one model is trained and used for three modalities in this work.
4. The transform technique used is simple and efficient.

3   Proposed Methodology

As shown in Fig. 1, after preprocessing the input biometric image, features are extracted from the convolutional autoencoder (CAE). Random noise is added to the obtained feature vector which is then convolved using a random kernel for generating the cancelable template.

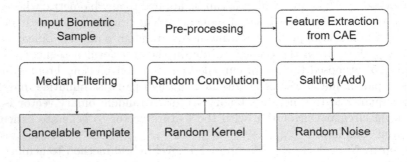

Fig. 1. Block diagram of the proposed method

3.1   Architecture and Training

The architecture of CAE is shown in Fig. 2. Two CNNs are used to construct the CAE. The first is an encoder (Enc) used for compressing the input image by extracting the features using *convolution* layers. The second is a decoder (Dec) used for reconstructing the image from the extracted features using *transposed convolution* layers. Every block of *convolution* or *transposed convolution* is followed by *LeakyReLU* and *batch normalization* layer. This network is implemented using *tensorflow* and *python*. Convolution blocks conv2, conv3, and conv4 have stride as 2×2 in each of their first convolution layer. The same is true for transposed convolution blocks convT2, convT3, and convT4.

The network is trained on the CASIA - palm print, CIEPUT - palm vein, CIEPUT - wrist vein, and PolyU - palm print datasets combined together. Adamax [14] is used as optimizer with default parameters, mean squared error (MSE) is used as loss and a random seed value is also used. The CAE is trained for 196 epochs with early stopping. Train and validation loss can be seen in Fig. 3.

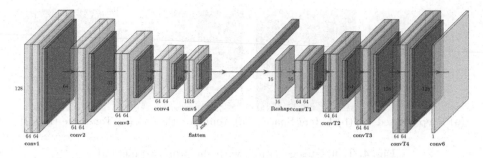

Fig. 2. Architecture of the proposed CAE

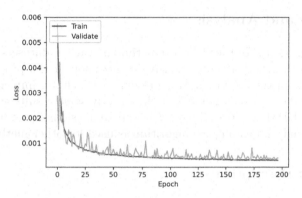

Fig. 3. Train and validation loss of CAE

3.2 Preprocessing and Feature Extraction

Input biometric image is preprocessed for noise removal and region of interest (ROI) is extracted. Extracted ROI is converted to gray scale to obtain image I_g, which is re-sized to the required size of $M \times N$ (here, $128 \times 128 \times 1$). The image is then made ready for input to CAE by normalising it in the range $(0, 1)$ to obtain I_p (Fig. 4a). To extract the features of the preprocessed biometric image, encoder (Enc) is used by passing the biometric image as input and output received is the feature vector (latent space).

3.3 Cancelable Template Generation

A random key (user specific token) from a uniform distribution in the range $(-4, 4)$ of the same size as the feature vector (here, 4096) is generated. This key (random noise) is added to the obtained feature vector from the CAE. A random kernel of size 7×7 is generated from a uniform distribution and convolved over the salted feature vector. Median filtering is performed to obtain the final cancelable template. The sample templates for a user with different keys can be seen in Fig. 4.

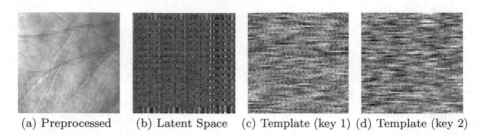

(a) Preprocessed   (b) Latent Space   (c) Template (key 1) (d) Template (key 2)

Fig. 4. Templates generated with the proposed method

4 Results and Analysis

The qualitative results for the proposed method on various datasets are presented in this section. Further, a comprehensive comparison of the proposed method with some state-of-the-art methods is presented, which are implemented in the same environment and may not reflect the exactly same results as presented in the literature. RDM [12] is evaluated without dimensionality reduction (kernel discriminant analysis) as no such algorithm is used for other methods.

4.1 Dataset Description

Table 1. Details of datasets used for experimentation

Name	Modality	Subjects	Samples
CIE-PUT	Palm Vein [2]	100	12
	Wrist Vein [3]	100	12
Poly-U	Palm Print [9]	400	20
CASIA	Palm Print [1]	428	6

Experiments are carried out on a number of publicly available palm vein, wrist vein, and palm print image datasets shown in Table 1. Some datasets provide images of left and right hands separately, which are merged considering both hands as different subjects. Some of these datasets consist of ROI images. Images from other datasets are subjected to ROI extraction while preprocessing.

4.2   Assessment Protocol

To evaluate performance of the proposed work in different scenarios, four type of templates, namely, genuine (GEN), imposter (IMP), pseudo-genuine I (PG1), and pseudo-genuine II (PG2) are generated [16] by using a set of keys, say K.

- GEN templates are generated for all subjects, with the genuine keys assigned to them. K_{Gen}^S is the genuine key assigned to a Subject S.
- IMP templates are generated for all subjects with keys other than those genuinely assigned to these subjects. For a subject S, the key assigned will be from K_{Gen} but not same as K_{Gen}^S.
- PG1 templates are generated for all subjects with a single key assigned to all of them, i.e., all subjects are assigned K_P but it has not been used for GEN or IMP templates.
- PG2 templates are generated with a single sample from all subjects using the same K_k keys. These keys are not used for GEN, IMP, or PG1 templates.

The scores are generated in three scenarios. GEN-IMP refers to the performance of the system in the normal situation where the user and key are both authentic (general scenario). GEN-PG1 shows the performance of the system when users' keys are stolen (stolen token scenario). GEN-PG2 refers to the situation where a user is enrolled at multiple devices using different keys (changeable or unlinkable scenario).

4.3   Performance Evaluation

Different cancelable biometric methods can be used in different devices, and at the same time a method can also be used in multiple devices. An individual's template from one device must be unlinkable from another device, each generated from a different key. Even different individuals can be assigned a common key when each individual is enrolled at only one of the devices. In both the cases, where either the key is same or an individual is same, system's performance should not deteriorate. Therefore, this work has been evaluated in three scenarios to explore such possibilities.

Performance is observed on three Metrics. **False accept rate (FAR)** is the percentage of subjects (imposter) who are falsely accepted. Such users should not be accepted at all and therefore, FAR must be minimized. **False reject rate (FRR)** is the percentage of subjects (genuine) who are falsely rejected. Such users, making claims of their authenticity must not be rejected. Therefore, FRR should also be low. **Equal error rate (EER)** is the point where FAR and FRR are equal. In this work, the templates are matched using threshold based cosine distances between them. The scores lie in the range $[0, 1]$, which are then scaled by 100 for better distinction. The scores for genuine users are close to 0, whereas the scores for imposter users are far and lie towards 100.

Table 2. Comparison of EER (GEN-IMP) at 95% CI (general scenario)

Modality method	CIEPUT		PolyU	CASIA
	PV	WV	PP	PP
RDM [12]	30.89 ± 0.007	32.61 ± 0.008	02.52 ± 0.001	05.44 ± 0.003
XOR [11]	00.00 ± 0.000	00.00 ± 0.000	00.00 ± 0.000	00.00 ± 0.000
LBP-RP [6]	00.00 ± 0.000	00.00 ± 0.000	00.00 ± 0.000	00.00 ± 0.000
BF [7]	00.00 ± 0.000	00.00 ± 0.000	00.00 ± 0.000	00.00 ± 0.000
Proposed	00.00 ± 0.000	00.00 ± 0.000	00.00 ± 0.000	00.00 ± 0.000

PV, WV, and PP stands for palm vein, wrist vein, and palm print respectively

Table 3. Comparison of EER (GEN-PG1) at 95% CI (stolen token scenario)

Modality method	CIEPUT		PolyU	CASIA
	PV	WV	PP	PP
RDM [12]	41.85 ± 0.008	43.48 ± 0.008	03.52 ± 0.002	06.72 ± 0.003
XOR [11]	00.00 ± 0.000	00.00 ± 0.000	00.00 ± 0.000	00.00 ± 0.000
LBP-RP [6]	68.07 ± 0.008	60.77 ± 0.008	10.34 ± 0.003	12.78 ± 0.005
BF [7]	40.67 ± 0.008	49.39 ± 0.008	03.65 ± 0.002	05.65 ± 0.003
Proposed	47.68 ± 0.008	54.68 ± 0.008	19.17 ± 0.003	11.21 ± 0.005

Table 4. Comparison of EER (GEN-PG2) at 95% CI (unlinkable scenario)

Modality method	CIEPUT		PolyU	CASIA
	PV	WV	PP	PP
RDM [12]	99.99 ± 0.000	99.99 ± 0.000	99.99 ± 0.000	99.99 ± 0.000
XOR [11]	63.89 ± 0.021	75.80 ± 0.018	31.51 ± 0.011	32.08 ± 0.013
LBP-RP [6]	00.00 ± 0.000	00.00 ± 0.000	00.00 ± 0.000	00.00 ± 0.000
BF [7]	00.00 ± 0.000	00.00 ± 0.000	00.00 ± 0.000	00.00 ± 0.000
Proposed	00.00 ± 0.000	00.00 ± 0.000	00.00 ± 0.000	00.00 ± 0.000

4.4 Experimental Results

Ideal case for a biometric device is when EER is 0. This work also tries to bring the error rates close to 0 and all experimental results are presented in terms of EER. The performance is evaluated in three scenarios, i.e., GEN-IMP (Table 2), GEN-PG1 (Table 3), and GEN-PG2 (Table 4). The results are shown at 95% confidence interval (CI) for better analysis [20]. The EER scores shows that the proposed method has promising results when compared to some state-of-the-art methods XOR and RDM based on log-gabor filters [11,12], LBP-RP method based on random salting [6], and bloom filters (BF) [7]. The results of the proposed method are 0 in all modalities for GEN-IMP and GEN-PG2 scenarios.

The performance of the proposed method is low in GEN-PG1 as the network is trained on multiple datasets combined due to the large data size requirement for training a neural network. The features generated from the autoencoder depends on the data it is trained on. Here, it is trained on a combination of different datasets of different modalities. Since these datasets have a varying number of samples (data imbalance), the features learned by the network are not uniform. Therefore, it leads to generation of features in the non-uniform range during testing. This also makes the distinction in inter-dataset higher than inter-class features.

The results of the proposed method are comparable to LBP-RP and BF in GEN-PG1 scenario. EER of proposed method is lower from LBP-RP in CIEPUT PV, WV, and CASIA PP, whereas slightly higher in PolyU PP. Proposed method has slightly higher EER when comparable to BF for all modalities. EER are high for XOR in GEN-PG2 scenario and RDM in GEN-PG1 and GEN-PG2 scenarios.

4.5   Unlinkability Analysis

Transformed templates should be unlinkable, if they are generated from the same biometric instance and transformed using different keys. To evaluate unlinkability, the protocol defined in [7] is used as benchmark. Unlinkability of the proposed method depends on the random noise and random kernel used for the transformation. Scores GEN-IMP and GEN-PG2 are used to evaluate unlinkability. GEN-PG2 act as mated scores whereas GEN-IMP act as non-mated scores. $D_{\leftrightarrow}^{sys}$ is global score-wise measure. Unlinkability score is defined as $D_{\leftrightarrow}^{sys} \in [0,1]$, where $D_{\leftrightarrow}^{sys} = 1$ denotes a fully linkable system, i.e., no overlap in score distribution and $D_{\leftrightarrow}^{sys} = 0$ denotes a fully unlinkable system, i.e., complete overlap in score distribution. Figure 5 shows the unlinkability plots for modalities used in this work satisfy unlinkability upto a large extent.

4.6   Non-invertibility Analysis

Non-invertibility is an important property to fulfil for every cancelable transformation as this factor determines the security of the templates. Even if the key, transformation function, and transformed templates are compromised, *invertibility* should not be possible (computationally hard).

In the proposed method, the final template has been reduced to $1/4^{th}$ size of the original biometric image, i.e., from $M \times N$ (here, 128×128) to $M/2 \times N/2$ (here, 64×64). Once a template is generated, regeneration of the original biometric image is not possible without the use of the trained network with known weights [26]. During the training of the CAE, a seed value has been used. Without this seed value, even if another CAE is trained, it will not result in the exact reconstructed image from the templates of this CAE. The generated template is median filtered, which is a *non-invertible* operation [11,12]. Therefore, the templates generated in the proposed work are non-invertible.

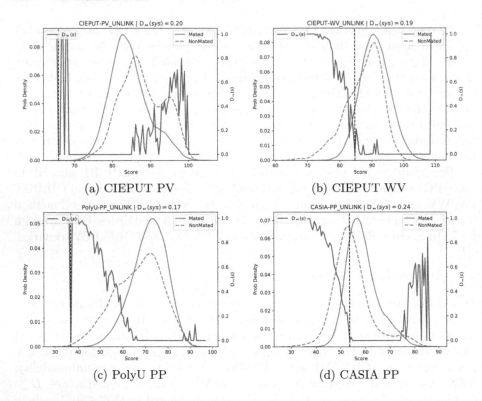

Fig. 5. Graphs for unlinkability analysis of the proposed method

5 Conclusion

The proposed method adopts CAE for feature extraction and cancelable biometric template generation. The method proves to be efficient, non-invertible, and privacy preserving but does not prove to be fully unlinkable for all modalities used for experimentation. The size of the cancelable template is also reduced to $1/4^{th}$ to the size of the original biometric image, which makes the biometric system storage and computationally efficient. This method can be optimized for its unlinkability and to increase the accuracy of the network.

References

1. Casia palmprint database. http://biometrics.idealtest.org/
2. Cie biometrics palmvein database. https://biometrics.cie.put.poznan.pl
3. Cie biometrics wristvein database. https://biometrics.cie.put.poznan.pl
4. Ali, M.A., Tahir, N.M.: Cancelable biometrics technique for iris recognition. In: 2018 IEEE Symposium on Computer Applications & Industrial Electronics (ISCAIE), pp. 434–437. IEEE (2018)

5. Cao, X., Shen, W., Yu, L.G., Wang, Y., Yang, J.Y., Zhang, Z.: Illumination invariant extraction for face recognition using neighboring wavelet coefficients. Pattern Recogn. **45**(4), 1299–1305 (2012)
6. Deshmukh, M., Balwant, M.K.: Generating cancelable palmprint templates using local binary pattern and random projection. In: 13th International Conference on Signal-Image Technology & Internet-Based Systems (SITIS), pp. 203–209. IEEE (2017)
7. Gomez-Barrero, M., Galbally, J., Rathgeb, C., Busch, C.: General framework to evaluate unlinkability in biometric template protection systems. IEEE Trans. Inf. Forensics Secur. **13**(6), 1406–1420 (2017)
8. Jang, Y.K., Cho, N.I.: Deep face image retrieval for cancelable biometric authentication. In: 16th IEEE International Conference on Advanced Video and Signal Based Surveillance (AVSS), pp. 1–8. IEEE (2019)
9. Kanhangad, V., Kumar, A., Zhang, D.: Contactless and pose invariant biometric identification using hand surface. IEEE Trans. Image Process. **20**(5), 1415–1424 (2010)
10. Kaur, H., Khanna, P.: Biometric template protection using cancelable biometrics and visual cryptography techniques. Multimed. Tools Appl. **75**(23), 16333–16361 (2015). https://doi.org/10.1007/s11042-015-2933-6
11. Kaur, H., Khanna, P.: Cancelable features using log-Gabor filters for biometric authentication. Multimed. Tools Appl. **76**(4), 4673–4694 (2017)
12. Kaur, H., Khanna, P.: Random distance method for generating unimodal and multimodal cancelable biometric features. IEEE Trans. Inf. Forensics Secur. **14**(3), 709–719 (2018)
13. Kim, J., Teoh, A.B.J.: One-factor cancellable biometrics based on indexing-first-order hashing for fingerprint authentication. In: 24th International Conference on Pattern Recognition (ICPR), pp. 3108–3113. IEEE (2018)
14. Kingma, D.P., Ba, J.: Adam: a method for stochastic optimization. arXiv preprint arXiv:1412.6980 (2014)
15. Kumar, N., Rawat, M.: RP-LPP: a random permutation based locality preserving projection for cancelable biometric recognition. Multimed. Tools Appl. **79**(3), 2363–2381 (2020)
16. Lee, D.H., Lee, S.H., Cho, N.I.: Cancelable biometrics using noise embedding. In: 24th International Conference on Pattern Recognition (ICPR), pp. 3390–3395. IEEE (2018)
17. Maiorana, E., Campisi, P., Fierrez, J., Ortega-Garcia, J., Neri, A.: Cancelable templates for sequence-based biometrics with application to on-line signature recognition. IEEE Trans. Syst. Man Cybern. Part A Syst. Hum. **40**(3), 525–538 (2010)
18. Nguyen, T.A.T., Dang, T.K., Nguyen, D.T.: A new biometric template protection using random orthonormal projection and fuzzy commitment. In: Lee, S., Ismail, R., Choo, H. (eds.) IMCOM 2019. AISC, vol. 935, pp. 723–733. Springer, Cham (2019). https://doi.org/10.1007/978-3-030-19063-7_58
19. Patel, V.M., Ratha, N.K., Chellappa, R.: Cancelable biometrics: a review. IEEE Signal Process. Mag. **32**(5), 54–65 (2015)
20. Petrovska-Delacrétaz, D., Chollet, G., Dorizzi, B.: Guide to Biometric Reference Systems and Performance Evaluation. Springer, London (2009). https://doi.org/10.1007/978-1-84800-292-0
21. Phillips, T., Zou, X., Li, F., Li, N.: Enhancing biometric-capsule-based authentication and facial recognition via deep learning. In: Proceedings of the 24th ACM Symposium on Access Control Models and Technologies, pp. 141–146 (2019)

22. Pillai, J.K., Patel, V.M., Chellappa, R., Ratha, N.K.: Secure and robust iris recognition using random projections and sparse representations. IEEE Trans. Pattern Anal. Mach. Intell. **33**(9), 1877–1893 (2011)
23. Ratha, N., Connell, J., Bolle, R.M., Chikkerur, S.: Cancelable biometrics: a case study in fingerprints. In: 18th International Conference on Pattern Recognition (ICPR 2006), vol. 4, pp. 370–373. IEEE (2006)
24. Srinivasan, A., Balamurugan, V.: Occlusion detection and image restoration in 3D face image. In: TENCON 2014 IEEE Region 10 Conference, pp. 1–6. IEEE (2014)
25. Wang, S., Hu, J.: Design of alignment-free cancelable fingerprint templates via curtailed circular convolution. Pattern Recogn. **47**(3), 1321–1329 (2014)
26. Zhu, J., Kaplan, R., Johnson, J., Fei-Fei, L.: HiDDeN: hiding data with deep networks. In: Ferrari, V., Hebert, M., Sminchisescu, C., Weiss, Y. (eds.) ECCV 2018. LNCS, vol. 11219, pp. 682–697. Springer, Cham (2018). https://doi.org/10.1007/978-3-030-01267-0_40

A Novel Method for Cephalometric Landmark Regression Using Convolutional Neural Networks and Local Binary Pattern

S. Rashmi$^{(\boxtimes)}$ (iD) and Vani Ashok (iD)

Department of Computer Science and Engineering,
Sri Jayachamarajendra College of Engineering, Mysuru, India
vanisj@sjce.ac.in

Abstract. A cephalogram analysis is a clinical application that includes evaluation of anatomical landmarks and their skeletal relationship in the craniofacial area of the human skull. In this paper, a novel deep learning method is proposed to automatically identify the anatomical landmarks. A Convolutional Neural Network (CNN) based framework is designed to regress the landmark location from the Local Binary Patterns (LBP) image of cephalogram. A U-Net based CNN model and multi-resolution down-sampling models together process the LBP feature map of cephalogram. LBP helps in fast convergence of the framework. U-Net and three down-sampling models contribute towards eliminating the week candidate locations predictions thereby improving the robustness of the system. LBP images when trained using CNN learns the spatial relationship and intensity changes at the landmark position better than training the original image. The proposed framework showed a mean landmark error of 1.17 mm and success detection rate of 85.36% that is about 10% higher than state-of-art results in a 2 mm precision range.

Keywords: Cephalometric analysis · Deep learning · Convolutional Neural Network · Heatmap regression · Local Binary Pattern

1 Introduction

A cephalogram analysis includes locating anatomical reference points and measuring the scientific distances between those identified points in lateral cephalometric radiographs. In orthodontic practices, manual tracing of the cephalometric landmarks is an important and necessary step as it provides essential information regarding bony and soft tissue structures of the patient's skull. Cephalometric analysis is usually carried out in medical cases like orthognathic diagnosis, maxillofacial treatment planning and craniofacial growth prediction. Tracing the anatomical landmarks manually is time-consuming work and is error-prone. The annotation process takes around 20 min for an experienced professional. In addition, manual annotation is subject to inter and intra-observer variability. To address these issues many clinical researchers are trying to automate the landmark annotation process.

© Springer Nature Singapore Pte Ltd. 2021
S. K. Singh et al. (Eds.): CVIP 2020, CCIS 1376, pp. 315–326, 2021.
https://doi.org/10.1007/978-981-16-1086-8_28

It started with handcrafted algorithms like edge detection and template matching by Ferreira [1]. The performance was highly dependent on image quality. Later relatively high landmark detection accuracy obtained in model-based approaches like principal component analysis and pattern matching by Yue [2]. As proved by Kaur [3], significant performance gain obtained from computer vision algorithms like Active appearance modeling (AAM), Active shape modeling (ASM).

More recently, IEEE International Symposium on Biomedical Imaging (ISBI) held a grand challenge of anatomical landmark detection in the year 2015. The challenge was to detect the cephalometric landmarks in a clinically accepted precision range of 2 mm radial distance in the benchmark dataset [4, 5]. The Random Forest regression-voting method by Lindner et al. [6, 7] won the challenge with success detection rate of 74.84%. Imbragimov et al. [8] applied game theory with shape based model and achieved higher accuracy. Later, Wang [9] proposed an ensemble tree-based method to regress the landmarks. Lee et al. [10] proposed deep learning methods for cephalometric landmark localization, 38 independent CNN structures were trained to regress 19 x-coordinates and 19 y-coordinates separately. This deep learning experiment was followed by several CNN's models experiments [11–13]. Payer et al. [14] transformed the coordinate regression problem to the heatmap regression problem. His results indicated that regressing pixel-to-pixel as a heatmap intrinsically results in more accurate landmark detection. A multimodal CNN model optimized by transfer learning based on 5,890 lateral cephalograms by Yu [15]. An experiment reported for 219 Cephalograms collected through internet, manually traced for ground truth and trained using deep learning by Nishimoto [16]. In his experiment despite different image quality, an average prediction error of 1.7 mm is achieved. Qian et al. [17] proposed a new architecture called CephaNet using Faster R-CNN and achieved an accuracy 6% higher than existing state of art methods. Zhong [18] proposed two-stage u-net model that achieved state of art results with less manual tuning. The recent experiments by Song [19] and Lee [20] showed satisfying results on successful detection rate.

The proposed work is a combination of image processing (LBP visual descriptors) and deep learning methods [21]. Higher detection accuracy is obtained in recent r searches using CNN. LBP is a simple and powerful image transformation operation to extract spatial features, which reduces the workload of CNN and it increases the detection accuracy [22, 23]. The current study is inspired by the work of Payer et al. [24] for data augmentation and heatmap regression.

2 Materials and Methods

This section explains the proposed landmark localization model. Section 2.1 describes dataset used for the experiment. Section 2.2 describes image and ground truth data pre-processing employed before the training. In Sects. 2.3 and 2.4 two deep CNN architectures used for landmark regression are described. In Sect. 2.5 the proposed end-to-end architecture and methodology are summarized.

2.1 Experimental Data

A larger clinical data containing lateral cephalogram radiographs is built for ISBI Dental image analysis grand challenge. The dataset contains 2-dimension lateral cephalometric radiographs of 400 patients. The statistical details of the patients are as follows, mean age of patients is 27.0 years; patient's age ranges between 7 to 76 years. Out of 400 patients, 235 are females, and 165 are males. The images are acquired using the Soredex CRANEX® Excel Ceph machine (Tuusula, Finland) and Soredex SorCom software (3.1.5, version 2.0). The pixel resolution of each image is 1935 × 2400 pixels in .bmp format with 0.1 mm pixel size. The ground truth for evaluation of landmarks locations for all the images are manually marked and inspected by two experts. The individual image in the dataset is available with 19 landmarks annotations. One such manual annotation of 19 cephalometric landmark positions on a sample cephalogram radiograph is shown in Fig. 1.

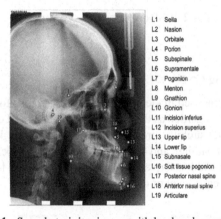

L1	Sella
L2	Nasion
L3	Orbitale
L4	Porion
L5	Subspinale
L6	Supramentale
L7	Pogonion
L8	Menton
L9	Gnathion
L10	Gonion
L11	Incision inferius
L12	Incision superius
L13	Upper lip
L14	Lower lip
L15	Subnasale
L16	Soft tissue pogonion
L17	Posterior nasal spine
L18	Anterior nasal spine
L19	Articulare

Fig. 1. Sample training image with landmark name list.

2.2 Data Preprocessing

- The mean value of the landmark coordinates of the manual annotations from two experts is calculated as ground truth coordinate value for localization.
- The image is cropped to square shape with resolution 1935 × 1935 towards the bottom of the image, as it is the landmarks distribution area in the cephalograms. This lessens the computational time.
- 1935 × 1935 pixels resolution is considered as 193.5 × 193.5 mm^2 resolution.
- From mean landmark coordinates, corresponding Y-coordinate values are subtracted by 46.5 mm as the upper portion of each image is cropped by 465 pixels.
- Input images are scaled to 512 × 512 mm^2 using bi/tricubic interpolation to make it compatible with the network input size. The final landmark predictions are generated by rescaling the network outputs to original size of 193.5 × 193.5 mm^2.
- Spatial data augmentation is done using SimpleITK. It includes a random translation by [−20, 20] pixels, rotation by [−15∘, 15∘], and scale by [−0.6, 1.4].

- Uniform LBP feature map is constructed from augmented images and is used to train the deep learning model. The grey value of the individual pixel is compared with its surrounding 8 pixel's gray value to generate 8-bit binary number. This binary number is the LBP value of the individual pixel [25]. The LBP operation is explained in Fig. 2.
- The cropping and rescaling gray scale image contributed to noise reduction. As LPB are sensitive to noise, the transformation operation is performed after image resizing that makes the model noise robust.

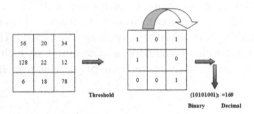

Fig. 2. LBP operation in 3×3 window

2.3 U-Net Model Using CNN

The U-Net model was first used in electron microscopic stacks for the neural structures segmentation, and it was regarded as the best method of the ISBI cell tracking challenge in 2015 [26]. The U-Net architecture used in our framework is shown in Fig. 3. It includes 4 contracting, 4 parallel, and 4 expanding levels in 3 blocks. As the input image is processed, height and width is halved (down-sampled) at each level of the contracting block and is doubled at each level of the expanding path.

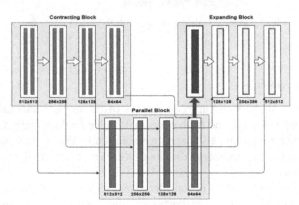

Fig. 3. Schematic representation of the U-net architecture. Gray colored boxes represent convolution layers, arrows represents down sampling and up sampling in contracting block and expanding block respectively.

In each level of contracting block, two standard convolutional layers with a kernel size of 3×3 are used in a successive sequence. Leaky- rectified linear unit (Leaky-ReLu) is employed to ease the convergence during training. After 2 convolution sequences, an average pooling layer is placed to down-sample input at half the resolution for the next level in the contracting path. Drop-out of 0.5 is introduced after first convolution at each level in the contracting path to avoid over-fitting. The parallel block contains a single convolutional layer at each level. This block receives input from contracting block levels and feeds it to expanding block levels. The name parallel represents input resolution as received is as processed using convolutional layers. Expanding block linearly up-samples the previous layer output and adds it to the output of the corresponding parallel block node. There are two primary tasks performed by expanding block to retain the information related to the spatial representation of unique features extracted in previous levels: Up-sampling the previous level's low-resolution image to their corresponding level image dimension via bi-linear interpolation technique; shaping it to a proper output format by adding respective parallel block convolutional layer outputs [27]. Due to contracting and expanding nature of the convolutional layer's framework, the model is able to hold unique features from substantial image regions using small kernel sizes. Multiple convolution outputs produced from LBP input image contribute to fast feature learning.

2.4 Down-Sampling Multi-resolution Model Using CNN

In the current work, we propose 3 multi-scale models with the same architecture (Fig. 4) that are used to regress the heatmaps of the localization points. There are two major advantages of having individual down-sampling networks. The first advantage is reducing the number of parameters will contribute to increasing the computation speed. The second advantage is any pooling layer like max-pooling or average pooling ensures translational equi-variance. The redundancy in feature learning helps in the fast convergence of the neural network.

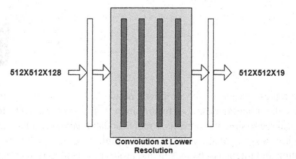

512X512X128   512X512X19

Convolution at Lower
Resolution

Fig. 4. Schematic representation of the down-sampling network architecture. Average pooling and tricubic interpolation with kernel size equal to the down-sampling factor are employed during entry and exit of the block respectively.

Feature response from the U-Net is reduced to different resolutions to 3 individual down-sampling networks (512 × 512 feature map output from U-Net is reduced by scale factors 1/8, 1/16, 1/32). Average pooling with kernel size equal to the scaling factor is used to fit the U-Net output to down-sampling networks. The individual down-sampling networks fine-tunes the feature learning in and around the landmark localization points. The architecture consists of 4 consecutive convolutional layers with 11×11 kernel size. The first 3 convolutional layers use leaky-ReLu activation function and produce 128 outputs. The last convolutional layer uses Tanh activation function and produces 19 outputs that are equal to the number of landmarks. These outputs are up-sampled again back to input resolution using tri-cubic interpolation to produce heatmaps. Feature response from the 3 down-sampling networks are multiplied together to produces strong contenders of heatmap localization points. Multiplication eliminates week candidate landmark points and retains the landmark points present in all the three network's output. The structure is named as multi-resolution local regression component as it regresses the landmark points at different resolution levels.

2.5 Methodology

The framework consists of the image pre-processing component, U-NET component, and multi-resolution local appearance component as shown in Fig. 5. The approach is to regress heatmaps directly from input LBP images for multiple landmark localization.

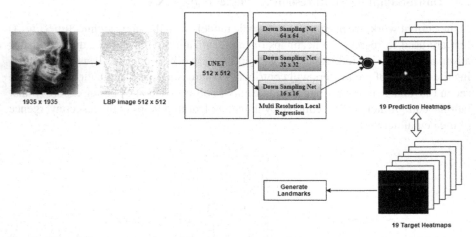

Fig. 5. Schematic representation of the proposed network. In U-Net component, LBP feature map is transformed into a landmark global feature map that is transformed to local heatmaps by multi-resolution local regression components. Prediction landmarks heatmaps are compared with target heatmaps, with back-propagation and parameter tuning the entire network is trained to learn the spatial co-relation and intensity changes in and around the landmark locations.

Individual heatmaps are the Gaussians distributions located at the position of the landmarks. Set of training images are given as an input to the CNN framework while their corresponding 19 landmark's heatmaps are used as target images for training framework. As a first step, input image is converted into LBP feature map. Next, the deep learning module regress the heatmaps of landmarks at 19 channels from coarse to fine in a two stage process. Stage 1 includes training the U-Net structure that helps in fast feature learning from the LBP image for landmark regression. The output of stage 1 is given as input to stage 2 which is assigned as "multi-resolution local regression" that contains 3 down-sampling networks. Guided by the coarse training from U-NET, down-sampling net refines the output at different resolutions. Down-sampling factors 1/8, 1/16, 1/32 are used which produces the images at resolution 64×64, 32×32, 16×16 respectively to down-sampling networks. The output from all down-sampling networks are combined in such a way to obtain maximum feature response within all obtained heatmaps produced using different resolution feature input. The final predicted heatmaps are calculated as shown below. The output vector's element-wise multiplication is done to produce final heatmaps.

$$\text{HeatmapTarget} = \text{Heatmap}_8 \odot \text{Heatmap}_{16} \odot \text{Heatmap}_{32}$$

The Gaussian distribution with a standard deviation of 0.001 is used to draw the initial weights of the network. The bias values are initialized with 0. For backpropagation heatmap regression loss is calculated using L2 normalization. Momentum optimizer with momentum value of 0.99 and a learning rate of 10^{-06} are employed. Predicted heatmaps at 19 different channels are again Gaussian distributions centered at predicted landmark locations. Finally, landmark coordinates are extracted from the final predicted heatmap. The network is tested with a validation set at regular intervals during training. Test error reached a constant plateau after 15,000 to 20,000 of training iterations. A tensor-flow session object with a multi-threading environment is used to speed up and utilize the GPU resources. U-Net along with multi-resolution regression model learns spatial local correlation patterns in order to regress the 19 different heatmaps of the landmarks.

3   Results and Discussion

The framework is implemented using TensorFlow open-source platform on a machine with an NVIDIA TESLA K80 Titan 1X with 12 GB of RAM. Training and testing data are divided in the ratio 3:1. In each epoch, an image is given as an input to the network. Increasing the number of images per epoch showed an increase in training time and memory consumption. Training the model took approximately 2 h for 20,000 iterations. Single image testing took approximately 2 s. All landmarks are identified with 100% accuracy within radial error 10 mm. However, for results comparison and analysis the landmarks identified within a clinically acceptable range of 2 mm radial error are considered. The absolute difference between manually annotated landmark and predicted landmark is calculated using Eq. (1).

$$\|D\| = \left[\text{abs}(X_T - X_P)^2 + \text{abs}(Y_T - Y_P)^2 \right]^{1/2} \tag{1}$$

Where X_T, Y_T represent target x and y coordinate values, X_P and Y_P represent predicted x and y coordinate values. This standard measurement for calculating the error is in accordance with the guidelines mentioned in the ISBI challenge. For a given test image, outliers are calculated as the number of landmarks located outside given radial error range. Mean radial error (MRE) for a landmark is calculated as shown in

Eq. (2). It is the sum of distances of the landmarks of that type identified within given radial distance, divided by the number of landmarks identified.

$$MRE = \left(\sum_i^n Di\right)/n \tag{2}$$

Where Di is the distance between target and predicted landmark, n being the number of landmarks identified in the validation set within a given radial distance. The successful detection rate (SDR, in %) given by the Eq. (3) is the percentage of landmarks detected within a certain precision range (radial distance) $z \epsilon \{2.0\,mm, 2.5\,mm, 3.0\,mm, 4.0\,mm\}$.

$$SDR = \#\{(D_i < z)/n\} \times 100 \text{ for } 1 \leq i \leq n \tag{3}$$

The localization results of individual landmarks using our framework are listed in Table 1. MRE and SD values listed in the table are for 2 mm precision range.

Table 1. Localization results on individual landmarks

Landmark	MRE (mm)	SD (mm)	SDR (%)			
			2.0 mm	2.5 mm	3.0 mm	4.0 mm
L1	0.65	0.68	99%	99%	99%	99%
L2	1.17	0.81	86%	95%	97%	99%
L2	1.39	0.94	80%	85%	92%	99%
L4	1.61	1.06	70%	80%	88%	96%
L5	1.4	0.71	82%	90%	98%	100%
L6	1.6	1.12	71%	79%	86%	94%
L7	0.82	0.61	95%	98%	98%	100%
L8	0.82	0.61	93%	98%	100%	100%
L9	0.76	0.45	99%	100%	100%	100%
L10	1.65	1.22	70%	84%	91%	97%
L11	1.01	0.81	89%	94%	96%	98%
L12	0.88	0.79	96%	98%	98%	98%
L13	1.21	0.80	84%	93%	96%	100%
L14	0.94	0.57	95%	100%	100%	100%
L15	0.81	0.57	98%	99%	99%	99%
L16	1.73	1.44	69%	74%	81%	90%
L17	0.89	0.64	96%	96%	99%	99%
L18	1.36	1.05	80%	88%	91%	97%
L19	1.61	1.18	70%	80%	88%	96%
Average	1.17	0.85	85.36%	91%	94.57%	97.9%

The average mean radial error between predicted landmark and actual landmark is 1.179 mm, with a median value of 0.951 mm and a standard deviation of 0.85 mm.

Overall detection accuracy in 2 mm precision range is 85.36% with 14.64% of landmarks detected outside the 2 mm radial distance. About 91% of landmarks identified within a radial distance of 2.5 mm that infers that with further modification and improvements the much better results can be achieved with our proposed work. The accuracy of a few landmarks localizations is reducing the overall localization accuracy. The reason behind is, these landmarks lack intensity distribution changes surrounding them which is difficult to capture both in LBP feature extraction and Neural network feature leaning. LBP is a powerful image descriptor to identify the texture pattern in an image. It is known that LBP sometimes miss the local structure and are sensitive to noise. The cropped gray scale image is resized to network input size. This rescaling will further help in reducing the noise. Hence, experiment yielded higher accuracy. Since LBP image is used as an input, the model can also be used to train the test the images with varying intensity as LBP remains invariant regardless of the illumination changes. This makes LBP entirely appropriate for real-time applications [28]. In general, when an original image is used for training the CNN, the network learns the feature from each pixel; the process starts from the lowest level. When the local texture feature calculated using LBP is given as an input to CNN, learning is better than original pixel-level processing. In addition, when original image is used for training the model convergence took 3 h of time but with LBP transformed image the model convergence took only 2 h of time. The landmark annotation image obtained from the framework are visualized in Fig. 6.

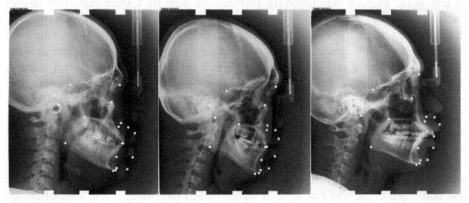

Fig. 6. Results of cephalometric landmark localization. Yellow spots represent the landmark identification points using our framework.

It is also found that when individual landmarks are regressed without considering spatial co-relation of the other landmarks, the performance was different for different landmarks. Landmark numbers 4, 6, 10, 16, and 19 are giving low localization accuracy compared to other landmarks. In addition, training time is different for all landmarks, few landmarks namely 1, 3, 7, 11, 12, 13 converge in very less time. The trained model for few landmarks like 7, 8, 9 and 5, 18 is saved and re-used for other landmarks, which saves the time for training as these landmarks are distributed in a close proximity.

The benchmark dataset is evaluated with 4-fold cross-validation. The proposed framework results are compared with the results obtained in ISBI 2015 Grand challenge's state of art methods and other recent experiments on the same dataset. Comparisons are quoted in Table 2.

Table 2. Comparison of localization results of proposed framework with existing methods. O_r stands for outliers in radius range.

Method	#O_r (in %)			
	r = 2 mm	r = 2.5 mm	r = 3 mm	r = 3.5 mm
Proposed method	14.64%	8.9%	5.3%	2.2%
Qian [17]	17.5%	13.8%	10.7%	9.4%
Zhong [18]	13.26%	8%	5.29%	2.18%
Payer et al. [24]	26.67%	21.24%	16.76%	10.25%
Linder et al. [6]	29.35%	23.07%	17.83%	10.15%

4 Conclusion

In this work, we have considered the LBP feature map for texture extraction around the landmarks. Texture features around the landmarks are obtained from a set of pixels in the image surrounding the landmark and their relationship. This eliminated the need for single-pixel value consideration during training. Landmarks in cephalograms show less or no difference with its surrounding pixels when the individual pixel value is considered. This drawback is not only concerning cephalograms radiographs but also with other anatomical landmark identification tasks that have the same problem that causes neural network training convergence to take time. From the literature survey done this is the first experiment reported using the LBP feature extraction method for landmark annotation.

Results of our proposed methodology show that a fully convolutional neural network model trained with LBP transformed images at different resolution feature maps and combined at the end can achieve higher localization results than state-of-the-art localization by regressing heatmaps. The use of LBP feature map reduced the training time as well as the percentage of outliers. Given its very less runtime and high accuracy of 85.36%, our framework exhibits great promise for the computer-assisted cephalometric tracing application. It is concluded from the experienced medical professor that the cephalometric localization position differs depending on the age range as well as sex of the patient. The dataset used in the current experiment lacks individual patient's age or sex information from whom cephalogram radiographs are captured. In future work, we plan to evaluate datasets available with above-mentioned information. The proposed method can be extended to other landmarks detection problems like chest X-ray, fetal X-ray, hand X-ray, etc.

References

1. Ferreira, J.T.L.: Evaluation of the reliability of computerized profile cephalometric analysis. Braz. Dent. J. **13**(3), 201–204 (2002). ISSN 0103-6440
2. Yue, W., Yin, D., Li, C., Wang, G., Xu, T.: Automated 2-D cephalometric analysis on X-ray images by a model-based approach, vol. 9010900, pp. 1615–1623. IEEE (2006)
3. Kaur, A., Singh, C.: Automatic cephalometric landmark detection using Zernike moments and template matching. SIViP **9**, 117–132 (2015). https://doi.org/10.1007/s11760-013-0432-7
4. Wang, C.-W., Huang, C.-T., Hsieh, M.-C.: Evaluation and comparison of anatomical landmark detection methods for cephalometric X-Ray images. A grand challenge ISBI. IEEE Trans. Med. Imaging **34**, 1890–1900 (2015)
5. Wang, C.W., et al.: A benchmark for comparison of dental radiography analysis algorithms. Med. Image Anal. **31**, 63 (2016)
6. Lindner, C., Cootes, T.F.: Fully automatic cephalometric evaluation using random forest regression-voting. In: IEEE International Symposium on Biomedical Imaging. Citeseer (2015)
7. Lindner, C., Wang, C.-W., Huang, C.-T., Li, C.-H., Chang, S.-W., Cootes, T.F.J.S.R.: Fully automatic system for accurate localisation and analysis of cephalometric landmarks in lateral cephalograms. Sci. Rep. **6**, 33581 (2016)
8. Ibragimov, B., Likar, B., Pernuš, F., Vrtovec, T.: Computerized cephalometry by game theory with shape and appearance-based landmark refinement, pp. 1–8 (2014)
9. Wang, S., Li, H., Li, J., Zhang, Y., Zou, B.: Automatic analysis of lateral cephalograms based on multiresolution decision tree regression voting. J. Healthc. Eng. **2018**, 1–15 (2018). https://doi.org/10.1155/2018/1797502
10. Lee, H., Park, M., Kim, J.: Cephalometric landmark detection in dental X-ray images using convolutional neural networks. In: Medical Imaging 2017, Computer-Aided Diagnosis, p. 101341W. International Society for Optics and Photonics (2017)
11. Arık, S.Ö., Ibragimov, B., Xing, L.: Fully automated quantitative cephalometry using convolutional neural networks. J. Med. Imaging **4**, 014501 (2017). https://doi.org/10.1117/1.jmi.4.1.014501
12. Dai, X., et al.: Locating anatomical landmarks on 2D lateral cephalograms through adversarial encoder-decoder networks. IEEE Access **7**, 132738–132747 (2019)
13. Li, Y., et al.: Fast multiple landmark localisation using a patch-based iterative network. In: Frangi, A.F., Schnabel, J.A., Davatzikos, C., Alberola-López, C., Fichtinger, G. (eds.) MICCAI 2018. LNCS, vol. 11070, pp. 563–571. Springer, Cham (2018). https://doi.org/10.1007/978-3-030-00928-1_64
14. Payer, C., Štern, D., Bischof, H., Urschler, M.: Regressing heatmaps for multiple landmark localization using CNNs. In: Ourselin, S., Joskowicz, L., Sabuncu, M.R., Unal, G., Wells, W. (eds.) MICCAI 2016. LNCS, vol. 9901, pp. 230–238. Springer, Cham (2016). https://doi.org/10.1007/978-3-319-46723-8_27
15. Yu, H.J., Cho, S.R., Kim, M.J., Kim, W.H., Kim, J.W., Choi, J.: Automated skeletal classification with lateral cephalometry based on artificial intelligence. J. Dent. Res. **99**, 249–256 (2020). https://doi.org/10.1177/0022034520901715. 002203452090171
16. Nishimoto, S., Sotsuka, Y., Kawai, K.-I., Ishise, H., Kakibuchi, M.: Personal computer-based cephalometric landmark detection with deep learning, using cephalograms on the Internet. J. Craniofac. Surg. **30**, 1 (2018). https://doi.org/10.1097/scs.0000000000004901
17. Qian, J., Cheng, M., Tao, Y., Lin, J., Lin, H.: CephaNet: an improved faster R-CNN for cephalometric landmark detection, pp. 868–871 (2019). https://doi.org/10.1109/isbi.2019.8759437

18. Zhong, Z., Li, J., Zhang, Z., Jiao, Z., Gao, X.: An attention-guided deep regression model for landmark detection in cephalograms. In: Shen, D., et al. (eds.) MICCAI 2019. LNCS, vol. 11769, pp. 540–548. Springer, Cham (2019). https://doi.org/10.1007/978-3-030-32226-7_60
19. Song, Y., Qiao, X., Iwamoto, Y., Chen, Y.-W.: Automatic cephalometric landmark detection on X-ray images using a deep-learning method. Appl. Sci. **10**(7), 2547 (2020)
20. Lee, J., Yu, H., Kim, M., et al.: Automated cephalometric landmark detection with confidence regions using Bayesian convolutional neural networks. BMC Oral Health **20**, 270 (2020)
21. Kafieh, R., Sadri, S., Mehri, A., Raji, H.: Discrimination of bony structures in cephalograms for automatic landmark detection. In: Sarbazi-Azad, H., Parhami, B., Miremadi, S.-G., Hessabi, S. (eds.) CSICC 2008. CCIS, vol. 6, pp. 609–620. Springer, Heidelberg (2008). https://doi.org/10.1007/978-3-540-89985-3_75
22. Wei, X., Yu, X., Liu, B., Zhi, L.: Convolutional neural networks and local binary patterns for hyperspectral image classification. Eur. J. Remote Sens. **52**, 448–462 (2019)
23. Anwer, R.M., Khan, F.S., van de Weijer, J., Molinier, M., Laaksonen, J.: Binary patterns encoded convolutional neural networks for texture recognition and remote sensing scene classification. ISPRS J. Photogramm. Remote Sens. **138**, 74–85 (2018)
24. Payer, C., Štern, D., Bischof, H., Urschler, M.: Integrating spatial configuration into heatmap regression based CNNs for landmark localization. Med. Image Anal. **54**, 207–219 (2019)
25. Zhang, H., Qu, Z., Yuan, L., Li, G.: A face recognition method based on LBP feature for CNN. In: 2017 IEEE 2nd Advanced Information Technology, Electronic and Automation Control Conference (IAEAC), Chongqing, pp. 544–547 (2017). https://doi.org/10.1109/iaeac.2017.8054074
26. Ronneberger, O., Fischer, P., Brox, T.: U-Net: convolutional networks for biomedical image segmentation. In: Navab, N., Hornegger, J., Wells, W.M., Frangi, A.F. (eds.) MICCAI 2015. LNCS, vol. 9351, pp. 234–241. Springer, Cham (2015). https://doi.org/10.1007/978-3-319-24574-4_28
27. Goutham, E.N.D., Vasamsetti, S., Kishore, P.V., Sardana, H.K.: Automatic localization of landmarks in cephalometric images via modified U-Net. In: 10th International Conference on Computing, Communication and Networking Technologies (ICCCNT) (2019). https://doi.org/10.1109/icccnt45670.2019.8944411
28. Yang, X., Li, M., Zhao, S.: Facial expression recognition algorithm based on CNN and LBP feature fusion. In: IRJET, pp. 33–38 (2017). https://doi.org/10.1145/3175603.3175615

Multi-class Glioma Classification from MRI Images Using 3D Convolutional Neural Networks

Subin Sahayam$^{(\boxtimes)}$ ⓘ, Umarani Jayaraman, and Bhaskara Teja

Indian Institute of Information Technology Design and Manufacturing,
Kancheepuram, Chennai 600127, India
{coe18d001,umarani,coe16b004}@iiitdm.ac.in

Abstract. Glioma is a prevalent and deadly form of brain tumor. Most of the existing models have used 2D MRI slices for general tumor classification. In this paper, a 3D convolutional neural network has been proposed to automatically classify gliomas namely, astrocytoma, oligodendroglioma, and glioblastoma from MRI images. MRI modalities like T1, T1ce, FLAIR, and T2 are used for glioma classification. This step is essential for diagnosis and treatment planning for a patient. Manual classification is costly, time-consuming, and human-error prone. So, there is a need for accurate, robust, and automatic classification of glioma. Convolution neural networks have achieved state-of-the-art accuracy in many image processing classification tasks. In this work, 3D and 2D CNN models have been studied with multiple (T1, T1ce, FLAIR, and T2) and single (T1ce) MRI image modalities as input. The effect of segmentation of glioma on the classification accuracy has also been studied. The CNN models have been validated on the publicly available CPM-RadPath2019 dataset. It has been observed that the 3D CNN with segmented glioma along with multiple MRI modalities (T1, T1ce, FLAIR, and T2) has achieved an overall accuracy of 75.45%.

Keywords: Glioma/Brain tumor classification · 3D convolutional neural network · Segmentation · MRI images

1 Introduction

Glial cells support neurons and have various structural and functional roles throughout the nervous system. Some of the main types of glial cells in the brain are astrocytes, oligodendrocytes, microglia, Schwann cells, and ependymocytes [2]. A brain tumor is the uncontrolled growth of brain cells and is the leading cause of death for men and women below the age of 40 and 20 respectively. Glioma is the most common and deadly form of a brain tumor that originates from glial cells. According to the WHO classification of brain tumors of the central nervous system, based on the origin of the glial cell, they are mainly classified into astrocytoma, oligoastrocytoma, oligodendroglioma, and ependymoma.

© Springer Nature Singapore Pte Ltd. 2021
S. K. Singh et al. (Eds.): CVIP 2020, CCIS 1376, pp. 327–337, 2021.
https://doi.org/10.1007/978-981-16-1086-8_29

Glioblastoma is a glioma for which the origin glial cell is not known [12,17]. The proposed model is trained to classify astrocytoma, oligodendroglioma, and glioblastoma.

Generally, tumors are diagnosed using magnetic resonance imaging (MRI). They are further classified based on studying tumorous tissues under a microscope or, by molecular testing. This diagnosis and classification of the tumor are important for treatment planning. The diagnosis task is tedious, expensive, time-consuming, and human error-prone [12]. So, there is a need for an accurate, robust, and automatic classification model which can increase the efficiency of tumor diagnosis and classification.

There exist several models for brain tumor classification in the literature. Cheng et al. [7] explored various data augmentation and partitioning preprocessing models for classification and studied their performance on support vector machine (SVM), the sparse representation-based classifier (SRC), and k-nearest neighbor (KNN) based classifier. They validated their models on Nanfang hospital's dataset which consists of 3064 selective 2D slices of T1ce MRI modality to perform ternary classification, namely, 708 meningiomas, 1426 gliomas, and 930 pituitary tumors. They showed that SVM performed best after performing data augmentation and partitioning. Usually, a patient undergoes MRI with several modes of operation. This motivated us to study whether the usage of a single MRI modality (T1ce) is sufficient to perform classification without additional MRI modalities (T1, T1ce, FLAIR, and T2). In [1,16], the authors used the same dataset and classified a deep convolution neural network (CNN) and capsule networks, respectively. Ge et al. [9] implemented a 2D deep convolutional neural network for glioma classification. They validated their model on BraTS2019 [3,4] dataset, which has two classes namely high and low-grade glioma. Also, it has been validated on the Mayo Clinic dataset [8] which has glioma with and without 1p19q codeletion. The input for their model used 2D slices from the MRI images in the respective datasets. Ge et al. [10] also proposed a non-invasive classification model to classify IDH mutant and IDH wildtype classes from MRI images. They used a pairwise generative adversarial network (GAN) to perform the classification task on 2D MRI slices. MRI images are usually 3D in nature. The usage of 2D image slices over 3D image volumes of MRI images motivated us to studied whether usage of 3D volumes would result in better classification accuracy when compared to the usage of 2D image slices. Table 1 gives an overview of brain tumor classification problems available in the literature.

The important contributions of this paper are (i) A 3D CNN to incorporate volume information of MRI modalities, (ii) Compare the performance of 3D CNN with 2D CNN which takes 2D slices from 3D MRI images, (iii) Performance study between a single MRI modality (T1ce) vs four MRI modalities (T1, T1ce, FLAIR, and T2) and (iv) Performance study of the proposed model with and without tumor (glioma) segmentation.

Table 1. Overview on various types of tumor classification problems in the literature.

Year	Method	Dataset	Target classes
2015	Tumor Classification using Support Vector Machines with Augmentation and Partition [7]	Public [7]	Meningioma, Glioma, Pituitary Tumor
2018	Capsule Networks for Brain Tumor Classification [1]	Public [7]	Meningioma, Glioma, Pituitary Tumor
	Deep 2D Convolutional Neural Network with Data Augumentation for Multi-grade Brain Tumor Classification [16]	Public [7]	Meningioma, Glioma, Pituitary Tumor
		Radiopaedia [16]	Grade I, II, III, IV
	Multistream 2D Convolutional Networks for Glioma Classification [9]	BraTS2017 [5, 13]	High and Low Grade Glioma
		Mayo Clinic [8]	1p19q with and without co-deletion
2019	Pairwise Generative Adversarial Network for Glioma Classification from Brain MRI images [10]	TCGA [3,4]	IDH - Mutation, IDH - Wildtype
–	Proposed Model	CPM- RadPath [11]	Astrocytoma, Oligodendroglioma, Glioblastoma

2 Proposed Model

The proposed model consists of a training and testing phase. Each phase consists of three steps namely, (i) Preprocessing, (ii) Segmentation, and (iii) Classification. The flow diagram of the proposed model is shown in Fig. 1.

2.1 Pre-processing

MRI images suffer from intensity inhomogeneity. This is because of several factors such as varying magnetic field strength among MRI scanners, different acquisition scanners, MRI a bias field distortion, the expertise of the radiologist, and so on [15]. This results in the varying mean and standard deviation of voxel intensity values in and across all slices in a single 3D MRI image. This effect can also be observed in MRI images captured from the same acquisition scanner across different time frames. Several bias correction methods have been discussed in the literature. The simplest of which is zero mean and unit standard normalization, which is also called z-score normalization. To achieve this, the mean (M_o) of each MRI image modality (I_o) has been normalized to zero. Further, to normalize the distribution of intensities across MRI images, voxels in the zero-mean images have been divided by the standard deviation (Sd_o) of

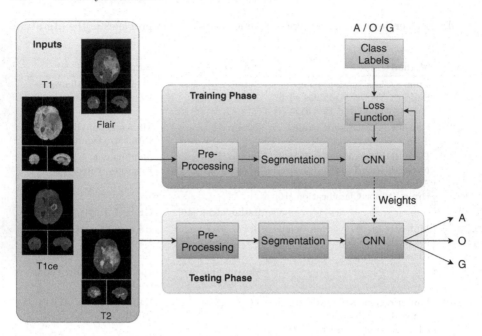

Fig. 1. The flow diagram of the proposed model. Here, A - Astrocytoma, O - oligodendroglioma and G - Glioblastoma.

the original image. The resultant normalized image is used for segmentation and is given by,

$$\text{Normalized Image, } I_n = \frac{I_o - M_o}{Sd_o}$$

2.2   Segmentation

As segmentation is not the main focus of this work, the autoencoder regularization model proposed by Andriy [14] has been used to implement the segmentation of gliomas. The autoencoder regularization is the winner of the brain tumor segmentation (BraTS) challenge 2018. The study has been done using the CPM-RadPath2019 dataset. The segmentation ground truth is not available in the dataset. So, the BraTS2019 dataset [3–5] which has the segmentation ground truth has been used for training the autoencoder regularization model. Due to memory constraints, a few modifications have been done to the hyperparameters of the segmentation model. The original MRI modalities are of size $(240 \times 240 \times 155)$ and the resultant segmented images are of size $(80 \times 96 \times 64)$ which, are further used in classification.

2.3 Convolution Neural Network

Recently, convolution neural network (CNN) and its variants have performed well for various classification problems [1, 9, 16]. In this paper, a 3D convolutional neural network for glioma classification namely, Astrocytoma, Oligodendroglioma, and Glioblastoma has been used to capture information from MRI images. Four MRI modalities namely, T1 - weighted (T1), post-contrast T1-weighted (T1ce), T2 weighted (T2), and T2- Fluid Attenuated Inversion Recovery (T2-FLAIR) modalities have been given as input to the 3D CNN of size $(80 \times 96 \times 64)$, parallelly as shown in Fig. 2.

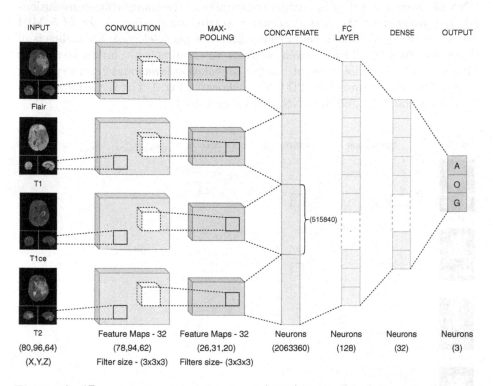

Fig. 2. The 3D convolutional neural network (CNN) architecture where, A - Astrocytoma, O - oligodendroglioma and G - Glioblastoma.

The CNN layer has 32 feature maps obtained by applying a $3 \times 3 \times 3$ filter on each input modality with the stride of 1. The output of the convolution layer is of size $(78 \times 94 \times 62)$. This has been given as input to a max-pooling layer obtained by applying a $3 \times 3 \times 3$ filter on each input modality with the stride of 3. The output consists of 32 feature maps each of size $(26 \times 31 \times 20)$. The max-pooling layer captures the voxel with the highest intensity value in a given filter space. This will reduce the size of the input space and also reduces the computational time. The output of the max-pooling layer has been concatenated into a column vector, each of size 5,15,840 respectively. The total number of concatenated neurons are 20, 63, 360. This has been followed by three fully connected layers, each consisting of 128, 32, and 3 neurons respectively. The last layer gives a probability value ranging from 0 to 1 for each class. The neuron with the highest value has been considered as the tumor class. Rectified linear unit (ReLU) is used in all the layers as an activation function, while softmax is used in the last layer. Additional 3D convolution and pooling layers could not be added due to a lack of sufficient memory.

The 2D CNN consists of 4 sets of convolution-convolution-pooling layers followed by a concatenation layer and 2 fully connected layers. The depth of the CNN has been decided by increasing the number of the convolution-convolution-pooling layers until the overall accuracy started decreasing. A set of 5 MRI slices consisting of the maximum tumor area has been selected. Each slice is of dimension 80 × 96 which is given as input to the first convolution layer. The filter size is 3 × 3 with a stride of 1 in the convolution layers and 2 in the pooling layers. The architecture of the 2D CNN is shown in Fig. 3. The Hyperparameters for the proposed 2D and 3D CNN is given in Table 2.

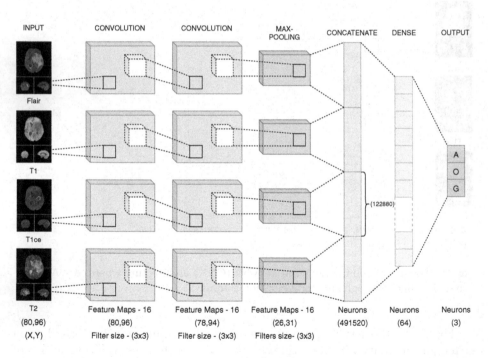

Fig. 3. The 2D convolutional neural network (CNN) architecture where, A - Astrocytoma, O - oligodendroglioma and G - Glioblastoma.

Table 2. Hyperparameters used for training the 3D CNN model

Stage	Hyperparameter	Value
Initialization	Bias	0
	Weights	Xavier uniform
Adam Optimizer	Alpha	0.001
Training	Epochs	20
	Batch size	10

3   Experimental Result

3.1   Dataset

The above proposed model has been validated on Computation Precision Medicine Radiology - Pathology 2019 (CPM-RadPath) dataset [11]. It consists of three classes namely, (i) 54 astrocytoma, IDH-mutant (Grade II or III), (ii) 34 oligodendroglioma, IDH-mutant, 1p/19q co-deleted (Grade II or III) and (iii) 133 glioblastoma and diffuse astrocytic glioma with molecular features of glioblastoma, IDH-wildtype (Grade IV).

The dataset has radiology and pathology images collected from 256 patients. Out of which, MRI images of 221 patients are used for training while the remaining MRI images (35 patients) are used for validation. Each patient has a T1, T1ce, FLAIR, and T2 MRI images. All the images have been obtained from different institutions across the world with different image acquisition protocols and scanners. The images are skull-stripped and have been preprocessed by co-registration to the same anatomical template which is then interpolated to the same resolution of ($1\,mm^3$).

3.2   Results

To conduct experiments with the CPM-RadPath dataset, the MRI images are divided into two different sets namely C1 and C2. C1 consists of T1ce modality, whereas C2 consists of all modalities such as T1, T1ce, FLAIR, and T2. The study has been conducted on these two different modality sets (C1 and C2) with the proposed models (3D and 2D CNN) as discussed in Sect. 2. For 2D CNN, a set of 5 MRI slices (frames) consisting of maximum tumor area has been selected manually, whereas in 3D CNN all the slices (frames) are considered as an input to the proposed models. The experiments have also been conducted by taking MRI images with and without tumor (glioma) segmentation for glioma classification. All the above experiments are executed on the Keras platform on the GPU environment provided by Google Colaboratory. The classification accuracy obtained with these experiments is tabulated in Table 3.

When using T1ce modality alone, the same 3D CNN architecture Fig. 2 and 2D CNN architecture have been used with the same level of depth for a fair

Table 3. Shows the validation accuracy obtained by each model. The accuracy given as C1 is trained only on T1ce MRI modality whereas, C2 is trained on T1, T1ce, FLAIR and T2 MRI modalities.

	2D CNN		3D CNN	
	C1	C2	C1	C2
Without segmentation	57.60%	59.20%	62.20%	65.00%
With segmentation	**62.50%**	**65.44%**	**63.15%**	**75.45%**

comparison. The difference is that the parallel pathways corresponding to the other modalities namely, T1, FLAIR, and T2 have been removed and the concatenation layer is replaced with a 3D, or 2D to 1D flattening layer.

Table 4. Comparison with other existing models in the literature for the same CPM-RadPath Dataset

Model	Accuracy
2D CNN + Seg + All Mod	65.00%
3D CNN + Seg + All Mod	75.45%
3D CNN + Res [18]	69.80%
3D CNN + Res + Seg [18]	77.10%
VGG16 [6]	76.20%

From Table 3, it has been observed that the classification accuracy is better in the 3D CNN model as compared to 2D CNN in both with and without tumor segmentation. This is probably because, in 3D CNN, all the slices are related to its neighboring slice whereas the selective slices considered in 2D CNN do not capture the 3D temporal related information about the tumor. Table 4 gives the comparison between the best performing 2D CNN and 3D CNN models with some state-of-the-art algorithms in the literature on the same CPM-Radpath dataset. Also, it can be observed that within models (2D and 3D CNN), C2 (T1, T1ce, FLAIR and T2) modality set produces better results when compared to C1 modality set (T1ce only), which is 59.20% and 65.00% without segmentation and 65.44% and 75.45% with segmentation, respectively. This shows the importance of segmentation and the usage of additional MRI modalities (T1, T1ce, FLAIR and T2) when classifying the gliomas. Also, it can be noted that the overall classification accuracy has improved with segmented tumor than without segmented tumor and it is highlighted in Table 3. The best overall classification accuracy is 75.45% and is achieved with the help of segmented T1, T1ce, FLAIR and T2 MRI images. The curve obtained between "Number of Epoch" and "Accuracy" during the training of 3D CNN with and without segmentation using C2 modality set is shown in Fig. 4.

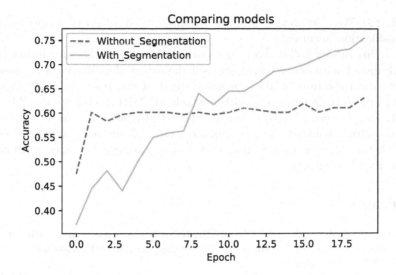

Fig. 4. Number of epoch vs accuracy plot of the proposed 3D CNN model.

4 Conclusions and Future Works

The proposed 2D and 3D CNN model has been tested on the CPM-RadPath dataset (C1 and C2) with and without tumor segmentation. It is observed that for 2D and 3D CNN models C2 (T1, T1ce, FLAIR, and T2) modality set produces better results as compared to C1 modality set (T1ce only) which is 59.20% and 65.00% without segmentation while it is 65.44% and 75.45% with segmentation, respectively. This shows the importance of segmentation and the usage of additional MRI modalities (T1, T1ce, FLAIR, and T2) while classifying gliomas. It is found that the 3D CNN with segmented glioma along with multiple MRI modalities (T1, T1ce, FLAIR, and T2) has achieved an overall accuracy of 75.45% while the 2D CNN model has achieved 65.00% which shows the importance of neighboring slice information and the learning capability of 3D CNN. One probable reason for the lower results is that the dataset size is comparatively small, so the trained CNN models may not generalize well. Another, possible could be the bias-field distortion which may affect the neighborhood property of the MRI images. This loss could be amplified in the pooling layers which could lead to poor results. Capsule nets tend to overcome this problem so it can be explored as future work.

From the obtained results, we conjecture that usage of 3D MRI images with 3D neural networks can achieve better results than 2D slices of MRI images with 2D neural networks. Hence, classification results from [1,7,16] can improve with the incorporation of 3D MRI images with 3D neural networks. Also, the usage of a single MRI modality (T1ce) [7] may not achieve optimal classification results when compared with the usage of additional MRI modalities (T1, T1ce,

FLAIR, T2). We also provide positive evidence on the effect of segmentation on the classification accuracy.

As a part of our future work, we aim to replace the 3D convolution neural network model with other recent state-of-the-art models like capsule networks with the incorporation of 3D capsules instead of the traditional 2D capsules. Also, we aim to train the model with multiple 3D MRI modalities like T1, T1ce, FLAIR, and T2 images. Additionally, the CPM-RadPath dataset consists of detailed histopathological images. So, as a part of our next work, we aim to study whether the incorporation of such histopathological images will improve the classification accuracy.

References

1. Afshar, P., Mohammadi, A., Plataniotis, K.N.: Brain tumor type classification via capsule networks. In: International Conference on Image Processing (ICIP), pp. 3129–3133. IEEE (2018)
2. Allen, N.J., Barres, B.A.: Glia—More than just brain glue. Nature **457**(7230), 675–677 (2009)
3. Bakas, S., et al.: Segmentation labels and radiomic features for the pre-operative scans of the TCGA-GBM collection. The Cancer Imaging Archive (2017)
4. Bakas, S., et al.: Segmentation labels and radiomic features for the pre-operative scans of the TCGA-LGG collection. The Cancer Imaging Archive, vol. 286 (2017)
5. Bakas, S., et al.: Advancing the cancer genome atlas glioma MRI collections with expert segmentation labels and radiomic features. Sci. Data **4**, 170117 (2017)
6. Chan, H.-W., Weng, Y.-T., Huang, T.-Y.: Automatic classification of brain tumor types with the MRI scans and histopathology images. In: Crimi, A., Bakas, S. (eds.) BrainLes 2019. LNCS, vol. 11993, pp. 353–359. Springer, Cham (2020). https://doi.org/10.1007/978-3-030-46643-5_35
7. Cheng, J., et al.: Enhanced performance of brain tumor classification via tumor region augmentation and partition. PLoS ONE **10**(10), e0140381 (2015)
8. Erickson, B., Akkus, Z., Sedlar, J., Kofiatis, P.: Data from LGG-1p19qDeletion. The Cancer Imaging Archive (2017)
9. Ge, C., Gu, I.Y.H., Jakola, A.S., Yang, J.: Deep learning and multi-sensor fusion for glioma classification using multistream 2D convolutional networks. In: Engineering in Medicine and Biology Society (EMBC), pp. 5894–5897. IEEE (2018)
10. Ge, C., Gu, I.Y.H., Jakola, A.S., Yang, J.: Cross-modality augmentation of brain MR images using a novel pairwise generative adversarial network for enhanced glioma classification. In: International Conference on Image Processing (ICIP), pp. 559–563. IEEE (2019)
11. Kurc, T., et al.: Segmentation and classification in digital pathology for glioma research: challenges and deep learning approaches. Front. Neurosci. **14**, 27 (2020)
12. Louis, D.N., et al.: The 2016 world health organization classification of tumors of the central nervous system: a summary. Acta Neuropathol. **131**(6), 803–820 (2016)
13. Menze, B.H., et al.: The multimodal brain tumor image segmentation benchmark (BRATS). IEEE Trans. Med. Imaging **34**(10), 1993–2024 (2014)
14. Myronenko, A.: 3D MRI brain tumor segmentation using autoencoder regularization. In: Crimi, A., Bakas, S., Kuijf, H., Keyvan, F., Reyes, M., van Walsum, T. (eds.) BrainLes 2018. LNCS, vol. 11384, pp. 311–320. Springer, Cham (2019). https://doi.org/10.1007/978-3-030-11726-9_28

15. Nyúl, L.G., Udupa, J.K., Zhang, X.: New variants of a method of MRI scale standardization. IEEE Trans. Med. Imaging **19**(2), 143–150 (2000)
16. Sajjad, M., Khan, S., Muhammad, K., Wu, W., Ullah, A., Baik, S.W.: Multi-grade brain tumor classification using deep CNN with extensive data augmentation. J. Comput. Sci. **30**, 174–182 (2019)
17. Siegel, R.L., Miller, K.D., Jemal, A.: Cancer statistics, 2020. CA Cancer J. Clin. **70**(1), 7–30 (2020)
18. Xue, Y., et al.: Brain tumor classification with tumor segmentations and a dual path residual convolutional neural network from MRI and pathology images. In: Crimi, A., Bakas, S. (eds.) BrainLes 2019. LNCS, vol. 11993, pp. 360–367. Springer, Cham (2020). https://doi.org/10.1007/978-3-030-46643-5_36

Accounting for Demographic Differentials in Forensic Error Rate Assessment of Latent Prints via Covariate-Specific ROC Regression

Emanuela Marasco[1(✉)], Mengling He[2], Larry Tang[2], and Sumanth Sriram[1(✉)]

[1] Center for Secure and Information Systems, George Mason University, Fairfax, USA
emarasco@gmu.edu, ssriram@masonlive.gmu.edu
[2] Department of Statistics, Central Florida University, Orlando, USA
menglinghe@knights.ucf.edu, ltang1@ucf.edu

Abstract. The challenge of understanding how automated tools might introduce bias has gained a lot of interest. If biases are not interpreted and solved, algorithms might reinforce societal discrimination and injustices. It is also not clear how to measure fairness in algorithms. In biometrics disciplines such as automatic facial recognition, examining images pertaining to male subjects has been proven does not yield the same error rates as when examining images from female subjects. Furthermore, recent studies found that automatic fingerprint match scores vary based on an individual's age and gender. Although ROC curve has been essential for assessing classification performance, the presence of covariates can affect the discriminatory capacity. It might be advisable to incorporate these covariates in the ROC curve to exploit the additional information that they provide. More importantly, the ROC regression modeling discussed in the paper can handle both continuous covariates such as age and discrete covariates such as gender and race. The resulting adjusted ROC curve provides error rates which account for demographic information pertaining to each subject. Thus, a better measure of the discriminatory capacity is generated compared to the pooled ROC curve.

1 Introduction

Fairness is the absence of any prejudice toward an individual or a group based on their inherent characteristics. Scientists are currently confronting complex research questions about what it means to make an algorithm fair. Potential sources of unfairness in machine learning outcomes arise from biases in the data as well as from the algorithms [8, 15]. For biometric systems, systematic research is needed to understand, explain and minimize the biases that can compromise the invariance of the features representing the identity of an individual [10, 13]. In biometric disciplines such as facial recognition, examining images from male subjects does not yield the same error rates as examining images from female subjects, and it is unclear whether the pooled error rates lead to the same error rates in subgroups of subjects with different demographics. Recent studies on operational fingerprint databases found that fingerprint decision scores vary with covariates such as subjects' demographic information (e.g., age and gender). Furthermore, several approaches for gender estimation from fingerprints have been explored

S. K. Singh et al. (Eds.): CVIP 2020, CCIS 1376, pp. 338–350, 2021.
https://doi.org/10.1007/978-981-16-1086-8_30

[12–14]. In particular, logistic regression models have been applied for this task and found that image quality features, such as ridge valley uniformity, minimum foreground pixels and minutiae counts, are significant covariates associated with gender [14].

In forensic science and criminal investigations, fingerprints are one of the most important sources of evidence left at a crime scene. It generally consists of latent prints, unintentional reproductions of the ridge configuration made by the transfer of materials such as amino acids to a surface, see Fig. 1. The examination of a latent print involves a comparison of the latent print to a known (or exemplar) print. The FBI's Criminal Justice Information Services (CJIS) Division developed and incrementally integrated a new system the Next Generation Identification (NGI) [1] to improve the effectiveness of latent fingerprint searches. NGI provides the criminal justice community with the world's largest and most efficient electronic repository of biometric and criminal history information. An examiner usually must do a full comparison while a demographic indicator may refine the search and narrow down the huge pool of candidates. Although fingerprints are extremely accurate, the technology is still probabilistic [4]. Furthermore, when interpreting evidence in a forensic casework, results can be affected by factors such as the experience or expertise of the forensic examiner. Forensic examiners with different training and demographics may not result in the same error rates. More experienced examiners may tend to have higher confidence and lower individualization error rates than newly recruited examiners.

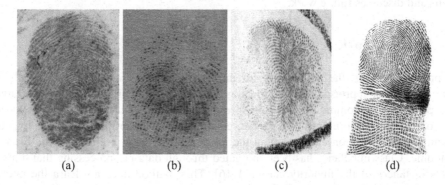

(a)   (b)   (c)   (d)

Fig. 1. Sample images pertaining to the FBI Biometric Collection (BioCoP) Next Generation Identification Phase 1 (2008–2009) collected at West Virginia University: (a), (b) and (c) are latent fingerprint impressions of different quality, (d) is an exemplar used as an identity reference.

The Receiver Operating Characteristic (ROC) curve is a popular way to evaluate and compare the accuracy of classification markers when the outputs are continuous. A matching score is obtained by comparing two copies of the same biometric sample. The accuracy of any given threshold value can be measured by the probability of a true positive (sensitivity) and the probability of a true negative (specificity). The ROC curve is a plot of the sensitivity ($Se(c)$) versus 1-specificity ($1-Sp(c)$) over all possible threshold values (c) of the marker. Although ROC curves are very useful to assess fingerprint matching algorithms, the ROC estimation has rarely accounted for covariates from the known source. Whether a specific demographic covariate is associated with matching status, the pooled ROC curve needs to incorporate the proportion of discrimination attributable to the covariate. As covariates for source demographics vary with different known sources, accounting for them provides a way to utilize the background information which may yield more accurate evidence interpretation as more information is integrated.

The contribution of this paper is two-fold. First, to the best of our knowledge there is no experimental evidence showing the impact of demographic biases in automated matching of latent fingerprints used in forensic casework. We assess the impact of age, gender and ethnicity on a large-scale FBI database. Second, we study ROC regression techniques to incorporate such covariates into the ROC curve. The resulting covariate-specific ROC curves provide the interpretation of error rates specific to the demographics of source subjects, and error rates which account for them. *The importance of the ROC regression is that it allows the estimating of ROC curve for continuous covariates.* These ROC curves are compared with the pooled ROC curves commonly studied in the scientific literature. The significance of the focus on latent fingerprints pertains to generating a decision score by an algorithm automatically. Such a score is related to the subject and not to the examiner. The paper is organized as follows: Sect. 2 reviews research conducted on the analysis of demographics in fingerprint images, Sect. 3 describes the proposed approach, Sect. 4 presents the experimental results, Sect. 5 draws our conclusions and discusses future work.

2   Related Work

In previous studies, the problem of mitigating unfairness of machine learning algorithms has been approached by introducing fairness before, during and after the training process [2]. Common countermeasures to discovered biases consist of exposing machines to more fresh data, feature engineering, algorithm selection, hyper-parameter optimization and retraining the machine to reduce or eliminate the biased outcome. Class imbalance has been mitigated through data pre-processing that duplicates instances of the minority class [11, 16]. This method does not learn the latent structure of the data. Some solutions focused on producing data that are less biased than the original dataset via generative models or data transformation [3]. Artificially generated data may not provide realistic examples for training.

An important study on an operational fingerprint database by Yoon and Jain also found that fingerprint decision scores vary with subjects' demographic covariates [22]. Variations pertaining to fingerprint matching features over time were analyzed. They experimentally confirmed that, for a given individual, genuine match scores decrease over time, impostor scores do not significantly vary, and that the accuracy remains stable. Image quality was considered as being the best covariate to explain the changes in the genuine match scores. The data used in the study was collected from records of the Michigan State Police with TenPrint cards as acquisition type. The focus was on observing fingerprint matching features changes over time and their experiments are carried out to demonstrate this aspect. Their model considers genuine and impostors separately and focuses on regression only. Our investigation starts from finding out that gender, age and ethnicity impact automatic tools designed for identifying finger marks. Our model provides a more general approach applicable to any relevant demographic information available for each individual. We first execute a linear regression based on match scores, next we analyse the covariates age, gender and ethnicity from these scores, and then we model them directly in the ROC curve producing covariates-specific ROC curves.

A dependence of fingerprint features on age group (individuals born at a similar time), gender (physical characteristics that distinguish males from females) and ethnicity (common culture and origin) has been reported [6,9,12]. Methods for demographics estimation from fingerprints have searched for gender clues in the ridge density structure that can be encoded by the local texture [12,18]. Marasco *et al.* [14] recently applied logistic regression models to data acquired from four optical sensors. Gender was the response variable and NFIQ2 score the independent variable as well as four minutiae features including ridge valley uniformity, image contrast, minutiae count, and minimum foreground pixels. For fingerprints from L1 Identify Solutions, subjects with higher ridge valley uniformity ($p < .0001$), higher Image Contrast ($p = .023$) and higher foreground pixels ($p < .0001$) exhibited a higher chance of coming from female subjects. Similar results were observed for Cross Match Guardian while for the i3 digID, subjects with higher ridge valley uniformity ($p = .013$) and higher foreground pixels ($p < .0001$) had a higher chance coming from female subjects. Lower minutiae count ($p < .001$) was also associated with a higher chance of female subjects for all the sensors.

3   The Proposed Approach

Source identification problems aim to determine the link between the known evidence (e.g., suspect) and an unknown evidence (e.g., evidence from the crime scene). The common-source problem relates to whether two evidences are from the same source. Errors in evidence interpretation are mainly related to individualization and exclusion decisions [19]. The term individualization means that, among all the possible suspects, the analyst confidently can state that the defendant is the source of the latent print. Exclusion indicates the determination by an examiner that two friction ridge impressions did not originate from the same source. When the decision scores from examiners or computer algorithms are ordinal or continuous, the accuracy can be assessed with the ROC curve. The associated error rates are related to the decision on the following two propositions for how the evidence has arisen:

H_0: The unknown and known evidence are from different sources;
H_1: The unknown and known evidence are both from a common source.

Since the presentation by forensic scientists in courts has influence over decisions made by the judge and the jury, as consequences of these errors, an innocent person could be wrongly accused and a criminal could be mistakenly claimed innocent [5]. These error rates and the ROC curve are obtained by pooling all the decisions from examiners or computer algorithms with same-source or different-source prints. These measures report the average error rates across a population of examiners for evidence sources. Ideally, the error rates tend to provide guidance for the error rates for interpreting a given evidence source if error rates are consistent for sources with various aspects and for examiners with various background. Further research is necessary to identify the attributes of prints associated with false positive or false negative errors. ROC regression methodology offers the opportunity to investigate how factors such as characteristics of study subjects influence test accuracy [17]. A method for applying generalized ordinal regression models to categorical rating data to estimate and analyze ROC curves is presented. This model permit adjustment of ROC curve parameters for relevant covariates through two regression equations that correspond to location and scale [20]. The proposed model accounts for both sets of covariates such as source subjects' covariate information including their demographics and/or source images' attributes and quality, and potentially examiners' covariate information such as their training background and demographics.

We recall the definition of the ROC curve without covariates. Let T denote the real-valued random variable associated with a continuous biometric measurement (score) for assessing the above two propositions, and let further D be a $\{0, 1\}$-valued status variable, with $D = 1$ indicating a genuine pair (H_1 is true), and $D = 0$ indicating an imposter pair (H_0 is true). Let $F_0(t) = P(T \leq t | D = 0)$ and $F_1(t) = P(T \leq t | D = 1)$, $t \in$, denote the cumulative distribution functions of T conditional on $D = 0$ and $D = 1$, respectively, and let further $S_j(t) = 1 - F_j(t)$, $j \in \{0, 1\}$, and $F_j^{-1}(u) \inf \{t \in: F_j(t) \geq u\}$, $j \in \{0, 1\}$, denote the corresponding survivor and quantile functions, respectively.

Mathematically, without the covariates, the ROC curve can be defined by:

$$\mathrm{ROC}(u) = 1 - F_1(F_0^{-1}(1 - u)), u \in (0, 1) \tag{1}$$

where F_i denotes the cumulative distribution function (CDF) conditioning on the value of label, ROC(u) is the sensitivity at u, and u is the false positive rate (FPR).

3.1 Covariate-Specific ROC Curve

Covariate-specific ROC curves model the covariate effects on the ROC curves and are commonly used in medical diagnostics [23]. Although rarely used in forensics, it provides a useful tool for the interpretation of error rates specific to the demographics of source subjects and covariates of examiners. Using the covariate information, the population of examiners are no longer considered as a homogeneous group with only random variation in their error rates. Instead, the error rates will account for examiners' training background and their demographics. Second, important covariates related to the evidence that impact the corresponding error rates will be identified and explored. Third, the covariate specific model provides an intuitive tool to incorporate background information on the known source. The weight of evidence with covariate information essentially account for more information from a case than the model without. Finally, quantification of the uncertainty will present forensic scientists with better understanding on the trade-off between variation and sample sizes involved in the error rate assessment.

Accounting for a set of covariates $X = (X_1, \ldots, X_p)$ that may represent subject demographics, information on quality of the measurement on the process, etc., it is often of interest to examine how the ROC curve varies conditional on observed covariates $X = \mathbf{x}$. We define the covariate-specific ROC curve by:

$$\text{ROC}_{\mathbf{x}}(u) = 1 - F_{1,\mathbf{x}}(F_{0,\mathbf{x}}^{-1}(1-u)), \quad u \in (0,1) \tag{2}$$

where $F_{1,\mathbf{x}}(t) = P(T \leq t | D = 1, X = \mathbf{x})$, is the distribution of scores in the genuine group conditional on the covariates, and $F_{0,\mathbf{x}}^{-1}(u) = \inf\{t \in: F_{0,\mathbf{x}}(t) \geq u\}$ is the quantile function of the imposter group conditional on the covariates [23].

In order to model the conditional distributions $F_{j,\mathbf{x}}(t)$, and $F_{j,\mathbf{x}}^{-1}(u)$, it is common to use linear regression models on genuine and imposter match scores as follows:

$$T_j = \mu_j(\mathbf{x}) + \sigma_j(\mathbf{x})\epsilon_j, j \in \{0,1\} \tag{3}$$

where, $\mu_j(\mathbf{x}) = E(T | D = j, X = \mathbf{x})$ and $\sigma_j^2(\mathbf{x}) = var(T | D = j, X = \mathbf{x})$ are the conditional mean and the conditional variance of T given observed covariates $X = \mathbf{x}$, respectively. And the error term ϵ_j is independent of $\mathbf{x}$. Then, for a given covariate $\mathbf{x}$, the covariate-specific ROC curve can be expressed as:

$$\text{ROC}_{\mathbf{x}}(u) = 1 - G_1[G_0^{-1}(1-u)\frac{\sigma_0(\mathbf{x})}{\sigma_1(\mathbf{x})} - \frac{\mu_1(\mathbf{x}) - \mu_2(\mathbf{x})}{\sigma_1(\mathbf{x})}] \tag{4}$$

where, for $i \in 0,1$, $G_i(z) = P(z \leq \epsilon_j)$ is the distribution function of the regression error term which is independent of covariates. The derivation for this expression can be found in [17] and [20].

In this paper, the unknown source (i.e., the latent fingerprint evidence) is referred to as Query Q while the one pertaining to the known source as Reference R. Subsequently, the demographic covariate pertaining to them will adopt a similar nomenclature. For instance, the age variable pertaining to the unknown source is referred to as Age_Q while the one pertaining to the known source as Age_R. This scheme is also used for the gender and ethnicity covariates.

The match scores are modeled according to linear regression as follows:

$$\text{Model A} : Score = \beta_0 + \beta_L * label + \beta_{11} * Age_Q + \beta_{12} * Age_R + \beta_{21} * Gender_Q$$
$$+ \beta_{22} * Gender_R + \beta_{L11} * Age_Q * label + \beta_{L21} * Gender_Q * label \tag{5}$$

where the variable $label$ equals '1' if the two images are from the same subjects, while it equals to '0' otherwise. Age_Q and Age_R indicate the age category of the two images being compared, while $Gender_Q$ and $Gender_R$ represent their gender category. Specifically, when the subject is male then gender equals to '1'.

In the regression model, we only consider the interaction term $Age_Q*label$ and $Gender_Q*label$ given that the case $label$ is '1' indicates that the two images pertain to the same identity, subsequently, Age_Q equals Age_R as well as $Gender_Q$ equals $Gender_R$. Whether $label$ corresponds to '0', the two interaction terms are also equal to '0'. Therefore, it is not meaningful to include four interaction terms in the model.

After the model above is estimated, the regression results can be used to compose the covariate-specific ROC curve in Eq. 4, then the accuracy of the examiners or computer algorithms can be estimated. The ROC curve based on Model A can be expressed as follows:

$$\text{ROC}_{\mathbf{x}}(u) = 1 - G_1[G_0^{-1}(1-u)\frac{\sigma_0(\mathbf{x})}{\sigma_1(\mathbf{x})} - \frac{\beta_L + \beta_{L11} * Age_Q + \beta_{L21} * Gender_Q}{\sigma_1(\mathbf{x})}] \quad (6)$$

We build models based only on one covariate. The model with only variable age is reported below:

Model B : $Score = \beta_0 + \beta_L * label + \beta_{11} * Age_Q + \beta_{12} * Age_R + \beta_{L11} * Age_Q * label$
$$(7)$$

The model with only variable gender is defined below:

Model C : $Score = \beta_0 + \beta_L * label + \beta_{21}*Gender_Q + \beta_{22} * Gender_R$
$$+ \beta_{L21} * Gender_Q * label$$
$$(8)$$

The corresponding ROC curves based on Model B and Model C can be expressed as:

$$\text{ROC}_{\mathbf{x}}(u) = 1 - G_1[G_0^{-1}(1-u)\frac{\sigma_0(\mathbf{x})}{\sigma_1(\mathbf{x})} - \frac{\beta_L + \beta_{L11} * Age_Q}{\sigma_1(\mathbf{x})}] \quad (9)$$

$$\text{ROC}_{\mathbf{x}}(u) = 1 - G_1[G_0^{-1}(1-u)\frac{\sigma_0(\mathbf{x})}{\sigma_1(\mathbf{x})} - \frac{\beta_L + \beta_{L21} * Gender_Q}{\sigma_1(\mathbf{x})}] \quad (10)$$

We discuss the impact on the error rate assessment of the demographic ethnicity. The model based only on the ethnicity covariate is expressed as follows [23]:

Model D : $Score = \beta_0 + \beta_L * label + \beta_{31}*Ethnicity_Q + \beta_{32} * Ethnicity_R$
$$+ \beta_{L31} * Ethnicity_Q * label \quad (11)$$

The ROC curve model can be expressed as:

$$\text{ROC}_{\mathbf{x}}(u) = 1 - G_1[G_0^{-1}(1-u)\frac{\sigma_0(\mathbf{x})}{\sigma_1(\mathbf{x})} - \frac{\beta_L + \beta_{L31} * Ethnicity_Q}{\sigma_1(\mathbf{x})}] \quad (12)$$

Finally, all the three demographics analysed in this study are incorporated in the model below:

Model E : $Score = \beta_0 + \beta_L * label + \beta_{11} * Age_Q + \beta_{12} * Age_R + \beta_{21} * Gender_Q$
$$+ \beta_{22} * Gender_R + \beta_{31} * Ethnicity_Q + \beta_{32} * Ethnicity_R + \beta_{L11} * Age_Q * label$$
$$+ \beta_{L21} * Gender_Q * label + \beta_{L31} * Ethnicity_Q * label \quad (13)$$

and the corresponding ROC curve becomes:

$$\text{ROC}_{\mathbf{x}}(u) = 1 - G_1[G_0^{-1}(1-u)\frac{\sigma_0(\mathbf{x})}{\sigma_1(\mathbf{x})} - (\beta_L + \beta_{L11} * Age_Q + \beta_{L21} * Gender_Q$$
$$+ \beta_{L31} * Ethnicity_Q)/\sigma_1(\mathbf{x})] \quad (14)$$

4 Experimental Results

4.1 Dataset

The dataset used in this study is a subset of the FBI Biometric Collection of People (BioCoP) Next Generation Identification Phase 1 (2008–2009) [7]. The data collection involved the acquisition of latent-deposited fingerprints on common materials as well as standard ink and paper methods. The ink and paper data was used as an exemplar set for both electronic capture performed using BioCOP and the latent substrate capture. Each scanned image is saved as a grayscale type image with a resolution of 1000 ppi. These fingerprints pertain to a total of 1504 subjects and were collected at West Virginia University. There was a nearly equal amount of male to female participants with 52% to 48% ratio. Also, among the participants, the age group between 18–29 was highest accounting for 74% percent of people, 8% between 30–39 years old, 7% between 40–49 years old and 11% above 50 years old. Among the ethnicity, Caucasians accounted for 79% of the people, only 6.2% Asian, 3.8% Asian Indian, 3.7% African American, 2.4% African, 2.1% Hispanic. For the experiments of this paper, we considered only right index.

The latent fingerprints collection was carried out by gloving the subject's hands with nitrile gloves that induce sweating required for the development of the first latent fingerprints. Three quality sets were needed, good, bad and ugly, so that three whole or partial impressions for each finger were made on each of the substrates. Three different substrates were used: paper, plastic, and glass/porcelain. The items were separated based on substrate type and processed in one of three ways: *i)* chemical (ninhydrin) processing, *ii)* cyanoacrylate processing, *iii)* lift cards (processed with black fingerprint powder at the collection site). All fingerprints processed with cyanoacrylate were digitally photographed, while all ninhydrin and black powder fingerprints were scanned.

Latent-to-reference Print Comparison. Latent print studies mainly analyze examiners' binary decisions and discuss error rates including false positive rate (FPR) indicating the probability of incorrect individualization on imposter pairs and false negative rates (FNR) corresponding to the probability of incorrect exclusion from the same source [21]. The match scores were obtained using the fully automated, end-to-end latent fingerprint search system recently released publicly by Anil Jain's research group at Michigan State University [4]. This algorithm executes automated region of interest (ROI) cropping, latent image pre-processing, feature extraction, feature comparison, and outputs a candidate list. Two separate minutiae extraction models provide complementary minutiae templates. Furthermore, to compensate for poor quality latents, an additional texture template is also generated. Each reference fingerprint template consists of one minutiae template and one texture template. Two matchers, i.e., minutiae template matcher and texture template matcher are used for comparison between the query latent and reference prints. Three latent minutiae templates are compared to one reference minutiae template, and the latent texture template is compared to the reference texture template. Four comparison scores are fused to generate the final comparison score.

4.2 Results

We consider a confidence score for a pair of images based on whether the images come from the same source. The score obtained by comparing two images of the same source is referred to as genuine score, while that generated by comparing two different sources as an impostor score. The distributions of genuine and impostors match scores are shown in Fig. 2. Error rates such as the FPR and the FNR are calculated for all the possible thresholds. For a specific threshold, the FPR is the percentage of the impostor scores greater than the threshold in the non-genuine pairs, and the FNR is the percentage of genuine scores less than or equal to the threshold in the genuine pairs. As the threshold increase, the FPR decreases while the FNR increases. The accuracy is assessed by the receiver operating characteristic (ROC) curve reported in Eq. 2 which can also be summarized using the area under the ROC curve (AUC) [17]. Figure 3 (a) shows how ethnicity affects the genuine match scores. The class Non-Caucasian appears not to be able to reach the highest values of genuine scores as it happens for the Caucasian population. Figure 3 (b) illustrates the distributions of the genuine match scores with respect to gender. Male subjects exhibit higher values of genuine match scores compared to female subjects. Figure 3 (c) shows the scatter plot of the genuine match scores with respect to age values. We can see that younger individuals exhibit higher values of genuine match scores.

We examine how the ROC curve varies conditioning on observed covariates by reporting the regression results for the three covariate-specific ROC models described in Sect. 3. Figure 4 (a) compares ROC curves of Model A considering both gender and age covariates. Figure 4 (b) compares ROC curves of Model B with only the covariate age. As age increases, the model's identifying ability decreases at a modest trend. Figure 4 (c) compares ROC curves of Model C with only the covariate gender. We can observe that the model performs significantly better for male subjects. The results obtained from the integration of both age and gender covariates are consistent with the corresponding univariate modes. For male subjects, the model performs significantly better in source identification problems, and for younger subjects, the performance seems to be further slightly improved. Nevertheless, pooling the data regardless of the values of the covariate yields a ROC curve that is below the specific ROC curves for each of the populations determined by a given demographic covariate. Similarly, Fig. 5 (c) compares ROC curves conditioned only on the ethnicity covariate. The performance observed for Non-Caucasian subjects is worse than the Caucasian ones. This trend can also be seen in Fig. 5 (a) that compares ROC curves considering both gender and age covariates for the Caucasian population as well as in Fig. 5 (b) that compares them for the Non-Caucasian population. The results shown in Table 1 were used to compute the Sensitivity.

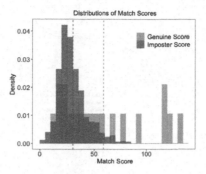

Fig. 2. Distributions of the genuine and impostor match scores

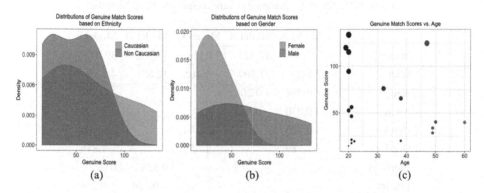

Fig. 3. Distributions of genuine match scores with respect to the demographic covariates considered in this study: (a) density plot of the genuine match scores by ethnicity, (b) density plot of the genuine match scores by gender, and (c) scatter plot of the genuine scores vs. age.

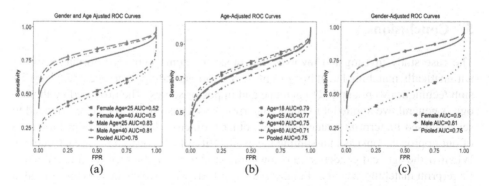

Fig. 4. Comparison between the proposed covariate-specific ROC curves conditioned on demographic covariates: (a) Conditional ROC Curve corresponding to Model A, (b) Conditional ROC Curve corresponding to Model B, and (c) Conditional ROC Curve corresponding to Model C.

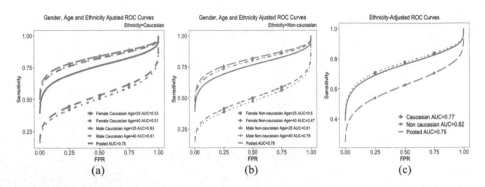

Fig. 5. Comparison between the proposed covariate-specific ROC curves conditioned on the demographic covariates observed in this study, including ethnicity.

Table 1. Result of the designed covariate-specific ROC Models

	Model A	Model B	Model C	Model D	Model E
Intercept	38.893	37.024	31.131	30.002	39.012
label	7.141	37.709	−0.105	12.851	4.125
Age_Q	−0.214	−0.204	-	-	−0.214
Age_R	−0.070	−0.065	-	-	−0.069
$Gender_Q$	−0.496	-	−0.294	-	−0.505
$Gender_R$	−1.789	-	−1.252	-	−1.815
$Ethnicity_Q$	-	-	-	0.323	0.096
$Ethnicity_R$	-	-	-	−0.154	−0.254
Age_Q*label	−0.185	−0.242	-	-	−0.173
$Gender_Q$*label	36.970	-	36.856	-	36.416
$Ethnicity_Q$*label	-	-	-	17.769	3.470

5   Conclusions

The case study investigated involves the impact of demographics information when automatically matching latent fingerprints to the corresponding references. ROC regression techniques were applied to genuine and impostor scores. The proposed methodology is general, we applied it to latent fingerprints as a case study. It can be extended to sensor-based fingerprint matching and to other biometric data. An inherent limitation of our approach consists in assuming the availability of the covariates for each subject. Whether the age and gender are unknown, the model cannot be applied in a real latent fingerprint matching scenario. Future research efforts will investigate the causes related to the demographic differentials analysed in this paper.

Acknowledgments. The authors thank Dr. Anil Jain at the Michigan State University for the latent fingerprints matcher. This work was funded by the NIJ grant #2019-DU-BX-0011.

References

1. Next generation identification (NGI). https://www.fbi.gov/services/cjis/fingerprints-and-other-biometrics/ngi
2. Amini, A., Soleimany, A.P., Schwarting, W., Bhatia, S.N., Rus, D.: Uncovering and mitigating algorithmic bias through learned latent structure. In: AAAI/ACM Conference on AI, Ethics, and Society, pp. 289–295 (2019)
3. Calmon, F., Wei, D., Vinzamuri, B., Ramamurthy, K., Varshney, K.: Optimized preprocessing for discrimination prevention. In: Advances in Neural Information Processing Systems, pp. 3992–4001 (2017)
4. Cao, K., Nguyen, D., Tymoszek, C., Jain, A.: End-to-end latent fingerprint search. arXiv preprint arXiv:1812.10213 (2018)
5. Cole, S.A.: More than zero: accounting for error in latent fingerprint identification. J. Crim. Law Criminol. **95**, 985 (2004)
6. Gnanasivam, P., Muttan, D.S.: Estimation of age through fingerprints using wavelet transform and singular value decomposition. Int. J. Biometr. Bioinform. (IJBB) **6**(2), 58–67 (2012)
7. Hornak, L., et al.: FBI biometric collection of people (BioCoP): next generation identification phase 1 (2008–2009). In: 2008 Biometric Collection Project 08–06-2008 to 12–31-2009 FINAL REPORT (2009)
8. Hutchinson, B., Mitchell, M.: 50 Years of Test (un) fairness: lessons for machine learning. In: Proceedings of the Conference on Fairness, Accountability, and Transparency, pp. 49–58 (2019)
9. Huynh, C., Brunelle, E., Halaìmkovaì, L., Agudelo, J., Halaìmek, J.: Forensic identification of gender from fingerprints. Anal. Chem. **87**(22), 11531–11536 (2015)
10. Jain, A.K., Ross, A., Prabhakar, S.: An introduction to biometric recognition. IEEE Trans. Circuits Syst. Video Technol. **14**(1), 4–20 (2004)
11. Lu, Y., Guo, H., Feldkamp, L.: Robust neural learning from unbalanced data samples. In: International Joint Conference on Neural Networks, vol. 3, pp. 1816–1821 (1998)
12. Marasco, E., Lugini, L., Cukic, B.: Exploiting quality and texture features to estimate age and gender from fingerprints. In: SPIE Defense and Security (2014)
13. Marasco, E.: Biases in fingerprint recognition systems: where are we at? In: IEEE Biometrics: Theory, Applications and Systems - Special Session on Generalizability and Adaptability in Biometrics (BTAS-SS GAPinB)
14. Marasco, E., Cando, S., Tang, L., Tabassi, E.: Cross-sensor evaluation of textural descriptors for gender prediction from fingerprints. In: 2019 IEEE Winter Applications of Computer Vision Workshops (WACVW), pp. 55–62 (2019)
15. Mehrabi, N., Morstatterd, F., Saxena, N., Lerman, K., Galstyan, A.: A survey on bias and fairness in machine learning. arXiv preprint arXiv:1908.09635 (2019)
16. Miller, C.: When algorithms discriminate. New York Times **9**, 2015 (2015)
17. Pepe, M.: An interpretation for the ROC curve and inference using GLM procedures. Biometrics **56**(2), 352–359 (2000)
18. Rattani, A., Chen, C., Ross, A.: Evaluation of texture descriptors for automated gender estimation from fingerprints, pp. 764–777 (2014)
19. Ray, E., Dechant, P.: Sufficiency and standards for exclusion decisions. J. Forensic Ident. **63**(6), 675–697 (2013)
20. Tosteson, A., Begg, C.: A general regression methodology for ROC curve estimation. Med. Decis. Making **8**(3), 204–215 (1988)
21. Ulery, B., Hicklin, R., Buscaglia, J., Roberts, M.: Accuracy and reliability of forensic latent fingerprint decisions. Proc. Natl. Acad. Sci. **108**(19), 7733–7738 (2011)

22. Yoona, S., Jain, A.: Longitudinal study of fingerprint recognition. Proc. Natl. Acad. Sci. **112**(28), 8555–8560 (2015)
23. Zhou, X., McClish, D., Obuchowski, N.: Statistical Methods in Diagnostic Medicine. Wiley, New York (2009)

A Semi-supervised Generative Adversarial Network for Retinal Analysis from Fundus Images

A. Smitha and P. Jidesh[(⊠)]

Department of Mathematical and Computational Sciences,
National Institute of Technology Karnataka, Mangalore, India
jidesh@nitk.edu.in

Abstract. Retinal disorders are the prominent diseases causing visual impairments to a large population across the globe. A prompt diagnosis can address this problem to a large extend. Moreover, AI-enabled devices help ophthalmologists in the timely diagnosis of the disorders and initiate appropriate treatment. In this work, we develop a GAN based semi-supervised model to extract the prominent retinal structures and classify the fundus images as normal or abnormal using data from multiple repositories. The dice coefficient of 0.9 across various datasets affirms the good performance on source independent data. Such a model can be extended to incorporate additional features and be integrated into the ophthalmoscopes for quick retinal examination through telemedicine.

Keywords: Generative Adversarial Networks · Semi-supervised GANs · Fundus imaging · Retinal disorders

1 Introduction

Several preventable disorders manifest themselves in the retina. Ophthalmologists predominantly rely on fundus imaging to diagnose retinal disorders. In general, the specialists locate various structural indicators on the fundus image; some are depicted in Fig. 1 ([3]). Diabetic retinopathy, glaucoma, and retinitis pigmentosa are some of the retinal disorders that can be easily diagnosed using fundus images. Glaucoma is indicated by a widening of the optic cup, leading to an optic cup disc ratio above 0.3. Diabetic retinopathy is a condition swamped with hemorrhages, weak blood vessels, microaneurysms, and exudates around the macula region. Thus optic disc, macula, and blood vessels are keenly observed to locate the clinical findings in the retina. A plethora of works exist that perform segmentation of blood vessels, localization of fovea, or annotate the optic disc and optic cup from fundus images. The majority of the works perform either classification of retinal disorders using transfer learning or perform segmentation using deep learning models. The works which perform both these tasks are directed specifically to a single disorder grading. In this work, our prime focus

© Springer Nature Singapore Pte Ltd. 2021
S. K. Singh et al. (Eds.): CVIP 2020, CCIS 1376, pp. 351–362, 2021.
https://doi.org/10.1007/978-981-16-1086-8_31

is to develop a model that can extract all generic features from fundus images and classify the state as normal or abnormal. The main contributions of our proposed work are listed below.

- Generative Adversarial Networks (GANs) are used to process the fundus images from various datasets and extract the structural indicators, namely the fovea region, optic disc, and blood vessels. Along with this, the model predicts the probability that the retinal image is normal. Thus, the clinicians can use both segmentation and classification results to validate the predictions.
- Using heterogeneous datasets to train the model makes it scalable and adapts to source and camera independent image analysis.
- The proposed model does not use any mask to perform segmentation. Thus the manual grading and input images are sufficient to train the models and achieve acceptable results.

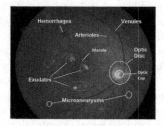

Fig. 1. A fundus image with prominent structural indicators.

2   Literature Review

The automatic detection of retinal disorders has been a prime focus in recent years. Several works exist on segmentation from fundus images (Refer [1,5,15,19,24]). A distance regression approach is implemented by authors in paper [12] for the fovea and optic disc center detection. Combining Resnet blocks to the UNet model is yet another recently introduced deep learning architecture. This model is used for the segmentation of blood vessels from fundus images by authors in [25]. A global and local residual Unet is proposed for blood vessel extraction by the authors in [11]. Semi-supervised Generative Adversarial Networks are explored by authors in [8] to generate synthetic fundus images and classify the images into glaucoma or normal categories using heterogeneous datasets. VGAN [21,22] gives promising results in optic disc segmentation and retinal blood vessel extraction. However, fovea localization is unexplored using VGAN. Additionally, the model is trained using a small number of images from old datasets. In our proposed work, we attempt to improvise this work by incorporating classification and fovea localization. These works reveal that deep learning models can be extensively useful in an automatic diagnosis of retinal disorders.

3   Proposed Work

3.1   Dataset

Publicly available datasets used for training are listed in Table 1. As evident from this Table, the images available are diverse in terms of resolution, format, and field of view. All the images are converted to JPG format since the majority of the datasets are of this format. One approach to finding the optimum size of all images would be to compute the weighted average image resolution (approx. 1220×1400). However, the size of the input images is restricted to 512×512 in our work. This size is selected considering the smallest resolution of images in the dataset. The nearest power of 2 is chosen as the image size to reduce the computational time complexity during the training process. Based on the available ground truth data, the entire collection of datasets are divided into three groups. Images from REFUGE [14] and IDRiD [16–18] grand challenges are considered as first group. These are labeled datasets and have groundtruth data for fovea localization and optic region segmentation. The second group of images involved all other listed datasets, excluding the ODIR-2019 repository. These datasets purely provide the gold standard manual segmentation of retinal blood vessels. Therefore, this combined group of images are used for the blood vessel segmentation task. The final group of images from the ODIR dataset is used for performing classification. Data augmentation on the fly is incorporated in every phase to increase the number of samples. Random rotation by $2°$, horizontal and vertical flip, and brightness variations are the augmentation considered. All images are normalized and mean-centered before feeding it to the model. Training the GANs using such a heterogeneous dataset enables them to learn multiple features from the retina, irrespective of the source.

3.2   Block Diagram of Model

Multiple feature extraction from retinal images, like fovea, optic disc, and blood vessels, and the classification into the abnormal and normal category, is the significant contribution of the proposed work. GAN is the ideal deep learning model to perform multiple tasks. Additionally, traditional retinal image analysis methods necessitate mask to extract the region of interest from fundus images. However, semi-supervised GAN models are trained directly using groundtruth images. The overall block diagram of the proposed work is shown in Fig. 2. The training stage includes two GAN models, namely, VGAN for segmentation and semi-supervised GAN for classification. Segmentation further includes three tasks namely, fovea region localization, optic disc region selection, and blood vessel segmentation which is explained in the following subsections. Notations used throughout this paper are as follows:

- (X_l, Y_l): Image and corresponding label pair.
  where $\forall X_l \in$ REFUGE, IDRiD, ODIR, $Y_l(X_l) = \begin{cases} 0 & \text{if } X_l \text{ is Normal,} \\ 1 & \text{Otherwise.} \end{cases}$
- (X_{ul}, Y_{ul}): Image and corresponding ground truth image pair where,
  $Y_{ul}(X_{ul}) = \begin{cases} \text{Fovea or optic disc region} & \text{if } X_{ul} \in \text{REFUGE, IDRiD,} \\ \text{blood vessel manual} & \text{Otherwise; and } X_{ul} \notin \text{ODIR.} \end{cases}$
- N_z: Random 1D Noise vector.
- G_V: Generator of VGAN that tries to map $X_{ul} \mapsto Y_{ul}$.
- $Z_{ul} = G_V(X_{ul})$: Fake images generated by VGAN with X_{ul} as input.
- D_V: Discriminator of VGAN such that $D_V(f(X_{ul} \parallel Y_{ul}, Z_{ul})) = \begin{cases} 0 & \text{fake,} \\ 1 & \text{real.} \end{cases}$
- G_S: Generator of semi-supervised GAN that maps $N_z \mapsto X_l$.
- $Z_l = G_S(N_z)$: Fake images generated by Semi-supervised GAN with noise vector as input.
- C_S: Supervised discriminator of semi-supervised GAN that maps $X_l \mapsto Y_l$.
- D_S: Unsupervised discriminator of semi-supervised GAN such that
  $D_S(X_{ul}, Z_{ul}) = \begin{cases} 0 & \text{fake,} \\ 1 & \text{real.} \end{cases}$
- $f(\theta) = \frac{e^\theta}{\sum_{j=0,1}(e_j^\theta)}$: Sigmoid activation function for binary classification.
- $\mathbb{E}_{a \sim b}$: Expectation of 'a' having the data distribution 'b'.

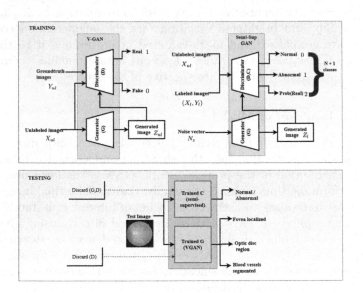

Fig. 2. Block diagram of the combined GAN models.

VGAN consists of a generator and a discriminator. The generator accepts input images and generates fake segmented images. Discriminator tries to distinguish between the ground truth segmentation images and fake images generated by

Table 1. List of datasets combined to train the model.

Sl. No.	Challenge-Year	No. images	Description	Size	Type	Link
1	REFUGE-2018 & 2020 [14]	2000	Grand challenge that involves three tasks: Classification of Glaucoma and normal, segmentation of Optic Disc region and Fovea localization. images are aquired from 2 types of devices	2056 × 2124	jpg	https://refuge.grand-challenge.org/Home/
2	IDRiD-2018 [16–18]	400	Images of diabetic retinopathy grading were acquired from Eye Clinic in Maharashtra, India, using a Kowa VX-10 alpha digital fundus camera with 50-degree field of view. The challenge tasks are similar to REFUGE	1204 × 1500	jpg	https://idrid.grand-challenge.org/
3	Mendeley-2020 [2]	100	Images are taken from Armed Forces Institute of Ophthalmology (AFIO), Rawalpindi, Pakistan. Annotated arteries, veins and combined vessels are provided along with fundus images	1504 × 1000	jpg	https://data.mendeley.com/datasets/3csr652p9v/2
4	IOSTAR-2016 [26]	30	The images in the IOSTAR vessel segmentation dataset are acquired with an EasyScan camera (i-Optics Inc., the Netherlands), which is based on a SLO technique with a 45° Field of View (FOV)	1024 × 1024	jpg, tif	http://www.retinacheck.org/datasets
5	HRF-2013 [6]	45	Fundus images of 15 healthy patients, 15 diabetic retinopathy and 15 glaucomatous patients are aquired using a Canon CR-1 fundus camera with a field of view of 45 degrees. Binary gold standard vessel segmentation images are available for each image	3504 × 2336	jpg	https://www5.cs.fau.de/research/data/fundus-images/
6	CHASE-DB-2012 [9]	28	Retinal image analysis is the major focus of this project. Blood vessel manuals for 14 left and 14 right eye fundus images are provided in this repository	1280 × 960	jpg	https://www.idiap.ch/software/bob/docs/bob/bob.db.chasedb1/master/index.html
7	DRIVE-2004 [23]	40	33 normal and 7 mild diabetic fundus images and corresponding manual segmentation is available as ground truth. Images are aquired from The Netherlands. Masks to obtain the region of interest is also provided	768 × 584	tif	https://drive.grand-challenge.org/https://drive.grand-challenge.org/
8	STARE-2000 [10]	20	Images acquired from Shiley Eye Center at the University of California, for blood vessel segmentation from retinal fundus images. Manually annotated blood vessels are provided	700 × 605	tiff	https://cecas.clemson.edu/~ahoover/stare/
9	ODIR-2019	7000	Images are collected from various hospitals by Peking University in China. At present, this is the largest diverse repository of fundus images available publicly for classification. However, only 1000 images, belonging to glaucoma and normal condition are used in our work	vary	jpg	https://odir2019.grand-challenge.org/background/

the generator. The detailed architecture of the generator and discriminator used for segmentation is shown in Fig. 3. In the proposed model, the number of filters begins from 16, and doubles in every layer. It was observed from multiple trials that the number of filters less than or equal to 256 gives a good performance. The discriminator and generator loss functions of VGAN are given in Eq. 1 and 2, respectively.

$$
\begin{aligned}
L(D_V) = &-\mathbb{E}_{u,v \sim p_{\text{fundus}} (X_{ul}, Y_{ul})}[\log D_V(f(u \parallel v))] \\
&-\mathbb{E}_{u \sim p_{\text{fundus}} (X_{ul})}[\log(1 - D_v(f(u \parallel G_V(u))))],
\end{aligned}
\tag{1}
$$

$$
L(G_V) = \mathbb{E}_{u \sim p_{\text{fundus}} (X_{ul})}[\log(1 - D_v(f(u \parallel G_V(u))))].
\tag{2}
$$

Considering the segmentation problem to be a mapping of input to groundtruth images, it can be associated with binary cross entropy loss as given in Eq. 3.

$$
L_{Seg} = \mathbb{E}_{u,v \sim p_{\text{fundus}} (X_{ul}, Y_{ul})} - v \log(G_V(u)) - (1 - v) \log G_V(u)].
\tag{3}
$$

Thus combining Eqs. 1, 2, and 3, the objective function of VGAN is rendered in Eq. 4, where α is a constant parameter, balancing the objective functions of D_V and G_V.

$$
VGAN = \arg \min_{G_V} \left[\max_{D_V} L(D_V) \right] + \alpha L_{Seg}.
\tag{4}
$$

The trained model is used on the test dataset. In order to perform segmentation, only the generator of VGAN is used and hence the discriminator is discarded. The segmentation output images obtained for a randomly picked fundus image from ODIR dataset is shown in Fig. 5.

3.3   Fovea Localization

Consider a fundus image, I of size (M×N) picked from the REFUGE and IDRiD grand challenge datasets. Let the pixel location of fovea be denoted as $F(p_f, q_f)$. A distance map is created by computing the Euclidean Distance of every pixel to this point, as given in Eq. 5. Since the distance of a point to itself is zero, it is the brightest pixel marked in white color, and as the pixel around this point is equidistant, the color gradually turns gray. The image is then normalized using Eq. 6. Such distance maps (feature maps) are used as ground truth data. One such feature map and its corresponding input fundus image are shown in Fig. 6a and 6b, respectively. Now the GAN is trained to generate such fovea localized images for any given input image. Once the model is trained, for any given test fundus image, it generates a fovea distance map. The centroid of the blob region, B, in the generated feature map, is computed using Eq. 7, and it is marked on the test image.

$$E_D(F, I) = \sqrt{(p_i - p_f)^2 + (q_j - q_f)^2};$$
(5)

$\forall (p_i, q_j) \in I$, where $1 \le i \le M \& 1 \le j \le N$.

$$I(p, q)^N = \left[1 - \frac{I(p, q)}{max(I(p, q))} \right]^{\alpha},$$
(6)

where $0 < \alpha \le 1$.

$$C_{p,q} = \left[\frac{1}{n} \sum_{k=1}^{n} p_k, \frac{1}{m} \sum_{k=1}^{m} q_k \right].$$
(7)

3.4   Optic Disc Segmentation

For the optic disc, the ground truth images are provided by REFUGE and IDRiD grand challenge. Hence, the GAN model is trained using these ground truth images. For a sample given input image (Fig. 6c), it generates the optic disc, as shown in Fig. 6e. The corresponding ground truth is shown in Fig. 6d. As a next step, the centroid of the blob region is computed. This central pixel marks the center of the optic disc. A region of 100×100 is cropped around this center from the original input image as shown in Fig. 6f.

3.5   Vessel Extraction

The groundtruth data from various resources are combined. Similar to optic disc segmentation, here, the GAN hyperparameters are fine-tuned, and the model is trained to extract the vessels from the fundus image. Apart from data augmentation, the histogram equalization (CLAHE) is incorporated during data augmentation. Since only 200 images are available with ground truth data, the model experiences overfitting when tested on the ODIR dataset. Thus it is necessary to incorporate preprocessing in the GAN model. A non-local retinex framework for image enhancement and restoration could be incorporated during image pre-processing to enhance the visibility of thick and thin blood vessels similar as explained by authors in [20]. A sample input image, corresponding ground truth manual segmentation and generated images are shown in Fig. 6g, 6h, and 6i, respectively.

3.6   Classification

The semi-supervised GAN comprises of a generator and discriminator. It works with partially labeled data. Here, the segmentation images mentioned in the above subsection are used as an unlabeled dataset. A subset of images from ODIR, REFUGE, and IDRiD datasets are used as the labeled dataset. Since the labeled category consists of different retinal disorder grading, we combine the disorders and design a binary classifier with Normal and Abnormal retinal classes. Although the ODIR dataset consists of nearly 7000 training images, the images are acquired from various hospitals, and they are not preprocessed. Hence, for semi-supervised GANs, to maintain an equal ratio of unlabeled and labeled data, around 500 images are considered each from normal and abnormal categories. The generator maps the noise vector to fake images that resemble the unlabeled data. The discriminator performs two tasks. The first task is to classify the labeled images into normal or abnormal (C_S). This is termed as a supervised discriminator. The second task is to discriminate between real and fake images (D_S), called as an unsupervised discriminator. This is achieved by extending the N-category classification problem into N+1 level classification. The additional level is obtained by normalizing the outputs of the final layer in the discriminator model. Readers are suggested to refer [7] for more details. The architecture of the proposed semi-supervised GAN is depicted in Fig. 4. The loss functions of C_S, D_S and G_S are given in Eq. 8, 9, and 10 respectively.

$$L(C_S) = -\mathbb{E}_{u,v \sim p_{\text{fundus}} (X_l, Y_l)} \log(P(v|u, v < N + 1), \tag{8}$$

where, N = Number of classes; (in our work N = 2 referring to normal or abnormal categories).

$$L(D_S) = -\mathbb{E}_{u \sim p_{Z_l}} \log(P(v|u)v{=}N{+}1 - \mathbb{E}_{u,v \sim p_{\text{fundus}} (X_{ul}} \log(1 - P(v|u), \tag{9}$$

where, P denotes the conditional probability.

$$L(G_S) = \mathbb{E}_{u,v \sim p_{\text{fundus}} (X_{ul})} \log(1 - P(v|u). \tag{10}$$

The combined objective function of the semi-supervised GAN is given as:

$$Semi - supGAN = \arg\min_{G_S} \left[\max_{C_S, D_S} L(D_S), L(C_S) \right]. \tag{11}$$

Unlike VGAN, once the semi-supervised GAN is trained only the supervised discriminator (C_S) is retained to perform classification on different test datasets and the rest of the model is discarded.

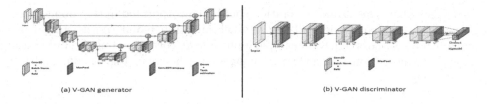

(a) V-GAN generator

(b) V-GAN discriminator

Fig. 3. Architecture of V-GAN.

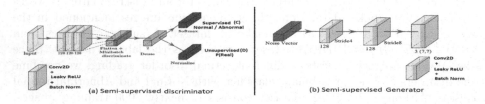

(a) Semi-supervised discriminator

(b) Semi-supervised Generator

Fig. 4. Architecture of Semi-supervised GAN.

4   Implementation and Result Analysis

Implementation is done using Keras and python on Tesla V100 DGX station with 4 GPUs, each having a memory capacity of 32478MiB. The CPU configuration employed is Intel Xeon E5-2698 v4 @2.2 GHz, with 51.2 MB cache size, 20 cores, and has 265 GB RAM. Hyperparameters are tuned using a Random search, and the final values are listed in Table 2. Earlystopping is included, and the learning rate is reduced to half for every 50 epochs. The data is split in the ratio of 60:20:20 for training, validation, and testing, respectively. Training the GAN model for every stage took around 8 to 10 h when the task was scheduled on a single GPU.

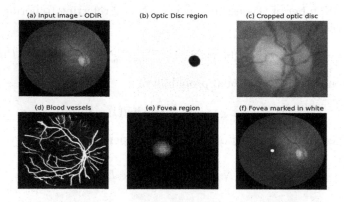

Fig. 5. Output of GAN for a randomly picked image from ODIR dataset.

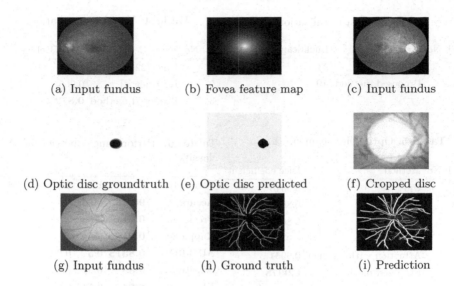

(a) Input fundus   (b) Fovea feature map   (c) Input fundus

(d) Optic disc groundtruth   (e) Optic disc predicted   (f) Cropped disc

(g) Input fundus   (h) Ground truth   (i) Prediction

Fig. 6. Segmentation of DRIVE, REFUGE and IDRiD images.

Table 2. List of hyperparameters.

Hyperparameter	VGAN	Semi-sup GAN
Number of layers	5	3
Optimizer	Adam	Adam
Initial learning Rate	3E-4	0.001
Number of filters	16,32,64,128,256	128,128,128
Kernel initializer	he normal	Glorot uniform
Epochs	200	300
Batch size	32	32
Stride	2	1,4,8
Kernel Size	3×3	4×4

Performance: Tables 3, 5, and 4 summarize the segmentation results obtained using the proposed combined GAN model (marked in bold) and compare it with related works. Since REFUGE and IDRiD grand challenges provide the fovea locations, the Euclidean distance between predicted and actual fovea location is measured. To compare the results, the pretrained weights provided by authors in [12] was used. Dice Coefficient is measured for optic disc and vessel segmentation. The results obtained by research works discussed in the literature review are based on the performance of the model on the homogeneous dataset. However, in our work, we use a heterogeneous repository. For the semi-supervised classification, accuracy, precision, Kappa score, AUC-ROC, sensitivity, and F1-scores are measured and tabulated in Table 6. The test set for proposed method was

Table 3. Fovea Localization.

Sl. No	Method	Euclidean Distance
1	Model in [12]	23
2	Proposed method	**49**

Table 4. Vessel segmentation.

Sl. No	Method	Dice Coefficient
1	Unet [22]	0.834
2	R2 Unet [4]	0.965
3	Proposed method	**0.872**

Table 5. Optic Disc segmentation.

Sl. No	Method	Dice coefficient
1	Unet [19]	0.9340
2	CNN [1]	0.88
3	AttUnet [13]	0.8631
4	R2Unet [4]	0.9723
5	Attention with R2Unet	0.9964
6	Proposed method	**0.9978**

Table 6. Performance metrics of the classifier.

Parameter	P1	P2	Method in [8]
Accuracy	**90.63**	50.32	–
Precision	**0.911**	0.56	–
Kappa Score	**0.717**	0.64	–
AUC-ROC	**0.8315**	0.5	0.9017
Sensitivity	**0.83**	0.51	0.8290
F1 score	**0.94**	0.53	0.8429

grouped into two parts. First parts, consisting of images randomly selected from REFUGE and IDRiD dataset, denoted as 'P1'. The second had fundus images from the ODIR dataset denoted as 'P2'. The classification results obtained for ODIR images are inferior probably because this dataset has a high variance in terms of image quality. The classification results are compared with results obtained in [8], although the classes considered in [8], is glaucoma and normal. Transfer learning using VGG16 and Resnet101 models was attempted; however, the ODIR classification accuracy was less than the semi-supervised classifier approach.

5 Conclusion

This paper designs a model that segments and classifies retinal disorders from fundus imagery using a semi-supervised GAN architecture. The visual and statistical quantification highlights the performance of the model. The future expansion possibilities of the work include extraction of retinal abnormalities such as hemorrhages and exudates around the fovea and measuring the thickness of blood vessels from fundus images. Further, it is necessary to integrate homogeneity correction and image enhancement techniques in the ODIR dataset. This work can be extended further by considering manifestations of other retinal disorders available in the ODIR dataset.

Acknowledgements. Ms. Smitha A. expresses her gratitude to the Ministry of Education, Government of India, for providing financial support (as fellowship) for carrying out the research at National Institute of Technology Karnataka, Surathkal. She is also thankful to the Department of Information Technology, NITK, for providing the access to computational resources. Authors would like to thank the authors of [7,12,22] for making their code available publicly. Authors acknowledge all the grand challenge organizers mentioned in this paper, for making their datasets available on public domain.

References

1. Agrawal, V., Kori, A., Alex, V., Krishnamurthi, G.: Enhanced optic disk and cup segmentation with glaucoma screening from fundus images using position encoded CNNs (2018)
2. Akhbar, S., Akram, M.U., Hassan, T., Yasin, U., Basit, I.: Data on fundus images for vessels segmentation, detection of hypertensive retinopathy, diabetic retinopathy and papilledema. Mendeley Data v2 (2020). https://doi.org/http://dx.doi.org/10.17632/3csr652p9y.2
3. Akil, M., Elloumi, Y., Kachouri, R.: Detection of Retinal abnormalities in Fundus image using CNN Deep learning networks. Hal-02428351 (01 2020)
4. Alom, M.Z., Hasan, M., Yakopcic, C., Taha, T.M., Asari, V.K.: Recurrent residual convolutional neural network based on u-net (r2u-net) for medical image segmentation. CoRR abs/1802.06955 (2018). http://arxiv.org/abs/1802.06955
5. Bajwa, M.N., Malik, M.I., Siddiqui, S.A., et al.: Two-stage framework for optic disc localization and glaucoma classification in retinal fundus images using deep learning. BMC Med. Inform. Decis. Mak. **19**, 136 (2019). https://doi.org/https://doi.org/10.1186/s12911-019-0842-8
6. Budai, A., Bock, R., Maier, A., Hornegger, J., Michelson, G.: Robust vessel segmentation in fundus imagesrobust vessel segmentation in fundus images. Int. J. Biomed. Imaging **2013** (2013)
7. Das, V., Dandapat, S., Bora, P.K.: A data-efficient approach for automated classification of oct images using generative adversarial network. IEEE Sens. Lett. **4**(1), 1–4 (2020). https://doi.org/10.1109/LSENS.2019.2963712
8. Diaz-Pinto, A., Colomer, A., Naranjo, V., Morales, S., Xu, Y., Frangi, A.F.: Retinal image synthesis and semi-supervised learning for glaucoma assessment. IEEE Trans. Med. Imaging **38**(9), 2211–2218 (2019)
9. Fraz, M.M., Remagnino, P., Hoppe, A., Uyyanonvara, B., et al.: An ensemble classification-based approach applied to retinal blood vessel segmentation. IEEE Trans. Biomed. Eng. **59**(9), 2538–2548 (2012). https://doi.org/10.1109/TBME.2012.2205687
10. Hoover, A., Kouznetsova, V., Goldbaum, M.: Locating blood vessels in retinal images by piecewise threshold probing of a matched filter response. IEEE Trans. Med. Imaging **19**(3), 203–210 (2000)
11. Lian, S., Li, L., Lian, G., Xiao, X., Luo, Z., Li, S.: A global and local enhanced residual u-net for accurate retinal vessel segmentation. IEEE/ACM Trans. Comput. Biol. Bioinform. 1 (2019)
12. Meyer, M.I., Galdran, A., Mendonça, A.M., Campilho, A.: A pixel-wise distance regression approach for joint retinal optical disc and fovea detection. In: Frangi, A.F., Schnabel, J.A., Davatzikos, C., Alberola-López, C., Fichtinger, G. (eds.) MICCAI 2018. LNCS, vol. 11071, pp. 39–47. Springer, Cham (2018). https://doi.org/10.1007/978-3-030-00934-2_5

13. Oktay, O., et al.: Attention u-net: Learning where to look for the pancreas. CoRR abs/1804.03999 (2018). http://arxiv.org/abs/1804.03999
14. Orlando, J.I., Huazhu, F., Barbosa Breda, J., et al.: Refuge challenge: a unified framework for evaluating automated methods for glaucoma assessment from fundus photographs. Med. Image Anal. **59**, 101570 (2020). https://doi.org/https://doi.org/10.1016/j.media.2019.101570, http://www.sciencedirect.com/science/article/pii/S1361841519301100
15. Park, K., Kim, J., Lee, J.: Automatic optic nerve head localization and cup-to-disc ratio detection using state-of-the-art deep-learning architectures. Sci. Rep. **10**(5025) (2020). https://doi.org/https://doi.org/10.1038/s41598-020-62022-x
16. Porwal, P., Pachade, S., Kamble, R., Kokare, et al.: Indian diabetic retinopathy image dataset (idrid): a database for diabetic retinopathy screening research. data. IEEE Dataport 3(3), 25 (2018). Available (Open Access): http://www.mdpi.com/2306-5729/3/3/25
17. Porwal, P., Pachade, S., Kokare, M., Girish Deshmukh, J.S., Bae, W., Liu, L., et al.: Idrid: diabetic retinopathy–segmentation and grading challenge. Med. Image Anal. **59**, 101561 (2020). https://doi.org/https://doi.org/10.1016/j.media.2019.101561
18. Prasanna, P., Samiksha, P., Ravi, K., et al.: Indian diabetic retinopathy image dataset (idrid). IEEE Dataport (2018) http://dx.doi.org/10.21227/H25W98
19. Singh, V.K., et al.: Refuge Challenge 2018-task 2: deep optic disc and cup segmentation in fundus images using u-net and multi-scale feature matching networks. CoRR abs/1807.11433 (2018). http://arxiv.org/abs/1807.11433
20. Smitha, A., Jidesh, P., Febin, I.P.: Retinal vessel classification using the non-local retinex method. In: Tiwary, U.S., Chaudhury, S. (eds.) IHCI 2019. LNCS, vol. 11886, pp. 163–174. Springer, Cham (2020). https://doi.org/10.1007/978-3-030-44689-5_15
21. Son, J., Park, S., Jung, K.: Towards accurate segmentation of retinal vessels and the optic disc in fundoscopic images with generative adversarial networks. J. Digit. Imaging **32**, 499–512 (2019). https://doi.org/10.1007/s10278-018-0126-3
22. Son, J., Park, S.J., Jung, K.: Retinal vessel segmentation in fundoscopic images with generative adversarial networks. CoRR abs/1706.09318 (2017). http://arxiv.org/abs/1706.09318
23. Staal, J., Abramoff, M., Niemeijer, M., et al.: Ridge-based vessel segmentation in color images of the retina. IEEE Trans. Med. Imaging **23**(4), 501–509 (2004)
24. Wu, C., Zou, Y., Yang, Z.: U-GAN: generative adversarial networks with u-net for retinal vessel segmentation. In: 2019 14th International Conference on Computer Science & Education (ICCSE), pp. 642–646 (2019)
25. Xiuqin, P., Zhang, Q., Zhang, H., Li, S.: A fundus retinal vessels segmentation scheme based on the improved deep learning u-net model. IEEE Access **7**, 122634–122643 (2019)
26. Zhang, J., Dashtbozorg, B., Bekkers, E., Pluim, J.P.W., Duits, R., ter Haar Romeny, B.M.: Robust retinal vessel segmentation via locally adaptive derivative frames in orientation scores. IEEE Trans. Med. Imaging **35**(12), 2631–2644 (2016)

A Graph Spectral Approach for Restoring Images Corrupted by Shot-Noise

P. Jidesh[1]([✉])[iD] and A. A. Bini[2]

[1] Department of Mathematical and Computational Sciences,
National Institute of Technology Karnataka, Mangalore, India
jidesh@nitk.edu.in
[2] Indian Institute of Information Technology Kottayam, Pala, Kerala, India

Abstract. Image restoration is a fundamental problem in image processing. Usually, images gets deteriorated while storing or transmitting them. Image restoration is an ill-posed inverse problem, wherein one has to restore the original data with a priori information or assumption regarding the degradation model and its characteristics. The literature is too elaborate for various restorations under different assumptions on the degradation-architecture. This paper introduces a strategy based on graph spectral theory to restore images with non-local filters controlled by a loss function. The non-local similarity-based weight function controls the restoration process resulting in the preservation of local image features considerably well. The parameter controlled adaptive fidelity term helps to re-orient the diffusion to handle data correlated shot-noise following a Poisson distribution, which is pretty common in many medical and telescopic imaging applications. Experimental results are conforming to the fact that the proposed model performs well in restoring images of the different intensity distributions.

Keywords: Spectral Graph theory · Graph Laplacian · Image restoration · Regularization · Variational formulation

1 Introduction

Spectral graph theory mainly deals with the study of the properties of a graph with reference to the Eigenvalues and Eigenvectors of the matrix (such as adjacency matrix or graph Laplacian) associated with the graph [1–3]. Borrowing the definitions from graph theory we recall a graph G as a set of vertices V and a set of edges E denoted as $G(V, E)$. For most of the practical problems in signal and image processing, one has to deal with undirected weighted graphs. The weight may be either associated with vertices or edges or both. The adjacency matrix A associated with a graph is a real and symmetric matrix. In the usual sense, an adjacency matrix A is:

$$A(i, j) = \begin{cases} 1 \text{ if there is an edge between the vertices i and j} \\ 0 \text{ otherwise.} \end{cases} \quad (1)$$

© Springer Nature Singapore Pte Ltd. 2021
S. K. Singh et al. (Eds.): CVIP 2020, CCIS 1376, pp. 363–373, 2021.
https://doi.org/10.1007/978-981-16-1086-8_32

For a given graph $G(V, E)$ with total number of vertices $|V| = n$, the degree matrix D (of size $n \times n$) is a diagonal matrix defined as

$$D(i, j) = \begin{cases} deg(i) & \text{if i}=\text{j} \\ 0 & \text{otherwise,} \end{cases} \tag{2}$$

where $deg(i)$ denotes the number of times an edge terminates at the vertex i. Now we can define a graph Laplacian L as a symmetric matrix $(n \times n)$

$$L(i, j) = \begin{cases} deg(v_i) & \text{if i}=\text{j} \\ -A(i, j) & \text{otherwise.} \end{cases} \tag{3}$$

Here L is an unnormalized matrix. Some applications demand L be normalized, see [2,3] for the details. The symmetric normalized Laplacian is defined as

$$L^{sym} = D^{-1/2}LD^{-1/2} = I - D^{-1/2}AD^{-1/2}. \tag{4}$$

Since the Laplacian matrix is symmetric and positive semidefinite the Eigenvalues are non-negative (≥ 0). The multiplicity of Eigenvalue "zero" represents the number of connected components in the graph. Since zero being in the spectrum of the Laplacian operator a formal inversion process is ill-posed. Further, the row and columns sums of the matrix are always zero, which indicates the average energy is preserved while it is used as an operator. Since the row-sum or column-sum results in a null vector, a vector with all 1's is the Eigenvector corresponding to the zero Eigenvalue. This shows an analogy with the Fourier Transform therefore sometimes referred as Graph Fourier Transform [2].

2   Representation of an Image

The image can be considered as a weighted graph G with weights on vertices and edges. The vertex weight corresponds to the intensity value of the pixel, and the edge weight $w(u, v)$ indicates the connectedness of the pixels (u and v), and this plays a vital role while designing a heat kernel to perform a graph based diffusion [1,4–6]. One common function used to represent the edge weight of an image is:

$$w(u, v) = exp^{-\frac{(d(u,v))+\|(I_\sigma(u)-I_\sigma(v))\|_2^2)}{2\sigma_1^2}}, \tag{5}$$

where u and v denote the pixel locations and $d(u, v) = \|u - v\|_2^2$, is the Euclidean distance between u and v. I_σ in the above expression denotes the Gaussian convolved version of the image I, (since we do not possess the original image we initialize I with I_0 in the initial step and it gets updated in subsequent steps) where σ is spread of the Gaussian kernel. The smoothed version of the distance measure is more robust in case of noisy data. The weight matrix defined above incorporates both spatiometric and radiometric information as in the case of a Bilateral filter [7] and subsequently supports the non-local behaviour of the filtering process [8]. The adjacency matrix defined in (1) can be rewritten using the above mentioned expression as $A(i,j) = w(i,j)$. Subsequently the graph Laplacian matrix also changes its definition. An analogy of the graph Laplacian under the variational formulation has been considered in the rest of the paper to define the relation between the image pixels.

Consider a graph $G(v, E, w)$ where v is a set of vertices and $E \subset v \times v$ is a relation between vertices, represented by edges with weights w, where w is a function returning positive real values i.e. $w \colon v \times v \to \mathcal{R}^+$. An image can be viewed as a set of vertices representing the pixel values connected by some pre-defined relation or the edges. The edge weight denotes the magnitude of the relation. In many image processing problems, the relation is represented as the similarity among the pixels.

3   The Graph Spectral Approach for Short Noise

Under the above assumptions, we may formulate an image restoration problem using the variational formulation borrowing the concepts from graph spectral theory as introduced in [5]:

$$\min_I \{E_w^p(I, I_0, \lambda) = \frac{1}{p}\sum_{v \in V}|\nabla_w I_{(v)}|^p + \frac{\lambda}{2}\|I_{(v)} - I_{0(v)}\|_2^2\}, \tag{6}$$

where I denotes the image function and I_0 is the function representing the observed image. The symbol p denotes the order of the function which regulates the smoothing of data. A higher value of p denotes a higher magnitude of smoothing. Here λ is a scalar regularization parameter and $\nabla_w I$ is the local variation of the image weighted by the function w given as below:

$$\nabla_w I \stackrel{def}{=} \sqrt{w(u,v)}\left(I_{(u)} - I_{(v)}\right), \tag{7}$$

$$|\nabla_w I| \approx \left[\sum_{u \sim v} w(u,v)\left(I_{(u)} - I_{(v)}\right)^2\right]^{1/2}. \tag{8}$$

In (8), $u \sim v$ denotes there exists an edge between u and v nodes in the image and $w(u,v)$ is given in (5). The functional given in (6) can be re-formulated to an optimization problem under a non-local regularization framework given as below:

$$\min_I E_w^p(I, I_0, \lambda) = \min_{I,\lambda} \{R_w^p(I) + \frac{\lambda}{2}\sum_{u \sim v}(I - I_0)^2\}, \tag{9}$$

where $R_w^p(I)$ denotes the regularization prior (as given in (10)) and the second term denotes the data fidelity aspects of the model. Therefore, we have the following

$$R_w^p(I) = \frac{1}{p}\sum_{u \in V}|\nabla_w I(u)|^p$$

$$\approx \frac{1}{p}\left(\sum_{u \in V}\left(\sum_{u \sim v} w(u,v)(I_{(u)} - I_{(v)})\right)^2\right)^{p/2}. \tag{10}$$

Now, consider the images corrupted by shot-noise following a Poisson process. So, the data fidelity term in the above functional gets modified as $I - I_0 log(I)$. The functional is derived using the Bayesian MAP estimator as done in [18]. The modified data fidelity under the regularization framework takes the form:

$$\min_{I, \lambda} R_w^p(I) + \frac{\lambda}{2} \sum_{u \sim v} (I - I_0 log(I)). \tag{11}$$

Further, assuming a spatially adaptive scalar regularization parameter $\lambda(x)$, where $\lambda(x)$ is evaluated as :

$$\lambda(x) = e^{-\left(\frac{G_{(*)} \ \rho(I(x))}{K}\right)}, \tag{12}$$

where $\rho(I(x)) = \frac{(I - I_0)}{I}$ is a function which denotes the residual image or the data fidelity term of the functional which is related to the noise distribution and is a positive scalar value, and G_* denotes a convolution operation with a Gaussian Kernel with spread K. With the above modification to λ the final objective functional takes the form

$$\min_{I, \lambda} R_w^p(I) + \frac{\lambda(x)}{2} \sum_{u \sim v} (I - I_0 log(I)). \tag{13}$$

The parameter $\lambda(x)$ is a matrix whose value changes with the noise characteristics of the image in each iteration, and there exists one value for each pixel in the image. If the residue is less or close to zero, the data fidelity term has less contribution to the overall process. In other words, the regularization tends to be dominant. On the other hand, if the residual value is high, then the data fidelity dominates the diffusion process leading to a low magnitude diffusion.

The shot-noise being data correlated its distribution follows the model such as Poisson. In other words, the shot-noise common in areal and telescopic images are modeled as a Poisson process. The image thus formed under a Poisson process heavily depends on the number of photons that hit on the imaging surface [9]. Among the various restoration models introduced to handle shot-noise present in images, variational ([9–11]) and PDE [12] are more prominent. Apart from these, a set of data-driven approaches are also introduced lately in the literature (see [13] and the references therein for the details). Moreover, non-local framework motivated by [14], has been incorporated in variational methods to design non-local variational models such as the one in [15]. Combining principal component analysis and non-local scheme was found to improve the restoration process in [16]. A variance stabilization transform which stabilizes the transform and makes the noise data independent has been demonstrated in [17]. More recently the authors in their work [18] have proposed a p Laplacian model for the restoration of images from Poisson corruption using a scalar regularization parameter. In all these models the regularization parameter remains constant throughout the iteration process leading to an improper smoothing in the course of iteration. This issue has been addressed considerably well in the proposed model using a controlled regularization parameter leading to an effective restoration of image details. Considering a Poisson distribution of the noise in the image formation process, the model reformulation amounts to

$$\min_I \{E_w^p(I, I_0, \lambda) = R_w^p(I) + \frac{\lambda(x)}{2} \sum_{u \sim v} \left(I - I_0 log(I)\right). \tag{14}$$

The minimization of the above functional is done using the EL method and yields:

$$\frac{\partial E_w^p(.)}{\partial I} = \frac{\partial R_w^p(I)}{\partial I} + \frac{\lambda(x)}{2}\left(1 - \frac{I_0}{I}\right)$$
$$= \frac{\partial R_w^p(I)}{\partial I} + \frac{\lambda(x)}{2}\left(\frac{I - I_0}{I}\right). \tag{15}$$

Here, $\frac{\partial R_w^p(I)}{\partial I} = \sum_{u \sim v} w(u, v) \ (I_{(u)} - I_{(v)}) \ (|\nabla_w I(u)|^{p-2} + |\nabla_w I(v)|^{p-2}).$

Therefore, the functional now takes the form:

$$0 = \sum_{u \sim v} w(u, v) \ (I(u) - I(v)) \ (|\nabla_w I(u)|^{p-2} + |\nabla_w I(v)|^{p-2})$$
$$+ \frac{\lambda(x)}{2} \sum_{u \sim v} \frac{I(u) - I_0(u)}{I(u)}, \tag{16}$$

so,

$$0 = \sum_{u \sim w} w(u, v)I(u) \left(|\nabla_w I(u)|^{p-2} + |\nabla_w I(v)|^{p-2}\right)$$
$$- w(u, v)I(v) \left(|\nabla_w I(u)|^{p-2} + |\nabla_w I(v)|^{p-2}\right)$$
$$+ \frac{\lambda(x)I(u) - \lambda(x)I_0(u)}{I(u)}. \tag{17}$$

Now let $\gamma_w^{I^t}(u, v) = \sum_{u \sim v} w(u, v) \ (|\nabla_w I(u)|^{p-2} + |\nabla_w I(v)|^{p-2})$, then the above expression transforms to

$$0 = \sum_{u \sim w} \gamma_w^{I^t}(u, v)I(u) - \gamma_w^{I^t}(u, v)I(v) + \frac{\lambda(x) \ (I(u) - I_0(u))}{I(u)}, \tag{18}$$

i.e.

$$\sum_{u \sim w} \gamma_w^{I^t}(u, v)I(v) = \sum_{u \sim w} I(u) \left(\gamma_w^{I^t}(u, v) + \lambda(x)/I(u)\right)$$
$$- \lambda(x)\frac{I_0(u)}{I(u)}. \tag{19}$$

The gradient descent solution for the above expression amounts to

$$I(u) = \frac{\lambda(x)\frac{I_0}{I(u)} + \sum_{u \sim w} \gamma_w^{I^t}(u, v)I(v)}{\lambda(x)/I(u) + \sum_{u \sim w} \gamma_w^{I^t}(u, v)}. \tag{20}$$

Here $\lambda(x)$ (evaluated using (12)) is a regularization function that controls the magnitude smoothing at each pixel location based on the noise variance of the data in each iteration. As already pointed out, the value of $\lambda(x)$ changes in each iteration with reference to the residual function $\rho(.)$ (in (12)). Since the function λ is attached to the data fidelity term in the functional defined here, the high value of the function indicates domination of the data fidelity over the regularization aspects of the functional. The low value of the residual function (due to high intensity homogeneity in the region) results in a high lambda value.

4   Experimental Results

Different test images corrupted by shot-noise intervention are employed for testing and comparing the performance of various methods described in this paper along with the one proposed here. Four state of the art Poisson restoration methods are compared and demonstrated in this paper. The models used for comparison are the Fast TV model in [10], Variance Stabilization Transform (VST) in [17], PDE model for Poisson noise removal [12], non-local PCA model for Poisson noise [16], non-local TV regularization model for Poisson noise [15], p Laplacian based Poisson model in [18] along with the proposed model. These models are implemented and tested using Matlab running on Intel® Core™ i7-3770 CPU @ 3.40 GHz × 8 processor with 8 GB RAM (Os: Ubuntu 16.04 LTS, 64 bit). Typically the parameter p can take any positive real value between [1–2], the outputs are shown only for the value 1.5. As evident from the literature, if the value is close to 1 the edges are duly preserved, however, piecewise linear approximation makes the outputs apparently artificial, on the other hand, if the value is close to 2, then the results are over-smoothed. Therefore, the parameter value is set to 1.5 (empirically) in order to set a trade off between over-smoothing and piecewise patch formation.

The original test images are observed to be corrupted by shot-noise distortions following a Poisson PDF (as observed from the distribution of the affected pixels in homogeneous regions, where the oscillations are predominantly due to the noise features). Apart from the real noisy test images an artificial synthetic image (manually corrupted with Poisson noise) is also used for testing and verification purpose. The statistical measures used in this paper are performed on this synthetic data as the ground truth is readily available for this image unlike the original noisy images (it may be noted that the ground truth is needed to evaluate the statistical measures discussed hereafter). Statistical quantification of the model is performed using Peak Signal to Noise Ratio (PSNR) and Structural Similarity Measure (SSIM) [19]. The visual representation of the performances

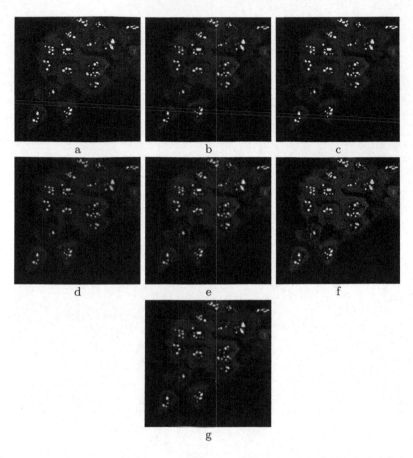

Fig. 1. (a) Confocal image restored using the model in (b) [10], (c) [17] (d) [12] (e) [15], (f) [18] and (g) the proposed one with $p = 1.5$.

of various methods is shown in Figs. 1, 2 and 3 for confocal, CT and synthetic images, respectively. The last sub-figures of each figure represent the results of the proposed model for different test data. As evident from these figures, the proposed model outperforms other counterparts with regard to image restoration and denoising. The fine details are well preserved. The method was tested for low and high peak Poisson noise distributions, and the restored results are found intact for the proposed strategy (Fig. 4).

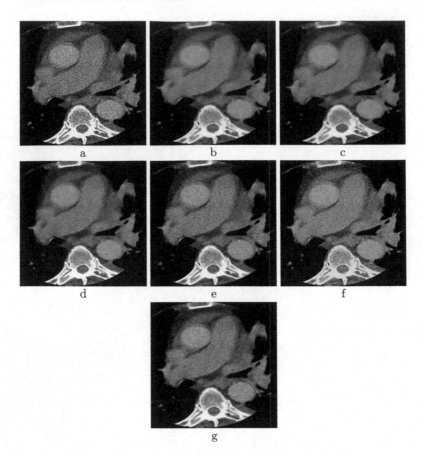

Fig. 2. (a) CT image of a human chest, restored using the model in (b) [10], (c) [17] (d) [12] (e) [15], (f) [18] and (g) the proposed one with $p = 1.5$.

The Statistical results are provided in Table 1 for the measures PSNR and SSIM. A higher PSNR denotes better noise preservation. The SSIM denotes the structure and contrast preservation capability of the model. The ideal performance under this measure is in the range [0–1]. The proposed model is found to perform pretty well in terms of the statistical measures and the visual representations. As inferred from the table, the PSNR value increases with increase in the value of the parameter p, however the SSIM values decreases with increase in the value of p. Therefore, there should be a trade-off between the noise removal and structure preservation. Hence the value of p is chosen as 1.5 for our experiments so that the results are more promising in terms of visual representation and statistical analysis.

Fig. 3. (a) Original Synthetic image (b) The image corrupted with Poisson noise, peak = 30, restored using the model in (c) [10], (d) [17] (e) [12] (f) [15], (g) [18] and (h) the proposed one with $p = 1.5$.

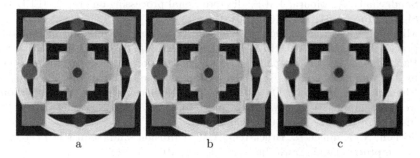

Fig. 4. Restored images using the proposed method with different values of the parameter p (a) $p = 1$ (b) $p = 1.5$ (c) $p = 2$.

Table 1. Quality metrics for Poisson noise with peak value 30 for different p values, applied on the synthetic image.

The value of p name	Metric	Noisy	Model in [10]	Model in [17]	Model in [12]	Model in [15]	Model in [18]	Proposed
1	PSNR	19.08	19.63	20.05	21.03	20.04	20.25	22.45
	SSIM	0.19	0.29	0.43	0.22	0.42	0.51	0.55
1.5	PSNR	19.78	20.16	21.26	21.83	20.84	21.05	23.15
	SSIM	0.16	0.22	0.33	0.18	0.38	0.46	0.51
2	PSNR	20.08	20.63	21.05	21.93	21.04	21.25	23.45
	SSIM	0.059	0.19	0.33	0.12	0.32	0.41	0.43

5   Conclusion

A non-local adaptive restoration method based on spectral graph approach with $p - norm$ is proposed in this paper for images corrupted by shot-noise. The selection of value of the parameter p affects the restoration process. As this value increases, the smoothness of the output also increases. The selection of an optimal p value is pretty challenging, as it depends on the application under consideration. The results shown in favour of the proposed model among the comparative results endorse the efficiency of the model in terms of the demonstrated qualitative and quantitative results.

Acknowledgements. The author Dr. Jidesh would like to thank Department of Atomic Energy, Govt. of India for providing financial support under Grant No: 02011/17/2020NBHM(RP)/R&DII/8073 for carrying out the research work.

References

1. Zhang, F., Edwin, R.: Hancock Graph spectral image smoothing using, the heat kernel. Pattern Recogn. **41**, 3328–3342 (2008)
2. Sandryhaila, A., Moura, J.M.F.: discrete signal processing on graphs. IEEE Trans. Signal Process. **61**, 1644–1656 (2013)
3. Milanfar, P.: A Tour of modern image filtering: new insights and methods, both practical and theoretical. IEEE Signal Process. Mag. **30**, 106–128 (2013)
4. Pang, J., Cheung, G.: Graph Laplacian regularization for image denoising: analysis in the continuous domain. IEEE Trans. Image Process. **26**, 1770–1785 (2017)
5. Elmoataz, A., Lezoray, O., Bougleux, S.: Nonlocal discrete regularization on weighted graphs: a framework for image and manifold processing. IEEE Trans. Image Process. **17**, 1047–1060 (2008)
6. Sochen, N., Kimmel, R., Bruckstein, A.M.: Diffusions and confusions in signal and image processing. J. Math. Imaging Vis. **14**, 195–209 (2001)
7. Barash, D.: A fundamental relationship between bilateral filtering, adaptive smoothing, and the nonlinear diffusion equation. IEEE Trans. Pattern Anal. Mach. Intell. **24**, 844–847 (2002)
8. Kindermann, S., Osher, S., Jones, P.W.: Deblurring and denoising of images by nonlocal functionals. Technical Report, UCLA (2005)

9. Le, T., Chartrand, R., Asaki, T.J.: A variational approach to reconstructing images corrupted by Poisson noise. J. Math. Imaging Vision **27**, 257–263 (2007)
10. Wang, W., He, C.: A fast and effective algorithm for a Poisson denoising model with total variation. IEEE Sig. Process. Lett. **24**, 269–273 (2017)
11. Lanza, A., Morigi, S., Sgallari, F., Wen, Y.-W.: Image restoration with Poisson-Gaussian mixed noise. Comput. Meth. Biomech. Biomed. Eng. Imaging Vis. **2**, 12–24 (2014)
12. Srivastava, R., Srivastava, S.: Restoration of Poisson noise corrupted digital images with nonlinear PDE based filters along with the choice of regularization parameter estimation. Pattern Recogn. Lett. **34**, 1175–1185 (2013)
13. Anwar, S.: Data-Driven Image Restoration, Ph.D. thesis submitted to The Australian National University (2018)
14. Buades, A., Coll, B., Morel, J.-M.: A non-local algorithm for image denoising. In: 2005 IEEE Computer Society Conference on Computer Vision and Pattern Recognition (CVPR 2005), vol. 2, pp. 60–65. IEEE (2005)
15. Zhang, Z.R., Huang, L.L., Fei, X., Wei, Z.: Image Poisson denoising model and algorithm based on nonlocal TV regularization. J. Syst. Simul. **26**, 2010–2015 (2014)
16. Salmon, J., Harmany, Z., Deledalle, C.-A., Willett, R.: Poisson noise reduction with non-local PCA. J. Math. Imaging Vision **48**, 279–294 (2014)
17. Makitalo, M., Foi, A.: Optimal inversion of the generalized Anscombe transformation for Poisson-Gaussian noise. IEEE Trans. Image Process. **22**, 91–103 (2013)
18. Holla, S., Jidesh, P.: Non-local total variation regularization approach for image restoration under a Poisson degradation. J. Modern Optics **65**, 2265–2276 (2018)
19. Wang, Z., Bovik, C.A., Sheikh, R.H., Simoncelli, E.P.: Image quality assessment: from error visibility to structural similarity. IEEE Trans. Image Process. **13**, 600–612 (2004)

ECASR: Efficient Channel Attention Based Super-Resolution

Sameeran Borah and Nilkanta Sahu(✉) (iD)

IIIT Guwahati, Guwahati, India
nilkanta@iiitg.ac.in
http://iiitg.ac.in/faculty/nilkanta/

Abstract. Despite recent advancements in single image super-resolution (SISR) methodologies, reconstruction of photo-realistic high resolution (HR) image from its single low resolution (LR) counterpart remains a challenging task in the fraternity of computer vision. In this work, we approach the problem of SR using a modified GAN with specialized Efficient Channel Attention (ECA) mechanism. CA mechanism prioritizes convolution channels according to there importance. The ECA mechanism, an extension of CA, improves model performance and decreases the complexity of learning. To capture the image texture accurately low-level features are used for reconstruction along with high-level features. A dual discriminator is used with GAN to achieve high perceptual quality. The experimental result shows that the proposed method produces better results for most of the dataset, in terms of Peak Signal-to-Noise Ratio (PSNR), Structural Similarity Index Measure (SSIM), and mean-opinion-score (MOS) over the state-of-the-art methods on benchmark data-sets when trained with same parameters.

1 Introduction

Image Super-Resolution (SR), is the process of reconstructing an HR image from one or more LR image. SR is inherently a challenging ill-posed problem since there exist multiple HR image that corresponds to a single LR image. SR has its application in various image processing and computer vision tasks ranging from surveillance, medical imaging, object detection, satellite imaging to different image restoration and recognition tasks.

The SR algorithms can be broadly classified into two categories, one based on the number of input LR images the other based on the principle used to construct the HR image. Further, based on the principles used in the construction of SR image, the SR algorithms can also be categorized into three categories [24]: interpolation-based, model-based, and deep learning-based algorithms. Interpolation-based algorithms like bi-linear or bi-cubic interpolation use local information in an LR image to compute pixel values in the corresponding SR image, which are characterized by high computational efficiency. Prior knowledge is used in model-based algorithms such as the Maximum a Posteriori (MAP) to constrain the solution space whose performance is improved compared to the interpolation-based approach.

S. K. Singh et al. (Eds.): CVIP 2020, CCIS 1376, pp. 374–386, 2021.
https://doi.org/10.1007/978-981-16-1086-8_33

Supervised machine learning approaches learn the mapping function that maps LR images to it's corresponding HR images from a large number of examples. The mapping function learned during the training phase is inverse of the down-sample function that is used to transform the HR image to its corresponding LR image, which can be known or unknown. With the help of known downgrade functions like bi-cubic, bi-linear down-sampling, the LR-HR pair can automatically be generated. This allows the creation of large training data-sets from a vast amount of freely available HR images which can be used for self-supervised learning (Figs. 1 and 2).

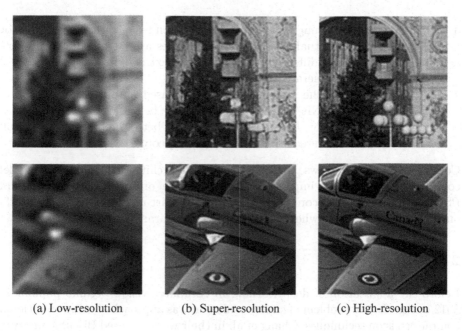

(a) Low-resolution   (b) Super-resolution   (c) High-resolution

Fig. 1. Reconstructed Super-resolution images comparison with Original High-resolution and Low-resolution images.

This work proposes a GAN based SISR model that produces HR image with realistic texture details. Our contributions can be summarized as follows.

1. The generator architecture consists of multiple ECA blocks which emphasize on certain channels, along with it a 3-layer CNN network is added to the generator that extracts sufficient low-level features. The ECA block avoids dimensionality reduction step which destroys the direct relation with a channel and it's weight, instead, we use 1D convolution to determine the cross channel interaction. The generator achieves state-of-the-art PSNRs when it is trained alone without discriminators.

2. The proposed SISR framework utilizes a dual discriminator network inspired by SRFeat [12] architecture, one that works on image domain that uses Mean Square Error (MSE) loss, the other that works on feature domain that uses perceptual feature loss.

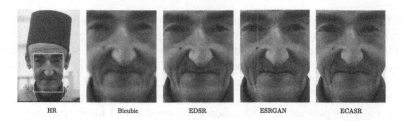

Fig. 2. Example of super-resolution images from different models.

3. During the GAN training phase, the generator and the feature discriminator are trained on perceptual loss [12], which utilizes a pre-trained VGG19 network to calculate the difference of feature map extracts between the original HR image and the generated HR image.
4. The performance of the system is measured based on objective evaluation indicators such as PSNR/SSIM on several public benchmarks data-sets Set5, Set14, and BSD100 [16]. To find the perceptually better image, Mean Opinion Score (MOS) is calculated with the help of 10 people.

Comparative study shows that the proposed architecture with low model complexity significantly improve the performance of the model in terms of PSNR/SSIM and MOS score over the state-of-the-art methods [12,13,17,22,25] on benchmark data-sets when trained with same parameters.

2   Related Work

Before the application of deep learning in computer vision became popular in 2012 on-wards, the problem of super-resolution was approached using traditional computer vision techniques. Chang et al. in their work [3], used Bi-cubic interpolation for super-resolution. Bi-cubic interpolation and Lanczos re-sampling [15] are very computationally effective techniques, but they suffer from the drawback that they can't produce an accurate super-resolution image. The Markov Random Field (MRF) [23] approach was first embraced by Freeman et al. to investigate the accessible real images. Similarly, scientists applied sparse coding techniques to SISR [8] problems. Random forest [14] additionally accomplished a lot of progress in the reconstruction of the SISR. Many use a combination of reconstruction based as well as a learning-based approach to decrease the artifacts produced by external training examples.

In recent years, Deep Learning based Image Super-resolution models has demonstrated noteworthy improvement to reconstruction based and other learning-based methods. Dong et al. [5] first presented CNN for SISR reason, from that point forward there have been different enhancements to SISR methods utilizing Deep learning-based methodology [6,10,12,13,17,21,22,25]. SRCNN had its downside since it utilized a shallow three-layer architecture, thus highlight features couldn't be caught. Kim et al. proposed VDSR [10], which was an improvement to SRCNN by increasing the number of convolution layers to 20. Influenced by ResNet engineering Lim et al. [13] presented EDSR model which had long and short skip associations that helped to prepare profound SISR systems. Also removing Batch Normalization (BN) layers in the lingering residual network, they improved computational advantages. Even though the models so far created a high Peak Signal-to-Noise Ratio (PSNR) and Structural Similarity (SSIM) score, they couldn't produce SR image with realistic feature details.

Ledig et al. [12] were probably the first to use GAN for the purpose of SR. A GAN [7] generally consists of two networks, one generates a fake/new image where the other one tries to find whether it's fake or not. Ledig et al. [12] used SRResNet as generator of GAN. SFTGAN [21] demonstrated that it is conceivable to recoup sensible surfaces by tweaking highlights of a couple halfway layers in a single system adapted on semantic division likelihood maps. SRFeat [17] is another GAN-based SISR strategy where the creators previously proposed the double discriminator, one chip away at picture space and other on highlight areas to deliver perceptually practical HR picture. Xintao et al. introduced ESRGAN [22], which is an improved version of SRGAN, where they use Residual in Residual (RIR) generator architecture. Also, they added realistic discriminator that estimates the probability that the given real data is more practical than fake data. They enhanced the SRGAN model by using features before activation to calculate the perceptual loss of the generator during the adversarial learning phase.

Attention Mechanism. Recent studies show that the uses of attention mechanisms enhance the performance of CNN networks for various tasks. Attention mechanism was first introduced in CNN for image classification task [9,19,20]. Hu et al. [9] utilized channel-wise inter-dependencies among various feature channels. [4,25] used channel attention mechanism for SISR purpose. The dimensionality reduction step used in channel attention mechanism makes correspondence between the channel and its weight indirect. This limitation was surmounted by [18] with the attention mechanism that introduced a local cross channel interaction method using 1D convolution.

3   Network Architecture

The network architecture as shown in Fig. 3 utilizes a GAN based approach with a generator that produces super-resolution images along with a dual discriminator architecture that classifies the produced SR images into real and fake classes which helps the generator to produce realistic-looking images. The efficient channel attention mechanism used by the generator allows the network to focus on certain channels by modeling their inter-dependencies. The feature maps of the CNN network are then passed through two sub-pixel convolution layers where HR images are generated by upsampling.

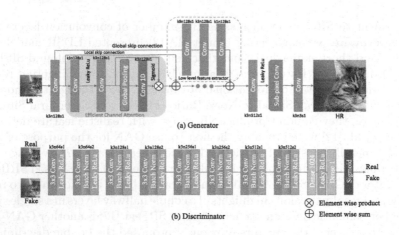

(a) Generator

(b) Discriminator

$\otimes$ Element wise product
$\oplus$ Element wise sum

Fig. 3. ECASR architecture.

3.1 Generator

The LR image after passing through the first convolutional layer of the generator enters the high-level and low-level feature extractors

$$F_0 = H_{SF}(I_{LR}), \tag{1}$$

where F_0, H_{SF} and I_{LR} denotes initial feature map, first convolutional layer and input low-resolution image respectively.

$$F_{HF} = H_{ECA}(F_0) \tag{2}$$
$$F_{LF} = H_{3CN}(F_0) \tag{3}$$

H_{ECA} denotes a deep feature extractor consisting of multiple ECA blocks which extract high-level features (F_{HF}) and H_{3CN} denotes the 3-layer shallow convolutional feature extractor that controls the flow of low-level features (F_{LF}) to the final output.

$$F_{Total} = F_{HF} + F_{LF} \tag{4}$$

F_{Total} is the total feature after adding both the features maps element-wise, the total feature map is then passed through the upsampling layer.

$$I_{SR} = H_{REC}(H_{UP}(F_{TF})) \tag{5}$$

H_{UP} and H_{REC} denotes the upsampling and reconstruction layer respectively that generates the super-resolution image.

Channel Attention. The resultant weight of the channel attention mechanism introduced in SENet [9] also utilized by [4, 25] can be expressed as

$$\omega = \sigma(\mathcal{W}_2\delta(\mathcal{W}_1\mathcal{G}(\chi)), \tag{6}$$

$\mathcal{G}(\chi)$ is the channel-wise global average pooling (GAP) of the output of a convolution block, $\chi \in \mathbb{R}^{W \times H \times C}$, where W, H and C are width, height and channel dimension. GAP can be expressed as

$$\mathcal{G}(\chi) = \frac{1}{WH} \sum_{i=1,j=1}^{W,H} \chi_{ij} \qquad (7)$$

where $\delta(\cdot)$ and $\sigma(\cdot)$ indicates the Rectified Linear Unit [1] and Sigmoid activation function respectively. In order to avoid high computational complexities dimension of the channels are first reduced into $(\frac{C}{r})$ and then transformed back into (C). This step of first reducing the dimension of channels into a low dimension space and then mapping it back to the original dimension makes indirect correspondence between the channel and it's weight which degrades performance by losing valuable information. In this paper we use Leaky ReLU over ReLU activation which fixes the "dying ReLU" problem, as it doesn't have zero-slope parts, also it provides additional benefit in training speed.

Efficient Channel Attention (ECA) [18]. Instead of using dimensionality reduction to reduce model complexity which destroys the direct correspondence between the channel and its weight, this work uses channel attention mechanism by efficiently using 1D convolution of kernel size k which. Given an output of a convolution block, χ, the resultant weight of efficient channel attention can be expressed as

$$\omega = \sigma(\mathcal{W}\mathcal{G}(\chi)), \qquad (8)$$

where $\mathcal{W}$ is a C×C parameter matrix. Let $y = \mathcal{G}(\chi)$ and $y \in \mathbb{R}^C$ where the weight of ith channel (y_i) can be calculated by considering the interaction among y_i and its k neighbors that can be given as,

$$\omega_i = \sigma\left(\sum_{j=1}^{k} \omega^j y_i^j\right), y_i^j \in \Omega_i^k \qquad (9)$$

where Ω_i^k indicates the set of k adjacent channels of y_i, ω_i is weight of y_i and ω^j is convolutional kernel. Equation (9) can be efficiently achieved by using 1D convolution as shown in Eq. (10)

$$\omega = \sigma(Conv1D_k(y)), \qquad (10)$$

The size of the kernal can be determined with the Eq. (11) as mentioned in [18].

$$k = \left| \frac{log_2(C)}{\gamma} + \frac{b}{\gamma} \right|_{odd}, \qquad (11)$$

here γ and b are constants, we use 2 and 1 respectively in our training process. $|x|_{odd}$ denotes the nearest odd integer to x. Let F_{ECA-1} be the input to our ECA block, the weighted output based on channel attention mechanism can be finally expressed as

$$F_{ECA} = \omega \otimes (F_{ECA-1}) \qquad (12)$$

3.2 Discriminator

The generator is coupled with a dual discriminator network which is similar to the architecture proposed by SRFeat [17]. One discriminator works on the image domain and the other works on the feature domain. The image discriminator is similar to the discriminator network used by SRGAN [12] while the feature discriminator has the same architecture as the image discriminator but the only difference is that the inputs to the feature discriminators are feature map extracts

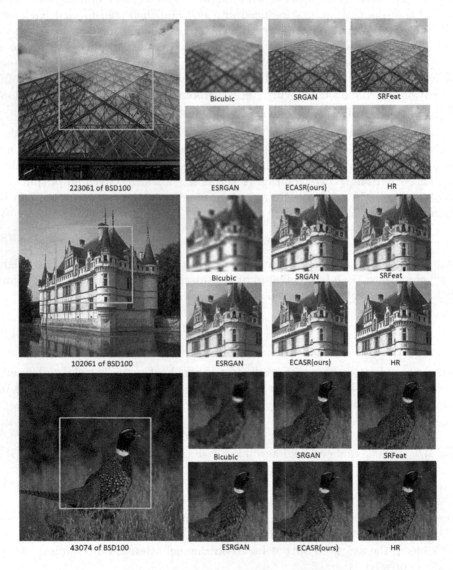

Fig. 4. Visual comparison of 4× SR on BSD100.

of the HR image and the super-resolved image from Conv5 of VGG-19 network. Both of them try to classify an image into a real and a fake class.

3.3   Loss Functions

A network that minimizes MSE loss tends to produce excessively smooth images. The generator network thus is pre-trained on Mean Absolute Error (MAE) loss that produces perceptually better-looking images to human eyes.

$$L_{MAE} = \frac{1}{WH} \sum_i^W \sum_j^H |I_{i,j}^h - I_{i,j}^g| \tag{13}$$

Here W, H indicates the dimension of the image. The objective of utilizing GAN system here is to improve the perceptual quality. GAN structure can be explained as a minmax game where the generator tries to minimize the discriminator's gain and the discriminator tries to minimize the generator's gain which can be characterized as below:

$$\min_g \max_d (E_{y \sim P_{data}(y)}[log(d(y))] + E_{x \sim P_x(x)}$$
$$[1 - log(d(g(x)))]) \tag{14}$$

Here g(x) is the output of a generator network g for x where x is irregular noise. On the other hand d(y) is the output of discriminator for y, where y is an example of genuine information distribution. $P_{data}(y)$ refers to distribution of real data and $P_x(x)$ is the distribution of generator output.

The discriminators, d^i and d^f denotes a pair of dual discriminators taking a shot at picture and feature area, separately. The generative adversarial procedure with a pre-trained generator and discriminators follows the loss-function characterized as:

$$L_g = L_p + \lambda(L_a^i + L_a^f) \tag{15}$$

where L_p is a perceptual similarity loss, L_a^i is a image GAN loss for the generator L_a^f is a feature GAN loss for the generator and λ is the weight for the GAN loss terms. To prepare discriminators d_i and d_f , we minimize the loss of L_d^i and, L_d^f which corresponds to L_a^i and L_a^f. The generator and discriminators are trained by thus limiting L_g, L_d^i and L_d^f. For adversarial learning, the discriminator uses loss functions introduced in [21]. There are by and large three-loss terms adding to the all-out loss, to be specific, perceptual similarity loss, image GAN loss, and GAN loss calculated based on features obtained by passing the super-resolution and high-resolution images through a VGG19 network. The description of each loss will be expressed as follows.

Perceptual Similarity Loss L_p. This loss processes the difference between two pictures in the feature area, rather than the pixel space, prompting all the more perceptually fulfilling outcomes. The perceptual loss is characterized as:

$$\frac{1}{W_m H_m C_m} \sum_{i}^{W_m} \sum_{i}^{H_m} \sum_{i}^{C_m} (\phi_{i,j,k}^m(I^h) - \phi_{i,j,k}^m(I^g))^2 \tag{16}$$

where W_m, H_m, C_m describes the dimensions of the m-th feature map extract from a pre-trained VGG network with $\phi_{i,j,k}^m$ indicating the feature map obtained by the j-th convolution (after activation) before the i-th maxpooling layer within the VGG network.

Image GAN Losses L_a^i and L_d^i. The image GAN loss term L_a^i for the generator and the loss function L_d^i for the image discriminator are characterized as:

$$L_a^i = -log(d^i(I^g)), \tag{17}$$

$$L_d^i = -log(d^i(I^h)) - log(1 - (d^i(I^g))), \tag{18}$$

where $d^i(I)$ is the yield of the image discriminator d^i.

Feature GAN Losses L_a^f and L_d^f. The element GAN loss term L_a^f for the generator and the capacity L_d^f for the element discriminator are characterized as:

$$L_a^f = -log(d^f(\phi^m(I^g))), \tag{19}$$

$$L_d^f = -log(d^f(\phi^m(I^h))) - log(1 - (d^f(\phi^m(I^g)))), \tag{20}$$

where $d^f(\phi^m)$ is the yield of the feature discriminator d^f.

4   Experiments

Experiments are done in two phases, in the first phase generator alone is trained on MAE loss, in the second phase the generator is trained on perceptual loss along with the dual discriminators. The performance of the pre-trained generator is evaluated and compared with other state-of-the-art approaches in terms of PSNR and SSIM score. Finally, the results obtained from the GAN based SISR network are evaluated and compared on PSNR/SSIM and MOS score, which proves the efficiency of our network.

Table 1. Comparison of PSNR/SSIM score with and without Low-level feature extractor after 64000 iterations.

PSNR/SSIM	w/o Low level feature extractor	with Low level feature extractor
Set4	30.06/0.8520	**30.12/0.8544**
Set14	27.22/0.7485	**27.27/0.7501**
BSD100	26.74/0.7098	**26.76/0.7110**

The training data-sets are obtained by bi-cubic down-sampling of the HR images. The cropped HR images are of the size 296×296, while the LR images are of the size 74×74, which are then again normalized to $[-1,1]$ intensity. DIV2K [2] data-set is used for training which consists of 800 HR training images and 100 HR validation images. The data-set is augmented into 160000 images by random cropping, rotating ($90°, 180°$, and $270°$) and horizontally flipping. Publicly available data-sets Set5, Set14, BSD100 are used for validation. We train the generator network on Nvidia Titan X GPU for 3.2×10^6 iterations with a batch size of 16 which is optimized by Adam [11] optimizer. The learning rate is initialized 1×10^{-4} with a decay of 0.5 for every 1×10^5 iterations.

Table 2. Comparison with PSNR oriented pre-trained models SRGAN, EDSR, ESRGAN, SRFeat, RCAN and our proposed model ECASR on benchmark data [12, 13, 17, 22, 25]. [$4\times$ upscaling]

PSNR/SSIM	Set5	Set14	BSD100
Bicubic	28.42/0.8104	26.00/0.7027	25.96/0.6675
SRCNN	30.48/0.8628	27.50/0.7513	26.90/0.7101
VDSR	31.35/0.8830	28.02/0.7680	27.29/0.7260
SRGAN	31.67/0.8864	28.30/0.7770	27.40/0.7318
EDSR	32.01/0.8917	28.48/**0.7832**	27.53/**0.7373**
ESRGAN	31.83/0.8892	28.44/0.7801	27.46/0.7340
SRFeat	31.45/0.8821	28.14/0.7719	27.26/0.7271
RCAN	32.05/0.8920	28.57/0.7821	**27.60**/0.7360
ECASR	**32.12/0.8924**	**28.58**/0.7830	27.54/0.7371

Table 3. Comparison of GAN-trained models, SRGAN [12], SRFeat [17], ESRGAN [22] and the proposed model ECASR on benchmark data-set.

PSNR/SSIM	Set5	Set14	BSD100
SRGAN	29.158/0.8643	26.165/0.7791	25.459/0.5775
ESRGAN	29.752/0.8665	26.323/**0.7854**	**25.505**/0.6279
SRFeat	29.420/0.8245	26.100/0.7850	25.417/0.5675
ECASR	**29.864/0.8677**	**26.436**/0.778	25.461/**0.6454**

5   Results

In order to prove the effectiveness of the shallow low-level feature extractor, we do an ablation study. The network is trained and tested with and without the low-level feature extractor. Results are tabulated in Table 1. It shows that the use of the low-level feature extractor helps in achieving a high PSNR/SSIM score.

Table 4. MOS ratings of SRGAN, ESRGAN, SRFeat [12,17,22] and our Proposed Model ECASR on BSD100 [16].

Models	SRGAN	SRFeat	ESRGAN	**ECAS (ours)**
MOS	3.72	3.87	4.08	**4.12**

The performance of the generator network is evaluated and compared to bicubic interpolation and other state-of-the-art models which proves the efficiency of our proposed network. Quantitative results are summed in Table 2 that shows our model produces comparable results. EDSR and RCAN have higher values for Set14 and BSD100 which is because of their deeper architecture, if we stack up more ECA blocks in our network it should necessarily produce a higher benchmark score. Though the generator produces images that have high PSNR/SSIM values, they lack in perceptual quality. We then compare the performance of our GAN trained network as shown in Table 3 and Fig. 4 provides visual examples that show considerably better performance. The dip in the PSNR/SSIM score of our GAN trained network is presumably for the competition between the MSE based content loss and adversarial loss. We further obtained MOS ratings from a group of 10 people, who rated the images from 1 to 5 based on the reconstruction quality of the images, higher the better. Table 4 shows our proposed model has better MOS ratings compared to SRGAN, SRFeat, and ESRGAN.

6   Conclusion

In this paper, we have proposed a new GAN based SR scheme. In the proposed scheme, ECA method has been used, probably for the first time to solve SR problem. ECA tends to produce higher PSNR results with a smaller number of parameters. Considering low-level features with high-level features for super-resolution, both the fine texture details as well as overall description of the image are captured accurately. Dual discriminator helps the generator to create photo-realistic SR images. Comparison with various models with the same training data-set and parameters show the superiority of our proposed method. There is always a trade-off between model complexity and quality. Stacking up more ECA layers into our model, expected to result better SR images but it will also increase the training complexity.

References

1. Agarap, A.F.: Deep learning using rectified linear units (relu). arXiv preprint arXiv:1803.08375 (2018)
2. Agustsson, E., Timofte, R.: Ntire 2017 challenge on single image super-resolution: dataset and study. In: The IEEE Conference on Computer Vision and Pattern Recognition (CVPR) Workshops, July 2017

3. Chang, H., Yeung, D.Y., Xiong, Y.: Super-resolution through neighbor embedding. In: Proceedings of the 2004 IEEE Computer Society Conference on Computer Vision and Pattern Recognition. CVPR 2004, vol. 1, pp. I-I. IEEE (2004)

4. Dai, T., Cai, J., Zhang, Y., Xia, S.T., Zhang, L.: Second-order attention network for single image super-resolution. In: Proceedings of the IEEE Conference on Computer Vision and Pattern Recognition, pp. 11065–11074 (2019)

5. Dong, C., Loy, C.C., He, K., Tang, X.: Image super-resolution using deep convolutional networks. IEEE Trans. Pattern Anal. Mach. Intell. **38**(2), 295–307 (2015)

6. Dong, C., Loy, C.C., Tang, X.: Accelerating the super-resolution convolutional neural network. In: Leibe, B., Matas, J., Sebe, N., Welling, M. (eds.) ECCV 2016. LNCS, vol. 9906, pp. 391–407. Springer, Cham (2016). https://doi.org/10.1007/978-3-319-46475-6_25

7. Goodfellow, I., et al.: Generative adversarial nets. In: Advances in Neural Information Processing Systems, pp. 2672–2680 (2014)

8. Gu, S., Zuo, W., Xie, Q., Meng, D., Feng, X., Zhang, L.: Convolutional sparse coding for image super-resolution. In: Proceedings of the IEEE International Conference on Computer Vision, pp. 1823–1831 (2015)

9. Hu, J., Shen, L., Sun, G.: Squeeze-and-excitation networks. In: Proceedings of the IEEE Conference on Computer Vision and Pattern Recognition, pp. 7132–7141 (2018)

10. Kim, J., Kwon Lee, J., Mu Lee, K.: Accurate image super-resolution using very deep convolutional networks. In: Proceedings of the IEEE Conference on Computer Vision and Pattern Recognition, pp. 1646–1654 (2016)

11. Kingma, D.P., Ba, J.: Adam: A method for stochastic optimization. arXiv preprint arXiv:1412.6980 (2014)

12. Ledig, C., et al.: Photo-realistic single image super-resolution using a generative adversarial network. In: Proceedings of the IEEE Conference on Computer Vision and Pattern Recognition, pp. 4681–4690 (2017)

13. Lim, B., Son, S., Kim, H., Nah, S., Mu Lee, K.: Enhanced deep residual networks for single image super-resolution. In: Proceedings of the IEEE Conference on Computer Vision and Pattern Recognition workshops, pp. 136–144 (2017)

14. Liu, Z.S., Siu, W.C., Huang, J.J.: Image super-resolution via weighted random forest. In: 2017 IEEE International Conference on Industrial Technology (ICIT), pp. 1019–1023. IEEE (2017)

15. Madhukar, N.: Lanczos resampling for the digital processing of remotely sensed images. In: Proceedings of International Conference on VLSI, Communication, Advanced Devices, Signals & Systems and Networking (VCASAN-2013), pp. 403–411 (2013)

16. Martin, D., Fowlkes, C., Tal, D., Malik, J.: A database of human segmented natural images and its application to evaluating segmentation algorithms and measuring ecological statistics. In: Proceedings of the 8th International Conference on Computer Vision, vol. 2, pp. 416–423, July 2001

17. Park, S.-J., Son, H., Cho, S., Hong, K.-S., Lee, S.: SRFeat: single image super-resolution with feature discrimination. In: Ferrari, V., Hebert, M., Sminchisescu, C., Weiss, Y. (eds.) ECCV 2018. LNCS, vol. 11220, pp. 455–471. Springer, Cham (2018). https://doi.org/10.1007/978-3-030-01270-0_27

18. Wang, Q., Wu, B., Zhu, P., Li, P., Zuo, W., Hu, Q.: ECA-net: efficient channel attention for deep convolutional neural networks. In: The IEEE Conference on Computer Vision and Pattern Recognition (CVPR) (2020)

19. Wang, F., et al.: Residual attention network for image classification. In: Proceedings of the IEEE Conference on Computer Vision and Pattern Recognition, pp. 3156–3164 (2017)
20. Wang, X., Girshick, R., Gupta, A., He, K.: Non-local neural networks. In: Proceedings of the IEEE Conference on Computer Vision and Pattern Recognition, pp. 7794–7803 (2018)
21. Wang, X., Yu, K., Dong, C., Loy, C.C.: Recovering realistic texture in image super-resolution by deep spatial feature transform. In: The IEEE Conference on Computer Vision and Pattern Recognition (CVPR), June 2018
22. Wang, X., et al.: ESRGAN: enhanced super-resolution generative adversarial networks. In: Leal-Taixé, L., Roth, S. (eds.) ECCV 2018. LNCS, vol. 11133, pp. 63–79. Springer, Cham (2019). https://doi.org/10.1007/978-3-030-11021-5_5
23. Wu, W., Liu, Z., Gueaieb, W., He, X.: Single-image super-resolution based on Markov random field and contourlet transform. J. Electron. Imaging **20**(2), 005–023 (2011)
24. Xu, Y., Yu, L., Xu, H., Zhang, H., Nguyen, T.: Vector sparse representation of color image using quaternion matrix analysis. IEEE Trans. Image Process. **24**(4), 1315–1329 (2015)
25. Zhang, Y., Li, K., Li, K., Wang, L., Zhong, B., Fu, Y.: Image super-resolution using very deep residual channel attention networks. In: Ferrari, V., Hebert, M., Sminchisescu, C., Weiss, Y. (eds.) ECCV 2018. LNCS, vol. 11211, pp. 294–310. Springer, Cham (2018). https://doi.org/10.1007/978-3-030-01234-2_18

Transfer Learning Based COVID-19 Patient Classification

Vrinda Rastogi[1], Sahima Srivastava[1], Chandra Prakash[2(✉)], and Rishav Singh[2]

[1] Indira Gandhi Delhi Technical University for Women, Delhi, India
[2] National Institute of Technology, Delhi, India
cprakash@nitdelhi.ac.in

Abstract. The COVID-19 pandemic has had drastic global effects and has severely influenced our daily lives. One way to lessen the impact is by integrating Artificial Intelligence technology in medical imaging. It is vital to accurately and quickly assess positive COVID-19 patients, which can be done using their Chest X-Rays (CXR). In this study, a CXR dataset containing three classes namely: normal, viral pneumonia, and COVID-19 is used. After preprocessing the dataset, Transfer Learning methods are applied to the dataset. Re-training ResNet 50 gave the overall highest accuracy of 99.2%. Meanwhile, the Support Vector Machine (SVM) classifier performed the best with InceptionResNetV2 model giving an accuracy of 98.424%. This paper aims to provide a robust and accurate method to classify positive COVID-19 patients.

Keywords: COVID-19 · Transfer learning · Deep learning

1 Introduction

The coronavirus pandemic is one of the largest global concerns the world has faced since the second world war. According to the World Health Organisation (WHO), it is first discovered in December 2019 in China's Wuhan province According to Fauci et al. [1], it seems to be caused by a new coronavirus which induces severe acute respiratory syndrome (SARS). Hence this type of strain of the virus has been coined as "severe acute respiratory syndrome coronavirus 2 (SARS-CoV-2) [2]. Due to the rapid spread of this disease, the WHO declared it as a global public health emergency on 30th January 2020 As of August 2020, there has been no clinically approved medicine or vaccine effective against COVID-19. The pandemic has just not affected the health of the global community but also has posed challenges in the economic, environmental, and social sector [3]. It has truly changed the world as we know it. Therefore it is vital to stop or at least slow down the spread of the virus which can be done by detecting COVID-19 positive patients quickly and efficiently.

One of the primary techniques which can be used to detect COVID-19 is medical imaging. Both Chest X-rays (CXR) imaging or Computed Tomography (CT) scans can be utilized to detect COVID-19. CXR is more preferred due to

© Springer Nature Singapore Pte Ltd. 2021
S. K. Singh et al. (Eds.): CVIP 2020, CCIS 1376, pp. 387–397, 2021.
https://doi.org/10.1007/978-981-16-1086-8_34

their reliability, accessibility, and complementary to the virus's symptoms [4,5]. With the recent emerging discoveries in Artificial Intelligence (AI), technology has the power to strengthen imaging tools and aid the plight of medical workers [6]. The integration of deep learning with medical imaging can help to detect COVID-19 accurately as well as curb the challenges of expensive equipment or availability of physicians in remote locations.

As this virus is very novel, data is scarce. This may result in AI generalizing its observations or giving biased output [7]. Deep learning has been heavily applied in the medical industry [8]. Similarly, these techniques have now been applied to detect COVID-19.

Ozturk et al. [9] implemented the DarkNet model by customizing You Only Look Once (YOLO) for real-time COVID-19 detection. It is applied to both binary and multi-class classification. It achieved 98.08% accuracy for binary and 87.02% for multi-class by using an imbalanced dataset.

'COVIDX-Net' is constructed by Hemdan et al. [10] using a combination of seven state-of-the-art deep learning models namely: VGG19, InceptionV3, DenseNet121, InceptionResNetV2, Xception, ResNetV2, and MobileNetV2. This model used 50 images where 25 images represented positive COVID-19 cases and the other 25 images are normal CXR. According to the study, VGG19 achieved the highest accuracy of 90%.

For COVID-19 detection, Abbas et al. [11] proposed a convolutional neural network named Decompose, Transfer, and Compose (DeTraC). It is a three-step process. The first step is feature extraction. The next step is to train the model by using an optimizing method. The last step is to enhance the filtering of the classification of images. The advantage of this method is that it is able to leverage class boundaries to deal with irregularities. The model is trained on a large dataset composed of CXR images collected from numerous hospitals. It achieved an accuracy of 95.12%.

In another study, the acquired X-ray images are first made uniform in terms of image data via histogram equalization [11]. After this, lung segmentation and image intensity equalization are carried out. Tartaglione et al. [12] then applied multiple CNN and deep learning-based approaches for the purpose of classification on different combinations of the datasets used.

Transfer Learning for the purpose of COVID-19 prediction is applied to X-ray Images by Minaee et al. [13]. They trained their dataset on four popular CNN's: ResNet18, ResNet50, SqueezeNet, and DenseNet-121. However, the dataset used in this study also contained a skewed number of COVID-19 positive against COVID-19 negative cases yet achieved a 97% sensitivity rate.

Henceforth, deep learning techniques are applied to curb this imbalance. Six deep learning models namely: VGG-16, ResNet 50, InceptionV3, Xception, VGG-19, and InceptionResNetV2 have been used to both re-train weights and to extract crucial features from CXR imaging.

In this study, Deep-Learning models are explored for multi-class classification (COVID-19, Pneumonia, and normal) on X-ray images of the subjects. The contributions of this paper presents are as follows:

1. A comprehensive study of two different methods namely; re-train existing deep learning models and transfer learning using feature extraction.
2. A variation of different types of datasets are used to analyze the results. Also, a larger dataset is used in comparison to other works.

This paper is organized with the second section explaining the methodology applied and the third section explaining the results. The fourth section concludes the work.

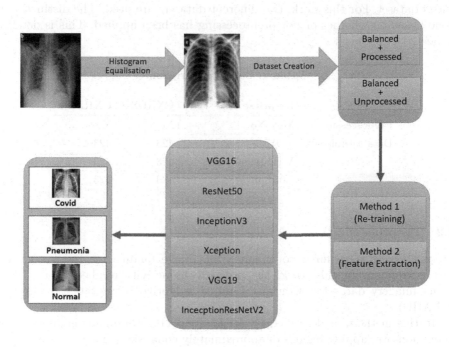

Fig. 1. The methodology employed in order to identify COVID-19 positive patients.

2   Methodology

This section details the methodology applied in this work which aims to create a flexible and accurate approach to detect COVID-19. Figure 1 showcases the workflow used in this study. CXR imagery is collected and then used to build four different types of datasets. Prepossessing is applied to some of the images in order to enhance their features. After which, two methods are applied. Firstly, deep learning models are re-trained based on the dataset. Secondly, transfer learning via feature extraction is performed on which Machine Learning algorithms are applied.

2.1 Datasets

Chest X-ray images used in this study are taken from publicly available datasets. Cohen et al. [14] created a large dataset where images both CXR and CT scans, are taken from various resources. This dataset is used to extract COVID-19 positive CXR imaging. For Viral Pneumonia and Normal imagery, the open dataset constructed by Kermany et al. [15] is taken.

A balanced dataset is constructed having an equal number of CXR images for each class. This is done in order to overcome the bias introduced by an unbalanced dataset. For this work, two different datasets are used. The distinction is done based on whether or not preprocessing has been applied. This is detailed in Sect. 3.2 (Table 1).

Table 1. Dataset description.

	DataBase case-study	CXRDS-1	CXRDS-2
Preprocessing	Yes/ No	No	Yes
Data sample size	COVID	423	423
	Viral pneumonia	423	423
	Normal	423	423

2.2 Preprocessing

Pre-processing is required to enhance the image quality for the better feature extraction. In this work, the pre-analysis activity applied to the chest X-ray imagery dataset is Contrast Limited Adaptive Histogram Equalization (CLAHE).

In this method, as described by Ali M. Reza [16], the image is divided into many non-overlapping regions of approximately equal sizes. Then the area's histogram is calculated. Thereafter, a clip limit for the clipping histograms is found based on the prescribed limit for contrast expansion. This is followed by redistribution of all the histograms so that its height remains below the clip limit. In the last step, grayscale mapping is done using the histogram's cumulative distribution functions (CDF). These pixels are linearly mapped based on the results of the nearest neighboring regions.

This work uses the following two methods:

1. Re-training existing deep learning models
2. Transfer Learning via Feature Extraction

2.3 Method 1: Re-Training Models

This technique utilises six existing deep learning models namely: VGG16, ResNet 50, InceptionV3, Xception, VGG19, and InceptionResNetV2. These models are applied without using their top layer. Instead, new fully connected layers are included where the last layer had three nodes and a softmax activation function. In order to find each of their numerous parameters for each model, they are trained on the two different datasets. The training of models are carried out on 100 epochs which are subjected to callbacks like early-stopping and model-checkpoint. The learning rate used for training the models is consistent for all, $1e-4$.

The following showcases the deep learning models in more detail.

VGG16. This model is first introduced via the ImageNet Challenge in 2014 where produced extra-ordinary results [17]. VGG16 is created by Karen Simonyan and Andrew Zisserman. In order to feed images into this model, some pre-processing is required such as resizes the images into 224×224 sizes. After which, these images go through 16 layers which vary in size and type. The first two layers the images go through are of 224×224 size which are then fed into a pooling layer. The images again go through another stack of convolutional layers of size 112×112 which meets another pooling layer. This process in continued for three more stacks of convolutional and pooling layers where the convolutional layers size changes to 56×56 to 28×28 to finally, 14×14. Spatial pooling occurs due to the five max pooling layers prevalent in this model [18]. The images then go through three dense layers which uses a softmax activation function. In short, images of size 224×224 are converted to an one-dimensional array. A limitation of VGG16 is that it has 160 million parameters which the fully connected layers may consume.

ResNet 50. Residual Neural Networks are very useful as they utilise shortcuts in order to skip convolutional layer blocks [19]. These networks have a uniform amount of filters for the output maps. Also if the feature map is reduced to half, the number of filters may double [20]. In ResNet 50, the images are fed into 50 layers which contain over 20 million training parameters. This model is created using residual building blocks. These blocks are created with several convolutional layers, rectified linear unit activation function, batch normalisations, and one shortcut [21]. As displayed in Fig. 3, the images are fed into a 112×112 convolutional layer. After which, the images go through numerous residual building blocks of varying sizes such as 56×56, 28×28, 14×14, and 7×7. While re-training this model, the images would then go through dense layers, yet for feature extraction a machine learning classifier is placed in its stead. The distinctive feature of these neural networks is that they learn the residual [22].

InceptionV3. Similar to VGG16, InceptionV3 also performed exceptionally well in the ImageNet Challenge. This model is established from the works of Szegedy et al. [23]. This model is constructed of alternate symmetrical and asymmetrical building blocks. It contains many types of layers such as convolutional, dropouts, fully connected, and average pooling. InceptionV3 architecture is built in a progressive manner. There are instances of smaller convolutions which replaces bigger convolutions, making the training process more rapid. There are asymmetric convolutions such as 1×3 followed by 3×1, which replaces 3×3. Auxillary classifier is also inserted within this architecture which performs as a regularizer. The model also performs grid size reductions efficiently without the use of pooling layers [22]. All of these techniques are amalgamated to create InceptionV3.

Xception. Xception is considered to be an extention of InceptionV3 as it is highly influenced by it. The same number of parameters lie in both models, yet their implementation is different. Xception is introduced by Francois Chollet [24] where a new deep convolutional neural network is constructed based on the Inception model's interpretation. In this models, Inception modules are replaced with depth-wise separable convolution layers. This model is built using 14 modules which are connected using ResNet type of residual connection [19]. In the beginning, the architecture is built to down sample the images and reduce the spatial dimensional. In the middle, Xception tries to learn crucial features. In the end, the model consolidates and summarize the features using a softmax activation function.

VGG19. VGG19 is introduced by K. Simonyan and A. Zisserman [17]. As the name prescribes, this model has 19 layers of various types such as convolutional, fully connected, max pooling, and dropout. The model emphasises on expanding the depth by the utilisation of small convolutional filters. In terms of architecture, both VGG16 and VGG19 are similar except for the occurrence of three extra layers in three convolutional stacks. These extra layers add extra convolution operations over the images. VGG19 performed well as it achieved high accuracy from the ImageNet dataset, therefore concluding that representation depth can be crucial to garner optimal results [25].

InceptionResNetV2. InceptionResNetV2 is a seamless integration of Microsoft's ResNet model and the Inception model. It is constructed by Szegedy et al. [26] where they found that using the residual structure's shortcuts, the Inception blocks would be more simplified. It is found that this model performed better than Inception yet IneceptionResNetV2 is more expensive in comparison. The architecture of InceptionResNetV2 is divided into four components [27]. In the encoding component, the images undergo dimension reduction whereas in the feature extraction stage, high level features are procured. These features are then consolidated in the fusion layer. Finally, the last component known as the "decoder" uses the extracted feature to classify the images.

2.4   Method 2: Transfer Learning via Feature Extraction

In this method, existing deep learning models are applied to the dataset. Images are fed into the model which is responsible for extracting important and distinct features from these images. Machine Learning classifiers are then applied on these extracted features. Support Vector Machine (SVM) and Random Forest(RF) are utilised in this work as these algorithms can handle the high dimensionality of the CXR extracted feature data given [28,29].

Grid search algorithm is used to tune parameters. According to [30], this algorithm is advantageous as it greatly improves the predictive performance and the overall stability of the classification model. Moreover, applying grid search with SVM also helps prevent over-fitting. Thus, this work utilises grid search algorithm to find the optimum values and carry out hyperparameter tuning. The learning parameters for the two classifiers used are given in Table 2.

Table 2. Learning parameters for machine learning classifiers.

Parameter	Value
n_estimators	100
Criterion	Entropy
C	1
Kernel	Linear
random_state	0

Figures 2 and 3 depict two of the models with the Machine Learning classifier.

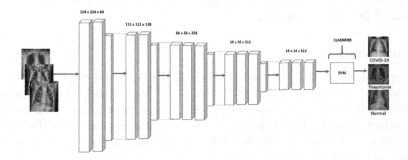

Fig. 2. Use of VGG16 as Feature Extractor with Support Vector Machine as classifier.

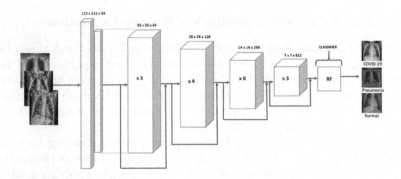

Fig. 3. Use of ResNet50 as Feature Extractor with Random Forest as classifier.

3   Results

This section details the results achieved using the various techniques.

3.1   Method 1

The performance for re-training existing models is given in Table 3. Without pre-processing, InceptionResNetV2 performed the best attaining 98.4% in accuracy. The CLAHE method applied to the CXR dataset aided in getting the highest accuracy via the ResNet 50 model. This model and method attained the highest accuracy overall: 99.2%. ResNet 50 has the advantage of residual networks which works to learn the residual instead of learning the features.

In terms of methodologies, generally re-training existing models performed better in comparison to transfer learning. This may be due to the fact that in Method 1, the models alter millions of parameters based specifically on the CXRDS dataset whereas in transfer learning the parameters remained unchanged from the original model.

3.2   Method 2

The performance of this technique is given in Tables 3 and 4 are for both Support Vector Machine and Random Forest as classifier. Using SVM as classifier, InceptionResNetV2 model acquired the best accuracy of 98.43%. On the other hand, when Random Forest is used to classify images into COVID-19, Viral Pneumonia, and Normal, both VGG16 and InceptionResNetV2 showcased the highest classification accuracy, i.e., 95.67%. Overall, SVM performed better for balanced unprocessed data as compared to processed data. The same cannot be said for Random Forest, as the performance fluctuated. InceptionResNetV2 is the only model that showed an approximate 3% jump in accuracy for both the classifiers when applied on a unprocessed dataset. It went up from 95.65% to 98.43% and from 92.49% to 95.67% for SVM and Random Forest, respectively. This model has the advantage of being a hybrid of both ResNet and Inception, therefore it contains residual learning and shortcuts.

Table 3. Balanced dataset accuracy for method 1 and method 2

Dataset	Model	Accuracy (%)		
		Re-train	SVM	Random forest
CXRDS-1	VGG16	96.9	97.6377	**95.669**
	ResNet 50	97.3	97.6377	94.8818
	Inception V3	97.3	96.85	94.094
	Xception	96.5	94.489	93.307
	IncecptionResNetV2	98.4	**98.425**	**95.669**
	VGG19	98	98.0314	93.7007
CXRDS-2	VGG16	97.6	96.047	93.2806
	ResNet 50	**99.2**	96.443	95.65
	Inception V3	98.8	94.071	92.095
	Xception	96.1	95.6522	95.652
	IncecptionResNetV2	97.6	95.65	92.49
	VGG19	92.9	96.838	92.49

Table 4. Balanced dataset result for method 2: precision, recall, F1-score

Dataset	Model	SVM			Random forest		
		Precision	Recall	F1-score	Precision	Recall	F1-score
CXRDS-1	VGG16	1	0.99	0.99	0.99	1	0.99
	ResNet 50	1	0.99	0.99	0.97	0.99	0.98
	Inception V3	1	0.99	0.99	0.99	0.99	0.99
	Xception	0.99	0.99	0.99	0.95	0.96	0.95
	IncecptionResNetV2	1	1	1	0.99	1	0.99
	VGG19	1	0.99	0.99	0.97	0.99	0.98
CXRDS-2	VGG16	1	1	1	0.97	0.99	0.98
	ResNet 50	1	1	1	1	1	1
	Inception V3	0.99	0.99	0.99	0.92	1	0.96
	Xception	0.97	1	0.99	0.99	0.99	0.99
	IncecptionResNetV2	0.97	1	0.99	0.97	0.97	0.97
	VGG19	1	1	1	0.95	0.99	0.97

4 Conclusion and Future Works

In this work, two different types of balanced dataset is utilised: one with CLAHE applied and the other sans it. Using these two datasets, two different methods are applied: re-training existing deep learning models and transfer learning via feature extraction. For the first method, ResNet 50 performed the best attaining 99.2%. In the second method, two machine learning classifications are also applied namely: SVM and Random Forest. SVM performed the best with IncecptionResNetV2 model attaining a 98.425% on the dataset without preprocessing.

There are some limitations in this work which should be addressed in the future. Firstly, CXR images for COVID-19 positive images are very limited which decreases the efficiency of the deep learning techniques applied. Another application of this work could be the integration of the patient's past medical history to more quickly predict COVID-19 and its aftermath on the patient. Regardless of the accuracies attained via these processes, clinical trials should be implemented to correctly assess their performance.

The COVID-19 pandemic has affected the globe, hence it is imperative that Artificial Intelligence be applied to quickly and accurately predict the virus.

References

1. Fauci, A.S., Lane, H.C., Redfield, R.R.: Covid-19–navigating the uncharted. New Engl. J. Med. **382**(13), 1268–1269 (2020)
2. Zheng, Y.-Y., Ma, Y.-T., Zhang, J.-Y., Xie, X.: Covid-19 and the cardiovascular system. Nat. Rev. Cardiol. **17**(5), 259–260 (2020)
3. Chakraborty, I., Maity, P.: Covid-19 outbreak: Migration, effects on society, global environment and prevention. Sci. Total Environ. **728**, 138882 (2020)
4. Self, W.H., Courtney, D.M., McNaughton, C.D., Wunderink, R.G., Kline, J.A.: High discordance of chest x-ray and computed tomography for detection of pulmonary opacities in ed patients: implications for diagnosing pneumonia. Am. J. Emerg. Med. **31**(2), 401–405 (2013)
5. Nair, A., et al.: A british society of thoracic imaging statement: considerations in designing local imaging diagnostic algorithms for the covid-19 pandemic. Clin. Radiol. **75**(5), 329–334 (2020)
6. Shi, F., et al.:. Review of artificial intelligence techniques in imaging data acquisition, segmentation and diagnosis for covid-19. IEEE Rev. Biomed. Eng. 1–1 (2020). https://doi.org/10.1109/RBME.2020.2987975
7. Breslow , N.E., Lin, X.: Bias correction in generalised linear mixed models with a single component of dispersion. Biometrika **82**(1), 81–91 (1995)
8. Litjens, G.: A survey on deep learning in medical image analysis. Med. Image Anal. **42**, 60–88 (2017)
9. Ozturk, T., Talo, M., Yildirim, E.A., Baloglu, U.B., Yildirim, O., Acharya, U.R.: Automated detection of covid-19 cases using deep neural networks with x-ray images. Comput. Biol. Med. **121**, 103792 (2020)
10. Hemdan, E.E.D., Shouman, M.A., Karar. , M.E.: Covidx-net: a framework of deep learning classifiers to diagnose covid-19 in x-ray images (2020)
11. Abbas, A., Abdelsamea, M.M., Gaber, M.M.: Classification of covid-19 in chest x-ray images using detrac deep convolutional neural network (2020). arXiv:2003.13815
12. Tartaglione, E., Barbano, C.A., Berzovini, C., Calandri, M., Grangetto, M.: Unveiling covid-19 from chest x-ray with deep learning: a hurdles race with small data (2020). arXiv:2004.05405
13. Minaee, S., Kafieh, R., Sonka, M., Yazdani, S., Soufi, G.J.: Deep-covid: Predicting covid-19 from chest x-ray images using deep transfer learning (2020). arXiv:2004.09363
14. Cohen, J.P., Morrison, P., Dao, L., Roth, K., Duong, T.Q., Ghassemi, M.: Covid-19 image data collection: Prospective predictions are the future (2020). arXiv:2006.11988

15. Kermany, D.S., et al.: Identifying medical diagnoses and treatable diseases by image-based deep learning. Cell **172**(5), 1122–1131 (2018)
16. Reza, A.M.: Realization of the contrast limited adaptive histogram equalization (clahe) for real-time image enhancement. J. VLSI Signal Process. Syste. Signal, Image and Video Technol. **38**(1), 35–44 (2004)
17. Simonyan, K., Zisserman, A.: Very deep convolutional networks for large-scale image recognition (2014). arXiv:1409.1556
18. Dhankhar, P.: Resnet-50 and vgg-16 for recognizing facial emotions. Int. J. Innov. Eng. Technol. **13**(4), 126–130 (2019)
19. He, K., Zhang, X., Ren, S., Sun, J.: Deep residual learning for image recognition. In: Proceedings of the IEEE Conference on Computer Vision and Pattern Recognition, pp. 770–778 (2016)
20. Rezende, E., Ruppert, G., Carvalho, T., Ramos, F., De Geus, P.: Malicious software classification using transfer learning of resnet-50 deep neural network. In: 2017 16th IEEE International Conference on Machine Learning and Applications (ICMLA), pp. 1011–1014. IEEE (2017)
21. Wen, L., Li, X., Gao, L.: A transfer convolutional neural network for fault diagnosis based on resnet-50. Neural Comput. Appl. **31**, 1–14 (2019)
22. Reddy, A.S.B., Juliet, D.S.: Transfer learning with resnet-50 for malaria cell-image classification. In: 2019 International Conference on Communication and Signal Processing (ICCSP), pp. 0945–0949. IEEE (2019)
23. Szegedy, C., Vanhoucke, V., Ioffe, S., Shlens, J., Wojna, Z.: Rethinking the inception architecture for computer vision. In: Proceedings of the IEEE Conference on Computer Vision and Pattern Recognition, pp. 2818–2826 (2016)
24. Chollet. F.: Xception: Deep learning with depthwise separable convolutions. In: Proceedings of the IEEE Conference on Computer Vision and Pattern Recognition, pp. 1251–1258 (2017)
25. Jaworek-Korjakowska, J., Kleczek, P., Gorgon, M.: Melanoma thickness prediction based on convolutional neural network with vgg-19 model transfer learning. In: Proceedings of the IEEE/CVF Conference on Computer Vision and Pattern Recognition (CVPR) Workshops (2019)
26. Szegedy, C., Ioffe, S., Vanhoucke, V., Alemi, A.A.: Inception-v4, inception-resnet and the impact of residual connections on learning. In: Thirty-First AAAI Conference on Artificial Intelligence (2017)
27. Baldassarre, F., Morín, D.G., Rodés-Guirao, L.: Deep koalarization: Image colorization using cnns and inception-resnet-v2 (2017). arXiv:1712.03400
28. Kumar, M., Thenmozhi, M.: Forecasting stock index movement: A comparison of support vector machines and random forest. In: Indian Institute of Capital Markets 9th Capital Markets Conference Paper (2006)
29. Rodriguez-Galiano, V., Sanchez-Castillo, M., Chica-Olmo, M., Chica-Rivas M.: Machine learning predictive models for mineral prospectivity: An evaluation of neural networks, random forest, regression trees and support vector machines. Ore Geol. Rev. **71**, 804–818 (2015)
30. Lameski, P., Zdravevski, E., Mingov, R., Kulakov, A.: Svm parameter tuning with grid search and its impact on reduction of model over-fitting. In: Rough Sets, Fuzzy Sets, Data Mining, and Granular Computing, pp. 464–474. Springer (2015)

Automated Scoring of Metaphase Cell Images and Identification of Dicentric Chromosomes

Muhammad Ubadah[1]($\boxtimes$), Kishore K. Singh[2], Anil Sao[2], Arnav Bhavsar[2], Shuchi Bhagi[3], Amit Alok[3], and N. K. Chaudhury[3]

[1] Electrical Engineering, Indian Institute of Technology Delhi, New Delhi, India
[2] School of Computing and Electrical Engineering, Indian Institute of Technology Mandi, Mandi, India
[3] Division of Radiation Biodosimetry, Institute of Nuclear Medicine and Allied Sciences, Delhi, India

Abstract. The absorbed dose of radiation can be estimated by a dicentric chromosomal assay using blood culture in the Biodosimetry lab. The process requires specialized skills and competency and is time-consuming. In the case of large samples during a radiation emergency, a lab will not be able to handle the radiation-exposed subjects. In this study, we propose a method to identify the dicentric chromosomes in each metaphase image which is based on the intensity profile of the segmented chromosome. Also, we have developed an automated computerized image processing based scheme to rank the metaphase cell images according to their quality based on the inputs from the biodosimetry (accredited) lab of the Institute of Nuclear Medicine and Allied Sciences (INMAS), India. We have evaluated the performance of the system for different ranked images. Experimental results demonstrate that if we use the ranking module with the detection of the dicentric chromosome, the performance of the system improves because the false detection of DC reduces as we use only good quality images.

Keywords: Cytogenetic biodosimetry · Dicentric chromosomes · Intensity profile

1 Introduction

Cytogenetic Biodosimetry is the process of estimating the absorbed dose of radiation by estimating the number of dicentric chromosomes (DCs) per metaphase cell image [1]. This assay is the Gold standard and recommended by the World Health Organization (WHO) and the International Atomic Energy Agency (IAEA) [2]. Until now, the biodosimetry process in the lab is manual and thus

---

This work was supported by grants (Project No: IITM/INMAS-DRDO/ASO/194) from the Institute of Nuclear Medicine and Allied Sciences lab, Defence Research and Development Organization, India.
M. Ubadah and K.K. Singh—The authors have contributed equally to this work.

© Springer Nature Singapore Pte Ltd. 2021
S. K. Singh et al. (Eds.): CVIP 2020, CCIS 1376, pp. 398–406, 2021.
https://doi.org/10.1007/978-981-16-1086-8_35

the process of estimation of DCs in metaphase spreads is very tedious and time-consuming [3]. This method may not be scalable in case of a large-scale disaster such as a nuclear power plant accident [4]. Hence, a fast and robust computerized automated DC detection system needs to be developed.

Figure 1(a) illustrates the normal chromosomes and a dicentric chromosome (DC) in a typical metaphase cell image. A normal chromosome has only one centromere while a DC has two centromeres [1]. In cytogenetic biodosimetry, the goal is to count all 46 or more chromosomes in a given metaphase image and detect DCs as per the scoring criteria of IAEA [2]. However, the detection of DC becomes challenging because chromosomes may be touching or overlapping, or the chromosomes in the cell may not be in the analyzable phase (metaphase) [5] (see Fig. 1(c)). It can be referred to as a non-analyzable metaphase cell image. A scorer avoids non-analyzable metaphase cells for counting of DCs. Thus, before doing any biodosimetry process it is necessary to identify the cells with ana-lyzable chromosomes and only a requisite number of metaphase spreads are necessary for dose estimates and required to be done manually [5].

Figures 1(a) and (c) are two extreme examples of metaphase images in terms of analyzability but some metaphase cell images lie between them (shown in Fig. 1(b)) which can be used by a scorer to conclude in case of insufficient good analyzable metaphase images. Hence, if we can develop a computerized algorithm to rank each cell image according to some characteristics of the chromosomes present in the image, we will be able to select the desired number of images by choosing images up to a particular rank.

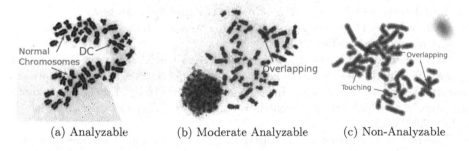

(a) Analyzable   (b) Moderate Analyzable   (c) Non-Analyzable

Fig. 1. Examples of metaphase cell images collected from the biodosimetry laboratory (accredited) of INMAS, India.

Some researchers have attempted to automate the process of classification of metaphase cell images into analyzable and unanalyzable images. For example, in [5] the authors proposed a scheme, based on an artificial neural network (ANN) and decision tree to classify cell images into good and bad metaphase images. Most of the researchers and research groups have attempted to address individual problems in a cell image. For example, Grisan *et al.* [6] compared the results of the segmentation of human chromosomes for different threshold-ing methods while Keerthi *et al.* [7] used the connected component concept for the segmentation of human chromosomes. Shen *et al.* [8] used K-means clustering for segmentation. Also, to segment the chromosome clumps, they combined the K-means clustering algorithm with the watershed algorithm. Monika Sharma *et al.* [9] reported a method to segment out and classify chromosomes for healthy patients using a combination of crowdsourcing, preprocessing and deep learning, wherein the nonexpert crowd from CrowdFlower is utilized to segment out the chromosomes from the cell image, which are then straightened and fed into a (hierarchical) deep neural network for classification. Gajendran *et al.* [10] reported a digital image analysis based approach for counting of the chromosomes present in cell images. To find the centromere in individual chromosomes, Mohammadi *et al.* [11] used concavity degree of chromosome's boundary pixels while to identify the DCs, Wilkins *et al.* [3] developed a Support Vector Machine (SVM) based classifier.

This paper proposes a novel approach to rank the given metaphase images. The objective has been achieved by combining the three criteria (suggested by experts) – (a) separation between arms of chromosomes, (b) the number of chromosomes in a cell, and (c) the number of overlapping chromosomes. The hypothesis is that by selecting the most analyzable metaphase cell images (having a good rank), we can reduce the false detection of DCs and improve the system performance.

Secondly, we also propose a novel approach to detect DCs. In a DC, there are two centromeres and a centromere is the most constricted part of a chromosome. We have used an intensity-based approach to find the DC in which we compute the intensity profile of the segmented chromosome and from it, we differentiate the DC from a normal chromosome. It has to be noted that the proposed approach of detection of DC doesn't require any training data. Moreover, to the best of our knowledge, this is the first work in this area which shows the dependency of ranking on the detection of DCs.

Experimental results in this paper are demonstrated using the image data set provided by the biodosimetry lab (accredited) of INMAS, India. The data set contains 470 metaphase images. In these images, more than 21,000 chromosomes are present of which 90 are dicentric chromosomes. The size of each image is 2048 * 2560 pixels.

The rest of the paper is organized as follows. Section 2 provides the proposed method which includes identification of DCs and ranking of metaphase cell images. Experimental results are reported in Sect. 3. Finally, Sect. 4 presents the conclusion and future work.

2   The Proposed Method

This paper proposes a fully automated image processing based approach to detect the DCs in metaphase cell images with the ranking of metaphase images. It exploits the unique characteristic of DC that it has two centromeres and are observed as two peaks in intensity profile along with the height of chromosomes. This approach does not require any training sample, which is desirable in most of the pattern recognition methods. It has been observed that there are several false detections of DCs, which come mostly from non-analyzable metaphase cell images. Hence, a novel approach is proposed to rank the given metaphase images according to their suitability for further analysis. If we select only good rank metaphase images for the detection of DCs, we will be able to reduce the false detection of DCs, and hence, the system performance will improve. Proposed approaches of DC detection and the ranking of metaphase images are explained in the following subsections.

2.1 Preprocessing of Images

First, a Gaussian filter is applied to the given metaphase image to remove noise. Then Otsu thresholding is used for binarization of metaphase image. The number of background pixels is much higher than the foreground pixels in the given metaphase images. As a result, the threshold value is skewed towards higher intensity background pixels. So, for better segmentation, pixel values higher than a certain intensity have been discarded. We then find all the contours in the binarized image. These contours are then subjected to area parameters to separate potential chromosomes from non-chromosomes (e.g. stain debris). Using the coordinates of the contours, a rectangular box of minimum area enclosing the contour is drawn around it. These rectangles are then cropped out from the original image, brought into their vertical orientation by rotating around their center points, and saved for further analysis.

2.2 Identification of Dicentric Chromosomes

Due to the radiation exposure, chromosomes break and the broken end of one chromosome may join with a broken end of another, resulting in the formation of a dicentric chromosome (DC) [12]. Thus, we need to detect two centromeres in a chromosome for labeling a chromosome as dicentric. A centromere, most constricted region of a chromosome where the sister chromatids (arms) join can be seen in Figs. 2(a) and (c). We have computed the sum of pixel values along the width of the segmented chromosome at all points over the height of it (except an alpha number of points at the bottom and the top) and project it on the XY-plane as shown in Figs. 2(b) and (d). Along with the height of the segmented chromosome image, most of the white pixels are present at the centromere, and thus, we get a peak at the centromere.

In the proposed algorithm, we consider two conditions to label a chromosome as DC. (1) There should be two peaks (maxima) such that the difference between the two peak values is less than the difference between the minimum of these two peak values and the average sum of intensity value. (2) The sum of the intensity value of these two peaks (maxima) should be comparable. Then it is considered as a dicentric chromosome. Figure 2(a) illustrates a typical DC and its sum of intensity profile is shown in Fig. 2(b). On the contrary, a normal chromosome and its intensity profile are depicted in Figs. 2(c) and (d).

It is to be noted that for highly bent chromosomes, this algorithm gives false results but such chromosomes are very less in number especially in analyzable metaphase images.

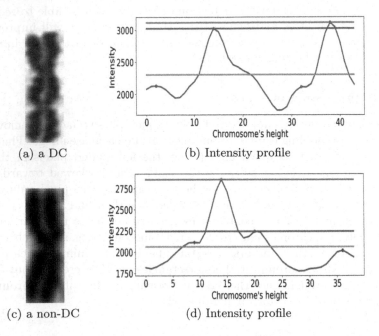

(a) a DC   (b) Intensity profile

(c) a non-DC   (d) Intensity profile

Fig. 2. Detection of DC by analyzing the sum of the intensity profile. In the plots, the orange line, the green line, and the red line represents the average sum of intensities value, the maximum sum of intensities value, and the second maximum sum of intensities value, respectively. The blue curve represents the sum of intensities along the width. (Color figure online)

2.3   Ranking or Scoring of Metaphase Cell Images

The detection of a DC is good if two centromeres of a dicentric chromosome are perceptually visible. But the performance starts degrading if chromosomes are very thin, blurred, or overlapped. This behavior comes due to two reasons, (a) the natural behavior of the cell and (b) error in slide preparation. This issue can be addressed by eliminating the metaphase images which are not suitable for further analysis. It can be achieved by giving a rank to each metaphase image because classifying them into two classes of analyzable and unanalyzable (as performed in literature) can be very strict. Thus, classifying into more classes (ranks) will give the advantage to a scorer to select images up to a particular rank according to the need of images.

We have used the following three criteria after consultation with experts to rank the given metaphase cell images, a) the sister chromatids (arms) of chromosomes in a cell image should be separated, b) the chromosomes should be well separated and overlapped chromosomes are as small as possible and c) the metaphase spread should have 46 chromosomes. These three criteria are explained below.

– **Separation between arms:** In cells of the analyzable metaphase stage, one can see the chromosome's structure, and hence, the separation between arms of chromosomes is visible. Thus, the ranking module uses arm separation as one of the criteria of ranking. Figure 3(b) illustrates the intensity profile of a chromosome with separated arms while Fig. 3(d) shows the intensity profile of a chromosome with unseparated arms. The sum of intensities along the height is projected for each point along the width of the segmented chromosome. Along the width of the image, we find a global maximum (peak). If the value of this global maxima is greater than the average sum of the intensity value, then it is considered that it has separated arms.

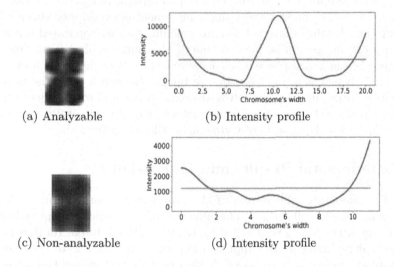

(a) Analyzable   (b) Intensity profile

(c) Non-analyzable   (d) Intensity profile

Fig. 3. Examples of a good and bad chromosome in terms of arm separation. Figures (a) and (c) show the original images of chromosomes while (b) and (d) represent their intensity profile. In the plot, the orange line represents the average sum of intensities whereas the green curve represents the sum of intensities along with the height. (Color figure online)

– **Overlapped chromosomes:** A metaphase cell image is considered as a bad image if it has touching or overlapping chromosomes. The width of a segmented touching or overlapping chromosome is always more than the width of a segmented normal chromosome. Hence, the scheme uses the median width of the chromosomes in an image as the threshold. If the width of a segmented chromosome is more than the median width then it is assumed that it is a touching or overlapping chromosome. As the number of such segments increases in a metaphase image, its analyzability gets reduced.

– **Number of segmented chromosomes:** Ideally, a metaphase cell should have 46 number of chromosomes but due to overlapping or overspreading, the number of chromosomes may be large or less than 46. The total number of segments in a cell image is considered as the number of chromosomes in the image. The scheme increases the assigned score (rank) of a metaphase image as the variation of the number of segmented chromosomes in a metaphase image increases from 46.

We have combined these three criteria to rank a given metaphase image. First of all, we see the number of chromosomes present in a metaphase image. If a metaphase image has 46 number of chromosomes then we assign it as rank1. If the number of chromosomes is 44, 45, 47, or 48, then we assign it as rank2. Similarly, as the variation of the number of chromosomes increases, the rank of the image decreases. Next, we note the number of overlapping chromosomes. Since the number of overlapping chromosomes in each metaphase image is very less. So, we decrease the rank by one for every single increment in overlapped chromosomes. Next, we consider the number of chromosome images with separated arms. After analyzing cell images, it is decided that if the number of chromosomes with separated arms in a metaphase image is more than 50% of the total chromosomes of that cell then it is a good metaphase image. In such a case, the rank does not change. However, for every 10% decrease of such chromosomes, the rank decreases by one. These parameters are determined experimentally and set after consultation with the experts of Cytogenetic Biodosimetry Lab.

3   Experimental Results and Discussion

Figure 4 demonstrates the results of the automated identification of dicentric chromosomes in the cell images. The efficiency of the proposed approach is evaluated using 470 cell images provided by INMAS DRDO, India. Rank is given to each metaphase image by the approach explained in Sect. 2.2. In this study, we classify input images into 10 ranks. A high rank (score) means less analyzable. The performance of the algorithm is demonstrated using the True Positive Rate (TPR) and False Positive Rate (FPR) for each rank and shown in Table 1. Rank 10 denotes that all the metaphase cell images are analyzable and subjected further to detect DC. In this case, TPR is 62.2% and FPR is 2.07% (it should be noted that the FPR is estimated for 21,000 segmented chromosome images). If we select images of only good ranks, then non-analyzable metaphases are discarded. This removes the false detection of DC and hence, FPR improves. For example, TPR becomes 86.6% and FPR reduces to .39% if we select images only up to rank 2 as shown in Table 1. Thus, the experimental results indicate the performance of the DC detection system can be improved by incorporating the ranking module in it.

It has been observed that only very few research papers are available for the research problem addressed in this paper. We have not come across any work in the literature which performs ranking at the coarser level. Besides, the published works have quoted the results using images acquired by themselves and those images are not publicly available. Hence, we have not given any comparison with the existing approaches.

Table 1. Performance of complete system of dicentric chromosome detection (Each cell is having on an average 46 number of chromosomes)

Rank (upto)	No. of cell images	No. of chromosomes	No. of DCs	TPR (%)	FPR (%)
1	24	1104	5	83.7	0.27
2	72	3371	14	86.6	0.39
3	119	5543	17	80.5	0.56
4	148	6891	25	68.7	0.67
5	182	8454	37	67.4	0.86
6	248	11575	62	66.0	1.26
7	279	12979	67	65.4	1.35
8	303	14053	72	64.1	1.42
9	338	15706	82	63.4	1.61
10	470	21949	90	62.2	2.07

(a)   (b)

Fig. 4. Some results of the proposed algorithm to find out the DCs. Colour coded contours are used to classify the chromosomes as either dicentric chromosomes (red) or normal chromosomes (green). (Color figure online)

4   Summary and Future Work

This paper proposed a novel approach to rank given metaphase cell images together with the identification of the dicentric chromosome. The proposed approach used three criteria based on the inputs from the experts to rank given metaphase images. Further, the detection of DC was performed by exploiting the unique characteristic of a DC that it had two centromeres. The experimental results demonstrate that FPR improves if only good rank metaphase images are considered for the detection of DC. In the future study, we wish to optimize and test our system for a large metaphase cell image dataset. Our future work will make a huge corpus of annotated metaphase images and made available in public for improving the performance of the detection of DC.

References

1. Wong, K.F., Siu, L.L., Ainsbury, E., Moquet, J.: Cytogenetic biodosimetry: what it is and how we do it. Hong Kong Med. J. **19**(2), 168–173 (2013)
2. Brewen, J.G., Preston, R.J., Littlefield, L.G.: Radiation-induced human chromosome aberration yields following an accidental whole-body exposure to ^{60}co γ-rays. Radiat. Res. **49**(3), 647–656 (1972)
3. Liu, J., Li, Y., Wilkins, R., Flegal, F., Knoll, J.H.M., Rogan, P.K.: Accurate cytogenetic biodosimetry through automated dicentric chromosome curation and metaphase cell selection. F1000research **6**, 1396 (2017)
4. Sullivan, J.M., et al.: Assessment of biodosimetry methods for a mass-casualty radiological incident: medical response and management considerations. Health Phys. **105**(6), 540–554 (2013)
5. Wang, X., Li, S., Liu, H., Wood, M., Chen, W.R., Zheng, B.: Automated identification of analyzable metaphase chromosomes depicted on microscopic digital images. J. Biomed. Inform. **41**(2), 264–271 (2008)
6. Poletti, E., Zappelli, F., Ruggeri, A., Grisan, E.: A review of thresholding strategies applied to human chromosome segmentation. Comput. Methods Programs Biomed. **108**(2), 679–688 (2012)
7. Keerthi, V., Remya, R.S., Sabeena, K.: Automated detection of centromere in G banded chromosomes. In: International Conference on Information Science (ICIS), pp. 83–86 (2016)
8. Shen, X., Qi, Y., Ma, T., Zhou, Z.: A dicentric chromosome identification method based on clustering and watershed algorithm. Sci. Rep. **9**(1), 1–11 (2019)
9. Sharma, M., Saha, O., Sriraman, A., Hebbalaguppe, R., Vig, L., Karande, S.: Crowdsourcing for chromosome segmentation and deep classification. In: Proceedings of the IEEE Conference on Computer Vision and Pattern Recognition Workshops, pp. 34–41 (2017)
10. Gajendran, V., Rodriguez, J.J.: Chromosome counting via digital image analysis. In: International Conference on Image Processing, ICIP 2004, vol. 5, pp. 2929–2932 (2004). https://doi.org/10.1109/ICIP.2004.1421726
11. Mohammadi, M.R.: Accurate localization of chromosome centromere based on concave points. J. Med. Signals Sens. **2**(2), 88 (2012)
12. Vyas, R.C., Darroudi, F., Natarajan, A.: Radiation-induced chromosomal breakage and rejoining in interphase-metaphase chromosomes of human lymphocytes. Mutat. Res. **249**, 29–35 (1991)

Clustering of Writers and Cluster Dependent Classifier Selection for Offline Signature Verification

H. Annapurna[1]($\boxtimes$), K. S. Manjunatha[2], and D. S. Guru[1]

[1] Department of Studies in Computer Science, University of Mysore, Manasagangothri,
Mysuru 570006, Karnataka, India
dsg@compsci.uni-mysore.ac.in
[2] Maharani's Science College for Women, Mysuru 570001, Karnataka, India

Abstract. Identity establishment on handwritten signature is a promising research area in biometrics. This work is based on an approach for verification of offline signatures through the recommendation of classifiers for each group of likelihood writers. Initially, a single representative sample is created for each writer which exhibits maximum similarity with all other samples of the same writer. Once the representative signatures are created, we cluster them through k-means clustering to find groups of likelihood writers. Further, features most relevant for a writer are selected through computationally simple feature selection criteria which results in selection of suitable features for each writer. A suitable classifier is selected from a pool of classifiers based on the EER estimated with each of the classifier through k-fold cross-validation. We recommend same classifier for all writers of a particular cluster which yields lowest EER for majority of writers in that cluster. The genuineness of the test signature of a writer is established using the set of features and the classifier selected for the cluster for which the claimed writer is a member. The applicability of the proposed approach is validated through extensive experiments on two benchmarking datasets namely MCYT-75 and CEDAR. Comparison of the obtained results is also brought out against several other existing contemporary methods.

Keywords: Offline signature · Representative signature · Clustering of writers · Signature verification

1 Introduction

Establishing person's identity either through physiological traits like fingerprint, face, hand geometry, retina, and iris etc., or by means of behavioral characteristics such as handwritten signature, voice and gait etc., is referred to as biometrics [6]. Handwritten signature is a commonly used behavioral trait for authentication purpose. It has been widely used as identity proof in many of our day-to-day applications. Signatures can be verified through static (offline) or dynamic (online) mode. In an offline mode, signatures are verified using static information obtained from handwritten signatures image. In

© Springer Nature Singapore Pte Ltd. 2021
S. K. Singh et al. (Eds.): CVIP 2020, CCIS 1376, pp. 407–419, 2021.
https://doi.org/10.1007/978-981-16-1086-8_36

case of online mode, verification is done considering majorly dynamic features extracted through the acquisition device [10].

Some of commonly used features in offline signature verification are component oriented such as graphometric features, curvature [2], geometric features [24], stroke thickness [12], directions [25] and pixel oriented features such as texture features [30] and grid-based features [33]. For classification, researchers have adopted many classifiers such as Neural Networks [7, 15], Support Vector Machine [8, 22] and Hidden Markov Model [13]. The literature survey clearly indicates that majority of the existing models are based on the usage of a set of features and a suitable classifier which are common across all signatories. But a human expert uses entirely different strategies for different writers during verification depending on the specific characteristics of the representative signatures. The signature samples of all the writers may not fit the same distribution and also the consistency of writing differs from signer to signer. These two factors demand the application of different classifiers and also distinctive set of features for different writers for effectively verifying the signatures. Further, instead of training a separate classifier for each writer, we cluster the writers with similar characteristics and all writers within a cluster are trained with common classifier.

The paper is organized into five sections. The architecture of the proposed model is discussed in Sect. 2. Experimentation details, datasets used and results obtained is presented in section. In Sect. 4, the performance of our model is compared against the state-of-the-art models. Conclusions are inferred in Sect. 5.

2 Proposed System

Following are the major steps in our model:

1. Preprocessing
2. Extraction of features
3. Representative signatures selection
4. Clustering based on representative signatures
5. Selection of writer-specific features and classifiers
6. Selection of cluster dependent classifier
7. Signature verification

The block diagram of the proposed approach is shown in Fig. 1.

2.1 Preprocessing

Preprocessing is necessary to improve the quality of signature images. In this step, the input images are binarized using Otsu's method [21]. After binarization, the images are resized to 192×192. To remove the noise from the resized images, a 3×3 median filter [31] is applied. The two morphological operations named as closing and thinning are performed on filtered images. The preprocessed images are used for feature extraction.

2.2 Extraction of Features

Extraction of features is a key step in offline signature verification system because features of offline signature image depending on the psychophysical state of the signer and conditions under which the signature acquisition process takes place [6]. In this approach, global and grid features are considered. Global features provide characteristics of entire signature image, whereas grid features give structural information of particular parts of the signature image [24]. In the proposed work, 25 global features are extracted namely, signature area [26], perimeter of the signature, outline signature area, normalized area, convex area, filled area, total number of background pixels, length of minor axis, length of major axis, major plus minor axis length, center feature, horizontal center of the signature, vertical center of the signature [26], maximum horizontal projection plus maximum vertical projection, number of end points, diameter, equi-diameter, radii, global centroid, baseline shift [24], mean of row vector and variance of row vector [18], homogeneity, energy and correlation [30]. In order to extract the structural information of the signature image, nine different 3 × 3 grids are super imposed on an input signature image which allows the division of the signature into identical sectors. From each sector we have extracted statistical features such as standard deviation, skewness, variance, contrast and homogeneity. Totally, 70 features are extracted from each input image.

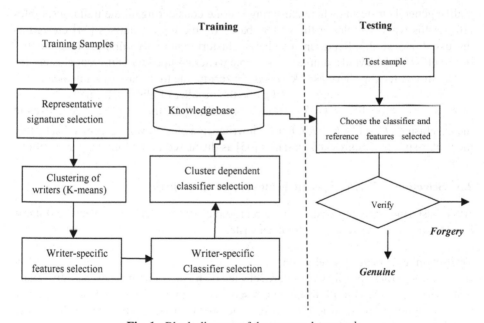

Fig. 1. Block diagram of the proposed approach

2.3 Representative Signatures Selection

Given set of training samples, we select unique representative signature for each writer from the available training samples [34]. The representative sample selected will exhibit the maximum similarity with the rest of the signatures. The reason being when all the samples of a writer are considered for clustering may not go to the same cluster. In such situation, it is difficult to fix up the classifier for the respective writer. This can be avoided through clustering based on representatives. For instance, the representative R_{W_i} for i^{th} writer $W_i (1 \leq i \leq N)$, N being the total number writers is selected as follows. Let $\{S_1^i, S_2^i, S_3^i, \ldots\ldots, S_n^i\}$ be the set of n training samples considered for training the writer W_i. The representative for W_i is selected by estimating the pair-wise distance between the training signatures of W_i and finally, selecting the training sample with minimum average distance to the rest of the signatures as the representative of W_i. The representative selected serves as a centroid among training samples of the respective writer. Similarly, the representative for every writer is selected in the manner discussed above. Let $\{R_{W_1}, R_{W_2}, R_{W_3}, \ldots\ldots, R_{W_N}\}$ denotes the set of representatives created for individual writers.

2.4 Clustering Based on Representative Signatures

Unlike general clustering where clustering is done considering all the training samples [10] in this work, we cluster the writers based on the representatives [34] created as discussed in Sect. 2.3. Representative based clustering not only minimizes the number of samples but also avoids samples of the same writer grouped into different clusters. To cluster the writers, we have used k-means clustering due to its ease of implementation. Let $CL = \{CL_1, CL_2, CL_3, \ldots\ldots, CL_K\}$ be the number of clusters formed. The value of K is set empirically. $\{R_{W_1}, R_{W_2}, R_{W_3}, \ldots\ldots, R_{W_S}\}$ be the set of representatives in the kth cluster CL_k, $(1 \leq k \leq K)$. For each writer in a cluster, we recommend selecting the writer-specific features and classifier [35] as discussed in the following subsection.

2.5 Selection of Writer-Specific Features and Classifiers

After clustering all writers based on their representative signatures, we select the suitable features and a suitable classifier for each writer.

Writer-Specific Features Selection

In this work, writer-specific features are selected by means of a filter-based multi-cluster feature selection (MCFS) [4] technique. A score is computed for every feature based on its contribution in preserving the cluster structure of the respective writer. The score denotes the relevancy of a feature. We sort the selected features based on its relevancy. The top d ranked features selected for the ith writer $W_i (1 \leq i \leq N)$ is denoted as $\{f_1^i, f_2^i, f_3^i, \ldots\ldots, f_d^i\}$. Here, for every writer the features indices which have been selected vary from one writer to another. In the knowledgebase, indices of writer-specific features of each writer are stored for use during verification.

Selection of Writer-Dependent Classifier

In this section, we discuss the methodology adopted for fixing the classifier suitable for a particular writer [35]. We estimate the EER (Equal Error Rate) obtained with each of the classifier through the application of k-fold cross-validation (here the value of k is 3). For instance, $\left\{ EER^i_{C_1}, EER^i_{C_2}, EER^i_{C_3}, \ldots\ldots, EER^i_{C_t} \right\}$ be the EER obtained for the ith writer W_i from the each of classifier $C_t (1 \leq t \leq M)$, M denotes the number of classifiers used. The classifier with least EER is selected as the appropriate classifier for writer W_i. Finally, out of m number of trials the classifier which yields lowest EER in maximum trials is fixed as the writer-dependent classifier for writer W_i. In a similar way, we fix up a classifier for all writers. The classifier selected for each the writer is preserved in the knowledgebase along with the indices of features selected and cluster index.

2.6 Selection of Cluster Dependent Classifier

Once the classifier for every writer is selected as discussed in Sect. 2.5, the classifier for a particular cluster $C_k (1 \leq k \leq K)$ is decided based on the majority voting. That means the classifier which yields least EER for highest number of writers in a cluster is recommended to be the classifier for all writers of that cluster. For instance, $\left\{ C_1^1, C_2^2, C_3^3, \ldots\ldots, C_M^K \right\}$ denotes the list of classifier chosen for each of the cluster where K indicates the number of clusters and M represents the number of classifiers.

2.7 Signature Verification

In this step, we discuss the methodology adopted for deciding whether the given test signature is genuine or forgery. When a test signature is to be tested, first the label of cluster to which the test signature belongs is identified. After identifying the cluster label, the classifier and feature which have been selected for that writer is identified and retrieved from the knowledgebase. Then test signature is given to the cluster dependent classifier with the writer specific features. Finally, the genuineness of the test signature is determined.

3   Experimentation Details and Results

Here, we discuss details of datasets used to validate our model and the obtained results.

Database: We have used two different standard bench marking datasets namely, CEDAR [14] and MCYT-75 [20] for experimentation. CEDAR contains signatures of 55 users with 24 samples of original signature and 24 skilled forgery signatures from each writer. Thus, it consists of 2640 signatures (1320 original and 1320 skilled forgeries). MCYT-75 consists of signatures of 75 users with 15 original signature samples and 15 skilled forgeries per user. Thus it consists of 2250 signatures (1125 original and 1125 skilled forgery samples).

Experimental Setup: The system is trained with 30%, 40%, 50%, 60% and 70% of genuine signatures of each writer. 50% of training samples and the equal number of random forgeries are considered to decide the cluster dependent classifier for each cluster. Remaining genuine and all forgeries samples of each writer are used for testing. The experimentations are repeated for 10 times. Signatures for training purpose are randomly chosen in different trials. In this work, the most commonly used classifiers [34, 35] in signature verification systems are considered namely, Naïve Bayesian (NB), Linear Discriminant Analysis (LDA), Nearest Neighbor (NN), Principal Component Analysis (PCA), Probabilistic Neural Network (PNN) and Support Vector Machine (SVM). We have used the symbols to represent these classifiers as C_1, C_2, C_3, C_4, C_5 and C_6 respectively.

Experimental Results: Here, the experimentation is conducted by varying number of clusters from 2 to 10. For each cluster selected features are also varied from 5 to 50 in steps of 5. In Table 1 and Table 2, the lowest EER obtained for varying number of clusters on CEDAR and MCYT datasets shown respectively.

Table 1. Minimum EER obtained with writer-specific features and cluster dependent classifiers on CEDAR dataset

No. of clusters	No. of signature samples for training									
	S_07	S_10	S_12	S_14	S_17	R_07	R_10	R_12	R_14	R_17
2	7.66	6.91	6.29	5.78	5.58	6.12	4.09	3.50	3.12	2.84
3	7.66	7.36	5.91	5.52	5.45	7.49	5.88	4.77	3.55	2.79
4	7.82	7.14	6.52	6.36	5.52	6.36	4.51	3.77	3.31	2.73
5	8.13	7.40	7.05	6.69	6.64	4.92	4.28	3.38	3.09	2.21
6	9.09	7.66	6.89	6.00	5.71	4.55	3.56	3.38	3.31	3.09
7	7.50	7.10	7.01	6.64	6.10	5.78	4.45	4.39	3.96	3.27
8	8.24	7.42	7.09	6.82	6.49	4.97	4.47	3.96	3.82	2.92
9	7.40	7.14	6.74	6.29	5.73	5.21	4.16	3.32	3.25	2.61
10	7.73	7.43	7.34	6.75	5.91	4.68	4.05	3.86	3.57	3.25
Min	7.40	6.91	5.91	5.52	5.45	4.55	3.56	3.32	3.09	2.21

As a curiosity, we further conducted experimentation by selecting writer-specific features and using a same classifier for all writers. The minimum EER obtained is presented in Table 3 and Table 4 respectively. In Tables 1, 2, 3 and Table 4, S and R denote skilled forgeries and random forgeries respectively.

Table 2. Minimum EER obtained with writer-specific features and cluster dependent classifiers on MCYT dataset

No. of clusters	No. of signature samples for training									
	S_05	S_06	S_08	S_09	S_10	R_05	R_06	R_08	R_09	R_10
2	22.40	17.33	15.00	13.71	13.33	8.07	7.60	6.78	4.67	4.75
3	22.53	16.33	15.56	14.86	10.67	8.74	7.83	7.28	5.00	4.90
4	23.00	16.00	15.26	14.29	11.67	10.28	8.40	6.57	6.50	6.26
5	20.93	15.11	14.67	14.67	11.00	8.80	5.24	4.83	5.00	5.00
6	21.00	17.00	15.48	14.48	12.00	8.81	8.10	7.67	6.48	6.06
7	23.27	15.56	14.76	14.33	12.33	9.00	8.00	7.50	7.42	5.43
8	22.53	16.96	15.81	15.00	13.83	8.80	7.57	6.15	5.58	4.78
9	22.00	15.67	14.74	14.38	12.17	6.27	6.00	5.62	5.44	4.33
10	20.27	18.67	17.33	14.67	12.17	8.07	7.57	5.42	5.00	4.76
Min	20.27	15.11	14.67	13.71	10.67	6.27	5.24	4.83	4.67	4.33

Table 3. Minimum EER achieved with writer-dependent features and the usage of common classifiers on CEDAR dataset

Classifier label	No. of signature samples for training									
	S_07	S_10	S_12	S_14	S_17	R_07	R_10	R_12	R_14	R_17
C1	8.34	8.12	7.88	7.73	7.10	6.30	5.68	5.19	4.63	4.58
C2	9.35	8.09	7.04	6.68	6.36	8.59	8.07	7.63	6.95	4.81
C3	12.86	12.60	11.95	11.55	11.14	9.22	9.16	7.69	7.59	6.30
C4	14.22	13.51	12.55	12.27	11.95	9.44	9.00	8.73	8.26	6.30
C5	5.88	13.64	13.03	12.79	12.73	13.16	12.23	11.14	10.62	9.09
C6	7.98	7.65	6.74	6.55	6.09	5.19	4.20	4.12	3.68	2.60
Min	7.98	7.65	6.74	6.55	6.09	5.19	4.20	4.12	3.68	2.60

From Tables 1, 2, 3 and 4, it can be observed that EER achieved with the classifier specific to a cluster is lower than the EER obtained when a common classifier is used. The Fig. 2 and Fig. 3 clearly shows the effectiveness of the cluster specific classifier (Table 5).

Table 4. Minimum EER achieved with writer-dependent features and the usage of common classifiers on MCYT dataset

Classifier label	No. of signature samples for training									
	S_05	S_06	S_08	S_09	S_10	R_05	R_06	R_08	R_09	R_10
C1	26.47	16.81	16.11	15.71	12.67	10.57	9.30	7.67	7.17	5.96
C2	21.60	17.19	17.00	15.17	14.67	8.17	7.13	6.28	5.48	4.42
C3	31.40	29.04	22.57	20.78	19.83	12.27	11.05	9.59	8.72	7.83
C4	31.67	25.63	23.67	22.86	18.50	13.77	9.48	9.43	7.56	7.25
C5	45.33	35.93	27.52	26.33	20.67	23.07	20.87	15.19	13.25	9.28
C6	20.80	15.33	15.24	15.11	11.83	7.13	6.20	5.22	4.90	4.42
Min	20.80	15.33	15.24	15.11	11.83	7.13	6.20	5.22	4.90	4.42

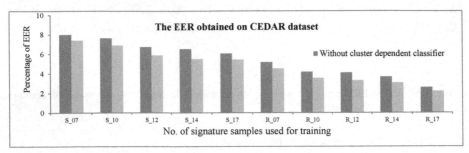

Fig. 2. Minimum EER obtained with the usage of common classifiers and cluster dependent classifiers on CEDAR dataset

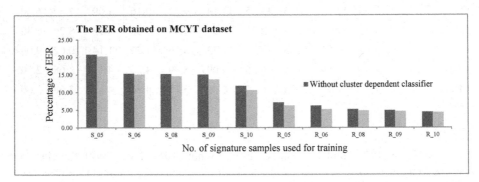

Fig. 3. Minimum EER obtained with the usage of common classifiers and cluster dependent classifiers on MCYT dataset

Table 5. The indices of top 5 writer specific features and writer-dependent classifier selected for the first 10 users of CEDAR dataset in different clusters

Writer_Id	Indices of top 5 writer specific features					Cluster_Id	Selected classifier label
1	46	40	26	60	15	2	5
2	5	3	36	6	11	3	3
3	40	15	3	18	6	6	1
4	60	6	19	31	3	7	1
5	2	19	10	15	26	4	3
6	2	6	60	11	4	6	3
7	6	5	15	36	46	2	6
8	2	60	11	3	26	2	3
9	5	11	19	46	36	2	2
10	40	46	57	26	15	4	1

4 Comparative Study

In this section, the performance of our model is compared with other state-of-the-art works on CEDAR and MCYT-75 separately in Table 6 and Table 7 and the last rows indicate the EER of our model, while the figure within the parenthesis denotes the feature dimension at which the obtained EER is the lowest.

From Table 6, it is observed that EER of the proposed approach is lower than EER of the various offline signature models on CEDAR dataset [5, 8, 14–17] and [3] even though EER obtained is higher when compared to [9, 27, 28] and [33]. The models [9, 27, 28] and [33] works in higher dimension while our model is based on selecting features specific to individual writers. During verification we consider only those features which are specific for the claimed writer which results in minimized testing time. In addition, the models [9, 16] and [28] are based on convolutional neural networks and genetic algorithm respectively where we need to tune number of parameters to train the model which is quite a difficult task which is not there in our model.

Even in Table 7, the models which have reported lower EER compare to ours works in much higher feature dimension.

Further, alternative ways of clustering can be explored for further reduction of EER which is our future target. Further, as we select features specific to writer, our model work in lower dimension compare to other works reported in Table 6 and Table 7 and hence results in reduction of computational burden during testing.

When compared other writer dependent model, where the number of classifier to be trained depends on the number of writer, in our model it depends on the number of cluster formed. This after reduces the number of classifier to be trained.

Table 6. EER of the different methods on CEDAR dataset

Method reference #	No. of signature samples for training	EER
[14]	24	21.90
[15]	24	8.33
[5]	16	7.90
[17]	14	7.66
[16]	10	5.91
[8]	12	5.60
[3]	12	5.50
[9]	12	4.63
[28]	12	4.17
[27]	16	3.54
[33]	10	2.74
Proposed	**17**	**5.45**(35)

Table 7. EER of the different methods on MCYT dataset

Method reference #	No. of signature samples for training	EER
[23]	05	26.31
[1]	10	20.00
[32]	05	15.02
[19]	10	9.87
[29]	10	9.86
[3]	10	9.26
[30]	10	7.08
[28]	10	5.96
[33]	10	3.45
Proposed	10	**10.67**(40)

5 Conclusions

A model is designed for an offline signature verification exploiting cluster dependent characteristics. To reduce the number of classifiers to be trained, clustering is done considering representative of each writer. Authentication of test signature is done through the usage of features and classifier specific to a writer.

To demonstrate the effectiveness of the recommended model, we accomplished extensive experiments on CEDAR and MCYT datasets. The result achieved indicates the effectiveness of the proposed methodology.

References

1. Alonso-Fernandez, F., Fairhurst, M.C., Fierrez, J., Ortega-Garcia, J.: Automatic measures for predicting performance in off-line signature. In: 2007 IEEE International Conference on Image Processing, vol. 1, pp. I-369. IEEE (2007)
2. Bertolini, D., Oliveira, L.S., Justino, E., Sabourin, R.: Reducing forgeries in writer-independent off-line signature verification through ensemble of classifiers. Pattern Recogn. **43**(1), 387–396 (2010)
3. Bhunia, A.K., Alaei, A., Roy, P.P.: Signature verification approach using fusion of hybrid texture features. Neural Comput. Appl. **31**(12), 8737–8748 (2019)
4. Cai, D., Zhang, C., He, X.: Unsupervised feature selection for multi-cluster data. In: Proceedings of the 16th ACM SIGKDD International Conference on Knowledge Discovery and Data Mining, pp. 333–342 (2010)
5. Chen, S., Srihari, S.: A new off-line signature verification method based on graph. In: 18th International Conference on Pattern Recognition (ICPR'06), vol. 2, pp. 869–872. IEEE (2006)
6. Diaz, M., Ferrer, M.A., Impedovo, D., Malik, M.I., Pirlo, G., Plamondon, R.: A perspective analysis of handwritten signature technology. ACM Comput. Surv. (CSUR) **51**(6), 1–39 (2019)
7. Drouhard, J.P., Sabourin, R., Godbout, M.: A neural network approach to off-line signature verification using directional PDF. Pattern Recogn. **29**(3), 415–424 (1996)
8. Guerbai, Y., Chibani, Y., Hadjadji, B.: The effective use of the one-class SVM classifier for handwritten signature verification based on writer-independent parameters. Pattern Recogn. **48**(1), 103–113 (2015)
9. Hafemann, L.G., Sabourin, R., Oliveira, L.S.: Learning features for offline handwritten signature verification using deep convolutional neural networks. Pattern Recogn. **70**, 163–176 (2017)
10. Jain, A.K., Griess, F.D., Connell, S.D.: On-line signature verification. Pattern Recogn. **35**(12), 2963–2972 (2002)
11. Jain, A.K.: Data clustering: 50 years beyond K-means. Pattern Recogn. Lett. **31**(8), 651–666 (2010)
12. Ji, J.W., Chen, C.B., Chen, X.S.: Off-line Chinese signature verification: using weighting factor on similarity computation. In 2010 2nd International Conference on E-business and Information System Security, pp. 1–4. IEEE (2010)
13. Justino, E.J., El Yacoubi, A., Bortolozzi, F., Sabourin, R.: An off-line signature verification system using hidden markov model and cross-validation. In Proceedings 13th Brazilian Symposium on Computer Graphics and Image Processing (Cat. No. PR00878), pp. 105–112. IEEE (2000)
14. Kalera, M.K., Srihari, S., Xu, A.: Offline signature verification and identification using distance statistics. Int. J. Pattern Recogn. Artif. Intell. **18**(07), 1339–1360 (2004)

15. Kumar, R., Sharma, J.D., Chanda, B.: Writer-independent off-line signature verification using surroundedness feature. Pattern Recogn. Lett. **33**(3), 301–308 (2012)
16. Maergner, P., Pondenkandath, V., Alberti, M., Liwicki, M., Riesen, K., Ingold, R., Fischer, A.: Combining graph edit distance and triplet networks for offline signature verification. Pattern Recogn. Lett. **125**, 527–533 (2019)
17. Manjunatha, K.S., Guru, D.S., Annapurna, H.: Interval-valued writer-dependent global features for off-line signature verification. In: International Conference on Mining Intelligence and Knowledge Exploration, pp. 133–143. Springer, Cham (2017)
18. Mhatre, P.M., Maniroja, M.: Offline signature verification based on statistical features. In: Proceedings of the International Conference and Workshop on Emerging Trends in Technology, pp. 59–62 (2011)
19. Ooi, S.Y., Teoh, A.B.J., Pang, Y.H., Hiew, B.Y.: Image-based handwritten signature verification using hybrid methods of discrete Radon transform, principal component analysis and probabilistic neural network. Appl. Soft Comput. **40**, 274–282 (2016)
20. Ortega-Garcia, J., Fierrez-Aguilar, J., Simon, D., Gonzalez, J., Faundez-Zanuy, M., Espinosa, V., Escudero, D.: MCYT baseline corpus: a bimodal biometric database. IEE Proc.-Vis. Image Signal Process. **150**(6), 395–401 (2003)
21. Otsu, N.: A threshold selection method from gray-level histograms. IEEE Trans. Syst. Man Cybern. **9**(1), 62–66 (1979)
22. Pal, S., Pal, U., Blumenstein, M.: Hindi and English off-line signature identification and verification. In: Proceedings of International Conference on Advances in Computing, pp. 905–910. Springer, New Delhi (2013)
23. Prakash, H.N., Guru, D.S.: Relative orientations of geometric centroids for off-line signature verification. In: 2009 Seventh International Conference on Advances in Pattern Recognition, pp. 201–204. IEEE (2009)
24. Qi, Y., Hunt, B.R.: Signature verification using global and grid features. Pattern Recogn. **27**(12), 1621–1629 (1994)
25. Rivard, D., Granger, E., Sabourin, R.: Multi-feature extraction and selection in writer-independent off-line signature verification. Int. J. Doc. Anal. Recogn. **16**(1), 83–103 (2013)
26. Saikia, H., Sarma, K.C.: Approaches and issues in offline signature verification system. Int. J. Comput. Appl. **42**(16), 45–52 (2012)
27. Serdouk, Y., Nemmour, H., Chibani, Y.: Handwritten signature verification using the quad-tree histogram of templates and a Support Vector-based artificial immune classification. Image Vision Comput. **66**, 26–35 (2017)
28. Sharif, M., Khan, M.A., Faisal, M., Yasmin, M., Fernandes, S.L.: A framework for offline signature verification system: best features selection approach. Pattern Recogn. Lett. **18**(11), 3872 (2018)
29. Soleimani, A., Araabi, B.N., Fouladi, K.: Deep multitask metric learning for offline signature verification. Pattern Recogn. Lett. **80**, 84–90 (2016)
30. Vargas, J.F., Ferrer, M.A., Travieso, C.M., Alonso, J.B.: Off-line signature verification based on grey level information using texture features. Pattern Recogn. **44**(2), 375–385 (2011)
31. Wang, Z., Zhang, D.: Progressive switching median filter for the removal of impulse noise from highly corrupted images. IEEE Trans. Circuits Syst. II: Analog Digital Signal Process. **46**(1), 78–80 (1999)
32. Wen, J., Fang, B., Tang, Y.Y., Zhang, T.: Model-based signature verification with rotation invariant features. Pattern Recogn. **42**(7), 1458–1466 (2009)
33. Zois, E.N., Alewijnse, L., Economou, G.: Offline signature verification and quality characterization using poset-oriented grid features. Pattern Recogn. **54**, 162–177 (2016)

34. Manjunath, S., Manjunatha, K.S., Guru, D.S., Somashekara, M.T.: Cluster dependent classifiers for online signature verification. In: International Conference on Mining Intelligence and Knowledge Exploration, pp. 58–69. Springer, Cham (2015)
35. Manjunatha, K.S., Annapurna, H., Guru, D.S.: Offline signature verification: An approach based on user-dependent features and classifiers. In: Data analytics and learning, pp. 235–243. Springer, Singapore (2019)

Evaluation of Auto-encoder Network with Photoacoustic Signal for Unsupervised Classification of Prostate Cancer

Megha Patil[1], Saugata Sinha[1(✉)], Nikhil Dhengre[1], Bhargava Chinni[2], Vikram Dogra[2], and Navalgund Rao[2]

[1] Department of Electronics and Communication Engineering, Visvesvaraya National Institute of Technology, Nagpur, India
saugata.sinha@ece.vnit.ac.in
[2] Department of Imaging Science, University of Rochester Medical Center, Rochester, USA
{bhargava_chinni,vikram_dogra}@urmc.rochester.edu,
rao@cis.rit.edu

Abstract. Photoacoustic imaging can potentially be used for early detection of prostate cancer. Photoacoustic imaging, which is a hybrid of pure optical and ultrasound imaging technique can potentially detect malignant lesions at early stage. In this study, unsupervised classification was performed with photoacoustic data, generated by freshly excised prostate specimens from actual human patients. An auto-encoder network, specifically tuned for clustering, was employed for unsupervised classification of malignant and nonmalignant prostate tissue. The performance of the auto-encoder algorithm was compared with that of K-means with original as well as compressed photoacoustic data. The preliminary results show that it is possible to perform unsupervised classification with moderate accuracy for prostate cancer detection using photoacoustic imaging. The performance of this network was compared with various implementations of K-means algorithm. While the specifically tuned auto-encoder provided the maximum accuracy and sensitivity, K-means with auto-encoder code space representation of photoacoustic data provided the maximum specificity.

Keywords: Photoacoustic imaging · Prostate cancer detection · Unsupervised classification · Auto-encoder · K-means

1 Introduction

In India, prostate cancer is among the ten major leading cancers [1]. In some of the top metropolitan cities in India, prostate cancer is the second largest cancer type among males [2]. For American males, it has been estimated that every one in nine persons will be affected by prostate cancer in his lifetime [3]. Timely detection of prostate cancer at early stage improves the survival rate of the patients [4]. Typical screening protocol for prostate cancer detection involves looking for abnormalities in prostate specific antigen (PSA) levels and/or digital rectal examination (DRE). If abnormalities are found in

© Springer Nature Singapore Pte Ltd. 2021
S. K. Singh et al. (Eds.): CVIP 2020, CCIS 1376, pp. 420–429, 2021.
https://doi.org/10.1007/978-981-16-1086-8_37

these tests, the patient is referred for the transrectal ultrasound (TRUS) guided biopsy procedure, which is the gold standard for prostate cancer detection.

However, TRUS guided biopsy procedure may not always provide the accurate information due to low sensitivity of ultrasound imaging for detecting malignant prostate lesions [5]. Several ultrasound based imaging techniques have been tried by researchers to improve the accuracy of prostate cancer detection.

Photoacoustic (PA) imaging, which is a hybrid of pure optical and ultrasound imaging technique can potentially detect malignant lesions at early stage. PA imaging is based on photoacoustic effect. In photoacoustic effect, nanosecond duration pulsed laser beam falls on the light absorbing material. At the sites of light absorption, additional pressure is created and released in the form of high frequency ultrasound waves [6]. These high frequency ultrasound waves are known as PA waves. Different PA images are formed using PA waves captured by ultrasound detectors. These PA images provide the functional information of tissue in terms of spatially varying optical absorption coefficient. As PA imaging is a hybrid imaging, it preserves the advantages of both purely optical as well as ultrasound imaging while it does not suffer from some of their limitations. Due to excessive scattering of light, pure optical imaging provides poor resolution at a significant depth inside soft tissue. The resolution of PA imaging inside soft tissue is better than that of pure optical imaging [6, 7]. Pure ultrasound imaging provides mechanical property based contrast which is inadequate for soft tissue characterization. On the other hand, PA imaging provides optical property based contrast which can potentially be used for soft tissue characterization [6, 7]. PA images acquired at multiple wavelengths can produce functional information in terms of spatially varying chromophores i.e. light absorbing tissue constituents inside soft tissue. This functional information can be used further for efficient detection of different pathologies like cancer. In multi-wavelength PA imaging, the different wavelengths are selected such that each wavelength matches with the absorption peak of a particular chromophore. In this study, photoacoustic data captured at five different wavelengths were analyzed for prostate cancer detection. These PA data were generated by freshly excised prostate tissue specimens of actual human patients.

Human experts such as radiologists perform medical image interpretation in the clinic. However, the potential fatigue of human experts and the wide variations in pathology may become an obstacle in efficient image interpretation [8]. Recent advances in deep learning overcome this obstacle by exploiting hierarchical feature representations learned from data instead of using hand-picked features [8]. Deep learning techniques can therefore be used for identification, quantification and classification of patterns in medical images. Deep models such as auto-encoders, deep belief networks and convolutional neural networks can be used for applications like image registration, lesion segmentation, computer-aided diagnosis and unsupervised classification in medical imaging.

Unsupervised classification or clustering is the task of finding similarities in the data and grouping similar data together. The performance of clustering algorithms depend on factors such as the type and separation of the input data. The techniques like dimension reduction or representation learning can be used for clustering. Many researchers have implemented unsupervised classification using various deep learning models such as auto-encoder and its variations.

Shin et al. implemented a single-layer sparse auto-encoder with visual and temporal features learned for unsupervised organ identification using Dynamic contrast-enhanced magnetic resonance imaging (DCE-MRI) data [9]. In [10], a model for Alzheimer's disease (AD) or Mild Cognitive Impairment (MCI) classification was proposed which combined original features of the data and latent feature representation of a stacked auto-encoder. In [11], Cheng et al. proposed computer-aided diagnosis based on stacked denoising auto-encoder for unsupervised classification of lung CT nodules and breast ultrasound lesions. Wang et al. employed a stacked denoising auto-encoder for classification of breast lesions by analyzing microcalcifications with or without masses [12]. In [13], the detection of Alzheimer's disease was done using sparse auto-encoder with soft-max output layer. Kim et al. combined the sparse denoising auto-encoder with support vector machine (SVM) for unsupervised classification of pulmonary nodules in lung CT [14]. In [15], Sevakula et al. implemented a stacked sparse auto-encoder along with feature selection and normalization techniques for molecular cancer classification. Qiu et al. proposed an algorithm for EEG classification and analysis of nonstationary epileptic EEG signals using denoising sparse auto-encoder and logistic regression classifier [16]. Wen et al. implemented a model for unsupervised feature learning and classification of EEG in epilepsy by combining deep convolution network and auto-encoder network using common classifiers like K-means, support vector machine and others [17].

Song et al. used auto-encoder network for clustering and compared it with existing clustering algorithms using standard datasets [18]. In this study, we implemented a clustering model based on an auto-encoder network for prostate cancer detection with photoacoustic data and compared its performance with different implementations of K-means algorithm.

2 Methodology

PA data were acquired from freshly excised human prostate tissue specimens at five different wavelengths as a part of a detailed multi-wavelength PA imaging study in our laboratory. This study was performed on 30 patients. In the acquired 3D PA dataset, the region of interests (ROI), corresponding to different tissue pathologies were selected using digital images of histology slides, marked by a genitourinary pathologist. A total of 53 different ROIs were identified. Out of these 53 ROIs, 19 ROIs were generated by malignant prostate tissue, 8 ROIs were generated by benign prostatic hyperplasia (BPH) and remaining 26 ROIs were generated by the normal prostate. Our earlier reports provide all details about PA imaging system, imaging protocol and different wavelengths used [19–21]. This report contains the results of analysis performed on PA data acquired at 850 nm wavelength. Figure 1A shows a freshly excised prostate tissue sample. Figure 1B shows the C-scan photoacoustic image formed using PA data acquired at 850 nm wavelength. The ROIs corresponding to malignant and normal prostate region for the prostate specimen are shown in Fig. 1B by blue and white circles respectively. Figure 1C shows the A line PA signal corresponding to a particular pixel in the malignant region in Fig. 1B.

A total of 807 data vectors were generated from the 53 ROIs identified from the PA data. Among these, 398 data vectors belonged to malignant ROIs, 133 belonged to BPH ROIs and 276 belonged to normal ROIs. For our problem, the data vectors were

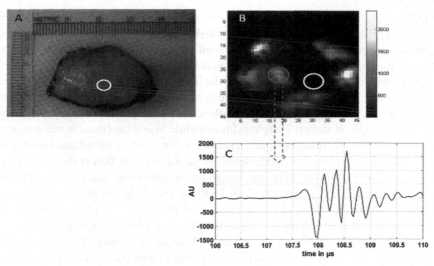

Fig. 1. A. Freshly excised prostate tissue specimen. B. C-scan photoacoustic image at 850 nm wavelength. C. A line photoacoustic signal generated by tissue corresponding to the marked pixel in 1B. In figure B, blue and white circles denote the photoacoustic image pixels corresponding to malignant and normal prostate region respectively. (Color figure online)

classified into malignant class and nonmalignant class. The data vectors corresponding to BPH and normal ROIs were combined to form the nonmalignant class.

We performed unsupervised classification with this dataset using four different algorithms. These algorithms are auto-encoder, standard K-means algorithm, K-means with code space output of auto-encoder and K-means with data projected onto principal components.

2.1 Clustering Using Auto-encoder

The auto-encoder network consists of two parts – encoder and decoder. The encoder maps an input to its latent space representation and the decoder reconstructs the input from this representation. The latent space representation is the code space mapping from the original data.

Our first clustering model is based on a three-layer auto-encoder network. The number of neurons in the input layer is 105. The three hidden layers have 29 neurons, 11 neurons and 29 neurons respectively. Figure 1 shows the auto-encoder structure used for our algorithm implementation. The cancer database used for evaluation of our algorithm contains 802 observations each having 105 features. The database comprises of two categories – malignant class with 398 observations and nonmalignant class with 404 observations. The algorithm is implemented in Python v3.5 using tensorflow library.

The algorithm minimizes the objective function which is given in Eq. 1.

$$\min_{W,b}\left[\left\{\frac{1}{N}\left(\sum_{a=1}^{N}\left\|x_a - x'_a\right\|^2\right)\right\} + \lambda\sum_{a=1}^{N}\left\|y_a - c\right\|^2\right] \qquad (1)$$

In Eq. 1, x_a represents input data vector, x_a' is the corresponding decoder output vector, y_a is the activation output vector of the last encoding layer, c is the cluster center for x_a input data vector and N is the total number of observations. The parameter λ assigns weight to the second term. The first term in the objective function is the L_2 norm between the reconstructed output and the input. The second term gives the distance between the data and their corresponding cluster centers in the code space. This objective function ensures that the proximity between the code layer representation of data and their corresponding cluster centers is high and meanwhile also minimizes the reconstruction error. In this network, features from each data vector were extracted and then used to calculate the distance between the cluster center and data point. Before the first iteration, the weight matrix of the network was initialised and the code space representation of all the data points were computed. Each of these coded data points were distributed randomly into two clusters. The total number of data-points were evenly distributed among the two clusters. The mean of all coded data points belonging to a specific cluster was computed and used as the cluster center for that specific cluster. After each iteration, the distance between each coded data point and the two cluster centers was computed. The data points were reassigned to the clusters based on their proximity to the cluster centers. Once all the data points were rearranged, the new cluster centers were calculated. This whole process was repeated for all the iterations. The network was executed using batch method. The whole dataset was considered as one batch and the weights and biases were updated after every iteration. The activation of each hidden unit was hyperbolic tangent function. The learning rate for the network was 0.05 while the parameter λ was set as 0.1.

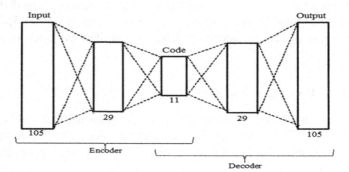

Fig. 2. Auto-encoder structure

2.2 Standard K-means Algorithm

Unsupervised classification was performed using standard K-means algorithm with value of K = 2. The iterative rearrangements of the data points were done following the same procedure as adopted in the clustering with auto-encoder network. In this case, the cluster centers were calculated by computing the mean of actual data points instead of the coded representation of the data points. The clusters were decided based on the input data and the cluster centers were updated accordingly.

2.3 PCA and K-means

Each PA data vector contained 105 sample values. Principal component analysis (PCA) was performed on the complete data matrix [802 × 105] and 11 principal components were selected. The complete original PA data set was projected on a new space formed by the 11 principal components. This way, the 105 dimensional original data were compressed to 11 dimensional data. Unsupervised classification with this newly formed dataset was then performed using standard K-means algorithm.

2.4 Auto-encoder and K-means

An identical auto-encoder network, as shown in Fig. 1, was used to compress the dimensions of the PA data from 105 to 11. Here, the coding layer of the auto-encoder network provided the compressed representation of the original PA dataset. Clustering was performed with the compressed data using standard K-means algorithm. Batch method was used for training the auto-encoder network and the weights and biases were updated after every iteration. The differences between the auto-encoder used for clustering and the auto-encoder used here is in the objective function. While for clustering, the objective function as given in Eq. 1 was used, the objective function shown in Eq. 2 was used here.

$$\min_{W,b}\left[\left\{\frac{1}{N}\left(\sum_{a=1}^{N}\|x_a - x_a'\|^2\right)\right\}\right] \tag{2}$$

In Eq. 2, x_a represents input data vector, x_a' is the corresponding decoder output vector and N is the total number of observations. Once the auto-encoder was completely trained, its code space representation was stored. The standard K-means algorithm was performed with it for unsupervised classification.

3 Result

Three performance metrics are used to evaluate the experimental results. For an observation x_a, let g_a be the ground truth cluster label and r_a be the resolved cluster label. The accuracy of the algorithm is defined as,

$$\text{Acc} = \frac{1}{N}\sum_{a=1}^{N}\delta(g_a, r_a) \tag{3}$$

In Eq. 3, $\delta(x, y)$ is the delta function that equals to one if $x = y$ and zero otherwise and N is the total number of observations.

Sensitivity or true positive rate is defined as the ratio of number of correct positive predictions to the total number of positives. Specificity or true negative rate is defined as the ratio of number of correct negative predictions to the total number of negatives.

The variation of accuracy with respect to the number of iterations is evaluated for all the four algorithms. Figures 2, 3, 4 and 5 shows the accuracy plots of clustering using auto-encoder, standard K-means algorithm, K-means with projected principal components and K-means with auto-encoder code space representation. For standard K-means algorithm, accuracy decreased for first 4 iterations and then increased gradually to saturate at 48.87% after 25 iterations. In case of K-means with projected principal components, accuracy increased for 10 iterations, then decreased for next 4–5 iterations and finally saturated at 54.24%. The accuracy of K-means with auto-encoder code space representation increased for first 15 iterations, then decreased for next 4 and finally attained saturation at 57.1%. The auto-encoder tuned for clustering showed the highest accuracy of 59.85% which was attained after gradual increase for 10 iterations.

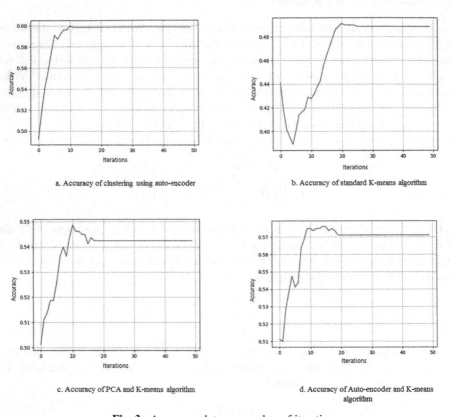

a. Accuracy of clustering using auto-encoder

b. Accuracy of standard K-means algorithm

c. Accuracy of PCA and K-means algorithm

d. Accuracy of Auto-encoder and K-means algorithm

Fig. 3. Accuracy plots vs. number of iterations

We compared the performance metrics of all four algorithms in Table 1. The results showed that the auto-encoder network specially tuned for clustering performed better than all the other three algorithms, whereas the performance of the standard K-means algorithm was the poorest among all. The auto-encoder complexity vs. accuracy is explored in Table 2. Four different structures were implemented for clustering using auto-encoder. These included two structures with 3 layers each in encoder and decoder along with 1 code layer and two structures with 2 layers each in encoder and decoder along with 1 code layer. The auto-encoder structure which gave the best results among all 4 was selected for comparison with other 3 algorithms.

Table 1. Performance comparison of four algorithms

Metrics	Accuracy	Sensitivity	Specificity
Auto-encoder	0.5985	0.5954	0.6015
K-means	0.4887	0.5251	0.453
PCA + K-means	0.5424	0.5427	0.542
Auto-encoder + K-means	0.571	0.4824	0.6584

Table 2. Exploration in auto-encoder layer complexity vs accuracy

Encoder structure	Code layer	Decoder structure	Accuracy
105-52-25	12	25-52-105	0.5512
105-35-12	4	12-35-105	0.5334
105-40	15	40-105	0.5864
105-29	11	29-105	0.6015

4 Discussion

In this study, a specifically tuned auto-encoder network was used for unsupervised classification of PA data generated by excised prostate specimens of actual human patients. The performance of this network was compared with various implementations of K-means algorithm. The dimensionality of compressed data used for different implementations of K-means algorithm was kept same as the code space dimension of the auto-encoder network tuned for clustering. The accuracy of clustering using auto-encoder was observed to be the highest whereas that of standard K-means algorithm was the lowest. However, the accuracy obtained for clustering using auto-encoder was moderate. Initial inspection of PA data revealed that there was significant overlap among the histograms formed using PA data corresponding to malignant and nonmalignant prostate. This might have resulted in poor clustering accuracy. Careful preprocessing which involves reduction of overlapping regions in the two histograms may be implemented to improve the accuracy.

The sensitivity obtained for clustering using auto-encoder was highest while it was least for K-means with auto-encoder code space representation. The specificity of K-means with auto-encoder code space representation was observed to be highest and it was least for the standard K-means algorithm. The algorithms were implemented with PA data acquired at 850 nm wavelength. The specificity was expected to be greater than the corresponding sensitivity for this wavelength. It was observed that the specificity achieved with auto-encoder designed for clustering was greater than the sensitivity provided by it. The sensitivity was observed to be greater than specificity for standard K-means algorithm while both values were nearly same for K-means with projected principal components. However, K-means with auto-encoder code space representation provided very large specificity than sensitivity.

Although our study showed that unsupervised classification for prostate cancer detection was possible using tuned auto-encoder network, the accuracy value was observed to be around 60%. In future, advanced auto-encoder networks such as sparse auto-encoder, stacked auto-encoder and convolutional auto-encoder will be implemented with same dataset for improving the accuracy.

5 Conclusion

The preliminary results indicate that unsupervised classification with moderate accuracy is possible to achieve for prostate cancer detection with PA data. The auto-encoder network, specially tuned for unsupervised classification, provided better accuracy and sensitivity than that of K-means algorithm with original and compressed PA data. Reduction of cluster overlap in the PA data by careful preprocessing may be performed in future to improve the accuracy of unsupervised classification.

References

1. Ferlay, J., et al.: GLOBOCAN 2012 v1.0, Cancer Incidence and Mortality Worldwide: IARC CancerBase No. 11 [Internet]. International Agency for Research on Cancer, Lyon (2013)
2. Anon.: Three year report of population based cancer registries 2009–2011. National Cancer Registry Programme, Indian Council of Medical Research, Bangalore, India (2013)
3. American Cancer Society. https://www.cancer.org/cancer/prostate-cancer/about/key-statis tics.html
4. American Cancer Society. https://www.cancer.org/acs/groups/cid/documents/webcontent
5. Presti Jr., J.C.: Prostate biopsy: current status and limitations. Reviews in Urology 9(3), 93 (2007)
6. Beard, P.: Biomedical photoacoustic imaging. Interface Focus 1(4), 602–631 (2011)
7. Valluru, K.S., Chinni, B.K., Rao, N.A., Bhatt, S., Dogra, V.S.: Basics and clinical applications of photoacoustic imaging. Ultrasound Clin. 4, 403–429 (2009)
8. Shen, D., Guorong, W., Suk, H.-I.: Deep learning in medical image analysis. Annu. Rev. Biomed. Eng. 19, 221–248 (2017)
9. Shin, H.-C., Orton, M.R., Collins, D.J., Doran, S.J., Leach, M.O.: Stacked auto-encoders for unsupervised feature learning and multiple organ detection in a pilot study using 4D patient data. IEEE Trans. Pattern Anal. Mach. Intell. 35(8), 1930–1943 (2013)
10. Suk, H.-I., Lee, S.-W., Shen, D.: Latent feature representation with stacked auto-encoder for AD/MCI diagnosis. Brain Struct. Func. 220, 841–859 (2015)
11. Cheng, J.-Z., et al.: Computer-aided diagnosis with deep learning architecture: applications to breast lesions in US images and pulmonary nodules in CT scans. Sci. Rep. 6, 24454 (2016)
12. Wang, J., Yang, X., Cai, H., Tan, W., Jin, C., Li, L.: Discrimination of breast cancer with microcalcifications on mammography by deep learning. Sci. Rep. 6, 27327 (2016)

13. Jha, D., Kwon, G.-R.: Alzheimer's disease detection using sparse auto-encoder, scale conjugate gradient and softmax output layer with fine tuning. Int. J. Mach. Learn. Comput. **7**(1), 13–17 (2017)
14. Kim, B.-C., Sung, Y.S., Suk, H.-I.: Deep feature learning for pulmonary nodule classification in a lung CT. In: 4th International Winter Conference on Brain-Computer Interface (2016)
15. Sevakula, R.K., Singh, V., Verma, N.K., Kumar, C., Cui, Y.: Transfer learning for molecular cancer classification using deep neural networks. IEEE Trans. Comput. Biol. Bioinform. **16**, 2089–2100 (2018)
16. Qiu, Y., Zhou, W., Nana, Yu., Peidong, D.: Denoising sparse autoencoder-based ictal EEG classification. IEEE Trans. Neural Syst. Rehabil. Eng. **26**(9), 1717–1726 (2018)
17. Wen, T., Zhang, Z.: Deep convolution neural network and auto-encoders based unsupervised feature learning of EEG signals. IEEE Access **6**, 25399–25410 (2018)
18. Song, C., Liu, F., Huang, Y., Wang, L., Tan, T.: Auto-encoder based data clustering. In: CIARP 2013, pp. 117–124 (2013)
19. Saugata, S., Rao, N.A., Chinni, B.K., Dogra, V.S.: Evaluation of frequency domain analysis of a multiwavelength photoacoustic signal for differentiating malignant from benign and normal prostates. J. Ultrasound Med. **35**(10), 2165–2177 (2016)
20. Sinha, S., Rao, N., Chinni, B., Moalem, J., Giampolli, E.J., Dogra, V.: Differentiation between malignant and normal human thyroid tissue using frequency analysis of multispectral photoacoustic images. In: IEEE Western New York Image Processing Workshop (WNYIPW 2013), pp. 5–8. IEEE (2013)
21. Saugata, S., Rao, N.A., Valluru, K.S., Chinni, B.K., Dogra, V.S., Helguera, M.: Frequency analysis of multispectral photoacoustic images for differentiating malignant region from normal region in excised human prostate. In: SPIE Medical Imaging, pp. 90400P–90400P. International Society for Optics and Photonics (2014)

An Efficient Approach for Skin Lesion Segmentation Using Dermoscopic Images: A Deep Learning Approach

Kishore Babu Nampalle$^{(\boxtimes)}$ (iD) and Balasubramanian Raman (iD)

Computer Science and Engineering Department, Indian Institute of Technology Roorkee, Roorkee, India
{kbabu89,bala}@cs.iitr.ac.in

Abstract. Segmentation is a process of detecting boundaries of an object to extract the object of interest within a given image. There are different techniques like CT scan, MRI scan, X-ray scan, and so on those can be used to get these medical images. Processing of these medical images is laborious because of variation in size and shape, and contrast. Hence, Skin lesion segmentation became a challenging task for researchers and dermatologists. The Segmentation of medical images plays a vital role in medical diagnosis and further treatment. Although there are many proposed image segmentation techniques, there is no perfect segmentation method that supports different datasets. This paper presents an efficient skin lesion segmentation model using a Convolutional Deconvolutional Neural Networks (CDNN). The proposed framework is developed based on Convolutional Neural Networks (CNN) by replacing the classification network with a segmentation network. The proposed model has used International Skin Imaging Collaboration (ISIC) 2017 challenging data set and PH2 dataset, and results are compared with State of Art models U-Net and SegNet.

Keywords: Skin lesion segmentation · Convolutional Neural Network(CNN) · Dermoscopic images · Convolutional Deconvolutional Neural Networks(CDNN)

1 Introduction

The outer region of the body is known as the skin, which is the largest organ. The total area is 20 square feet. It helps in regulating the body temperature and provides sensations like touch, cold, and heat. It is exposed more to the surrounding environment and may get in touch with pollution, dust, and radiation. These are the reasons for skin diseases and affect the functionality of the body. The skin has three layers. Dermis (Inner Layer), which is having Connective tissue, hair follicles. Epidermis (Outer Layer), which provides a waterproof barrier and forms skin tone. Deeper layer (Hypodermis), which has fat and connective tissue. The outer layer epidermis, which is composed of three types of cells. (1) SQUAMOUS: These are residing on the surface. The shape of these cells is flat

© Springer Nature Singapore Pte Ltd. 2021
S. K. Singh et al. (Eds.): CVIP 2020, CCIS 1376, pp. 430–439, 2021.
https://doi.org/10.1007/978-981-16-1086-8_38

and scaly. (2) BASAL: These are round cells. (3) MELANOCYTES: These cells provide color and save from skin damage identified at an early stage. It can spread deeper into the body and will affect other parts of the body. Firstly, the diagnosis of melanoma segmentation of a lesion followed by the extraction of features and then classification. Samples of images of skin lesion images are shown below in Fig. 1.

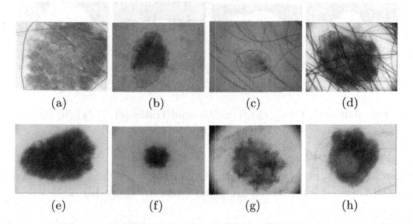

(a)   (b)   (c)   (d)

(e)   (f)   (g)   (h)

Fig. 1. Sample Dermoscopic images for Lesion segmentation. (a) with large sizes; (b) with irregular borders; (c) low contrast with surrounding part; (d) artifacts and few other sample images of ISIC 2017 data set.

Nowadays, Medical Image Processing is one of the fast upcoming research fields. Getting results with more accuracy is more desirable in any research field. Segmentation with more accurate results plays a vital role in disease diagnosis, disease monitoring, and further treatment and planning. Segmentation [26] of an image by humans is laborious, tedious, and time-consuming. Segmentation by automated algorithms for segmentation with more accuracy is preferable. There are few factors for measuring the performance of a segmentation method. They are Region of Interest, Behavior of a segmentation algorithm, Performance of technique in terms of previous results. There are many advantages and disadvantages to each segmentation technique. There are benchmark measurements to evaluate the results.

Segmentation plays a vital role in Registration, image labeling, and tracking the motion. For example, in the heart-related segmentation, segmentation [7]of left ventricular (LV) in cardiac images. To find out the output of the heart and volume ratio of ventricular, segmentation of left ventricular is mandatory, and in the same way to get the information about the thickness of the wall it requires analysis of wall motion which in turn requires details of segmentation of left ventricular [11]. Implementation of required segmentation methods requires a good knowledge of the data and underlying problem. Validation and acceptance of segmentation techniques depend on simplicity in computations and supervision of the user. Semi-automatic and automatic segmentations are proposed

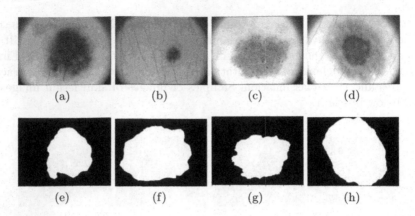

Fig. 2. Original images (a),(b),(c),(d) and Ground Truths (e),(f),(g),(h) from PH2 data set ((a)(b)(e)(f)) and ISIC 2017 ((c),(d),(g),(h)) data set.

and mostly used in the medical image segmentation process. Samples of original images and their Ground truths are given below in figure Fig. 2.

Validation and acceptance of segmentation techniques depend on simplicity in computations and supervision of the user. Semi-automatic and automatic segmentations are proposed and mostly used in the medical image segmentation process. Manual segmentation of an object involves manually drawing the borders by experts. Usually, manual segmentation takes more time so, it is tedious and time taking. It depends on experts like more number of experts do the work differently at a time (Inter-rater) [18,25] or the same expert does the same in different ways in different time of intervals (Intra-rater), and it will not be a reproducible [25]. Manual segmentation provides ground truth for fully automatic and semi-automatic segmentation techniques. It is still mostly used in clinical diagnosis if there is no time constraint [2,6]. In the Semi-automatic segmentation method, less human interactions will be there for the initialization process and correcting results [3]. This method combines human services and computer services. These semi-automatic segmentation methods depend on intra and inter rate reliability. In the case of the fully automatic segmentation [4], work will be performed without human involvement. Mostly model-based methods are involved besides soft computing methods. In these techniques, automatic information like image size, image color, brightness, etc. is required to have robust algorithms. Developing the automatic segmentation algorithm to get high accuracy [23] is a challenge because the human mind is having special knowledge with high visual processing. Nowadays, automatic segmentation methods are not accepted in clinical diagnosis but they are advantageous in processing.

Artificial Neural network is one of the supervised clustering methods, which involves mathematical operations to be applied to the inputs (Features) and results are obtained at output nodes. Parameter values should be computed while training Artificial Neural Networks in such a way that prediction error is minimized.

3D image segmentation [13] is a difficult and challenging task and it can be handled by model-based segmentation techniques. Deformable methods are used to segment anatomic structural mages by building a model that takes priority information like size, location, orientation, and shape. The main property of deformable methods is the capability of adjusting with a change in biological structures over time and among the different individuals [10].

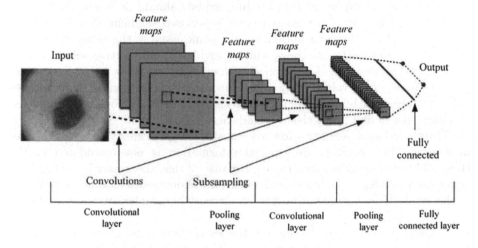

Fig. 3. Basic Structure of CNN

Artificial Neural Network [21] includes a non-parametric method, so no parametric distribution is considered for the data. Modeling of nonlinear dependencies in the given data is done using hidden layers of ANN. The training process in ANN is very complex, still, the ability of modeling non-trivial distributions includes practical advantages.

The other sections of the paper are arranged as follows: Sect. 2 represents a survey on research. The proposed method has been described in Sect. 3. Implementation, Results have been presented in Sect. 4, Sect. 5 and Concludes in Sect. 6 along with the highlighting the directions for future research.

2   Literature Survey

Medical Image Segmentation is an active topic of research with more challenging datasets. Traditionally, skin lesion segmentation methods mainly include clustering region-based method, and model-based methods [2,3,6].

In general, the first step in the image segmentation process is threshold-based segmentation because it is not useful to segment all images desirably [14]. As a solution for this drawback, the threshold technique based on the gradient for the segmentation [20] was proposed. In this method, first of all, parameters will be estimated with the help of the iterative process. The further process will be carried out by using these estimated parameters and the obtained results are more accurate compare to previously used threshold methods.

Labeling is an important task because experts should do it and it will take more time. Hence, it is not good to use supervised segmentation for a large amount of data. A better solution for the same issue is the usage of a semi-supervised segmentation method, which provides an alternative solution from a cost point of view. Semi-supervised segmentation methods give good results in terms of accuracy values compared to unsupervised segmentation techniques [13]. Clustering will be done using unsupervised segmentation based on unlabeled training data to find the decision boundaries [9,15,17].

Threshold-based segmentation will consider only intensity values, no other information like location. So, special information is not considered in the threshold-based segmentation. Hence, Because of this, there may be a chance to suffer from problems like noise sensitivity and inhomogeneity in intensity values of the image. These problems lead to an increase in complexity in segmentation and false results [1,24].

Region growing method leaks the tissues if there is no proper information about boundaries and if contrast is low. This method works fine with homogeneous regions. The drawback of the region-based method is noise sensitivity and it results in disconnected regions due to the noise. This method is useful in radiology applications like bone, lung, and tumor segmentation and is used in extracting lesions [12].

The fuzzy C-means method is used for the segmentation of different body parts [22]. Due to iterative nature, the Fuzzy C-means method will take more time to process and to solve this problem Bias corrected Fuzzy C-means (BCFCM) clustering method is proposed. BCFCM is used to segment brain images and provides results with good quality, in this way it is very much useful for brain tumor segmentation [5]. MRF is one of the unsupervised clustering methods, which is used to integrate information in the clustering techniques and it reduces the effect of problems like clusters overlapping and noise effect [8]. It can handle complex data dependencies and results in high accuracy in segmentation [16]. The segmentation of the cone-beam CT images of the tumor can be done by hidden MRFs.

3   Proposed Technique

3.1   Proposed Lesion Segmentation Algorithm

The structure of CDNN of the proposed model is developed from the basic architecture of the Convolutional neural network (CNN) by modifying the classification part with the segmentation part. It means that a fully Convolutional network [19] is replaced with Deconvolutional networks to provide symmetric up sampling architecture (Fig. 4).

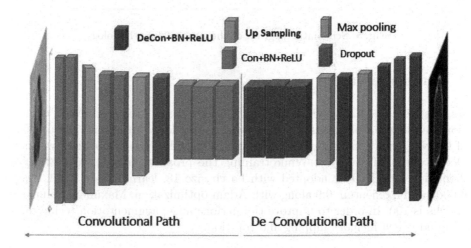

Fig. 4. Schematic diagram of the proposed Architecture

The proposed algorithm which is presented below is successful for the problem of skin lesion segmentation with data sets PH2 and ISIC 2017 and it relies on the convolutional part (Convolutional layers with different kernel sizes (5×5, 4×4, 3×3, Batch normalization, ReLU activation function and dropout layer (0.5) as well) and Deconvolutional part(Deconvolutional layers with kernel size 3×3, Batch normalization, ReLU activation function, dropout layer (0.5) and Upsampling as well) and the performance metrics IOU, Accuracy, and Loss functions. The complete diagrammatic representation of the proposed method is shown in figure Fig. 5.

The algorithm applied in steps as follows:

- 1. Resize the images and convert label images to indexed images.
- 2. Hyper parameters tuning
- 3. Tune the hyper parameters of the networks.
- 4. Pre-processing: Augmentation(Rotation, Flipping)
- 5. Performing Train, Test, and Validation based on splitting the data.
- 6. Apply the metrics IOU, Accuracy, and Loss Function.
- 7. Examine the performance.

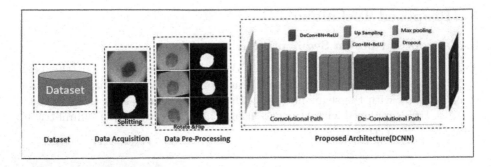

Fig. 5. Schematic diagram of the proposed methodology

4 Implementation

As it is mentioned in previous sections. The Proposed Architecture of Convolutional and Deconvolutional neural network is developed from basic architecture of CNN as shown in figure Fig. 3., by modifying fully convolutional networks to Deconvolutional networks. While training the proposed model, stochastic gradient descent (SGD) is adopted with batch size 18, learning rate 0.001, decay 0.0005 and momentum 0.9 along with Adam optimization. Maximum number of epochs is 100. In order to improve the performance, augmentation technique is adopted which includes flipping and rotation.

4.1 Experimental Setup

Model training has been performed on Nvidia Quadro P5000 GPU with a 10.2 CUDA version and Driver Version 440.100, 16 GB RAM CPU machine with a 64-bit Ubuntu Linux OS machine. The PH2 data set is having 200 images and 25% of these are given for testing. ISIC 2017 data set is having 2000 images, 500 images are given for testing.

4.2 Evaluation Metrics

Quality of emotion labeling is generally subjective. It is challenging to correlate any evaluation metric with human judgement quality. A possible way to mitigate this challenge is to use diverse evaluation metrics. With this aim, the following metrics have been considered to evaluate the translations.

- **Accuracy**: Accuracy can be defined as the mean value of all predictions and it is the ratio of the accurate value of predictions and total predictions.
- **Intersection over Union(IOU)**: It is also known as Jaccard index and measured as the ration of intersection and the union of true and predicted values.

- **Loss**: Cross-entropy loss is used as loss measurement and ranges from 0 to 1. Probability of prediction diverges if Loss is more else converges. Overall Loss and corresponding accuracy are shown in figure Fig. 7 and results of proposed methods are shown qualitatively and quantitatively in Table 1 and Fig. 6.

5   Results and Evaluation

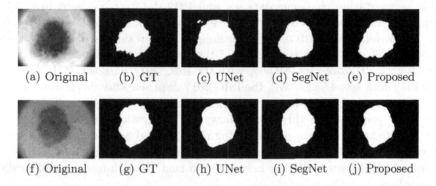

(a) Original   (b) GT   (c) UNet   (d) SegNet   (e) Proposed

(f) Original   (g) GT   (h) UNet   (i) SegNet   (j) Proposed

Fig. 6. Qualitative results of Proposed method from ISIC 2017 (Top Row) and PH2 (Bottom Row) Data sets.

Table 1. Quantitative results of proposed technique.

S.No	Method	IOU	Accuracy	Loss	Data set	Epochs
1	UNet	46.88	77.46	53.12	ISIC 2017	100
	Proposed	**47.42**	**80.56**	**52.58**		
2	SegNet	90.10	91.57	27.00	PH2	100
	Proposed	**90.94**	**92.66**	**9.06**		

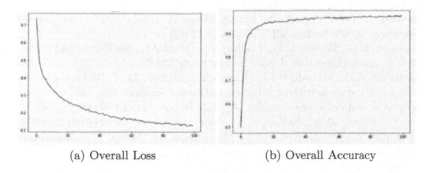

(a) Overall Loss   (b) Overall Accuracy

Fig. 7. Graphical representation of over all loss and accuracy values.

438   K. B. Nampalle and B. Raman

6 Conclusion

The Literature survey and experiment and results, presented in this paper regarding the segmentation of skin lesion with the help of Dermoscopic images, will have a good impact on medical applications like diagnosis and further treatment with more accuracy. The development of a good segmentation technique is always necessary to find out the segments with the help of labeled data while using supervised techniques for segmentation. The famous data sets ISIC 2017 lesion segmentation challenge data set and PH2 data set are used in order to train, test, and examine the performance of the proposed method and to compare the performance with different techniques. The results, which are obtained in this model, shows the superiority of the proposed technique with accuracy 92.66% with PH2 data set, 80.56% with the ISIC 2017 data set, IOU is 90.94% with PH2 data set, 47.42% with the ISIC 2017 data set, and also in case of Loss, the proposed method is showing promising results shown above, Table 1. The case study presented in this paper shows few suggestions like the increase in data set size and change in preprocessing methods and architecture can improve the overall performance. Future work can be carried out on new data sets by including failed cases with the help of optimized algorithms for more medical applications.

References

1. Anand, P., Bharanitharan, K., Wu, J.: Algorithm and architecture for adaptive motion estimation in video processing. IETE Techn. Rev. **30**(1), 24–30 (2013)
2. Bae, K., et al.: Intra-and inter-observer reproducibility of volume measurement of knee cartilage segmented from the OAI MR image set using a novel semi-automated segmentation method. Osteoarthr. Cartil. **17**(12), 1589–1597 (2009)
3. Bankman, I.: Handbook of Medical Image Processing and Analysis. Elsevier, Amsterdam (2008)
4. Bezdek, J.C., Hall, L., Clarke, L.: Review of MR image segmentation techniques using pattern recognition. Med. Phys. **20**(4), 1033–1048 (1993)
5. Dheeba, J., Singh, N.A., Selvi, S.T.: Computer-aided detection of breast cancer on mammograms: a swarm intelligence optimized wavelet neural network approach. J. Biomed. Inform. **49**, 45–52 (2014)
6. Gaonkar, B., et al.: Automated tumor volumetry using computer-aided image segmentation. Acad. Radiol. **22**(5), 653–661 (2015)
7. Gonzalez, R.C., Woods, R.E., Eddins, S.L.: Digital Image Processing using MATLAB. Pearson Education, Upper Saddle River (2004)
8. Hassanien, A.E., Moftah, H.M., Azar, A.T., Shoman, M.: MRI breast cancer diagnosis hybrid approach using adaptive ant-based segmentation and multilayer perceptron neural networks classifier. Appl. Soft Comput. **14**, 62–71 (2014)
9. Lee, C., Unser, M.A., Ketter, T.A.: Automated connectivity-based thresholding segmentation of midsagittal brain MR images. In: Visual Communications and Image Processing, vol. 2727, pp. 713–724. International Society for Optics and Photonics (1996)
10. Malladi, R., Sethian, J.A., Vemuri, B.C.: Shape modeling with front propagation: a level set approach. IEEE Trans. Pattern Anal. Mach. Intell. **17**(2), 158–175 (1995)

11. McInerney, T., Terzopoulos, D.: Deformable models in medical image analysis: a survey. Med. Image Anal. **1**(2), 91–108 (1996)
12. Moores, M., Hargrave, C., Harden, F., Mengersen, K.: Segmentation of cone-beam CT using a hidden Markov random field with informative priors. In: Journal of Physics: Conference Series, vol. 489, p. 012076. IOP Publishing (2014)
13. Ni, T., Xie, L., Zheng, H., Fishman, E.K., Yuille, A.L.: Elastic boundary projection for 3D medical image segmentation. In: 2019 IEEE/CVF Conference on Computer Vision and Pattern Recognition (CVPR), pp. 2104–2113 (2019)
14. Oliver, A., et al.: A review of automatic mass detection and segmentation in mammographic images. Med. Image Anal. **14**(2), 87–110 (2010)
15. Ostu, N.: A threshold selection method from gray level histogram. IEEE Trans. Syst. **9**(1), 62–66 (1979)
16. Parmar, H., Talati, B.: Brain tumor segmentation using clustering approach. In: 2019 Innovations in Power and Advanced Computing Technologies (i-PACT), vol. 1, pp. 1–6. IEEE (2019)
17. Pham, D.L., Xu, C., Prince, J.L.: Current methods in medical image segmentation. Ann. Rev. Biomed. Eng. **2**(1), 315–337 (2000)
18. Ramkumar, A., et al.: User interaction in semi-automatic segmentation of organs at risk: a case study in radiotherapy. J. Digit. Imaging **29**(2), 264–277 (2016)
19. Rohlfing, T., Maurer, C.R.: Multi-classifier framework for atlas-based image segmentation. In: Proceedings of the 2004 IEEE Computer Society Conference on Computer Vision and Pattern Recognition, CVPR 2004, vol. 1, p. I (2004)
20. Sajadi, A.S., Sabzpoushan, S.H.: A new seeded region growing technique for retinal blood vessels extraction. J. Med. Signals Sens. **4**(3), 223 (2014)
21. Saxena, N., Raman, B.: Semantic segmentation of multispectral images using Res-Seg-Net model. In: 2020 IEEE 14th International Conference on Semantic Computing (ICSC), pp. 154–157 (2020)
22. Schmidt, M.: Automatic brain tumor segmentation (2005)
23. Sharma, N., Aggarwal, L.M.: Automated medical image segmentation techniques. J. Med. Phys. **35**(1), 3 (2010). Association of Medical Physicists of India
24. Sun, K.: Development of segmentation methods for vascular angiogram. IETE Tech. Rev. **28**(5), 392–399 (2011)
25. White, D.R., Houston, A.S., Sampson, W.F., Wilkins, G.P.: Intra-and interoperator variations in region-of-interest drawing and their effect on the measurement of glomerular filtration rates. Clin. Nucl. Med. **24**(3), 177–181 (1999)
26. Zhou, Y., et al.: Collaborative learning of semi-supervised segmentation and classification for medical images. In: 2019 IEEE/CVF Conference on Computer Vision and Pattern Recognition (CVPR), pp. 2074–2083 (2019)

SigVer—A Deep Learning Based Writer Independent Bangla Signature Verification System

Sk Md Obaidullah[1(✉)], Himadri Mukherjee[2], Kaushik Roy[2], and Umapada Pal[3]

[1] Aliah University, Kolkata, India
[2] West Bengal State University, Barasat, India
[3] Indian Statistical Institute, Kolkata, India
umapada@isical.ac.in

Abstract. Handwritten signature is one of the most popular biometric traits which have been addressed by researchers since the last few decades. Scientists have proposed disparate handcrafted feature-based techniques for signature verification in the past. Presently there has been an interest towards deep learning-based approaches which has demonstrated promising results across different avenues of pattern recognition problems. In this paper, light-weight CNN architecture named SigVer is proposed for Bangla offline writer independent signature verification. The proposed network was built with only six layers with no pooling in between convolution layers to minimize information loss. Experiments were performed on 2956 signatures from 57 writers and a highest accuracy of 99.49% was obtained. Further, comparative analysis was performed with established CNN architectures as well as handcrafted feature-based techniques and SigVer produced better results.

Keywords: Bangla script · Signature verification · Deep learning

1 Introduction

In behavioral biometric signature is one of the most popular and widely used modality which is used as proof of identity. Over the last few decades researchers are paying attention to develop automatic signature verification system to reduce the uncertainty of manual authentication process [1]. Based on the input method signature verification can be operated in two ways: (i) static and (ii) dynamic. In static modality, writers first sign on paper, it is then digitized using a camera or scanner. Thereafter, a verification system verifies the signature image analyzing its shape or any other properties. Static method is also called *offline* as real time information processing is not done here. In dynamic modality, writer information is captured through specialized writing tablet, which capture the signature in real time. Stylus-operated PDAs are also used to capture this type of signature. Nowadays smart phones or tablets coupled with a capacitive screen are also used to capture dynamic signature. In dynamic modality the real time information that we can capture are mainly: spatial coordinates in x/y directions, pen or fingertip pressure,

© Springer Nature Singapore Pte Ltd. 2021
S. K. Singh et al. (Eds.): CVIP 2020, CCIS 1376, pp. 440–450, 2021.
https://doi.org/10.1007/978-981-16-1086-8_39

inclination angle etc. This dynamic method is also known as *online* as real time dynamic user writing style/patters are captured here. In general online system performs better compared to offline because of the ability to capture dynamic information while writers are writing. On contrary, offline system works on two dimensional image data where all kind of dynamic writer information is lost. That is why offline signature verification is more challenging compare to online one. In this paper, we worked on Bangla offline writer independent signature verification problem.

As per the 8th schedule of Indian constitution [2], Bangla is one of the major scripts used in India and also it is the native language of Bangladesh. In India, Bangla script is used by different languages like Bengali, Assamese, and Manipuri. Bangla script falls under the abugida family of writing system where its vowel graphemes are not used as independent letters, but as diacritics changing the vowel integral in the base letter they are added to. Research developments on Bangla signature verification system are very less in number as compared to other popular scripts like Roman, Arabic or Devanagari. Among few of the reported pieces of work handcrafted feature computation based system are mostly reported so far.

Offline signature verification problem can be approached into two ways: (i) writer dependent and (ii) writer independent. For the first scenario, the whole process is writer specific, means from a particular writer we collect the signature data and the classifier is trained with a subset of original signature data (training sample). During testing phase the trained classifier decides whether the given signature was written by that particular writer or not. So this approach is not a generic one rather writer specific verification. The shortcoming of such system is every time when there is a new writer; the system needs to be trained with the new writer's signature sample. Writer independent signature verification system is more generic in the sense that here during testing any writer's signature can be tested, that is not writer specific. Another advantage is maintaining this system is much easier as every time we need not to train the classifier if new writer signature comes.

This paper deals with offline signature verification system (OSVS). As discussed, for OSVS, there are either writer dependent approaches where writer specific system is built or writer independent approaches where a generic model is built considering all writers. In early days OSVS was reported mainly on western scripts like Roman. In recent years several works on scripts like Arabic, Chinese, Japanese and some Indic scripts can also be found. Signature verification system can be generic with respect to script considered but till date no such model is available. Script specific OSVS are common practice as during feature computation stage we used to collect many features which are script specific. For example, "Matra" or "Shirorekha" [3] is an inherent property for Bangla and Devanagari script. Now any feature computation based OSVS which focuses on writing style of "Shirorekha" by different writers will fail to perform as expected for signature written in Roman or Arabic scripts where "Shirorekha" is absent. Although the general signature writing and recognition process is invariant with respect to geographical and cultural traits, still script specific solution were more preferred choice among the researcher compared to script independent generic model.

Based on feature computation strategy several signature verifications tasks were reported in literature on non-Indic and Indic scripts. Global features like signature boundary, energy, projection information, size of signature box [4], geometric, centroid information [5], statistical texture measure [6], quad-tree structure [7], descriptor like SIFT [8], SURF [9], Discrete Wavelet Transform [10], geometric and grid based feature [11], feature fusion with fuzzy modeling [12], histogram of oriented gradients [13] were considered for signature verification from various non-Indic scripts. Among the various popular works on Indic scripts, features like Zernike moments and gradient [14], chain-code based contour information [15], local binary patterns [16] were considered. Since last couple of year deep learning based OSVS has become popular. Deep multitask metric learning (DMML) [17], deep convolutional generative adversarial networks (DCGANs) [18], writer independent CNN [19], convolutional siamese network [20] are some popular convolutional neural network based works on Indic and non-Indic scripts.

In this paper, a deep learning based Bangla offline writer independent signature verification system is proposed. A Light-weight CNN architecture is designed for the same. The computational cost of CNN is well known to be huge as it involves many convolutional layers. To minimize the computational cost, three lower dimensional convolution layers were used to design the proposed model. 2956 signatures from 57 writers were considered to train and test the model using k-fold cross validation strategy. Furthermore performance of the proposed network was compared with some popular CNN architecture and also with some state-of-the-art handcrafted features.

Rests of the papers are organized as follows: Sect. 2 describes the design of the proposed CNN architecture; Sect. 3 discusses about dataset considers, experimental setup, experimental outcome, error analysis and comparison with the state-of-the-arts; Sect. 4 concludes the paper mentioning some future plans.

2 Proposed Method

Considering the present problem of OSVS, to avoid handcrafted feature computation overhead we proposed deep learning based solution which computes the feature set automatically. CNN is a type of deep learning architecture where three type of layers namely: convolution, pooling and dense is present. Convolution is the first layer to extract features from an input image by applying some predefined filters. Pooling layer is used to reduce the spatial size of the feature map which in turn reduces the number of parameters and computation in the network. The dense layer feeds all outputs from the previous layer to all its neurons, each neuron providing one output to the next layer. In literature, different types of CNN architectures have been reported to solve disparate document analysis problems. Application of CNN for signature verification on Indic scripts is very limited as on date [1]. Computational cost and system overhead is another issue while designing CNN architecture. For present problem we have designed a light-weight CNN architecture which is efficient in terms for computational cost and performance. In the following subsection we will discuss the same.

2.1 SigVer Architecture

SigVer is a 6-layered CNN model designed for the present problem. The first 3 layers are convolution layers of 16, 32 and 48 dimensions. The number of convolution layers was chosen heuristically to keep the network lightweight. The filter sizes being $5 \times 5, 4 \times 4$ and 3×3 respectively. This is followed by a max pooling layer having a window size of 3×3 dimensions. No pooling was used in between the convolution layers in order to ensure propagation of unaltered feature maps to the next convolution layers which are the feature detectors. In order to ensure lower computation, lower dimensional convolution layers were used. The result was only pooled prior to feeding to the dense layers where high number of computations was involved. There were 2 dense layers; the first had a dimension of 256 and the second had a dimension of 57 (number of output classes, i.e. number of writers). All the convolution layers along with the first dense layer had a ReLU activation function which is presented in Eq. 1. ReLU is considered because it is computationally efficient to accomplish faster learning. The final layer had a softmax activation function which is presented in Eq. 2.

$$f(x) = \max(0, x) \tag{1}$$

where x is the input to a neuron.

$$\sigma(z)_j = \frac{e^{z_j}}{\sum_{k=1}^{K} e^{z_k}} \tag{2}$$

where z is the jth input vector of length K.

The proposed network is presented in Fig. 1. The initial image size, pooling window size and training iterations was set to 100×100 pixels, 3×3 pixels and 200 epochs and 50% dropout respectively (selected experimentally). The system was evaluated with n-fold cross validation scheme where n was set to 10. The parameters of the network were set based on experimental trials. The hyper parameters were further tuned to obtained performance gains which are presented hereafter:

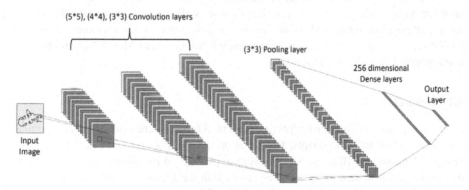

Fig. 1. Block diagram of the proposed CNN architecture with six layers (3 convolution, 1 pooling and 2 dense). No pooling was used in between the convolution layers in order to ensure propagation of unaltered feature maps to the next convolution layers which are the feature detectors.

The parameters generated by the proposed network are presented in Table 1. Number of parameters by three convolution layers are 1216, 8224 and 13872 respectively.

Then first dense layer (256 dimensional) performs highest computation with 5947648 parameters followed by 19789 parameters considered by the final dense layer. Total number of parameters considered is 5990749. Eventually the proposed architecture is called light-weight because:

Table 1. Number of generated parameters in different layers for the proposed network.

Layer	#Parameters
Convolution 1	1216
Convolution 2	8224
Convolution 3	13872
Dense 1	5947648
Dense 2	19789
Total	5990749

- Only three convolution layers were used with no pooling layer in between.
- The dimensions of the convolution layers used are 16, 32 and 48 only.
- During the parameters fine tuning less number of parameters were generated by the proposed network compared to other standard models (experimentally found).

3   Experimental Results and Analysis

First, we will talk about the dataset considered for present work; followed by experimental setup along with system configuration; then we will analyses the results obtained and error analysis. Finally we will show the comparative study of the proposed architecture with three state-of-the-arts namely InceptionV3, VGG16 and MobileNet and also with some popular handcrafted features.

3.1   Dataset

Signature dataset on Western scripts like Roman, Arabic, Chinese or Persian are available easily compared to Indic scripts. Bangla is one of the popular Indic scripts as well as national language of Bangladesh. We were in process of building a multi-script offline handwritten signature dataset and the present Bangla dataset is a subset of that. A total of 2956 Bangla signatures were collected from 57 different writers of varying sex with different cultural and social background. Each writer contributed 52 signature samples with few exceptions. The samples were collected in different time intervals to ensure the natural variability in the handwriting. No constrained on ink type, pen type was imposed on the writers. Few sample signatures from our dataset are shown in Fig. 2.

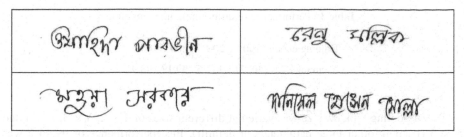

Fig. 2. Sample Bangla signatures of four different writers from our dataset which was built in-house

3.2 Setup

The experimentation was carried out in a system with configuration that includes: Intel Core i5-6200U processor with 2.30 GHz clock speed, 8 GB RAM and NVIDIA GeForce 940MX GPU with 4 GB memory. In software part Python 3.7.0 was used to write the code.

For performance measure we have computed overall recognition accuracy using the following Eq. 3:

$$accuracy = ((tp + tn)/(tp + fp + fn + tn)) \tag{3}$$

Where tp, tn, fp, and fn are the number of true positive, true negative, false positive, and false negative samples respectively. As mentioned the system was evaluated with n-fold cross validation where the value of n was set to 10. The parameters of the network were set based on experimental trials which are discussed below.

3.3 Results with Ablations Studies on Parameters

We started experimentation, setting default values of 100×100 pixels image dimension, 3×3 pixels pooling window, 200 epochs training iteration and 50% dropout rate. Then these parameters are varied to find the best result. In accordance with this experimental protocol, we tested four types of image dimension: 50×50, 100×100, 150×150 and 200×200. Table 2 shows the performance of the proposed network for four different image dimensions. The best performance of 98.65% verification accuracy was obtained for image size 100×100 pixels (keeping other three parameters at default).

Table 2. Performance of images resized to different dimensions

Image dimensions	50×50	100×100	150×150	200×200
Accuracy (%)	98.61	**98.65**	98.11	98.48

Next, training epoch was varied at different sizes of 100, 200, 300 and 400 (keeping other three parameters at default). Best performance of 99.19% was obtained using 300 epochs which is shown in Table 3.

Table 3. Performance of different training iteration

Training epoch	100	200	300	400
Accuracy (%)	98.71	98.65	**99.19**	98.91

Next, pooling window size was varied at different sizes of 2×2, 3×3, 4×4 and 5×5 (keeping other three parameters at default). Best performance of 99.46% was obtained at pooling window size of 4×4 which is shown in Table 4.

Table 4. Performance of different pooling window sizes

Pooling size	2×2	3×3	4×4	5×5
Accuracy (%)	97.94	98.65	**99.46**	99.36

Next dropout (%) values are varied to observe the best performance (keeping other three parameters at default). In Table 5, different dropout (%) values are shown which start from 10% and ends in 90% with 10% increase each time. Experimentally we found best performance of 99.49% at 80% dropout scenario. This is the overall highest result in our experiments.

Table 5. Performance for different dropouts (%)

Dropout (%)	10	20	30	40	50
Accuracy (%)	98.34	98.71	98.61	98.68	98.65
Dropout (%)	60	70	**80**	90	
Accuracy (%)	99.02	99.22	**99.49**	99.26	

3.4 Comparative Study

3.4.1 Comparison with Other CNN Models

First we compared the performance of proposed architecture with three popular CNN models which are presented as follows.

InceptionV3 [21], a 48-layered deep architecture was started as a module for Googlenet which was mainly used for image analysis and object detection. It has a series of convolution and pooling layers. There are 3 types of inception modules in this model namely mod1, mod2, and mod3 for parameter reduction and generation of differential features.

VGG16 [22] is a popular CNN architecture introduced by Simonyan and Zisserman in 2014. It uses only 3×3 convolutional layers stacked on top of each other in increasing depth. After that there are two fully-connected layers, each with 4096 nodes. Then the output is passed to a softmax classifier in order to normalize the classification vector. All the hidden layers in use ReLU as its activation function as it is computationally efficient for faster learning.

MobileNet [23] was proposed by Howard et al., in 2017 which uses depth-wise separable convolutions. This network requires very less computational power making it suitable for using at transfer learning based solutions.

Table 6 shows the performance of the proposed SigVer network with InceptionV3, VGG16 and MobileNet. Among the four, the proposed method produces highest accuracy of 99.49% followed by VGG16 which is only 0.1% lesser. While considering number of parameters taken during training process the proposed method is almost 2.8 times faster than VGG16. Thus, it proves when number of training sample is comparatively less (2661 in our experiment as 10-fold cross validation was used on total 2956 samples) then light-weight CNN model performs better and computationally efficient in comparison with state-of-the-art complex CNN architectures.

Table 6. Comparison of the proposed network with three existing models namely: InceptionV3, VGG16 and MobileNet

Model	#Parameters	Accuracy (%)
InceptionV3	26541421	99.05
VGG16	16831885	99.39
MobileNet	7443213	93.00
Proposed network (SigVer)	**5990749**	**99.49**

3.4.2 Comparison with Handcrafted Features

SigVer was also compared with some standard texture based handcrafted features extracted from Gray-level co-occurrence matrix (GLCM) [24], Histogram of oriented gradient (HOG) [13], Local binary pattern (LBP) [24], Weber local descriptor (WLD) [25] and Zernike moments [26]. Figure 3 shows the comparative chart of SigVer and texture based handcrafted features where we found, SigVer outperforms all the handcrafted features. Among the handcrafted features HOG performs the best with 2.89% lower than SigVer and GLCM performs the worst with 37.36% lesser from SigVer using Random Forest classifier (default parameters) [27]. Random forest was chosen as it performs well (fast training and good accuracy) during some of our earlier experiments [28].

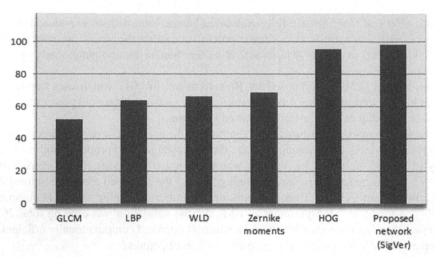

Fig. 3. Comparison of the proposed SigVer system with some of the state-of-the-art texture based handcrafted features based approach.

4 Conclusion

A lightweight CNN architecture named SigVer is proposed here for Bangla offline writer independent signature verification. Several variations of signature verification task are explored. Light-weight CNN architecture is designed without any pooling layers in between the convolution layers. Lower dimensional convolution layers were considered to ensure fast training. To find the best hyper-parameters, we conducted experiment varying four important parameters namely: image dimensions, pooling size, number of epochs and dropout rate. We obtained the highest accuracy of 99.49% with image dimension 200, pooling size 4 × 4, #epoch 300 and dropout rate 80%. Upon comparing other CNN models using these trainable parameters, we found the proposed method is efficient since computational complexity and light-weight design are our primary concern. Finally, the method is compared with some well-known texture based handcrafted feature-based approach and our proposed method outperforms all of them.

Considering future scopes of the present work there are two major directions. First, a common framework for multi-script signature verification is still an open area where we can contribute. We are in process of building multi-script signature dataset for official Indic scripts. Once the dataset is ready we will explore the performance of deep learning models [30] and check how the proposed light-weight architecture performs on such dataset. Applying some holistic approaches for signature verification is also in our mind [29]. Having access to more such multi-script signature data and more computational resources would likely allow us to accomplish stronger results. In addition we will also evaluate the performance of our method on different public datasets [31].

One limitation of the proposed work is: all experimentation was carried out without considering any forged signature data. Writer specific signature verification with forged signature data [32] need to explore as this task mirrors the situation of real world applications (especially for banking and legal sectors). Building such benchmark dataset for official Indic scripts is also an open area till date. Nevertheless, we are also planning to develop some handheld compatible solutions with light-weight CNN model for multi-script writer dependent/independent signature verification task.

Acknowledgement. The first author of this paper is thankful to Science and Engineering Research Board (SERB), DST, Govt. of India for funding this research through Teachers Associateship for research Excellence (TARE) grant TAR/2019/000273.

References

1. Diaz, M., Ferrer, M.A., Impedovo, D., Malik, M.I., Pirlo, G., Plamondon, R.: A perspective analysis of handwritten signature technology. ACM Comput. Surv. **51**(6) (2019). https://doi.org/10.1145/3274658. Article no. 117
2. https://rajbhasha.gov.in/en/languages-included-eighth-schedule-indian-constitution. Accessed 30 Aug 2020
3. Obaidullah, S.M., Goswami, C., Santosh, K.C., Halder, C., Das, N., Roy, K.: Separating Indic scripts with 'Matra' - a precursor to script identification in multi-script documents. In: International Conference on Computer Vision and Image Processing, pp. 205–214 (2016)
4. Nguyen, V., Blumenstein, M., Leedham, G.: Global features for the off-line signature verification problem. In: 10th International Conference on Document Analysis and Recognition (ICDAR 2009), pp. 1300–1304 (2009)
5. Schafer, B., Viriri, S.: An off-line signature verification system. In: International Conference on Signal and Image Processing Applications (ICSIPA 2009), pp. 95–100 (2009)
6. Vargas, J.F., Ferrer, M.A., Travieso, C.M., Alonso, J.B.: Off-line signature verification based on grey level information using texture features. Pattern Recogn. **44**(2), 375–385 (2011)
7. Serdouk, Y., Nemmour, H., Chibani, Y.: Handwritten signature verification using the quadtree histogram of templates and a support vector-based artificial immune classification. Image Vis. Comput. **66**(2017), 26–35 (2017)
8. Deng, H.-R., Wang, Y.-H.: On-line signature verification based on correlation image. In: International Conference on Machine Learning and Cybernetics, vol. 3, pp. 1788–1792 (2009)
9. Malik, M.I., Liwicki, M., Dengel, A., Uchida, S., Frinken, V.: Automatic signature stability analysis and verification using local features. In: 14th International Conference on Frontiers in Handwriting Recognition (ICFHR 2014), pp. 621–626. IEEE (2014)
10. Falahati, D., Helforoush, M.S., Danyali, H., Rashidpour, M.: Static signature verification for Farsi and Arabic signatures using dynamic time warping. In: 19th Iranian Conference on Electrical Engineering (ICEE 2011), pp. 1–6 (2011)
11. Mamoun, S.: Off-line arabic signature verification using geometrical features. In: National Workshop on Information Assurance Research, pp. 1–6 (2012)
12. Darwish, S., El-Nour, A.: Automated offline arabic signature verification system using multiple features fusion for forensic applications. Arab J. Forensic Sci. Forensic Med. **1**(4), 424–437 (2016)
13. Dutta, A., Pal, U., Lladós, J.: Compact correlated features for writer independent signature verification. In: 23rd International Conference on Pattern Recognition (ICPR) Cancún Center, Cancún, México, 4–8 December 2016 (2016)
14. Pal, S., Pal, U., Blumenstein, M.: Off-line verification technique for Hindi signatures. IET Biometrics **2**(4), 182–190 (2013)
15. Pal, S., Reza, A., Pal, U., Blumenstein, M.: SVM and NN based offline signature verification. Int. J. Comput. Intell. Appl. **12**(4), 1340004 (2013)

16. Pal, S., Alaei, A., Pal, U., Blumenstein, M.: Performance of an off-line signature verification method based on texture features on a large indic-script signature dataset. In: 12th IAPR Workshop on Document Analysis Systems (DAS 2016), pp. 72–77. IEEE, (2016)
17. Soleimani, A., Araabi, B.N., Fouladi, K.: Deep multitask metric learning for offline signature verification. Pattern Recogn. Lett. **80**(2016), 84–90 (2016)
18. Zhang, Z., Liu, X., Cui, Y.: Multi-phase offline signature verification system using deep convolutional generative adversarial networks. In: 9th International Symposium on Computational Intelligence and Design (ISCID 2016), vol. 2, pp. 103–107 (2016)
19. Hafemann, L.G., Sabourin, R., Oliveira, L.S.: Writer-independent feature learning for offline signature verification using deep convolutional neural networks. In: International Joint Conference on Neural Networks (IJCNN 2016), pp. 2576–2583. IEEE (2016)
20. Dey, S., Dutta, A., Toledo, J.I., Ghosh, S.K., Lladós, J., Pal, U.: SigNet: convolutional siamese network for writer independent offline signature verification. Corr (2017). arXiv:1707.02131
21. Szegedy, C., Vanhoucke, V., Ioffe, S., Shlens, J., Wojna, Z.: Rethinking the inception architecture for computer vision. arXiv:1512.00567 (2015)
22. Simonyan, K., Zisserman, A.: Very deep convolutional networks for large-scale image recognition. arXiv:1409.1556 (2015)
23. Howard, A.G., et al.: MobileNets: efficient convolutional neural networks for mobile vision applications. arXiv:1704.04861 (2015)
24. Wang, G.D., Zhang, P.L., Ren, G.Q., Kou, X.: Texture feature extraction method fused with LBP and GLCM. Comput. Eng. **38**, 199–201 (2012)
25. Chen, J., Shan, S., He, C., et al.: WLD: a robust local image descriptor. IEEE Trans. Pattern Anal. Mach. Intell. **32**, 1705–1720 (2010)
26. Sharma, N., Chanda, S., Pal, U., Blumenstein, M.: Word-wise script identification from video frames. In: ICDAR 2013, pp. 867–871 (2013)
27. Liaw, A., Wiener, M.: Classification and Regression by randomForest. R News **2**(3), 18–22 (2002)
28. Obaidullah, S.M., Santosh, K.C., Halder, C., Das, N., Roy, K.: Automatic Indic script identification from handwritten documents: page, block, line and word-level approach. Int. J. Mach. Learn. Cybern. **10**(1), 87–106 (2019)
29. Bhowmik, S., Malakar, S., Sarkar, R., Basu, S., Kundu, M., Nasipuri, M.: Off-line Bangla handwritten word recognition: a holistic approach. Neural Comput. Appl. **31**, 5783–5798 (2019)
30. Chowdhury, R.R., Hossain, M.S., ul Islam, R., Andersson, K., Hossain, S.: Bangla handwritten character recognition using convolutional neural network with data augmentation. In: Joint 8th International Conference on Informatics, Electronics & Vision (ICIEV) and 3rd International Conference on Imaging, Vision & Pattern Recognition (icIVPR), Spokane, WA, USA, 2019, pp. 318–323 (2019). https://doi.org/10.1109/iciev.2019.8858545
31. Jain, A., Singh, S.K., Singh, K.P.: Handwritten signature verification using shallow convolutional neural network. Multimedia Tools Appl. **79**, 19993–20018 (2020)
32. Gideona, S.J., Kandulna, A., Abhishek, A., Diana, K.A., Raimond, K.: Handwritten signature forgery detection using convolutional neural networks. Procedia Comput. Sci. **143**(2018), 978–987 (2018)

Colorectal Cancer Segmentation Using Atrous Convolution and Residual Enhanced UNet

Nisarg A. Shah[1(✉)], Divij Gupta[1], Romil Lodaya[2], Ujjwal Baid[2], and Sanjay Talbar[2]

[1] Department of Electrical Engineering, Indian Institute of Technology Jodhpur, Jodhpur, India
{shah.2,gupta.13}@iitj.ac.in
[2] Shri Guruji Gobind Singhji Institute of Engineering and Technology, Nanded, India
sntalbar@sggs.ac.in

Abstract. Colorectal cancer is a leading cause of death worldwide. However, early diagnosis dramatically increases the chances of survival, for which it is crucial to identify the tumor in the body. Since its imaging uses high-resolution techniques, annotating the tumor is time-consuming and requires particular expertise. Lately, methods built upon Convolutional Neural Networks(CNNs) have proven to be at par, if not better in many biomedical segmentation tasks. For the task at hand, we propose another CNN-based approach, which uses atrous convolutions and residual connections besides the conventional filters. The training and inference were made using an efficient patch-based approach, which significantly reduced unnecessary computations. The proposed AtResUNet was trained on the DigestPath 2019 Challenge dataset for colorectal cancer segmentation with results having a Dice Coefficient of 0.748. Its ensemble, with its simpler version, achieved a Dice Coefficient of 0.753.

1 Introduction

Cancer is the abnormal growth of cells that can invade or spread to other parts of the body. Colorectal cancer is a type of cancer that begins in the large intestine (colon). This cancer is often seen in old age people, but now it can even be seen in younger people due to lifestyle factors, with only a small number of cases due to underlying genetic disorders. Colorectal cancer is the fourth most common cancer diagnosed and the third leading cause of cancer death worldwide [21]. Chances of survival increase manifold if the cancer is diagnosed early. This cancer is diagnosed by obtaining tissue samples by Colonoscopy. These tissues are stained using hematoxylin and eosin(H&E) stain. The hematoxylin stains the cell nuclei blue, and eosin stains the extracellular matrix and cytoplasm pink, with other structures taking on different shades, hues, and combinations of these colors. The glass slides which contain the stained tissue are digitized and converted into high-resolution whole slide images(WSI). Their diagnosis

---

D. Gupta, R. Lodaya, U. Baid—These authors contributed equally to this article.

© Springer Nature Singapore Pte Ltd. 2021
S. K. Singh et al. (Eds.): CVIP 2020, CCIS 1376, pp. 451–462, 2021.
https://doi.org/10.1007/978-981-16-1086-8_40

requires experienced pathologists and is also a laborious task. Since the images are high-resolution, it is a challenging task to make an automatic segmentation tool that accurately predicts the tumor region. However, recently, Deep Learning(DL) approaches have shown to be much better than the conventional techniques for segmentation tasks, with many researchers worldwide publishing various work on the same. In this paper, we propose another Convolutional Neural Network(CNN)-based DL approach for the segmentation of the tumor wherein we used a patch-based, sliding window technique as the images used for the task were of high resolution. In this paper, we present a novel convolutional block based on the concept of atrous convolutions. The block can be easily integrated into other CNN-based approaches as well. We also make use of a simple pre-processing and post-processing approach for better results.

2 Related Work

The power of CNNs was first exhibited in the ImageNet challenge [7], and ever since then, CNNs have revolutionized the field of computer vision and have produced far better results than conventional techniques on numerous tasks. The same can be said in the case of medical imaging [20], particularly segmentation. The inherent property of CNNs to automatically find crucial and task-relevant structures in images account for their widespread use. The first revolutionary architecture was the UNet [22] introduced for the task of cell tracking and segmentation. The UNet [2,6,22] is a well known CNN architecture first introduced in 2015 primarily for cell segmentation. Since then, it has been the backbone of several biomedical segmentation architectures. The UNet [22] consists of a contracting path (encoder) and an expansion path (decoder), along with the skip connections in between the corresponding layers of the encoder-decoder to retain the spatial information between early and late layers for location precise segmentation maps. Many researchers have modified the UNet to produce impressive results on various biomedical segmentation tasks. In [1], the authors used a cascaded UNet for brain tumor segmentation, while in [13], the authors used attention-mechanism in the UNet for liver tumor segmentation. In [10], the author varied the kernel size of the filters in the UNet for bladder cancer cell segmentation. Researchers have recently shifted their focus on using deep learning techniques for histopathology analysis, especially colorectal cancer diagnosis. In [23], the authors have discussed the use of locality-sensitive deep learning with the use of Spatially Constrained CNN. In [14], the authors have discussed the prediction of the clinical course of patients diagnosed with colorectal cancer, while in [3], the authors have discussed estimating the patient risk score using LSTMs. Also, some work has also been done for incorporating adversarial or GAN-based approaches as in the work of [26] wherein the authors have also used concepts of attention, pyramid pooling, and atrous convolutions in their work. Another work by [8] uses adversarial approach for domain adaptation to detect the tumor in an unsupervised manner. Another popular approach is the use of ensembles such as in the work of [15] wherein the final prediction was obtained after averaging predictions from three FCN models.

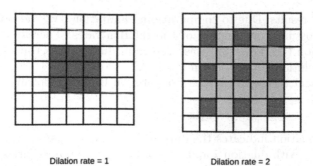

Fig. 1. Effect of change of dilation rate. With increasing the dilation rate, the space between the weights (dark red) increases and is filled with zeros. In this manner, the receptive field is increased (Color figure online)

3 Method

This section discusses the proposed method, which primarily uses CNNs with the UNet as the backbone. We provide an in-depth discussion about the various components of the architecture and their features and, finally, the whole architecture as one.

3.1 Atrous Convolution

Atrous convolution [4] is a convolutional operation wherein an extra parameter, the dilation rate, is used in addition to the convolutional layer (Fig. 1). The dilation rate determines the spacing between the values in a kernel. By dilating the convolutional kernel, a broader receptive field is acted upon for the same computational cost as that of a regular convolution operation. This type of convolution is particularly useful in segmentation, which requires feature extraction from various receptive fields. The atrous convolutions have been shown to decrease blurring in semantic segmentation maps. Additionally, they are indicated to produce the same effect as that of pooling by extracting long-range information.

3.2 Series Atrous Convolution Unit

The Series Atrous Convolution Unit makes use of series pixel-wise addition on the feature map obtained from a series of convolution operations done at a particular dilation rate, as shown in Fig. 3. This is similar to using residual connections [9]. Using residual connections also ensured that information was not diminished, as in the general case of deep networks. Experimentally, we found that a series connection of feature maps obtained at different dilation rates produced better results than a concatenation of convolution operations at different dilation rates. We tried different types of combination for the series Atrous Convolution Unit like (1,2), (1,2,4), (1,2,4,8), (1,2,4,8,16), (1,2,4,8,16,32), and the best combination among these experiments was obtained for (1,2,4,8,16,32), based on the segmentation results. Due to computational limitations, we did not experiment with every possible combination of the dilation rates. Therefore, the particular combination (1,2,4,8,16,32) was used in all further experiments. The Series Atrous Convolution Unit is shown in Fig. 2.

We represent the Series Atrous Convolution Unit as following :-

$$F_i(x) = w \oplus_i x + b$$

The above equation indicates the output F for input x after convolution with 3×3 kernel, w with dilation i and bias b. For the proposed Series Atrous Convolution Unit, i can take up values, 1,2,4,8,16,32.

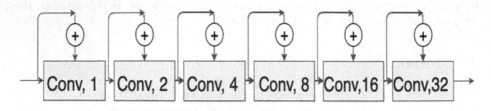

Fig. 2. The series atrous convolution unit

With the above terminology, we define the Series Atrous Convolution Unit as below.

$$Input = x_1$$

$$x_2 = F_1(x_1) + x_1$$

$$x_3 = F_2(x_2) + x_2$$

$$x_4 = F_4(x_3) + x_3$$

$$x_5 = F_8(x_4) + x_4$$

$$x_6 = F_{16}(x_5) + x_5$$

$$x_7 = F_{32}(x_6) + x_6$$

$$Output = x_7$$

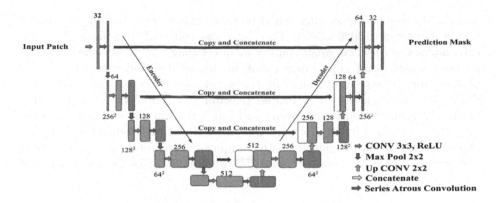

Fig. 3. The proposed AtResUNet

3.3   Proposed Architecture

In the proposed architecture depicted in Fig. 3, the UNet [22] is used as the base model, and the Series Atrous Convolution Unit is used for feature extraction. The input image is passed through a convolutional layer from which basic feature extraction occurs at that particular resolution. After that, the extracted primitive map is fed into the Series Atrous Convolution Unit having the same number of filters as the input feature map. The crucial information is extracted by 1×1 convolution, which decreases the number of channels in feature maps to that of the input to the Series Atrous Convolution Unit. The presence of Series Atrous Convolution Unit aids in extracting meaningful information required for the model training, as well as for proper convergence of the model. Moreover, the presence of the Series Atrous Convolution Units in the expansion region of the proposed model architecture helps in streamlining essential features present in the feature map obtained from the upsampling operation and enhances them considerably. Skip connections, inherent to UNet, share information at the same encoder-decoder level, which helps boost segmentation accuracy through the proper flow of gradient through the model. However, the apparent drawback to UNet-style architectures is that training of the intermediate layers of deeper models gets sluggish, which increases the risk of the network learning to scorn away the layers where abstract features are extracted. Conceivably, using a UNet architecture can improve the retention of fine detail features with fast training of deep networks. The benefits of the UNet outweigh its drawbacks, which prompted us to use it as our base model upon which we base our improvements.

4   Data Processing and Training

4.1   Dataset

The DigestPath, 2019 [17] dataset was used which consisted of colonoscopy images of 750 tissue samples from 450 patients. The challenge also provided another dataset on signet ring cell detection. The average size of the images in the dataset was 3000×3000. This data was collected from multiple medical centers from several small centers in developing countries/regions; hence, it shows a significant appearance variation. Image style differences can be an obstacle for the screening task. The tissue samples collected were first dehydrated and then embedded in melted paraffin wax. After that, the resulting block was mounted on a microtome and cut into thin slices. All whole slide images were stained by hematoxylin and eosin(H&E) and scanned at X20. We applied standard data augmentation techniques such as rotating, flipping, shear and stretch. The dataset was split into 75% for training, 15% for validation, and 10% for testing.

4.2   Preprocessing

In the training phase, the model was trained with 50% overlapping patches of size $512 \times 512 \times 3$. This was primarily done to mitigate the effects of class imbalance and the less availability of data. The data consists of a white background and tissue sample in the foreground. Therefore, when patches of $512 \times 512 \times 3$ were generated, many patches consisted of only the white background or very less useful portion (Fig. 4). These redundant patches would have misled the training, so they were discarded. The samples' discarding was based on thresholding the amount of tissue sample or the useful information present in the patch. The dataset was segregated by thresholding it for a minimum X% of tissue pixels. After thresholding for several percentages such as 40%, 30%, 20%, etc., it was observed that by thresholding with 30%, maximum redundancy was removed, and useful information was saved. Also, the patches with data less than 30% would be covered in other patches that share the same 50% overlap. Lastly, the patches were directly normalized to 0–1 by dividing each pixel by 255. This normalization has the effect of stabilizing the learning and converging of the model, requiring less training.

4.3   Post-processing

While predicting the given image, we predicted on patches of $512 \times 512 \times 3$ from the image with no overlapping and reconstructed the image. The predicted image, however, had block artifacts in it. Therefore, certain steps were taken as post-processing to overcome this and enhance the results. Firstly, the image of dimension $X \times Y$ was padded from all sides with a depth of 256, which resulted in the new dimensions $(X + 512) \times (Y + 512)$. Subsequently, the whole image was predicted upon with the above method by taking overlapping patches from 4 different starting points, (1) black:(0,0), (2) blue:(256,0), (3) red:(0,256) and (4) green:(256,256) as shown in Fig. 5. For representation, the center square is the original image, while the rest of the squares are padded regions. The four overlapping patches are then taken and predicted upon so that the original image is predicted upon four times. After this, the segmentation result corresponding

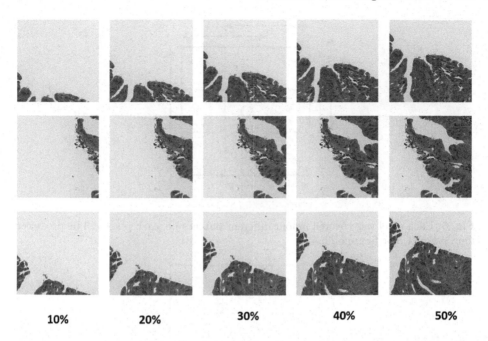

10%   **20%**   **30%**   **40%**   **50%**

Fig. 4. Sample patches extracted for training. % threshold indicates ratio of tissue pixels

to the original image in each of the four patches is extracted from the four predicted segmentation maps by removing the excess padding. The final result is then obtained by averaging the four segmentation maps and then thresholding for 50%. The averaging provides a more robust output. A more accurate representation can be seen in Fig. 6, wherein the center green square is the original image while the rest of the squares and rectangles are padded regions. Also, the above technique of post-processing can be easily implemented in clinical settings as it only makes use of a simple padding algorithm.

4.4 Loss Function

The loss function used for training of model was the Dice Loss, which is the complement of the Dice Coefficient(DC). DC is the measure of the intersection or similarity between the two representations. It ranges from 0 to 1, where a DC of 1 denotes precise and whole overlap. The DC was formerly stated for binary data and calculated as:

$$DC = \frac{2 * |X \cap Y|}{|X| + |Y|}$$
$$Loss = 1 - DC$$

where $X \cap Y$ represents the common elements between sets X and Y, and $|X|$, $|Y|$ represents the number of elements in set X and set Y, respectively.

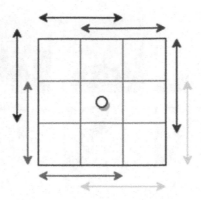

Fig. 5. Each pixel was covered in four different patches i.e. each pixel will be predicted four times (Color figure online)

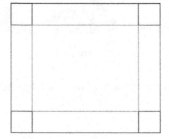

Fig. 6. The green box is whole slide image. All other regions are padded portions. Patches were taken from four different positions hence four different colors are used for depiction (Color figure online)

$|X \cap Y|$ was computed as the element-wise multiplication between the target and prediction mask and then adding the resulting matrix. The Dice Loss is a popular loss function used for various segmentation tasks, especially for medical image segmentation, and we used the same for training. The Dice Coefficient was used as the performance metric for comparison during testing.

4.5   Ensemble Modeling

The process of ensemble modeling remained reasonably straightforward. We used the self-ensemble [18] technique, where the results from six flipped/rotated versions of the same image were calculated. The final probability predictions were calculated by averaging all six predictions. We also ensemble the results obtained from our two best performing models, namely ResUNet and the proposed AtResUNet model.

5   Experiments and Results

We implemented our network using Keras [5] (version 2.2.4) with Tensorflow backend. For preprocessing, OpenCV(version 4.1.0) and Scikit-Learn(version 0.21.2) was used. All the networks were trained on two NVIDIA Tesla-V100 GPUs with a mini-batch size of four. Adam [16] optimizer was used to optimize the whole network, and the learning rate was initialized as 0.001 and decayed, according to cosine annealing. The patch initially extracted from the dataset has the shape of 512×512, max-pooling was performed in subsequent layers till the resolution of the feature map reduced to 1/8th of the original. For better training and reduction in overfitting of the model, batch-normalization [11], and twenty-five percent dropout [24] was applied before the max-pooling operation. Every convolution filter in the model is of size 3×3, and dilation rate, one unless specified. The activation function used is ReLU. In UNet [22], after every pooling operation, the output is passed through a 3×3 convolution, ReLU activation, and batch normalization layer. The model was trained for 100 epochs with data augmentation (as stated above) and a training dice coefficient of 0.96, and a validation dice coefficient of 0.87 was achieved. Lastly, even though the training was done using 30% as the threshold for white matter ratio, the model performed exceptionally well on images with a ratio up to the tune of even 70%.

Table 1. Comparison among the models evaluated on the basis of Accuracy(Acc.), Dice Coefficient, Sensitivity(Sen.), Specificity(Spe.).

Model/Architecture	Acc.	Dice	Sen.	Spe.
FCN [19]	0.473	0.497	0.461	0.502
DnCNN [25]	0.621	0.612	0.604	0.647
UNet [22]	0.725	0.684	0.713	0.737
ResUNet [12]	0.734	0.725	0.741	0.776
Proposed AtResUNet	0.762	0.748	0.759	0.794
Ensemble (AtResUNet+ResUNet)	**0.788**	**0.753**	**0.767**	**0.802**

Without limiting the study to UNet [22] and its variants, we also trained other models as given in the works of [19], and [25]. As for the UNet-based models, we trained and compared the results with UNet itself and ResUNet [12], which follows the idealogy of using residual connections in the UNet. For generalized results, self-ensembles of all the models were used for comparison. The winning team of the DigestPath 2019 Challenge achieved a dice score of 0.8075 on the testing dataset. However, we generated and compared our results using a five-fold cross-validation split of the training data itself. A considerable improvement from the UNet was noted with the use of residual connections, which was further improved upon using the novel Series Atrous Convolution Unit. It was found that the proposed model converges more effectively and can carry more information,

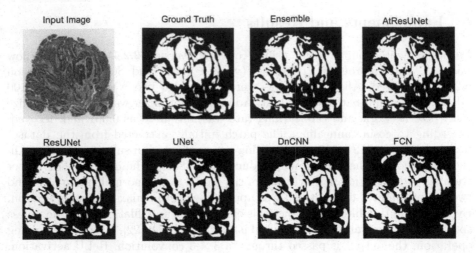

Fig. 7. Qualitative Results of the final model

which increased localization and segmentation accuracy of the model compared to that of UNet. Finally, the ensemble of the novel AtResUNet and the ResUNet was found to give the best results in our study as seen in Table 1, and Fig. 7.

6   Conclusion

In this work, we have proposed a novel CNN-based architecture for segmenting the tumor in colonoscopy images. The AtResUNet combines atrous convolutions and residual connections with the UNet as the base model. Our architecture outperformed the existing architectures to emerge as the state-of-the-art for the task. Also, the pre and post-processing techniques used provided for efficient patch-based processing of the high-resolution images, which comprised a substantial amount of white matter. For overall comparison and generalization, the self-ensembling of all the architectures was done. Finally, the ensemble of the novel AtResUNet and ResUNet was found to give the best of the result in our study. Further work on this task includes introducing adversarial networks for the generation of artificial data for improved training. The adversarial network could also be directly introduced in the training process for better performance on the segmentation predictions. Lastly, we aim to make the model more generalizable to be used for other biomedical segmentation tasks too.

References

1. Baid, U., Shah, N.A., Talbar, S.: Brain tumor segmentation with cascaded deep convolutional neural network. In: Crimi, A., Bakas, S. (eds.) BrainLes 2019. LNCS, vol. 11993, pp. 90–98. Springer, Cham (2020). https://doi.org/10.1007/978-3-030-46643-5_9

2. Baid, U., et al.: A novel approach for fully automatic intra-tumor segmentation with 3D U-Net architecture for gliomas. Front. Comput. Neurosci. **14**, 10 (2020)
3. Bychkov, D., et al.: Deep learning based tissue analysis predicts outcome in colorectal cancer. Sci. Rep. **8**(1), 1–11 (2018)
4. Chen, L.C., Papandreou, G., Kokkinos, I., Murphy, K., Yuille, A.L.: DeepLab: semantic image segmentation with deep convolutional nets, atrous convolution, and fully connected CRFs. IEEE Trans. Pattern Anal. Mach. Intell. **40**(4), 834–848 (2017)
5. Chollet, F., et al.: Keras (2015). https://keras.io
6. Çiçek, Ö., Abdulkadir, A., Lienkamp, S.S., Brox, T., Ronneberger, O.: 3D U-Net: learning dense volumetric segmentation from sparse annotation. In: Ourselin, S., Joskowicz, L., Sabuncu, M.R., Unal, G., Wells, W. (eds.) MICCAI 2016. LNCS, vol. 9901, pp. 424–432. Springer, Cham (2016). https://doi.org/10.1007/978-3-319-46723-8_49
7. Deng, J., Dong, W., Socher, R., Li, L.J., Li, K., Fei-Fei, L.: ImageNet: a large-scale hierarchical image database. In: 2009 IEEE Conference on Computer Vision and Pattern Recognition, pp. 248–255. IEEE (2009)
8. Figueira, G., Wang, Y., Sun, L., Zhou, H., Zhang, Q.: Adversarial-based domain adaptation networks for unsupervised tumour detection in histopathology. In: 2020 IEEE 17th International Symposium on Biomedical Imaging (ISBI), pp. 1284–1288. IEEE (2020)
9. He, K., Zhang, X., Ren, S., Sun, J.: Deep residual learning for image recognition. In: Proceedings of the IEEE Conference on Computer Vision and Pattern Recognition, pp. 770–778 (2016)
10. Hu, H., Zheng, Y., Zhou, Q., Xiao, J., Chen, S., Guan, Q.: MC-UNet: Multi-scale convolution UNet for bladder cancer cell segmentation in phase-contrast microscopy images. In: 2019 IEEE International Conference on Bioinformatics and Biomedicine (BIBM), pp. 1197–1199. IEEE (2019)
11. Ioffe, S., Szegedy, C.: Batch normalization: accelerating deep network training by reducing internal covariate shift. arXiv preprint arXiv:1502.03167 (2015)
12. Isensee, F., Maier-Hein, K.H.: OR-UNet: an optimized robust residual U-Net for instrument segmentation in endoscopic images. arXiv preprint arXiv:2004.12668 (2020)
13. Jin, Q., Meng, Z., Sun, C., Wei, L., Su, R.: RA-UNet: a hybrid deep attention-aware network to extract liver and tumor in CT scans. arXiv preprint arXiv:1811.01328 (2018)
14. Kather, J.N., et al.: Predicting survival from colorectal cancer histology slides using deep learning: a retrospective multicenter study. PLoS Med. **16**(1), e1002730 (2019)
15. Khened, M., Kori, A., Rajkumar, H., Srinivasan, B., Krishnamurthi, G.: A generalized deep learning framework for whole-slide image segmentation and analysis. arXiv preprint arXiv:2001.00258 (2020)
16. Kingma, D.P., Ba, J.: Adam: a method for stochastic optimization. arXiv preprint arXiv:1412.6980 (2014)
17. Li, J., et al.: Signet ring cell detection with a semi-supervised learning framework. In: Chung, A.C.S., Gee, J.C., Yushkevich, P.A., Bao, S. (eds.) IPMI 2019. LNCS, vol. 11492, pp. 842–854. Springer, Cham (2019). https://doi.org/10.1007/978-3-030-20351-1_66
18. Liu, X., Cheng, M., Zhang, H., Hsieh, C.J.: Towards robust neural networks via random self-ensemble. In: Proceedings of the European Conference on Computer Vision (ECCV), pp. 369–385 (2018)

19. Long, J., Shelhamer, E., Darrell, T.: Fully convolutional networks for semantic segmentation. In: Proceedings of the IEEE Conference on Computer Vision and Pattern Recognition, pp. 3431–3440 (2015)
20. Raj, A., Shah, N.A., Tiwari, A.K., Martini, M.G.: Multivariate regression-based convolutional neural network model for fundus image quality assessment. IEEE Access **8**, 57810–57821 (2020)
21. Rawla, P., Sunkara, T., Barsouk, A.: Epidemiology of colorectal cancer: incidence, mortality, survival, and risk factors. Przeg. Gastroenterologiczny **14**(2), 89 (2019)
22. Ronneberger, O., Fischer, P., Brox, T.: U-Net: convolutional networks for biomedical image segmentation. In: Navab, N., Hornegger, J., Wells, W.M., Frangi, A.F. (eds.) MICCAI 2015. LNCS, vol. 9351, pp. 234–241. Springer, Cham (2015). https://doi.org/10.1007/978-3-319-24574-4_28
23. Sirinukunwattana, K., Raza, S.E.A., Tsang, Y.W., Snead, D.R., Cree, I.A., Rajpoot, N.M.: Locality sensitive deep learning for detection and classification of nuclei in routine colon cancer histology images. IEEE Trans. Med. Imaging **35**(5), 1196–1206 (2016)
24. Srivastava, N., Hinton, G., Krizhevsky, A., Sutskever, I., Salakhutdinov, R.: Dropout: a simple way to prevent neural networks from overfitting. J. Mach. Learn. Res. **15**(56), 1929–1958 (2014). http://jmlr.org/papers/v15/srivastava14a.html
25. Zhang, K., Zuo, W., Chen, Y., Meng, D., Zhang, L.: Beyond a Gaussian denoiser: residual learning of deep CNN for image denoising. IEEE Trans. Image Process. **26**(7), 3142–3155 (2017)
26. Zhu, C., et al.: Multi-level colonoscopy malignant tissue detection with adversarial CAC-UNet. arXiv preprint arXiv:2006.15954 (2020)

Deep Learning Based Detection of Rhinoceros Beetle Infestation in Coconut Trees Using Drone Imagery

Atharva Kadethankar[1(✉)], Neelam Sinha[1], Abhishek Burman[2],
and Vinayaka Hegde[3]

[1] International Institute of Information Technology, Bengaluru, India
atharva.kadethankar@iiitb.org, neelam.sinha@iiitb.ac.in
[2] General Aeronautics Pvt. Ltd., Bengaluru, India
abhishek.burman@generalaeronautics.com
[3] ICAR-CPCRI, Kasaragod, Kerala, India

Abstract. This paper reports an end-to-end pipeline for detecting a specific infestation among coconut trees, caused due to the attack of rhinoceros beetle, which can critically harm the productivity, using drone imagery. The advantage of drone imagery lies in giving a bird's eye view of the plantation which cannot be seen from the ground level. However, the challenge in processing drone imagery stems from the lack of depth information. The main objective is to detect and extract the individual tree-crown from an image that might contain up to 30 tree-crowns, to enable further analysis. The challenges lie in separating the crown in the presence of textured soil, shadows, companion plants. The data-set generated is composed of 1212 drone images containing 9727 individual tree crowns. In this work, we use Invariant Risk Minimization (IRM) for the first time in object detection and classification approach. Faster R-CNN model was used to extract candidate regions containing all individual crowns in the drone image while VGG-16 model was used to classify the detected crowns based on their health. For crown detection, the precision and recall score obtained was 97.30% and 92% respectively, while the classification accuracy obtained was 84.64%. This illustrates that analyzing drone images can be effectively used to monitor the well-being of a large plantation.

Keywords: Rhinoceros beetle · Coconut trees · Drone · Faster R-CNN · VGG-16 · IRM

1 Introduction

In traditional coconut cultivation practices, to monitor crown health, farmers can see from the ground or climb trees, but only see the base level leaves of the crowns. Capturing images at higher altitude in large farms using traditional imaging techniques is a very difficult and time-consuming task. Manual intervention is required for this process, which is expensive and error prone. The drone

© Springer Nature Singapore Pte Ltd. 2021
S. K. Singh et al. (Eds.): CVIP 2020, CCIS 1376, pp. 463–474, 2021.
https://doi.org/10.1007/978-981-16-1086-8_41

image provides a bird's eye view of the farm at high altitude. Here, the map of the farm is entered into the drone system, and the drone captures images through an automated process, making this process fast, accurate and cost effective. Due to these advantages over conventional imaging, we are using drone images to analyze coconut crowns from top.

When rhinoceros beetles invade coconut and oil palm trees, they have a direct impact on the health and yield of the tree. New 'V-shaped' cuts due to rhino beetles are observed in the upper canopy, and old cuts are observed in the bottom of the canopy of coconut trees (Fig. 2). The images taken from the drone are fed into the crown localization and segmentation algorithm, where individual coconut crowns are detected and their location is stored. The detected coconut crown from the image is further subjected to classification algorithm where it is classified as healthy or rhino beetle affected.

In this paper we propose first of its kind a complete pipeline for detecting rhino beetle infestation in coconut palm trees, Fig. 1. We propose Invariant Risk Minimization (IRM) based coconut crown segmentation and classification technique, in which model overcomes the biases and spurious correlations which are learnt from Empirical Risk Minimization (ERM) training and gives better performance.

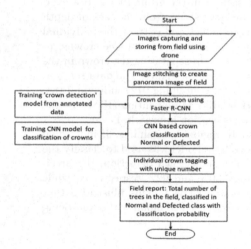

Fig. 1. Workflow of proposed method.

Fig. 2. V-shape cuts in coconut leaves due to Rhino Beetle attack (Showed with red arrows). (Color figure online)

2   Literature

Coconut tree (Cocos nucifera (L.)) is referred to as 'Kalpa Vriksha' in ancient Indian scripts due to its multipurpose use [2]. Between 2015 and 2019 alone coconut water industry has generated $4 billion in revenue globally [1]. India

(a) 40 m altitude, summer season   (b) 60 m altitude, rainy season

Fig. 3. Input RGB images collected from drone at different altitudes and in different seasons.

has coconut production over 119 million tons making it among the top three countries for coconut production [1].

Coconut rhinoceros beetle (Oryctes rhinoceros (Linnaeus)) is mostly found in Asia and the Pacific Islands region and its infestation is observed in both coconut and oil palm [3]. Rhino beetle bores into the base of the crown of palm trees making cuts in the unopened leaves which results in V-shaped cuts after unfolding of leaves. Boring of rhino beetle into meristem of palm trees results in severe damage to the plant resulting in loss of yield, delayed maturity in palm plants and death of plant in all ages [4]. Due to rhino beetle attack, around 3% loss in leaf area reduce nut yield by 5%, while 7% loss in leaf area results in 13% nut yield loss [4].

In recent years, use of image processing techniques along with deep learning has grown in precision agriculture field. In image processing based approaches for crown identification and segmentation, Salim Malek and et al. proposed a method for palm tree detection using UAV images in desert [7]. Authors are detecting palm trees from UAV images using SIFT for identifying key-points then classifying the key-points as palm vs non-palm using extreme learning machine (ELM) and finally to get the contour of palm tree, they used level sets over key-points. This method is specifically developed to detect palm trees, where the data-set images are captured at such a high altitude that it covers approximately 7600 m² field area, in this case the details of palm crown are not visible, which is not useful in case of identifying rhino beetle infestation. This method works best with background of palm trees as desert soil only, in case of compliment plantation or soil texture change, this method fails. Another approach in which Hung et al. [15] used vision band only (RGB) imagery acquired from UAVs to detect tree crowns using template matching. This method fails when there are different background scenarios also, the boundaries are rigid due to template which is not desirable as crown shapes change throughout the field.

In deep learning based approaches, Italos de Souza et al. [13] proposed a method in which they are classifying whether a given image contain coconut tree or not. Authors are proposing Feature Learning from Image Markers (FLIM) method in which first, user marks relevant features on the images which are subjected to training, layers of convolutional network learn features based on the marks and then model is trained to classify according to class. This method is introduced to reduce the number of images to train the fully connected layers by introducing user interface in the training process. This method fails in case multiple crown localization from single image and it's not robust to background changes. In another approach Ramesh Kestur et al. [14] proposed coconut crown detection in which supervised classification is carried out using extreme learning machine (ELM), a single hidden layer feed forward network neural network classifier. RGB images analyzed in this experiment are low spectral resolution, the ability to discriminate the tree crown pixels is constrained, leading to misclassification of pixels of crowns.

In the work done by M. Zakharova [8] the author used annotated data of coconut trees to train CNN models to find coconut trees from aerial images. In the work done by Steven Puttemans et al. [9] proposed fast and robust coconut crown tree detection using boosted cascade and deep learning. For boosted cascade approach, authors train object detection model using Viola and Jones boosted cascade with LBP features. For deep learning approach, authors use Darknet19 for coconut crown detection. Authors train models on manually annotated image taken from remote sensing sensor. The model accuracy using deep learning is remarkable. This work is targeting just localization of coconut crowns, due to which the model is trained on very high-altitude images. This approach is disadvantageous in case of observing details of coconut crown.

The proposed method in this paper detects high resolution coconut tree crowns from an image which have different background scenarios and different altitudes, and then classifies detected crown as healthy or defected based on the crown health condition.

3   Drone, Dataset and Annotations

The drone used for collecting data was built by General Aeronautics Pvt. Ltd., India. The model used for this purpose was 'GA-3 Multirotor ISR UAS'. Images were collected by GA-3 drone from two different locations of Central Plantation Crops Research Institute (CPCRI) situated at Kasaragod and Kayamkulam, Kerala, India. Total 1,212 images were collected from different coconut farms to create the dataset. Drone was flown at two different altitudes (40 m & 60 m) in different seasons (summer & rainy) for making the model robust to altitudes and different seasonal effects. In drone imagery, coconut crown visibility is clearer in clear or partially cloudy weather conditions due to which all data was collected considering these weather conditions.

Drone was flown in square wave pattern over the field to cover total of 25 hectors area with overlap score of 75% in each image. The images taken at an altitude of 40 m approximately covered 225 m^2 area per image which contain around 16 to 20 tree crowns. However, images taken at an altitude of 60 m approximately covered 400 m^2 area per image which contain around 24 to 30 coconut tree crowns. In 40 m and 60 m altitude images, pixels covered by each crown range from 1,60,000 to 4,90,000 pixels and 6,40,000 to 13,20,000 pixels respectively. In total, 1,212 images were collected from field, among which 547 images are captured at 40 m altitude and 665 images are captured at 60 m altitude, Fig. 3.

Annotation of captured images is being done by CPCRI scientists using 'labelImg' [11] image annotation tool. From each image, crowns were identified and labelled as 'crown' with rectangular bounding-box. In similar way, the annotation label used for normal/healthy coconut crowns was 'Healthy' and for coconut crowns with Rhinoceros Beetle attack was 'P_RB'. The following annotation strategy is followed to annotate different defected crowns, (1) if the defect is pest, then first letter in the annotation is 'P', (2) if the defect is disease, then first letter in the annotation is 'D', (3) For second part in the annotation, the initials of the disease/pest name are abbreviated together, e.g. Pest - Rhinoceros Beetle - P_RB. The total 'crown' annotations obtained over the whole dataset are 9427. Among 9427 annotated crowns, distribution of crowns labelled as 'Healthy' and 'P_RB' is 4200 and 5227 respectively.

4   Proposed Method

The proposed method for detecting Rhino beetle infestation can be divided into two parts: (1) Crown detection, (2) Crown classification. In this work, we are adapting newly introduced concept, Invariant Risk Minimization (IRM) a loss minimizing technique [12]. The performance comparison of IRM and Empirical Risk Minimization (ERM) based outputs for the proposed approach is done to see which method works better in the given scenario.

4.1   IRM Based Framework for Crown Detection and Segmentation

ERM learning rule targets on minimizing training error, this leads deep learning model into imprudently learning all the correlations found in training data. This kind of learning may lead model to learn some spurious correlations as causal correlation, based on which model may give undesirable results. To overcome this drawback, Martin Arjovsky et al. proposed Invariant Risk Minimization (IRM) technique that estimates invariant, nonlinear, causal predictors from various training environments, to enable out-of-distribution (OOD) generalization [12]. In Eq. 1, Φ represents dataset such that $\Phi : X \rightarrow H$, $\omega.\Phi$ is invariant predictor over all environments E where ω is classifier such that $\omega : H \rightarrow Y$, the function $D(\omega, \Phi, e)$ measures how close ω is to minimizing $R^e(\omega.\Phi)$, and $\lambda \epsilon [0; 1)$ is a hyper-parameter balancing predictive power and invariance.

$$L_{IRM}(\Phi, \omega) = \sum_{e \epsilon E_{tr}} R^e(\omega.\Phi) + \lambda.D(\omega, \Phi, e) \qquad (1)$$

L_{IRM} is IRM penalized loss such that initially, $\omega = 1$ is a pseudo classifier which is optimized using the gradient norm penalty at each environment e, and empirically λ was set to 1.6*(#epoch) which promotes low error. IRM promotes that the features learnt by the model over all the data is the same for every environment. The non-invariant features won't be ideal for all the environments so that the function will use invariant features only. In case of coconut crown detection and classification, as scenarios are complicated than regular detection and classification model, with IRM based approach we expect to get better relations of features to causal effects.

4.2   Crown Detection

Before the crown being classified as normal or defected, first task is to iden-tify each individual crown from every image where each image contain multiple coconut tree crowns. There are multiple challenges while identifying coconut crown from an image, (1) shadows of coconut crowns in the background, both shadow and crown have similar shape makes it hard to differentiate based on shape, (2) weed growth in the field can be seen in the background of coconut crown making it difficult to distinguish between foreground and background due to same color intensity, (3) texture of soil in the crown background brings lots of variations, (4) inter cropping or companion planting makes it difficult to differ-entiate between coconut crown and other plant as there is no depth information this which makes model difficult to spot coconut crown.

For identifying crown from an image, we have used 'Deep learning based object detection' approach. While training, model was trained over 7401 crown annotations and 2026 crown annotations were used for testing purpose. The annotations for 'crown' is represented by 1 and all other background with 0. The proposed IRM model was trained using 'Faster R-CNN with Inception-V2' architecture which was pre-trained on MS-COCO data-set, the network structure of Faster R-CNN can be seen in Fig. 4. The object detection and region proposal generation, both tasks are done by the same convolutional networks in Faster R-CNN [10]. The initial learning rate for model was 0.001, after 4000 steps it was reduced to 0.0001 and Adam optimizer was used. The training was done for 8,000 steps where minimum IRM loss obtained was 0.373, Fig. 5(a). Loss function used during all the experiments is 'Cross-Entropy-Loss' this function is combination of the 'logarithmic Softmax' function and 'Negative log likelihood loss' function, Eq. 2.

$$Crossentropy\ loss = L(x, class) = -\log\left(\frac{exp(x[class])}{\sum_i exp(x[i])}\right) \tag{2}$$

The results of crown detection process can be seen in, Fig. 6 and 7. It can be observed that, the model is able to detect crowns even when there is companion planting and green grassy background. In both cases of altitude variation, the model is able to detect crowns. From the output images it can be inferred that,

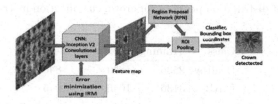

Fig. 4. Proposed crown detection architecture using IRM framework.

flying drone at 40 m altitude for collecting data for coconut farms is preferable as there are less number of unidentified crown cases near image border. Model performance is determined for IoU with threshold of 0.5 overlap. The precision obtained for IRM based model is 97.30 % mAP and Recall is 92%, Fig. 5(b) and Table 2.

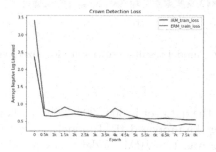

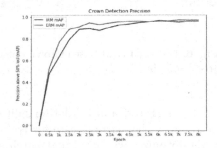

(a) Proposed IRM model & ERM model's crown detection loss plot.

(b) Proposed IRM model's & ERM model's crown detection precision plot.

Fig. 5. Comparison of proposed IRM crown detection model with ERM model w.r.t. loss and precision.

4.3 Crown Classification

To identify crown's health, each localized crown is then passed down to the classification model. The classification model is trained for two classes: 'Healthy' and 'P_RB'. For classification purpose, VGG-16 pre-trained model was chosen empirically. This architecture consists of 16 layers among which 13 are convolutional layers and 3 are fully connected layers [6]. Transfer learning was used to while training the model, the pre-trained model used was trained over ImageNet [5] data-set and the learned features from this model were used in the proposed model.

Table 1. Data-set distribution per class for crown classification in Training, Validation and Test data.

Class	Training	Validation	Test
Healthy	2530	840	840
P_RB	3136	1046	1045

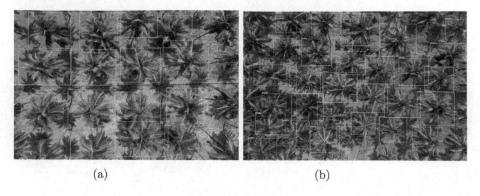

(a)   (b)

Fig. 6. Proposed IRM based Crown detection model results, crowns are localized with green bounding box.

Training, test and validation split on the data-set is 60%-20%-20% as shown in Table 1. The learning rate for training the proposed IRM model was 0.0001, SGD optimizer was used and batch size was 128. IRM model was trained for 150 epochs after which the training accuracy started to saturate, Fig. 8(a). For IRM based classification model, maximum training accuracy obtained is 91.55% and maximum validation accuracy obtained is 90.30%. Minimum IRM training and validation loss obtained is 0.44 and 0.351 respectively, Fig. 8(b). In case of training the model, training loss is calculated during every epoch while validation loss is calculated after every epoch. Dropout regularization technique was used during the training and not during validation. These methods of practice led the model to have lower validation loss than training loss.

To validate model performance, five fold cross validation was carried out for IRM based classification model. Stratified k-fold cross validation was used to preserve class distribution in each fold, the average training accuracy obtained was 86.7%. The IRM based model obtained classification accuracy of 84.64%, Table 4.

5   Results and Discussion

IRM based crown localization and classification methods are combined together thus creating the entire pipeline for localizing and detecting Rhinoceros beetle infestation in coconut trees. At 40 m altitude collected data, the crown localization model performed better as compare to 60 m altitude. IRM based model

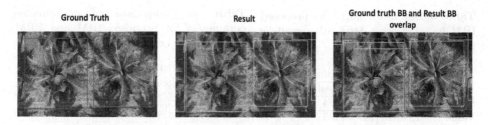

Fig. 7. Ground truth (red bounding box) and obtained result (green bounding box) comparison of crown localizing bounding boxes. (Color figure online)

Table 2. Comparison of proposed IRM architecture performance on private data with different coconut crown detection methods.

Methods	Number of training dataset annotations	Total dataset annotations	Precision (%)	Recall (%)
IRM crown localization	7401	9427	**97.30**	**92.0**
M Zakharova (2017)	500	1500	71.0	93.0
Steven P. et al. (2018)	2000	3798	97.31	88.58
de Souza et al. (2020)	200	13587	86.3	84.9

learnt features over different environments and learnt more causal relations learning more about invariant features. The data-set had huge impact of different background scenarios. Even in the foreground, there was not that much change in features as all were coconut crowns. In this scenario, IRM model learnt the real causal features and was able to perform better. In case of crown localization, our model got 97.30% precision and 92% recall, better performance than Steven P. et al. [9], Table 2. The crown classification approach is first of its kind making our result of 84.64% accuracy as benchmark, Tables 3 and 4.

We also compared IRM based model results with ERM based models. The learning rule to minimize the average training loss of deep learning architectures is known as 'Empirical Risk Minimization (ERM)' [16], Eq. 3.

$$argmin_{f \in F} R_{emp}(f) = \frac{1}{n} \sum_{i=0}^{n} L(f(x_i), y_i) \tag{3}$$

ERM models were trained with same parameters that were used in IRM models training. Minimum ERM loss obtained for training crown segmentation model was 0.5412, Fig. 5(a). For crown segmentation, the precision over the test data obtained for ERM based model was 96.26% mAP and Recall was 90.18%, Fig. 5(b). For ERM based crown classification model, maximum training accuracy obtained was 90.72% and maximum validation accuracy obtained was 86.26%. For crown classification, ERM based model obtained 80.31% accuracy, Table 4. Comparing the results of IRM based model with ERM model in both, crown segmentation and classification, IRM outperformed ERM approach.

472   A. Kadethankar et al.

Table 3. Confusion matrix for proposed IRM based crown classification model's performance of test data.

		True Value	
		P_RB	Healthy
Predicted Value	P_RB	821	224
	Healthy	147	693

Table 4. Comparison of performance parameters for proposed IRM and ERM based crown classification results.

Performance parameter	IRM based classification (%)	ERM based classification (%)
Accuracy	84.64	80.31
Precision	86.98	78.56
Sensitivity	85.51	84.81
Specificity	83.45	75.57
F1 score	86.24	81.56

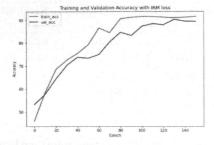

(a) Training-Validation accuracy plot for proposed IRM classification model.

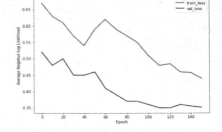

(b) Training-Validation loss plot for proposed IRM classification model.

Fig. 8. Proposed IRM classification model performance w.r.t. Training-Validation accuracy and loss.

For crown segmentation, IRM got 1.04% more precision than ERM model and in classification, IRM got 4.33% more accuracy than ERM model.

In earlier methods to detect coconut trees from aerial images, the authors used annotated data to train CNN models to find coconut trees [8,9]. This approach limits the robustness of the model against different background. In the proposed method, with developed detection technique, it is possible to detect coconut crown at different altitude scales with different backgrounds. In order to find the area and location of the tree, GPS tagging of the image via image metadata is done, Fig. 9. There is scope to increase the crown classification score with more data annotations. In case of crown classification, for future work, Feature Learning from Image Markers (FLIM) can be used to improve classification accuracy.

Fig. 9. Proposed IRM classification model output, red boxes for rhinoceros beetle damaged coconut trees and blue for healthy coconut trees, green value is classification probability crown and yellow value is GPS coordinates. (Color figure online)

6   Conclusion

The basic pipeline for the identification of coconut trees from field using drone imaging and classifying the identified coconut tree as normal or defected due to rhino beetle infestation is developed. For data-set, 1212 coconut field images were captured through drone which contain 9427 coconut crowns. The proposed IRM based coconut crown detection method produced results with 97.30% precision and 92% recall score. For crown detection, the proposed method gets upper hand compared to previous approaches while dealing with different background scenarios and different altitudes. The proposed work is first of its kind approach to identify rhino beetle infestation in coconut trees. The IRM based crown classification accuracy for localized coconut crown is 84.64%. Newly introduced concept IRM was adapted for the first time to train model for localization and classification. The IRM based model learnt deeper causal relations of foreground and background of coconut crown and performed better than ERM model.

For getting information from whole field, panorama image was developed for the field with GPS tagging. From the results, flying drones at 40 m altitude for analyzing coconut fields is preferable. This method can also get the count of coconut crowns from entire field which is helpful for farmers and scientists for quantitative analysis. The proposed work can be extended to develop other disease or pest infestation detection models in coconut trees.

References

1. Cuckoo for Coconuts: Demand Is Soaring, but Production isn't Keeping Up (2002). https://gro-intelligence.com/insights/articles/coconuts-growing-demand-stagnant-production
2. DebMandal, M., Mandal, S.: Coconut (Cocos nucifera L.: Arecaceae): in health promotion and disease prevention. Asian Pac. J. Trop. Med. **4**(3), 241–7 (2011)

3. Manjeri, G., Muhamad, R., Tan, S.G.: Oryctes rhinoceros beetles, an oil palm pest in Malaysia. Annu. Res. Rev. Biol. **4**(22), 3429 (2014). SCIENCEDOMAIN International

4. CABI: Invasive species compendium: Oryctes rhinoceros. CAB International, Wallingford (2018). www.cabi.org/isc

5. Deng, J., Dong, W., Socher, R., Li, L.-J., Li, K., Fei-Fei, L.: ImageNet: a large-scale hierarchical image database. In: 2009 IEEE Conference on Computer Vision and Pattern Recognition, pp. 248–255. IEEE (2009)

6. Simonyan, K., Zisserman, A.: Very deep convolutional networks for large-scale image recognition. arXiv preprint arXiv:1409.1556 (2014)

7. Malek, S., Bazi, Y., Alajlan, N., AlHichri, H., Melgani, F.: Efficient framework for palm tree detection in UAV images. IEEE J. Sel. Top. Appl. Earth. Obs. Remote Sens. **7**(12), 4692–4703 (2014). IEEE

8. Zakharova, M.: Automated coconut tree detection in aerial imagery using deep learning. Master's thesis, The Katholieke Universiteit Leuven, Löwen, Belgium (2017)

9. Puttemans, S., Van Beeck, K., Goedemé, T.: Comparing boosted cascades to deep learning architectures for fast and robust coconut tree detection in aerial images. In: Proceedings of the 13th International Joint Conference on Computer Vision, Imaging and Computer Graphics Theory and Applications, vol. 5, pp. 230–241 (2018)

10. Ren, S., He, K., Girshick, R., Sun, J.: Faster R-CNN: towards real-time object detection with region proposal networks. In: Advances in Neural Information Processing Systems, pp. 91–99 (2015)

11. Tzutalin: LabelImg, Free Software: MIT License (2015). https://www.bibsonomy.org/bibtex/24d72bded15249d2d0e3d9dc187d50e16/slicside

12. Arjovsky, M., Bottou, L., Gulrajani, I., Lopez-Paz, D.: Invariant risk minimization. arXiv preprint arXiv:1907.02893 (2019)

13. de Souza, I.E., Falcão, A.X.: Learning CNN filters from user-drawn image markers for coconut-tree image classification. arXiv preprint arXiv:2008.03549 (2020)

14. Kestur, R., et al.: Tree crown detection, delineation and counting in uav remote sensed images: a neural network based spectral-spatial method. J. Indian Soc. Remote Sens. **46.6**, 991–1004 (2018)

15. Hung, C., Bryson, M., Sukkarieh, S.: Multi-class predictive template for tree crown detection. ISPRS J. Photogramm. Remote Sens. **68**, 170–183 (2012)

16. Vapnik, V.: Statistical Learning Theory. Wiley, New York (1998)

Crop Classification from UAV-Based Multi-spectral Images Using Deep Learning

B. Sudarshan Rao$^{(\boxtimes)}$, Manjit Hota$^{(\boxtimes)}$, and Uttam Kumar$^{(\boxtimes)}$

Spatial Computing Laboratory, Centre for Data Sciences, International Institute of Information Technology Bangalore (IIIT-B), 26/C, Electronics City Phase-1, Bangalore 560100, India
{sudarshan.b,manjit.hota}@iiitb.org, uttam@iiitb.ac.in

Abstract. This work explores the suitability of various deep convolutional neural network (CNN) architectures for semantic segmentation of agricultural crops such as cotton, maize etc. from multi-spectral UAV (unmanned aerial vehicle) data. Initially, the UAV data were preprocessed and training samples for each crop type were manually annotated from multiple UAV scenes. Different CNN architectures such as U-Net, SegNet and PSPNet (Pyramid Scene Parsing Network) were trained with various combinations of input spectral bands along with select band derived indices such as NDVI (Normalized Difference Vegetation Index) and EVI (Enhanced Vegetation Index) as additional features. The experimental results indicated that inclusion of NIR (near-infrared) band and NDVI in the input data yielded high segmentation accuracy of more than 90%. U-Net proved to be the best among the three architectures with 97% overall accuracy while dealing with three classes separation problem. This study demonstrated the scope of deep neural network based semantic segmentation techniques in crop classification from multi-spectral UAV data.

Keywords: Crop classification · UAV (unmanned aerial vehicle) · Multi-spectral data · Deep learning · U-Net · SegNet · PSPNet · Image analysis

1 Introduction

Food is a primary part of everyone's life. It is one of the basic requirements of any human being as quoted in Abraham Maslow's theory of hierarchical needs. Agriculture, the art of cultivation satisfies the daily food necessities, therefore plays a pivotal role in providing livelihood to majority of the population for centuries and is considered to be the backbone of any country. India is no exception to this and more than 50% of the Indian population is employed in the agricultural sector. Agriculture as such contributes 16% to India's total GDP. Therefore, it is essential to modernize the field of agriculture using the latest technological advancements to effectively and efficiently manage the processes involved.

Traditional challenges in the agricultural field have ranged from timely detection of crop diseases to estimation of crop damages due to either natural calamities, or water and nutrient stress, or plant disease to finding suitable methods for crop yield estimation. Central to devising effective solutions to all these problems lies in the ability of a

© Springer Nature Singapore Pte Ltd. 2021
S. K. Singh et al. (Eds.): CVIP 2020, CCIS 1376, pp. 475–486, 2021.
https://doi.org/10.1007/978-981-16-1086-8_42

system to map large areas of the Earth's surface with high spatial, spectral and temporal resolution data which is not only quick but also economical. This would intensify the capability to identify crops and classify each crop type accurately, thereby enhancing the overall production. In this context, UAVs (unmanned aerial vehicles) are proving to be indispensable in providing images of the land surface in multi-spectral channels. Once the images are acquired, computer vision tasks such as detection, recognition, segmentation and classification can be performed with deep learning techniques.

Advancements in imaging and deep neural networks have attracted a lot of attention in image segmentation. Some of the notable works have focused on segmentation techniques using convolutional neural network (CNN) for object detection and recognition. For example, a unique architecture for semantic segmentation in the form of encoder decoder architecture was proposed for biomedical studies [1], which consists of two paths, contracting path used for feature extraction and the expanding path for precise localization of the features. SegNet [2] was proposed as a new deep fully convolutional network architecture based on encoder decoder architecture for pixel-wise classification. Scene parsing for diverse unrestricted open vocabulary was proposed using a network [3] that exploited the capability of global context information by different region-based context aggregation through pyramid pooling module. Sa et al., presented a modified SegNet architecture called weedNet [4] which differentiated crops from weeds using Micro Aerial Vehicle (MAV) imagery. Popular vegetation indices were used in this study and were shown to be successful in achieving a F1-score of 0.8 and area under the curve as 0.78 [5]. Nevertheless, this work was limited to an area of 150 m². In one of their later works, they studied the effect of multiple spectral combinations, however this work was limited to weedNet architecture and the experiments were carried out on a mosaic of images. CIR (Composite Infra-Red), NDVI and Red Edge band combination showed promising results for Red Edge-M dataset [6]. The aforementioned works attribute to a great deal of research in classifying the agricultural areas. However, classifying the agricultural areas with the help of UAV multi-spectral data is still a difficult problem to solve given the vegetation diversity, soil patterns and type of crops practiced in the area. Also, studies of the application of deep learning on locally grown crops like cotton and maize is limited. Therefore, a data driven deep learning method to understand the specifics of the input data requirements and best suited architectures have to be explored.

This work attempts to explore the application of CNN based architectures such as PSPNet, SegNet and U-Net in classifying the crops using multi-spectral UAV data. The objectives include: (i) to identify the best possible combination of input spectral bands for crop classification, and (ii) to evaluate state-of-the-art deep learning architectures for semantic segmentation and propose a framework to classify the agricultural crops. The paper is organized as follows. Section 2 discusses the data, preprocessing steps and methodologies used in the analysis. Results are discussed in Sect. 3 with concluding remarks and recommendations for future work in Sect. 4.

2 Data and Methods

Multi-spectral data used for the classification of crops were captured at the same instance from a UAV mounted Micasense® Altum camera [7]. Approximately, 200 GB of data were acquired over a small agricultural field (vegetation region) in Dharwad district, Karnataka state, India on 21st and 22nd October, 14th November and 4th December, 2019 consisting of single and combination of multiple crops in each scene of the study area. The camera captures data in six bands within specific wavelength range across the electromagnetic spectrum (Table 1) at 3 mega pixel resolution. A small subset of manually selected scenes were finally used in the study. Figure 1 shows a sample of an actual image captured over an agricultural field, where each image corresponds to one of the six bands with the naming convention as per Table 1.

Table 1. Bandwidth details of the images captured by the camera

Image number	Band	Centre wavelength	Bandwidth
IMG_1	Blue	475 nm	20 nm
IMG_2	Green	560 nm	20 nm
IMG_3	Red	668 nm	10 nm
IMG_4	Red edge	717 nm	10 nm
IMG_5	Near-infrared	840 nm	40 nm
IMG_6	Thermal	11 μm	6 μm

2.1 Image Pre-processing

The uncalibrated raw images had effects of light source, sensor, atmosphere and different surface materials. Initially, the raw values were converted to radiance and then to reflectance to observe the properties of various surface materials. Reflectance values are useful in spectral image analysis and for comparison of different image spectra. Therefore, image pre-processing was applied on different bands to obtain a dataset suitable for vegetation studies as depicted in Fig. 2.

Micasense provides a reflective surface (along with the camera) which acts as a reference for measuring the reflectance that were further used in calibration of the individual images. Raw images consisting of digital numbers were converted to radiance and then to reflectance values for analysis. The raw values to radiance conversion included compensation for dark pixel offset, imager-level effects, optical chain effects, and were finally normalized by exposure and gain settings. Dark pixel compensation is done to remove the effects of dark current generated due to electrical characteristics of transistors. Imager-level and optical chain effects like row gradient and vignette effects were compensated by using the camera's calibration metadata to correct the radial and directional effects of the lens. Image and optical distortions were normalized with the selected bit depth.

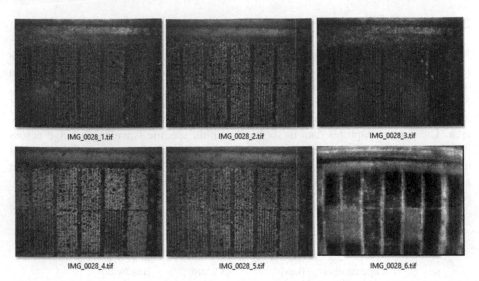

Fig. 1. Original images captured by the multi-spectral camera in different wavelength bands.

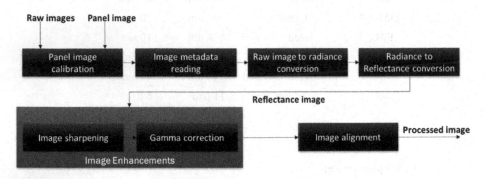

Fig. 2. Image pre-processing pipeline.

Exposure and gain settings were obtained from the image metadata and were applied to form the radiance measurements. Scale factor between radiance and reflectance was computed based on the calibration panel which was used as a reference parameter for calculation of the reflectance. Following the pre-processing stages, image sharpening and gamma correction were carried out. Sharpness correction was performed to enhance the edges in the image and Gamma correction improved the human eye perception.

Composite images were generated to obtain true-color (RGB) and false color (such as CIR - Composite Infra-Red) representations. CIR images are useful in studying the nature of vegetation which consist of three plane data with Green, Red and NIR (near-infrared) bands included. In addition, two popular vegetation indices viz. Normalized Difference Vegetation Index (NDVI) and Enhanced Vegetation Index (EVI) were computed that have been proved useful for vegetation studies and are given as Eq. (1) and (2) respectively.

$$NDVI = \frac{(NIR - RED)}{(NIR + RED)} \tag{1}$$

where, NIR and RED are the near-infrared and red bands of the electromagnetic spectrum. NDVI compensate for changes in lighting conditions, surface slope and exposure. It accounts for the amount of light reflected by a plant at certain frequencies to measure the plant's health because some energy are absorbed while some reflected back in the atmosphere by different plant structures. Chlorophyll, which is a health indicator of a plant absorbs visible light, and the cellular structure of the leaves strongly reflect NIR light. When the plant is dehydrated or distressed due to disease, the spongy layer deteriorates, and the plant absorbs more of the NIR light, rather than reflecting it. Therefore, changes in NIR band provides indication of the presence of chlorophyll, which correlates with plant health. NDVI values range from -1 to 1 where higher values from 0.5 towards 1 indicate dense vegetation, 0 to 0.5 represent agricultural farm, shrub and grassland while negative values show the presence of water, sand, cloud or snow [8]. On the other hand, EVI is used to quantify vegetation greenness. It corrects the atmospheric conditions and canopy background noise and is also more sensitive in areas with dense vegetation.

$$EVI = G \times \frac{(NIR - RED)}{(NIR + C1 \times RED - C2 \times BLUE + L)} \tag{2}$$

where, BLUE refers to the blue band of the electromagnetic spectrum, G is the gain factor with a value of 2.5, $C1 = 6$, $C2 = 7.5$, and $L = 1$. C1 and C2 are the coefficients for atmospheric resistance, and L adjusts the canopy background. Together they reduce the atmospheric and background noise, and saturation [9]. It is important to mention that NDVI is chlorophyll sensitive whereas EVI is more responsive to variations in canopy structure and their types.

Next, image alignment was done to reduce the mosaicing artifacts that may otherwise skew the analysis results. Figure 3 shows the RGB composite images generated before and after pre-processing of data.

In order to speed up the training process, the images were subdivided into 256×256 dimensions. NDVI and EVI were used along with the other spectral bands as input to the algorithms. A subset of images were labeled using an open source image annotation tool - GNU Image Manipulation (GIMP) for preparing the ground truth based on the domain knowledge and ancillary information. Image areas were manually labeled with different intensity values using the lasso tool in GIMP and stored in gray scale. Finally, a python script was used to remove any undesired values (noise) which were generated due to interpolation by the labeling software before saving the ground truth images.

Fig. 3. RGB composite images obtained from original and preprocessed data.

2.2 Class Balance

The proportion of different class types in the input data plays a key role in the neural network performance. Therefore, individual class distributions were assessed among all the labeled images. Figure 4 shows the percentage of cotton, maize and others classes among the 29 images used for training whereas Fig. 5 illustrates the total class distribution for the three classes considered.

Fig. 4. Class balance among the 29 training images.

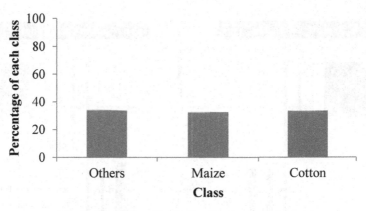

Fig. 5. Total class distribution for the three classes.

2.3 Training, Testing and Validation

PSPNet [3], SegNet [2] and U-Net [1] are based on encoder decoder architecture, which consist of two paths of operation. The contracting or down sampling path was used for feature extraction and the expanding or up sampling path was used for precise localization of the features. The encoder path forms the coarse features at every layer and the maps are retained that are later used by the decoder for translation of features from coarse to dense. Figure 6 shows the network architecture for U-Net. SegNet also follows similar principle as U-Net with added optimization for low memory usage. PSPNet adds not only local features but also adds global contextual information to differentiate between scenes by different region-based context aggregation through pyramid pooling. PSPNet and SegNet architectures are not shown due to space constraints.

Data pre-processing and generation were done using python and OpenCV library. Training and testing of the neural network was performed using TensorFlow library with Keras as wrapper in Python. The networks were trained in Google CoLab platform with GPUs where stochastic gradient descent was used with 50 epochs in a batch size of 16. The learning rate was 0.01 and cross entropy was used as a loss function. Testing and validation were done in personal computer with Intel CPUs. Accuracy assessment was done to evaluate the results. In a multi-class classification problem, when the predicted class label equals the ground truth it is considered as a true positive. Accuracy is computed as the fraction of the total number of true positives to the total number of samples which lies in the range of 0–1 with 1 representing most accurate classification.

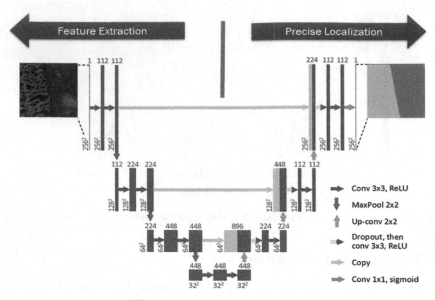

Fig. 6. U-Net network architecture.

3   Results and Discussion

The three classes namely, cotton, maize and others were used for all the experiments with various input spectral combinations on three different networks as summarized in Table 2. U-Net showed highest accuracy with different test cases.

Table 2. List of experiments carried on different input band combinations and networks architectures

	RGB	CIR	RGB + NDVI	CIR + NDVI	RGB + EVI
U-Net	✓	✓	✓	✓	✓
SegNet	✓	✓	✓	✓	✗
PSPNet	✓	✓	✓	✓	✗

Table 3 shows the accuracy assessment results across the networks which revealed that U-Net with CIR and NDVI performed best with highest average accuracy of 97.83% (highlighted in bold font in Tables 3 and 4) while dealing with three classes separation problem. U-Net achieved an overall accuracy improvement of 2.5% compared to the approach described in [10]. SegNet is based on U-Net with added optimization of low memory architecture, so it compromises the output while PSPNet might work well for cases that involve scene classification with related context.

Table 3. Average accuracy results across networks

	RGB	CIR	RGB + NDVI	CIR + NDVI
U-Net	0.9235	0.9677	0.9774	**0.9783**
SegNet	0.8362	0.6929	0.9734	0.9745
PSPNet	0.8501	0.9652	0.9457	0.9772

Table 4. Accuracy of U-Net results for 6 test cases with various spectral combinations

Scene Number	CIR	RGB	CIR + NDVI	RGB + NDVI	RGB + EVI
Crop scene 1	0.9597	0.9479	0.9673	0.9994	0
Crop scene 2	0.9123	0.7343	0.9686	0.9487	0.1165
Crop scene 3	0.9651	0.9807	0.9794	0.9833	0.5004
Crop scene 4	0.9999	0.9999	0.9999	0.9999	0.9999
Crop scene 5	0.9930	0.9334	0.9983	0.9603	0
Crop scene 6	0.9763	0.9447	0.9561	0.9730	0.6161
Average accuracy	0.9677	0.9235	**0.9783**	0.9774	0.3725

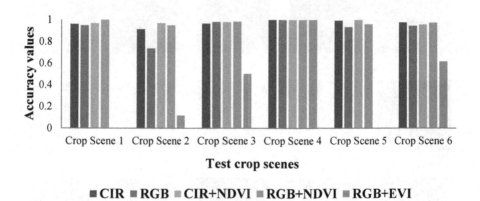

Fig. 7. Comparison of accuracies for different input spectral combinations on U-Net.

Table 4 lists the accuracy results for 6 test scenes on U-Net architecture. Figure 7 shows the graphical comparison of accuracies on 6 test crop scenes for various band combinations. Further, it was also observed that addition of EVI did not improve the test accuracy. Figure 8 shows the comparative results with original UAV image (column a), predicted crop classification from U-Net (column b), predicted crop classification from SegNet (column c), predicted crop classification from PSPNet (column d) and ground

484   B. Sudarshan Rao et al.

truth (column e) that indicates high visual accuracy in differentiating the three crop classes across experimented networks.

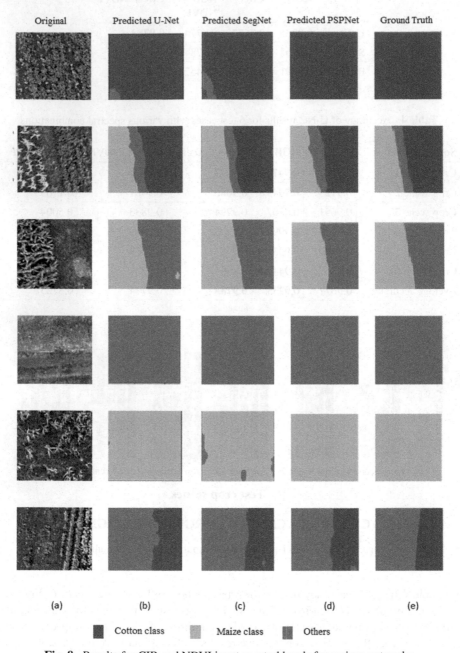

Original   Predicted U-Net   Predicted SegNet   Predicted PSPNet   Ground Truth

(a)   (b)   (c)   (d)   (e)

■ Cotton class   ■ Maize class   ■ Others

Fig. 8. Results for CIR and NDVI input spectral bands for various networks.

4   Conclusions

This study demonstrated the efficacy of deep learning based semantic segmentation techniques that rendered promising results for agricultural crop classification from multi-spectral UAV data. It was observed that class balance (similar proportions) of various input classes in the training data plays an important role in deep learning networks to achieve high classification accuracy. Further, inclusion of Green, Red, NIR band and derived index such as NDVI in the input dataset improved the class separability with highest classification accuracy. Among the deep learning networks, U-Net outperformed SegNet and PSPNet in achieving a classification accuracy of 97% with a latency of 2.6 s on a 3 mega pixel image for three classes. The skeletal methodology used for differentiating crops like cotton and maize in the current work could as well be extended to classify more number of crops, and also in detecting healthy versus diseased crops with balanced annotated data. Classifying the crops in an agricultural field with high accuracy would help in solving traditional agricultural issues like crop yield estimation, fertilizer utilization etc. Further, analysis of the effect of including other spectral bands obtained from the multi-spectral camera mounted on UAV for crop classification is a subject of our forthcoming research.

Acknowledgement. We thank CSIR-4PI (Fourth Paradigm Institute), Bangalore and University of Agricultural Sciences (UAS), Dharwad for providing the UAV data. We are grateful to International Institute of Information Technology Bangalore (IIIT-B), India for the infrastructure support and acknowledge Infosys Foundation for the financial assistance through the Infosys Foundation Career Development Chair Professor.

References

1. Ronneberger, O., Fischer, P., Brox, T.: U-Net: convolutional networks for biomedical image segmentation. In: Navab, N., Hornegger, J., Wells, William M., Frangi, Alejandro F. (eds.) MICCAI 2015. LNCS, vol. 9351, pp. 234–241. Springer, Cham (2015). https://doi.org/10.1007/978-3-319-24574-4_28
2. Badrinarayanan, V., Kendall, A., Cipolla, R.: Segnet: a deep convolutional encoder-decoder architecture for image segmentation. IEEE Trans. Pattern Anal. Mach. Intell. **39**(12), 2481–2495 (2017). https://doi.org/10.1109/TPAMI.2016.2644615
3. Zhao, H.S., Shi, J.P., Qi, X.J., et al.: Pyramid scene parsing network. In: Proceedings of the IEEE Conference on Computer Vision and Pattern Recognition (CVPR), Honolulu, pp. 2881–2890 (2017)
4. Sa, I., Popović, M., Khanna, R., Chen, Z., Lottes, P., Liebisch, F., et al. WeedMap: a large-scale semantic weed mapping framework using aerial multispectral imaging and deep neural network for precision farming. Remote Sens. **10**(9), 1423 (2018)
5. Sa, I., Chen, Z., Popović, M., Khanna, R., Liebisch, F., Nieto, J., et al.: weedNet: dense semantic weed classification using multispectral images and MAV for smart farming. IEEE Robot Autom. Lett. **3**(1), 588–595 (2017)
6. Lillesand, T.M., Kiefer, R.W.: Remote Sensing and Image Interpretation, 4th edn. Wiley, New York (2002). ISBN 9971-51-427-3
7. MicaSense, Inc. (2020). https://www.micasense.com. Accessed: 20 May 2020

8. Schowengerdt, R.A.: Remote Sensing: Models and Methods for Image Processing, 2nd edn. Academic Press, San Diego (1997)
9. Zhang, M., et al.: Classification of paddy rice using a stacked generalization approach and the spectral mixture method based on MODIS time series. IEEE J. Sel. Top. Appl. Earth Obs. Remote Sens. 1 (2020). https://doi.org/10.1109/jstars.2020.2994335
10. Ishida, T., et al.: A novel approach for vegetation classification using UAV-based hyperspectral imaging. Comput. Electron. Agric. **144**, 80–85 (2018)

A Novel Face Print Spoof Detection Using Color Scatter Measures in HSI Space

Pooja R. Patil$^{(\boxtimes)}$ (iD) and Subhash S. Kulkarni (iD)

PESIT - Bangalore South Campus, Hosur Road, Bengaluru 560 100, India
prpatil@pesit.pes.edu, sskul@pes.edu

Abstract. Face spoof detection has been a topic of interest in research in recent times. Here, a novel approach for face spoof detection addressing print spoof is presented. The novelty lies in distinct features derived from scatter and variance measures on HSI color space. The volumetric measures around the convex hull and geometric description have yielded compact and effective features. It works well with naturally available acquisition devices too. Spoof detection rate is highly significant and works well over inter database protocols too.

Keywords: Biometrics · Face recognition · Print spoof detection · Volumetric and statistical dispersion measures · Supervised learning · Binary classification

1 Introduction

Widely used recognition systems range from simple unlocking to criminal identi- fication. Among the range of biometrics face is the commonly exploited biometric trait in recognition systems. The ease of acquiring face images from social media combined with their inexpensive and manipulative reproducibility has led to the proliferation of various anti-spoofing methods.

Recognition systems using spoof detection methods can be fooled by pre- senting videos of high quality and hence pose a challenge either to detect or reject these replay attacks. Spoof analysis methods requiring users' response may fail when they fail to respond and hardware-based methods requiring aux- iliary devices such as sensors, cameras, etc. may become difficult for deployment and may incur additional costs. Finally, the descriptor or software-based meth- ods do not involve any installation requirements and hence are inexpensive and widely accepted. These methods are summarized in Table 1.

The central idea of this paper is, given a single image, how one can seek coherent interpretation by visualization. Such interpretation opportunistically includes the distinction of the ensemble of live and spoof images. Apart from this, our goal is to capture the sense of the whole image even if we do not get acquainted with its constituent parts. To tackle this difficult task, we propose a novel framework that aims to jointly model the pixels that make up an image

© Springer Nature Singapore Pte Ltd. 2021
S. K. Singh et al. (Eds.): CVIP 2020, CCIS 1376, pp. 487–499, 2021.
https://doi.org/10.1007/978-981-16-1086-8_43

within the geometric perspective of the 3D space they occupy. Because none of the anticipated features in the published works are completely reliable, all the elements of the image are considered coherently. This geometric representation will allow all these image elements to be physically placed within this contextual frame and permit reasoning between them and their 3D environment along with statistical characterization in a joint optimization framework.

Table 1. Different spoof detection methods

Si. No.	Type	Challenges
1	Based on human involuntary actions	These methods fail when video spoofs are presented
2	Based on user interactions	These methods fail when users refuse to respond
3	Hardware based methods	These methods become expensive due to additional auxiliary devices and are location dependent
4	Software-based methods	Widely accepted due to their non-intrusive nature and low-cost

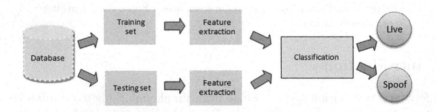

Fig. 1. Workflow of spoof analysis

The steps in spoof detection are depicted in Fig. 1. It is very challenging to select the features that effectively extract the underpinned patterns for accurate spoof detection while being invariant to affine transformations and dynamic external factors such as changing illumination conditions. A brief introduction to different anti-spoofing methods along with their limitations are given in Sect. 1, Sect. 2 focuses on the protocol modalities and literature review of the existing anti-spoofing procedures. Section 3 begins with the description of the proposed method with the proposed features exploiting discriminative inherent disparities between the real and the spoof face images followed by the description of the databases used for experimental evaluation of the proposed method in Sect. 6. In Sect. 5, the performance of some of the existing methods on the publicly available NUAA database is tested and the detailed analysis of the proposed features for print spoof detection along with the intermediate results on the obtained NUAA dataset are outlined. The paper is concluded in Sect. 6 with a summary of the contribution and possible future directions.

2 Background

Majority of anti-spoofing is focused on the software-based methods. Evaluation of recognition systems exploiting other hardware-based methods is sparsely covered in literature. Discussions focusing on the generalization issue of face anti-spoofing methods are covered in Sect. 2.1 and Sect. 2.2 focuses on the literature review of the published anti-spoofing procedures on different databases.

2.1 Protocol Modalities

Depending on the attack types, the process of producing spoofing attacks is time-consuming and sometimes requires a lot of resources and certain manufacturing skills. Therefore, it is not difficult to imagine that collecting attack data for many subjects become very demanding, and, for certain types of attacks such as 3D masks, is too expensive. Perhaps this is one main reason for creating database with limited subjects.

Common databases available such as CASIA FASD [1] use high-resolution videos and imposters printed on copper sheets, IDIAP's Replay Attack database [2] use high-resolution videos and imposters printed using a laser printer, in NUAA database, still images are printed on photographic sheets of two different sizes and A4 paper [3]. Although these databases contain images or video clips in various possible lighting conditions, they miss practical scenarios. Hence, in our work, we address the spoof detection problem using commonly available devices along with foreseen challenges.

2.2 Literature Review

In [4], the authors used (i) SIFT (ii) uniform LBP and (iii) the Gabor wavelet features with statistical moments for spoof analysis and applied to Replay Attack, CASIA FASD, and NUAA datasets for analysis. These works used SVM for classification. Among the three kernels used (linear, polynomial, and RBF), RBF is the most widely used kernel. In [5], the improved version of Local Binary Pattern (LBP), Multi-scale LBP (MLBP), SIFT and LUCID are analyzed, and LBP and color moments (mean, variance and skewness) are exploited as features for face liveness detection. The MSU USSA, CASIA FASD, IDIAP Replay Attack, MSU MFSD, and RAFS [5] databases are considered for analysis.

Some significant works with DA classifiers is presented below. In [6], the proposed nine pixel difference based measures, three correlation-based measures, and two edge-based measures have been used to generate feature vector and presented to a Linear Discriminant Analysis (LDA) classifier to assign one of the two classes: live or spoof. The authors report the same HTER as that obtained in [2] with the Replay Attack dataset but the speed and simplicity of the IQ measures make it more suitable for real-time applications. The accuracy of the classifier decreases when high-quality spoofing attacks are presented. In [7], authors extracted statistical textural features and evaluated their framework on their database of 25 subjects and measured the performance using accuracy, sensitivity, and specificity. Here, Quadratic Discriminant Analysis (QDA) is used for classification.

The k-NN based liveness detection is employed in [8]. Recent works use Convolutional Neural Networks (CNN) which can accept raw images (even with background) and make acceptable predictions. In [9], spectral energy density as a function of time is used as a feature.

3   Coherent Measurements in Perceptual Space for Spoof Detection

Color and shape are very intuitive to Human Visual System (HVS) enabling persuasive natural visualization of the Data. However, color descriptors of print spoofs, due to print/media range with assorted chromatic reproduction properties, makes it challenging for spoof detection. In this present work, we have explored the color scatter features and have found them as a valuable graphic representation. We have developed a framework that allows a geometrically coherent semantic interpretation for spoof analysis. Despite being simple, scatter plots serve as an influential means for data visualization. The properties pave a way for new features that are effective and useful for the classification of the ensemble. Our main insight is to model the contextual relationships between the image pixels in the 3D visual space. We also use variance as a feature in the image as an attribute. The categorization of the descriptors used and those in the literature is depicted in Fig. 2. A thorough quantitative evaluation of the proposed algorithm is also carried out with testing made on the NUAA database and naturally created database of faces to demonstrate its usefulness in spoof detection, especially print spoof. This section presents the features used in detail.

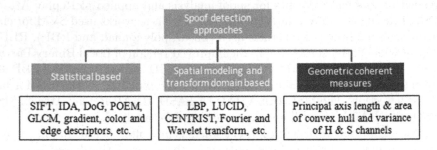

Fig. 2. Spoof detection approaches

3.1   Proposed Features for Print Spoof Detection

The representation of the whole image into an affine invariant and illumination independent feature vector while preserving the information in the original data and ensuring uniqueness to serve the purpose is a challenging task and requires proper exploration and investigation of the data. The selection of the feature extraction method depends on the type of attacks that the anti-spoofing method targets. As different types of attacks have different properties, the relevant information that differentiates them from real accesses may be different and may need to be extracted differently. As the impostor face used here is printed either on an A4 paper or a photographic sheet, all spoof images will have very high cohesion. But in the case of real face images, scattering is predominant than cohesion by being open to wide color combinational choices as illustrated in Fig. 3. This serves as a discrimination factor between the real and impostor classes and limited descriptors used to describe these characteristic features.

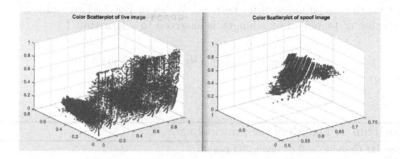

Fig. 3. Scatter plots of live (left) and spoof (right) face images

3.2   Principal Axis Length and Area of Convex Hull

In an attempt to explore new possible features based on geometric measures, the present work have experimented on a 3D surface generated over a virtual surface by convex hull with color dispersion obtained through occupancy of colors in real and spoof images. The 3D plot of this color space occupancy or dispersion is generally represented as scatter plots. All the geometric measures or features explored in this work correspond to the volumetric measures across the convex hull surface. Some of the features explored that assist in print spoof detection are principal axes of convex 3D object and relative surface area measures in scatter plots of real and print spoof images.

Because the data points in the scatter plot are randomly distributed in the 3D space, distribution characterization is more economical than pattern characterization. Hence, the problem is transferred from statistical space to geometrical space. In geometric space, one method is to restrict the geometrical shape to a regular shape, atleast to a convex shape. Modeling with an ellipsoid avoids the usage of computationally expensive local descriptors like curvature. Thus, an approximate model convex hull algorithm is used. The number of features are reduced and the distribution space in coarse characterization is also found sufficient to discern between live and spoof images.

A convex polygon is a polygon with all interior angles less than 180° The convex hull algorithm is to find the convex hull of a given set of data points. The Quickhull (Qhull) algorithm, which employs the divide and conquer approach that begins by sorting the points, is used to serve the purpose. The outline of the chosen algorithm is presented in [10].

Complicated volumes of such polyhedra can be computed approximately by subdividing the polyhedron into smaller pieces of known shapes for example, by triangulation i.e. by taking each known point of the known face inside the hull and triangulating each face. The result is a set of "thick" facets that contain all possible exact convex hulls of the input data consisting of solid tetrahedra. The convex hulls of live and spoof images for the scatter plots depicted in Fig. 3 are illustrated in Fig. 4. There is an easy formula for the volume of a tetrahedron given the coordinates of its vertices, V_i, as in Eq. 1. The summary for the computation of principal axis length is as given in Algorithm 1.

$$Area = \frac{1}{6}|(V_2 - V_1) \cdot (V_3 - V_1) \times (V_4 - V_1)| \tag{1}$$

Algorithm 1: Length of the principal axes

Result: Convex hull of given 3D points
Step 1: Get data ($N^2 \times 3$ for an image of size $N \times N$ in HSV space);
Step 2: Subtract mean from the data;
Step 3: Compute the Covariance matrix;
Step 4: Calculate the Eigen Vectors and Eigen Values of the Covariance matrix;
Step 5: Sort the Vectors in the descending order of maximum weight or Eigen Value;
Step 6: The principal axis length is the range of elements of these Vectors sorted according to their Eigenvalues;

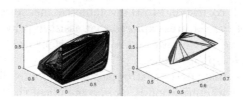

Fig. 4. Convex hull of live (left) and spoof (right) face images

3.3   Variance of H and S Channels

In print spoof detection, the imposter images lack high-frequency detail com-pared to live images due to multiple recaptures and various other factors such as environmental conditions and resolution of the spoofing media, in case of fixed spoofing attacks. While presenting handheld attacks, the bending of the photo paper may lead to skewed face shape in the spoof images. Additionally, the viewing direction of the camera will also lead to the deformation of the face shape in the spoof images. Hence, the statistical dispersion measure - variance, of H and S channels, is used to identify the differences in sharp details such as edges using first-order statistics which estimate the properties of individual pixel values, ignoring the spatial or neighborhood relationship between image pixels. The H and S channels of live and spoof face images are depicted in Fig. 5. The variance of an image x of size $\sqrt{N}$ is given by the Eq. 2.

$$V = \frac{1}{N-1} \sum_{i=1}^{N} |x_i - \mu|^2 \tag{2}$$

where μ is the mean of x given by

$$\mu = \frac{1}{N} \sum_{i=1}^{N} x_i \tag{3}$$

Fig. 5. Variance of Hue (first two columns) and Saturation (last two) channels of live (left) and spoof (right) face images

With all the features computed and concatenated to form a feature vector of size 1×6 (Principal axis length - 1×3, area - 1, and variance of H & S channels 1×2), we train an SVM classifier with an RBF kernel (using optimized parameters) to distinguish between live and spoof face images.

4   Test Databases for Experimentation

A brief description of the database used and the personally created database used in the experimentation is as follows:

4.1 NUAA Photograph Database

[1]The NUAA imposter database is a publicly available database for face spoof detection. Some sample images of the NUAA database are depicted in Fig. 6. The series of live images are captured using webcams and 500 images are collected for 15 distinct subjects. The spoof images are collected by first capturing face images using a Canon camera in such a way that the face covers 2/3 rd of the area of the photograph and are then printed on (i) photographic papers of size 6.8 cm × 10.2 cm and 8.9 cm × 12.7 cm using a traditional photo printing method, and 70 GSM A4 paper using a color HP printer and finally, these five categories of spoof images are recaptured using a webcam.

4.2 Naturally Created Test Database (NCTD)

Live images are captured for 14 subjects using three different devices (webcam on Dell laptop with Intel Core i3-4005U CPU @ 1.7GHz, Redmi Note 5 with 12MP camera, and Motorola G4x with 8MP camera) taken indoor daylight in

Fig. 6. Sample images of the NUAA dataset: Live images (first row) and Spoof images (second row)

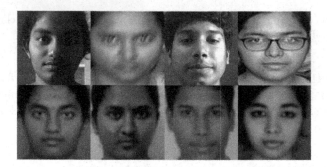

Fig. 7. Sample images of NCTD: live images (first row) and Spoof images (second row)

---

[1] http://parnec.nuaa.edu.cn/_upload/tpl/02/db/731/template731/pages/xtan/ NUAAImposterDB_download.html.

a naturally lit room and this test database is exhaustively used for testing the algorithm. For print spoofs, the subjects' photograph printed on a quality photographic sheet is used. For testing the algorithm, scanned versions of these photographs are used. Some of the images of NCTD are depicted in Fig. 7.

5   Experimental Results and Discussions

In the experimentation, the size of all the images is restricted to 180×180, and is assumed that the face is known apriori. SVM classifier with RBF kernel is used to compare the obtained predictions with the known labels, which is the procedure for supervised learning [11]. All the experimental evaluations are implemented in MATLAB 2018b.

We perform face spoof detection experiments using the NUAA database. The influences of some factors (e.g., image acquisition device, image region, and database size) have been studied on the proposed face spoof detection approach. The proposed approach is compared with the state of the art methods in intra-database testing scenarios. The protocol used is intra-database with a subject-exclusive five-fold cross-validation. In binary classification systems, a way to measure the performance accuracy and Half Total Error Rate (HTER) being defined using the Eqs. 4 and 5 with TP & TN representing the number of True Positives & True Negatives indicating correctly classified live and spoof images, and FP & FN representing the number of False Positives & False Negatives.

$$Accuracy = \frac{TP + TN}{TP + TN + FP + FN} \tag{4}$$

$$HTER = \frac{FPR + FNR}{2}; FPR = \frac{FP}{FP + TN}, FNR = \frac{FN}{TP + FN} \tag{5}$$

The proposed method achieved an accuracy of 96% which is greater than 92.7% in [12] and 87.5% in [3] and less than 98.8% [13] in and 98.45% in [14]. From the proposed approach, we obtained an HTER of 0.03 which is very less than 1.54 in [15] and 0.54 in [16]. Comparison of the state of the art methods with the proposed method using accuracy and HTER are tabulated in the Tables 2 and 3 respectively. These results support the claim that our approach can be seen to outperform the prevailing methods in literature.

In the literature, intra-database testing with a standard acquisition environment has been the norm for spoof detection. The proposed method characterizes realistic situations in acquisition and database generation. Further testing the proposed algorithm over inter-database with the goal to test with naturally acquired images under natural lighting conditions. The performance of the algorithm over NUAA and NCTD for print spoofing is tabulated in the Table 4.

The key attribute for performance variation over the two databases is that the NUAA database is made under standard lighting and standardized acquisition protocols. On the contrary, the performance of algorithms will have a huge

Table 2. Comparison of performance of existing methods using accuracy

Si. No.	Features used	Database used	Performance analysis Accuracy (in %)
1	Specular reflection ratio, color distribution and blurriness [13]	NUAA	98.80
2	Diffusion speed patterns [14]	NUAA	98.45
3	LBP + Fourier [17]	Wrbcam & ATM	96.72
4.	**Proposed method**	**NUAA**	**96**
5	DoG [18]	Yale recaptured and NUAA	94.5
6	LBP [12]	NUAA	92.7
7	Lambertian reflectance model [3]	NUAA	87.5
8	DoG [1]	CASIA FAS	81.8

Table 3. Comparison of performance of the proposed method using HTER (tested on NUAA database)

Si. No.	Features	HTER
1.	LUCID [15]	1.54
2	Reflectance [16]	0.54
3.	**Proposed method**	**0.03**

impact when these acquisition standards deviate. In this work, this impact is studied for naturally acquired images over the spoof detection features used in the literature. Classification performance using the proposed methodology tested over intra-database testing are shown in Figs. 8 and 9.

All the methods described above have been reported with different success rates, which cannot be easily compared because they are obtained on different types of attacks and on various databases some of which are not released publicly. Following the trend in computer vision, the research community, working on spoof detection, has started experimenting via deep learning (DL) to automatically extract and learn the features directly from the data. Although it can

Table 4. Results using inter-database testing protocol

Modality	Accuracy (in %)	HTER
Proposed method-with classifier trained using NUAA and tested on NCTD	46.43	0.53

Fig. 8. Spoof images misclassified as live images (false positives)

Fig. 9. Some live images misclassified as spoof images (false negatives)

Table 5. Comparison of the proposed approach with existing using Intra and Inter database testing protocols

Si. no.	Features used	Length of the feature vector per image of size 180 × 180	Accuracy (in %)	
			Intra-database testing protocol	Inter-database testing protocol
1	2D FFT [17]	90	36	25
2	LBP [17]	59	54	30
3	2D FFT + LBP [17]	149	36	25
4	**Proposed method**	**6**	**96**	**46**

be argued that countermeasures engineered this way are suitable only for the type of artifacts they are designed for, some recent works using DL reported lower performance than ML-based methods.

We evaluated the performance of the widely used LBP histogram with uniform mapping and spectral features using 2D FFT as in [17] on the NUAA database. We also implemented the method proposed in [17] which used both 2D Fourier Transform and LBP to extract features on Webcam and ATM databases and reported an accuracy of 98.6%. The accuracy of spoof detection using these Fourier and LBP features extracted from the images of the NUAA database with SVM + RBF classifier is observed to 37.42%. This indicates that the spectral and LBP features fail miserably in detecting the spoof images and the relative performance of these features compared with those of proposed methodology is tabulated in Table 5 In an attempt to explore the works based on edge detection, we implemented some edge detection methods such as DoG as in [18] and these methods are observed to fail when high-quality images are presented leading to increased false positives and for distorted live images to increased false negatives.

6 Conclusions and Future Work

An efficient spoof detection is proposed in this work with volumetric and statistical color dispersion of image on a publicly available NUAA database. The proposed print spoof detection method is unique exhibiting reduced feature dimension and computational cost (length = six). We also tested the performance on a generated database for print spoof with laptop and smartphone acquired subject faces in different lighting conditions. It is observed that HSV color channel features possess better discrimination characteristics over the RGB color channel. The proposed methodology effectively performs on print spoofs over full images without requiring the face detection step and hence requires less computation and is trait independent and can also be employed to scenic spoof detection.

Fulfilling the void in diverse database is one of the future challenges. Considering different materials in spoofing attacks, viz high-quality printing to match the quality of live images and to capture live and spoof images of different quality happen to be alternate ways that cause increased complexity for spoofing databases. Hence, there is a need to construct affine invariant features that can exploit the characteristics of spoofing attacks of different quality robust to illumination variations, facial occlusions, and other preprocessing techniques.

References

1. Zhang, Z., Yan, J., Liu, S., Lei, Z., Yi, D., Li, S.Z.: A face antispoofing database with diverse attacks. In: 2012 5th IAPR International Conference on Biometrics (ICB), pp. 26–31. IEEE (2012)
2. Chingovska, I., Anjos, A., Marcel, S.: On the effectiveness of local binary patterns in face anti-spoofing. In: 2012 BIOSIG-Proceedings of the International Conference of Biometrics Special Interest Group (BIOSIG), pp. 1–7. IEEE (2012)
3. Tan, X., Li, Y., Liu, J., Jiang, L.: Face liveness detection from a single image with sparse low rank bilinear discriminative model. In: Daniilidis, K., Maragos, P., Paragios, N. (eds.) Computer Vision – ECCV 2010. Lecture Notes in Computer Science, vol. 6316, pp. 504–517. Springer, Berlin, Heidelberg (2010). https://doi.org/10.1007/978-3-642-15567-3_37
4. Hassan, M.A., Mustafa, M.N., Wahba, A.: Automatic liveness detection for facial images. In: 2017 12th International Conference on Computer Engineering and Systems (ICCES), pp. 215–220. IEEE (2017)
5. Patel, K., Han, H., Jain, A.K.: Secure face unlock: spoof detection on smartphones. IEEE Trans. Inf. Forensics Secur. 11(10), 2268–2283 (2016)
6. Galbally, J., Marcel, S.: Face anti-spoofing based on general image quality assessment. In: 2014 22nd International Conference on Pattern Recognition, pp. 1173–1178. IEEE (2014)
7. Jayan, T.J., Aneesh, R.: Image quality measures based face spoofing detection algorithm for online social media. In: 2018 International CET Conference on Control, Communication, and Computing (IC4), pp. 245–249. IEEE (2018)
8. Yeh, C.-H. Chang, H.-H.: Face liveness detection with feature discrimination between sharpness and blurriness. In: 2017 Fifteenth IAPR International Conference on Machine Vision Applications (MVA), pp. 398–401. IEEE (2017)

9. Lakshminarayana, N.N., Narayan, N., Napp, N., S. Setlur, Govindaraju, V.: A discriminative spatio-temporal mapping of face for liveness detection. In: 2017 IEEE International Conference on Identity, Security and Behavior Analysis (ISBA), pp. 1–7. IEEE (2017)

10. Barber, C.B., Dobkin, D.P., Huhdanpaa, H.: The quickhull algorithm for convex hulls. ACM Trans. Math. Softw. (TOMS) 22(4), 469–483 (1996)

11. Marsland, S.: Machine Learning: An Algorithmic Perspective. CRC Press (2015)

12. Määttä, J., Hadid, A., Pietikäinen, M.: Face spoofing detection from single images using micro-texture analysis. In: 2011 International Joint Conference on Biometrics (IJCB), pp. 1–7. IEEE (2011)

13. Luan, X., Wang, H., Ou, W., Liu, L.: Face liveness detection with recaptured feature extraction. In: 2017 International Conference on Security, Pattern Analysis, and Cybernetics (SPAC), pp. 429–432. IEEE (2017)

14. Kim, W., Suh, S., Han, J.-J.: Face liveness detection from a single image via diffusion speed model. IEEE Trans. Image Process. 24(8), 2456–2465 (2015)

15. Akhtar, Z., Michelon, C., Foresti, G.L.: Liveness detection for biometric authentication in mobile applications. In: 2014 International Carnahan Conference on Security Technology (ICCST), pp. 1–6. IEEE (2014)

16. Kose, N., Dugelay, J.-L.: Reflectance analysis based countermeasure technique to detect face mask attacks. In: 2013 18th International Conference on Digital Signal Processing (DSP), pp. 1–6. IEEE (2013)

17. Kim, G., Eum, S., Suhr, J.K., Kim, D.I., Park, K.R., Kim, J.: Face liveness detection based on texture and frequency analyses. In: 2012 5th IAPR International Conference on Biometrics (ICB), pp. 67–72. IEEE (2012)

18. Peixoto, B., Michelassi, C., Rocha, A.: Face liveness detection under bad illumination conditions. In: 2011 18th IEEE International Conference on Image Processing, pp. 3557–3560. IEEE (2011)

FingerPIN: An Authentication Mechanism Integrating Fingerprints and Personal Identification Numbers

Emanuela Marasco[(✉)] and Massimiliano Albanese[(✉)]

Center for Secure Information Systems, Volgenau School of Engineering, George Mason University, 4400 University Drive, Fairfax, VA 22030, USA
{emarasco,malbanes}@gmu.edu

Abstract. Fingerprint-based authentication has been successfully adopted in a wide range of applications, including law enforcement and immigration, due to its numerous advantages over traditional password-based authentication. However, despite the usability and accuracy of this technology, some significant concerns still exist, which can potentially hinder its further adoption. For instance, a subject's fingerprint is permanently associated with an individual and, once stolen, cannot be replaced, thus compromising biometric-based authentication. To mitigate this concern, we propose a multi-factor authentication approach that integrates type 1 and type 3 authentication factors into a fingerprint-based personal identification number, or FingerPIN. To authenticate, a subject is required to present a sequence of fingerprints corresponding to the digits of the PIN, based on a predefined secret mapping between digits and fingers. We conduct a vulnerability analysis of the proposed scheme, and demonstrate that it is robust to the compromise of one or more of the subject's fingerprints.

1 Introduction

Robust authentication mechanisms are critical to protect the security of data and applications. While offering a high level of security, biometric-based authentication maintains convenience for the user. In particular, fingerprints provide well-known distinctiveness and persistence properties. Biometric technologies are widely adopted in various government applications such as National ID, border control, and passport control [18], as well as in forensics and in criminal investigations for the identification of terrorists and other criminals. Commercial applications include computer network login, ATMs, credit card and medical records management [7, 10]. Fingerprint systems are currently used for unlocking smartphones (e.g., iPhone 5S) or to engage in financial transactions and make purchases. However, if compromised, the same characteristics and advantages of biometrics present a potential threat to the owner of the biometric markers and risks to the businesses that use biometric data. Biometrics are biologically unique to the individual, therefore, once compromised, the individual has no recourse and they are at an increased risk for identity theft.

E. Marasco and M. Albanese—were partially supported by the National Science Foundation under award CNS-1822094.

Type 1, or *knowledge-based*, authentication is still the most widely adopted form of authentication, despite its many weaknesses. Most user create passwords that are easy to remember, therefore easy to guess or crack through a variety of means including social engineering and dictionary attacks. When longer or difficult-to-remember passwords are chosen, users tend to write them down in easily accessible places, effectively defeating the purpose of using authentication. Furthermore, compromising a single password may represent a risk for multiple applications, as users tend to reuse the same passwords across different applications [7].

To address these limitations, organizations are transitioning to multi-factor authentication, requiring users to provide at least two different authentication factors to prove their identity and be granted access to a system. A type 1 authentication factor (e.g., password, PIN) is typically paired with either a type 2 authentication factor (e.g., token) or a type 3 authentication factor (e.g., fingerprint). In traditional multi-factor authentication approaches, a user would need to *sequentially* prove knowledge of the PIN and validity of their biometrics features by entering the PIN on a keyboard and scanning one or more fingerprints. We propose a multi-factor authentication scheme that *integrates* a type 1 authentication factor (a PIN) and a type 3 authentication factor (fingerprints) into a fingerprint-based PIN, which we refer to as FingerPIN. In this paper, we push the boundaries of multi-factor authentication by combining type 1 and type 3 factors in such a way that a user must *simultaneously* prove knowledge of the PIN and validity of their biometrics features by scanning multiple fingers in a sequence determined by the PIN through a secret mapping between digits and fingers. While such secret mapping may be difficult to remember and may slow down user authentication, what a user really needs to recall is the sequence of fingers corresponding to the digits of the PIN, as both the PIN and the mapping are set once in the enrollment phase and may change infrequently. If either the PIN or the mapping changes, the user would need to determine the new sequence of fingers used for authentication.

The paper is organized as follows. Section 2 discusses related work in multi-factor authentication involving biometrics. Section 3 presents the proposed authentication scheme, whereas Sect. 4 presents metrics to evaluate the strength of FingerPIN, along with an assessment of vulnerabilities in different attack scenarios. Then, Sect. 5 discusses our experimental results. Finally, Sect. 6 gives some concluding remarks and indicates possible future research directions.

2   Related Works

Traditional authentication solutions based on passwords or graphical patterns suffer from credential theft (e.g., through shoulder surfing) [1,16]. Authentication mechanisms involving physiological biometrics (e.g., fingerprints, iris patterns and face) are less likely to suffer from credential theft. However, different biometric technologies require different devices having a range of costs. Furthermore, they may limit privacy for users [2]. Recent studies exploiting biometric features (e.g., a sequence of 2D handwriting and corresponding pressure) rely on touch screens for feature extraction and are not easy to extend to general security access systems [8,9]. In 2014, driven by the need for increasing robustness against reuse of a fingerprint by a malicious attacker,

Go *et al.* proposed a two-factor authentication system involving fingerprint information and a password [5]. During registration, the users input their fingerprint and a password. A decimal number is associated to each letter of the password by modular arithmetic. The fingerprint template is converted to a square of fixed size to generate a standardized template that is then partitioned into a 3×3 matrix indexed by a sequence number 1–9. The generated nine regions are extracted based on the decimal numbers corresponding to the characters of the password. Partial templates are then relocated into a 3×3 matrix to create a new virtual template from which minutiae points are extracted, which does not follow the traditional matching operation.

In 2017, Nguyen *et al.* presented an authentication mechanism in which the user is asked to draw their PIN through a touch interface instead of typing it on a keypad [19]. This approach offers better security by utilizing drawing traits or behavioral biometrics as an additional authentication factor and it is prone to usability by leveraging user familiarity with PINs. This scheme was evaluated under stronger threat models but experiments were carried out on a small set of subjects. Liu *et al.* proposed the Vib-Write system that involves novel algorithms to discriminate fine grained finger-input and that supports three independent passcode secrets including PIN number, lock pattern and gesture features extracted in the frequency domain [8]. However, gesture-based authentication is not as discriminative as the well-established minutiae-based recognition. Additionally, combining a vibration signal into an authentication procedure is vulnerable to blind attacks and the vibration signal itself may be easy to imitate and vulnerable to impersonation attacks.

In 2018, Souza *et al.* presented an optical authentication technique based on two-beam interference and chaotic maps used in conjunction with biometrics [15]. The user registers by recording a biometric template. He then chooses a base image that is encoded through two-beam interference to produce a phase key that is used to encrypt the biometric data. A chaotic sequence is generated from the password and used to scramble this phase key resulting in the possession factor. Cantoni *et al.* proposed an authentication scheme that combines behavioral gaze-based biometrics with a PIN. In particular, eye information is captured by means of an eye tracker when the user enters a PIN through a virtual keypad displayed on a screen [4]. In 2019, Henderson suggested the benefits of a multi-factor security device that would combine a fingerprinting sensor and an LED pulse oximeter which would eliminate most if not all threats to fingerprinting authentication technology [6]. A CNN-based anti-spoofing two-tier multi-factor authentication system was proposed in [14]. Tier I integrates fingerprint, palm vein print and face recognition to match with the corresponding databases, and Tier II uses fingerprint, palm vein print and face anti-spoofing convolutional neural networks (CNN) based models to detect spoofing. In the first stage, the hash of a fingerprint is compared with the fingerprint database. After a successful match of the fingerprint, a CNN-based model tests the fingerprint to verify whether it is a spoof or real.

3   The Proposed Authentication Scheme

The proposed authentication scheme combines type 1 and type 3 authentication factors into a new multi-factor authentication mechanism. We investigate the integration of fingerprints and Personal Identification Numbers (PINs), and develop FingerPIN, an authentication scheme using fingerprint-based PINs: to authenticate, the user is required to scan multiple fingers in a sequence determined by a secret mapping between the user's 10 fingers and digits from 0 to 9, based on the user's PIN. Adding one digit to FingerPIN increases the complexity for an attacker significantly more than adding a digit to a traditional PIN. The two authentication factors are combined in such a way that the user does not need to remember both the PIN and the secret mapping but only a specific sequence of fingers, which is as easy to remember as remembering a PIN.

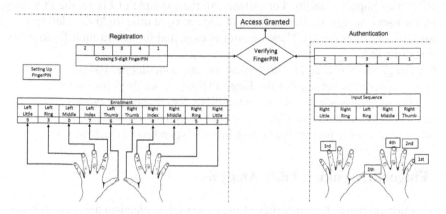

Fig. 1. After enrolling their ten fingerprints, a user chooses 2, 5, 3, 4, 1 as their PIN, which is converted into the sequence Right Little, Right Ring, Left Ring, Right Middle, Right Thumb.

A *finger-digit* is a single fingerprint component of the chosen sequence. The mapping between digits from 0 to 9 to fingers is set during enrollment. For instance, in the example of Fig. 1, the user chooses to map their left little finger to 9, left ring to 3, left middle to 0, and so on. The user then chooses a PIN – 25341 in our example – which determines the sequence of fingerprints to present for authentication. In our example, the first digit of the PIN is 2, which is mapped to the right little finger. The following four digits are mapped to right ring, left ring, right middle, and right thumb respectively. At authentication time, the user presents the sequence: right little, right ring, left ring, right middle, and right thumb. Intuitively, since the mapping between digits and fingers is not predefined, but rather determined by the user, an extra layer of protection is added. FingerPIN involves the execution of enrollment, registration, and authentication tasks. The *enrollment* module is responsible for storing the reference biometric data into the system database [7]. During this phase, the ten fingerprints of the subject are acquired by a sensor and a digital representation is produced. This digital representation is further processed by a feature extractor and a more compact representation, called a template, is obtained. Multiple templates of an individual are usually stored in order to account for variations observed in the biometric trait. Furthermore, the templates in the database may be updated over time. During this phase, the user also defines a mapping between digits and fingers, which can be changed at any time or with a predefined frequency for additional security. During *registration*, the user chooses a PIN, which determines the sequence of fingerprints to be used for authentication. During *authentication*, the system verifies the identity of a subject based on their FingerPIN. The process compares the biometric data captured from the subject attempting to authenticate with the biometric templates stored in the system database for that same subject. Authentication can operate in one of the two following modes.

- Standard Authentication Mode (Mode 1). All the fingerprints composing the Finger-PIN are sequentially matched, one by one, which makes the time required to verify the identity linear with the length of the FingerPIN. Consequently, longer Finger-PINs may impact usability. For instance, in the example of Fig. 1, the PIN chosen by the user is mapped to the sequence of fingers: right little, right ring, left ring, right middle, and right thumb. Thus, the user is expected to present their fingerprints in this exact order.
- Challenge Mode (Mode 2). The system presents a challenge, asking the user to provide a specific finger-digit of the FingerPIN (e.g., the third finger-digit). The processing time does not dependent on the PIN's length, and the burden on the user is limited. In the example of Fig. 1, when asked to provide the third finger-digit, the user is expected to present the fingerprint corresponding to their left ring finger.

4 FingerPIN Vulnerability Analysis

This section discusses the properties of the proposed mechanism and demonstrates its advantages over traditional multi-factor authentication.

In a brute-force attack against a traditional PIN, a randomly chosen five-digit sequence is guaranteed to be guessed in 100,000 attempts.

A brute-force attack to a fingerprint system is an indirect attack, e.g., a brute force attack to the feature extractor input or to the matcher input. A False Match Rate (FMR) of 0.001% corresponds to the success of 1 out of 100,000 attempts by using a large number of different fingerprints. Generating or acquiring a large number of biometric samples is much more difficult and time-consuming than generating a large number of PINs. The number of attempts to brute-force a single fingerprint is typically in the same order of magnitude of the number of attempts to brute-force a 5-digit PIN, in addition to the fact that comparing two fingerprints is computationally more demanding than comparing two 5-digit numbers.

A brute-force attack against FingerPIN is studied by estimating the probability of a success in different scenarios, based on the information available to the attacker. In Scenario 1, the ten fingerprints of the user are unknown to the attacker. In Scenario 2, one fingerprint template has been stolen by the attacker. In this case, we assume that the matching during authentication will occur with an accuracy of 100%. In Scenario 3, all the ten fingerprint templates are known to the attacker. Furthermore, for each case we consider when the secrecy of the mapping is compromised as well. In the following subsections, we will use k to denote the length of the PIN. We will also assume that the number of repetitions of a certain fingerprint in the chosen sequence is zero.

4.1   Scenario 1: Brute-Force Attack with No Fingerprint Compromised

In a brute-force attack, the attacker has no knowledge about any fingerprint of the genuine user. Given a FingerPIN, we compute the probability $P(Success)$ that a sequence of k arbitrary fingerprints presented by an attacker during a brute-force attack is successfully matched against the FingerPIN, allowing the attacker to achieve authentication. Let $P(FM_{ij})$ be the probability of False Match (FM) of the ith fingerprint used by the attacker against the ith finger-digit of the FingerPIN, with $P(F_{ij})$ indicating the probability that the ith finger-digit maps to digit j, and $\sum_{j=0}^{9} P(F_{ij}) = 1$. When the system operates in Mode 1, assuming that finger-digits are independent and equally distributed, $P(Success)$ is given by Eq. 1 below.

$$P(Success) = \prod_{i=1}^{k} P(Success_i) = \prod_{i=1}^{k} \sum_{j=0}^{9} P(FM_{ij}) \cdot P(F_{ij}) \qquad (1)$$

Regarding the term $P(FM_{ij})$, an empirical estimate of the probability with which the system incorrectly declares that a biometric sample belongs to the claimed identity when the sample belongs to a different subject (impostor) can be provided by the False Match Rate (FMR) [12]. FMR is typically selected based on the level of security required by the application and the corresponding threshold is set for the system.

It is clear from Equation 1 that the probability of k random fingerprints matching k finger-digits is much smaller than the probability of k random digits matching a k-digit PIN. When the attacker does not have any genuine fingerprints available, knowledge of the secret mapping or the PIN would not help the attacker increase this probability.

4.2   Scenario 2: Brute-Force Attack with One Fingerprint Compromised

In this scenario, one fingerprint of the genuine user has been stolen and a brute-force attack is attempted. We analyze how the probability $P(Success)$ changes when one fingerprint is compromised. The matching accuracy varies across different instances of an individual's fingerprints. A vulnerability in FingerPIN is found when the cross-instance match score is high for one or multiple fingerprint instances. In this case, the vulnerable instance can potentially be matched to more than one fingerprint which makes the scheme less secure. Although, in the scientific literature, there is not yet convergence for the term *non-zero effort attack*, in this paper it refers to the exploitation of any of the vulnerability points present in a typical fingerprint system [3, 11, 13]. Let $P(NFM_i^{SF})$ be the probability of Non Zero-Effort Attack Same-Finger False Match (NFM^{SF}) of the ith fingerprint in the FingerPIN sequence. Let $P(NFM_i^{CF})$ be the probability of Non Zero-Effort Attack Cross-Finger False Match (NFM^{CF}) of the ith fingerprint when the stolen fingerprint is from a different finger than the one chosen in the FingerPIN sequence. Let F_s indicate the fingerprint stolen. When the system operates in Mode 1, assuming that finger-digits are independent and equally distributed, $P(Success)$ is given by Eq. 2 below.

$$P(Success) = \prod_{i=1}^{k} \sum_{j=0}^{9} (P(F_{ij}, F_{sj}) \cdot P(NFM_j^{SF}) + P(F_{ij}, F_{s \neq j} \cdot P(NFM_j^{CF})) \qquad (2)$$

Whether the secrecy of the correspondence between fingers and digits is compromised, the probability that a brute-force attack can be simplified as follows:

$$P(Success) = \prod_{i=1}^{k}\sum_{j=0}^{9}(P(F_{sj}) \cdot P(NFM_j^{SF}) + P(F_{s \neq j} \cdot P(NFM_j^{CF})) \qquad (3)$$

4.3   Scenario 3: Brute-Force Attack with All the Fingerprints Compromised

In this scenario, all the ten fingerprints of the genuine user have been stolen and a brute-force attack is attempted. The FingerPIN is guaranteed to be guessed in 10^k attempts – corresponding to all possible sequences of length k of the 10 fingerprints – requiring a total of $10^k \cdot k$ fingerprint comparisons. By contrast, a brute a force attack against a traditional PIN would require only 10^k comparison between k-digit numbers. The secrecy of the mapping between the digits from 0 to 9 and the subject's fingers adds complexity to the scheme, making a brute-force attack more onerous. In fact, even when all fingerprints have been compromised, the attacker still needs to run a brute-force attack to compromise the FingerPIN, and every trial involves matching k fingerprints.

5   Experimental Results

5.1   Dataset

The dataset used in our experiments is a subset of the ManTech Innovations Fingerprint Study Phase I collection. It contains fingerprints of 500 subjects acquired using 7 optical sensors. We used images of the ten fingers acquired using the I3 digID Mini sensor. Among the participants, the age group between 20–33 was the largest, accounting for 60.6% percent of the subjects. With respect to ethnicity, Caucasians accounted for 57.2% of the subjects. There was a nearly equal number of male and female participants with a 51% to 48% ratio. Every subject provided two sets of rolled fingerprints for both hands, see sample images in Fig. 2.

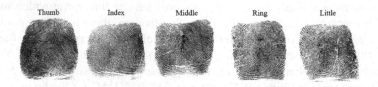

Fig. 2. Examples of fingerprint images from the ManTech Phase I collection used in this study

5.2   Evaluation Metrics

For a PIN Number-based scheme, the Attack Success Rate can be computed as the percentage of correctly verified PIN numbers entered by the attacker during the user authentication process. It includes the complete PIN sequence verification accuracy and the PIN digit verification accuracy. Biometric matching performance is assessed using: (i) False Match Rate (FMR), the proportion of instances where an impostor is incorrectly labelled as a genuine match with respect to the total number of impostor comparisons; (ii) False Non-Match Rate (FNMR), the proportion of instances where a genuine match is incorrectly labelled as an impostor with respect to the total number of genuine comparisons; and (iii) Detection Error Trade-off (DET) curve, which plots FMR and FNMR as a function of the decision threshold [7]. The inputs to the matcher are two fingerprint samples (e.g., gallery and probe images) and the output is a match score that indicates the proximity of the two samples. A threshold is applied to this match score to determine if the samples correspond to the same identity.

5.3   Experimental Results

Baseline. Match scores were extracted using Neurotechnology VeriFinger Version 10.0[1]. The quality measures were extracted using the NIST Fingerprint Image Quality (NFIQ 2.0) software[2], see Fig. 3(a) [17]. These distributions shows that right thumb, left thumb and right index exhibit a better image quality than other fingers.

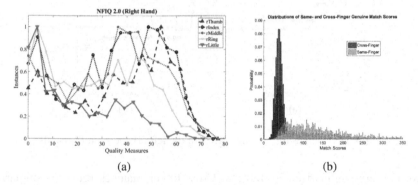

(a)   (b)

Fig. 3. (a) NFIQ 2 distribution of the fingers of the right hand. Little fingers exhibit lower image quality, a similar trend was observed for the left hand as well; (b) Distributions of same-finger and cross-finger match scores, fingerprints being compared pertain to the same identity

Figure 3(b) shows the probability distributions of the match scores output by comparing fingerprints pertaining to the same subject in both cross- and same-finger scenarios. In this graph, genuine match scores were generated by comparing same fingers of the same subject, while impostor scores were obtained by matching different fingers of the same subject. We can notice a relatively small overlap area between the two distributions. In the scientific literature, an analysis of cross-finger matching when the identity is the same is rarely carried out. The attack-resistance of a fingerprint system alone, expressed as the probability of successfully launching a brute-force attack, is 1

---

[1] https://www.neurotechnology.com/verifinger.html.
[2] http://www.nist.gov/services-resources/software/development-nfiq-20.

out of 100,000 attempts. The baseline fingerprint verification performance alone can depicted using the Detection Error Trade-off graph for all the ten fingers, see Fig. 4(a) and Fig. 4(b). For certain fingerprint instances such as left and right little fingers, error rates are higher. Thus, we wondered if the security of FingerPIN is affected when those instances are chosen as components of the authentication sequence.

System Performance of Verifying Legitimate User. We discuss experimental results related to scenarios 1 and 2 in which one or multiple fingerprints used in FingerPIN have been captured by an attacker. As case study, ten random 5-digit PINs with no repetitions were generated for every subject. For simplicity, the compromised fingerprint instance is assumed to be the same for all the authorized users. The FMR of the fingerprint system is 0.01%. Although such scenarios may seem critical, we found out that the success rate to break the FingerPIN scheme is very low.

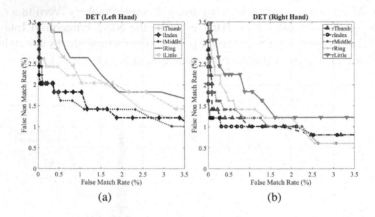

Fig. 4. DET curves for the fingerprints of the left (a) and right (b) hands.

Results are summarized in Table 1. Cross-finger matches refer to comparisons between different fingerprint instances carrying the same identity and they are high-lighted in bold. FM^{CF} indicates the proportion of the cross-finger matches wrongly accepted with respect to all the cross-finger matches. Findings show that with one compromised finger-digit, the additional four are able to keep high the level of protection. When the stolen fingerprint is the right index for all the subjects, only a few cross-finger false matches occur. The gallery was the right middle in 7 out of 8 false matches, while it was the left ring only in one case. These matches involved comparison between fingerprints pertaining to different identities.

Findings showed also that with two compromised finger-digits, the remaining three can guarantee robustness. When the stolen instance was the right thumb, only three cross-finger false matches among all the possible combinations were found. In two of these cases, the galleries were the right index and the left ring of the same subject, while in the third case the gallery was the left middle finger from a different subject. In this critical scenario, the proposed scheme would still be secure given the presence of the fifth component. Similar to the above, when the stolen fingerprint is the right middle finger for all the subjects, six cross-finger false matches were found. In two cases the galleries were right index and right little fingers pertaining to the same subject, while in four cases the galleries were right index, right ring (twice) and left ring fingers from different individuals. When the compromised finger-digit is the right ring, the gallery was the right middle finger in 5 out of 6 cross-finger false matches. When the right little finger is stolen, results are similar to the scenario previously encountered with the difference that the galleries are from different subjects. Regarding the fingers of the left hands, with the left index fingerprint compromised, there were eight occurrences of cross-finger false matches, in six of them the left middle finger was the gallery. Among the remaining fingers, the left thumb showed less risk with only one cross-finger found while the left ring the highest with 14 cross-finger false matches.

Table 1. Security results in Scenario 2: cross-finger false match rate for one stolen fingerprint.

Cross-Finger False Match FM^{CF} (%)

Stolen Fp	Rx Thumb	Rx Index	Rx Middle	Rx Ring	Rx Little	L Thumb	L Index	L Middle	L Ring	L Little
Rx Thumb	-	**0.0037**	-	-	-	-	-	0.0037	**0.0037**	-
Rx Index	-	-	0.0259	-	-	-	-	-	0.0037	-
Rx Middle	-	**0.0111**	-	0.0074	**0.0074**	-	-	-	0.0037	-
Rx Ring	-	-	0.0185	-	-	-	-	-	-	-
Rx Little	-	0.0037	-	-	-	-	-	-	0.0037	-
L Thumb	-	-	0.0037	-	-	-	-	-	-	-
L Index	0.0037	-	0.222	-	-	-	-	-	0.0037	-
L Middle	-	0.0074	-	-	-	-	0.0296	-	0.0111	-
L Ring	0.0037	-	0.0074	-	-	-	0.0111	0.0296	-	-
L Little	-	-	-	-	-	-	-	-	-	-

For a more user-friendly authentication, the constraint of choosing a sequence without repetitions can be relaxed. For instance, a user is allowed to repeat or not a particular finger-digit in the sequence. The repetitions are not expected but allowed. For every fingerprint instance, there is no constraint regarding the number of expected repetitions. The probabilities of repetitions of each stolen fingerprint are summarized in Table 2. The probability of choosing a given finger-digit five times in the sequence is always zero. One stolen fingerprint is repeated twice in the FingerPIN sequence in about 7% of the cases, in which three cross-finger false matches should occur for a brute force attack to succeed.

Based on a preliminary usability assessment involving our research group, applying FingerPIN does not require any change in the position of the hand given the acquisition of the next finger-digit can be done through the same sensing surface. No movement of the hand is necessary given that the user only need to change finger. In a traditional PIN, the (same) finger needs to be pressed on different keys of a keyboard requiring movement of the hand.

Table 2. Probability of repetitions for a given fingerprint instance.

Stolen Fp	P(Rep = 1)	P(Rep = 2)	P(Rep = 3)	P(Rep = 4)	P(Rep = 5)	P(Rep)
Rx Thumb	0.3300	0.0766	0.0088	$4\,e^{-4}$	0	0.4158
Rx Index	0.3272	0.0732	0.0064	$8\,e^{-4}$	0	0.4076
Rx Middle	0.3326	0.0768	0.0062	$4\,e^{-4}$	0	0.4160
Rx Ring	0.3208	0.0730	0.0104	0	0	0.4042
Rx Little	0.3326	0.0660	0.0062	$4\,e^{-4}$	0	0.4052
L Thumb	0.3324	0.0708	0.0082	$4\,e^{-4}$	0	0.4118
L Index	0.3226	0.0792	0.0086	$8\,e^{-4}$	0	0.4114
L Middle	0.3212	0.0758	0.0076	$8\,e^{-4}$	0	0.4054
L Ring	0.3290	0.0706	0.0084	$4\,e^{-4}$	0	0.4084
L Little	0.3266	0.0712	0.0084	$6\,e^{-4}$	0	0.4068

6   Conclusions

In this paper, we proposed a new approach to multi-factor authentication that integrates knowledge- and inherence-based authentication factors into a fingerprint-based PIN. Computing the probabilities for a brute-force attack to succeed, we demonstrated that FingerPIN is less vulnerable than a PIN or a fingerprint system used alone. The nature of the information integrated in the proposed authentication scheme challenges an attacker's success more than traditional mechanisms. FingerPIN is more secure against a brute-force attack with and without compromised fingerprints compared to existing approaches. In scenarios where the attacker steals one fingerprint of the genuine user, the success rate of a brute-force attack breaking a 5-digit FingerPIN was zero. The overall probability of cross-finger false match was 0.004% and, only with a maximum of two fingers pertaining to the same subject. We can conclude that, a 5 finger-digits scheme guarantees robustness to brute-force attacks even in the presence of one stolen fingerprint. This result demonstrates how the parallel integration of the two factors considered in this paper overcomes the limitations of both a PIN mechanism alone as well as an authentication purely based on fingerprints. In future efforts, we will: *i)* extend experiments to additional touch-based fingerprint databases as well as to contactless fingerprint technologies, *ii)* integrate additional biometric modalities to further improve security, *iii)* extend the analysis to scenarios featuring repetitions of finger-digits in the chosen FingerPIN sequence, *iv)* explore the security level of the proposed scheme when more than one fingerprint is compromised, and *v)* carry out a large-scale usability assessment to validate the preliminary evaluation discussed in this work and to explore potential behavioral patterns with respect to gender, age group and ethnicity.

References

1. Angeli, A.D., Coutts, M., Coventry, L., Johnson, G.I., Cameron, D., Fischer, M.H.: VIP: a visual approach to user authentication. In: Proceedings of the Working Conference on Advanced Visual Interfaces (AVI 2002), pp. 316–323. ACM, Trento, Italy (2002)

2. Arakala, A., Jeffers, J., Horadam, K.J.: Fuzzy Extractors for Minutiae-Based Fingerprint Authentication. In: Lee, S.-W., Li, S.Z. (eds.) ICB 2007. LNCS, vol. 4642, pp. 760–769. Springer, Heidelberg (2007). https://doi.org/10.1007/978-3-540-74549-5_80

3. Barkadehi, M.H., Nilashi, M., Ibrahim, O., Fardi, A.Z., Samad, S.: Authentication systems: A literature review and classification. Telematics and Informatics **35**(5), 1491–1511 (2018)

4. Cantoni, V., Lacovara, T., Porta, M., Wang, H.: A study on gaze-controlled PIN input with biometric data analysis. In: Proceedings of the 19th International Conference on Computer Systems and Technologies, pp. 99–103. ACM, Ruse, Bulgaria (2018)

5. Go, W., Lee, K., Kwak, J.: Construction of a secure two-factor user authentication system using fingerprint information and password. J. Intell. Manuf. **25**(2), 217–230 (2012). https://doi.org/10.1007/s10845-012-0669-y

6. Henderson, L.: Multi-factor authentication fingerprinting device using biometrics. Technical report, Villanova University (2019)

7. Jain, A.K., Ross, A., Prabhakar, S.: An introduction to biometric recognition. IEEE Trans. Circ. Syst. Video Technol. **14**(1), 4–20 (2004)

8. Liu, J., Wang, C., Chen, Y., Saxena, N.: VibWrite: towards finger-input authentication on ubiquitous surfaces via physical vibration. In: Proceedings of the 2017 ACM SIGSAC Conference on Computer and Communications Security (CCS 2017), pp. 73–87. ACM, Dallas, TX, USA (2017)

9. Luca, A.D., Hang, A., Brudy, F., Lindner, C., Hussmann, H.: Touch me once and I know it's you! implicit authentication based on touch screen patterns. In: Proceedings of the SIGCHI Conference on Human Factors in Computing Systems (CHI 2012), pp. 987–996. ACM, Austin, TX, USA (2012)

10. Maltoni, D., Maio, D., Jain, A.K., Prabhakar, S.: Handbook of Fingerprint Recognition, 2nd edn. Springer, London (2009)

11. Marasco, E., Ross, A.: A survey on antispoofing schemes for fingerprint recognition systems. ACM Comput. Surv. **47**(2) (2014)

12. Poh, N., Chan, C.H., Kittler, J., Fierrez, J., Galbally, J.: Description of metrics for the evaluation of biometric performance. Technical Report, D3.3, BEAT (2012)

13. Ratha, N.K., Connell, J.H., Bolle, R.M.: Enhancing security and privacy in biometrics-based authentication systems. IBM Syst. J. **40**(3), 614–634 (2001)

14. Sajjad, M., et al.: CNN-based anti-spoofing two-tier multi-factor authentication system. Pattern Recogn. Lett. **126**, 123–131 (2019)

15. Souza, D., Burlamaqui, A., Souza Filho, G.: Improving biometrics authentication with a multi-factor approach based on optical interference and chaotic maps. Multimedia Tools Appl. **77**(2), 2013–2032 (2017). https://doi.org/10.1007/s11042-017-4374-x

16. Suo, X., Zhu, Y., Owen, G.S.: Graphical passwords: a survey. In: Proceedings of the 21st Annual Computer Security Applications Conference (ACSAC 2005). IEEE, Tucson, AZ, USA (2005)

17. Tabassi, E., Grother, P.: Fingerprint image quality. In: Li, S.Z., Jain, A. (eds.) Encyclopedia of Biometrics, pp. 635–643. Springer, Boston, MA (2015). https://doi.org/10.1007/978-0-387-73003-5_52

18. Trader, J.: The top 5 uses of biometrics across the globe (2016). http://www.m2sys.com/blog/biometric-hardware/top-5-uses-biometrics-across-globe/

19. Van Nguyen, T., Sae-Bae, N., Memon, N.: DRAW-A-PIN: authentication using finger-drawn pin on touch devices. Comput. Secur. **66**, 115–128 (2017)

Author Index